Building a Dream

Fifth Edition

A Canadian Guide to Starting Your Own Business

Walter S. Good
Professor, Department of Marketing
University of Manitoba

McGraw-Hill Ryerson

Toronto Montréal Boston Burr Ridge, IL Dubuque, IA Madison, WI New York San Francisco St. Louis Bangkok Bogotá Caracas Kuala Lumpur Lisbon London Madrid Mexico City Milan New Delhi Santiago Seoul Singapore Sydney Taipei

McGraw-Hill
Ryerson Limited

A Subsidiary of The McGraw-Hill Companies

BUILDING A DREAM
Fifth Edition

ISBN: 0-07-089810-3

3 4 5 6 7 8 9 10 TRI 0 9 8 7 6 5

Printed and bound in Canada

Care has been taken to trace ownership of copyright material contained in this text; however, the publisher will welcome any information that enables them to rectify any reference or credit for subsequent editions.

Vice President and Editorial Director: Pat Ferrier
Sponsoring Editor: Lenore Gray Spence
Managing Editor, Development: Kim Brewster
Director of Marketing: Jeff MacLean
Supervising Editor: Carrie Withers
Copy Editor: Catherine Haggert
Proofreader: Jim Zimmerman
Production Coordinator: Jennifer Wilkie
Photos and Permissions: Alison Derry, Permissions Plus
Composition: Sharon Lucas
Cover and Interior Design: Sharon Lucas
Art Direction: Dianna Little
Printer: Tri-Graphic Printing

Canadian Cataloguing in Publication Data

Good, Walter S.
Building a dream: a Canadian guide to starting a business of your own

5th ed.
ISBN 0-07-08910-3 (higher education edition)
ISBN 0-07-091097-9 (trade edition)

New business enterprise. 2. Entrepreneurship. I. Title.

HD62.5.G66 2002 658.1'1 C2002-900402-0

Contents

Preface

This self-help guide and workbook is intended to provide a vehicle to lead prospective small-business people and potential entrepreneurs through the conceptual stages involved in setting up a business of their own in a logical and sequential way.

Many people fantasize about being self-employed and having a business of their own at some stage in their lives. For most, this dream never becomes a reality. They don't really know the risks involved and feel very uncomfortable with the uncertainty associated with taking the initial step. In addition, they don't entirely understand the tasks required to get a new business venture off the ground successfully.

For the past decade or two the number of people who have started their own business has increased dramatically across North America. People's level of interest in and awareness of the entrepreneurial option has virtually exploded. This has been fostered and reinforced by governments at all levels, who have come to recognize the positive impact small-business start-ups have on job creation and regional economic development. Business magazines, the popular press, and radio and television have also fuelled this interest with numerous items on the emotional and financial rewards of having a business of your own. They have glamourized the role of entrepreneurs in our society, and established many of them, such as Ted Rogers of Rogers Communications Inc., Terry Matthews, the founder of Newbridge Networks Corp. and Celtic House International Corp., Izzy Asper of CanWest Global Communications Corp., Gerry Schwartz of Onex and Indigo Books, Peter Nygard of Nygard International Ltd., Bobby Julien of Kolter Property Co., and Ron Joyce of Tim Hortons as attractive role models. This has been accentuated over the past couple of years with the phenomenal success and, in some cases, subsequent failure of many Internet-based companies. However, some businesses like Yahoo and eBay have made a number of young entrepreneurs such as Jerry Yang, Jeff Skoll, Dave Filo, and Pierre Omidyar as well as a number of their employees multi-millionaires or even billionaires within a very short period of time.

Building a Dream has been written for individuals who wish to start a business of their own or want to assess their own potential for such an option. This includes all men and women who dream of some type of self-employment, on either a full-time or a part-time basis. This book contains a comprehensive overall framework outlining the entrepreneurial process, descriptive information, practical outlines, checklists, screening questionnaires, and various other tools that will enable you to evaluate your own potential for this type of career and guide you through the early stages of launching a successful business of your own.

This book covers a range of topics that will increase your understanding of what it takes to succeed in an entrepreneurial career. From an overview of entrepreneurship and the entrepreneurial process, the book spreads outward to consider the skills, personality, and character traits possessed by most successful entrepreneurs, how to find and evaluate a possible idea for a business, buy an existing firm, or acquire a franchise. It provides a comprehensive outline for conducting a feasibility study to evaluate the potential of your concept and discusses the ways you can carry on your business and protect your product or service concept or idea. It concludes with a comprehensive framework for preparing a detailed and professional business plan.

Building a Dream is divided into "Stages," each of which provides a descriptive overview of a topic, some conceptual material indicating the principal areas to be considered or evaluated, and a series of outlines, worksheets, checklists, and other forms that can be completed in conducting a comprehensive assessment of that stage in the new venture development process. In addition, each Stage within this fifth edition is highlighted by a number of boxes. The "**Key Points**" boxes emphasize material in that Stage that is of particular importance and should be emphasized. The "**FYI**" (For Your Information) boxes refer you to a number of Web sites that have supplementary material specifically related to the topics discussed in that Stage. This enables you to readily obtain further information on subjects that may be of particular interest.

This fifth edition also contains an increased number of "**Entrepreneurs in Action**" examples illustrating how people are actually going about building their businesses and trying to make things work for them on a day-to-day basis.

Overall the book will provide a practical opportunity for you to realistically assess the potential opportunity for your concept or idea and enable you to develop a detailed program or plan for your own new venture.

STAGE ONE: WHAT IS ENTREPRENEURSHIP?

This Stage introduces you to the concept of entrepreneurship and provides an overview of the other elements that are required to launch a successful new business venture. In addition to the entrepreneur, these include a viable business idea or opportunity, an organization, resources, a strategy, and a business plan. It also discusses some of the myths and stereotypes that have evolved over time about entrepreneurs and entrepreneurship.

STAGE TWO: ASSESSING YOUR POTENTIAL FOR AN ENTREPRENEURIAL CAREER

This Stage provides you with an opportunity to assess your personal attitudes and attributes and to see how they compare with those of "practising" entrepreneurs. It will also enable you to evaluate your managerial and administrative skills and experience and determine your financial capacity for starting a business.

STAGE THREE: EXPLORING NEW BUSINESS IDEAS AND OPPORTUNITIES

This Stage describes a number of sources from which you might obtain ideas for your prospective new venture and identifies a number of areas of opportunity for the future on the basis of dynamic changes now taking place within Canadian society. It also outlines a six-step opportunity selection process, describes the characteristics of an "ideal" or "model" business, and presents a framework for assessing the attributes of your product or service idea in comparison to this ideal. A number of entry strategies are outlined as well that can help you decide on the best way to proceed.

STAGE FOUR: BUYING A BUSINESS

The obvious route to self-employment is to start a business of your own based on a new or distinctive idea. Another route to explore is the possibility of buying an existing firm. This Stage deals with such issues as finding a business to buy and the factors to consider in making the acquisition. It also discusses a number of ways to determine an appropriate price to pay for a business and the pros and cons of buying versus starting one. A comprehensive checklist is provided for considering a number of potential business acquisitions.

STAGE FIVE: CONSIDERING A FRANCHISE

In recent years franchising has been one of the fastest-growing sectors of North American business. More and more people are considering the franchise alternative as a means of getting into business for themselves. This Stage explores the concept of franchising in some detail. It defines franchising so that you know exactly what the concept means. The broad range of types of franchises available is presented, along with an overview of the legal requirements associated with franchising and the terms and conditions contained in a typical franchise agreement. This Stage also discusses how to find and apply for a franchise, and presents an extensive checklist for evaluating potential franchise opportunities.

STAGES SIX AND SEVEN: CONDUCTING A FEASIBILITY STUDY — PARTS 1 AND 2

Stages Six and Seven provide a step-by step process for transforming your chosen new venture concept from the idea stage to the marketplace. This is accomplished by means of a feasibility study. A typical feasibility study considers the following areas:

- The concept of your proposed venture
- The technical feasibility of your idea

- A detailed assessment of your market potential and preparation of your marketing plan
- Managing the supply situation
- Conducting a cost and profitability assessment
- Indicating your plans for future action

Comprehensive outlines are provided to enable you to assess each of these areas in a preliminary way and to put your thoughts and ideas down on paper. Much of this material can be incorporated into your subsequent business plan.

STAGE EIGHT: ORGANIZING YOUR BUSINESS

One of the principal issues to be resolved when starting a new business is the legal form of organization the business should adopt. The most prevalent forms a business might assume include individual or sole proprietorship, general or limited partnership, and incorporation. This Stage reviews each of these forms and discusses the advantages and disadvantages of each from the standpoint of the prospective entrepreneur. It discusses how to select and register a name for your business and presents an overview of such issues as the types of licences and permits your business might require, your responsibilities for collecting and remitting a variety of employee contributions and taxes, the impact of provincial employment standards on your business, and protecting your investment.

STAGE NINE: PROTECTING YOUR IDEA

Many entrepreneurs are also innovators and inventors, and are faced with the problem of how to protect the idea, invention, concept, system, name, or design that they feel will be the key to their business success. This Stage discusses the various forms of intellectual property such as patents, copyrights, trademarks, and industrial designs, and what is required to protect your interest in their development.

STAGE TEN: ARRANGING FINANCING

The principal question relating to any new venture is where the money is going to come from to get the new business off the ground. This Stage examines the major sources of funds for new business start-ups — personal funds, "love money," bank loans, government agencies and programs, and venture capital. It also provides a framework for you to determine just how much money you think you will need to launch your business and where you think that financing might possibly come from.

STAGE ELEVEN: PREPARING YOUR BUSINESS PLAN

This Stage, which serves as a capstone for the book, provides a framework for the development of a comprehensive business plan for your proposed new business venture, whether it is a retail or service business or a manufacturing company. It lays out the necessary steps in the business planning process such as:

- Developing a vision statement
- Formulating a mission statement
- Defining the fundamental values by which you will run your business
- Setting clear and specific objectives
- Developing a realistic business plan

It also explains what a business plan is, how long it should be, and why it is important that you develop such a plan for your proposed venture and actually write it yourself. It lays out the contents of a typical business plan and provides an outline to follow for developing a plan for a retail or service type business and a manufacturing company. This Stage also contains two examples of completed business plans. Alfa-B Pollination Services is an example of a plan for a relatively small service business to serve a niche market in the agricultural sector. LifeLink Ventures, on the other hand, illustrates a plan for a new medical technology product that will require a couple of years of testing and a significant initial investment to bring the concept to market successfully. These can serve as comprehensive and useful guides for you to follow in developing your business plan.

FURTHER INFORMATION CONTAINS:

- a list of useful reading material you can obtain for little or no cost from banks, accounting firms, government departments, and other sources,
- a number of useful contacts that can provide you with additional information on many of the topics discussed in the book,
- a comprehensive selection of Web sites that have a wealth of additional information you can use to help your business get off the ground successfully, and
- a Glossary of financial terms.

Following the framework outlined in *Building a Dream* will give you hands-on, practical experience with the entire new venture development process and enable you to come up with a comprehensive plan for a proposed venture of your own selection. This plan will not only give you a better understanding of the potential opportunity and success requirements of your new venture idea, but also put you in a much stronger position to attract the necessary external resources and support to get your proposed business off the ground. Good luck in successfully building your dream.

Acknowledgements

Developing a workbook of this type can only be accomplished with the co-operation and support of a great many people. Much of the material would not have been developed without the dedicated effort of Steve Tax of the University of Victoria, who was largely responsible for many of the ideas that were incorporated into the first edition and have been carried forward to the current one. I am also indebted to David Milstein of David Milstein & Associates of Brisbane, Australia for contributing the material on the "Big Picture" of strategic planning and to Vance Gough of Mount Royal College for the exercise on creative thinking. My appreciation also goes to Carole Babiak who's organizational and word processing skills enabled me to keep the material moving during the revision process.

Very comprehensive suggestions for changes and improvements to this and previous editions were received from Robert Warren of the University of Manitoba, Walter Isenor of Acadia University, Bryan MacKay of Confederation College, Vance Gough of Mount Royal College, Kyleen Myrah of Okanogan University College, Neil Beattie of Sheridan College, and Terry Zinger of Laurentian University. Their comments were very helpful in improving and polishing the material and refining the concept of the book to make it even more useful to students and prospective entrepreneurs.

My appreciation also goes to Lenore Gray Spence, Kim Brewster, and Carrie Withers, my editors in the Higher Education Division at McGraw-Hill Ryerson, and my copy editor, Cat Haggert and proofreader, Jim Zimmerman for keeping me on track, expediting the review and production of the material, and providing numerous useful comments and suggestions throughout the revision process. The support of Joan Homewood, the Vice President, Publishing, and Catherine Leek and Claudia Hawkins of the Trade, Professional, and Medical Division of the company is also much appreciated.

I would also like to thank Moe Levy of the Asper Foundation and Shannon Coughlan of the Canada/Manitoba Business Services Centre for their comments on several components of the book and their encouragement during the early stages of the development of the concept behind the workbook. Special thanks go to Dean Beleyowski for his assistance in compiling many of the Web sites and much of the other supplementary material included with the book. The belief of these individuals in entrepreneurship as a vehicle for successful economic development in Canada and their faith in the premise of the self-help concept may finally pay off.

Finally, I would like to thank the college and university students and others who have used the earlier editions of the book over the years and have gone on to start new business ventures of their own. Their insatiable desire to assess their personal capacity for a career in this area and their drive to explore the mysteries of franchising, venture capital, and similar topics associated with the formation of a successful new business has enabled many of them to build their dream. I hope all of us have been able to play a small part in that process.

What Is Entrepreneurship?

At 24 Jesse Rasch is the CEO of his own company, a company he grew from scratch into a multi-million dollar corporation with more than 150 employees. Despite his relatively young age, this was not Rasch's first entrepreneurial venture. He had owned and operated businesses since he was 17. He started this latest, and most successful venture, Webhosting.com, just as the Internet was beginning to take off in the mid-1990s and the business flourished practically overnight.

Jesse Rasch and other Canadians like him are starting businesses of their own more frequently than ever before. Of the more than 2.2 million businesses in Canada, over 99 per cent are small- and medium-sized. Every year more than 150,000 other Canadians join this number by initiating new start-ups, principally in the construction, retail, and business services sectors. This has led to a major entrepreneurial revolution across the country and caused the small business sector of the economy to become more widely acknowledged by all levels of government, the chartered banks and other financial institutions, and secondary and post-secondary educational institutions.

The overall economic impact of this revolution on the country is difficult to determine precisely, but it is substantial. It is being fuelled by such factors as structural changes in the economy, such as organizational downsizing or "rightsizing"; the loss of middle-management positions in many larger companies and government departments; younger people wanting more independence; and the increasing number of immigrants who would have difficulty with conventional employment because of their limited skills and/or language issues. The entrepreneurial revolution has also been propelled by the explosion in technology-based companies and the publicity surrounding the creation of many so-called "dot-com millionaires," although this bubble has burst for the moment at least. One thing that is clear, however, is that the proportion of total employment in the country accounted for by these smaller firms has increased dramatically. They have created the lion's share of new jobs, while employment levels in large businesses have remained constant or decreased.

This book has been developed for people who may be aspiring entrepreneurs and are giving some thought to the possibility of joining the many others who have started some kind of business of their own. Most of us have given some thought to owning and managing our own business at some point in our lives. Provided you know what it takes to be successful, it can be a very rewarding way of life. These rewards may be financial, in terms of providing you with a return for the time and money you and others may invest in the business and the risks you take in operating your own firm. Having an independent business also gives you the freedom to act independently, make your own decisions, and be your own boss. This can be a very important motivating factor for many people. It can also be a very satisfying way of life, full of the "fun" and personal satisfaction derived from doing something that you genuinely love to do.

Table 1.1 illustrates the principal reasons that Canadians have decided to go into business for themselves. The primary considerations were to achieve a strong sense of personal accomplishment and to be their own boss.

TABLE 1.1 WHY PEOPLE START BUSINESSES

To achieve a sense of accomplishment	82%
To be their own boss	73%
To have an element of variety and adventure	66%
To make better use of their training and skills	63%
To be able to adapt their own approach to their work	62%
To be challenged by new opportunities	61%

Source: *Royal Bank Reporter*, Fall, 1988

STAGES TO BUILDING YOUR DREAM

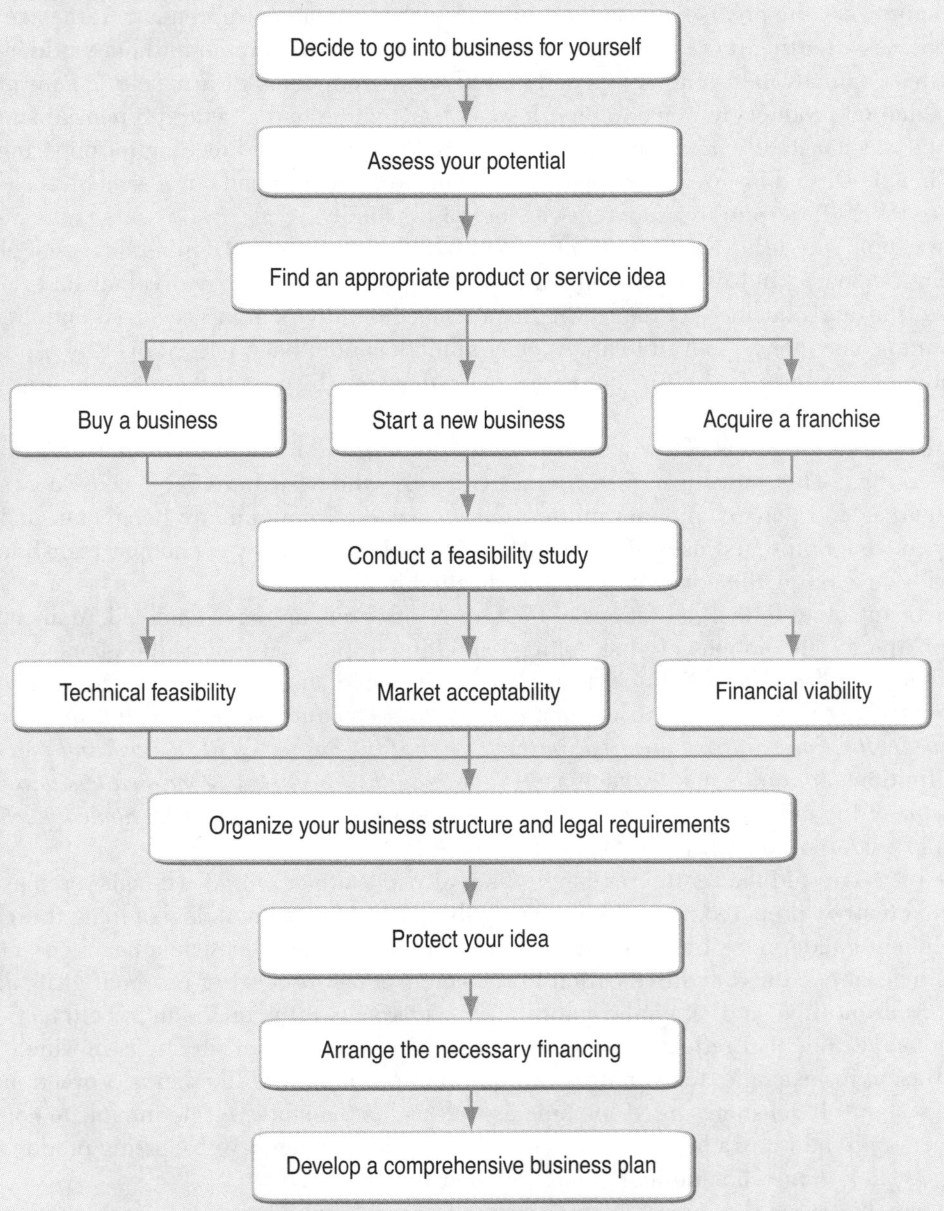

Starting a new business, however, can be very risky at the best of times. It typically demands long hours, hard work, a high level of emotional involvement and commitment, as well as significant financial risk and the possibility of failure. Your chances of succeeding, however, will be better if you spend some time carefully evaluating your personal situation and circumstances and trying to anticipate and work out as many potential problems as you can, before you invest any money.

Stage One will introduce you to the concept of entrepreneurship and give you some idea of what is required to be successful. It will also discuss some of the folklore and stereotypes that exist around entrepreneurship and, hopefully, dispel a few of the myths that have come to surround entrepreneurs.

WHAT IS ENTREPRENEURSHIP?

Entrepreneurship is difficult to define precisely. Entrepreneurs tend to be identified, not by formal rank or title, but in retrospect—after the successful implementation of an innovation or idea. The example of Jesse Rasch in Entrepreneurs in Action #1 may help to illustrate this definition problem for you.

It is difficult to say the precise moment at which Jesse became an entrepreneur. At the age of 17 he started his first business, putting up real estate signs on street corners in Toronto for homebuilders and developers. He sold that company to his employees and moved on to set up another firm selling natural gas and other recently deregulated products to homeowners. It was clear that he had an entrepreneurial spirit from a very early age as he was constantly dreaming up new ideas for businesses and looking for opportunities to be his own boss. When he started his Web site development business, he dropped out of school as soon as the business started to take off, despite the apparent concern of his family.

For some people like Jesse Rasch, entrepreneurship is a conscious and deliberate career choice. For others, there may be some kind of significant *triggering* event. Perhaps the individual had no better career prospects than starting a business of their own. Sometimes the individual has received an inheritance or otherwise come into some money, moved to a new geographic location, been passed over for a promotion, taken an early retirement, or been laid off or fired from their regular job. Any of these factors can give birth to a new business.

The word "entrepreneur" is of French origin, derived from the term "entreprendre," literally translated as "between-taking." This term describes the activities by which an individual takes a position between available resources and perceived opportunities and, because of some unique behaviour, makes something positive happen. One of the first uses of the word was in the late 1700s by economist Jean-Baptiste Say, who is credited with developing the concept of "entrepreneurship."

Over time many other formal definitions of the term "entrepreneur" have emerged. Many of these modern definitions incorporate the notions of "risk taking" and "innovation" as well as the elements put forward by Say. For example, the Fast Times Political Dictionary defines an entrepreneur as: *Someone who sets up a new business undertaking, raises the money necessary, and organizes production and appoints the management. The entrepreneur bears the financial risk involved, in the hope that the business will succeed and make a profit.*[1]

Other definitions are quite simple, such as: *An individual who starts his/her own business.*[2]

Perhaps one of the most straightforward definitions is that an entrepreneur is: *Someone who perceives an opportunity and creates an organization to pursue it.*[3]

Many people have said that entrepreneurship is really a "state of mind." Though you may be extremely innovative and creative, prepared to work hard, and willing to rely on a great deal of luck, these qualities may still be insufficient to guarantee business success. The missing element may be a necessary entrepreneurial mind-set: a single-mindedness and dedication to the achievement of a set of personal goals and objectives; confidence in your intuitive and rational capabilities; a capacity to think and plan in both tactical and strategic terms; and an attitude that reflects a penchant for action, frequently in situations in which information is inadequate. Rasch, for example, feels that sitting on top of a company is like being a proud mountaineer on top of a large summit. It consumes all of his time as well as his thoughts. Yet he intends to continue to build Webhosting.com into the world's largest provider of shared and dedicated Web-hosting products while, at the same time, give back to the community by helping other businesses.

Entrepreneurship is not the same as management. The principal job of professional managers is to make a business perform well. They take a given set of resources — such as money, employees, machines, and materials — and orchestrate and organize them into an efficient and effective production operation. Managers tend to delegate much of their authority and to rely on the use of formal control systems, and are usually evaluated on the basis of organizationally determined objectives. In contrast, entrepreneurs typically rely more on an informal, hands-on management style and are driven by their personal goals. Their principal job is to bring about purposeful change within an organizational context. They break new ground and, in many cases, each step is guided by some larger plan.

1 www.fast-times.com/political/dictE.html
2 investorwords.com/e2.htm#entrepreneur
3 William D. Bygraves, "The Entrepreneurial process" in William D. Bygraves, Ed., *The Portable MBA in Entrepreneurship*, Second Edition, John Wiley & Sons, Inc., 1997, p.2

1 Entrepreneurs in action

Conquering Cyberspace

At 24, Jesse Rasch is the CEO of Webhosting.com, a company he successfully grew from scratch into a multi-million dollar corporation with more than 150 employees. Don't let his age fool you, Rasch has owned and operated businesses since he was 17. He started his latest, and most successful venture, Webhosting.com, just as the Internet started to make its presence felt in the mid-1990s. His business flourished practically overnight as international commerce began using cyberspace.

While studying business at McGill University in Montreal, Rasch took notice of the growing number of companies joining the World Wide Web. He decided to continue studying business outside the classroom by starting a company in 1996 called DynamicWeb, which specialized in Web site development and catered to Canadian Fortune 500 clients.

Rasch explains that the more the company developed sites, the more his clients began asking him to host these sites. After partnering with third-party companies in the U.S. that provided similar services, Rasch soon learned that there were not many companies that specialized in hosting services. So Rasch quickly assembled a party of computer science students to help build a platform that would allow DynamicWeb to host these Web sites and empower its customers to manage their sites through the DynamicWeb's Web browser.

His business really took off after this expansion, leaving less time to devote to business school. Rasch would drop out before graduating.

"We decided we should focus on the Web hosting exclusively and forgo the Web site development because I didn't really see an opportunity for explosive revenue in that area," says Rasch. "And I needed to tell my mother that if I was going to drop out of school, I had something that had the potential of being very, very big."

But this was not the first time Rasch had demonstrated his talents as an entrepreneur. His first business venture was at age 17, when he started an A-frame real estate installation company called Signs Upright.

"To put it in simple terms, I had a truck and I drove around on the weekends and put up real estate signs on street corners for homebuilders and developers in the Greater Toronto Area."

He later sold the company to his six employees and moved on to start another organization that sold natural gas and other deregulated products in Canada. From an early age, Rasch had an entrepreneurial spirit that was constantly dreaming up new ideas for businesses, and he was always looking for opportunities to be his own boss.

After many entrepreneurial endeavours, it looked like his creativity and perseverance were starting to pay off. And it was only the beginning for DynamicWeb.

"When we started selling Web hosting products on the Internet, it was retail, 100 per cent," says Rasch. "[We told the companies:] we will put up a Web site for your company and we will give you Web-based tools so you can manage your E-mail accounts, security, and storefront hosting on-line, any time of the day you want. You don't have to pick up the phone and call. That differentiated us from others who could not provide that level of automation to their customers."

Already Rasch had made a better mousetrap that he could offer to his clients. Yet his real success came when he changed the company's name and domain to Webhosting.com, after a domain name conflict with another company called DynamicWeb in the U.S. in October of 1998.

"We went looking for a brand new domain name and found Webhosting.com, which is a very powerful generic domain name, and powerful generics on the Internet are very attractive because they can yield a lot of what's called 'type-in-traffic.' People type in a domain name not knowing who will be there, but they are looking for the product based on a generic phrase that describes the product, which in our case was Web hosting."

When DynamicWeb became Webhosting.com, sales quadrupled. The company started attracting the attention of large telecommunication providers and communication-service companies such as Bell Canada and SBC Communications, who wanted to expand their services. Rasch then co-branded the technology he was using, InQuent.

"InQuent is our wholesale brand that sells to our channel partners," explains Rasch. "Webhosting.com is our retail brand."

So, from two university students, Webhosting.com grew into a lucrative business employing more than 150 people, with plans to grow to a staff of some 250 employees before 2001. His partner from day one, Michael Apted, is still with Webhosting.com as the vice president of technical strategy.

Sitting on top of the company like a proud mountaineer on top of a large summit, Rasch says that being the president and CEO of a flourishing company consumes all of his time as well as his thoughts.

"You're always thinking about the company and it's always on your mind. When you have a vested interest financially, when you have given a commitment to your employees to keep them gainfully employed, and to your customers to always deliver the best product . . . it can consume you."

With so much time spent developing his company, at the age of 24, does Rasch feel he has missed out on anything?

"Academically, no," he says. "Socially, and from a personal human development perspective, I think so. [It's worthwhile] as long as you have your eyes wide open and you're conscious of the sacrifices you need to make to grow a company, knowing that one day, hopefully, it will all pay off."

And it does seem to be paying off. Rasch just sold a 51 per cent stake in his company to SBC Communications (the second-largest local telephone provider in the U.S.) for a record U.S.$115 million.

While Rasch may now be on easy street, starting a company is full of challenges. He worked 18-hour days to keep a tightly held equity structure, and he originally found it very difficult to recruit the talented people he needed.

"The challenge of being able to hire smart people was very difficult, especially when you are small and your name is not in the news," says Rasch. "You have to convince people you are a stable company and that the paycheques will clear. As CEO, it really becomes a sales job and you have to spend a lot of time telling people that this is a really great place to work."

Looking back at the whole process, the upsides and the downfalls, would Rasch recommend the life of an entrepreneur to someone else?

"I don't think that everyone that goes to business school wants to be an entrepreneur," says Rasch. "I don't think that most people understand the sacrifices that entrepreneurs need to make to grow companies and I don't think that many people could deal with the uncertainties and the constant risks of that. There is great risk in having to make decisions knowing only 60 per cent of the facts but having to live with 100 per cent of the consequences. I was willing to do that."

Rasch plans to continue to build Webhosting.com into the world's largest provider of shared and dedicated Web hosting products. At the same time, he also plans to give back to the community by helping other businesses. He intends to sponsor and support other start-ups in the Greater Toronto Area and, perhaps, the rest of Canada.

As the boundaries of cyberspace continue to expand, Rasch will continue to find new ground to break and new frontiers to conquer. It may be a small world, but it keeps growing for this visionary entrepreneur. (www.webhosting.com)

Source: "Conquering Cyberspace: Jesse Rasch Takes Web Hosting by Storm," by Tara Rose, *Business $ense*. Used with permission.

As agents of change, entrepreneurs play, or can play, a number of roles or perform a variety of different functions in the economy. They can, for example:

1. Create new product and/or service businesses
2. Bring creative and innovative methods to developing or producing new products or services
3. Provide employment opportunities and create new jobs as a result of growing their business consistently and rapidly
4. Help contribute to regional and national economic growth
5. Encourage greater industrial efficiency/productivity to enhance our international competitiveness

You should keep in mind, however, that other people also play a significant role in determining who will succeed or fail in our society. For example, entrepreneurs will succeed only when there are customers for the goods and services they provide. But, in many circumstances, it is the entrepreneurs themselves who play the principal role in determining their success or failure. Many still manage to succeed in spite of poor timing, inferior marketing, or low-quality production by combining a variety of talents, skills, and energies with imagination, good planning, and common sense. The entrepreneurial or self-employed option has many attractions, but along with these come risks and challenges and the possibility of failure.

THE ENTREPRENEURIAL PROCESS

The successful launch of new business ventures requires a number of other components in addition to an entrepreneur. For example, while there may be any number of specific parts, virtually every new start-up also requires:

- a viable business idea or opportunity for which there is a receptive market
- an organizational structure for the business
- access to financial and other resources, and
- a distinctive strategy that, if effectively implemented, will set the business apart from its competitors and enable it to become established

As illustrated in Figure 1.1, all of these elements are outlined and captured in the business plan.

THE ENTREPRENEUR It all begins with the entrepreneur, the driving force behind the business and the coordinator of all the activities, resources, and people that are needed to get it off the ground. This individual will have conducted some assessment of his or her own resources and capabilities and made a conscious decision to launch the business.

THE OPPORTUNITY The entrepreneur must then find a concept or idea that he/she feels has the potential to develop into a successful enterprise. The concept behind the business must be carefully evaluated to determine whether there is likely to be a market, and if it might represent a viable opportunity. The object is to determine the magnitude of the returns that might be expected with successful implementation.

ORGANIZATION To capitalize on any business opportunity, an organizational structure must be established, with a manager or management team and a form of ownership.

RESOURCES Some essential financial and other resources must be obtained. The key usually is money. It is the "enabler" that makes everything else happen. Other key resources typically include physical plant and equipment, technical capability, and human resources.

STRATEGY Once a start-up appears likely, a specific strategy must be developed and a feasibility study conducted. The feasibility study is a way to test your business concept to see whether it actually does have market potential. It is a series of tests you should conduct to discover more and more about the nature and size of your business opportunity. After each test you should ask yourself whether the opportunity still appears to be attractive and if you still want to proceed. Is there anything that has come up which would make the business unattractive or prevent you from going forward with its implementation? Throughout this process you probably will modify your concept and business strategy several times until you feel that you have it right.

FIGURE 1.1 THE COMPONENTS OF SUCCESSFUL ENTREPRENEURIAL VENTURES

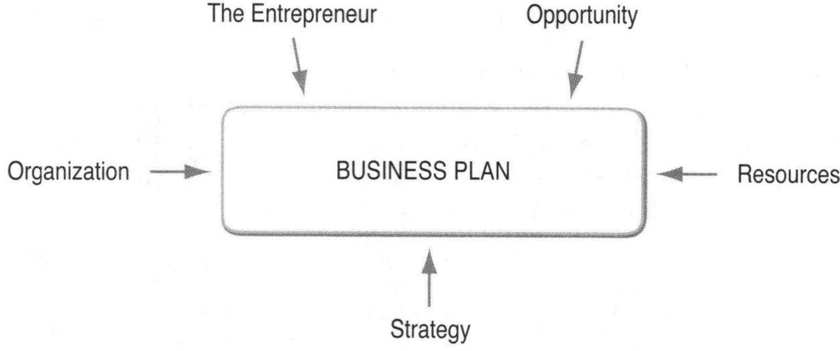

THE BUSINESS PLAN The business plan not only describes your business concept, but outlines the structure that needs to be in place to successfully implement the concept. The plan can be used to assist in obtaining the additional resources that may be necessary to actually launch the business and guide the implementation of the strategy. It assumes you have a feasible business concept and have now included the operational components needed to execute the strategy. It describes in some detail the company you are going to create.

Figure 1.2 illustrates how these components interrelate, the action required at each phase of the implementation of the process, and where these issues are addressed in the book.

This process proceeds in one manner or another to a conclusion, resulting in the implementation of the business. While the model gives the appearance that this is a linear process and that the flow is sequential from one stage to another, this has been done to provide a logical structure for the book and is not necessarily the case. For example, the entrepreneur may pursue two or three different elements at the same time, such as finalizing an organizational structure while also trying to compile the resources necessary to get the business off the ground.

MYTHS AND REALITIES CONCERNING ENTREPRENEURSHIP

According to noted author-lecturer-consultant Peter Drucker, entrepreneurs defy stereotyping. He states, "I have seen people of the most diverse personalities and temperaments perform well in entrepreneurial challenges."[4] This suggests that some entrepreneurs may be true eccentrics while others are rigid conformists; some are short and fat while others are tall and thin; some are real worriers while others are very laid-back and relaxed; some drink and smoke very heavily while others abstain completely; some are people of great wit and charm while others have no more personality than a frozen fish.

Despite all that is known about entrepreneurs and entrepreneurship, a good deal of folklore and many stereotypes remain. Part of the problem is that while some generalities may apply to certain types of entrepreneurs and certain situations, most entrepreneurial types tend to defy generalization. The following are examples of long-standing myths about entrepreneurs and entrepreneurship:[5]

- **Myth 1** Entrepreneurs are born, not made.
  Reality While entrepreneurs may be born with a certain native intelligence, a flair for innovation, a high level of energy, and a core of other inborn attributes that you either have or you don't, it is apparent that merely possessing these characteristics does not necessarily make you an entrepreneur. The making of an entrepreneur occurs through a combination of work experience, know-how, personal contacts, and the development of business skills acquired over time. In fact, other attributes of equal importance can also be acquired through understanding, hard work, and patience.

- **Myth 2** Anyone can start a business. It's just a matter of luck and guts.
  Reality Entrepreneurs need to recognize the difference between an idea and a real opportunity to significantly improve their chances of success. If you want to launch and grow a high-potential new venture, you must understand the many things that you have to do to get the odds in your favour. You cannot think and act like a typical bureaucrat, or even a manager; you must think and act like an entrepreneur. That often means initiating action even if conditions are uncertain and existing rules have to be pushed to the limit.

- **Myth 3** Entrepreneurs are gamblers.
  Reality Successful entrepreneurs only take what they perceive to be very carefully calculated risks. They often try to influence the odds by getting others to share the risk with them, or by avoiding or minimizing the risk if they have the choice. They do not deliberately seek to take more risk or to take unnecessary risks, but they will not shy away from taking the risks that may be necessary to succeed.

- **Myth 4** Entrepreneurs want to run the whole show themselves.
  Reality Owning and running the whole show effectively limits the potential for the business to grow. Single entrepreneurs can make a living, perhaps even a good one, but it is extremely difficult to grow a business by working single-handed. Most successful ventures typically evolve to require a formal organization, a management team, and a corporate structure.

---

4. Peter Drucker, *Innovation and Entrepreneurship: Practice and Principles* (New York: Harper and Row, 1985), p. 25.
5. Adapted from Jeffrey A. Timmons, *New Venture Creation: Entrepreneurship for the 21st Century*, 4th Edition (Homewood, IL: Richard D. Irwin, 1994), p. 23.

FIGURE 1.2 OUTLINE OF THE ENTREPRENEURIAL PROCESS

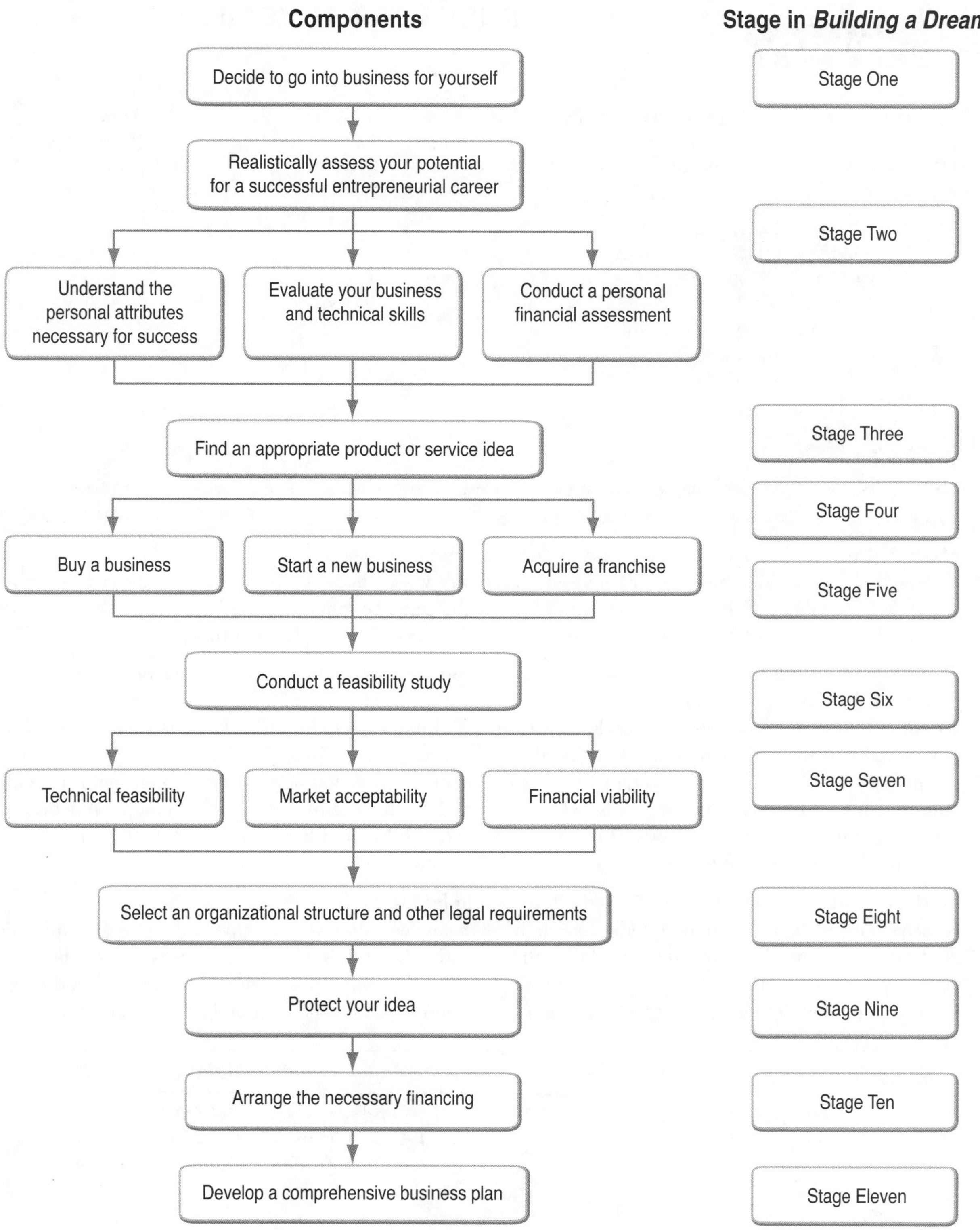

- **Myth 5** Entrepreneurs are their own bosses and completely independent.
  Reality Most entrepreneurs are far from independent and have to serve a number of constituencies and a variety of masters including partners, investors, customers, employees, suppliers, creditors, their families, and pressures from social and community obligations. They do have the choice, however, to decide whether and when to respond to these pressures.

RULES OF THE ROAD

Sarah Jane Baxter had just graduated from hospitality studies at Ryerson Polytechnic when she realized she had a great business idea: making accessories for bicycle helmets. "The trouble was," she said, "I had no experience in any of this. For the first year or so I used to wake up in a sweat wondering what I was doing." Here are 10 smart moves she made that other start-ups would do well to follow:

1. Spot the opportunity around you
2. Bring in the experts
3. Keep your options open
4. Be prepared to work
5. Learn when to hand off to suppliers
6. Look for value-added deals
7. Expand strategically
8. Think BIG
9. Lever relationships
10. Have a fallback

Source: Rick Spence and Richard Wright, "Canada's Hottest Start-ups," *PROFIT guide*, www.profitguide.com. Used with permission.

- **Myth 6** Entrepreneurs work longer and harder than corporate managers.
  Reality There is no evidence at all that entrepreneurs work harder than their corporate counterparts. Some do, some don't. Both are demanding situations that require long hours and hard work. However, as owners they are tied to the business and responsible in ways that are different than employees.

- **Myth 7** Entrepreneurs face greater stress and more pressures, and thus pay a higher personal price in their jobs than do other managers.
  Reality Being an entrepreneur is undoubtedly stressful and demanding. But there is no evidence it is any more stressful than numerous other highly demanding professional roles, such as being the principal partner in a legal or accounting practice or the head of a division of a major corporation or government agency. Most entrepreneurs enjoy what they do. They have a high sense of accomplishment. For them it is fun rather than drudgery. They thrive on the flexibility and innovative aspects of their job and are much less likely to retire than those who work for someone else.

- **Myth 8** Starting a business is risky and often ends in failure.
  Reality This statement is undoubtedly true in many instances. Some studies have indicated that upwards of 80 per cent of new business start-ups fail within their first five years. However, success tends to be more common than failure for higher-potential ventures because they tend to be directed by talented and experienced people able to attract the right personnel and the necessary financial and other resources.

Used by permission of Johnny Hart and Creators Syndicate, Inc.

Vince Lombardi, the well-known ex-coach of the Green Bay Packers, is famous for the quotation, "Winning isn't everything — It's the *only* thing." But a lesser-known quote of his is closer to the true entrepreneur's personal philosophy. Looking back on a season, Lombardi was once heard to remark, "We didn't lose any games last season, we just ran out of time twice." Entrepreneurs learn from experience and are inclined to believe they have failed if they quit.

Owning your own business is a competitive game, and entrepreneurs have to be prepared to run out of time occasionally. Businesses fail but entrepreneurs do not. Many well-known entrepreneurs experience failure, sometimes several times, before achieving success.

- **Myth 9** Money is the most important ingredient for success.
  Reality If the other important elements and the people are there, the money tends to follow. But it is not true that entrepreneurs are assured of success if they have enough money. Money is one of the least important ingredients of new venture success.
- **Myth 10** New business start-ups are for the young and energetic.
  Reality While youth and energy may help, age is absolutely no barrier to starting a business of your own. However, many people feel there is some threshold for an individual's perceived capacity for starting a new venture. Over time you gain experience, competence, and self-confidence: These factors increase your capacity and readiness to embark on an entrepreneurial career. At the same time, constraints such as increases in your financial and other obligations grow and negatively affect your freedom to choose. The trade-offs between individual readiness and these restraints typically result in most high-potential new businesses being started by entrepreneurs between the ages of 25 and 40.
- **Myth 11** Entrepreneurs are motivated solely by their quest for the almighty dollar.
  Reality Growth-minded entrepreneurs are more driven by the challenge of building their enterprise and long-term capital appreciation than by the instant gratification of a high salary and other rewards. Having a sense of personal accomplishment and achievement, feeling in control of their own destiny, and realizing their vision and dreams are also powerful motivators. Money is viewed principally as a tool and a way of "keeping score."
- **Myth 12** Entrepreneurs seek power and control over other people so that they can feel "in charge."
  Reality Successful entrepreneurs are driven by the quest for responsibility, achievement, and results rather than for power for its own sake. They thrive on a sense of accomplishment and of outperforming the competition, rather than a personal need for power expressed by dominating and controlling other people. They gain control by the results they achieve.

FYI FOR YOUR INFORMATION

ABOUT GUIDE TO SMALL BUSINESS: CANADA

An extensive source of information and links for Canadians running their own small business or thinking of starting one. This site will give you all the business resources, contacts, financial sources, and tools that you need to be a successful entrepreneur. *home.about.com/aboutcanada/index.htm*

CanadaOne

An on-line publication for Canadian businesses with articles, resources, promotional tools, a free directory for Canadian companies, and more. *www.canadaone.ca/*

PROFITguide

A site with articles, links, and quizzes of interest to Canadian entrepreneurs. *www.profitguide.com/*

Small Business Canada Magazine

This Web site includes selected articles from the magazine of the same name. Some additional features of the site are available on-line. *www.smallbusinesscanada.ca/*

Assessing Your Potential for an Entrepreneurial Career

The discussion in Stage 1 should have served to dispel many of the popular myths concerning entrepreneurship. This section will expand upon the theme of entrepreneurial characteristics by proposing and discussing two important questions which are vital to you if you are interested in an entrepreneurial career:

1. Are there certain common attributes, attitudes, and experiences among entrepreneurs that appear to lead to success?
2. If such attributes, attitudes, and experiences exist, can they be learned or are they inborn and thus available only to those with a "fortunate" heritage?

Research into these questions suggests that the answer to question 1 is yes, while the answer to question 2 is both yes and no. These answers, of course, are of little value to you on their own without some further explanation.

ENTREPRENEURS ARE BORN AND MADE BETTER

In 1980, Tom Wolfe wrote a perceptive bestseller that examined the lives of America's leading test pilots and astronauts. According to Wolfe, becoming a member of this select club meant possessing "The Right Stuff" — i.e., the proper mix of courage, coolness under stressful conditions, a strong need for achievement, technical expertise, creativity, etc. While Wolfe was not talking about entrepreneurs, his viewpoint is similar to the basic thesis held by many members of the "people school" of entrepreneurship: A person has to have the "right stuff" to become a successful entrepreneur.

There is considerable evidence, however, that a great deal of the ability and "right stuff" needed to become a successful entrepreneur can be learned (though probably not by everyone).

ENTREPRENEURIAL QUIZ

While most writers in the field of entrepreneurship agree that there is no single profile, no specific set of characteristics, that defines a successful entrepreneur, there do appear to be some common attributes, abilities, and attitudes. Prior to our discussion of these entrepreneurial characteristics, it is suggested that you take the Entrepreneurial Quiz that appears as Figure 2.1. This will enable you to compare your personal attitudes and attributes with those of "practising" entrepreneurs.

WHAT ATTRIBUTES ARE DESIRABLE AND ACQUIRABLE?

In a study of the 21 inductees into the Babson University Academy of Distinguished Entrepreneurs, only three attributes and behaviours were mentioned by all 21 as the principal reasons for their success, and they were all learnable:

1. Responding positively to all challenges and learning from mistakes
2. Taking personal initiative
3. Having great perseverance

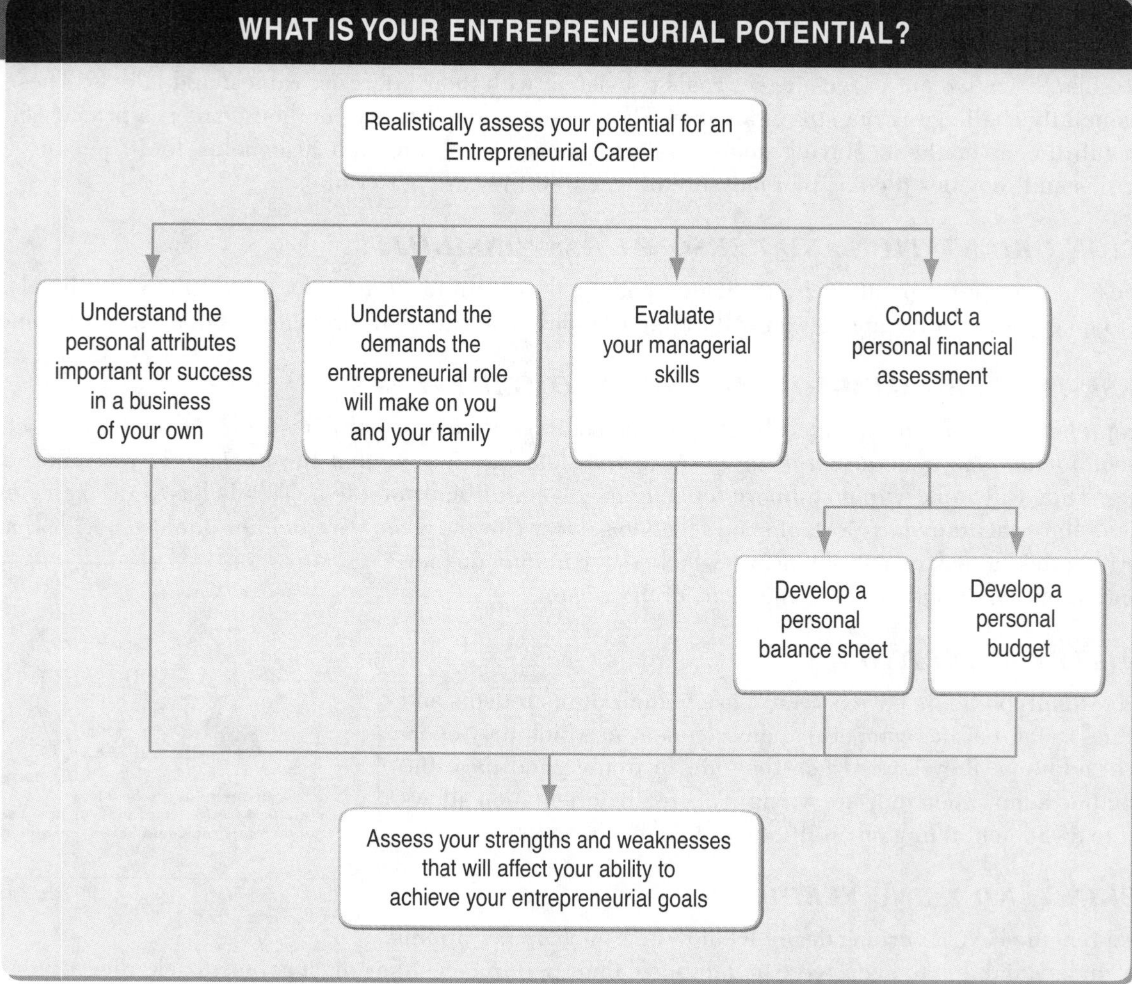

Other research has uncovered different lists of common learnable attributes. These qualities are also very desirable, in the people with whom entrepreneurs want to surround themselves in building a high-potential business.

Following is a summary of the attitudes and behaviours that can be valuable in turning a business dream into reality. The proposed characteristics represent the conclusions of over 50 separate research studies into the essential nature of the entrepreneur.

COMMITMENT, DETERMINATION, AND PERSEVERANCE

More than any other single factor, a combination of perseverance and total dedication is critical. In many cases these qualities have won out against odds considered impossible to overcome.

Determination and commitment can compensate for other weaknesses you may have. It requires substantial commitment to give up a well-paying job, with its regular paycheques, medical insurance, and pension and profit-sharing plans, and start out on your own.

SUCCESS ORIENTATION

Entrepreneurs are driven by an immense desire to achieve the goals they initially set for themselves and then to aim for even more challenging standards. The competitive needs of growth-minded entrepreneurs are to outperform their own previous best results, rather than just to outperform another person. Unlike most people, entrepreneurs do not allow themselves to be concerned with failure. What they think about is not what they are going to do if they don't make it, but what they have to do to succeed.

OPPORTUNITY AND GOAL ORIENTATION

Growth-minded entrepreneurs are more focused on the nature and extent of their opportunity rather than resources, structure, or strategy. They start with the opportunity and let their understanding of it guide these other important issues. Entrepreneurs are able to sense areas of unmet needs and their potential for filling these gaps. Effective entrepreneurs set goals consistent with their interests, values, and talents. These goals are generally challenging but still attainable. Their belief in the "reality" of their goals is a primary factor in their fulfillment of them. Having goals and a clear sense of direction also helps these persons define priorities and provides them with a measure of how well they are performing.

ACTION ORIENTATION AND PERSONAL RESPONSIBILITY

Successful entrepreneurs are action-oriented people; they want to start producing results immediately. They like to take the initiative and get on with doing it, today. The true entrepreneur is a doer, not a dreamer.

PERSISTENT PROBLEM-SOLVING, NEED TO ACHIEVE

Entrepreneurs are not intimidated by the number or severity of the problems they encounter. In fact, their self-confidence and general optimism seem to translate into a view that the impossible just takes a little longer. They will work with a stubborn tenacity to solve a difficult problem. This is based on their desire to achieve the goals they have established for themselves. However, they are neither aimless nor foolhardy in their relentless attack on a problem or obstacle that can impede their business, but tend to get right to the heart of the issue.

REALITY ORIENTATION

The best entrepreneurs have a keen sense of their own strengths and weaknesses and of the competitive environment in which they operate. In addition, they know when they are in trouble and have the strength to admit when they are wrong. This reality orientation allows them to avoid continuing on an ill-advised course of action.

"You don't have to be a loser, Todd. With hard work, determination, and a solid set of goals, you could become mediocre!"

SEEKING AND USING FEEDBACK

Entrepreneurs have a burning desire to know how they are performing. They understand that to keep score and improve their performance they must get feedback, digest the results, and use the information they receive to do a better job. In that way they can learn from their mistakes and setbacks and respond quickly to unexpected events. For the same reason, most entrepreneurs are found to be good listeners and quick learners.

SELF-RELIANCE

Successful entrepreneurs trust the fate of their ventures to their own abilities. They do not believe that external forces or plain luck determine their success or failure. This attribute is consistent with their achievement and motivational drive and desire to achieve established goals.

In a similar vein, entrepreneurs are not joiners. Studies have shown that the need for affiliation, or a high need for friendship, often acts as a deterrent to entrepreneurial behaviour.

SELF-CONFIDENCE

The self-confidence displayed by entrepreneurs is based on their feeling that they can overcome all the necessary challenges and attain their desired goal. They almost never consider failure a real possibility. While this self-confidence implies a strong ego, it is a different kind of ego — an "I know I'm going to do well" type of attitude.

TOLERANCE OF AMBIGUITY AND UNCERTAINTY

Entrepreneurs tolerate ambiguous situations well and make effective decisions under conditions of uncertainty. They are able to work well despite constant changes in their business that produce considerable ambiguity in every part of their operation.

Entrepreneurs take change and challenge in stride and actually seem to thrive on the fluidity and excitement of such undefined situations. Job security and retirement are generally not of great concern to them.

MODERATE RISK-TAKING AND RISK-SHARING

Despite the myth that suggests entrepreneurs are gamblers, quite the opposite is true. Effective entrepreneurs have been found, in general, to prefer taking moderate, calculated risks, where the chances of losing are neither so small as to be a sure thing nor so large as to be a considerable gamble. Like a parachutist, they are willing to take some measurable and predetermined risk.

The strategy of most entrepreneurs also includes involving other parties in their venture to share the burden of risk: Partners put money and reputations on the line; investors do likewise; and creditors and customers who advance payments, and suppliers who advance credit all share in the financial risk of the business.

RESPONSE TO FAILURE

Another important attribute of high-performance entrepreneurs is their ability to treat mistakes and failures as temporary setbacks on the way to accomplishing their goals. Unlike most people, the bruises of their defeats heal quickly. This allows them to return to the business world again soon after their failure.

Rather than hide from or dismiss their mistakes, entrepreneurs concede their errors and analyze the causes. They have the ability to come to terms with their mistakes, learn from them, correct them, and use them to prevent their recurrence. Successful entrepreneurs know that they have to take personal responsibility for either the success or the failure of their venture and not look for scapegoats when things do not work out. They know how to build on their successes and learn from their failures.

LOW NEED FOR STATUS AND POWER

Entrepreneurs derive great personal satisfaction from the challenge and excitement of creating and building their own business. They are driven by a high need for achievement rather than a desire for status and power. It is important, therefore, to recognize that power and status are a result of their activities and not the need that propels them.

In addition, when a strong need to control, influence, and gain power over other people characterizes the lead entrepreneur, more often than not the venture gets into trouble. A dictatorial and domineering management style makes it very difficult to attract and keep people in the business who are oriented toward achievement, responsibility, and results. Conflicts often erupt over who has the final say, and whose prerogatives are being infringed upon. Reserved parking spaces, the big corner office, and fancy automobiles become symbols of power and status that foster a value system and an organizational culture not usually conducive to growth. In such cases, the business's orientation toward its customers, its market, or its competitors is typically lost.

Successful entrepreneurs appear to have a capacity to exert influence on other people without formal power. They are skilled at "conflict resolution." They know when to use logic and when to persuade, when to make a concession and when to win one. In order to run a successful venture, entrepreneurs must learn to get along with many different constituencies, who often have conflicting aims — customers, suppliers, financial backers, and creditors, as well as partners and others inside the company.

INTEGRITY AND RELIABILITY

Long-term personal and business relationships are built on honesty and reliability. To survive in the long run, an approach of "Do what you say you are going to do!" is essential. With it the possibilities are unlimited. Investors, partners, customers, suppliers, and creditors all place a high value on these attributes. "Success" resulting from dishonest practices is really long-term failure. After all, anyone can lie, cheat, or steal and maybe get away with it once, but that is no way to build a successful entrepreneurial career.

TEAM BUILDER

Entrepreneurs who create and build successful businesses are not isolated, super-independent types of individuals. They do not feel they have to receive all of the credit for their success, nor do they feel they have to prove they did it all by themselves. Just the opposite situation actually tends to be true. Not only do they recognize that it is virtually impossible to build a substantial business by working alone, but they also actively build a team. They have an ability to inspire the people they attract to their venture by giving them responsibility and by sharing the credit for their accomplishments. This hero-making ability has been identified as a key attribute of many successful corporate managers as well.

TOP TEN CHARACTERISTICS OF SUCCESSFUL ENTREPRENEURS

1. **CREATIVITY** — have the ability to look at problems and needs from different angles and "think outside the box"
2. **GOAL ORIENTATED** — constantly set goals for themselves that challenge their creativity and strengths
3. **HARD WORKING** — willing to work long hours to complete tasks, go the extra mile
4. **COMMITMENT** — remain focused on an idea or task
5. **WILLING TO TAKE THE INITIATIVE** — always want to be first, do not sit back and wait for others to take the initiative
6. **SPIRIT OF ADVENTURE** — willing to try something new and different, pioneer
7. **POSITIVE ATTITUDE** — do no let minor setbacks hinder their progress towards their overall goal
8. **SELF-CONFIDENT** — believe in themselves and their idea
9. **PERSISTENCE** — keep working at a problem until they solve it or find an alternative
10. **NEED TO ACHIEVE** — strong desire to accomplish something in life and leave a legacy

In addition to these characteristics, other attributes that have been associated with successful entrepreneurs are the following:

1. They are determined to finish a project once it has been undertaken, even under difficult conditions.
2. They are dynamic individuals who do not accept the status quo and refuse to be restricted by habit and environment.
3. They are able to examine themselves and their ideas impartially.
4. They are not self-satisfied or complacent.
5. They are independent in making decisions while willing to listen to suggestions and advice from others.
6. They do not blame others or make excuses for their own errors or failures.
7. They have a rising level of aspirations and expectations.
8. They have a good grasp of general economic concepts.
9. They are mature, self-assured individuals who are able to interact well with people of varying personalities and values.
10. They are able to exercise control over their impulses and feelings.
11. They have the ability to make the very best of the resources at hand.

The consensus among most experts is that all of these personal characteristics can be worked on and improved through concerted practice and refinement. Some require greater effort than others, and much depends on an individual's strength of motivation and conviction to grow. Developing these attributes should not be very different from personal growth and learning in many other areas of your life.

THE NOT-SO-LEARNABLE CHARACTERISTICS

The attributes listed next are those that many experts consider to be innate, and thus not acquirable to any great degree. Fortunately the list is quite short. It is from these not-so-learnable characteristics that the conclusion that entrepreneurs are "born, not made" is principally derived. However, while possessing all these attributes would be beneficial, there are many examples of successful business pioneers who lacked some of these characteristics or who possessed them to only a modest degree:

1. High energy, good health, and emotional stability
2. Creativity and an innovative nature
3. High intelligence and conceptual ability
4. The ability to see a better future and a capacity to inspire others to see it

It is apparent from this discussion that entrepreneurs work from a different set of assumptions than most "ordinary" people. They also tend to rely more on mental attitudes and philosophies based on these entrepreneurial attributes than on specific skills or organizational concepts.

Many of these points are summed up in the "Entrepreneur's Creed," a general philosophy outlining the entrepreneurial approach to doing business.

AN ENTREPRENEUR'S CREED

1. Do what gives you energy—have fun.
2. Figure out how to make it work.
3. Anything is possible if you believe you can do it.
4. If you don't know it can't be done, then you'll go ahead and do it.
5. Be dissatisfied with the way things are—and look for ways to improve them.
6. Do things differently.
7. Businesses can fail. Successful entrepreneurs learn from failure—but keep the tuition low.
8. It's easier to beg for forgiveness than to ask for permission in the first place.
9. Make opportunity and results your obsession—not money.
10. Making money is even more fun than spending it.
11. Take pride in your accomplishments—it's contagious.
12. Sweat the details that are critical to success.
13. Make the pie bigger—don't waste time trying to cut smaller pieces.
14. Play for the long haul. It's rarely possible to get rich quickly.
15. Remember: Only the lead dog gets a change in scenery.

ANSWERS TO THE ENTREPRENEURIAL QUIZ

The answers provided in Table 2.1 for the Entrepreneurial Quiz represent the responses that best exemplify the spirit, attitudes, and personal views of proven, successful entrepreneurs. Here they are *not* arranged in numerical order (1–74) but by the characteristic that they are measuring (personal background, behaviour patterns, and lifestyle factors).

TABLE 2.1 ANSWERS TO ENTREPRENEURIAL QUIZ

Personal Background	
Most Desirable Response	*Question Number*
Rarely or No	30, 36, 37, 43
Mostly or Yes	17, 18, 23, 28, 32, 35, 28, 42, 44, 74
Behaviour Patterns	
Most Desirable Response	*Question Number*
Rarely or No	8, 9, 10, 11, 12, 14, 24, 39, 40, 48, 54, 57, 64, 65
Mostly or Yes	2, 4, 5, 6, 7, 13, 16, 20, 21, 22, 26, 27, 29, 31, 33, 41, 45, 46, 47, 49, 50, 52, 53, 55, 56, 58, 60, 61, 62, 66, 68, 69
Lifestyle Factors	
Most Desirable Response	*Question Number*
Rarely or No	25, 34, 51, 67, 71
Mostly or Yes	1, 3, 15, 19, 59, 63, 70, 72, 73

WHAT IS YOUR SCORE?

Answering this questionnaire will let you determine the extent to which your responses match those that best exemplify the spirit, attitudes, and personal views of proven, successful entrepreneurs. To determine your score, count the number of your responses that appear to be correct in Table 2.1 and mark it in Table 2.2. Your responses in Table 2.2 have also been arranged by the characteristic they are measuring (your personal background, behaviour patterns, and lifestyle factors).

TABLE 2.2 SELF-ASSESSMENT: RESULTS

	Number of Most Desirable Responses
Your Personal Background	/14
Your Behaviour Patterns	/46
Your Lifestyle Factors	/14
Total Number of Most Desirable Responses	/74

WHAT DOES YOUR SCORE MEAN?

The Entrepreneurial Quiz is *not* intended to predict or determine your likely success or failure. However, if you answer and score the questionnaire honestly, it will provide considerable insight into whether you have the attitudes, lifestyle, and behavioural patterns consistent with successful entrepreneurship.

The higher your number of most desirable responses, the more your responses agree with those of successful entrepreneurs. High levels of agreement indicate that you *may* have the "right stuff" to succeed in an entrepreneurial career. You should make certain, however, that your responses reflect your real opinions and attitudes.

The word *may* is highlighted above because of the overwhelming importance of one particular set of attributes/characteristics: commitment, determination, and perseverance. Scoring well on the test is not necessarily a guarantee of entrepreneurial success. Anything less than total commitment to your venture, and considerable determination and perseverance, will likely result in failure, regardless of the degree to which you may possess other important attributes. Your total commitment and determination to succeed helps convince others to "come along for the ride." If you are not totally committed, both financially and philosophically, to the venture, it is unlikely that potential partners, your employees, bankers, suppliers, and other creditors will have the confidence in you to provide the level of support your business will require.

FYI FOR YOUR INFORMATION

There are several other instruments available that will also enable you to assess your potential for an entrepreneurial career. You might check out:

"Am I an Entrepreneur?" Self-Assessment Quiz

This quiz will allow you to compare yourself with successful self-made business people on some key traits and characteristics. It provides a comprehensive individual assessment and will give you some insight into your own distinctive style. (www.wd.gc.ca/apps/amianent.nsf)

National Entrepreneurship Test

A light-hearted test from *PROFIT* magazine that enables you to rate your business potential. (www.profitguide.com/I/I1-01.asp)

Entrepreneurial Self Test

A questionnaire from the Business Development Bank of Canada on attitude and lifestyle that will enable you to assess how consistent your character is with that of proven successful entrepreneurs. (www.bdc.ca/scripts/site/display-tools.asp?&chk=1&language=eng&node_ID=40&module_ID=41&module_code=tools_self_assessment)

PERSONAL SELF-ASSESSMENT

The purpose of this discussion has been to have you evaluate your personal attitudes, behaviour tendencies, and views to determine the extent to which you seem to fit the typical entrepreneurial profile. Now you should complete Figure 2.2, the Personal Self-Assessment Questionnaire, which will help you summarize your feelings regarding your potential for self-employment.

Many of these attitudes are illustrated by the comments made by Tom Poole in Entrepreneurs in Action # 2 and Elizabeth Scott in Entrepreneurs in Action #3. Poole, for example, feels the principal character trait common to himself and other entrepreneurs is the "act of faith"—their strong belief that their concept or idea is "fantastic," and their readiness to jump in with both feet. Is this approach always successful? Of course not. But by being flexible and driven by a strong desire to "make it," he feels these individuals succeed more often than they should.

For Scott, business is a "gritty reality" involving constant responsibility and considerable stress rather than the glamorous lifestyle commonly perceived by the general public. Yet she and others like her are continually prepared to undertake such burdens. Why? Perhaps, she comments, it's the need to challenge themselves, to test their potential, to push the boundaries, reach goals, fulfill a mission, and make this wonderful world better. After all, she reflects, is this not the essence of an unbridled human spirit?

2 Entrepreneurs in action

The Entrepreneur Exposed

Over the years, people have asked me many questions about my business. But there are two questions I have found myself answering most often: "Why did you give up a promising career to leap into the world of the entrepreneur?" (which my father-in-law continues to ask me weekly) and, "Would you do it again?" For the longest time I was unable to provide good answers, and quite frankly, I never gave them much thought. However, as I grow older and perhaps more philosophical, I have pondered these questions. The answers are slowly beginning to take shape, and I believe my conclusions might shed some light on entrepreneurs in general.

I think the answers lie in a character trait common to most, if not all, entrepreneurs. By "entrepreneur," I do not mean the corporate executive who takes an early retirement package to start a home-based consulting business (not that there's anything wrong with that). I am talking about that crazy s.o.b. who quits his job as a C.A. and sells his mother to secure the capital needed to start a rubbish-collection company. Take a look around you at the entrepreneurs that you know. What do these people have in common? Are they all a little wacky? Eccentric? Unorthodox? Most likely; it goes with the territory.

If the prospective entrepreneur were reasonable and orthodox, he or she would use conventional methods of measuring the risk associated with giving up everything for a leap into the unknown. The consequence of conducting a proper "decision-tree" analysis would be that no one would ever take the step.

So how does an entrepreneur approach the "go/no-go" decision-making process? Well (at the risk of revealing that I never really had a master plan), I think the typical entrepreneur does some initial research, becomes absolutely convinced that his or her idea is fantastic, and jumps. This act of faith is the litmus test for entrepreneurs. Some people may decide that an idea is great but requires more research, and some spend years explaining to their friends how they had developed the concept long before Ms. X (who went on to make a fortune with the idea). But true entrepreneurs leap in with both feet.

I decided to jump in February 1989. I quit my high-paying, secure job with a multinational company, moved my wife and two and one-half children into a camper van, and set out to find a business to run. My gamble paid off — the company I eventually bought has grown from three employees, a 1,800 square-foot "factory" and $350,000 in annual sales to the current 800 employees, five production facilities and $80 million-plus in revenue.

Do entrepreneurs always succeed? Of course not. We simply don't hear as much about the failures. But entrepreneurs do succeed more often than circumstances suggest they should. Why? Often for what business schools call the "wrong" reasons: the speed of their decision-making, the dearth of analysis and the fact that they hold nothing back, financially, physically or emotionally. How do these seemingly irrational actions improve the chances of success? By acting quickly, the entrepreneur reduces the likelihood of having the idea "stolen"; the cursory analysis allows the entrepreneur to avoid an analysis-paralysis affliction; and by investing everything, the consequences of failure are so dire that . . . well, they just cannot afford to fail!

Am I suggesting that entrepreneurs are not always insightful business geniuses? Yes. Just take a look at how many entrepreneurs started out to make horse blankets and ended up making evening gowns. Their re-focus is seldom the unfolding of an elaborate business plan; rather, it is the result of the survival instinct kicking in. From experience I can tell you that there is no adage truer than "necessity is the mother of invention." When the wolf is at the door, ingenuity is indeed at its best.

Now back to the questions that I have been asked so many times over the years. First, why did I do it? Well, it was a "mix" of about one part crazy and two parts ignorance. And once I had taken the plunge, it was about 100 per cent fear. Most entrepreneurs, if pressed for an honest response, would likely acknowledge that their early days were not unlike mine.

Would I do it again? The answer is complicated. In this hypothetical situation, assuming I had the knowledge I have now, the answer is a categorical "No." Of course not. I would know that what I was undertaking was probably close to impossible. Equipped with this information, my analysis would result in a "no-go" decision. I may be crazy, but I'm not stupid!

But if you re-phrase the question and ask whether I would take another entrepreneurial plunge, the answer is "Yes, of course." Why? I think the Steve Martin film "Parenthood" contains the best answer to that question. Toward the end of the movie, a mother explains life to her risk-averse son (Martin). She tells of being young and going to the fair with his father. He always wanted to ride on the merry-go-round, while she preferred the roller coaster. On the merry-go-round, she explained, you saw the same things go by again and again. It became rather boring. The roller coaster, on the other hand, was exhilarating, sometimes even frightening. But once she had ridden the roller coaster, she could never go back to the merry-go-round.

So, having taken the plunge and ridden the roller coaster, I can never return to the merry-go-round. And to those of you who are riding the merry-go-round, mix yourself a cocktail consisting of one part crazy and two parts ignorance. Drink it in one gulp and go for the ride of your life.

Source: The Entrepreneur Exposed—Tom Poole of Sepp's Gourmet Foods Ltd. Profit Magazine Online, www.profitguide.com/firstperson/F1_poole.html. 12-07-01. Used with permission.

3 Entrepreneurs in action

Planet Entrepreneur

What galaxy was I visiting when I decided to become an entrepreneur!?

I ask this question every once in a while to relieve stress. For all the hype associated with entrepreneurship, the reality is anything but glamorous. The idea that entrepreneurs have plenty of time to enjoy foamy lattes, schmooze and parlay acquaintanceships into cash is largely fiction. Managing my business more often involves lunches at Taco Bell or Wrap-n-Go, with the odd flourish of warmth from a Second Cup coffee.

For an entrepreneur, responsibility, as Cervantes' Don Quixote says of death, perches forever upon the shoulder. It is a constant companion, an ever-present reminder of the impact decisions and actions can have on the business and on others.

Running a company is much like caring for a family — I have one of those too. Mornings begin with getting everyone organized and making sure my two sons get to school with full knapsacks and lunchbags. I then step delicately through the blanket of paper that is my office floor and begin the day. My relationship with WOMAN newsmagazine is my third 24-hour-a-day commitment. Since each was born, Ben and Byron have rested on one shoulder, WOMAN on the other.

Why do entrepreneurs undertake such burdens? Why are we compelled to initiate action, solve problems, produce results? I suspect every entrepreneur has a unique response. Perhaps it's the need to challenge ourselves, to test our potential, to push the boundaries, reach goals, fulfill a mission, make this wonderful world better. Is this not, after all, the essence of an unbridled human spirit?

In 1996 I launched WOMAN as a home-based business; I wanted to be in my own environment, accessible to my kids, do what I love and solve child-care dilemmas all at once. (Writing off the rent was also appealing.) But working from home is not for everyone. I sometimes long for a quiet place to go. But I've learned to work in close quarters with Super Nintendo. I've perfected focus, which has helped me manage the workload.

And there are small rewards. Ben and Byron sometimes join me at work-related events. Earlier this year, they came to a conference in Ottawa to listen to world-renowned women leaders. They found some speakers less than relevant, but not U.S. comedian Kathy Buckley. As she told of facing such monumental challenges as deafness, abuse and a tragic accident, her strength of spirit made a distinct impression, and may have instilled in them a new understanding of how I was able to launch WOMAN in the face of daunting odds.

Sharing the entrepreneurial experience with "the guys" somehow makes the responsibilities feel less onerous. Maybe the load seems lighter because I'm sharing it with people I care about. Which is why I've started to think maybe there is some truth in the perceptions that non-business owners have of entrepreneurs. For all the time we spend schmoozing and talking, negotiating and forming strategic alliances, underneath it all perhaps we're really reaching out to connect with someone to whom we think we may relate, to share our experiences, thoughts and self with another human being. (www.womanmag.com)

Source: Planet Entrepreneur by Elizabeth Scott. ***Profit Magazine***, November 1999. Used with permission.

WHAT KIND OF ENTREPRENEUR ARE YOU LIKELY TO BE?

As you can see from these few examples, not all entrepreneurs are the same. John Warrillow, a Toronto-based marketing consultant, spent three years interviewing more than 500 small business owners. He used that research to develop attitudinal profiles for three entrepreneurial archetypes:

CRAFTSPEOPLE: Comprise 60 per cent of small business owners and derive their sense of self-worth from their mastery of a craft or trade. While they don't think of themselves as entrepreneurs, they still have the resources and confidence to operate independently. They are more interested in developing their skills than growing their revenue and generally work alone or employ one other person, often a spouse.

FREEDOM FIGHTERS: They work hard to control their own destiny. That's because their prime motivator isn't growth, but simply being in business for themselves. They comprise 30 per cent of all small businesses and typically employ 3 to 50 staff and grow less than 30 per cent a year. More than half the freedom fighters are college educated, and 30 per cent are women. They are more likely to hire family and tend to treat their staff as family members.

MOUNTAIN CLIMBERS: They are the 10 per cent of growth-oriented business owners who are motivated almost solely by achievement, usually measured in terms of company growth. You can usually identify mountain climbers by the fact that their companies grow by more than 30 per cent annually. As a result, they are the most high profile and high-profit group. More than 75 per cent have college or university degrees. These go-getters work long hours, and expect a lot from themselves and their staff. Eighty-three per cent claim to be married.[1]

If you are planning to go into a business of your own, into which of these three groups do you think you would fall? Mountain climbers are the people we tend to read about in the newspapers and financial magazines and are likely to be the kind of individuals profiled throughout this book. It is important to recognize, however, that not everyone can or wants to be a mountain climber and there are many other opportunities for you to start a business and still be quite happy and do very well.

1. Kara Kuryllowicz, "What Kind of Entrepreneur are You?," *PROFIT: The Magazine for Canadian Entrepreneurs* (2000)

EVALUATING YOUR BUSINESS SKILLS

There is a lot more to succeeding as an entrepreneur than just having the proper background, attitudes, and lifestyle. This next section discusses another factor you should consider in assessing your potential for becoming a successful entrepreneur: Do you have the requisite managerial and administrative skills needed to manage and operate a business?

Possessing the necessary managerial skills is an essential ingredient to succeeding in any small venture. It is estimated the principal reason for the failure of small firms is poor management. Witness the experience of restaurateurs Richard Jaffray and Scott Morison (Entrepreneurs in Action #4). They thought they had learned a lot in building up their chain of Cactus Club Cafes in the lower mainland of British Columbia. They figured they "could do no wrong," decided to branch out, and opened four additional Clubs, two each in Calgary and Edmonton. Within six months, they knew they had a problem, and six months later it all fell apart.

What could have gone wrong for these relatively seasoned entrepreneurs? "Everything," says Jaffray. Restaurant locations were selected by price rather than by location as they had been in B.C. They changed the original concept of the restaurants and abandoned their long-time practice of grooming existing employees to take over the management of new restaurants. They neglected to take local culture into account and charged B.C. prices, which were 10 per cent to 20 per cent higher than comparable price levels in Alberta. In the end, three of the four Alberta locations were closed and the whole experience ended up costing them about $3 million.

Having learned their lesson and rebuilt the business in B.C., the pair are now looking to take their concept back into Alberta and also to the United States. This time they are not too worried. They feel they have been through it before and can be successful now. "Had we not gone right to the very bottom, I don't think we'd be as successful as we are today," says Jaffray.

4 Entrepreneurs in action

Rock Bottom and Back

It's 4:00 p.m. on a Monday, and business is booming in the newest uptown Vancouver location of Cactus Club Cafe. Hip young 20-somethings lounge in leather armchairs at tables surrounding a massive centrepiece mahogany bar, drinking Cactus Bellinis, a peach/rum/champagne/sangria slurpie billed as "better than sex." Others relax in plush leather booths next to massive windows framed with crushed velvet drapes. Still others gather around glowing-eyed gargoyle fountains, kibitzing with service staff as they sample diverse cuisine, ranging from jerk chicken and sea-salted fries to the Millionaire's Cut filet mignon.

It's an opulent yet informal, eclectic atmosphere that's become the tongue-in-cheek trademark of restaurateurs Richard Jaffray and Scott Morison. From the bawdy paintings in heavy gilt frames to the glass-enclosed courtyard, river-rock fireplaces and signature moose heads, the new $1.8-million restaurant is fanciful and fun. And that's a key component in Cactus Club's recipe for success, says Jaffray. The other ingredients? Innovative, high-quality food at a reasonable price, he says, and a service culture bent on entertaining customers. It's a formula that's proving popular with West Coast consumers, fuelling Cactus Club's growth into a 10-chain restaurant with 1998 sales of $20 million — up from $17 million in 1997.

But that success hasn't come without challenges. In 1996 an overzealous expansion into Alberta

PERRY ZAVITZ

brought the company to the brink of ruin. Opening four restaurants in less than 15 months without adequate research and preparation proved nearly fatal, says Jaffray. Undaunted by the near-disaster, the ambitious partners rolled up their sleeves to retrench and reorganize. The firm's 1999 sales are expected to climb to $24 million, says Jaffray, and the partners have set Cactus Club on a new course for steady yet cautious growth. Their long-term goal? No less than 200 restaurants across Western Canada and the U.S. in the next 20 years. "Our objective," says Jaffray, "is to be the best upscale, casual, fun restaurant in North America." A lofty ambition, perhaps, but one the partners are confident they can meet by learning from their past mistakes and adhering to the first rule of business: know thy customers.

In fact, that axiom was instrumental in Jaffray's decision to abandon his initial idea of launching a company that would offer party cruises upon arriving in Vancouver from Calgary in 1984. After living in his '74 Dodge Dart at a local beach for a month, he discovered that Vancouver's often inclement weather isn't well suited to cruising.

Instead Jaffray began waiting tables for Earl's Restaurants Ltd., a popular family-restaurant chain. It was there he met Morison, a fellow waiter and would-be entrepreneur. Eager to strike out on their own, two years later the then 21-year-olds hatched a plan to capitalize on the popularity of Expo 86, launching an ice cream and cappuccino bar called Café Cucamongas.

Revenues reached $250,000 in the first year, enough to attract the attention of the pair's former boss at Earl's, Stan Fuller. Impressed with the duo's enthusiasm and commitment, Fuller approached them in 1987 about a potential partnership in a new restaurant geared to a younger clientele. His timing was perfect, since Jaffray and Morison were already looking beyond Cucamongas. It was win-win, explains Jaffray. The partnership provided them with the capital they needed to develop a full-scale restaurant chain, plus access to Fuller's expertise and experience. In return, Earl's got an investment in a new market without having to manage it. The pair were even given access to Earl's budgets and financial statements. "It allowed us to see some of the inner workings of another organization," says Jaffray, "and the struggles they were going through."

Morison and Jaffray sold Cucamongas and wrangled a $225,000 bank loan, giving them enough cash to finance their half-share in the new venture. In March 1988, the first Cactus Club Café opened in club-starved North Vancouver. The concept was simple: to combine the best attributes of a pub, restaurant and nightclub in a single nightspot. The vision, says Jaffray, was to establish a restaurant that would become a local neighborhood handout, with its own character and vitality. A place where the food and atmosphere would entice customers into making a full night of it — not merely stop in for a drink or dinner.

Cactus Club seemed to fit the bill. Its quirky decor, music, party atmosphere and progressive menu proved popular with hip consumers. The menu featured Vancouver firsts such as tortilla wraps and microbrewed beer on tap. Staff, hired as much for their outgoing personalities as their waiting skills, were encouraged to engage and entertain customers. One waiter proved especially adept, for instance, at organizing an impromptu limbo contest. By 1995 Cactus Club had grown to include five restaurants in the lower mainland. "We could do no wrong," says Jaffray.

Emboldened, in 1996 Jaffray and Morison decided to branch out, opening four Cactus Clubs, two each in Calgary and Edmonton. "Within six months, we knew we were headed for trouble big time," says Jaffray. "Six months later, it all fell apart."

What went wrong? "Everything," says Jaffray. For starters, restaurant locations were chosen not by market research as they were in B.C., says Jaffray, but by price. They tweaked their original concept and ended up with more of a bar than a fun eatery. A longtime practice of grooming existing staff to take over the management of new restaurants was abandoned; they neglected to take into account local cultures such as Edmonton's tradition of "happy hour" discount drinks. Plus, they charged B.C. prices — 10% to 20% above local price points — despite the fact that Alberta costs were lower. Unimpressed by the West Coast whiz kids, customers stayed away.

Staunching mounting losses in Alberta consumed the pair's attention. The inevitable result — sales flatlined and even dropped for their B.C. locations. "We were trying to put out a fire in the corner," says Jaffray, "but in the meantime the whole house was burning down." Within a year of opening in Alberta, they realized they would have to cut their losses or lose everything.

In the end, three of the four Alberta locations were closed. "The whole exercise cost about $3 million." says Jaffray. "We've been paying it off for four years."

Fuller is impressed with the pair's courage. "To their credit, they rolled up their sleeves and changed direction," he says. "They went back to what they knew and then made it better, and worked themselves out of the hole." Indeed, getting back on track meant building change into the company's overall management philosophy. The menu for example, which had remained the same for two years, is now changed twice a year. Menu covers are updated every six weeks. To foster a team spirit and keep their 800 employees informed on the company's progress, Jaffray and Morison now practice open-book management. Staff are encouraged to use their own creativity when it comes to service, and managers are responsible for establishing and regularly updating goals. These initiatives seem to be working. Today Cactus Club's nine restaurants are all profitable, and posting annual sales increases of 5% to 22% for the past three years.

While Jaffray and Morison remain cautious about again expanding into a new market, they aren't overly worried. They've been through this before. "Had we not gone right to the very bottom, I don't think we'd be as successful as we are today," says Jaffray. "We now know all the things that can go wrong."

Source: Diane Luckow, "Rockbottomandback," *PROFIT*, April, 1999, pp. 53-55. Reprinted with permission.

WHAT SKILLS ARE NEEDED BY SMALL-BUSINESS OWNERS?

Businesses, whether large or small, have to perform a number of diverse functions to operate successfully. An entrepreneur, because of the limited amount of resources (human and financial) at his or her disposal, faces a particularly difficult time.

The business skills required by an entrepreneur (or some other member of the organization) can be broken down by function, as shown in Table 2.3.

TABLE 2.3 BREAKDOWN OF ENTREPRENEURIAL BUSINESS SKILLS

1. **Managing Money**
   a. Borrowing money and arranging financing
   b. Keeping financial records
   c. Managing cash flow
   d. Handling credit
   e. Buying insurance
   f. Reporting and paying taxes
   g. Budgeting
2. **Managing people**
   a. Hiring employees
   b. Supervising employees
   c. Training employees
   d. Evaluating employees
   e. Motivating people
   f. Scheduling workers
3. **Directing business operations**
   a. Purchasing supplies and raw materials
   b. Purchasing machinery and equipment
   c. Managing inventory
   d. Filling orders
   e. Managing facilities
4. **Directing sales and marketing operations**
   a. Identifying different customer needs
   b. Developing new product and service ideas
   c. Deciding appropriate prices
   d. Developing promotional strategies
   e. Contacting customers and making sales
   f. Developing promotional material and media programs
5. **Setting up a business**
   a. Choosing a location
   b. Obtaining licences and permits
   c. Choosing a form of organization and type of ownership
   d. Arranging initial financing
   e. Determining initial inventory requirements

WHERE CAN YOU ACQUIRE THE NECESSARY SKILLS?

It should be apparent from this lengthy list that few people can expect to have a strong grasp of all of these skills prior to considering an entrepreneurial career. The key question then becomes where and how you can acquire these skills. The available means for developing these business skills are outlined below.

JOB EXPERIENCE

Every job you have had should have contributed to the development of some business skills. For example, working as an accountant might teach you:

1. How to prepare financial statements
2. How to make financial projections and manage money
3. How to determine the business's cash requirements, among other things

Working as a sales clerk might teach you:

1. How to sell
2. How to deal with the public
3. How to operate a cash register

Perhaps the best experience, however, is working for another entrepreneur. In that case you will learn to understand the overall process and skills required to operate your own business.

CLUB ACTIVITIES

Many of the functions that service clubs and similar organizations perform in planning and developing programs are similar to those performed by small businesses. Some examples of what can be learned from volunteer activities are:

1. How to organize and conduct fundraising activities
2. How to promote the organization through public service announcements and free advertising
3. How to manage and coordinate the activities of other members of the organization

EDUCATION

Universities, community colleges, and high schools, and government agencies such as local business development organizations and the Business Development Bank of Canada, provide many programs and individual courses in which essential business-related skills can be acquired. Some examples of applicable skills which can be learned from these programs include:

1. Business skills (from particular business classes)
2. Socialization and communication skills (from all school activities)
3. Bookkeeping and record-keeping skills (from accounting classes)

YOUR FRIENDS

Most of us have friends who through their job experience and education can teach us valuable business skills. Some examples of useful information we may acquire from this source are:

1. Possible sources of financing
2. Assistance in selecting an appropriate distribution channel for your products
3. Information on the availability of appropriate sites or locations for your business
4. Sources for finding suitable employees

YOUR FAMILY

Growing up with an entrepreneur in the family is perhaps the best learning experience of all, even though you may not be aware of the value of this experience at the time. Some examples of what you might learn from other members of your family are:

1. How to deal with challenges and problems
2. How to make personal sacrifices and why
3. How to keep your personal life and business life separate
4. How to be responsible with money

HOME EXPERIENCES

Our everyday home experiences help us develop many business skills. Some examples of such skills are:

1. Budgeting income
2. Planning finances
3. Organizing activities and events
4. Buying wisely
5. Managing and dealing with people
6. Selling an idea

It can be hard for a single individual to wear all these "hats" at once. Partnerships or the use of outside technical or general business assistance can be an excellent supplement for any deficiencies in characteristics and skills a small business owner may have. Thus, it often becomes essential to identify an individual, or individuals, who can help you when needed. This outside assistance might come from one of the following sources:

1. A spouse or family member
2. A formal partnership arrangement
3. Hired staff and employees
4. External professional consultants
5. A formal course or training program
6. Regular idea exchange meetings or networking with other entrepreneurs

INVENTORY OF YOUR MANAGERIAL AND ADMINISTRATIVE SKILLS

Now that you understand the range of skills necessary to enable your new business to succeed, the Managerial Skills Inventory in Figure 2-3 can be used to develop an inventory of your skills and capabilities in several aspects of management. Your present level of expertise may be anything from minimal to having a great deal of skill. The goal of the inventory is to assess your present skills, with the purpose of identifying areas that may need improvement. Since each of these management skills is not required at an equivalent level in all new business situations, completing this inventory might also provide you with some insight into the type of business opportunities for which you are best suited.

ASSESSING YOUR PERSONAL FINANCIAL SITUATION

In addition to your managerial capabilities, your financial capacity will be a very important consideration in your decision as to whether an entrepreneurial career is right for you. It will certainly be a critical factor to those you may approach for a loan to provide investment capital for your venture.

YOUR PERSONAL BALANCE SHEET

Your personal balance sheet provides potential lenders with a view of your overall financial situation so they can assess the risk they will be assuming. Generally, if you are in a strong financial position, as indicated by a considerable net worth, you will be considered a desirable prospect. On the other hand, an entrepreneur with a weak financial position and a large number of outstanding debts may not meet the standards of most lenders.

From a personal standpoint, you might also want to reconsider becoming a small-business owner if you cannot afford a temporary or perhaps even a prolonged reduction in your personal income.

Your personal balance sheet includes a summary of all your assets — what you own that has some cash value — and your liabilities or debts. Preparing a personal balance sheet is a relatively simple process:

- **Step 1** Estimate the current market value of all your "assets" — the items you own that have cash value — and list them.
- **Step 2** Add up the value of these assets.
- **Step 3** List all your debts, also known as "liabilities."
- **Step 4** Add up your liabilities.
- **Step 5** Deduct your total liabilities from your total assets to find your "net worth."

Figure 2-4 shows a Sample Balance Sheet Form that you can use to help organize your assets and liabilities. The items listed are not exhaustive; the form is provided only as a guide for thinking about your present position. Since every business opportunity has its own unique capital (money) requirements, there is no specific dollar value for the personal net worth necessary to start a business. However, you should keep in mind that most private lenders or lending institutions typically expect a new small-business owner to provide at least 40 to 50 per cent of the capital required for start-up. In addition, lenders consider the net worth position of prospective borrowers to determine their ability to repay the loan should the new business fail.

In Entrepreneurs in Action #5 for example, consider the "Financial Snapshot" provided for Carlyle Jansen. Jansen is a young person who has recently gone into a business of her own. The Snapshot illustrates a typical financial position for someone in that situation with relatively few other assets. She does, however, have the advantage of having received a small inheritance from a number of great-aunts, which has been invested in a variety of mutual funds and used as collateral for a line of credit to provide the working capital to run her business. Her only liability is a $10,000 loan she obtained from her family to acquire the equity interest in her business. Her balance sheet shows a nominal net worth of just over $27,000, which leaves her a long way from her long-term goal of being able to retire and not be poor.

5 Entrepreneurs in action

A Business for Her

Visit Toronto's Harbord Street between Spadina and Bathurst and you'll find one of the city's most intriguing retail strips. Among the shops are the venerable Toronto Women's Book Store, which opened nearly a quarter-century ago, along with Parentbooks, WonderWorks (which focuses on nature and spirituality), Drum Travel Co-operative, responsible-tourism experts, and, since May 1997, Good For Her, a store devoted to "Celebrating Women's Sexuality."

Discreetly tucked into a house-turned-retail-outlet, Good For Her offers "women and their admirers a cozy, comfortable place" to buy educational and erotic books, videos and magazines, condoms, lubricants and the like. The store also hosts workshops and seminars (sample titles: "Women's Sex Toys 101," "Herbal Aphrodisiacs and Sensual Oils," "Midlife, Menopause and Sexuality").

Good For Her is the dream child of 32-year-old Carlyle Jansen, and it's a business that's very much an outgrowth of its founder's story. Born in Toronto to two doctors, Jansen grew up in middle-class comfort. Inheritances from five great-aunts financed her arrival in 1984 at the University of British Columbia. She recalls, "I didn't know what I wanted to do, but I knew I didn't want to go into business." She embarked on an arts degree, then laughs heartily as she explains, "I really don't remember applying, but in second year, I found myself in the Faculty of Commerce."

Here, Jansen discovered her interest in small business. She graduated in 1990 with a Bachelor of Commerce and a specialization in organizational behavior. By then, she'd also spent time with the Canada World Youth Program in Prince Edward Island and on a cultural exchange in Sri Lanka. In addition, she had lived at L'Arche Daybreak in Richmond Hill, Ont., a community for adults with developmental disabilities and those who wish to live and learn with them.

Jansen went on to complete the Canadian Securities Course. Her first job on graduation was in Old Crow, a Yukon community north of the Arctic Circle, where she worked for the local First Nations government, helping to establish sound accounting practices and later with land-claims negotiations. In Old Crow, Jansen met a number of people dealing with alcoholism and other social challenges, and inspired by their work, she went to Edmonton in 1992 to take the training required to become a life-skills coach. However, work in the field did not materialize, and after stints as a bicycle courier and waitress, she moved to Seattle in January 1993. Financed by an RESP held by her parents, Jansen took a master's degree at Antioch University in whole-systems design, focusing on how more effective interaction can be encouraged in educational settings.

In May 1995, Jansen attended a bridal shower in Toronto for her sister. Her gift was a selection of sex toys—definitely an unconventional choice—but far from being shocked, her sister's friends wanted to know all about them. In fact, they were so impressed by Jansen's knowledge and ease, they told her she should start giving seminars on the topic.

At the same time, her studies at Antioch were helping her hone the communication and education skills she'd been developing ever since taking up her specialty in organizational behavior at UBC.

When she realized her chosen field was overcrowded, she decided to take her sister's friends' advice. That group of women became the first to attend one of what Jansen called "Playshops in Sensuality for Women." Although the playshops never brought in a proper income, Jansen still had inheritance money from her UBC days, and an inexpensive living arrangement with her mother.

Meanwhile, the playshop participants repeatedly told Jansen they wanted to be able to buy the products she was showing them in an environment they found comfortable. Jansen's life changed yet again. In May 1996, she began doing the research that culminated in the opening of Good For Her. She designed a two-year business plan that accurately predicted her sales and expenses to date, and she has recently updated the plan.

Good For Her was launched with family money — Jansen holds personal liability for $10,000 she borrowed to buy her own common shares (and thus all voting rights) in the business. In addition, preferred shares were sold to family members. Jansen plans to buy them back at some point; she realizes she'll need a consultation with her accountant to determine whether the buyback should be done by herself or the corporation. The preferred shares will eventually be repaid with dividends — in a relaxed kind of way. "That's the great thing about family," says Jansen. "I'll pay dividends when I can afford it."

While the store isn't turning much of a profit yet, Jansen is able to support herself on its proceeds and has hired some part-time help as well. The salary she draws is modest — $1,200 per month — but her current low rent of $400 per month in the apartment she shares with a roommate helps her make do.

The inheritance money she's husbanded so carefully over the years also comes in handy now that Jansen's in business. Invested in mutual funds with a current value of $25,000, Jansen uses it as collateral against a line of credit. The corporation, she explains, pays prime plus 1%, but her fund earns money at a higher rate. In addition, Jansen has $11,000 in RRSPs: 80% held in the Ethical Growth fund, the remainder in foreign vehicles. She admits she's "not really able to save money right now." But she doesn't have grand plans for old age: "I just want to be able to retire and not be poor."

Jansen isn't driven by money, but she does want also eventually to garner enough spare money and time to raise a family. Currently she puts in a 60-hour week handling sales, managing relations with over 100 suppliers and organizing workshops and seminars hosted by the store. She hopes that as Good For Her becomes established, she'll be able to whittle that commitment down to 30 hours per week. She wants her future children to have "access to what I had access to." That means, at the very least, a university education. Her plan doesn't involve a family homestead, though. She has no desire for home ownership, considering herself better off with extra cash and no repair bills. "Houses sometimes appreciate and sometimes don't," she explains. "That's true for mutual funds, too, but I think the batting average there is better."

As is obvious by now, Jansen isn't driven by money. In fact, she asserts, "I can live cheaply," and she doesn't mind doing it. What's really important is having enough to allow her to fulfil her dreams of raising a family and continuing the work that Good For Her represents: "I see women's sexuality as always being important to me. So many women want resources and information to feel comfortable about their sexuality." (www.goodforher.com/)

FINANCIAL SNAPSHOT

Income	
14,000	Income from business
1,200	Income from investments
$15,600	**Total income**
Expenses	
4,800	Rent
240	Deductions
1,369	Income tax
1,200	RRSP contributions
2,400	Food
1,800	Entertainment
635	Household expenses
600	Clothing
900	Investments
240	Gifts
600	Vacation
240	Educational expenses
576	Club memberships
$15,600	**Total expenditure**
Assets	
1,200	Furnishings
11,000	RRSPs
25,000	Investments
$37,200	**Total**
Liabilities	
10,000	Family loan
$10,000	**Total**
$27,200	**Net worth**

Source: Sibylle Preuschat, "A Business for Her," *The Financial Post Magazine*, February, 1999, pp. 63-65. Reprinted with permission.

DEVELOPING A PERSONAL BUDGET

As well as determining your present net worth, you must also consider your personal living expenses when assessing your ability to provide the total financing needed to start a new business. In fact, you should evaluate your personal financial needs while in the process of determining whether an entrepreneurial career is right for you.

In some situations you will need to take money from the business each month to pay part or all of your personal living expenses. If such is the case, it is crucial that this amount be known and that at least that much be set aside to be paid out to you each month as a salary.

If your new business is starting off on a limited scale, you might wish to continue holding a regular job to cover your basic living expenses and provide some additional capital to your fledgling operation. In some cases, your spouse's income may be sufficient to cover the family's basic living expenses and it may not be necessary to consider your personal financial needs in making a go/no go decision.

Carlyle Jansen's Financial Snapshot also illustrates her annual expenses in relation to her annual income of $15,600. She only takes a modest salary of $1,200 a month from the business since her living expenses are very low and she figures she can live "cheaply" and doesn't mind doing it. Her largest expenses are for rent ($400/month), food ($200/month) and income tax ($150/month). Her other expenses are very small and probably much lower than a typical middle-class person living in Toronto. She has recently sold her car but has not made any financial provision for transportation. This may create a real problem for her should she decide to replace it. It is estimated that it costs roughly $4,000 a year to maintain a car in the city and she hadn't made any provision for this level of expense in her budget.

The Personal Living Expenses Worksheet shown in Figure 2.5 is an effective means of estimating your present cost of living. From the totals on the worksheet, you can calculate the minimum amount of money you and your family will require on a regular monthly basis and determine from what sources this regular income will be obtained.

ARE YOU READY FOR AN ENTREPRENEURIAL CAREER?

EXTERNAL ROLE DEMANDS

It is not enough simply to possess a large number and high level of the characteristics previously discussed as prerequisites for a successful entrepreneurial career. There are also certain external conditions, pressures, and demands inherent in the small-business ownership role itself.

While successful entrepreneurs may share several characteristics with successful people in other careers, entrepreneurs' preference for and tolerance of the combination of requirements unique to their role is a major distinguishing feature.

Many of these requirements have been alluded to earlier. What follows is a discussion of a few of the most relevant issues you should consider concerning your degree of readiness and preparedness for such a career.

NEED FOR TOTAL COMMITMENT

As an entrepreneur you must live with the challenge of trying first to survive in the business world, then to stay alive, and always to grow and withstand the competitive pressures of the marketplace. Almost any venture worth considering requires top priority on your time, emotions, and loyalty. As an entrepreneur you must be prepared to give "all you've got" to the building of your business, particularly during the initial stages of its development. Anything less than total commitment will likely result in failure.

MANAGEMENT OF STRESS

Stress, the emotional and physiological reaction to external events or circumstances, is an inevitable result of pursuing an entrepreneurial career option. Depending on how it is handled, stress can be either good or bad for an entrepreneur. The better you understand how you react to stressful situations, the better you will be able to maximize the positive aspects of these situations and minimize the negative aspects, such as exhaustion and frustration, before they lead to a serious problem.

Stress, in the short term, can produce excellent results, because of its relationship to the type of behaviour associated with entrepreneurial activities, especially during the start-up stage of a new business. There is some evidence that once individuals become accustomed to producing under stressful conditions, they seem to continue to respond in a positive manner; entrepreneurs tend to create new challenges to replace the ones they have already met, and to continue to respond to those challenges with a high level of effectiveness.

ECONOMIC AND PERSONAL VALUES

Entrepreneurs engaged in "for-profit" as opposed to social or "not-for-profit" organizations must share the basic values of the free enterprise system: private ownership, profits, capital gains, and growth. These dominant economic values need not exclude social or other values. However, the nature of the competitive market economy requires belief in, or at least respect for, these values.

A FINAL ANALYSIS

The Entrepreneurial Assessment Questionnaire in Figure 2.6 is designed to help you recap your thinking concerning what you need to become a successful entrepreneur. The questions involve considerations at various stages of a business's development, and some may not be applicable to the stage you have currently reached in your business planning. However, you should answer all applicable questions.

If you have answered all the questions carefully, you've done some hard work and serious thinking. That's a positive step. If your answer to most of the questions was yes, you are on the right track. If you answered no to some questions you have more work to do; these questions indicate areas where you need to know more or that you need to do something about. Do what you can for yourself, but don't hesitate to ask for help from other sources.

This assessment of your entrepreneurial potential is based on a series of self-evaluations, and for it to reveal anything meaningful an absolute requirement is for you to be completely honest with yourself. This, however, is only the first step. The road to entrepreneurship is strewn with hazards and pitfalls and many who start on it fall by the wayside for one reason or another. However, those who persevere and reach the end by building a successful venture may realize considerable financial and psychological rewards as well as a lot of personal satisfaction.

The remainder of this book can help you evaluate other important parts of this process and improve your chances for success. It will help you decide what else you need to consider and enable you to go after it. Good luck!

FIGURE 2.1 ENTREPRENEURIAL QUIZ

Below are a number of questions dealing with your personal background, behavioural characteristics, and lifestyle patterns. Psychologists, venture capitalists, and others believe these to be related to entrepreneurial success. Answer each question by placing an X in the space that best reflects your personal views and attitudes. The most important result of this exercise will be an honest, accurate self-assessment of how you relate to each of these dimensions.

	Rarely or no	Mostly or yes
1. Are you prepared to make sacrifices in your family life and take a cut in pay to succeed in business?	____	____
2. Are you the kind of individual that once you decide to do something you'll do it and nothing can stop you?	____	____
3. When you begin a task, do you set clear goals and objectives for yourself?	____	____
4. When faced with a stalemated situation in a group setting, are you usually the one who breaks the logjam and gets the ball rolling again?	____	____
5. Do you commonly seek the advice of people who are older and more experienced than you are?	____	____

	Rarely or no	Mostly or yes
6. Even though people tell you "It can't be done" do you still have to find out for yourself?	______	______
7. When you do a good job, are you satisfied in knowing personally that the job has been well done?	______	______
8. Do you often feel, "That's just the way things are and there's nothing I can do about it"?	______	______
9. Do you need to know that something has been done successfully before, prior to trying it yourself?	______	______
10. Do you intentionally try to avoid situations where you have to converse with strangers?	______	______
11. Do you need a clear explanation of a task before proceeding with it?	______	______
12. Are you a good loser in competitive activities?	______	______
13. After a severe setback in a project, are you able to pick up the pieces and start over again?	______	______
14. Do you like the feeling of being in charge of other people?	______	______
15. Do you enjoy working on projects which you know will take a long time to complete successfully?	______	______
16. Do you consider ethics and honesty to be important ingredients for a successful career in business?	______	______
17. Have you previously been involved in starting things like service clubs, community organizations, charitable fund-raising projects, etc.?	______	______
18. Did your parents or grandparents ever own their own business?	______	______
19. When you think of your future do you ever envision yourself running your own business?	______	______
20. Do you try to do a job better than is expected of you?	______	______
21. Do you make suggestions about how things might be improved on your job?	______	______
22. Are you usually able to come up with more than one way to solve a problem?	______	______
23. Are you between 25 and 40 years of age?	______	______
24. Do you worry about what others think of you?	______	______
25. Do you read a lot of books, particularly fiction?	______	______
26. Do you take risks for the thrill of it?	______	______
27. Do you find it easy to get others to do something for you?	______	______
28. Has someone in your family shared his or her experience in starting a business with you?	______	______
29. Do you believe in organizing your tasks before getting started?	______	______
30. Do you get sick often?	______	______
31. Do you enjoy doing something just to prove you can?	______	______
32. Have you ever been fired from a job?	______	______

continued

Entrepreneurial Quiz — continued	**Rarely or no**	**Mostly or yes**
33. Do you find yourself constantly thinking up new ideas?	______	______
34. Do you prefer to let a friend decide on your social activities?	______	______
35. Did you like school?	______	______
36. Were you a very good student?	______	______
37. Did you "hang out" with a group in high school?	______	______
38. Did you actively participate in school activities or sports?	______	______
39. Do you like to take care of details?	______	______
40. Do you believe there should be security in a job?	______	______
41. Will you deliberately seek a direct confrontation to get needed results?	______	______
42. Were you the firstborn child?	______	______
43. Was your father or another older male generally present during your early life at home?	______	______
44. Were you expected to do odd jobs at home before 10 years of age?	______	______
45. Do you get bored easily?	______	______
46. Are you sometimes boastful about your accomplishments?	______	______
47. Can you concentrate on one subject for extended periods of time?	______	______
48. Do you, on occasion, need pep talks from others to keep you going?	______	______
49. Do you find unexpected energy resources as you tackle things you like?	______	______
50. Does personal satisfaction mean more to you than having money to spend on yourself?	______	______
51. Do you enjoy socializing regularly?	______	______
52. Have you ever deliberately exceeded your authority at work?	______	______
53. Do you try to find the benefits in a bad situation?	______	______
54. Do you blame others when something goes wrong?	______	______
55. Do you enjoy tackling a task without knowing all the potential problems?	______	______
56. Do you persist when others tell you it can't be done?	______	______
57. Do you take rejection personally?	______	______
58. Do you believe you generally have a lot of good luck that explains your successes?	______	______
59. Are you likely to work long hours to accomplish a goal?	______	______
60. Do you enjoy being able to make your own decisions on the job?	______	______
61. Do you wake up happy most of the time?	______	______
62. Can you accept failure without admitting defeat?	______	______
63. Do you have a savings account and other personal investments?	______	______
64. Do you believe that entrepreneurs take a huge risk?	______	______
65. Do you feel that successful entrepreneurs must have advanced college degrees?	______	______

	Rarely or no	Mostly or yes
66. Do you strive to use past mistakes as a learning process?	______	______
67. Are you more people-oriented than goal-oriented?	______	______
68. Do you find that answers to problems come to you out of nowhere?	______	______
69. Do you enjoy finding an answer to a frustrating problem?	______	______
70. Do you prefer to be a loner when making a final decision?	______	______
71. Do your conversations discuss people more than events or ideas?	______	______
72. Do you feel good about yourself in spite of criticism by others?	______	______
73. Do you sleep as little as possible?	______	______
74. Did you ever have a small business of your own while in school?	______	______

Adapted from Judy Balogh et al., *Beyond a Dream: An Instructor's Guide for Small Business Explorations* (Columbus: Ohio State University, 1985), pp. 26–28.

FIGURE 2.2 PERSONAL SELF-ASSESSMENT QUESTIONNAIRE

1. What personal weaknesses did you discover from analyzing your responses to the questionnaire?

____

____

____

____

2. Do you feel you can be an entrepreneur in spite of these weaknesses?

____

____

____

____

____

3. What can you do to improve your areas of weakness?

____

____

____

____

4. What did the questionnaire indicate as your strengths?

____

____

____

____

____

5. Do your strengths compensate for your weaknesses?

6. Does your lifestyle appear to be compatible with the demands of an entrepreneurial career?

FIGURE 2.3 MANAGERIAL SKILLS INVENTORY

The following questionnaire can be used to develop an inventory of your skills and capabilities in each of the five areas of management outlined in this Stage. For each management area, the questionnaire lists some corresponding skills. Rate your present level of expertise for each skill listed by placing an "X" under the appropriate number in the charts below (1 indicates minimal skill, while 5 indicates a great deal of skill). Beneath each section, in the space provided, briefly describe where and when you obtained this experience.

The goal of this inventory is to assess the level of your present skills, with the purpose of identifying areas which may need improvement.

MONEY MANAGEMENT	1	2	3	4	5
Borrowing money and arranging financing	☐	☐	☐	☐	☐
Keeping financial records	☐	☐	☐	☐	☐
Cash flow management	☐	☐	☐	☐	☐
Handling credit	☐	☐	☐	☐	☐
Buying insurance	☐	☐	☐	☐	☐
Reporting and paying taxes	☐	☐	☐	☐	☐
Budgeting	☐	☐	☐	☐	☐

Describe where and when you obtained this expertise.

MANAGING PEOPLE	1	2	3	4	5
Hiring employees	☐	☐	☐	☐	☐
Supervising employees	☐	☐	☐	☐	☐
Training employees	☐	☐	☐	☐	☐
Evaluating employees	☐	☐	☐	☐	☐
Motivating people	☐	☐	☐	☐	☐
Scheduling workers	☐	☐	☐	☐	☐

Describe where and when you obtained this expertise.

DIRECTING BUSINESS OPERATIONS	1	2	3	4	5
Purchasing supplies and raw materials	☐	☐	☐	☐	☐
Purchasing machinery and equipment	☐	☐	☐	☐	☐
Managing inventory	☐	☐	☐	☐	☐
Filling orders	☐	☐	☐	☐	☐
Managing facilities	☐	☐	☐	☐	☐

Describe where and when you obtained this expertise.

DIRECTING SALES AND MARKETING OPERATIONS	1	2	3	4	5
Identifying different customer needs	☐	☐	☐	☐	☐
Developing new product and service ideas	☐	☐	☐	☐	☐
Deciding appropriate prices	☐	☐	☐	☐	☐
Developing promotional strategies	☐	☐	☐	☐	☐
Contacting customers and making sales	☐	☐	☐	☐	☐
Developing promotional material and a media program	☐	☐	☐	☐	☐

Describe where and when you obtained this expertise.

SETTING UP A BUSINESS	1	2	3	4	5
Choosing a location	☐	☐	☐	☐	☐
Obtaining licences and permits	☐	☐	☐	☐	☐
Choosing a form of organization and type of ownership	☐	☐	☐	☐	☐
Arranging initial financing	☐	☐	☐	☐	☐
Determining initial inventory requirements	☐	☐	☐	☐	☐

Describe where and when you obtained this expertise.

FIGURE 2.4 SAMPLE BALANCE SHEET FORM

Name: ______________________________

BALANCE SHEET
as of

______________ ________ ________
(Month) (Day) (Year)

ASSETS

Cash & cash equivalents

Cash	________	
Chequing/savings	________	
Canada Savings Bonds	________	
Treasury bills	________	
Short-term deposits	________	
Money market funds	________	
Other	________	
Subtotal		________

Business/property

Investment property	________	
Business Interests	________	
Subtotal		________

Registered assets

RRSPs	________	
Employer's pension plan (RPP)		
RRIFs	________	
DPSPs	________	
Other	________	
Subtotal		________

Personal Property

Home	________	
Seasonal home	________	
Cars and/or other vehicles	________	
Equipment	________	
Collectibles (art)	________	
Jewelry	________	
Household furnishings	________	
Subtotal		________

Investments

GICs and term deposits	________	
Mutual funds	________	
Stocks	________	
Bonds	________	
Life insurance (cash surrender value)	________	
Provincial stock savings plan	________	
Subtotal		________
TOTAL		________**(A)**

LIABILITIES

Short-term

Credit card debt	______	
Personal line of credit, margin account	______	
Instalment loans (e.g., car, furniture, personal loans)	______	
Demand loans	______	
Loans for investment purposes	______	
Tax owing (income and property)	______	
Other	______	
Subtotal		______

Long-term

Mortgage — home	______	
Mortgage — seasonal home	______	
Mortgage — investment property	______	
Other	______	
Subtotal		______
TOTAL		______**(B)**

NET WORTH ANALYSIS

Liquid assets vs. short-term debt

Total assets	______(A)	
Total liabilities	______(B)	
Assets exceed debt by	______	
(Debt exceeds assets by)	______	
Debt-equity ratio (liabilities/net worth)	______	
Net worth (assets less total liabilities)		______**(A-B)**

FIGURE 2.5 PERSONAL LIVING EXPENSES WORKSHEET—DETAILED BUDGET*

1. REGULAR MONTHLY PAYMENTS	
Rent or house payments (including taxes)	$________
Car payments (including insurance)	________
Appliances/TV payments	________
Home improvement loan payments	________
Personal loan payments	________
Health plan payments	________
Life insurance premiums	________
Other insurance premiums	________
Miscellaneous payments	________
Total	**$________**
2. FOOD EXPENSE	
Food at home	$________
Food away from home	________
Total	**$________**
3. PERSONAL EXPENSES	
Clothing, cleaning, laundry, shoe repair	$________
Drugs	________
Doctors and dentists	________
Education	________
Union or professional dues	________
Gifts and charitable contributions	________
Travel	________
Newspapers, magazines, books	________
Auto upkeep, gas, and parking	________
Spending money, allowances	________
4. HOUSEHOLD OPERATING EXPENSES	
Telephone	$________
Gas and electricity	________
Water	________
Other household expenses, repairs, maintenance	________
Total	**$________**
GRAND TOTAL	
1. Regular monthly payments	$________
2. Food expense	________
3. Personal expenses	________
4. Household operating expenses	________
Total Monthly Expenses	**$________**

*This budget should be based on an estimate of your financial requirements for an *average* month based on a recent 3- to 6-month period, and should not include purchases of any new items except emergency replacements.

FIGURE 2.6 ENTREPRENEURIAL ASSESSMENT QUESTIONNAIRE

WHAT ABOUT YOU?	**YES**	**NO**
1. Are you the kind of person who can get a business started and run it successfully?	____	____
2. Think about why you want to own your own business. Do you want it enough to work long hours without knowing how much money you'll end up with?	____	____
3. Does your family go along with your plan to start a business of your own?	____	____
4. Have you ever worked in a business similar to the one you want to start?	____	____
5. Have you ever worked for someone else as a supervisor or manager?	____	____
6. Have you had any business training in school?	____	____
WHAT ABOUT THE MONEY?		
7. Have you saved any money?	____	____
8. Do you know how much money you will need to get your business started?	____	____
9. Have you figured out whether you could make more money working for someone else?	____	____
10. Have you determined how much of your own money you can put into the business?	____	____
11. Do you know how much credit you can get from your suppliers — the people from whom you will buy?	____	____
12. Do you know where you can borrow the rest of the money needed to start your business?	____	____
13. Have you figured out your expected net income per year from the business? (Include your salary and a return on the money you have invested.)	____	____
14. Can you live on less than this so that you can use some of it to help your business grow?	____	____
15. Have you talked to a banker about your plans?	____	____
YOUR BUSINESS AND THE LAW		
16. Do you know what licences and permits you need?	____	____
17. Do you know what business laws you have to obey?	____	____
18. Have you talked to a lawyer about your proposed business?	____	____
HOW ABOUT A PARTNER?		
19. If you need a partner who has money or know-how, do you know someone who will fit — someone with whom you can get along?	____	____
20. Do you know the good and bad points about going it alone, having a partner, and incorporating your business?	____	____
WHAT ABOUT YOUR CUSTOMERS?		
21. Do most businesses in your community seem to be doing well?	____	____
22. Have you tried to find out how well businesses similar to the one you want to open are doing in your community and in the rest of the country?	____	____
23. Do you know what kind of people will want to buy what you plan to sell?	____	____
24. Do such people live in the area where you want to open your business?	____	____
25. Do you feel they need a business like yours?	____	____
26. If not, have you thought about opening a different kind of business or going to another neighbourhood?	____	____

Exploring New Business Ideas and Opportunities

In Stage Two you had an opportunity to evaluate your own potential for an entrepreneurial career from the standpoint of your personal fit with the requirements for success, the business skills required to start and run a business of your own, and the adequacy of your financial resources. Assuming that you feel you have the "right stuff" to continue to explore this career option, you will need an idea — the seed that will germinate and, hopefully, grow and develop into a profitable enterprise. This is the topic of Stage Three.

An idea is the first thing you will require to start a business. Ideas that succeed are difficult to find and evaluate, but they are critical to the entire process. It is rare for extraordinary amounts of money or effort to overcome the problems associated with what is fundamentally a bad idea.

While at the centre of every opportunity is an idea, not every idea represents a viable business opportunity. That relationship is illustrated below.

Initial New Venture Ideas → Potential New Opportunities → Decision to Start a New Venture[1]

Some people may come up with any number of initial new venture *ideas*. After some additional thought and evaluation, they may recognize that some of their ideas are potential new venture *opportunities*. With even further thought and consideration they may then decide to start a new venture. Perhaps only one idea in one hundred will possess the elements required to make it a success. But how do you tell an idea from an opportunity? Harvard professor J.A. Timmons says *an opportunity has the qualities of being attractive, durable, and timely and is anchored in a product or service that creates or adds value for its buyer or end user.*[2] Many ideas for prospective new business do not add much value for customers or users. To help you distinguish between a list of ideas and real opportunities you might start by asking yourself the following questions:

- Does the idea solve some fundamental consumer want or need?
- Is there a demand? Are there enough people who will buy the product to support a business and how much competition exists for that demand?
- Can the idea be turned into a business that will be *profitable*?
- Do you have the skills needed to take advantage of the opportunity? Why hasn't anyone else tried this concept? If anyone has, what happened to them?

In some instances what was felt to be a good idea was the key element stimulating an individual to think of going into business. In others it was the lack of an acceptable concept that was the principal factor holding back an aspiring entrepreneur. Perhaps you fall into this category. If so, it is important not to be impatient. It may take several years to fully develop and evaluate an idea which is suited to your particular circumstances and which you feel represents a real opportunity. Don't try to force the issue. Actively pursue a range of possible options, but wait until the right situation presents itself before investing your time and money.

There is no shortage of real opportunities. For example, the winners of the Business Development Bank of Canada's Young Entrepreneurs Awards for 2000 were involved in a wide range of activities including a dance school, a company that specializes in database application development, a garden-supply store, a publishing company, a computer service firm, and a number of other very diverse businesses:

---

1. R.P. Singh, G.E. Hills, and G.T. Lumpkin, "New Venture Ideas and Entrepreneurial Opportunities: Understanding the Process of Opportunity Recognition," Paper presented at the United States Association for Small Business and Entrepreneurship Annual Conference, 1999. (www.sbaer.uca.edu/Research/1999/USASBE/99usa657.htm)
2. Timmons, J.A., *New Venture Creation*, 4th ed. (Irwin, 1994), 87.

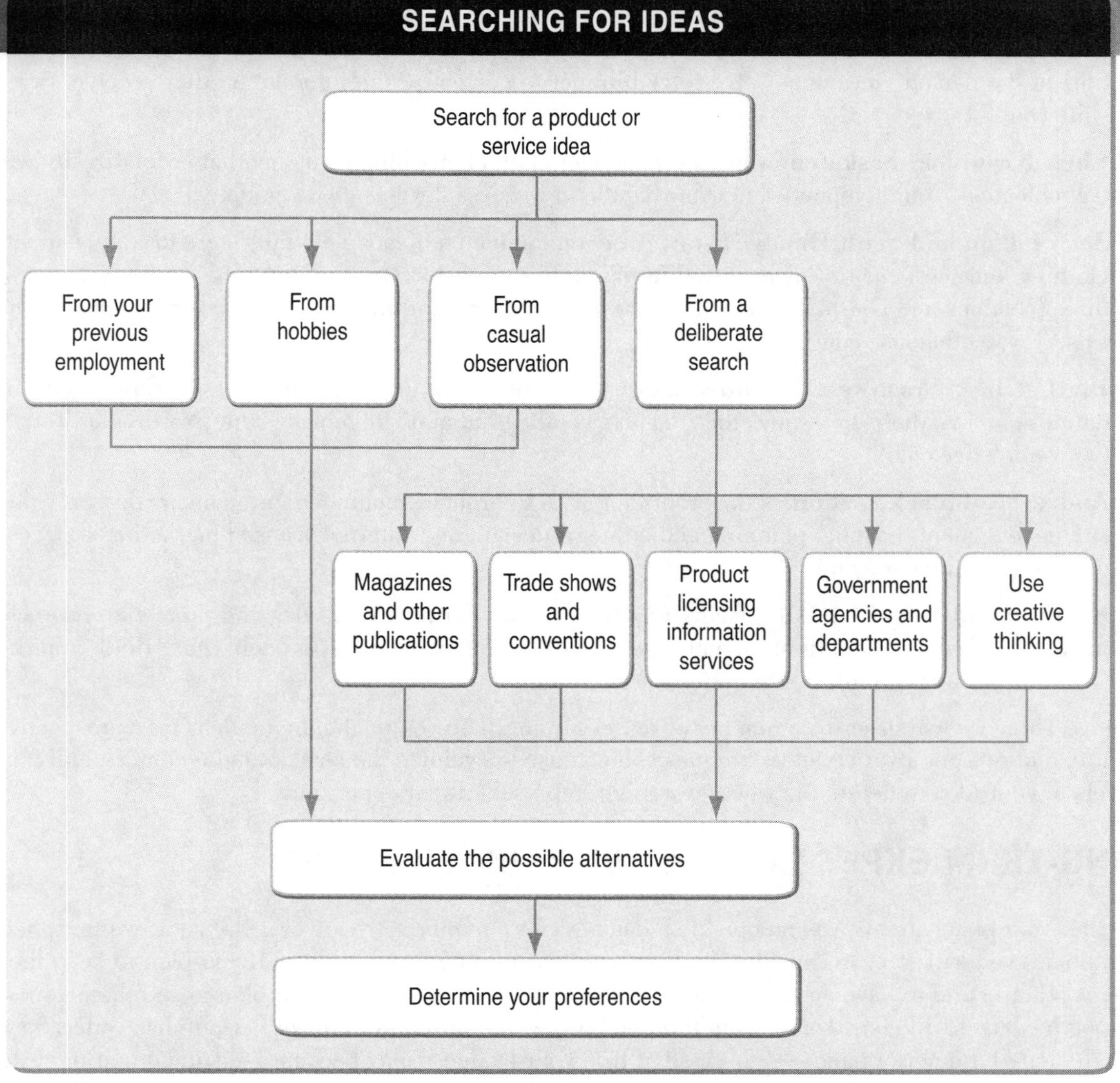

- **Connie Parsons, Newfoundland and Labrador**, operates the Connie Parsons School of Dance, a successful studio that offers classes in ballet, tap, jazz, modern stage, and ballroom dance.
- **Jason McNeill, Prince Edward Island**, is the owner and operator of two Jumbo Video stores.
- **Jason McGrath, Nova Scotia**, is the founder and president of a Halifax company that specializes in database application development. (www.kljsolutions.com)
- **Andy Buyting, New Brunswick**, is the owner and operator of the Green Village garden-supply store in Fredericton, the largest operation of its kind in Atlantic Canada. Green Village is a unique outlet, with attractions that include a Butterfly House, an in-store ice cream parlour, and a separate play area for children. (www.greenvillage.net)
- **Chris Emerqui and Dwayne Dear, Quebec**, are the joint operators of an Internet advertising company that has a staff of 25 and has recently expanded to Toronto. (www.bamsolutions.com)
- **Nathan and Mark Laurie, Ontario**, are the founders of a publishing company that focuses on helping companies reach the student market to promote their products and recruit for job openings. This is accomplished through providing poster wall calendars to student residents across North America, publishing a monthly magazine full of jobs for students, and maintaining a job-oriented Web site.

- **Patrick Akpalialuk, Nunavut**, is the founder of a dynamic high-tech company that manufactures and services computers in the far north.
- **Lisa Bako and Sigrid Froese, Manitoba**, are the founders of a computer software company that has developed a highly innovative Internet content management and filtering program that utilizes user profiles of the person viewing a Web site or Intranet to customize the information they receive. (www.pht-suite.com)
- **Chris Krywulak, Saskatchewan**, is the founder of an eight-outlet company that specializes in wireless technologies—from telephones to other handheld wireless devices. (www.jump.ca)
- **Sean Fillion and Scott Hendrickson, Alberta**, founded a lifestyle clothing store to supply street-style clothing and footwear to Calgary's California-style surf and skateboard set. The business has grown to three locations and boasts the largest and best selection of clothing and footwear for skateboard enthusiasts. (www.echohouse.com)
- **Ria Letcher, Northwest Territories**, owns and operates a lodge that provides world-class accommodations for visitors to enjoy the beauty of the Nahanni region of the Northwest Territories. (www.nnnlodge.com)
- **Andrew Robulack, Yukon**, is the proprietor of an Internet communications company that provides Web site development, hosting, planning and strategy, design, and Internet-focused marketing services to its clients. (www.pixelar.com)
- **Brenton and David Nichols, British Columbia**, are partners in a sales and promotion business that provides major Canadian companies with a creative approach to field marketing. (www.inventaworld.com)[3]

In Stage Three we will describe a number of sources from which you might obtain ideas for a prospective new venture, and present a variety of techniques you can use to evaluate the conceptual, technical, and financial aspects of your idea to determine whether it might represent a real opportunity.

LONG-TERM EXPECTATIONS FOR YOUR BUSINESS

Whether your plans are to own and operate a business for a number of years or sell it shortly after it becomes operational, you will want to consider the long-term prospects of your venture. If you plan to keep the business, you are bound to have an interest in how it is expected to prosper; if you plan to sell the business, the prospective buyer will consider the long-term viability of the business in his or her purchase offer. So, either way, the long-term performance — the kind of firm your business may become — is important in evaluating alternatives. Opportunities with higher growth potential generally offer greater economic payoffs. However, those are not the only kind of payoffs that are important. Some small but stable ventures provide very enjoyable situations and lucrative benefits to their owners.

For purposes of assessing the expected long-term prospects of your venture, three types of possibilities should be considered:

1. Lifestyle ventures
2. Small, profitable ventures
3. High-growth ventures

LIFESTYLE VENTURES

These include most "one-man shows," mom-and-pop stores, and other lifestyle businesses such as gas stations, restaurants, drycleaning shops, and small independent retail stores. Typically, their owners make modest investments in fixed assets and inventory, put in long hours, and earn considerably less income than the average unskilled auto worker or union craftsperson. The profit in reselling these businesses tends to be quite low.

3. Business Development Bank of Canada,"Young Entrepreneurs in the Spotlight, BDC Honours the Achievement of 13 Entrepreneurs under the ago of 30 in the Presence of Minister Brian Tobin," press release, Oct. 17, 2000 (www.bdc.ca/bdc/home/Default.asp).

The operator of a lifestyle business often risks his or her savings to capitalize the enterprise, and works longer hours with less job security than the average employee. Most lifestyle businesses have a high risk of failure. Unless you are willing to put up with these inherent conditions, such types of businesses should probably be avoided in favour of staying with your job until a more attractive opportunity can be identified.

SMALL, PROFITABLE VENTURES

Small manufacturing firms, larger restaurants and retail firms, small chains of gas stations, and other multi-establishment enterprises commonly fall into this category. Usually they involve a substantial capital investment — $100,000 or more. Some owners put in long hours, others do not. Once established, many owners enjoy a comfortable living. The profit in reselling the business can be high to a buyer who sees both an attractive job and a profitable investment.

You might be surprised at how many small, virtually unnoticed businesses around your city or town have managed to provide a very comfortable living for their founders. Almost always there is a very particular reason that they are able to do so: a contract the entrepreneur was able to land at favourable terms, or a market that was unknown to others or too small to attract competitors which therefore permitted a high profit margin, or special skills or knowledge on the part of the proprietor which enabled him or her to charge high rates for his or her time. The business's advantage may be its location, perhaps purchased for a low price many years earlier, or a patented process others are not able to copy. It may even be simply a brand that is protected by trademark and which has become well known by the passage of time or through successful advertising.

HIGH-GROWTH VENTURES

Much rarer than lifestyle ventures or small, profitable ventures, but typically more highly publicized, are small firms that have the capability of becoming large ones. They include many high-technology companies formed around new products with large potential markets, and also some of the small, profitable firms which, due to such factors as having amassed substantial capital or having hit upon a successful formula for operating, can be expanded many times. Ventures of this type are often bought up and absorbed by larger companies. The potential for significant capital gain on resale of the business can be substantial.

A key factor in starting a high-growth venture is choosing the right industry to enter. The rate of growth of the industry as a whole often plays a large role in determining the growth patterns of start-ups within it. In addition, however, there has to be some property of the business that can readily be multiplied by that company but cannot easily be duplicated by others for there to be significant growth potential. In franchising, for example, it can be a format for doing business which has proven exceptionally effective and can be taught. In high-technology firms, it is specialized know-how in creating something at a hard-to-reach frontier of engineering for which there is a demand. If a technology is common knowledge and not too capital-intensive, then companies providing it generally do not grow very rapidly.

SOURCES OF IDEAS FOR A NEW BUSINESS

In Stage Two it was suggested that your previous jobs, hobbies, personal experiences, and the like could provide you with some of the requisite business and technical skills needed to operate your own business. Similarly, your past work experience, hobbies, and acquaintances can provide a starting point for developing a list of business ventures you might wish to consider for further investigation. The following is a brief description of some of the sources most often used by entrepreneurs in search of new business opportunities.

YOUR JOB

Prior work experience is the most common source of new business ideas. It has been estimated that as many as 85 per cent of new businesses started are based on product ideas similar to those of prior employers of the founders. When you think about it the attractions of starting a business in a field in which you have experience and expertise are obvious. You are already familiar with the products and services you will provide, you understand the competitive environment, you have some knowledge and understanding of customer requirements, you may already know several prospective clients, and so on.

Ideas from your previous employment can take several forms. For example, you might set yourself up as a consultant in some technical area using the background and experience you acquired in a previous job. You might develop a product or service for which your prior employer might be a prospective customer. You might even be interested in providing a product or service similar or related to that provided by your previous employer. In this last case you should check with a lawyer to ensure your plans do not violate the legal rights of that employer. You must be certain your actions do not infringe on any patent, trademark, or other proprietary rights, break any non-competition clause or other agreements you may have signed, involve the direct solicitation of your former employer's customers, or raise similar legal or ethical problems. You might even set yourself up as a distributor of your employer's products, as illustrated by the case of Janine DeFreitas who quit her position as Rubbermaid Canada's sales and merchandising manager to open The Rubbery, North America's first, independent, full-line Rubbermaid store (Entrepreneurs in Action #6).

In other instances, the relationship with your previous employment situation may not be quite so direct as DeFreitas. Judson Marcor, for example, had a strong interest in flying since he was very young. By the time he was 19 he already had his private pilot's licence and subsequently graduated from university with a degree in aeronautical studies. After flying small planes around northern Canada for five years he returned to school to complete a combination law degree/MBA at the University of Alberta. Despite a brief detour to article and practise law, with his strong interest and extensive background in aviation it is not surprising that he would be one of the principals involved in starting a business to offer a fractional ownership of a commercial aircraft to western Canadian companies (Entrepreneurs in Action #7).

6 Entrepreneurs in action

When the Rubber Hits the Road

While Rubbermaid Inc. is recognized as one of the world's most innovative companies, its employees show similar flair. When Janine DeFreitas, Rubbermaid Canada's sales and merchandising manager, saw Rubbermaid's first-ever complete housewares display sell out at Kmart in four weeks, she decided to do what no one had tried before. In September 1996, with a 100-page business plan and a $180,000 loan (from the third bank she approached), DeFreitas opened The Rubbery, North America's first independent, full-line Rubbermaid store.

Almost instantly, her Mississauga, Ont. outlet proved too small. "It was just crazy," she says. "Every week we were backlogged." Eight months after opening, the 34-year-old DeFreitas doubled her floor space to 20,000 square feet. After 11 months, The Rubbery had done more than $3 million in sales — twice DeFreitas's initial projections. And she says she hasn't even begun to grow.

Strategically situated in a "power centre" near Price Club and Home Depot, the colorful store offers products from all seven Rubbermaid divisions: housewares, Little Tykes toys, office products, Graco infant products, home health-care supplies, commercial products for industry, and specialty products such as sheds and lawn carts. "I'm doing what no other retailer can do," says DeFreitas. "I'm showing the breadth of the product."

The only threat DeFreitas sees is the big discounters who price Rubbermaid products to lure customers. "Rubbermaid is typically used as a loss leader. We try to price ourselves about 10% lower than the average retailer, but my strength is the selection."

Now DeFreitas plans to roll out her concept across Canada. "You've got to admit the retail industry is kind of stale," she says. "This is a great new concept that's proven to work." First step: a store next spring in Toronto's east end, and a tad more emphasis on the bottom line. So far the Rubbery's profit margin is running about 6%, but for next year she's targeting 8% to 10% — enough, she hopes, to begin attracting equally innovative franchisees.

Source: Donna Green, "When the Rubber Hits the Road," *PROFIT*, September 1997, p. 38. Reprinted with permission. Donna Green specializes in small business and personal finance.

7 Entrepreneurs in action

Wanna Be a Jetsetter?

"We are the first company in Canada to offer fractional ownership of an airplane under a commercial certificate basis," says Judson Macor, a 33-year-old commercial pilot and president of AirSprint Fractional Ownership. "For $630,000, you can own a one-eighth interest in a Pilatus CP-12."

The concept of fractional ownership was originally conceived by American businessman Richard Santulli. The idea was simple; there were many individuals and corporations that couldn't rationalize the purchase of an entire jet but could afford part of one and the cachet of a private plane would still be theirs. "The manufacturers saw the light; instead of trying to sell a $16 million jet to an individual, you could open up a broader market by selling one-sixteenth of a jet for $1 million," says Macor.

Fractional ownership worked in the United States because U.S. Federal Aviation Administration regulations treated it as private ownership, instead of a commercial arrangement. "It meant less onerous crew duty terms, takeoff and landing restrictions, and maintenance schedules," says Macor.

Unfortunately, the same regulations weren't available in Canada. When you buy a portion of an aircraft in this country, Transport Canada does not consider it a private transaction, and owners must apply for the more stringent commercial operating certificate.

If there was anyone in Canada who was destined to make fractional ownership take flight however, it was Judson Macor. "I had the flying bug in me since I was five," he recalls. He obtained his private licence in high school, and by the age of 19, had qualified for his commercial pilot's ticket.

After high school, Macor attended the University of North Dakota, graduating in 1989 with a BSc in aeronautical studies. For five years, he flew Twin Otters and other small airplanes throughout northern Canada, before a downturn in the industry dried up work. Returning to school, he pursued a combined law degree/MBA at the University of Alberta. After graduating in 1997, he moved to Calgary and articled with a firm specializing in corporate law.

But, try as he might, Macor couldn't get the flying bug out of his system. When Phil Dewsnap, a friend from law school, called up and offered to help start a new company, Macor jumped at the chance. He quit his law job and, working from a spare bedroom in his house, the pair pored over various business plans, trying to decide what kind of company to start.

Knowing of the success of fractional ownership in the U.S., Macor and Dewsnap analyzed the Transport Canada rules and realized that they could make the concept work on a profitable economic basis within Canadian commercial regulations.

The key to their plan was the Pilatus CP-12 passenger plane. The Swiss-built turboprop is equipped with a 1,200 HP engine capable of transporting seven passengers and a quarter tonne of cargo for 3,500 kilometres at 500 km/hr. Designed to land and take off of very short, snow-covered gravel strips, it was ideal for northern Canadian destinations.

But, most of all, the price tag was under $5 million. "One quarter of a Pilatus 12 costs $1.26 million," he says. "That guarantees 200 hours per year of flight time. You pay a further $685/hr of flight time, and a monthly management fee of $6,900."

GREG GERLA PHOTOGRAPHY INC.

Macor and Dewsnap needed at least two aircraft to launch their endeavour. They contacted Bob MacLean in Edmonton, the western Canada distributor for the Pilatus, and struck up a 50/50 deal to merge their respective companies in exchange for two planes that MacLean owned. Macor then applied for the proper authorization and, after six months of paperwork, was finally granted commercial certification in May 2000.

The next step was to track down corporate clientele. AirSprint focused on western Canada-based companies with over $50 million in gross revenues,

150 employees, and a need to travel. "If you're flying less than 100 hours (per year), it's better to charter," says Macor. "If you're flying more than 500 hours, buy your own. The people who need 80 to 500 — that's who we're after."

AirSprint partly marketed their service based on cost comparisons to chartering. According to Macor, commonly quoted fares for a trip to Norman Wells, NWT, puts the cost of a charter in the $12,000 range, while the cost of a flight on your own plane, including monthly management fees, is under $8,000. "You only pay (the hourly fee) when you're onboard the aircraft," says Macor. "If it comes back empty, there's no extra charge. You don't pay holding fees for the aircraft or crew, either."

Soon after opening up for business in May, they managed to pre-sell their first aircraft. "Businesses like it because they get a huge tax deferral due to capital cost allowance," says Macor. "We minimize the effect of cash flow. The investment is also quite liquid, and you can sell anytime. The book value after five years is 95%."

Much to AirSprint's pleasant surprise, several individuals also stepped forward to buy portions. "Half of our clientele are high net-worth individuals who like the convenience of owning their own aircraft," says Macor. "We recently flew four and a half hours to Palm Springs. Compare that to showing up an hour in advance, and another hour at the other end clearing customs and collecting your baggage."

By the time AirSprint had their third plane delivered in August, it had been fully sold to fractional clients. "We have another one being delivered the second week of December, and we're pre-selling now," says Macor. He believes that there is a mature market for about 10 fractional ownership Pilatus aircraft in western Canada. "After that, we'll bring in jets with longer range."

* Some names and personal details have been changed to ensure anonymity. (www.airsprint.com)

Source: "Wanna Be a Jetsetter?" by Gordon Cope, *Alberta Venture*, (January/February 2001): 109–110.

YOUR HOBBIES

Some people are deeply involved with their hobbies, often devoting more time to them than to their regular job. There are many instances of such secondary interests leading to new business ventures. For example, serious athletes may open sporting goods stores, amateur photographers open portrait studios, hunters offer guiding services and run hunting lodges and game farms, pilots start fly-in fishing camps, philatelists open coin and stamp stores, and so forth.

Witness the case of Chris Griffiths in Entrepreneurs in Action #8. Chris got his first guitar at age 2 and was fascinated to see how it worked. By age 20 he had opened his first custom guitar-making and repair shop in St. John's. Now he is trying to raise $3 million to establish a plant to make mass-market guitars.

Many such ventures do very well, but there can be considerable conflict. Hobbies are typically activities that you and others are prepared to do at your own expense. This can exert downward pressure on the likely profitability of your business. As a result, margins are quite low in such areas as the production of arts and crafts, small-scale farming, trading in stamps, coins, and other collectibles, antique automobile restorations, and similar hobby-based operations.

PERSONAL OBSERVATION

For many people personal observation is the most practical way of identifying a business idea. Personal observations may arise from either casual observation or deliberate search.

CASUAL OBSERVATION

Often, ideas for a new product or service result from chance observation of daily living situations. This commonly occurs when people travel and observe product or service concepts being provided that are not yet available in the United States, Canada, or, perhaps, the person's local market area.

Restaurant themes and concepts, such as Thai, Mexican, health food, and salads, typically are only established in most cities after they have proven to be successful somewhere else. Sporting trends, such as sailboarding and rollerblading, and fashion colours and styles are also usually imported from outside the country.

8 Entrepreneurs in action

Sharing the Vision

Chris Griffiths of St. John's, Nfld. got his first electric guitar for Christmas at the age of 12. On Boxing Day he pulled it apart to see how it worked.

Griffiths' little experiment cost $200 to fix, but that investment paid off. Griffiths' interest in instruments landed him a job in a music store at age 16. But it was packing up damaged or broken guitars for shipment to Ontario that changed his life. "The bell went off," he says. "I wondered, if there's this much work going around, why isn't anyone here doing it?" In a vivid illustration of the entrepreneurial proverb, "Do what you love and the money will follow," Griffiths apprenticed at a "guitar hospital" in Michigan before opening his own custom guitar-making and repair shop four years ago at the age of 20.

Of course, it wasn't easy. Told he needed a business plan, Griffiths wrote a five-page essay. ("People kind of giggled at it," he says now.) With the help of St. John's Y Enterprise Centre, he spent five months working on a 75-page plan that spelled out the full opportunity—and his need for $40,000 in capital. A Youth Ventures Loan provided $30,000, but the Atlantic Canada Opportunities Agency turned him down twice for the rest. Finally Griffiths wrote his MP and Newfoundland power broker John Crosbie, outlining his experiences with ACOA. He never heard from either politician, but the federal agency soon called to say it had reviewed his application and would cough up $10,000.

When Griffiths opened his shop in a strip mall in May 1993, he quickly proved his instincts right. Newfoundlanders flocked to buy his $2,000 to $3,000 custom guitars, or to have their own models repaired on-site. Griffiths hired his first employee after just three weeks —about 11 months earlier than forecast.

At first Griffiths worked 90-hour weeks without pay, but today Griffiths Guitar Works is a clear winner. It boasts 2,000 square feet, seven employees and sales of about $250,000. Griffiths, who stopped making guitars himself two years ago, is now investing his newfound profits into his own real-estate management company. Plus, he's just opened a rock-and-roll music camp for Atlantic Canada youth which he hopes will become a year-round venture—and of course groom new customers.

But now Griffiths is looking at his biggest deal yet: establishing a new plant to make mass-market guitars. He has visited trade shows and factories to study new processes for revolutionizing the low-tech industry. "We will be building guitars like nobody else in the world," he says. Using robotics and CAD/CAM technology, "we'll be able to do it faster, we'll offer higher standards of raw materials, and we'll cost less than imported models." This time his business plan is 800 pages long. Griffiths has circulated it among venture capitalists "from here to Toronto" to try to obtain $3 million in backing. With the new teens of the baby-boomer "echo" generation boosting demand for guitars again, he's confident the money will come, even if it means giving up sole ownership of the venture. As Griffiths concludes, with the flair of a songwriter and the maturity of a veteran entrepreneur: "The more you share your vision, the better chance you have of seeing it come true." (www.griffiths.nfld.net)

Source: Rick Spence, "Sharing the Vision," *PROFIT*, September, 1997, pp 48-49. Reprinted with permission.

For this type of observation to yield results, you have to recognize the need for a new type of product or service offering and then work out some kind of solution. Myles Kraut, for example, recognized that animals were reacting negatively to preservatives in dog food (Entrepreneurs in Action #9). He also recognized that the treats used as rewards in the training of dogs were moist products that stained the clothes of the dog owners and were high in fat content. His Dr. Dean's line of dog treats and snacks have no moisture, so they overcome this problem and are healthier for the animals as well.

Similarly, Brian Scudamore was astute enough to recognize that trash collection could be a growth industry (Entrepreneurs in Action #10). While still a teenager he printed up cards and flyers and set up his own garbage disposal firm with a beat-up pickup truck. Since 1993 his business has grown to nearly $1.3 million in sales and he is looking to franchise his idea to other major centres across North America.

9 Entrepreneurs in action

He's a Dog's Best Friend

After years of struggling to start a business, a young Winnipeg entrepreneur is seeing his company go to the dogs — and he's loving it.

Myles Kraut, 24, is the sole proprietor of Dr. Dean's, a line of dog snacks and treats made in Manitoba and sold across Canada. Kraut says that after a long start-up process, he's finally seeing results.

"We can't make them fast enough," Kraut says of the dog treats.

Dr. Dean's (Dean is Kraut's middle name) are available in 475 pet stores nationwide, including Best West stores and Petland.

More to the point, Kraut is doing something he enjoys. He's his own boss, works hours he wants to work and is in control of his own destiny. It's a dog-eat-dog world, and he's loving it.

He's not the only one. A recent Angus Reid poll for the Royal Bank shows that one-third of young Canadians want to be entrepreneurs. The Royal Bank report shows that the top career choice of Canadians between the ages of 18 and 35 is entrepreneur.

Kraut says he wasn't sure what he wanted. He drifted a bit in school, never completing his science degree at the University of Winnipeg. He jokes that he's the only one in his family, including in-laws, who hasn't finished university.

But the business world is no stranger to him. His dad owns the Charleswood Department Store, his older brother co-owns the auto store Canadian Super Shop, and his mom owns a children's clothing store in Corydon Village mall.

Kraut didn't know what he wanted, but he knew what he didn't want — he didn't want to work in retail.

He says that three years ago, he spent a horrible six months struggling with what he was going to do. Sleeping in until noon and going to bed at 4 a.m. were commonplace.

Then it came to him.

"I don't want this to sound cheesy, but I truly love animals," Kraut says.

He's always had a dog and loved them. The family had two terriers, and one had to be put down because of a seemingly incurable skin condition. It was only after that dog was gone that they discovered the animals were reacting to preservatives in dog food.

That episode launched Kraut into an eight-month investigation of the world of pet food and accessories marketing. He quickly discovered that making food was too capital intensive. So he did his own market research — on foot.

"I went in store after store and found out what products were made that had the biggest margins on them," he recalls. "I never thought anything would come of it."

But he quickly discovered that the market didn't have an all-natural dog treat in a dry formula.

Specifically, Kraut went after the rewards market — the treats used to train dogs. He says the only things out there were moist products that stained the pockets of dog owners and were high in fat content.

When he knew he had an idea that worked, Kraut sold his car for his initial capital. He then took some chicken liver he bought at Safeway and other ingredients up to the Swiss Alex Bakery in Gimli.

Kraut says that after trial and error, they came up with a dried dog treat. Because there's no moisture, the treats have a long shelf life and dogs also crave them. He says garlic is the key — dogs love the smell and taste, and Kraut says it kills germs that cause doggy breath. Honest.

He sold his house on Borebank Street to move into his parents' basement when the business became a reality.

Today, he has the packaging made in Vancouver, a national distributor in Toronto and his manufacturer is still the Swiss Alex Bakery.

Kraut is rarely home. He says he's in Winnipeg five days a month. The rest of the time he's on the road with sales reps in pet stores across Canada. He also jets down to the United States frequently. Next week he's at a trade show in Chicago.

And he's making money. He's repaid his family the money they lent him to get the business going, and now sales are picking up in pet stores.

"Our next step is the U.S. Canada has 1,500 stores. Chicago alone has 1,500 stores," he says.

As for picking his hours, well, Kraut just laughs. He's working hard to get his business established, but he's not too concerned now.

"This is the time you work — when you're 24 or 25."

Source: Paul McKie, "He's A Dog's Best Friend," © *Winnipeg Free Press*, October 3, 1997, pp. B8-B9. Reprinted with permission.

10 Entrepreneurs in action

Dial 1-800-GOT-JUNK

One person's trash is another one's treasure. That adage proved true for Brian Scudamore. The Vancouver native has developed a Midas touch when it comes to junk, turning a summer job into a million-dollar business.

Scudamore was just 18 when he was struck by the sight of a truck hauling away rubbish. "I've always been entrepreneurial," says Scudamore. "It just struck me that [trash collection] could be a growth industry." He quickly printed up cards and flyers and with a beat-up $700 pickup truck launched his own garbage-disposal firm, The Rubbish Boys. Despite the name, it was actually a one-man show that Scudamore ran during his summers off from university. It wasn't until 1993 that Scudamore went at it full-time. Since then, it's been full speed ahead. With 1998 sales of nearly $1.3 million, revenues have grown 1,169% from 1993.

The move into garbage disposal proved prescient, as Vancouver, like many other North American cities, has passed regulations that allow residents to turf just two bags of trash per week — forcing them to look for other alternatives when tackling big jobs such as renovations or yard work. From the get-go, Scudamore's plan was to differentiate himself from competitors by being more, well, professional. "Service standards were missing," he says, "and the industry is notorious for people charging whatever they like. If you've got a Jag in the driveway, you'll pay more." Instead Scudamore — who changed the company name in 1998 to 1-800-GOT-JUNK? — puts a premium on service: he offers shiny trucks, uniformed drivers and a printed, up-front price list. Appointments are scheduled by a central office, and staff telephone customers for comments on their service. "Our approach really is different," he says, "and we get a lot of positive feedback about it."

Now Scudamore is taking that good will further afield. "We're planning to grow faster than we've grown," he says. He recently sold franchises in Seattle, Portland and Toronto. "We're expanding with other people and with other people's money," says Scudamore. "I believe that franchise owners have more of a drive to succeed than a corporate office does." Franchising is also a quick route to rapid growth, he says. "There are 30 major centres

PERRY ZAVITZ

in North America that we want to be in by 2003 — and they are all markets that are larger than Vancouver." And that's not trash talk. (www.1800gotjunk.com)

Source: Hilary Davidson, "5 Entrepreneurs You Need to Know," *PROFIT*, June, 1999, pp. 91-92. Reprinted with permission.

While he was a university student, Steve Debus observed that students wanted a casual pant that was congruent with their lifestyle. They often sat in front of a computer for hours on end so, wanted something that was comfortable and easy-wearing. They also wanted a pant they could wear during the day but still go out in at night. They wanted something they could fall asleep in in their rooms but could still wear to class the next day without looking wrinkled. His answer was the "Exam Pant" which he initially sold for $20 each but has parlayed into a $2 million clothing design and marketing business employing 26 people. His company, Modrobes, has since expanded to include skirts, jackets, and hip bags, but his designs have not strayed from the basic premise upon which the original Exam Pant was based—to provide young people with clothes that are comfortable, have a street-wise look, and are reasonably priced (Entrepreneurs in Action #11).

11 Entrepreneurs in action

Out of the Mainstream

Steven Debus wants you in his pants, and he's not afraid to tell you so. Clearly, the founder of Toronto-based Modrobes Saldebus Lounge Clothing Inc. knows a good catchphrase when he hears one. With eyebrow-raising slogans like "I want you in my pants" and "Saving the world one crotch at a time," the 29-year-old Debus has parlayed a lifelong interest in fashion into a $2-million clothing design and marketing business employing 26 people. He's shown that if you speak loudly enough in your customers' language, both consumers and conventional business partners will sit up and listen.

Debus formed Modrobes in 1995 to sell Exam Pants, a concept he'd developed as a business case study in university. Exam Pants were comfortable, easy-wearing pants designed by Debus for students who sit in front of computers for hours. "Students want a pant they can wear during the day and to go out in at night," says Debus. "They want to be able to fall asleep in them and go to class the next day without the pant wrinkling."

Borrowing money from a relative to start, Debus went straight to his customers, touring universities with a table piled high with Exam Pants, which he sold for $20 apiece. He went wherever students congregated, such as the travelling Edgefest rock music festival. Debus stuck to his strengths — design and marketing — contracting out manufacturing.

Modrobes' line expanded to include skirts, jackets and hip bags. Most new product ideas came from the customers Debus was careful to stay close to. His designs included all his young clientele wanted: comfort, a streetwise look and reasonable prices — usually under $50.

Selling out of the back of a truck, though, only takes you so far. Debus wanted to break into retail. When sales calls didn't work, Debus tried the unconventional. "When I was in a town and people asked me where they could get the pants, I told them to call a certain local store," he recalls. "Then 30 or 40 people would call the store, and then the store would call me back." Small independent retailers picked up his line and their customers bought. By 1998, chains such as Athlete's World and Jean Machine came knocking. Today, Modrobes fashions are sold in 350 stores across Canada, including two company-owned outlets in Toronto that allow Debus to stay close to customers, his source of inspiration.

Despite the retail success, Debus remains committed to guerrilla marketing. Chains have asked him to do more traditional advertising, but he's ignoring them. He believes that his approach — creating a "wow factor" by designing cutting-edge clothes and speaking directly to his young customers in unconventional ways — drives sales. He prefers distributing Modrobes stickers students can put on their snowboards over conventional advertising. As long as his clothes sell, he says, the stores should be happy.

© NADIA MOLINARI

Debus won't comment on Modrobes' profitability except to say that the company is 100% self-financed and has zero bank debt. He hopes to build a $60-million company in five years by selling on the Net and in the U.S., where he believes his "wow factor" will work as it has here. Debus appeared at last summer's Woodstock '99 festival in Rome, N.Y., but he hasn't yet done formal planning for his entry into the American market.

Debus is stepping up his grassroots efforts. "We want to do our own tour," he says. "It would be like a house party, with bands, DJs and a fashion show rolled into one. We want to entertain." It will also give him another chance to tell people he wants them in his pants — and his skirts, and his jackets. . . (www.modrobes.com)

Source: Hilary Davidson, "Out of the Stream," *PROFIT*, (November, 1999): 71–73. Reprinted with permission.

The observation may emerge from your own experience in the marketplace, be expressed by someone else who has recognized some opportunity or problem, or be the result of observing the behaviour of other people. Regardless of its source, this type of simple observation can be the source of numerous excellent new business ideas.

DELIBERATE SEARCH

While deliberate search may seem to be the most rational way of finding viable business ideas, in fact most new ventures do not start in this manner. The majority of business start-ups arise almost incidentally from events relating to work or everyday life. However, this approach should not be completely ignored, as it can be fruitful if you are committed to investigating the possibilities of starting a new business but lack the seed of any real, likely idea. For example, Michel Korwin came across the basic idea on which he based his business after spending long hours browsing through technological reviews at a local university library. There he came across an article about a metal heat-treating process that had never been developed to its full potential, despite its superior ability to render metals resistant to corrosion and wear. After further investigation and consultation with specialists he decided to go ahead with the project and established Nitrex Metal Inc. (Entrepreneurs in Action #12)

A deliberate search process can be initiated by consulting the following sources:

Improving on a Good Thing

I have always admired people and companies that were able to arrive at a revolutionary, successful and profitable product through careful analysis and re-engineering of an existing one. I am not talking about little, obvious improvements that bring little value added to end users; I am referring to such improvements that, once implemented, leave the user wondering how he or she used to get by without them.

So many opportunities lie under our noses, but we often fail to notice them when searching for ground-breaking business ideas. We tend to think that a revolutionary product is necessarily a new product, but this is not always the case. Many products are underdeveloped, and new or enhanced commercial applications can arise from their improvement. I think Japanese firms are particularly good at recognizing such opportunities. As a result, and in awe of some of these firms' accomplishments, I embarked on my search for that golden opportunity . . . to improve.

The economic uncertainty, job insecurity, and lack of control over my own destiny I experienced during the 1981–1983 recession led me to the point where I felt I needed to be my own man. This was not an easy decision, as I had no savings, my wife was studying, both our children were in a private school, and I was under great pressure to find a way to support them. However, since we had managed to gather the courage and strength to leave our country of birth in search of a better life — first on one continent and then on another — I knew our family could pull through the first crazy years of a company startup. Still, I could not afford to fail.

My quest led me to get very well acquainted with a local university library, where I spent long hours browsing through technological reviews, shelf by shelf. I went through more articles than I care to remember, but none ignited my imagination. As fatigue and discouragement began to slowly settle where enthusiasm and determination had once ruled, an article finally caught my eye.

The article, published in a German metallurgical journal, discussed "gas nitriding," a metal heat-treating process invented in 1928 that had never been developed to its full potential, despite its superior ability to render metals resistant to corrosion and wear. One of the main reasons this process had not received proper attention from the industry was that no one was able to fully control and duplicate its results. This article I had stumbled on was written by a Polish scientist who claimed to have achieved just that. But from behind the iron curtain, he had little means of commercializing his discovery.

This news appeared exciting to me, but as with many underdeveloped products, gas nitriding's broader application was also stifled by another major problem: its high cost. In fact, the process was so expensive that it was only used for military or aerospace purposes. Still, I gathered further information on the topic and forwarded it to George Tymowski, a friend who had a Ph.D. and extensive experience in metallurgy, for a second opinion. He was so enthused with the idea that he offered to invest if I decided to go ahead with it. He believed that the greatest impediment to the technology's success had been overcome by this scientist, and that a commercially sponsored development of his method would actually lower the cost of the process, making it commercially viable and opening up a whole new spectrum of applications.

After further consultations with specialists, I decided to get in touch with the Polish scientist and go ahead with the project. However, I knew I could not make it alone, so I began to look for associates that could help professionally or invest in the company. Unfortunately, I did not know people in the business community, so I feared the search would be difficult. Still, I was so excited about the project that I talked about it constantly, and this is how some of my bridge buddies came to hear of it. My enthusiasm must have been contagious, because after hours of heated discussions (our bridge games often lasted into the wee hours of the morning) many of them decided to invest, and one even decided to join the company.

This is how Nitrex was born. The first few years were very difficult. We had to overcome many problems and obstacles, but we kept on growing. By the time the next recession rolled around in the early 1990s, we were ready. In fact, while so many other companies were struggling to survive or going out of business, we were thriving. In a time when every one was looking for savings, we were able to provide a process of such high quality that it eliminated the need for further processing of parts treated, which often represented a 15% reduction in production costs.

Most groundbreaking improvements originate with recognizing the needs of end users and adapting a given product to suit those needs. Nitrex fulfilled and even at times pre-empted customer needs, and I believe this has been the secret of our success for the past 15 years. As our product satisfied users to a level they did not think possible, others gained interest in our process and became users themselves. Through the years, we have been able to supply a product that corresponds so well to many companies' needs that they come looking for us, rather than us having to look for them — a marketer's dream. Our future strategy is thus based on making sure we continue to pay attention to our worldwide customers, as they are our greatest source of inspiration. (www.nitrex.com)

Source: Michel Korwin, "Improving on a Good Thing," Profit Magazine Online www.profitguide.com/firstperson/FI_Korwin.html 12-07-01. Used with permission.

PUBLICATIONS

Reading business publications and other printed sources such as newspapers, specialty magazines, newsletters, and trade publications can provide ideas that might stimulate your entrepreneurial thinking. Some of the more important of these sources are listed below.

NEWSPAPERS AND MAGAZINES The *Wall Street Journal* (www.wsj.com), the *Globe and Mail* (www.theglobeandmail.com) and the *National Post* (www.nationalpost.com) offer business and classified sections that provide a listing or make other reference to available small-business opportunities. A number of Canadian magazines such as *Canadian Business* (www.canadianbusiness.com), *PROFIT: The Magazine for Canadian Entrepreneurs* (www.profitguide.com/), and the *Financial Post Magazine* (www.finpost.com), and U.S. publications such as *Inc.* (www.inc.com), *Entrepreneur* (www.entrepreneur.com), and *Fortune* (www.fortune.com) provide further descriptions of a range of business possibilities.

NEWSLETTERS Thousands of newsletters are available, covering almost every conceivable subject. The information they contain is current and specialized, and can provide invaluable access to opportunities in any field. For further information, contact the reference librarian at your public library, and ask for Newsletters in Print (Gale Research Company, www.gale.com). It lists every major publication.

TRADE PUBLICATIONS A list of available trade publications can be obtained from *Standard Rate and Data Service* (www.srds.com), *Canadian Advertising Rates and Data* (www.cardmedia.com), or similar publications available in most libraries. Trade magazines are usually the first to publicize a new product. In many cases the manufacturer is looking for help in distributing a new line. The ads will also provide information about potential competitors and their products. These trade publications are some of the best sources of data about a specific industry, and frequently print market surveys, forecasts, and articles on needs the industry may have. All this information can serve as a stimulating source of ideas.

INVENTORS' SHOWS, TRADE SHOWS, AND CONVENTIONS

INVENTORS' SHOWS These shows provide inventors and manufacturers with a place to meet to discuss potential products for the marketplace. There are major inventors' shows held annually in the larger cities throughout Canada and the United States. Information on upcoming shows may be available from online sources like InventNET, the Inventor's Network (www.inventnet.com/tradeshows.html), which provides a list of the major shows held throughout the United States.

TRADE SHOWS Shows covering the industry you want to enter can also be an excellent way to examine the products and services of many of your potential competitors. It can also be a way for you to meet distributors and sales representatives, learn of product and market trends, and identify potential products or services for your venture. Trade shows usually take place several times a year, in various locations. You will find trade show information in the trade magazines servicing your particular field or industry, or you may refer to the following sources:

- *Trade Shows Worldwide*, Gale Research Company, (www.gale.com).
- Tradeshowbiz.com (www.tradeshowbiz.com) provides a detailed listing of trade shows and conventions in all areas of the economy that can be searched by industry.

CONVENTIONS Fairs or conventions are also an excellent place to stimulate your creative thinking. At a convention you are exposed to panels, speakers, films, and exhibitions. You also have an opportunity to exchange ideas with other people attending. Information on conventions and meetings scheduled to take place around the world can be obtained from:

- AllConferences.net (www.allconferences.net) is a directory focusing on conferences, conventions, trade shows, and workshops. Their information ranges from specialized scientific, medical, and academic conferences to all kinds of general events.

PATENT BROKERS AND PRODUCT LICENSING INFORMATION SERVICES

An excellent way to obtain information about the vast number of new product ideas available from inventors, corporations, or universities is to subscribe to a service that periodically publishes data on products offered for licensing. Licensing means renting the right to manufacture or distribute a product within agreed rules or guidelines. For example, you might purchase the right to manufacture T-shirts and sweaters with the logo of Batman, Dilbert, or other popular fictional characters, or use the trademark of a popular product such as Labatt's or Coca-Cola on similar apparel. The owner of the licence retains ownership and receives a royalty or fixed fee from you as the licensee. Here are some of the information services you can contact to locate product or service licensing opportunities:

National Technology Index
Industry Canada
Innovation and Policy Branch
C.D. Howe Building
235 Queen Street
Ottawa,Ontario K1A 0H5
(strategis.ic.gc.ca/sc_innov/nti/engdoc/search.html)

Government Inventions Available for Licensing
National Technical Information Service (NTIS)
U.S. Department of Commerce
Springfield, VA 22161
(www.ntis.gov)

Also:

The World Bank of Licensable Technology available through
The Canadian Innovation Network
Waterloo, Ontario
(www.innovationcentre.ca)

The Canadian Intellectual Property Office administers the Canadian Patent Database (patents1.ic.gc.ca) as one vehicle for inventors and entrepreneurs to get together. This database includes the full content of all patent files including an indication of which patent-holders wish to make their patents available for sale or licensing. For more information, contact:

Canadian Intellectual Property Office
Place du Portage I
50 Victoria Street
Hull, Quebec K1A 0C9
(cipo.gc.ca)

FRIENDS, ACQUAINTANCES, AND OTHER SOCIAL CONTACTS

Discussions with those you know should not be overlooked as a source of insight into needs that might be fulfilled by a new venture. Comments such "wouldn't it be nice if someone came up with something to do away with ..." or "what this place needs is ..." and other complaints and observations can provide a number of potential ideas.

FEDERAL AND PROVINCIAL GOVERNMENT AGENCIES AND DEPARTMENTS

Industry Canada, the provincial departments of economic development, the Business Development Bank (BDC), university entrepreneurship centres, small-business development centres, community colleges, and various other federal and provincial government agencies are all in the business of helping entrepreneurs by means of business management seminars and courses, advice, information, and other assistance. See the listing of Some Useful Contacts in the back of the book. You can also get feedback on the viability of your business idea, or even suggestions. The cost in most cases is nominal.

Numerous other government agencies, such as the Canada Business Services Centres of Industry Canada (www.cbsc.org) also have publications and resources available to stimulate ideas for new business opportunities. Your public library can provide you with further information on all the government departments relevant to your area of interest. It is possible to get your name on mailing lists for free material, or even a government source list so that others can find out about goods or services that you may want to provide.

USE CREATIVE THINKING

Tremendous opportunities can materialize from the simple exchange of ideas among a number of people. There are a variety of analytical techniques and creative thinking concepts that can be used to facilitate this exchange. They help to generate and subjectively evaluate a number of prospective new business opportunities. These include such approaches as the use of decision trees, force field analysis, PMI — Plus/Minus/Interesting assessment — and similar concepts (see www.mindtools.com/page2.html). Perhaps the most popular approach used for this purpose is "brainstorming."

Brainstorming is a method for developing creative solutions to problems. It works by having a group of people focus on a single problem and come up with as many deliberately unusual solutions as possible. The idea is to push the ideas as far as possible to come up with distinctly creative solutions. During a brainstorming session there is no criticism of the ideas that are being put forward—the concept is to open up as many ideas as possible, and to break down any previously held preconceptions about the limits of the problem. Once this has been done the results of the brainstorming session can be explored and evaluated using further brainstorming or other analytical techniques.

Group brainstorming requires a leader to take control of the session, encourage participation by all members and keep the dialogue focused on the problem to be resolved. It is helpful if participants come from diverse backgrounds and experiences, as this tends to stimulate many more creative ideas. A brainstorming session should be fun as the group comes up with as many ideas as possible from the very practical to the wildly impossible, without criticism or evaluation during the actual session.

Ross McGowan and his friends used a brainstorming session to generate ideas for a prospective golf-related business they might start. Eventually someone hit on the idea of establishing a golf-training centre devoted entirely to the short game (Entrepreneurs in Action #13). From there they were able to go out and do a market analysis to see if the concept had any potential and the nature and extent of the competition. That analysis revealed that outside of one school in Florida, no one had thought to open a short game facility anywhere in North America and there seemed to be a tremendous need for such a centre. That was the motivation McGowan and his group needed to move forward with the implementation of their plan and the opening of their first centre.

Here is an example of a modified brainstorming exercise that you could use to help identify opportunities you might choose to develop for a new business.

A FOUR-STEP PROCESS:

1. Meet with someone you trust (a close friend, relation, or other person) for one hour. With this individual discuss your strengths, weaknesses, personal beliefs, values, and similar topics. In other words, focus on what you enjoy doing because you do it well (jobs, hobbies, sports, pastimes, etc.) and where your limits are in terms of interests, ethics, capabilities.

13 Entrepreneurs in action

Short Game, Big Ideas

Helping players get up and down appears to be on the upswing these days. That's what a group of golf-minded Winnipeggers guessed would be the case a little over four years ago.

Intent on starting a golf-related business but unsure about what that enterprise might be, the group convened a brainstorming session to determine what form their prospective business should take. Eventually, someone finally hit on an idea — why not open a golf training centre devoted entirely to the short game?

"The concept evolved from an idea put forth by one of our Toronto-based partners, Richard Donnelly," explained Ross McGowan, president of Winnipeg-based Short Game Golf Corporation. "The next step was to go out and do a market analysis to see if it had any potential."

What that analysis revealed was that outside of Dave Pelz's short game school in Boca Raton, Fla., no one had thought to open a short game-only practice facility anywhere in North America. Furthermore, the research showed that an untapped continental market of over 30 million golfers was there for the taking. And there was more, said McGowan.

"Our research also uncovered some other facts that underscored the need for a short game facility. First, 80 per cent of a golfer's handicap is created from 60 yards and in. Second, 65 per cent of the strokes taken in an average round occur from 60 yards and in. We also found that putting makes up 43 per cent of the strokes in an average round of golf."

Elated by its discovery, the group knew that it had to move fast to take advantage of the niche opportunity it had unearthed. The first step was to find a backer for the project.

"We got things started in the summer of 1995," recalls McGowan. "We went to Charlie Spiring (president and CEO of Wellington West, a Manitoba-based investment firm) to put together the initial financing to get the company going. After that, it was a matter of determining how to design the facility, and conducting site selection."

Although it took 14 months to refine the concept and find a suitable location, the wait proved to be worthwhile. A 3.8-acre parcel of land was purchased in South Winnipeg, and by May 1997, the first PGX Short Game and Golf Training Centre was open for business.

Though confident in its product, the group, which had grown to 12 partners, approached the opening with a cautious optimism. Winnipeg, after all, carries a reputation for being one of the toughest test markets in the country, so where better to make a trial run, noted McGowan.

"Winnipeg is a representative example of a mid-sized city, and the originating partners are from Winnipeg, as well. Plus there's the saying: 'If it works in Winnipeg, it will work anywhere,'" said McGowan, referring to the thrifty spending habits of the city's residents.

Apparently, Winnipeggers have liked what they've seen.

"The reception has been excellent and is continuing to build in a positive way," McGowan said. "Membership has increased in each of the three years, and we expect to keep building on that."

The major reason for the centre's success lies in its thoughtful layout. The complex contains four large USGA-standard greens, two silica sand bunkers, and two large water hazards. Both the greens and surrounding terrain have been contoured to provide golfers with similar conditions they would face during a typical round of golf. The emphasis is clearly on finesse, as no shot measures longer than 60 yards. Hitting stations are strategically placed around the greens to provide a variety of challenges and ensure no one shot is the same.

Unlike other practice facilities that leave customers to their own devices, there is plenty of expert advice readily available at the Short Game Centre. Each of the six major hitting stations features a video kiosk, where instruction on any facet of the short game is only a touch of a video screen away.

A new site was slated to open in Calgary in mid-July, with another in Oakland, Calif., by the end of the year, and seven more are planned for the San Francisco Bay area. Sites in Toronto and Vancouver are projected to be in place by the end of 2000, while keen interest in the short game concept has been shown by several other cities in the southern U.S. Expansion to far-off locales such as Australia, Eastern Europe and the Orient is a long-term goal.

"This year is going to be our break-out year," said McGowan. "We're currently working with groups in Vancouver and Toronto. We're also working with the city of Oakland to build a short game facility next to the Oakland Coliseum (home of major league baseball's Athletics, and the NFL's Raiders). That will provide us with a year-round market (Winnipeg is only open 125 days a year).

While the short game concept is attractive to communities not only because centres pay taxes, often reclaim derelict land and provide the average public player an opportunity to refine what is traditionally the worst part of his or her game, McGowan is also cognizant of the fact that the facility makes a great venue to stage corporate golf outings.

"Corporate events are a huge part of our business in Winnipeg, and we see it being no different elsewhere," he said. "Staging an event at a centre is an excellent alternative to a golf tournament. It's less costly and everyone is in one place. We close the centre down from 4–8 p.m., put on a nine-hole challenge along with a skills competition, and then cap off the day with a barbeque and drinks. Our goal is to have 40 corporate outings this year. We already had 25 booked by May."

The 1999 season will also see Short Game Centres get into the retail side of the game, something McGowan sees as a natural progression.

"We need to provide a full-service retail operation with custom-fitting of wedges and putters. Of course, there will be nuances unique to each market area. Seeing as we specialize in short game instruction, the next step is to specialize in fitting short game equipment."

While McGowan and his cohorts want to take the concept worldwide, their main goal remains a simple one.

"Where Dave Pelz is the Rolls Royce of the short game business, we want to be the Henry Ford of the short game. We want to give the average golfer access to the finest golf and training facility in the world." (www.shortgame-golf.com)

Source: Todd Lewys, "Short Game, Big Ideas," *Score*, Aug/Sept, p. 29. Reprinted with permission of *SCORE GOLF* Magazine.

2. After considering your strengths and weaknesses, pick the activity (job, hobby, etc.) that you enjoy the most. Think of a number of problem areas that affect you when you engage in that activity. Then meet with a group of personal acquaintances (3-5) and actively brainstorm a number of potential products or services that could solve those problems (no criticism or negative comments). In an hour you should be able to come up with 80–100 potential product/service ideas.
3. Take this list of potential ideas back to the same person you met with in (1). Reflect back on what you previously identified as your strengths and weaknesses and use that information to develop a framework to narrow the 80–100 ideas down to what you think are the five best new business ideas for you.
4. By yourself, take the five ideas and refine them down to the *one* that you feel relates most closely to your individual interests. Answer the following questions about that top idea:
   - Why did you select it?
   - Where did the idea come from?
   - What are the principal characteristics or attributes of the idea?
   - In what context did it come up during the brainstorming session?
   - What is your ability to carry out the idea?
   - What resources would you need to capitalize on the idea?
   - How profitable is a business venture based on the idea likely to be?
   - Who else might you need to involve?
   - What do you feel is the success potential of the idea you have proposed on a scale of 1 to 5 (with 5 being a very profitable venture)?[4]

The range of sources discussed here is certainly not exhaustive. Through careful observation, enthusiastic inquiry, and systematic searching, it is possible to uncover a number of areas of opportunity.

As you go about this kind of search it is important to write down your ideas as they come to mind. If you don't, a thought that might have changed your life may be lost forever.

4. I would like to thank Vance Gough of Mount Royal College for permission to include this exercise.

WHERE DO NEW VENTURE IDEAS COME FROM?

A survey of over 300 entrepreneurs asked them to provide the sources of the initial ideas for their business. The results are shown in Table 3.1.

TABLE 3.1 WHERE ENTREPRENEURS GET THE IDEAS FOR THEIR NEW VENTURES?[5]

SOURCE OF IDEA	PER CENT OF RESPONDENTS*
Prior Business Experience	73.0%
Business Associates	32.8%
Saw a Similar Business Somewhere Else	25.8%
Suggestion by Friends or Relatives	19.1%
Hobby/Personal Interest	17.2%
Personal Research	11.3%
It Just Came to Mind	10.9%
Saw Something in a Magazine/Newspaper	2.3%
Saw or Heard Something on Radio/Television	0.4%
Other Sources	4.7%

* Sums to more than 100% since respondents could indicate more than one source.

Prior experience was by far the most important source of new venture ideas that led to the founding of these firms (73 per cent). However, social contacts were also very important in identifying the ideas on which their businesses were based. A large percentage of entrepreneurs identified business associates (32.8 per cent) and friends and family (19.1 per cent) as important sources of the ideas for their business.

A substantial percentage also reported that they had seen a similar business somewhere else and used that as the basis for their firm (25.8 per cent). Most of those who reported that they had seen a similar business somewhere else also based their business on their prior personal experience. This indicates that that by far the majority of entrepreneurs model their firms in some way upon companies in which they have previously worked; for example, after working for some information technology company, these individuals may have realized they could provide some aspect of that or a similar service to clients themselves or provide a service to their employer and similar companies on a contract basis. Working in an industry provides individuals with information and access to professionals within that industry that can help prospective entrepreneurs identify new venture opportunities.

AREAS OF FUTURE OPPORTUNITY

In searching for a unique business idea the best thing to keep in mind is the dynamic changes taking place within our society, our economy, and our everyday way of doing things. These changes are usually difficult to get a handle on, and it is hard to understand their implications for new business possibilities, but they represent the principal areas of opportunity available today. If you think about it for a minute, most of the major growth areas in business — such as computers and information technology; cable television systems; fast food; a wide range of personal services; and direct selling by mail, telephone, and television — did not even exist just a few years ago. But now they are so commonplace we take them for granted. Getting information on emerging trends and assessing their implications for various business situations can be a major road to significant business success.

What can we expect in the future? No one has a crystal ball that can predict these changes with 100 per cent accuracy, but many books and business publications provide projections of future trends and changes that could be useful to the insightful observer. For instance, Faith Popcorn, the consumer-trend diva who first labelled the "cocooning" trend, has identified a number of others that she sees being reflected in modern North American society. These include:

5. Singh, Hills, and Lumpkin (1999).

FYI FOR YOUR INFORMATION

TOP 10 BUSINESS OPPORTUNITIES FOR 2001

1. Personal coaches: someone to organize our lives
2. Sex Toys: accessories that enhance the romance
3. Teen gadgets: video games, kiddy PDAs, and anything wireless
4. Outsourced business services: from distribution to Internet strategy
5. Specialist financial advisors: from tax experts to lifestyle confidantes
6. Vanity products for aging boomers
7. Escape Inc.: adventure travel and extreme sports
8. E-biz security: privacy and encryption software to foil prying eyes
9. High-tech marketers: wizards who can understand and explain it
10. Youth education: private-sector, after-school tutoring

Source: Richard Worzel, Rhea Seymour, Jennifer O'Connor, Rick Kang, Peter MacDonald, Kara Kuryllowicz, "Best Bets 2001," *PROFIT: The Magazine for Canadian Entrepreneurs* (December/January 2001): 27, www.profitguide.com/startups/issues_article.asp?ID=322, accessed December 22, 2001.

- **99 Lives** Too fast a pace and too little time causes societal schizophrenia and forces us to assume multiple roles. Popcorn says that time is the new money — people would rather spend money than time — and predicts that by 2010, 90 per cent of all consumer goods will be home-delivered.
- **Anchoring** A reaching back to our spiritual roots, taking what was secure from the past to be ready for the future. Popcorn notes that more and more people are returning to traditional Western religions, feeling that religion is an important part of their lives or are exploring non-Western alternatives in their search for spirituality and healing.
- **AtmosFEAR** Polluted air, contaminated water, and tainted food stir up a storm of consumer doubt and uncertainty. Headlines scream about E. coli, mad cow disease, anthrax threats, and other environmental problems. Bottled water has become a billion-dollar business in North America alone.
- **Being Alive** Awareness that good health extends longevity and leads to a new way of life. Look at the tremendous surge in the sales of organic products, herbal additives and remedies, and the popularity of fitness clubs and gyms, acupuncture, magnets, meditation, and other forms of alternative medicine.
- **Cashing Out** Working women and men, questioning personal/career satisfaction and goals, opt for simpler living. Stressed consumers, she says, are searching for fulfillment and simplicity but going back to basics in their lifestyles, consciously opting for more leisure time or getting out of the rat-race by starting a home-based or other small business.
- **Clanning** Belonging to a group that represents common feelings, causes, or ideals; validating one's own belief system. People are banding together to form common interest clubs, groups, and other organizations where they can share opinions, beliefs, complaints, or whatever else they are feeling with other like-minded individuals.
- **Down-Aging** Nostalgic for their carefree childhood, baby boomers find comfort in familiar pursuits and products from their youth. Music, automobile brands, movies, and a variety of other names and products from the 1960s and 1970s are all being resurrected in response to this demand.
- **Egonomics** To offset a depersonalized society, consumers crave recognition of their individuality. This has created opportunities for improved customer service by increasingly recognizing the specific needs of individuals or for the "ultracustomization" of products and services to the specific requirements of particular customers.
- **EVEolution** The way women think and behave is impacting business, causing a marketing shift away from a traditional, hierarchical model to a relationship model. As Popcorn notes, women have far more financial influence then has traditionally been recognized. They own one-third of all North American

businesses and control 80 per cent of all household spending in the country. As a consequence, marketing to them in an appropriate manner can mean a significant business opportunity.

- **Fantasy Adventure** The modern age whets our desire for roads untaken. Exotic theme hotels in Las Vegas are exploding, theme parks are booming, cruise lines are expanding, adventure and eco-tourism are growing, and theme rooms and suites in hotels are becoming increasingly popular as people strive to satisfy their exotic fantasies.
- **Icon Toppling** A new socioquake transforms mainstream North America and the world as the pillars of society are questioned and rejected. Increasingly skeptical consumers are ready to bring down the long-accepted monuments of business, government, and society. Large companies no longer hold our trust. Loyalty to a single employer has gone the way of the dinosaur. Governments are now a reminder of cynicism and distrust. And the views of doctors, lawyers, and other professionals are no longer accepted without question.
- **Pleasure Revenge** Consumers are having a secret bacchanal. They're mad as hell and want to cut loose again. They are tired of being told what's good for them, so are indifferent to rules and regulations and want to enjoy some of the more "forbidden" aspects of life. Steakhouses, martini bars, and cigar clubs are all popular reflections of this trend.
- **Small Indulgences** Stressed-out consumers want to indulge in affordable luxuries and seek ways to reward themselves. Premium-priced products such as ice cream, sunglasses, chocolate, liqueur, toothpaste, and similar items have become one way for consumers to reward themselves at moderate expense at the end of a hard day or week.
- **SOS (Save Our Society)** The country has rediscovered a social conscience of ethics, passion, and compassion. We are seeing more corporations make a commitment to return some proportion of their profits to the community; consumers are becoming more responsive to companies that exhibit a social conscience attuned to ethical concerns, education, or the environment; and there has been a dramatic increase in the popularity of "ethical" mutual funds.
- **Vigilante Consumer** Frustrated, often-angry consumers are manipulating the marketplace through pressure, protest, and politics. Consumers seek real products, benefits, and value. When they are disappointed, they can be formidable enemies. At any one time there are typically a number of boycotts in progress against some company. This has really been facilitated by the growth of the Net where consumers can set up chat rooms, news groups, and Web sites to carry on their complaint against some particular company or brand.[6]

The kind of social changes mentioned by Popcorn help define the future orientation of our society and can all spell potential opportunity for an aggressive entrepreneur.

In a similar vein, Canadian Shirley Roberts, in her book *Harness the Future: The Nine Keys to Emerging Consumer Behaviour*, says that the future will be bright for those entrepreneurial companies that move first out of the gate just as demand starts to rise for products and services to meet consumers' changing needs. That, she says, means figuring out tomorrow's buyers today.

Predicting consumer demand, Roberts feels, lies in understanding the nine drivers of consumer behaviour:

1. Demographics
2. The economy
3. Technology
4. Globalization
5. Government
6. Environmental issues
7. Wellness
8. The retail environment
9. The consumer psyche[7]

6. www.faithpopcorn.com/trends
7. Shirley Roberts, *Harness the Future: The Nine Keys to Emerging Consumer Behaviour*, John Wiley and Sons, 1998

For example, rising personal health concerns as reflected in the "Being Alive" trend mentioned by Popcorn mean future consumers will take a more proactive approach to maintaining their personal wellness. In addition, trends like increasing globalization are exposing more people to products and cultures, and changing their tastes as a result.

Any one of these trends could represent an area of significant opportunity for an observant individual. Keeping on top of these shifts can provide the inspiration for many significant new business opportunities. As the futurist John Naisbitt has said, "trends, like horses, are easier to ride in the direction they are going."

SOME SPECIFIC IDEAS AND CONCEPTS FOR THE FUTURE

In view of all these evident trends a number of specific business ideas are expected to do well in the marketplace of the future. Roberts, for example, provides a list of her best businesses for the future:

1. Self-diagnostic medical tools
2. Affordable organic foods
3. Educational books, videos, and CD-ROMs
4. Technology-training centres
5. Customized information services
6. Anti-aging cosmetics
7. Pet-related products and services
8. Financial services tailored to women
9. Activewear for aging adults
10. Home-safety devices[8]

The list that follows will expand upon some of the possible implications of these trends and give you some idea of specific businesses they indicate should be potential opportunities. The list is by no means complete, but it will give you a few things to think about.

BIOTECHNOLOGY will become a significant growth area as we expand our knowledge of genetic engineering. The world population is exploding, and feeding these additional people with our existing land base will require biotechnological intervention. There will be many business opportunities in agriculture, landscaping, and other food-related industries. Biotechnology will also come into play in products to extend and improve the quality of human life. Possible new venture opportunities include:

- Blood tests to screen for genetic diseases
- Genetic engineering and the development of alternative medicines
- Bionic parts and artificial replacement organs
- DNA modifications to improve disease resistance or increase plant and animal yields
- Implantable microchips in animals

THE INTERNET is growing explosively and interest is likely to continue to be strong despite the recent problems and failures of a number of business-to-consumer (B2C) Web-based companies. These were largely situations where the business model had not been well defined and developed, where they had underestimated the financial and technical resources required to get their business to the break-even point, or that were simply poorly managed and squandered the financial reserves that were available for them to get the business off the ground. Despite this shakeout, use of the Internet continues to grow rapidly and e-commerce still presents a large number of potential opportunities for either new or existing businesses. Many forecasters predict that business-to-business (B2B) e-commerce will grow more than ten times faster then B2C commerce, so most of the attractive opportunities are likely to be found in this arena.

There is no doubt the Internet will continue to change the way we communicate and conduct business. Regardless of whether your venture is Web-based or not, you will still likely have a Web page for customer

8. As reported in "Know Thy Next Customer," *PROFIT The Magazine for Canadian Entrepreneurs*, (December-January, 1999), 40.

support and communication, to complement your advertising and marketing program, to offer product information, to conduct research and competitive intelligence, or to network with other business owners. New venture opportunities using the Net could include:

- Designing, hosting, and maintaining Web sites
- Internet marketing consulting services
- Software development for very specific applications
- Selling specialty products such as small business equipment, health-related equipment and supplements, cosmetics and anti-aging products, home-delivered meals and specialty foods, gaming services and related products, travel and leisure products and services, multimedia packages and programs, and a wide range of other products that serve narrow markets around the globe, 24 hours a day, 7 days a week.

Key points

WHY AN E-BUSINESS TODAY?

1. The Internet is the fastest growing market opportunity today, promising a remarkable growth curve for entrepreneurs who like to think big.
2. The Net can make things better, faster, and cheaper, all in one place.
3. The number of Canadians with access to the Internet is soaring and they represent an affluent group.
4. The Web loves entrepreneurs, particularly women, because it's an ideal equalizer. It allows the breakdown of gender, geographic, and other barriers and enables small businesses to compete against big firms.
5. E-commerce makes your domestic market everyone's export market. It blurs the distinction between domestic and international markets.

Source: Based on Royal Bank, "Champions: Breakthroughs and Resources for Women Entrepreneurs," 3, no. 1 (Summer 2000).

ANATOMY OF A TYPICAL E-COMMERCE TRANSACTION

Here is an example of how a typical commercial transaction happens online. There are any number of ways in which this sequence of events can be facilitated, but once you understand what has to take place you can find the right solution for your business.

1. You must first develop a Web site that allows potential customers to find your products or services. A customer can browse through your electronic catalog and select items to add to their shopping cart.
2. Once customers have finished selecting their items, they can fill out an on-line order form. This usually includes entering their name, address, etc.
3. Order processing software will then calculate the totals, taxes and shipping information (usually based on delivery destination), credit card number, expiry date, and delivery address. This form must be secure.
4. Payment processing software encrypts the order total and payment information and contacts the credit card company to verify that the card number is valid and the total amount within the cardholder's limit.
5. Once authorized, a message is usually transmitted immediately to the customer and the merchant verifying the order, and the order is processed.

Source: Based on "E-Commerce: Exploring Your Options," The Business Link, Business Service Centre, Edmonton, Alberta, (www.cbsc.org/alberta).

FYI FOR YOUR INFORMATION

Here are a few Web sites you might want to check out for more information on doing business on the Internet:

ELECTRONIC COMMERCE INFO-GUIDE

A document designed to help you navigate through the different government programs, services, and regulations that deal with electronic commerce, and identify those of interest.
(www.cbsc.org/english/search/display.cfm?CODE=2842&Coll=FE_FEDSBIS_E)

NET GAIN

All the information you need to help your business get started on the Internet.
(strategis.ic.gc.ca/SSG/ee00209e.html)

E-COMMERCE—EXPLORING YOUR OPTIONS

An overview of what you need to know to set up an on-line store to do business on the Internet.
(www.cbsc.org/english/search/display.cfm?Code=4021&Coll=FE_FEDSBIS_E)

ESTABLISHING A PRESENCE ON THE INTERNET

A overview of Internet business application and what you need to know to conduct business on the Web.
(www.cbsc.org/alberta/tbl.cfm?fn=web_index)

BEFORE YOU START YOUR E-BUSINESS

What you need to consider before you start an e-business of your own.
(www.gosolocanada.com/ecom_start.html)

WEBMONKEY E-COMMERCE TUTORIAL

A tutorial that will show you how to generate a realistic e-business plan; create a site design that caters to your on-line customers; deal with things like credit cards, tax, shipping, and security; and decide whether you should build, buy, or rent an e-commerce solution to manage your site's transactions.
(hotwired.lycos.com/webmonkey/e-business/building/tutorials/tutorial3.html)

EXPLORING BUSINESS OPPORTUNITIES

A comprehensive overview for finding and developing business opportunities, including starting an on-line business.
(www.ei.gov.bc.ca/Publicinfo/publications/smallbuspubs/ebo2000.pdf)

TRAINING AND PROFESSIONAL DEVELOPMENT is also an important growth area, particularly in regards to corporate, consumer, and computer training. The explosion in Internet usage, new technology and operating systems, and modified software programs will continue to fuel the need for training to keep computer skills current. In addition, more and more small businesses are becoming computerized and need the support. Consumers are also looking to renew and improve themselves, and seminars and other educational programs designed to facilitate this personal growth are likely to do well. Some specific training and development opportunities include:

- Customized on-site computer training and centralized computer training centres
- Image consultants
- Professional organizers
- Video conferencing specialists
- Programming consultants
- Personal financial planning programs
- Internet-based training and educational programs

MAINTAINING "WELLNESS" is an emerging theme that will create a growing demand for a variety of fitness and health-related products. People are focusing on experiencing a better quality of life by shaping up and healing their minds and bodies. New venture opportunities exist in the following areas:

- Healthier and organically-grown food products
- Alternative medicine and homeopathic remedies
- Spas and cosmetic surgery centres
- Holistic health clubs and fitness centres
- Holistic healing and the use of ancient remedies
- Stress relief programs
- Restaurants emphasizing low-fat and other types of "healthy" foods

PERSONAL INDULGENCE is almost the opposite of the "wellness" trend, with people wanting to reward themselves periodically with small, affordable luxuries. New venture opportunities here could include:

- Individual portions of gourmet foods
- Specialty ice cream and other exotic desserts
- Specialty coffee, tea, and wine shops
- Imported cigars, smoking rooms, or a cigar-of-the-month type of club
- Outlets for specialty breads, bagels, and other baked goods
- Exotic meats such as elk, wild boar, bison, ostrich, and venison
- Bed-and-breakfast places or small hotels with specialty services
- Designer clothes for children
- Aromatherapy

CHILDREN'S PRODUCTS AND SERVICES will increase in demand with an increasing birth rate due to the "echo" from the baby boom, two-income families, and single-parent households trying to balance work and home. Young people, including teens and pre-teens, have also become a significant market in their own right, with considerable exposure to conventional media and billions of dollars of discretionary income of their own. In addition, parents and grandparents increasingly want their children and grandchildren to have "everything" and are prepared to pay for the "best." New business opportunities in this area include:

- Childcare centres and camps
- Juvenile safety products
- Fitness centres and play zones for kids
- Healthy food products for infants and children
- Home health care for newborns
- Designer clothing for children
- Educational toys, games, and puzzles
- Programs for children with learning disabilities
- Children's bookstores

HOME HEALTH SERVICE AND ELDERCARE will continue to be a rapidly growing market with the aging of the baby boom and the ever-increasing costs and declining quality of health care. Opportunities for businesses in this area include:

- Home health care providers such as physiotherapists, occupational therapists, and nursing assistants
- Door-to-door transportation services for the elderly
- Homemaking services
- Daycare centres for the elderly
- Seniors' travel clubs

- Independent, residential, and assisted-living centres
- Products and services for the physically challenged

WORK-AT-HOME PRODUCTS AND SERVICES will grow in popularity as the stay-at-home-and-work trend continues to sweep the country. Increasing numbers of telecommuters from the corporate world and home-based entrepreneurs want to provide a comfortable, secure environment for themselves to work effectively from home. Opportunities for new business ventures include:

- Decorating and furnishing of home offices
- Home safety and protection devices
- Home-office furniture and technical equipment
- On-site equipment repair services
- Home delivery services for office equipment, furniture, and supplies

PET CARE AND PAMPERING represents a significant market opportunity as well for specialized care products and services. Some opportunities for businesses here include:

- Pet day-care centres and hotels
- Pet snacks and treats
- Home grooming services for pets
- 24-hour veterinary care
- Entertainment products and videos for pets
- Baked products for dogs
- Pet furniture and clothing stores
- Restraining systems for pets

RETAIL BOUTIQUES with narrow sales niches will increase in number as the category killer, box stores, and discount department stores expand across the country and come to dominate most conventional retail markets like building materials, lawn and garden supplies, books, computers and office supplies, consumer electronics, food products, music, video rentals, and other categories. Opportunities for one-of-a-kind stores include:

- Second-hand goods
- Optometry
- Bakery cafés
- Specialty shoe stores
- Personal financial services
- Home decorating
- Birding
- Gardening centres
- Stress relief
- Paint-your-own pottery and similar craft stores
- Travel-related products and services
- Homeopathic remedies
- Microbreweries

PERSONAL SERVICES OF ALL TYPES will grow in popularity as people spend more time at work and have fewer leisure hours. As a result they will be willing to pay others to run their errands and handle many time-consuming home and family-related matters. These personal errand services could perform a variety of tasks such as grocery shopping, picking up laundry, theatre tickets, shoe repairs, and other items. They could also arrange for the repair and servicing of cars, taking care of pets, choosing gifts, consulting on the selection of clothes, and similar personal matters. Other opportunities in this area include:

- Personal concierge service
- Gift services
- Pickup and delivery service for guests and clients
- Rent-a-driver
- Rent-a-chef
- Personal escort service

DILBERT reprinted by permission of United Feature Syndicate, Inc.

These are just a few of the possibilities that are available to you for starting a business of your own. Becoming a successful entrepreneur means becoming a trend spotter so that you are aware of potential sources of opportunity. To this end you must be observant, listen to other people, and ask lots of questions. Keeping abreast of these changes will help you identify any number of prospective business opportunities.

EVALUATING YOUR IDEAS

As you have seen, generating ideas for a prospective new business is a relatively simple procedure—the end result of which is a number of potential business opportunities that may, or may not, have a chance of becoming successful ventures.

Discovering ideas is only part of the process involved in starting a business. The ideas must be screened and evaluated, and a selection made of those that warrant further investigation. It is essential that you subject your ideas to this analysis to find the "fatal flaws" if any exist (and they often do). Otherwise, the marketplace will find them when it is too late and you have spent a great deal of time and money.

But how can you determine which ideas you should evaluate? Of the multitude of possible alternatives, which are likely to be best for you? Knowles and Bilyea suggest that you think of the process of selecting the right opportunity for you as a huge funnel equipped with a series of filters. You pour everything into this funnel — your vision, values, long-term goals, short-term objectives, personality, problems, etc. — and a valuable business idea drains out the bottom.[9] This opportunity selection process contains six steps:

1. Identify your business and personal objectives.
2. Learn more about your favourite industries.
3. Identify promising industry segments.
4. Identify problem areas and brainstorm solutions.
5. Compare possible solutions with your objectives and opportunities in the marketplace.
6. Focus on the most promising opportunities.

9. Ronald A. Knowles and Cliff G. Bilyea, *Small Business: An Entrepreneur's Plan*, 3rd Canadian ed. (Harcourt Brace & Company, 1999), 55.

STEP 1: IDENTIFY YOUR BUSINESS AND PERSONAL GOALS

List your personal and business goals. What do you want from your business? Money? Personal fulfillment? Independence? To be your own boss? Freedom? Control over your own destiny? Think back to what stimulated your interest in thinking about going into a business of your own in the first place. List everything you would like to accomplish and what you expect your business to be able to provide.

At this stage it might help to meet with someone whom you trust — a close friend, relation, or other person — for an hour or so. With this individual you can discuss your strengths and weaknesses, goals, values, ethical standards, and similar personal issues. She/he can help you focus your goals and refine your thinking in relation to what you enjoy doing, what you are good at, and where your limits are in terms of interests and capabilities.

STEP 2: RESEARCH YOUR FAVOURITE INDUSTRIES

As you considered the variety of trends we discussed earlier in this Stage, there were undoubtedly a number of possibilities that captured your interest. Now you should explore a couple of these situations in more detail. These industries should be ones that interest you and about which you have some first-hand knowledge. They could be food service, travel, manufacturing, retailing, construction, or whatever.

After you have picked your industries, investigate all the information you can find about them from business publications, government agencies and departments, trade magazines, the Internet, and similar sources. The Industry Canada Web site (strategis.ic.gc.ca) and on-line databases such as ABI/Inform and Canadian Business and Current Affairs (CBCA) available at your local university library can point you to hundreds of articles related to almost any field. Focus on such areas as the history of the business, the nature and degree of competition, recent industry trends and breakthroughs, number and distribution of customers, and similar topics. It will help to write a brief industry overview of each situation after you have completed your investigation.

STEP 3: IDENTIFY PROMISING INDUSTRY SEGMENTS

With a thorough understanding of one or more industry situations you are now in a position to identify possible market segments where you think you could survive and prosper. Profile your typical target customer — a person or business who needs a particular product or service you could provide.

If you are looking at the consumer market, identify what this prospect will look like in terms of demographic factors such as age, sex, location, income, family size, education, and so on, and in terms of psychographic and other factors such as interests, values, lifestyle, leisure activities, and buying patterns. If you are looking at a commercial/industrial market, use company size, industry, geographic location, number of employees, and so on.

STEP 4: IDENTIFY PROBLEM AREAS AND BRAINSTORM SOLUTIONS

Identify the problem areas for some of these groups of customers that you feel are currently being met ineffectively. What "gaps" are there in terms of the needs of these customers that you feel you can address? Get together with a group of people who know something about business and the industry. Try to actively brainstorm up a list of products and services that could represent potential ways to solve these problems. Keep your discussion positive. Let your imaginations roam. Don't be concerned with the merits or demerits of an idea at this stage. Just try to make note of as many potential ideas as you can. You should be able to come up with 80–100 or more prospective ideas in an hour.

Refine your list. Try to narrow it down to the five or ten best ideas for you based on your interests, goals and objectives, strengths and weaknesses, and available resources.

STEP 5: COMPARE POSSIBLE SOLUTIONS WITH YOUR OBJECTIVES AND OPPORTUNITIES IN THE MARKETPLACE

Richard Buskirk of the University of Southern California has designed a framework you can use to evaluate the pros and cons of your potential business ideas.[10] It is built around what he calls the "Ideal" or "Model" business. The framework contains 19 distinct factors that affect the chances of success for any new business.

10.Richard Buskirk, *The Entrepreneur's Handbook* (Los Angeles: Robert Brian, Inc., 1985), 41–45.

Very few ideas will conform precisely to the specifications of the model, but the more a business idea deviates from the "ideal," the more difficulties and greater risks you will encounter with that venture. Testing your concepts against the model will also help identify the areas in which you might expect to have difficulties with your business.

The model is presented in Table 3.2. Let us briefly discuss each of the factors listed.

REQUIRES NO INVESTMENT If you don't have to put any money into your business, then you can't lose any if it fails. You only lose the time you have invested. The more money that must be committed to the venture, the larger the risk and the less attractive the business becomes. Some new businesses, such as fancy theme restaurants, may require so much initial capital there is really no way they can be financially profitable. Smart business people tend to avoid businesses that require a large investment of their own money.

TABLE 3.2 CHARACTERISTICS OF THE "IDEAL" BUSINESS

- Requires no investment
- Has a recognized, measurable market
- A perceived need for the product or service
- A dependable source of supply for required inputs
- No government regulation
- Requires no labour force
- Provides 100 percent gross margin
- Buyers purchase frequently
- Receives favourable tax treatment
- Has a receptive, established distribution system
- Has great publicity value
- Customers pay in advance
- No risk of product liability
- No technical obsolescence
- No competition
- No fashion obsolescence
- No physical perishability
- Impervious to weather conditions
- Possesses some proprietary rights

HAS A RECOGNIZED, MEASURABLE MARKET The ideal situation is to sell a product or service to a clearly recognized market that can be relied on to buy it. This may require doing a preliminary investigation of the market acceptance of your idea or concept. Look for some market confirmation of what you propose to offer before proceeding any further.

A PERCEIVED NEED FOR THE PRODUCT OR SERVICE Ideally, your intended customers should already perceive a need for what you intend to sell them. They should know they need your product or service now, thus simplifying your marketing efforts. If they don't recognize their need, you have to first persuade them they need the product and then convince them to buy it from you. Try to avoid products or services that require you to educate the market before you can make a sale.

A DEPENDABLE SOURCE OF SUPPLY FOR REQUIRED INPUTS Make certain you can make or provide what it is you plan to sell. Many businesses have failed because they were unable to obtain essential raw materials or components under the terms they had originally planned. Sudden changes in price or availability of these key inputs can threaten the viability of your entire venture. Large corporations commonly try to directly control or negotiate long-term contracts to assure reliable and consistent supplies. You have to be just as concerned if there are only one or two sources for the materials you require.

NO GOVERNMENT REGULATION The ideal business would not be impacted at all by government regulation. This is impossible in today's world, but some industries are more subject to government involvement than others. Food, drugs, financial services, transportation, communications, etc. are all examples of businesses that require extensive government approval. If your business falls into this category, make sure you understand how government regulations will affect you in terms of time and money.

REQUIRES NO LABOUR FORCE The ideal business would require no labour force. This is possible in one-person operations — the "one-man show." Once you hire an employee you have a lot of government paperwork to deal with relating to employment insurance, Canada Pension, and other legal requirements. You are also subject to a broad range of regulations concerning such things as occupational health and safety, human rights, and pay equity. Few small-business people enjoy dealing with these requirements, and they can be quite time-consuming. If your business demands the hiring of additional employees you must be prepared to take on the responsibility for managing these people effectively.

PROVIDES 100 PER CENT GROSS MARGIN While virtually no businesses provide a 100 per cent gross margin, the idea is that the larger the gross margin, the better the business. Gross margin is what you have left after paying the *direct* material and labour costs for whatever it is you are selling. For example, say you are running an appliance repair business. A typical service call takes one hour, for which you charge the customer $50. However, this call costs you $15 in direct labour and $5 in parts and materials; therefore, your gross margin is $30, or 60 per cent. Service industries like this generally have larger gross margins than manufacturing businesses.

In businesses with low gross margins, small errors in estimating costs or sales can quickly lead to losses. These businesses also tend to have a high break-even point, making it very difficult to make a lot of money. High-margin businesses, on the other hand, can break even with very small sales volumes and generate profits very quickly once this volume of business is exceeded.

BUYERS PURCHASE FREQUENTLY The ideal business would provide a product or service that customers purchase very frequently. This gives you more opportunities to sell to them. Frequent purchasing also reduces their risk in case your offering doesn't live up to their expectations. You are much more likely to try a new fast food restaurant that has opened in town than you are to purchase a new brand or type of washing machine, fax machine, home theatre system, or other such item.

RECEIVES FAVOURABLE TAX TREATMENT Firms in certain industries may receive tax incentives such as accelerated depreciation on capital assets, differential capital cost allowances, investment tax credits, or various other tax breaks. The ideal business will receive some sort of favourable or differential tax treatment. This sort of advantage can make your business more profitable and attractive to other investors should you require outside capital.

HAS A RECEPTIVE, ESTABLISHED DISTRIBUTION SYSTEM Ideally, your business would sell to established middlemen and distributors who are eager to handle it. If you have to develop a new method of distribution or are unable to obtain access to the existing one, getting your product to market can be a long and costly process. If traditional wholesalers and retailers are not prepared to carry your line, achieving any reasonable level of market coverage can be extremely difficult.

HAS GREAT PUBLICITY VALUE Publicity in magazines, in newspapers, and on television has great promotional value, and what's more, it's free. If your offering is sufficiently exciting and newsworthy, the resulting publicity may be sufficient to ensure a successful launch for your business. The publicity given to fashion concepts like Modrobes, the radio and television coverage of Al Pooper Scoopin', a business to clean up the "doggie doo" in one's backyard, and favourable reviews of local restaurants by newspaper food critics are all examples of tremendously helpful public notice of new products.

CUSTOMERS PAY IN ADVANCE A major problem facing most new businesses is that of maintaining an adequate cash flow. Typically, small firms are chronically short of cash, the lifeblood they require to pay their employees, their suppliers, and the government on an ongoing basis. The ideal business would have customers who pay in advance. This is in fact the case for many small retail service firms, the direct mail industry, and manufacturers of some custom-made products. Businesses where customers pay in advance are usually easier to start, have smaller start-up capital requirements, and don't suffer the losses due to bad debts incurred on credit sales.

NO RISK OF PRODUCT LIABILITY Some products and services are automatically subject to high risk from product liability. Anything ingested by the customer, amusement facilities such as go-cart tracks and water slides, and many manufactured products which possibly could cause injury to the user — all are loaded with potential liability. Liability can occur in unexpected situations, such as the serious injury recently sustained by a golfer whose golf club shattered and impaled him in the chest.

Try to avoid such high-risk businesses, or take every precaution to reduce risk, and carry lots of insurance.

NO TECHNICAL OBSOLESCENCE The ideal product or service would not suffer from technical obsolescence. The shorter the product's expected technical life expectancy, the less desirable it is as an investment. Products like popcorn, shampoo, garden tools, and electric drills seem to have been with us for as long as most of us can remember. On the other hand, the DVD player, MP3 Player, and laptop computer are of recent origin and are undergoing rapid technological transformation. Businesses built around these products are extremely risky for smaller firms and have a very high probability of failure.

NO COMPETITION Too much competition can be a problem, since aggressive price competitors can make it very difficult for you to turn a profit. Not having any competition can certainly make life much easier for a new small business. But if you should ever find yourself in this happy situation, you should ask yourself why. True, your offering may be so new to the marketplace that no other firms have had a chance to get established. But maybe it is just that other firms have already determined there really is no market for what you are planning to provide.

NO FASHION OBSOLESCENCE Fashion products usually have extremely short life cycles. You must be sure you can make your money before the cycle ends, or be prepared to offer an ongoing series of acceptable products season after season, if you hope to build your business into a sizeable enterprise. Fashion cycles exist not only for clothing and similar products but also for items like toys — witness what happened with the hula hoop, Wacky Wall Walker, Rubik's Cube, and Cabbage Patch dolls.

NO PHYSICAL PERISHABILITY Products with a short physical life have only a limited window available for their disposition. This applies not only to most food items but also to a wide variety of other goods such as photographic film. If your product is perishable, your business concept must include some method of selling your inventory quickly or a contingency plan to dispose of aged merchandise before it spoils.

IMPERVIOUS TO WEATHER CONDITIONS Some businesses are, by their very nature, at the mercy of the weather. If the weather is right for them, they prosper; if not, they may go broke. Pity the ski resort owner without any snow, the waterslide operator with a year of unseasonably cold weather, the beach concession during a summer of constant rain, the market gardener in the midst of an unexpected drought. The ideal business would not be impacted by these unpredictable changes in the weather.

POSSESSES SOME PROPRIETARY RIGHTS The ideal business would possess significant proprietary rights that give it some unique characteristic and protection against competition. These rights can be in the form of registered patents, trademarks, copyrighted material, protected trade secrets, licensing agreements that provide some sort of exclusive manufacturing arrangements, or perhaps rights for exclusive distribution of certain products in particular markets. Gendis Corporation, for example, was largely built on the rights to distribute first Papermate pens and then Sony products in Canada on an exclusive basis.

Of the ideas that you have generated you might want to pick three and evaluate each of them against the factors described in the Buskirk model in Figure 3.1. This evaluation will illustrate how well these ideas fit with all the characteristics of the "Ideal" business. How would you rate each idea on each of Buskirk's nineteen factors? On the basis of this evaluation, which of these ideas do you feel represents the most significant new venture opportunity for you? Can you justify your response? Did the idea you picked score less than five on any of Buskirk's factors? If so, can you think of any way to overcome the situation or find other solutions to the problem?

For a more formal evaluation of an invention, software concept, or other innovative idea, the Canadian Innovation Centre will conduct a comprehensive assessment to assist you in the decisions you must make regarding your idea. For more information, contact Canadian Innovation Centre, A1-490 Dutton Dr., Waterloo, Ontario, N2L 6H7, Phone 1-800-265-4559 or (519) 885-5870 (www.innovationcentre.ca).

FIGURE 3.1 COMPARE YOUR IDEAS TO THE "IDEAL" BUSINESS

Directions: Evaluate your concept in comparison with a model business by indicating how well each of the ideal characteristics below applies to your concept. Use a scale from 1 to 10, where 1 means the ideal trait is not at all true for your concept, and 10 means it is perfectly true.

FIT WITH MODEL BUSINESS

Requires no investment	1	2	3	4	5	6	7	8	9	10
Has a recognized, measurable market	1	2	3	4	5	6	7	8	9	10
A perceived need for the product or service	1	2	3	4	5	6	7	8	9	10
A dependable source of supply for required inputs	1	2	3	4	5	6	7	8	9	10
No government regulation	1	2	3	4	5	6	7	8	9	10
Requires no labour	1	2	3	4	5	6	7	8	9	10
Provides 100 per cent gross margin	1	2	3	4	5	6	7	8	9	10
Buyers purchase frequently	1	2	3	4	5	6	7	8	9	10
Receives favourable tax treatment	1	2	3	4	5	6	7	8	9	10
Has a receptive, established distribution system	1	2	3	4	5	6	7	8	9	10
Has great publicity value	1	2	3	4	5	6	7	8	9	10
Customers pay in advance	1	2	3	4	5	6	7	8	9	10
No risk of product liability	1	2	3	4	5	6	7	8	9	10
No technical obsolescence	1	2	3	4	5	6	7	8	9	10
No competition	1	2	3	4	5	6	7	8	9	10
No fashion obsolescence	1	2	3	4	5	6	7	8	9	10
No physical perishability	1	2	3	4	5	6	7	8	9	10
Impervious to weather conditions	1	2	3	4	5	6	7	8	9	10
Possesses some proprietary rights	1	2	3	4	5	6	7	8	9	10

Total points =
160–190 = A concept; 130–159 = B; 110–129 = C; 80–109 = D; Below 80, drop concept.

After completing this evaluation, does it make sense to proceed with the venture?
Explain your answer.

STEP 6: FOCUS ON THE MOST PROMISING OPPORTUNITIES

Which of the ideas you have evaluated seems to be the best fit with the "Ideal" business and is most consistent with your goals and values? This is probably the one you should be looking to pursue. However, no matter how exhaustive your evaluation, there is no guarantee of success. The challenge is to do the best you can in conducting an assessment of each of your principal ideas, knowing that at some point you will have to make a decision with incomplete information and less than scientific accuracy. As a good friend of mine commented during a dinner speech not long ago, "Entrepreneurship is like bungee jumping. Both require an act of faith."

DECIDING HOW TO PROCEED

Once satisfied you have identified an idea that represents a significant business opportunity, you must determine the best way to proceed. There are all sorts of *entry strategies* — ways people start new enterprises.

Reflecting on these alternatives and judging how they fit with your specific idea and your particular abilities and circumstances will enable you to turn them into real opportunities. No general rules have been developed to guarantee success, or even to indicate which concepts and strategies will work best in different situations, but being aware of the possibilities will give you a clearer picture of the job you need to do to succeed.

BUY A BUSINESS

One possibility is to find a business presently operating in your area of interest, buy it, and take over its operations. You may want to buy the business either because it is already quite successful but the current owners want to get out for some reason, or because the business is not doing very well under the current owners and you feel you can turn it around.

This can be a good entry strategy. A good deal of time and effort are involved in the startup phase of any business. This stage can be bypassed when you buy a going concern. You also acquire a location, customers, established trade relationships, and a number of other positive elements.

These advantages don't come for free, however. Buying an existing business may cost you more than getting into a similar business on your own. The current owner may expect to receive "goodwill" for certain assets already acquired or the effort devoted to the business so far. You may also inherit some problem, such as obsolete equipment, the bad image and reputation of the previous owners, or labour difficulties.

For a more complete discussion of this entry strategy refer to Stage Four of this book.

ACQUIRE A FRANCHISE

Another alternative is to buy the rights to operate a business that has been designed and developed by someone else, i.e., to acquire a *franchise*. Under a franchise agreement, an established company, the *franchisor*, with one or more successful businesses operating in other locations, provides assistance to a new firm in breaking into the marketplace. In return, the new owner, or *franchisee*, pays a fee for the assistance, invests money to set up and operate the business, pays a percentage of sales as a royalty to the franchisor, and agrees to operate the business within the terms and conditions laid out in the franchise agreement.

The assistance provided by the franchisor can take many forms, such as:

- The right to use the franchisor's brand names and registered trademarks
- The right to sell products and services developed by the franchisor
- The right to use operating systems and procedures developed by the franchisor
- Training in how to run the business
- Plans for the layout of the business facilities and the provision of specialized equipment
- A regional or national advertising program
- Centralized purchasing and volume discounts
- Research and development support

While the failure rate of franchised businesses is reported to be lower than that for independently established firms, there are a number of disadvantages associated with the concept.

For more detailed information refer to Stage Five of this book.

START A BUSINESS OF YOUR OWN

The third and probably most common means of getting into business for yourself is to start a business of your own from scratch. This is the route most frequently travelled by the true entrepreneur who wants a business that is really his or her own creation. Starting your own business can take many forms and involve a variety of entry strategies. While we are unable to discuss all the possibilities here in any detail, a few alternatives will be mentioned to get you thinking about their fit with your particular situation. Some of the possibilities available for you are:

a. Develop an entirely new product or service unlike anything else available in the market.

b. Acquire the rights to manufacture or sell someone else's product or use someone else's name or logo under licence. These rights could be exclusive to a product category, a geographic area, or a specific market.

c. Find a customer who wants to buy something. Then create a business to make that sale or serve that need.

d. Take a hobby and develop it into a business.

e. Develop a product or service similar to those currently on the market but which is more convenient, less expensive, safer, cleaner, faster, easier to use, lighter, stronger, more compact, or has some other important, distinguishing attribute.

f. Add incremental value to a product or service already available by putting it through another production process, combining it with other products and services, or providing it as one element in a larger package.

g. Become an agent or distributor for products or services produced by someone else. These may be domestically produced or imported from other countries.

h. Open a trading house or become a selling agent for Canadian firms who may be interested in selling their products or services abroad.

i. Develop a consulting service or provide information to other people in a subject area you know very well.

j. Become a supplier to another producer or large institutional customer. Large organizations require an extensive range of raw materials, supplies, and components to run their business. A small portion of their requirements could represent a significant volume of sales for you. This type of "outsourcing" is an excellent opportunity to pursue either through a contract or a strategic alliance with a larger organization.

k. Identify a situation where another firm has dropped what may be profitable products or product lines. They may have abandoned customer groups or market segments that are uneconomic for them to serve effectively but which may still be quite lucrative for a smaller company.

l. Borrow an idea from one industry or market and transfer it to another. A product or service that has been well accepted in one situation may well represent a substantial opportunity in other circumstances as well.

m. Look for opportunities to capitalize on special events and situations or unusual occurrences. You may be able to "piggyback" your business on to these situations.

Stage four

Buying a Business

Stages Two and Three of this book have provided you with a means of evaluating your personal potential for an entrepreneurial career and a procedure for generating and evaluating the basic attractiveness of an idea upon which to base your own business. The obvious route to self-employment is to start a business of your own based on this idea. Another route which should be explored is that of buying an existing firm. For many people this may even be their preferred course of action. How do you decide which route to take?

Stage Four discusses the various aspects that should be evaluated in considering whether you should start a new business or buy an existing one.

ADVANTAGES AND DISADVANTAGES OF BUYING AN EXISTING BUSINESS

The case for buying an existing firm, as against setting up a new one of your own, is not clear-cut either way. Each situation must be decided on its merits. There are distinct advantages and disadvantages to each course of action. You must consider how well your personal preferences fit into each of these options.

REASONS FOR BUYING AN ESTABLISHED BUSINESS

Here are some reasons why one *should* consider buying an established business:

1. Buying an existing business can reduce the risk. The existing business is already a proven entity. And it is often easier to obtain financing for an established operation than for a new one.
2. Acquiring a "going concern" with a good past history increases the likelihood of a successful operation for the new owner.
3. The established business has a proven location for successful operation.
4. The established firm already has a product or service that is presently being produced, distributed, and sold.
5. A clientele has already been developed for the product or service of the existing company.
6. Financial relationships have already been established with banks, trade creditors, and other sources of financial support.
7. The equipment needed for production is already available and its limitations and capabilities are known in advance.
8. An existing firm can often be acquired at a good price. The owner may be forced to sell the operation at a low price relative to the value of the assets in the business.

DISADVANTAGES OF BUYING AN ESTABLISHED BUSINESS

Here are some reasons why one may decide not to buy an existing business:

1. The physical facilities (the building and equipment) and product line may be old and obsolete.
2. Union/management relationships may be poor.
3. Present personnel may be unproductive and have a poor track record.

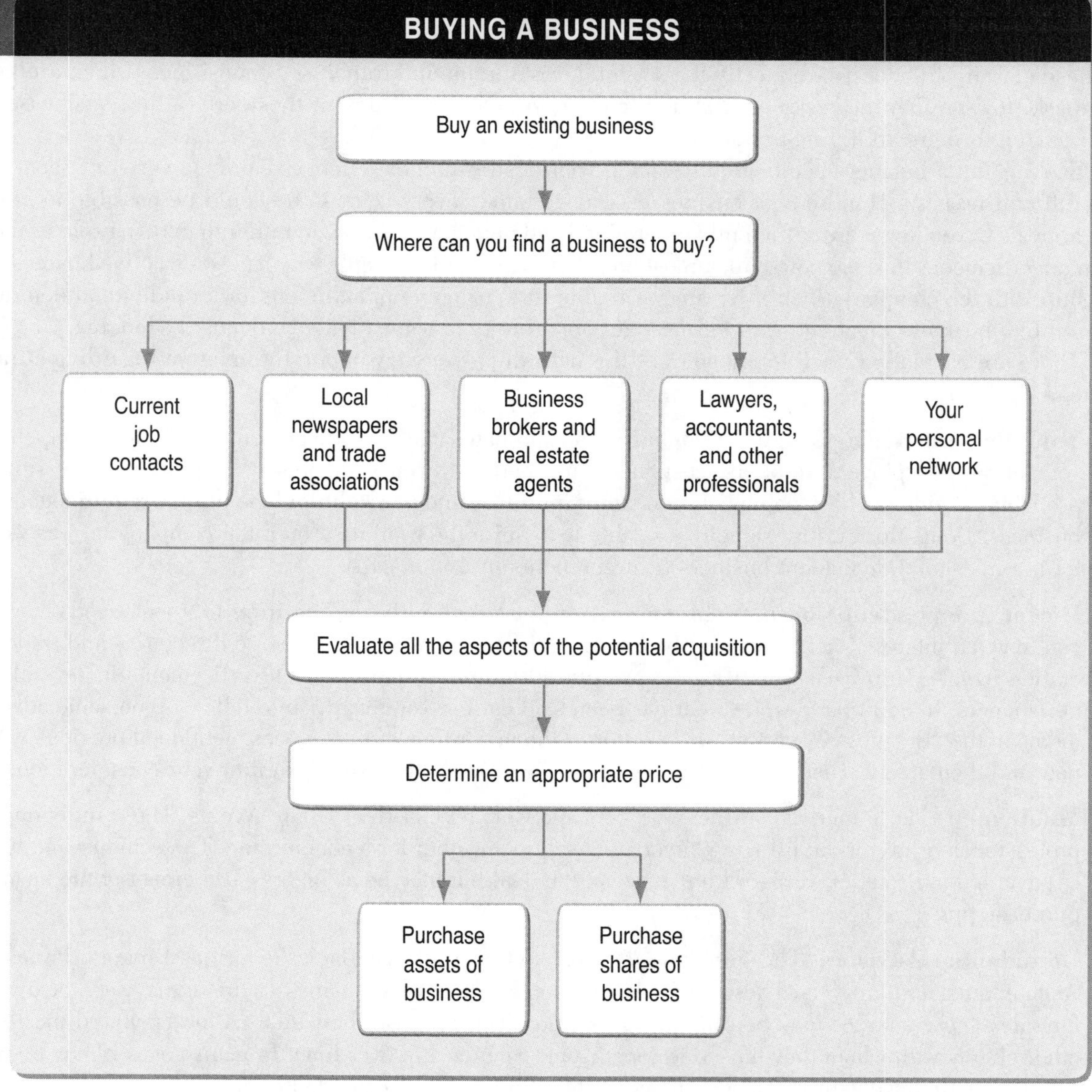

4. The inventory may contain a large amount of "dead" stock.
5. A high percentage of the assets may be in poor-quality accounts receivable.
6. The location of the business may be bad.
7. The financial condition of the business, and its relationships with financial institutions, may be poor.
8. As a buyer, you inherit any ill will that may exist toward the established firm among customers or suppliers.
9. As an entrepreneur, you have more freedom of choice in defining the nature of the business if you start one of your own than if you purchase an existing firm.

As you can see, there are both pluses and minuses in choosing to acquire an established business. You should view this option in terms of whether it will enable you to achieve your personal objectives. How do these advantages/disadvantages compare with those of starting a new business of your own? In buying an existing business do you see a reasonable opportunity to succeed? No one else can really advise you what to do. Instead, you must "do your own thing" and match the alternatives with your abilities and interests.

HOW TO FIND THE RIGHT BUSINESS TO BUY

Just finding a business to buy is easy. Dozens are listed every day in the "Business Opportunities" classified section of your local newspaper as well as the major business newspapers. However, what tends to be found in these classified sections are mostly hotel, motel, restaurant, and franchise propositions, which are largely high-risk, low-profit ventures generally unattractive to investors. Many of these are failing businesses that their current owners are trying to unload.

Seeking out a business acquisition to match your desires and experiences can be a very time-consuming and difficult process. Hundreds of businesses change hands every year, so it should be possible to find one that appeals to you if you are sufficiently determined and persistent. However, rather than being sold as a result of an advertisement in some newspaper, most businesses are sold to people who had some active business relationship with the company when it became available. It is usually not sufficient for an individual determined to acquire a business to sit and wait for the right opportunity to come along. One must go looking.

There are basically five different sources through which you may obtain information regarding attractive companies to buy:

1. **Your Present Business Activity** Acquisition candidates may include present or potential competitors of your current employer; suppliers; customers; and perhaps even your present employer. These situations probably provide the best match between your experience and strengths and the unique requirements of the business. Doug Morley, for example, was able to acquire the training arm of the company he was working for to run as an independent business (Entrepreneurs in Action #14).

2. **Direct Independent Contact** This may involve making "cold calls" on firms that look good or in which you have an interest; such firms may be identified from Chamber of Commerce directories and trade association membership lists. Another way is to place "Acquisition Wanted" advertisements in several major newspapers. In addition, despite what has been said earlier, you may wish to follow up on some advertisements in the "Business Opportunities" section of the major financial papers as mentioned previously. Every now and then an advertisement may appear in these sections that would warrant your consideration.

3. **Middlemen** These include Business Brokers and Commercial Real Estate Agents. These individuals are professionals who work at bringing buyers and sellers together for a commission. The commission, typically payable by the seller, varies with the size of the deal but may be as high as 10 percent of the negotiated purchase price.

4. **Confidential Advisors** These include the Loans Officer at your Bank, Securities Brokers, Professional Accountants, and Lawyers. These advisors are often aware of what businesses are or may soon be available for sale. These sources may be difficult to use, however, because their information is shared mostly with other clients with whom they have developed some relationship over time. In many cases it may be necessary for you to have gained the confidence of the source over an extended period.

5. **Other Sources** These include Venture Capital Firms, Personal Friends and Acquaintances, and Insurance Brokers and Agents. Essentially you should consider all individuals within your personal network of business contacts who may have access to information on attractive businesses for sale. This requires letting many of these people know about your search and the kind of business for which you are looking. You will need to keep reminding them about your interest, so that when the information comes along there is a good probability that it will make its way back to you. This was how Jim Iredale came to buy Ware House Hobbies (Entrepreneurs in Action #15).

Which of these lead sources you should utilize depends on many factors, such as the time you have available, whom you know within the business community, and the kind of company you are looking for. You should experiment with each of these sources and decide on the one or two that work best for you.

IMPORTANT FACTORS TO CONSIDER

An essential requirement for the successful purchase of an existing firm is knowing how to assess and evaluate the operation. This is a complicated process, so you are well advised to have professionals such as an accountant, lawyer, or business evaluator assist you in negotiations when considering buying a business. As

14 Entrepreneurs in action

Taking a Gamble on Education

A "company man" for almost 25 years, Doug Morley left the giant Honeywell Bull organization in 1990 when he saw middle-management jobs being squeezed by the recession.

An entrepreneur at heart, if not in practice, he bought the computer arm of Honeywell Bull, called the Institute for Computer Studies, a division he helped establish in the early 1980s to educate computer programmers and systems analysts.

In the past five years, the 53-year-old businessman has seen the institute grow from an organization that employed four trainers, taught 100 students a year and had revenue under $1 million, to one that has eight full-time instructors (plus 14 on contract), 350 students, a corporate education division, and annual revenue of about $7 million.

When he made the move, Morley remembers, some friends and colleagues questioned his decision. Under Honeywell Bull, the institute was basically a break-even operation, he says. "It did one thing: computer programming and systems analysis."

He was convinced there was room for growth in this fast-changing field. He also believed he could expand the business in a privately owned organization in ways he could not inside a large corporation.

First, Morley became the self-described chief cook and bottlewasher. "When we started I was the bookkeeper, janitor, I fixed the computers, ... I did everything." That helped chop about $100,000 off the overhead.

Hard work and quality training account for the rest of the institute's success, says Morley.

The Institute offers two courses: the career college geared at individuals who want to enhance their computer skills, and the other at corporations that want employees brought up to speed with advanced technology training.

Individuals pay about $8,800 for an intensive five-month program for which the institute is licensed by the Ontario Ministry of Education and Training to issue diplomas. Corporate education costs about $375 a day (usually for three- to five-day stints) in classes of eight people. (That compares with 30 students a class in the five-month course.)

Clients include Bell Canada, Ontario Hydro, and Bank of Montreal.

Morley says that, since opening the doors of his own business, he has not looked back. The timing, he adds, was just right.

"Large companies have changed in the past five years. When I left they were downsizing and everybody was scrambling.

"I just didn't want to be in that environment. So I decided to create an environment of my own, where I can do what I like in an organization with people I like."

Source: Excerpted from Gayle MacDonald, "Taking an Educated Gamble on Learning," *The Financial Post*, 13 May 1995, p. 34.

a potential buyer, you should also have a good understanding of the nature of the target business and the industry in which it competes to be able to assess its future performance, strengths, weaknesses, unexploited market opportunities, and other factors. Learning about a business after the fact can be a sure recipe for failure. A number of basic factors must be considered in determining the value of the business to you. Some of these are more complex and involved than others, but each one must be carefully investigated and studied. The most important of these concerns are discussed below.

WHY IS THE BUSINESS FOR SALE?

You should have this question in mind at all times during the evaluation of a possible acquisition. When the owner of a business decides to dispose of it, the reason presented to the public may be somewhat different from the facts of the situation. Owners may be quite willing to express some reasons for wanting to sell their businesses. They wish to retire, or they want to move to another city, or illness is pressuring the owner to leave the business. But there are a number of others that the current owner may not be quite so likely to volunteer. For example, they may be experiencing family pressures or marital problems, or perhaps they see a better business opportunity somewhere else. None of these reasons is cause for concern. But what if the company

15 Entrepreneurs in action

Model Railroader Makes Tracks

Jim Iredale is what you might call an entrepreneur by chance.

Three years ago, Iredale was holding down a regular nine-to-five job as a Winnipeg accountant/comptroller when the owner of a hobby shop he frequented — Ware House Hobbies —mentioned that he was looking for someone to buy his business.

Although he'd never harboured any entrepreneurial aspirations, the avid model railroader said he became intrigued by the notion of owning his own hobby shop.

He also realized that after 13 years as an accountant/comptroller, he was growing tired of just working with numbers. He wanted to work with people, too.

So after kicking the idea around for a couple of months, Iredale took the plunge. He quit his job, bought Ware House Hobbies, and he and his wife, Bev, became full-time small business operators.

"This was a situation that could not easily be repeated. It was the right opportunity at the right time."

Iredale said he's also surprised at how well the business has done.

"I thought I was buying a small, sleepy little business and that appealed to me," he said. "But it didn't turn out to be a slow, sleepy business at all. It's very busy."

So busy, in fact, that earlier this month he and Bev moved the store into larger quarters at 1870 Portage Ave. They've also hired a part-time helper.

The new store is twice the size of the old one, and gives them more room to display the more than 5,000 model-railroad related items they keep in stock. It also gives them room to expand their mail-order operations and their doll houses and miniatures department.

On the mail-order front, Iredale said although the bulk of the orders come from rural Manitoba, Saskatchewan and northwestern Ontario, the shop also regularly receives orders from as far as B.C. and the Northwest Territories.

In fact, mail order sales now account for about 20 per cent of the shop's total sales, he added.

"I'm not making as much money as I used to make as an accountant," he conceded. "But there are other rewards. I like my lifestyle a lot better."

Source: Murray, McNeill, "Model Railroader Makes Tracks After Turning Hobby Into Career," © *Winnipeg Free Press*, 22 October 1996, p. B1. Reprinted with permission.

needs more financing than the owner can raise, or the current market for the firms' products is depressed? What if competitors are moving in with more effective products or methods, or the current plant and equipment is worn out or obsolete, and the firm is no longer able to compete successfully? And what if the firm is having to contend with new government regulations that are creating some difficulties, or certain key employees are leaving the firm to set up a similar business of their own?

As you can see, there are many possible reasons why a business may be up for sale. It is important that you retain a skeptical attitude, because behind each of the offered explanations may be a number of hidden ones. A skeptical attitude forces you to examine the situation from all angles and not necessarily accept everything you are told at face value. When the real reasons for selling are factors that may lead to the eventual collapse of the company, the present owner may be hard-pressed to justify your purchase of the enterprise.

This is not to say that all businesses for sale are bad buys. Many companies are sold for very plausible and honest reasons. However, to keep from losing your shirt as well as your savings, a detailed evaluation should be conducted to determine the true character of the business.

FINANCIAL FACTORS

An analysis of the financial statements of the firm being sold, preferably with the help of a professional accountant, can help you assess its current health. You should not fall into the trap, however, of accepting these statements as the absolute truth. Even in those situations where the statements have been audited, many accounting techniques allow business owners to present a less than accurate picture of the financial situation of their company. You must be careful to ensure that the statements have not been biased in favour of the seller.

The most important financial factors are: (1) the trend in profits, (2) ratio analysis, (3) the value of the business's tangible assets, (4) the value of the business's intangible assets, and (5) cash flow. Let us discuss each in turn.

THE TREND IN PROFITS

A study of the records of the business will indicate whether sales volume and profits have been increasing or decreasing. If they have been going up, it is useful to know which departments within the business, or products within the firm's product line, have accounted for this increased sales and/or profitability.

If sales and profits are declining, the question may arise as to whether this is due to a failure by the firm to keep up with the competition, to its inability to adjust to changing circumstances, or perhaps to a lack of selling effort. Some experience with this type of business situation, plus a few questions directed to appropriate sources, may elicit an explanation.

RATIO ANALYSIS

For every size and type of business there are certain financial ratios that have become generally accepted as reasonable for that kind of operation. Some information on these ratios is collected and published by trade organizations and associations such as the National Retail Hardware Association or the National Association of Retail Grocers. Ratios have been developed by various manufacturers for use by retailers that handle their product lines. Ratios for firms in a wide variety of retail, service, and manufacturing sectors are published by Dun & Bradstreet (www.dnb.com), the Risk Management Association (formerly Robert Morris Associates) (www.rmahq.org), and other companies. Industry Canada, as part of its Performance Plus Small Business Profiles (sme.ic.gc.ca), can provide information as well. A study of the ratios of any business offered for sale, compared with standard ratios for that industry and size of company, will quickly indicate any discrepancies. These discrepancies may be due to mismanagement, neglect, carelessness, or perhaps even the lack of appropriate financing. The most frequently considered ratios are:

1. **Current ratio** The current ratio is defined as current assets divided by current liabilities. It is a measure of short-term solvency. Current assets normally include cash, marketable securities, accounts receivable, and inventories. Current liabilities consist of accounts payable, short-term notes payable, income taxes payable, and accrued expenses. A general rule of thumb is that a current ratio of 2:1 could be considered satisfactory for a typical manufacturing business. Service firms typically have a lower ratio, since they tend to have less inventory. However, as with any rule of thumb, extreme care should be exercised in evaluating this ratio. A cash-poor firm may be unable to pay its bills even though its ratio appears to be acceptable. On the other hand, many businesses with a current ratio less than the rule of thumb are quite solvent.

   Too high a ratio can indicate the business is not utilizing its cash and other liquid assets very efficiently; too low a ratio may raise questions about the firm's ability to meet its short-term obligations. In practice, however, what is more important than the absolute level of the current ratio is how the ratio is changing over time. An improving current ratio would tend to indicate improved short-term financial solvency unless the business is building up excessive or obsolete inventories.

   $$\text{Current Ratio} = \frac{\text{Current Assets}}{\text{Current Liabilities}}$$

2. **Quick ratio** The quick ratio is obtained by dividing current liabilities into current assets minus inventories. The quick ratio can be used to estimate the ability of a firm to pay off its short-term obligations without having to sell its inventory. Inventories tend to lose their value faster than other assets if disposed of in a hurry. The quick ratio is probably a more valid test of the firm's ability to meet its current liabilities and pay its bills than the current ratio.

   $$\text{Quick Ratio} = \frac{\text{Current Assets} - \text{Inventories}}{\text{Current Liabilities}}$$

3. **Debt to net worth** The debt-to-net-worth ratio indicates the firm's obligations to its creditors relative to the owner's level of investment in the business. Debt includes current liabilities, long-term loans, bonds, and deferred payments; the owner's net worth includes the value of common stock, preferred stock, any capital surplus, and retained earnings. Any outstanding shareholders' loans to the business should be considered part of the owner's net worth rather than as part of the business's present debt. This ratio is commonly used by creditors to assess the risk involved in lending to the firm. For example, if the debt-to-net-worth ratio is too high, say about 2:1 or 3:1, you may find it difficult to borrow additional funds for the business. Too low a ratio, on the other hand, may indicate the business is not being operated very efficiently and some profits are being sacrificed.

$$\text{Debt-to-Net-Worth Ratio} = \frac{\text{Total Outstanding Current and Long-Term Debt}}{\text{Net Worth}}$$

4. **Gross profit to sales** This ratio is determined by dividing gross profit or gross margin by net sales. Gross profit is determined by deducting costs of goods sold from net sales. No general guidelines exist for this ratio, or even among companies within an industry, as it can vary substantially.

$$\text{Gross-Profit-to-Sales Ratio} = \frac{\text{Gross Profit}}{\text{Net Sales}}$$

5. **Net profit to sales** This ratio is calculated by dividing net profit by net sales. You may use net profit either before or after taxes. As with the previous ratio, no general guidelines exist because of the variability among companies and industries. This figure can be as low as 1 per cent or less for retail food stores and supermarkets, and as high as 8 or 9 per cent in some service sectors.

   However, you might evaluate how these ratios compare with those of other, similar companies or how they have been changing over time. If the ratio has recently been declining, why? This may indicate that the firm's costs have been increasing without a commensurate increase in prices, or perhaps competition may have increased and the company is forced to keep its prices low in order to compete.

$$\text{Net-Profit-to-Sales Ratio} = \frac{\text{Net Profit (Before or After Taxes)}}{\text{Net Sales}}$$

6. **Return on assets** This ratio is determined by dividing net profit (before or after taxes) by total assets. It is an excellent indicator of whether all the firm's assets are contributing to its profits and how effectively the assets are being employed — the real test of economic success or failure. Unfortunately, this is not an easy ratio to apply, because it is a measure of the movement of assets in relation to sales and profits during a particular period of time. The methods used by accountants to determine the level of total assets in the business can have a great effect on this ratio, and there are no real general or convenient rules of thumb for finding out whether the current return on assets is acceptable.

$$\text{Return on Assets} = \frac{\text{Net Profit (Before or After Taxes)}}{\text{Total Assets}}$$

7. **Sales to inventory** This ratio is determined by dividing annual net sales by the average value of inventories. This does not indicate actual physical turnover since inventories are usually valued at cost while sales are based on selling prices, including markups, but this ratio does provide a reasonable yardstick for comparing stock-to-sales ratios of one business with another or with the average values for the industry.

$$\text{Sales-to-Inventory Ratio} = \frac{\text{Net Sales}}{\text{(Beginning Inventory + Ending Inventory) / 2}}$$

8. **Collection period** To determine the average collection period for the business's outstanding accounts receivable, annual net sales are divided by 365 days to determine the business's average daily credit sales. These average daily credit sales are then divided into accounts receivable to obtain the average collection period. This ratio is helpful in assessing the collectability of any outstanding receivables.

$$\text{Average Collection Period} = \frac{\text{Accounts Receivable}}{\text{Net Sales / 365}}$$

All these ratios are calculated from information on the firm's income statement or balance sheet. Figures 4.1 and 4.2 illustrate simplified financial statements for a hypothetical firm called The Campbell Co. The value of each of these ratios for that company would be as follows:

1. Current ratio $= \dfrac{\$158{,}000}{\$95{,}000} = 1.66$

2. Quick ratio $= \dfrac{\$78{,}000}{\$95{,}000} = 0.82$

3. Debt to net worth $= \dfrac{\$135{,}000}{\$50{,}000} = 2.70$

4. Gross profit to sales $= \dfrac{\$133{,}000}{\$425{,}000} = 0.31$ or 31%

5. Net profit to sales $= \dfrac{\$13{,}500}{\$425{,}000} = 0.03$ or 3%

6. Return on assets $= \dfrac{\$13{,}500}{\$185{,}000} = 0.07$ or 7%

7. Sales to Inventory Ratio $= \dfrac{\$425{,}000}{(\$75{,}000 + 80{,}000)/2} = 5.48$

8. Average Collection Period $= \dfrac{\$53{,}000}{\$425{,}000/365} = 45$ days

FIGURE 4.1 EXAMPLE OF SIMPLIFIED BALANCE SHEET

THE CAMPBELL CO. BALANCE SHEET
AS OF DECEMBER 31, 200Y

		(000s)	
ASSETS			
Current Assets			
Cash		$ 25	
Accounts receivable		53	
Inventory		80	
Total current assets			$ 158 **(A)**
Fixed Assets			
Machinery	$ 40		
Less: Accumulated depreciation	25	15	
Equipment and fixtures	30		
Less: Accumulated depreciation	18	12	
Total fixed assets			27 **(B)**
Total Assets (C = A + B)			**$185 (C)**
LIABILITIES AND OWNER'S EQUITY			
Current Liabilities*			
Accounts payable	$ 60		
Notes payable	35		
Total current liabilities		95	
Long-Term Liabilities			
Notes payable†	$ 40		
Total long-term liabilities		40	
Total liabilities			$135 **(D)**
OWNER'S EQUITY			
Capital investment		20	
Retained earnings		30	
Total owner's equity			50 **(E)**
Total Liabilities and Owner's Equity (F = D + E)			**$185 (F)**

* Debt is due within 12 months.
† Debt is due after 1 year.

FIGURE 4.2 EXAMPLE OF SIMPLIFIED INCOME STATEMENT

THE CAMPBELL CO.
INCOME STATEMENT
FOR YEAR ENDING DECEMBER 31, 200Y

		(000s)	
Gross sales	$428		
Less: Returns	3		
Net Sales		**$425**	**(A)**
Cost of goods sold:			
Beginning inventory	$ 75		
Plus: Net purchases	297		
Cost of goods available	372		
Less: Ending inventory	80		
Cost of Goods Sold		**292**	**(B)**
Gross Profit (C = A – B)		**$133**	**(C)**
Selling expenses		**$ 29**	**(D)**
Administrative expenses:			
Office salaries	$ 60		
Interest	9		
Depreciation	10		
Other administrative expenses	7		
Total Administrative Expenses		**86**	**(E)**
Profit Before Income Tax (F = C – D – E)		**$ 18**	**(F)**
Income Tax (G = 25% of F)		**4.5**	**(G)**
Net Profit (G = F – G)		**$ 13.5**	**(H)**

It would appear from these ratios that The Campbell Co. is in reasonably sound shape financially. Its debt-to-net-worth ratio is within acceptable limits, and the business is quite solvent as indicated by the current and quick ratios. The other ratios are more difficult to evaluate, but they would be quite acceptable for firms in many lines of business.

To illustrate the range of possible values for each of these ratios, some typical examples for Canadian companies in a number of industries are shown in Table 4.1. Notice that there can be considerable variation in the value of each ratio within economic sectors as well as between sectors. Within a sector these ratios represent an average for each industry code and, therefore, may be somewhat misleading. These figures include a range of firms, some of which may be doing extremely well and others of which may be on the verge of bankruptcy. The variations from sector to sector are largely due to structural differences that impact the financial profile of firms in each line of business in quite different ways.

This data as well as other detailed financial and employment data on small businesses by industry in Canada is available from the Performance Plus Small Business Profiles database of Industry Canada at sme.ic.gc.ca. These profiles are usually produced every two years, with 1997 being the most current available. These data can provide performance benchmarks for the financial planning of both start-up and established businesses.

Keep in mind that financial ratios are open to wide interpretation and should only be relied on to get a general perspective on the relative financial health of the business, to measure the financial progress of the business from one time period to another, or to flag major deviations from an industry or sector norm.

VALUE OF TANGIBLE ASSETS

In assessing the balance sheet of the prospective acquisition, you must determine the actual or real value of the tangible assets. A physical count of the inventory must be taken to determine if the actual level corresponds to the level stated on the balance sheet. This inventory must also be appraised in terms of its age, quality, saleability, style, condition, balance, freshness, etc. Most large inventories will have some obsolescence.

You must determine whether the present inventory is consistent with current market conditions. Also, take care that the seller does not sell this inventory after you have checked it. Any consignment goods in inventory should be clearly identified as well. This evaluation is best performed by someone with considerable experience in the industry involved. Perhaps you can hire the services of the owner of a similar but non-competing firm to assist you in this appraisal.

TABLE 4.1 KEY BUSINESS RATIOS IN CANADA — CORPORATIONS

SIC Category	Line of Business	I Current Ratio (Times)	III Debt/ Net Worth (Times)	IV Gross Profit/ Sales (%)	V Net Profit/ Sales (%)	VI Return on Assets (%)	VII Sales to Inventory (Times)	VIII Collection Period (Days)
Z000	**TOTAL ALL INDUSTRIES**	1.3	3.3	33.7	3.1	6.2	12.5	39.4
J0000	**RETAIL TRADE**	1.5	3.1	19.1	1.0	4.9	7.0	14.9
J6511	Book & Stationary Stores	1.4	2.4	19.6	1.6	6.4	5.4	17.9
J6130	Women's Clothing Stores	1.3	4.1	22.5	0.8	4.7	5.6	13.2
J6520	Florists, Lawn and Garden Centres	1.2	—	25.3	1.1	7.4	9.4	22.2
J6230	Household Furnishing Stores	1.3	4.4	22.0	0.9	4.1	4.9	15.3
J6110	Shoe Stores	1.7	7.0	22.8	—	—	2.8	3.8
Q9200	**FOOD AND BEVERAGE SERVICES**	1.0	16.0	33.1	-0.8	1.1	53.9	5.1
Q9221	Taverns, Bars and Night Clubs	0.9	7.2	34.8	0.8	5.7	37.2	5.2
Q9211	Restaurants, Licensed	1.0	34.9	31.0	0.4	3.7	52.6	4.4
Q9212	Restaurants, Unlicensed	1.0	12.4	37.0	-6.7	-8.4	50.2	—
I0000	**WHOLESALE TRADE**	1.5	2.8	17.5	1.9	5.5	7.9	49.2
I5210	Food	1.3	2.2	12.8	1.3	4.7	18.1	31.9
I5610	Metal and Metal Products	1.4	0.9	25.0	6.5	11.6	10.6	46.0
I5110	Petroleum Products	1.3	4.1	16.9	3.1	8.9	28.0	48.8
E0000	**MANUFACTURERS**	1.4	2.3	24.2	3.3	7.1	9.2	56.8
E1070	Bakery Products	1.3	7.5	23.2	1.3	5.8	17.5	15.6
E2440	Women's Clothing	1.4	12.6	18.7	—	—	15.5	50.9
E1030	Fruit and Vegtable Industries	1.8	1.4	21.3	—	—	2.4	49.6
E3070	Heating Equipment	2.2	0.6	23.7	—	—	5.2	71.7
E3090	Other Metal Fabricating	1.6	1.7	25.8	5.4	10.2	11.3	63.5
E2512	Sawmill and Planing Mill Products	2.0	1.5	21.1	4.0	9.9	4.4	43.7
F0000	**CONSTRUCTION INDUSTRIES**	1.5	7.4	25.6	2.6	5.1	9.6	47.6
F4010	Residential Building	1.4	-7.9	14.4	1.4	3.2	5.0	32.3
M0000	**BUSINESS SERVICES**	1.1	2.0	45.7	7.7	10.5	226.3	62.0
R9730	Funeral Services	1.0	2.5	60.2	8.3	4.4	95.8	47.8
Q9111	Hotels and Motor Hotels	0.6	—	48.8	1.8	5.6	69.7	6.9
R9650	Sports and Recreation Clubs	1.0	4.4	52.8	-0.8	2.6	24.0	21.5
G0000	**TRANSPORTATION AND STORAGE**	1.1	2.7	58.4	3.4	8.0	356.3	39.2
H4811	Radio Broadcasting	1.0	1.5	50.6	2.9	4.9	—	77.8
G4581	Taxicab Industry	1.1	1.8	55.2	1.6	4.1	—	26.2
G4560	Truck Transport	1.0	3.0	59.1	3.0	8.4	781.5	37.1

Source: Key Business Ratios in Canada — Corporations: Calculations partially based on data from the Statistics Canada, CANSIM database http://cansima.statcan.ca/cgi-win/CNSIMCGL.EXE, Small Business Profile.

You must also check the age of any outstanding accounts receivable. Some businesses continue to carry accounts receivable on their books that should have been charged off to bad debts, resulting in an overstatement of the firm's profit and value. Generally, the older the receivables, the lower their value. Old outstanding accounts may reveal a slack credit policy by the present owner. These old accounts will have to be discounted in determining the present value of the business.

The fixed assets of the business must also be scrutinized. You should determine if the furniture, fixtures, equipment, and building are stated at their market or depreciated value. Some questions you should ask include: How modern are these assets? Are they in operating condition? How much will it cost to keep these assets in operation? Are the assets all paid for? You must be aware of any liens or chattel mortgages which may have been placed against these assets. This pledging of assets to secure a debt is a normal business practice; however, you should know about any such mortgages. Other liabilities such as unpaid bills, back taxes, back pay to employees, and so on, may be hidden; you must be aware of the possibility of their existence, and contract with the seller that all claims not shown on the balance sheet will be assumed by him or her.

VALUE OF INTANGIBLE ASSETS

In addition to the more obvious physical goods and equipment, certain intangible assets may also have a real value to a prospective purchaser. Among the most important of these are goodwill, franchise and licensing rights, and patents, trademarks, and copyrights.

You must be very realistic in determining what you can afford or are prepared to pay for goodwill. Is the public's present attitude toward the business a valuable asset that is worth money, or is it a liability? Typically, few businesses that are for sale have much goodwill value. Is any goodwill associated with the business personal to the owner or largely commercial due to the location, reputation, and other characteristics of the business? If largely personal, this goodwill may not be transferable to a new owner, so you should not pay very much for it. Many business owners, however, often have very unrealistic and inflated ideas of the goodwill associated with their business because they have built it up over the years with their own "sweat equity" and, therefore, are not very objective. So you should be careful, and talk to customers, suppliers, neighbours, employees, and perhaps even competitors, to determine if this level of goodwill does actually exist.

In fact, quite often things are not always as they appear. When Jeanne Lawrence bought what she thought was a reputable and thriving fashion design business and retail store, she expected business to carry on as usual. It was only after she had taken over the firm that she discovered that the company's once reputable name had become tarnished in the past year. She was bombarded with a litany of customer service complaints ranging from poor workmanship, to ill-fitting clothing, to people who had paid in full for work that hadn't been done. The situation was so bad she was spending all the money she was taking in on new business repairing the damage that had been done before she took over the company. Eventually Lawrence realized that she could repair the merchandise that had been sold before she took over but she couldn't repair the reputation of the business, so she changed the name (Entrepreneurs in Action #16).

If franchise, licensing, or other rights are involved in the business, you should make certain that you understand the terms and conditions associated with such rights, and that these rights will be transferred to you upon acquisition of the company. An effort should also be made to determine the market value of any patents, trademarks, or copyrights the company may hold, and make sure these are part of the sale — i.e., do not remain with the current owner upon completion of the transaction.

CASH FLOW

You must also observe the cash flows generated by the operation. A business can be very profitable, but chronically low in cash due to overly generous credit terms, excessive inventory levels, or heavy fixed interest payments. You must assure yourself that upon your entry into the business you will have sufficient inflows of cash to meet your cash outflow requirements. Constant cash problems can indicate that the business is possibly being run by ineffective management or that the firm's resources have generally been badly allocated. You must ask yourself if you have the know-how to overcome this misallocation of resources. If the firm's cash flow is very low, and the long-term debt is quite high, the business may be eating up its capital to pay the debt, or possibly defaulting on its debt. If you are to contend with such issues, you may have to increase the firm's debt or be prepared to invest more capital in the business to ease the cash flow problem.

16 Entrepreneurs in action

Buyer Beware Doesn't Only Apply to Customers

CLOTHING STORE OWNER BOUGHT BAD REPUTATION

When Jeanne Lawrence bought a reputable and thriving company this year, she expected business would carry on as usual.

Lawrence bought a fashion design and retail store earlier this fall that specializes in made-to-order evening wear, bridal gowns and daytime apparel. Clothing ranges from $100 lingerie sets to $2,000 evening gowns. Lawrence is a designer with 25 years' experience and has also operated a store before.

SERVICE COMPLAINTS

But when she took over from the previous owner she was bombarded with a litany of customer service complaints. So many in fact that she says she's spending all the money she's taking in on new business repairing damage done before she took control Nov. 1.

"I've been trying to repair the reputation this place had at one time," says Lawrence.

Lawrence says customer complaints range from poor workmanship to poor-fitting clothing, to people who paid in full for work that hadn't been done. Since she has taken over, Lawrence discovered the business's once reputable name has fallen in the last year.

Lawrence estimates about 75 per cent of the clientele was lost in the last year or two.

"Complaints were never redressed. I've been contacted by the Better Business Bureau with horror stories."

Lawrence wouldn't reveal the purchase price of the business but said it was considerable. She said she thought she was also buying the goodwill that went with the company's name.

"To buy a name that's reputable — that doesn't come cheap," she comments.

Marty Eakins is a partner with the Winnipeg office of KPMG. Eakins says when buying a business, it's very much caveat emptor.

"The whole notion of due diligence is critical."

He says that means hiring an experienced financial person to review financial statements both current and past. But Eakins says even at that, no firm can give 100 per cent assurance that what you're buying is solid gold.

Lawrence says she had her accountant look at the books (her accountant recommended she buy the company). And financially, the business was solid. It was the company's reputation that wasn't what she expected.

Eakins says goodwill is difficult to assess. In purely financial terms, goodwill is the excess of the purchase price over the tangible assets. Eakins says if a company has assets valued at $500,000 and someone pays $1 million, then the goodwill they've purchased is $500,000.

Eakins says prospective buyers should learn as much about the business they're buying as possible, looking at macroeconomic factors such as the industry and the national economy as well as the business itself. He says checking customer lists and talking to a few customers is also helpful.

WAYNE GLOWACKI/WINNIPEG FREE PRESS. REPRINTED WITH PERMISSION.

Lawrence is sticking with the business, but she's already made changes. Along with her associate, designer Karen Dolan, she's bringing in more seasonal wear and gift items. Lawrence says they've even started selling ready-to-wear that's 80 per cent completed and then can be altered to the individual.

CHANGED THE NAME

Most importantly, Lawrence realizes that she can repair merchandise sold previously, but she can't repair the reputation associated with the name. So the store name has been changed to Loiselle.

Unfortunately, Lawrence has spent so much money fixing mistakes that for the moment she can't afford a new sign.

Source: Paul McKie, "Clothing Store Owner Bought Bad Reputation," © *Winnipeg Free Press*, 1 December 1997, P. B5. Reprinted with permission.

MARKETING CONSIDERATIONS

The previous section dealt with the internal aspects of the firm's profitability; there has been no discussion of the external determinants of these conditions. But you must be concerned with analyzing markets, customers, competition, and various other aspects of the company's operating environment.

You must carefully examine the company's current market situation. Each market segment served by the firm must be analyzed and understood. Studying maps, customer lists, traffic patterns, and other factors can help you to determine the normal market size for the business. Once the market and its various segments are understood, the composition of these segments should be determined to identify the approximate number of customers in the total market. As a buyer, you should be concerned with:

1. The company's trading area
2. Population demographics
3. The trend and size of the market
4. Recent changes in the market
5. Future market patterns

All these factors help in determining whether the firm's market area is changing, or there is a declining relevant population, or technological or other changes may be creating an obsolete operation.

This kind of information can assist you in assessing trends in the level of the business's market penetration. For example, if its market share has been increasing, then perhaps you should anticipate further growth. But if the business's market penetration has been declining or static, you should be aware that something could be wrong with the operation. It may be that the business is nearing the end of its life cycle. A shrewd seller, aware that the operation is approaching a natural decline, may be bailing out.

At the same time, a business that is not presently being marketed very well may represent a significant opportunity with the right management. John and Elisa Tait bought a store, Elements of Nature, that was little more than a museum gift boutique (Entrepreneurs in Action #17). Sales were often as low as $50 per day. In the five years since their acquisition they have turned the business around so that in-store sales have grown to as much as $4,000 on some days and have developed a thriving Web-based business as well, attracting orders from all over the world. The business has become so successful the Taits have expanded to Calgary where they can pursue not only new business opportunities but more personal interests as well.

Competition facing the business must also be evaluated and understood. First and foremost, you should make sure that the present owner will not remain in competition with you. Very often an owner will dispose of a business only to open up a similar operation. If the business is largely based on the personality and contacts of the owner, you may be hard-pressed to maintain the necessary rapport with customers, suppliers, and financial sources. A legal agreement may help ensure that the vendor will not go on to compete with you.

Another aspect of assessing competition is to look at that presently faced by the firm. You should be aware of the business's major competitors and what trends can be foreseen in the nature of their activity. Most of this information can be obtained either from direct observation or by talking with other people in the business.

Other aspects of the environment also should not be overlooked. You must be tuned in to developments in the economy, changes in technology, government policy and regulations, and trends in society at large that can affect your business situation. Your banker or other professionals may be able to tell you what the experts are saying about such variables. Both national and regional economic factors must be studied to develop accurate projections as to the size of the market opportunity available to the business.

HUMAN FACTORS

When a business is being purchased, personnel must be considered equal in importance to financial and marketing factors, for usually it is desirable to retain certain key people to provide some continuity. As a prospective buyer, you should assess the value of the company's personnel and try to become acquainted with the attitudes of the present employees. For example, will key employees continue to work for the firm under your management? If these key people are likely to leave, you must anticipate the consequences.

Both the quality and the quantity of trained personnel must be evaluated. The skill level of the employees has some bearing on the sale value of the business. Highly trained staff, for example, can increase the seller's bargaining power. On the other hand, inefficient and poorly trained staff may permit you to negotiate a lower purchase price because of the long-term expense involved in retraining or hiring additional employees.

17 Entrepreneurs in action

Kids-stuff connoisseurs find a niche in Calgary

John and Elisa Tait weren't monkeying around when they decided to take their Winnipeg toy store's concept out west.

The owners of Elements of Nature, located adjacent to the Manitoba Children's Museum, saw both a business and personal opportunity in Calgary.

Not only would the mountain bike addicts be able to get their fix in the nearby Rockies, but the Taits felt they could fill a void in the toy store market.

"We looked at Calgary and were amazed at how few stores there were in the marketplace. We were really encouraged by some of our suppliers. They told us if we opened a store in Calgary, we'd kick butt," said John Tait in an interview.

In April, the Taits moved west and, a month later, they opened The Discovery Hut in the Chinook Centre mall. The 2,400-square-foot store has a tropical theme similar to the slightly smaller Elements of Nature and likewise comes complete with scores of toy monkeys on the walls and world-beat music on the stereo.

Tait said such a move wouldn't have been possible if it weren't for the success of Elements of Nature. When they bought the store five years ago, it was more of a museum gift boutique. Customers were scarce and sales of some of its goods, such as rocks and magnifying glasses, were even more scarce, sometimes as little as $50 per day.

Slowly, the store was transformed into an interactive, bright, upbeat destination specializing in high-quality and educational toys such as beanie baby plush dolls, the Thomas the Tank Engine line, Brio Trains from Sweden, Felt Kids, Lamaze toys for infants and more than 2,000 CDs, tapes and videos of children's music, featuring the likes of local stars such as Al Simmons, Fred Penner and Heather Bishop.

As quickly as Elements of Nature sales have grown — to as much as $4,000 per day — its website business (www.elementsofnature.com) has grown even faster.

Eilef Ausland, Elements' manager, said web sales are consistently up more than 60 per cent year-over-year.

"This Christmas, we'll need to double our staff levels. It's going to be crazy," he said in an interview, as he thumbed through the day's Internet orders from Poland, England, California, Illinois, Ohio and Vancouver.

Tait said the Discovery Hut website is under construction but once it is up and running, its orders will be filled from his Winnipeg shipping hub.

Both Ausland and Tait agree that the biggest challenge facing a specialty toy store is carving out a niche in the face of big box retailers such as Toys R Us and Wal-Mart.

"Traditionally, we stay away from their product lines," Tait said. "Most of their products are from major suppliers and a lot of them are war-related or violent toys. We focus on toys that provide a real quality playing and learning experience for kids."

Terry Napper, manager of the Chinook Centre, said thus far the Discovery Hut has proven to be an excellent fit for the mall, which recently underwent a $300-million facelift.

"We have a lot of families that shop here. This store is bang-on for what we need. This concept would work in 70 to 80 per cent of the shopping centres in the country," he said in an interview.

"Most malls have either a Toys R Us or Zellers or Wal-Mart with a strong toy department, but very few have educational toys, which suit a lot of the public."

Source: Geoff Kirbyson, "Kids-stuff connoisseurs find a niche in Calgary," ***Winnipeg Free Press***, August 20, 2001, p.B5. © Winnipeg Free Press. Used with permission.

OTHER CONCERNS

In assessing a business to buy, you will also have to take into account a number of other factors. These include various legal considerations as well as past company policies. The legal aspects of doing business are becoming increasingly more complex and the use of a lawyer is practically a fact of business life. A lawyer can help you in such areas as deciding on an appropriate form of legal organization; identifying real estate documents such as zoning restrictions and covenants that may put you at a disadvantage; labour laws and union regulations; complying with all licensing and permit requirements; the transferability of intangible assets such as copyrights, patents, dealerships, and franchises; and whether buying the shares or the assets of the firm is the most advantageous way of purchasing the company.

You should also have some understanding of the historical practices of the firm relating to employees, customers, and suppliers if future policies are to enhance your opportunities for business growth. An evaluation of these practices and policies will determine if you should continue with past practices or make modifications. If you fail to make this evaluation, you may eventually find yourself in a situation where you have to continue policies that are ill-advised in the long run. For example, it may be necessary to tighten credit policies or make a change in labour practices, even though this may cause a short-term loss of customers or employees.

Key points

KEY POINTS TO CONSIDER IN BUYING A BUSINESS

- Take your time and verify the information you are given before you commit yourself.
- Don't fall in love with the business before you do your homework.
- Be careful not to pay too much for goodwill.
- Buy a business within an industry you know well, with a product or service you are comfortable selling.
- Buy based on the return on investment not the price.
- Don't use all your cash for the purchase and then run into cash flow problems.
- Investigate before you buy.

Source: "Buying a Business: Questions to Answer Before You Buy" (www.cbsc.org/manitoba/index.cfm?name=buying), accessed December 26, 2001.

HOW TO DETERMINE AN APPROPRIATE PRICE TO PAY FOR A BUSINESS

Buying a business is a serious matter involving a substantial financial and personal investment. A business bought at the wrong price, or at the wrong time, can cost you and your family much more than just the dollars you have invested and lost. After you have thoroughly investigated a business opportunity according to the factors in the previous section, weighed the wealth of information you have gathered, and decided that your expectations have been suitably fulfilled, a price must be agreed upon with the seller.

Valuing a business is a very complex procedure, so it is impossible to do it justice here. Any explanation short of an entire book is probably insufficient. The process takes into account many variables and requires that you make a number of assumptions. Determining an appropriate price to pay for a business is a very technical process. If you are trying to make this determination on your own, you should either have a sound knowledge of general accounting principles or use the services of a professional accountant or business valuation expert who has taken formal training and is accredited by the Canadian Association of Business Valuators.

Setting the purchase price for a going concern typically involves two separate kinds of evaluations:

1. **Balance sheet methods** — evaluation of the firm's tangible net assets
2. **Earnings-based methods** — evaluation of the firm's expected future earnings

The balance sheet methods are generally less reliant on estimates and forecasts than the earnings-based methods; however, it should be remembered that they totally ignore the future earnings capability of the business.

BALANCE SHEET METHODS

This approach calls for making some evaluation of the assets of the business. It is used most often when the business being valued generates its earnings primarily from its assets, as with retail stores and manufacturing companies.

There are a number of balance sheet methods of evaluation including *book value, modified or adjusted book value*, and *liquidation value*. Each has its proper application, but the most useful is the adjusted book value method.

BOOK VALUE

If the company has a balance sheet, the quickest means of determining a valuation figure is to look at its net worth as indicated there. You simply take the total assets as shown in the financial statement and subtract total liabilities to get the *net book value*. The advantage of this method is that for most firms the numbers are readily available.

Its drawbacks, however, are numerous. The company's accounting practices will have a big impact on its book value. Similarly, book value does not necessarily reflect the fair market value of the assets or the liabilities. For example, buildings and equipment shown on the balance sheet may be depreciated below their actual market value, or land may have appreciated above its original cost. These differences will not be reflected on the company's balance sheet. Despite these drawbacks, however, net book value may be useful in establishing a reference point when considering the asset valuation of a business. This approach is illustrated in Section I of Figure 4.3 on the basis of the balance sheet for The Campbell Company presented in Figure 4.1, and shows a value of $50,000.

ADJUSTED BOOK VALUE

The adjusted book value method is the most useful balance sheet method. It is simply the book value adjusted for differences between the stated book value and the fair market value of the business's fixed assets and liabilities. Adjustments are most frequently made to the book values of the following items on the balance sheet:

- Accounts Receivable—often adjusted downward to reflect the fact that some receivables may be uncollectible.
- Inventory—usually adjusted downward, since some of it may be dated or stale and difficult to sell off at prices sufficient to cover its cost.
- Real Estate—often adjusted upward since it has commonly appreciated in value since being acquired by the business.
- Furniture, Fixtures, and Equipment—adjusted upward if they are relatively new and have been depreciated below their market value or adjusted downward if they are older and worn out or technologically obsolete.

This refinement of the plain book value approach still has a number of drawbacks, but it does give a more accurate representation of the value of the company's assets at current market value than book value does. The application of this method is illustrated in Section II of Figure 4.3, and shows a value of $85,000.

LIQUIDATION VALUE

A third approach is to go beyond the books of the company to get a more detailed evaluation of specific assets. Generally this involves determining the *liquidation value* of the assets or how much the seller could get for the business or any part of it if it were suddenly thrown onto the market. This approach is ordinarily a highly conservative evaluation and, as such, is frequently useful in determining the lowest valuation in a range of values to be considered. The liquidation value approach is presented in Section III of Figure 4.3, and shows a value of $43,000. Note that the liquidation value of the firm's fixed assets may be considerably less than their appraised market value largely due to the distress nature of their disposition.

INCOME STATEMENT METHODS

Although a balance sheet method is often the approach to valuing a business that can be most easily prepared, it is more common to use an income statement method, particularly for service type businesses. In most cases a going concern is much more than just the sum of its physical assets. Income statement methods are more concerned with the profits or cash flow produced by the assets of the business rather than the assets themselves.

While the cost of reproducing or liquidating the business assets can be closely determined, the cost of duplicating the firm's experience, management, technical know-how, and reputation is not so easily determined. These intangible factors will be reflected in the firm's past and expected future earnings.

FIGURE 4.3 APPLICATION OF BALANCE SHEET METHODS

BUSINESS VALUATION — THE CAMPBELL CO.
BALANCE SHEET METHODS

	(000s)
I. NET BOOK VALUE	
Total stockholder's equity*	$ 50
Net Book Value	**$ 50**
II. MODIFIED BOOK VALUE	
Net book value	$ 50
Plus:	
Excess of appraised market value of building and equipment over book value	25
Value of patent not on books	10
Modified Book Value	**$ 85**
III. LIQUIDATION VALUE	
Net book value	$ 50
Plus:	
Excess of appraised liquidation value of fixed assets over book value	9
Less:	
Deficit of appraised liquidation value of inventory over book value	(5)
Deficit due to liquidation of accounts receivable	(3)
Costs of liquidation and taxes due upon liquidation	(8)
Liquidation Value	**$ 43**

* Item E from Figure 4.1.

To study past earnings trends, it is important to select a time period that is true and representative. A period of five years is generally considered to be an appropriate length of time to observe an earnings trend; however, economic cycles and other factors must be taken into consideration.

Once earnings have been determined, various approaches can be used to determine an appropriate price. One approach is a simple *capitalization of an average of past profits or capitalization of earnings*. In this method, the profits for a selected period of years are adjusted for unusual items and an appropriate capitalization rate is applied to the average profit level derived. (See Figure 4.4, and Section I of Figure 4.6.)

A variation on this method is to weight the earnings of prior years to give greater emphasis to more recent profit levels (for example, the most recent year is given a weight of 5, the previous year 4, the next previous year 3, and so on).

The major advantage of this approach is that it is easy to use. However, the selection of an appropriate capitalization rate or multiple to apply to past or expected future earnings is not a simple, straightforward process. For illustrative purposes we have selected a desired rate of return of 16 per cent, or approximately six times earnings shown in Figure 4.6.

The rate that can be earned on secure investments usually serves as the "base" rate or minimum capitalization rate that would be used. The chosen capitalization rate is really an assessment of the risk you perceive to be related to the business in comparison to the risk related to obtaining the "base" rate. It is an indication of the rate of return you are prepared to accept for assuming that risk in relation to the rates of return you could earn from other, more secure investments such as bonds, guaranteed income certificates, etc.

The selection of a capitalization rate can have a large impact on your evaluation of a business. If, for example, your desired rate of return is increased from 16 per cent to 20 per cent in Figure 4.6, the estimated value of The Campbell Co. based on capitalization of their past earnings would be reduced from $60,000 to $48,000. The estimated values using discounted future earnings and discounted cash flow would be similarly reduced if we were to use a 20 per cent rather than a 16 per cent expected rate of return.

The *discounted future earnings* approach requires estimating after-tax earnings for a number of years in the future as well as determining an appropriate rate of return for the investor. Each future year's earnings are then discounted by the desired rate of return. A higher discount rate might be considered in this case since the estimates are based on projections of future earnings rather than historical results and may be very subjective in nature. In addition, since net earnings, after tax, are used as the basis for the projection, the discount rate used should be net of tax as well. The sum of these discounted values is the estimated present value of the company (Figure 4.5 and Section II of Figure 4.6).

FIGURE 4.4 EXAMPLE OF SUMMARY OF EARNINGS SHEET

THE CAMPBELL CO.
SUMMARY OF EARNINGS FOR PAST FOUR YEARS

Year	Earnings After Taxes (000s)
200Y	$13.5
200Y–1	12.1
200Y–2	10.8
200Y–3	7.2
200Y–4	4.6

FIGURE 4.5 EXAMPLE OF PROJECTED INCOME SHEET

THE CAMPBELL CO.
PROJECTED FIVE-YEAR EARNINGS AND CASH FLOW

Year	Projected Earnings After Taxes (000s)	Projected Cash Flow (000s)
200Y+1	$14.0	$16.9
200Y+2	16.8	21.1
200Y+3	20.2	26.4
200Y+4	24.2	33.0
200Y+5	29.0	41.2

Assumptions:
1. Earnings are expected to grow at a rate of 20% per year.
2. Cash flow is expected to grow at a rate of 25% per year.

The advantage of this approach is that future earnings potential becomes the principal investment criterion, taking into account the time value of money. The principal disadvantage is that in many situations, future earnings cannot be projected with any real accuracy because of the uncertainties of the operating environment and the marketplace.

The *discounted cash flow* approach is the valuation method most commonly used for smaller, privately held businesses. It is essentially the same as the discounted future earnings approach, except that future anticipated cash flows rather then earnings are used to determine the valuation, as can be seen in Section III of Figure 4.6. The difference between earnings and cash flow is that cash flow includes a number of non-recurring and non-cash items that may be reflected in the income statement such as:

- The net profit or loss of the business
- Any salary paid to the owner in excess of what a comparable manager might be paid
- Any perks or discretionary benefits paid to the owner such as a car allowance, travel and entertainment expenses, personal insurance, etc.
- Interest payments unless they will be assumed by the buyer
- Any non-recurring expenses such as legal or other fees
- Non-cash expenses such as depreciation and amortization

FIGURE 4.6 APPLICATION OF EARNINGS METHODS

BUSINESS VALUATION — THE CAMPBELL CO.
EARNINGS METHODS

I. CAPITALIZATION OF EARNINGS

	Average Earnings Over Past Five Years (Figures 4.2 and 4.4) (000s)
200Y–4	$ 4.6
200Y–3	7.2
200Y–2	10.8
200Y–1	12.1
200Y	13.5
Total	$48.2 in the previous 5 years

Average Earnings = $9.6
Divided By: Investor's desired rate of return = 16%*
Value of Company Based on Capitalization of Past Earnings = 9.6 x 100/16 = $60.0

II. DISCOUNTED FUTURE EARNINGS

	Projected After-Tax Earnings (Figure 4.5) (000s)	x	Present Value Factor Assuming 16% Return	=	Present Value of After-Tax Earnings (000s)
200Y+1	$ 14.0		0.862		$12.1
200Y+2	16.8		0.743		12.5
200Y+3	20.2		0.641		13.0
200Y+4	24.2		0.552		13.4
200Y+5	29.0		0.476		13.8
Total	$104.2			**Total**	$64.8

Value of Company Based on Discounted Future Earnings = $64.8

III. DISCOUNTED CASH FLOW

	Projected Cash Flow (Figure 4.5) (000s)	x	Present Value Factor Assuming 16% Return	=	Present Value of Cash Flow (000s)
200Y+1	$ 16.9		0.862		$14.6
200Y+2	21.1		0.743		15.7
200Y+3	26.4		0.641		16.9
200Y+4	33.0		0.552		18.2
200Y+5	41.2		0.476		19.6
Total	$138.6				$85.0

Value of Company Based on Discounted Cash Flow = $85.0

* The actual rate of return to use depends upon your cost of capital, as well as the perceived risk inherent in the investment.

Like the discounted future earnings approach, this method of valuation also depends upon highly uncertain estimates and assumptions. Many people feel, however, that this method typically provides the most reasonable estimate of a company's value. Both of these approaches require detailed year-to-year forecasts that can result in data that have the illusion of precision, but in fact may be quite speculative and unreliable.

Each of these evaluation methods is illustrated for the case of Campbell. The following assumptions are reflected in these calculations:

1. Future earnings are estimated with new management in place.
2. Earnings are expected to grow at a rate of 20 per cent per year.
3. The income tax rate, including federal and state or provincial income taxes, is 20 per cent.
4. Your desired return on investment is 16 per cent.

As illustrated in Figure 4.7, the values of The Campbell Company vary widely according to the valuation method used. The actual value of the company will depend upon which method is most appropriate for the circumstances. For example, the seller will argue that the valuation method yielding the highest value — modified book value or discounted cash flow — is the most appropriate one. However, you would argue that the one reflecting the lowest value for the business — liquidation value — is probably the most appropriate. The price actually agreed upon will result from extensive negotiation between you and the prospective seller, and will involve considering not only these formal evaluation methods but a host of other business and personal considerations as well.

FIGURE 4.7 CAMPBELL CO. VALUATIONS ACCORDING TO DIFFERENT METHODS

Method	Estimated Value (000s)
Net book value (Figure 4.3, I)	$50.0
Modified book value (Figure 4.3, II)	85.0
Liquidation value (Figure 4.3, III)	43.0
Capitalization of earnings (Figure 4.6, I)	60.0
Discounted future earnings (Figure 4.6, II)	64.8
Discounted cash flow (Figure 4.6, III)	85.0

RULE-OF-THUMB APPROACHES

In some situations, especially the purchase of service industries, certain rules of thumb have been developed to serve as useful guides for the valuation of a business. They typically rely on the idea of a "price multiplier." One common rule of thumb in firms where there are substantial assets is to add up:

(the fair market value of the company's fixed assets) +
(the owner's cost of current inventory) +
(approximately 90 per cent of what appear to be good accounts receivable) +
(a percentage of the company's net income before taxes as goodwill) =
Approximate Value of the Business

In companies where there are relatively few tangible assets, another rule of thumb is to calculate the selling price as a percentage of the net or gross annual receipts of the business. This method is illustrated in Table 4.3 for various types of businesses. In this table other important conditions to consider, and key things to watch out for, are listed as well.

One word of advice, however. Many valuation professionals discourage the use of such rule-of-thumb formulas. They contend that they don't address many of the factors that impact a business's actual value and rely on a "one size fits all" approach when no two businesses are ever actually alike. These rule-of-thumb formulas do, however, give you an easy way to at least get a ballpark figure on what a business might be worth.

WHAT'S A BUSINESS WORTH?

A CASE STUDY—THE BROWN CO.

On Dave Brown's 65th birthday, he decided to sell his business, The Brown Co., a manufacturer and importer of specialty leather products. Dave had worked hard all his life, and now he wanted time to travel. But he didn't know where to start in setting a price for his business. His lawyer suggested he contact a valuation firm to find out what his business was worth.

The valuation expert, George Smith, asked Brown to describe his business and its strengths and weaknesses. He also asked for such items as balance sheets, cash flow statements, and income statements for the past five years.

Brown Co.'s Profile

Brown Co., while somewhat cyclical, had a history of consistent profitability. The past year had provided an income of roughly $100,000 before taxes. Brown pays himself an annual salary of $100,000.

The Brown Co. has a stable and diverse customer base as well as an excellent reputation for quality service and product delivery. Its exclusive contracts with certain key suppliers also provide Brown Co. with a significant competitive advantage over its rivals.

Valuation Approaches

After considering all the information Brown provided and making his own investigation, Smith considered the two classic approaches to determining a value for the business:

THE INCOME APPROACH. This method capitalizes or discounts the company's expected earnings stream. One of the best approaches is discounted cash flow analysis, which estimates the present value of the future stream of net cash flows expected to be generated by the business. The net cash flows are forecast for an appropriate period and then discounted to present value using a discount rate that reflects the risks of the business.

THE ASSET APPROACH. This method considered the value or replacement cost of the company's assets as an indication of what a prudent investor would pay for this opportunity.

Using the Approaches

Smith used the discounted cash flow approach to provide what he thought was a realistic assessment of the business's expected selling price. He did not employ the asset approach because he felt a going concern business like The Brown Co. has significant "goodwill" value, such as brand equity or established customer relationships, which are very difficult to account for using the asset method.

To determine a value for the Brown Co., Smith first estimated the present value of future net cash flows. Cash flow forecasts require analysis of all variables influencing revenues, expenses, and capital investment. While projections of future operating results can sometimes be difficult to forecast reliably, the Brown Co. had a history of stable sales and profitability, both growing at an annual rate of about 3 per cent. Smith therefore chose the most recent twelve month's results as his base year forecast.

Computing Cash Flow

To obtain an accurate basis for his forecast, Smith first adjusted the income statement. As shown in Table 4.2, he added back into the net profit the difference between Brown's salary of $100,000 and a more typical manager's salary of $50,000 to run such a business. He also added back interest expenses because existing financing arrangements typically don't affect the value of a company unless they are going to be assumed by the buyer.

He then subtracted taxes at Brown's Co.'s average effective federal and provincial tax rate of 20 per cent and calculated the company's after-tax operating profitability.

Smith next added back depreciation expense, a non-cash expense of $25,000. He then subtracted the average annual capital expenditures, estimated at $35,000, and the $5,000 average increase in working capital, such as Accounts Receivable, needed to finance Brown Co.'s revenue growth.

Brown was a mechanical engineer by training and had collected a quantity of machinery not really needed in the business's operations. So, Smith had these hard assets appraised by an external firm that specialized in that business, with a resulting value of $50,000. He then added this appraised value of this excess machinery, which could be sold separately to the total value of Brown Co.'s operations.

Return on Investment

Would you buy a business if you could make as much simply by investing your money? Of course not, the risk in owning a business is much greater. So, Smith considered the fact that buyers expect to receive a higher return on the business than on more passive investments such as certificates of deposit and real estate. The valuation expert defines the rate at which cash flows were discounted as a competitive rate of return for Brown Co. given its inherent risk factors. Smith also examined the rates of return of comparable publicly held companies. Based on this analysis, Smith concluded 16 per cent was a fair cost of capital to use to discount Brown Co.'s after-tax net cash flow.

The discounted cash flow valuation conclusion for Brown Co. was approximately $800,000, consisting of $750,000 for the company's operations and $50,000 as the value of the excess machinery.

Happy Endings

Brown was pleasantly surprised by the final valuation. But, as Smith told him, a valuation is one thing, but the actual selling price can be quite another. He suggested that Brown ask $850,000 for the business including the extra equipment but be prepared to accept less, or possibly assist the buyer with some financing. Brown agreed, and at Smith's suggestion also offered to stay on for a few months after the sale to ensure a smooth management transition.

What was the actual price? After about nine months, The Brown Co. was sold for $820,000. The price was slightly greater than the valuation number due to the favourable terms Brown gave the buyer. He agreed to accept $300,000 in cash, provided a promissory note to the buyer for another $300,000 at 7 per cent and the remainder was the buyer's assumption of Brown Co.'s outstanding $220,000 of long-term debt and accrued expenses.

TABLE 4.2

Brown Co. Base Year Adjustments and Valuation

Income before taxes	$100,000
Excess salary	50,000
Interest on financing	25,000
Adjusted pretax income	175,000
Taxes @ 20%	(35,000)
Adjusted profit after tax	140,000
Plus depreciation	25,000
Less working capital invest.	(5,000)
Less capital expenditures	(35,000)
Total adjusted base year free cash flow	$125,000
Present value of discounted cash flow	$750,000
Plus excess machinery	50,000
Total value of Brown Co.	$800,000

Source: Adapted from "What's My Company Worth? A Case Study—'Colombo Company,'" BVS, www.bvs-inc.com

But keep in mind that using one of these rules of thumb does not mean that the balance sheet and the income statement for the business can be ignored. These rules are merely a starting point for business valuation and must be reviewed in the context of the other business factors discussed earlier in this section.

WHAT TO BUY — ASSETS OR SHARES?

The acquisition of a business may be structured under one of two basic formats:

1. You can purchase the seller's stock or shares in the business.
2. You can purchase part or all of the business's assets.

Although these alternatives are treated somewhat the same for financial reporting purposes, the tax consequences can differ significantly. A major consideration in the purchase or sale of a business may be the effect on the tax liability of both the buyer and the seller. The "best" form of a particular transaction will depend on the facts and circumstances of each case. Since the tax implications of acquiring or disposing of a business can be very complex, and a poorly structured transaction can be disastrous for both parties, it is suggested that you seek competent tax advice from your accountant or lawyer regarding this matter. Another factor to consider in deciding whether to buy assets or shares is "contingent liabilities." If assets are acquired, in most instances the buyer takes no responsibility for any contingencies that may arise subsequent to the sale such as lawsuits, environmental liabilities, or tax reassessments.

TABLE 4.3 VALUING A SMALL BUSINESS BY RULE OF THUMB

BUSINESS	PRICE MULTIPLIER	IMPORTANT CONDITIONS	WATCH FOR:
Apparel stores	0.75 to 1.5 times net plus equipment and inventory	Location, competition, reputation, specialization	Unfavourable shopping patterns, inadequate parking, outdated inventory
Beauty salons	0.25 to 0.75 times gross plus equipment and inventory	Location, reputation, boutique image	Excessive staff turnover
Car dealerships	1.25 to 2 times net plus equipment	Type of dealership, location, reputation of company	Brand new manufacturers, factory allocation policy
Employment agencies	0.75 to 1 times gross, equipment included	Reputation, specialization, client relations	Excessive staff turnover
Fast food stores	1 to 1.25 times net	Location, competition, neatness of premises, lease terms	Inadequate street traffic, inadequate servicing space or seating area
Gas stations	$1.25 to $2 per gallon pumped per month, equipment included	Gallons/month, lease terms, location, competition, other services	Poor traffic pattern, short lease
Grocery stores	0.25 to 0.33 times gross, equipment included	Location, lease terms, presence of liquor, condition of facilities	Nearby supermarkets or convenience stores
Insurance agencies	1 to 2 times annual renewal commissions	Client demographics and transferability, carrier characteristics	Agent turnover, account mix
Newspapers	0.75 to 1.25 times gross, equipment included	Location, demographics, economic conditions, competition, lease terms	Stagnant or declining area
Real estate offices	0.75 to 1.5 times gross, equipment included	Tenure of salespeople, franchised office, reputation	Intensity of competition
Restaurants	0.25 to 0.5 times gross, equipment included	Competition, location, reputation	Predecessor failures
Travel agencies	0.04 to 0.1 times gross, equipment included	Revenue mix, location, reputation, lease terms	Negative climate for international travel
Video shops	1 to 2 times net plus equipment	Location, competition, inventory	Obsolescence of tapes, match of tapes to customers

Excerpted from S. M. Pollan and M. Levine, *Playing to Win: The Small Business Guide to Survival & Growth*, advertising supplement to *U.S. News & World Report and The Atlantic*, 1988. Used by permission.

FYI FOR YOUR INFORMATION

FOR MORE INFORMATION ON BUYING A BUSINESS:

1. **BUYING A BUSINESS** An overview of the pros and cons, and the key questions you need to ask yourself about buying a business. (www.cbsc.org/english/search/display.cfm?CODE=4009&Coll=FE_FEDSBIS_E)
2. **HOW TO BUY A BUSINESS LIST** The steps you need to take in evaluating a business that is for sale. (http://www.cbsc.org/alberta/search/display.cfm?Code=4009&coll=FE_FEDSBIS_E)
3. **BUYING A BUSINESS WHY BUY?** A comprehensive discussion of the range of issues involved in buying a business. (strategis.ic.gc.ca/SSG/mi04329e.html)
4. **FINANCING THE BUSINESS ACQUISITION** A discussion of where to get the money to finance the acquisition of a business (from a U.S. perspective). (businessbookpress.com/articles/article144.html)
5. **BUSINESS VALUATION METHODS** An overview of several of the basic methods of evaluating a business. (home3.americanexpress.com/smallbusiness/resources/starting/valbiz.shtml)

In some cases there may not be any choice. If the company is a sole proprietorship, for example, there are no shares, only assets and liabilities accumulated in the course of doing business which belong to the proprietor personally. So when acquiring the company, you and the owner must decide which of these assets and liabilities are to be transferred and which are to stay with the present owner. You may feel that some of the assets are not really essential to carry on the business and the seller may desire to keep something — often the real estate, which you may be able to lease rather than buy from him. This may be one way of reducing the cost of the business to you. These are matters which would have to be discussed in detail between you and the prospective seller.

FINANCING THE PURCHASE

PERSONAL EQUITY

There are any number of sources of financing that can be used to purchase a business. Because you are buying something that already exists and has a track record, you may find this financing easier to obtain than if you were starting a business from scratch. However, the place to begin is with your own personal equity. In most transactions anywhere from 20 to 50 per cent of the money needed to purchase a business comes from the buyer and his or her family and close friends. The notion of buying a business by means of a highly leveraged transaction with a minimum amount of up-front cash is not a reality for most buyers.

SELLER FINANCING

If you do not have access to enough cash to make the purchase you might consider asking the seller to finance part of the purchase. This is very common in the sale of many small businesses. The seller's willingness to participate will be influenced by his or her own requirements such as tax considerations as well as cash needs. For example, the seller might carry a promissory note for part of the purchase price, or you might lease rather than buy a portion of the facilities, equipment, or other assets. Another option is that you may be able to get the seller to agree to tie repayments to the actual performance of the business after the sale. Terms offered by sellers are usually more flexible and often more favourable than those available from a third-party lender like a bank. In addition, there may be some real advantages to the sellers since many of these options will provide them with a steady source of revenue instead of a lump sum payment, so they don't immediately face a tax liability on any capital gains realized from selling the business.

THIRD PARTIES

Banks and other lending institutions may provide a loan to assist in the purchase of a business, although the rate of rejection tends to be quite high on these transactions. When a bank will consider financing an acquisition, its focus tends to be on the physical assets associated with the transaction. The bank might, for example, provide financing for up to 50 to 75 per cent of the value of any real estate, 75 to 90 per cent for any new equipment acquisitions, or 50 per cent of any inventory. The only other assets that might be attractive are the accounts receivable, which it may finance to 50 or 60 per cent as well.

With any of these financing options, buyers must be open to creative solutions. They must also be prepared to take some risks. There is no sure thing, even though the business may appear to have had a long and successful operating history.

CHECKLIST FOR A BUSINESS ACQUISITION

Should you start a new business or buy an existing one? At this point in your deliberations, this is the critical question. The material in the Business Acquisition Questionnaire, Figure 4.8, will aid you in making this choice.

If, after answering the questions in Part A, you decide to enter an established business rather than to start one of your own, then you should proceed to the questions in Part B. You may want to reproduce these pages and answer the same questions for several businesses you have in mind. Go through the questionnaire and answer the questions concerning each business as conscientiously as you can.

FIGURE 4.8 BUSINESS ACQUISITION QUESTIONNAIRE

PART A

Before deciding whether you will purchase an established business, you need to give consideration to the positive and negative features of this alternative. You should rate each point in the questionnaire as you perceive its significance and importance to you.

1. How would you define the nature of the business in which you are interested?

____

____

____

2. How important are each of the following factors to you in electing to buy an established business? Indicate the importance of each factor to you on a scale ranging from 0 (not important at all) to 10 (extremely important):

a. Having a business with a proven performance record in sales, reliability, service, and profits ______

b. Avoiding the problems associated with assembling the composite resources — including location, building, equipment, material, and people ______

c. Avoiding the necessity of selecting and training a new workforce ______

d. Having an established product line ______

e. Avoiding production problems typically associated with the start-up of a new business ______

f. Having an established channel of distribution to market your product ______

g. Having a basic accounting and control system already in place ______

h. Avoiding the difficulty of having to work out the "bugs" that commonly develop in the initial operation of a new business ______

i. Having established relationships with suppliers and financial institutions ______

j. Being able to acquire the assets of the business for less than their replacement value ______

Total ______

3. In checking back over the points covered in question 2, the closer your total score on all items is to 100, the more purchasing an established business is likely to be of interest to you as a means of going into business for yourself.

PART B

The following is a set of considerations to be assessed in evaluating an established business. Your responses, information from the present owner, and other information concerning the status of the business should guide you to a comfortable decision as to whether this business is for you.

1. Why Is the Business for Sale?

____

____

____

____

2. Financial Factors

a. Recent sales trend:

- ______ Increasing substantially
- ______ Increasing marginally
- ______ Relatively stable
- ______ Decreasing marginally
- ______ Decreasing substantially

b. Recent trend in net profit:

- ______ Increasing substantially
- ______ Increasing marginally
- ______ Relatively stable
- ______ Decreasing marginally
- ______ Decreasing substantially

c. Are the financial statements audited?
Yes ________No ________

d. Apparent validity of financial statements:
Accurate________Overstated ________Understated________

Check the following:

- Relationship of book value of fixed assets to market price or replacement cost
- Average age of accounts receivable and percentage over 90 days
- Bad debts written off in the past 6 months, 12 months

e. Ratio analysis:

		This Company		
	Industry Standard	*Year To Date*	*Last Year*	*Two Years Ago*
Current ratio	________	________	________	________
Quick ratio	________	________	________	________
Debt-to-net-worth ratio	________	________	________	________
Gross-profit-to-sales ratio	________	________	________	________
Net-income-to-sales ratio	________	________	________	________
Return on assets	________	________	________	________

Business Acquisition Questionnaire — continues

Business Acquisition Questionnaire — continued

3. Tangible Assets

a. Are the land and buildings adequate for the business?
Yes ________ No ________

b. Is the location acceptable?
Yes ________ No ________

c. Is the machinery and equipment worn and out of date?
Yes ________ No ________

d. How does it compare with the latest available?

____

____

____

e. What is the maintenance status of the plant and equipment?
Excellent ________ Good ________ Fair ________ Poor ________

f. Is the plant of sufficient size and design to meet your current and projected requirements?
Yes ________ No ________

g. Does the plant appear to be well laid out for the efficient use of people, machines, and material?
Yes ________ No ________

h. What is the approximate value of the company's inventory?

Raw material	$__________
Work-in-process	$__________
Finished goods	$__________
Total	**$**__________

i. Does the inventory contain a high proportion of obsolete or "dead" stock?
Yes ________ No ________

4. Intangible Assets

a. Does the company name or any of its trade names have any value?
Yes ________ No ________

b. What kind of reputation does the business have with its customers?
Positive ________ Neutral ________ Negative ________

c. What kind of reputation does the business have with its suppliers?
Positive ________ Neutral ________ Negative ________

d. Are any franchise, licensing, or other rights part of the business?
Yes ________ No ________

Are they included in the deal?
Yes ________ No ________

e. Are any patents, copyrights, or trademarks part of the business?
Yes ________ No ________

Are they included in the deal?
Yes ________ No ________

5. Marketing Factors

a. Is the market for the firm's product/service:

______ Increasing?

______ Stable?

______ Declining? If *declining*, this is principally attributable to:

____________ i. Decreasing demand due to lower popularity

____________ ii. A changing neighbourhood

____________ iii. A declining target population

____________ iv. Technological change

____________ v. Lack of effort by present owner

____________ vi. Other factors

6. Human Factors

a. Is the present owner in good health?
Yes ________ No ________

b. Does the present owner plan to establish a new business or acquire another business that would compete with yours?
Yes ________ No ________ Uncertain ________

What are the intentions of the present owner?

____

____

____

c. How efficient are current personnel?

i. What is the rate of labour turnover? ______%

ii. What is the rate of absenteeism? ______%

iii. What proportion of production is completed without rejects? ______%

iv. Can you accurately determine the cost of producing an individual unit of the product or service? Yes ______ No ______

v. How has this changed in the past year?
Increased ________ Stayed the same ________ Decreased ________

d. Has a union recently won an election to serve as a bargaining agent for the company's employees?
Yes ________ No ________

e. Will most of the key employees continue to work for the firm under your management?
Yes ________ No ________

f. Will you have to incur considerable costs in retraining or hiring additional employees?
Yes ________ No ________

7. Other Considerations

a. Are there any zoning restrictions or caveats on the property that may put you at a competitive disadvantage?
Yes ________ No ________

b. Can you satisfy all the federal and provincial licensing and permit requirements?
Yes ________ No ________

Business Acquisition Questionnaire — continues

Business Acquisition Questionnaire — continued

c. Have you considered what would be the most advantageous way of purchasing the company?
Buy shares ________ Buy assets ________ Don't know ________

d. Have you had a lawyer and an accountant review the material you received from the vendor and any other information you may have regarding the business?
Lawyer Yes ________ No ________
Accountant Yes ________ No ________

8. Your Evaluation of the Business

What have you determined to be the approximate value of the business based on the following valuation approaches?

a. Net book value $ __________
b. Modified book value $ __________
c. Liquidation value $ __________
d. Capitalization of past earnings $ __________
e. Discounted future earnings $ __________
f. Discounted cash flow $ __________

The areas covered by this checklist are not meant to be exhaustive; they are presented merely to guide and stimulate your own thinking about buying an existing business. The more information you can compile to assist you in making this decision the better.

Considering a Franchise

In addition to exploring the possibilities of starting your own business or buying an existing one, you may want to investigate the opportunities presented by *franchising*. Canada is said to be the franchise capital of the world. The sector is estimated to employ one million people and register sales of $100 billion a year, or almost 50 per cent of total retail sales in the country. Over 1,300 franchisors have nearly 64,000 outlets, giving Canada more franchised units per capita than any other place on the planet.[1]

Franchising allows you to go into business for yourself, and at the same time be part of a larger organization. This reduces your chances of failure, because of the support that the established company can provide. If this appears to be an attractive situation, then a franchise may be the answer for you. Let's look at what this means in the context of starting a business of your own.

AN INTRODUCTION TO FRANCHISING

Franchising has often been referred to as an industry or a business. However, it is neither. It can best be described as *a method of doing business* — a means of marketing a product and/or service that has been adopted and used by a wide variety of industries and businesses.

WHAT IS FRANCHISING?

There is no single, simple definition of franchising. For example, Statistics Canada defines it as "A system of distribution in which one enterprise (the franchisor) grants to another (the franchisee) the right or privilege to merchandise a product or service." The International Franchise Association, the major trade association in the field, defines it as "A continuing relationship in which the franchisor provides a licensed privilege to do business, plus assistance in organizing, training, merchandising, and management in return for consideration from the franchisee." These are just two of the many definitions that have been offered.

Regardless of the formal definition, however, it is best to think of franchising as a legal and commercial relationship between the owner of a trademark, trade name, or advertising symbol and an individual or group of people seeking the right to use that identification in a business. A franchisee generally sells goods and services supplied by the franchisor or that meet the franchisor's quality standards. Franchising is based on mutual trust and a legal relationship between the two parties. The franchisor provides business expertise such as a proven product or service offering, an operating system, a marketing plan, site location, training, and financial controls that otherwise would not be available to the franchisee. The franchisee brings to the franchise operation the motivation, entrepreneurial spirit, and often the money, to make the franchise a success.

Virtually all franchise arrangements contain the following elements:

1. A continuing relationship between two parties
2. A legal contract that describes the responsibilities and obligations of each party
3. Tangible and intangible assets (such as services, trademarks, and expertise) provided by the franchisor for a fee
4. The operation of the business by the franchisee under the franchisor's trade name and managerial guidance

---

1. C. Clark, "The New Face of Franchising," *PROFIT: The Magazine for Canadian Entrepreneurs* (December/January 2000): 37.

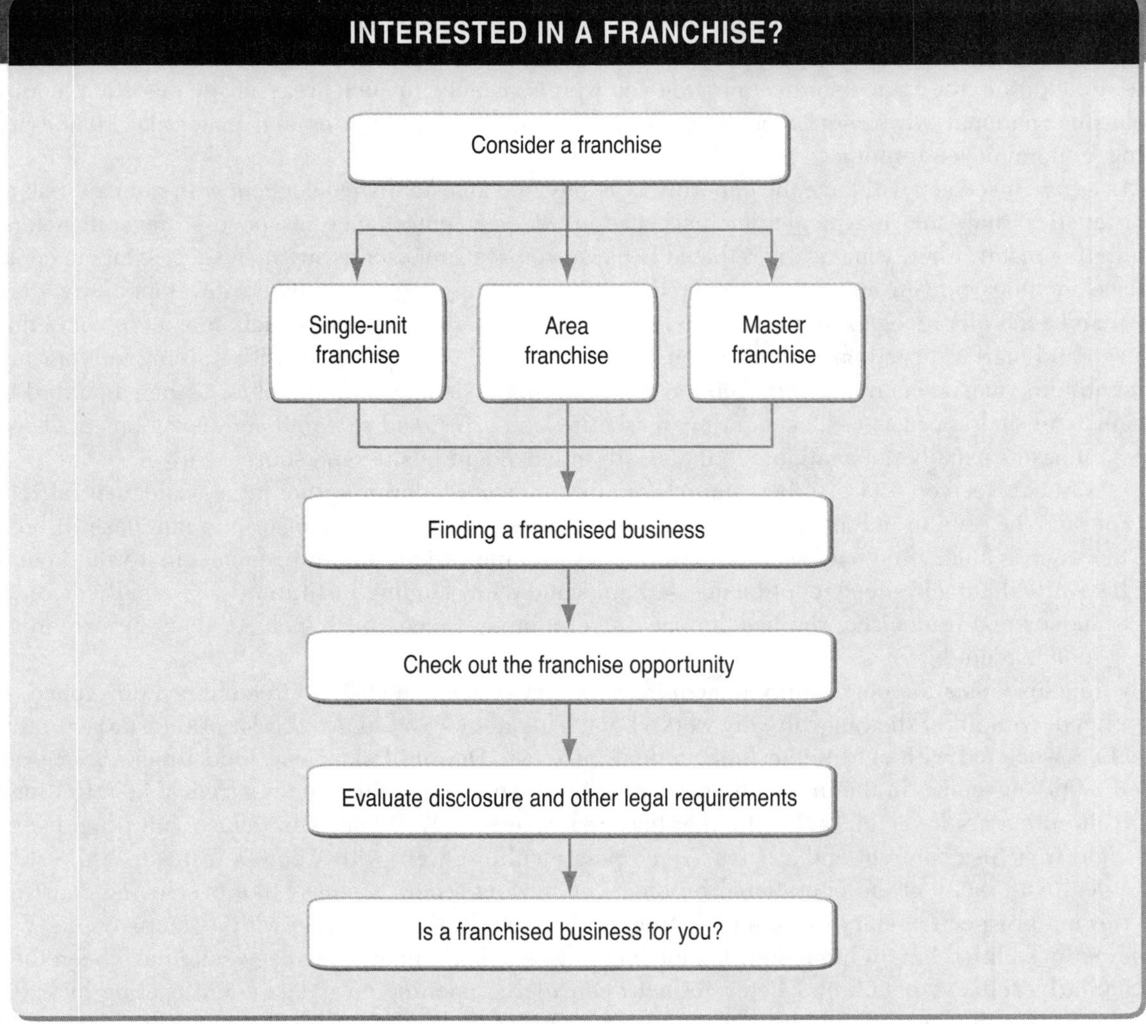

Franchise arrangements can be subdivided into two broad classes:

1. **Product distribution arrangements**, in which the dealer is to some degree, but not entirely, identified with the manufacturer/supplier
2. **Entire-business-format franchising**, in which there is complete identification of the dealer with the supplier

In a *product distribution arrangement*, the franchised dealer concentrates on one company's product line, and to some extent identifies his or her business with that company. Typical of this type of franchise are automobile and truck dealers, gasoline service stations, and soft drink bottlers.

Entire-business-format franchising is characterized by an ongoing business relationship between franchisor and franchisee that includes not only the product, service, and trademark, but the entire business format — a marketing strategy and plan, operating manuals and standards, quality control, and continuing two-way communications. Restaurants, personal and business services, rental services, real estate services, and many other businesses fall into this category.

Entire-business-format franchising has been primarily responsible for most of the growth of franchising since 1950. Most of our comments will relate to this form of franchising.

ADVANTAGES OF FRANCHISING

As has been pointed out, franchising is one means for you (the *franchisee*) to go into business for yourself, yet at the same time also be part of a chain, with the support of an established company (the *franchisor*) behind you. This can enable you to compete with other chains through the use of a well-known trademark or trade name. In addition, the franchisor may provide you with assistance in such areas as site selection, equipment purchasing, national advertising, bookkeeping, the acquisition of supplies and materials, business counselling, and employee training.

As a franchisee you will have the opportunity to buy into an established concept with reduced risk of failure. Statistics show that a typical franchisee has an 80 per cent chance of success. Several factors may explain this result. First, your risk is reduced because you are supposedly buying a successful concept. This package includes proven and profitable product or service lines, professionally developed advertising, a known and generally recognized brand name, the standardized design or construction of a typical outlet, and a proven and market-tested operating system. Second, you are often provided with training for your new job and continuing management support. You have the ongoing assistance of a franchisor, who can afford to hire specialists in such areas as cost accounting, marketing and sales, and research and development. These are important assets usually not available to the small, independent businessperson.

As a franchisee you may also be able to take advantage of the lower cost of large-scale, centralized buying. You may be able to purchase supplies at reduced cost, since the franchisor can purchase in bulk and pass the savings along. You may also have access to financing and credit arrangements that would not otherwise be available to an independent business. Banks and other lending institutions are usually more willing to lend money to a franchisee who has the backing of a large, successful franchisor than they are to a completely independent business.

A franchisee has the opportunity to acquire a proven system which has already been developed, tested and refined, with all of the bugs already worked out. This allows you to avoid a lot of the start-up problems typically associated with starting an independent business. Downhill ski racer Todd Brooker, for example, served 2,000 customers in the first couple of days after the opening of his Wendy's franchise in Collingwood, Ont. (Entrepreneurs in Action #18). Brooker had first coveted a McDonald's franchise, but when faced with their rigid franchise contract and a pervasive corporate culture, went with Wendy's instead. While still having to deal with many of the operational problems of starting a new business like overseeing construction, interviewing prospective employees, and setting up the payroll, the affiliation with a company like Wendy's undoubtedly enabled him to jump-start his business more quickly than otherwise would have been the case.

Similarly, Jeff Pylypchuk and Peter Tofinetti considered opening an independent cycling business but opted for a franchise instead, and were glad they did. Their Cyclepath franchise was profitable almost immediately and they credit much of this success to the franchise system. By buying into a franchise they were immediately set up with a complete system and had the advantage of being associated with a larger brand name company. (Entrepreneurs in Action #19).

DISADVANTAGES OF FRANCHISING

While franchising has a considerable number of advantages, there are also several disadvantages of which you should be aware. One of the principal complaints is the degree of control that franchisors exert over their franchisees. While you will be an independent businessperson, in effect you do not have complete autonomy and must operate within the operating system as defined by the franchisor. You are usually in a subordinate position to the franchisor and must abide by the often extremely rigid terms and conditions of the franchise agreement. All franchise contracts give the franchisor either an open right to terminate the contract or the right to terminate upon breach of the agreement. As a result, you may find yourself in a weak bargaining position.

Franchisees also have certain reporting obligations to the franchisor and may be subject to frequent inspection and constant supervision. To fit comfortably into such an arrangement, you must accept the necessity of such controls. These restrictions, however, may be unacceptable to some individuals. You must seriously assess your personal suitability for the role of a franchisee.

Another disadvantage of franchising is that the cost of the services provided to you by the franchisor is based on your total sales revenue. These costs can amount to 10 per cent or more of your total revenue

18 Entrepreneurs in action

Through the Gate

HOW TO JUMP-START A NEW FRANCHISE

Downhill ski racer Todd Brooker is accustomed to making split-second decisions at high speed, so he was in his element last winter when he opened his Wendy's restaurant in Collingwood, Ont. Looking back at his first months, however, he displays the perfectionism that served him well as a World Cup skier: "Now I know why everyone wants a second franchise," he says. "Everything you've done, you figure you could do better if you had another chance."

Don't be misled. Brooker's Wendy's franchise served 2,000 customers in the first couple of days after its December opening. Always competitive, he attributes the success of his grand opening to hard work and good technique.

After buying the land on a corner of Collingwood's main drag, Brooker got dirty quickly. Once Wendy's approved his blueprints, he found a contractor and donned a hard hat, appearing at the building site each day. By November, he was interviewing for the 90 positions he figured he needed for the first month over Christmas. "Drawing up a schedule was a big pain in the neck," he says. "You don't know how strong anyone will be, so you just schedule everyone three hours at a time."

Soon, it was time to ramp up to the Dec. 15 opening. "Cleaning was the big thing," he recalls. "Drywall dust just gets into everything." By Dec. 9, he started bringing in paper goods, cooking supplies and utensils, putting together tables and arranging the menu boards. Two days later, the food arrived — another Wendy's franchisee passed along his opening food supplies order as a guide — and Brooker was finally ready for three days of "practice runs."

Over the previous weeks he had made the rounds of every local business he could find, passing out free lunch and dinner coupons for the days leading up to the opening. "I told them to come over and help us train our employees," Brooker recalls. "Every coupon came back. I gave away $2,500 worth of food a day." The third day, he also invited the mayor, deputy mayor, councillors and municipal economic development people for a VIP dinner.

Opening day, the lineups went out the door. Brooker was thrilled. Then an employee asked when they would be paid. "I hadn't even thought about how to pay everyone," Brooker laughs. He quickly drove to the bank to set up a payroll, and calculated deductions and tax remissions by hand for about four months until he joined the bank's fully automated program. "Doing things the stupid way gives you an education about what it's all about," he says. "If I just went to the bank, I wouldn't understand half this stuff. So I'm glad I did it that way, but I'm also glad I'm not doing it any more."

Source: Based on material from the Canadian Franchising Association.

or an even larger share of your profits. A related complaint is that the markup which franchisors may add to the products you must buy from them can increase your operating costs, particularly if equally good products could be purchased elsewhere at lower prices. While you might initially feel that your operating costs are likely to be lower as a result of the franchisor's central purchasing program, it may not become apparent until later that you are actually paying a huge markup on the material, equipment, and supplies you acquire.

Acquiring a franchise is not necessarily a licence to print money. Besides an initial franchise fee, you will probably also have to make periodic royalty payments and advertising contributions based on a percentage of your gross revenues. Even with these expenditures, you still run the risk of not achieving the expected sales, and thus the profit, that the franchisor stated was possible.

It should also be remembered that the benefits available through franchising have not always materialized. Franchisors have not always supplied the services they promised or truthfully disclosed the amount of time and effort the franchisee would have to commit to the franchise. Termination policies of many franchisors have given franchisees little or no security in many cases.

19 Entrepreneurs in action

The Franchise Biz

Lifelong best friends Jeff Pylypchuk, 29, and Peter Tofinetti, 30, never thought they could turn their love of bike riding into a business. Just four years ago, the two were "socking away" cash at menial jobs in Thunder Bay, Ontario — Pylypchuk, waiting tables and Tofinetti, hawking insurance. Today, their bike shop, Cyclepath, pulls in an impressive $750,000 a year in sales.

How did they do it? By purchasing a franchise business that matched their interests.

"We started cycling together — road racing — when we were about 13, and we had always been unimpressed with the service we received in bike shops," says Pylypchuk. "So, we thought about starting our own business."

With their combined savings of about $75,000, Pylypchuk and Tofinetti considered opening an independent business, but that meant starting from scratch — coming up with a store name, finding real estate and attracting customers. Then they discovered Cyclepath, which, at the time, was a successful bicycle franchisor with 50 franchises. After extensive research, which included calling other franchisees, Pylypchuk and Tofinetti decided to buy into the system. They paid $40,000 for their franchise, and took out a small business loan to help with expenses such as rent and merchandise. "It just took off from there," says Pylypchuk.

Did it ever. Their Cyclepath franchise opened in 1996 and was almost immediately profitable. Halfway through its second year, the store was pulling in half a million dollars, "which is double what we ever imagined," says Tofinetti.

They credit their success, in part, to the franchise system. "There was good advertising support by a professional ad agency. The store looked polished; you could tell a lot of research had gone into these stores," says Pylypchuk. "There were a lot of things we could have figured out over time, but by buying into a franchise, we basically bought the package and, boom, we were set up."

Therein lies the lure of the franchise business: it's the same adrenaline rush that comes with starting an independent business, but with the instantaneous advantage of being associated with a larger brand name company.

However, if you're considering plunking your savings on a franchise, know that it can be a complex and risky proposition, but one that can be immensely rewarding. Just ask Jeff Pylypchuk: "The coolest thing is working with a product that is more than just a means to make money. Sometimes we'll just get up and go for a ride in the bush. Had we opened a doughnut franchise, I think after five years I'd be going nuts," he says. "Ultimately, it is about buying into a product that you enjoy."

Excerpted with permission from Real: Creating Work You Want™ Fall 2000, published by YES Canada-B.C. Available online at http://realm.net and in print by calling 1-877-REALM-99. For more information, Phone: (604) 412-4141 Fax: (604) 412-4144 E-mail: info@realm.net

TYPES OF FRANCHISES

FRANCHISE FORMATS

There are three major ways a franchise can be formatted:

- **Single-unit franchise** This is the most popular and simplest format. In it, the franchisor grants you the right to establish and operate a business at a single location. This has been the most popular means of franchise expansion and the method by which many independent entrepreneurs have become involved in franchise distribution.

- **Area franchise** This format involves a franchisor's granting you the right to establish more than one outlet within a specified territory. This territory can be as large as an entire state, a province, or even a country, or it can be as small as part of a city. To assure that this territory is adequately serviced, the franchisor will usually require the construction and operation of a specific number of outlets within a period of time. Area franchising may be a means of achieving certain economies of scale, and perhaps a lower average franchise cost. On the other hand, it requires a larger total capital outlay for plant and equipment. Area franchisees with a large number of outlets can sometimes acquire greater financial strength than their franchisors. This has happened in a number of instances in the fast food industry.

- **Master franchise** In this format, a franchisor grants you (the *master franchisee*) the right, not only to operate an outlet in a specific territory, but also to sell subfranchises to others within that same territory. Granting master franchises is the fastest way for a franchisor to expand, but it is also very complex and results in a division of fees and royalties between the franchisor and subfranchisor. A master franchisee may not need as much initial capital as an area franchisee, but he or she must learn not only how to open and operate a franchise business but also how to sell franchises.

RANGE OF AVAILABLE FRANCHISES

To give you an idea of the current scope of franchising, the *Canadian Franchise and Dealership Guide* provides information on over 1000 different franchisor organizations in 32 product/service categories. The range of possibilities available to a prospective franchisee includes opportunities in the following areas:

- Accounting and financial services
- Automotive products and services
- Beauty, health, and personal services
- Building products and services
- Business related/communication services
- Car rental and limo services
- Computer and Internet products and services
- Convenience & grocery stores and bakeries
- Educational training systems
- Employment and personnel services
- Fast food: takeout/sit-in
- Food retail: candy, coffee, yogurt, etc.
- Health aids and services and water treatment
- Hotels, motels, and campgrounds
- Interior decorating products and services
- Lawn care, landscaping, and hydroponic services
- Maid and janitorial services
- Maintenance, repair, restoration, and cleaning products
- Pet products and services
- Photography, art products, and services
- Printing, copying, and typesetting
- Publishing
- Real estate
- Recreation, sporting goods, and related services
- Restaurants: dining rooms/bars
- Retail apparel; footwear and fashion accessories
- Retail miscellaneous
- Security systems
- Support services
- Travel
- Vending and dispensing machine systems
- Video retail

Within this broad spectrum of available opportunities, the most popular areas have been fast food (takeout/sit-in), food retail (candy, coffee, yogurt, etc.), automotive products and services, and business related/communication services.

At the individual franchisor level, the Top 10 franchise organizations for 2001 based on an evaluation by *Entrepreneur*[2] magazine were:

Company	Description	Web Site	No. of Outlets Total	Canada
1. Subway	Submarine sandwich restaurant chain	www.subway.com	15,026	1,466
2. Mail Boxes Etc.	Postal/business/ communications services	www.mbe.com	4,393	260
3. McDonald's	Hamburgers, chicken, salad	www.mcdonalds.com	32,296	812

2. *Entrepreneur* 29, no. 29 (January 2001). The evaluation is based on a number of factors including length of time in business and number of years franchising, number of franchised units and company-owned operating units, start-up costs, growth rate, percentage of terminations, and financial stability of the company.

4. Jiffy Lube Int'l Inc.	Fast oil change centres	www.jiffylube.com	2,177	36
5. Taco Bell Corp.	Mexican quick-service restaurant	www.tacobell.com	5,670	0
6. The Quizno's Corp.	Submarine sandwiches, soups, salads	www.quiznos.com	1,182	121
7. Sonic Drive In Restaurants	Drive-in hamburger restaurant	www.sonicdrivein.com	2,268	0
8. RadioShack	Consumer electronics store	www.radioshack.com	7,356	0
9. General Nutrition Centers	Vitamin and nutritional products stores	www.gncfranchising.com	4,509	0
10.Jani-King	Commercial cleaning	www.janiking.com	8,188	429

It is interesting to observe that four of these top 10 franchise organizations presently have no outlets in Canada although two of them, Taco Bell and RadioShack, have had stores in this country but subsequently withdrew from the Canadian market.

CANADIAN LEGISLATION AND DISCLOSURE REQUIREMENTS

Many states in the United States have laws and regulations governing franchise companies, but the same is not true of Canada. Only Alberta and Ontario have legislation specifically relating to franchise disclosure, although other provinces are expected to soon adopt similar legislation. The Ontario legislation only came into effect completely on January 31, 2001. The legislation in both provinces is quite similar in that it requires franchisors (with some exceptions) to provide prospective franchisees with a disclosure document containing a lot of information that otherwise would be very difficult for the prospective franchisee to obtain. This information includes:

- the business background of the directors and officers of the franchisor
- details of any litigation against the franchisor
- details of bankruptcy, insolvency, or criminal proceedings against the franchisor or its directors
- the names and addresses of existing and former franchisees
- the particulars of any advertising fund expenditures
- a set of financial statements.

This information must be provided to the franchisee at least 14 days before signing any franchise agreement or paying any money to the franchisor. Otherwise the franchisee may have recourse to rescind the franchise agreement. The basic principle behind the legislation is that everyone entering into a franchise arrangement should have access to all the information necessary to make an informed decision. The presumption is that both parties "act in good faith and in accordance with reasonable commercial standards."

Prior to the recent passage of these regulations, Canada was known as the "Wild West" of franchising. The passage of these and similar laws may prevent further situations like that of Fereshteh Vahdati and her husband in Entrepreneurs in Action #20. They spent more than $100,000 to buy a Toronto pizza franchise and another $100,000 in legal costs in a court battle against the pizza-chain owner, and ended up losing it all.

In all other provinces, franchisors are still under no legal obligation to provide any specific information or file any material with a government agency or department. As a prospective franchisee, you are on your own for the most part. If your potential franchisor does operate in Alberta or Ontario, however, you should request a copy of the disclosure material they are obliged to provide to prospective franchisees in those provinces, although you may not be entitled to the same time for deliberation or legal recourse.

20 Entrepreneurs in action

Taken to the Cleaners

Fereshteh Vahdati and her husband spent more than $100,000 to buy a Toronto pizza franchise, invested thousands more on various fees—and worked 17 hours a day.

Their payoff?

"We didn't make any money," said a despondent Vahdati on Thursday.

"Everything goes to (the chain) ... These people cheat us and we've lost everything."

Vahdati said she and her husband spent $100,000 on legal costs in a fruitless court fight against the pizza-chain owner.

The couple immigrated from Iran eight years ago and heard about the business from an Iranian community newspaper here.

The owner, also of Iranian descent, asked them to pay a 10 per cent royalty and four per cent of sales for advertising, Vahdati said.

But after they bought the stores, they were told they also had to spend $65,000 a year to buy flyers from the owner.

They eventually ran out of money and the company seized the stores from them, Vahdati said.

Source: Adapted from Tom Blackwell, "New Bill Aims to Protect Franchise Owners," *Canadian Press Newswire*, (December 3, 1998). Used with permission.

THE U.S. SITUATION

Since 1979 the U.S. Federal Trade Commission (FTC) has required that every franchisor offering franchises in the U.S. have a *disclosure statement* called a "Uniform Franchise Offering Circular" (UFOC) ready to offer a prospective franchisee. A copy of any disclosure statement can be obtained from the Federal Trade Commission, Washington, DC 20580 (www.ftc.gov). This document discloses 20 categories of information:

1. Identifying information about the franchisor
2. Business experience of the franchisor's directors and key executives
3. The franchisor's business experience
4. Litigation history of the franchisor and its directors and key executives
5. Bankruptcy history of the franchisor and its directors and key executives
6. Description of the franchise
7. Money required to be paid by the franchisee to obtain or commence the franchise operation
8. Continuing expenses to the franchisee in operating the franchise business that are payable in full or in part to the franchisor or to a person affiliated with the franchisor
9. A list of persons who represent either the franchisor or any of its affiliates, with whom the franchisee is required or advised to do business
10. Real estate, services, supplies, products, inventories, signs, fixtures, or equipment that the franchisee is required to purchase, lease, or rent, and a list of any persons with whom such transactions must be made
11. Descriptions of consideration paid (such as royalties, commissions, etc.) by third parties to the franchisor or any of its affiliates as a result of a franchisee's purchase from such third parties
12. Description of any franchisor assistance in financing the purchase of a franchise
13. Restrictions placed on a franchisee's conduct of the business
14. Required personal participation by the franchisee
15. Information about termination, cancellation, and renewal of the franchise
16. Statistical information about the number of franchises and their rate of termination or failure

17. Franchisor's right to select or approve a site for the franchise
18. Training programs for the franchisee
19. Celebrity involvement with the franchise
20. Financial information about the franchisor

The FTC regulations also require that if the franchisor makes any claims regarding the level of earnings you might realize as a result of owning its franchise, a reasonable basis must exist to support the accuracy of these claims. When such claims are made, the franchisor must have prepared an "Earnings Disclosure Document" for prospective franchisees, explaining the basis and material assumptions on which the claims are made.

If the franchise you are investigating currently operates in the U.S., this information should be readily available.

THE FRANCHISE AGREEMENT

Because two independent parties participate in a franchise relationship, the primary vehicle for obtaining central coordination and control over the efforts of both participants is a formal contract. This *franchise agreement* is the heart of the franchise relationship. It differs from the typical contract in that it contains restrictive clauses peculiar to franchising that limit your rights and powers in the conduct of the business. Franchisors argue that these controls are necessary to protect their trademark and to maintain a common identity for their outlets.

A franchise agreement should cover a variety of matters. There should be provisions that cover such subjects as:

- The full initial costs, and what they cover
- Use of the franchisor's trademarks by the franchisee
- Licensing fees
- Land purchase or lease requirements
- Building construction or renovation
- Equipment needs
- Initial training provided
- Starting inventory
- Promotional fees or allowances
- Use of operations manuals
- Royalties
- Other payments related to the franchisor
- Ongoing training
- Cooperative advertising fees
- Insurance requirements
- Interest charges on financing
- Requirements regarding purchasing supplies from the franchisor, and competitiveness of prices with those of other suppliers
- Restrictions that apply to competition with other franchisees
- Terms covering termination of the franchise, renewal rights, passing the franchise on to other family members, resale of the franchise, and similar topics

In considering any franchise proposition, you should pay a great deal of attention to the franchise contract. Since it is a key part of the relationship, it should be thoroughly understood. The rest of this section discusses the evaluation of an agreement for a single-unit franchise within a business format franchise system. It is important to realize, however, that this is not a "typical" franchise agreement; there is really no such thing. While agreements may follow a fairly standard approach in terms of format, they do not do so in terms of content. Every agreement is specially drafted by the franchisor to reflect its particular objectives and the future of the business.

OBLIGATIONS UNDERTAKEN BY THE FRANCHISOR

The obligations undertaken by the franchisor may include any or all of the following:

1. To provide basic business training to you and your employees. This includes training in bookkeeping skills, staff selection, staff management, business procedures, and the systems necessary to control the operation. In addition, the franchisor may provide you with training relating to the operational aspects of the business.
2. To investigate and evaluate sites for the location of your franchise. You will be advised as to whether or not the site meets the franchisor's standards and what sort of performance might be expected at that location. In addition you may be assisted in the design and layout of your franchise operation.
3. To provide either the equipment or the specifications for any necessary equipment and furniture you require.
4. To provide promotional and advertising material to you, and some guidance and training on marketing and promotional principles.
5. The franchisor may provide you with a statement indicating the amount of opening inventory required, and may make arrangements for you to purchase inventory either from the franchisor's own purchasing department or from particular suppliers established for this purpose.
6. The franchisor may provide you with on-site assistance for the opening of your franchise outlet. Quite often the franchisor will provide a team of two to three people to assist you in getting the business off the ground.
7. The franchisor may also provide business operating manuals explaining the details of operating the franchise system and a bookkeeping/accounting system for you to follow. There may also be additional support through such things as business consultation, supervisory visits to your premises, and staff retraining.

OBLIGATIONS IMPOSED UPON A FRANCHISEE

Your obligations as a franchisee may include any or all of the following:

1. To build your franchise outlet according to the plan or specifications provided by the franchisor
2. To maintain construction and opening schedules established by the franchisor
3. To abide by the lease commitments for your franchise outlet
4. To observe certain minimum opening hours for your franchise
5. To pay the franchise fees and other fees specified in the franchise agreement
6. To follow the accounting system specified by the franchisor and to provide financial reports and payments of amounts due promptly
7. To participate in all regional or national cooperative advertising and to use and display such point-of-sale or advertising material as the franchisor stipulates (this would include having all your advertising materials approved by the franchisor)
8. To maintain your premises in clean, sanitary condition and redecorate when required to do so by the franchisor
9. To maintain the required level of business insurance coverage
10. To permit the franchisor's staff to enter your premises to inspect and see whether the franchisor's standards are being maintained
11. To purchase specific goods or services from the franchisor or specified suppliers
12. To train all staff in the franchisor's method and to ensure that they are neatly and appropriately dressed
13. Not to assign the franchise contract without the franchisor's consent
14. To maintain adequate levels of working capital and abide by the operations manual provided by the franchisor

These are only examples of some of the obligations you might expect to incur. There will probably also be clauses involving bankruptcy, transfer of the business, renewal of the contract, and provisions for the payment of royalties and other financial considerations.

FRANCHISE FEES AND ROYALTIES

In most cases you will be required to pay an initial franchise fee on signing the franchise agreement. This fee generally pays for the right to use the trade name, licences, and operating procedures of the franchisor, some initial training, and perhaps even assistance in site selection for your franchise outlet. The amount of the fee varies tremendously, according to the type of franchise business. For a large restaurant operation or hotel, for example, the fee may be as high as $50,000 or $60,000, but for a small service franchise (such as maid service or lawn care) it may be only $5,000 to $10,000. This fee is not all profit for the franchisor, as it must go to pay for franchisee recruitment, training, assistance with site selection, and other services normally provided to you. Some franchisors will charge a separate training fee, but this is usually established merely to recover the cost of providing the training to you and your employees.

In addition to this initial fee, ongoing fees may also be provided for in the franchise agreement. These will generally consist of royalties payable for ongoing rights and privileges granted by the franchisor. Royalties are usually calculated as a percentage of the gross sales, not profits, generated by your franchise. They may be paid either weekly, monthly, or quarterly, and represent the main profit centre for most franchisors. These royalties must continue to be paid even though the franchise may be losing money. For a fast food franchise, typical royalties range from 3 per cent to 8 per cent. For some service franchises, the royalty may run from 10 to 20 per cent or even higher.

While some franchisees come to resent having to continue to pay ongoing royalties to their franchisor, this payment may be preferable to the franchisor charging a higher initial fee to the franchisee. Ongoing royalty payments at least imply a continuing commitment to the success of the franchise by the franchisor, to the ultimate benefit of both parties.

As well as royalty fees, many franchise agreements require you to contribute a proportion of your business's gross revenues to a regional or national cooperative advertising fund. This contribution may be an additional 2 to 4 per cent of gross sales. These payments are used to develop and distribute advertising material and to run regional and national advertising campaigns. These, too, are typically not a source of profit for the franchisor.

The administration of these advertising funds has often been the subject of considerable concern to franchisees and one of the areas of greatest dispute between franchisors and franchisees. The advertising fund should be maintained as a separate trust account by the franchisor and not intermixed with its general operating revenues. The purpose of this fund should be specified in the franchise agreement. In addition, the agreement should also state how and by whom the fund will be administered.

In addition to requiring you to support a regional or a national advertising program, a franchisor may require you to support your own local advertising. Typically you must spend a specific amount on a periodic basis, calculated either on the basis of a percentage of gross sales or in terms of a fixed amount. Local advertising devised by you will normally require the prior approval of the franchisor.

In some cases the franchisor also provides you with special services such as bookkeeping, accounting, and management consulting services, which are billed on a fee-for-service basis. Before acquiring a franchise you should be sure that you understand all the fees that will be payable, including any extra fees that may not be mentioned in the franchise agreement.

PURCHASE OF PRODUCTS AND SUPPLIES

A key element in the success of many franchise organizations is the sameness of each of the franchise outlets. Therefore, franchisors will work to ensure the maintenance of a certain quality of product or service and to make sure that uniform standards are employed throughout their system. Consequently, many franchisors, in an attempt to exercise complete control over their operation, require you to purchase products and services from them or from designated sources. In some cases the approved suppliers may include affiliates of the franchisor. You may also be able to purchase items from other sources of supply, provided the franchisor has approved each of those sources in advance.

If the franchisor exerts tight control over such supplies, you should try to ensure beforehand that supplies are going to be readily available when required, that they are sold to you at fair market value and on reasonable terms, and that you have the ability to choose alternative sources for any non-proprietary items if the franchisor or the designated supplier is unable to provide them to you when required.

Many franchisors earn a profit from providing supplies to their franchisees. Often, however, because franchisors exercise enormous buying power they can supply goods and services at prices and under terms which are better than those you could negotiate for yourself. You should shop around to compare prices for comparable merchandise. If the prices being charged by the franchisor are out of line, this added cost can dramatically affect your business's future earnings.

Volume rebates are often paid to franchisors by suppliers of particular products. Rather than pocket the money themselves or distribute it back to their franchisees, some franchisors will contribute this to the advertising fund. As a potential franchisee you should ask how these rebates will be handled, as a considerable amount of money may be involved.

LEASED PREMISES

Many franchise operations require the use of physical facilities such as land and buildings. When these premises are leased rather than owned by the franchisee, there are a number of ways in which this lease arrangement can be set up:

1. The franchisor may own the land and/or buildings and lease it to you
2. You may lease the land and/or building directly from a third party
3. You may own the property, sell it to the franchisor, and lease it back under a *sale leaseback* agreement
4. A third party may own the property and lease it to the franchisor, who then sublets it to you

The franchise agreement should spell out who is responsible, you or the franchisor, for negotiating the lease, equipping the premises, and paying the related costs. If a lease is involved, its terms and renewal clauses should be stated and should correspond with the terms of the franchise. You must be careful not to have a 20-year lease on a building and only a 5-year franchise agreement, or vice versa.

Franchisors generally want to maintain control of the franchise premises. Accordingly they will often own or lease the property on which the franchise business is located, and then sublet these premises to you. In other situations the franchisor may assign a lease to you subject to a conditional reassignment of the lease back to the franchisor upon termination of the franchise for any reason.

With respect to other leasehold improvements, you may also be required to purchase, or lease from the franchisor or from suppliers designated by the franchisor, certain fixtures, furnishings, equipment, and signs that the franchisor has approved as meeting its specifications and standards.

TERRITORIAL PROTECTION

In many cases the franchise agreement provision with respect to your territory and protection of that territory may be subject to considerable negotiation prior to inclusion in the agreement. You will generally want to have the franchisor agree not to operate or grant a franchise to operate another franchised outlet too close to your operation. This restriction may be confined to a designated territory, or may be confined to a predetermined geographic radius from your premises.

Franchisors, on the other hand, like to see exclusive territorial protection kept to a minimum. As a result, some franchisors may restrict the protection provided to you to a grant of first refusal to acquire an additional franchise within your territory, or may subject you to a performance quota in terms of a prescribed number of outlet openings in order to maintain exclusivity within your territory. Another approach taken by some franchisors is to limit exclusivity to a formula based on population, with the result that when the population within your territory exceeds a certain number, the franchisor may either itself operate, or grant a franchise to operate, an additional outlet in the territory.

Some questions you might like to have answered in the franchise agreement are as follows:

1. Exactly what are the geographic boundaries of your territory, and are they marked on a map as part of the contract?
2. Do you have a choice of other territories?
3. What direct competition is there in your territory, and how many more franchises does the franchisor expect to sell in that area within the next five years?
4. If the territory is an exclusive one, what are the guarantees of this exclusivity?
5. Even with these guarantees, will you be permitted to open another franchise in the same territory?
6. Can your territory be reduced at any time by the franchisor?

7. Has the franchisor prepared a market survey of your territory? (If so, ask for a copy of it and study it.)
8. Has the specific site for the franchise within the territory been decided on? (If not, how and when will this be done?)

TRAINING AND OPERATING ASSISTANCE

Virtually every franchise agreement deals with the question of training the franchisee. Training programs may involve training schools, field experience, training manuals, or on-location training.

The franchise agreement should have some provision for an initial training program for you, and should specify the duration and location of this training and who is responsible for your related transportation, accommodation, and living expenses. This initial training is generally provided for you and the manager of your franchise business. The franchisor will usually require you and your managers to complete the training program successfully prior to the opening of your franchise business. If for some reason you should fail to complete the training program, the franchisor often reserves the right to terminate the agreement and refund all fees, less any costs incurred.

Many franchise agreements also provide for start-up advisory training at the franchise premises prior to or during the opening of the business. This typically involves a program lasting a specified number of days. The agreement should indicate who is expected to bear the cost for such start-up training, including who will be responsible for the payment of travel, meals, accommodation, and other expenses of the franchisor's supervisory personnel.

The franchise agreement may also make reference to periodic refresher training. It should specify whether attendance at such programs is optional or mandatory. If they are mandatory, you should ensure that a specified maximum number of such programs is indicated for each year of the franchise agreement. The duration and location of these programs should also be specified.

Most franchisors want tight control over the day-to-day operations of the franchise, and accordingly they provide extensive operating assistance to their franchisees. This assistance is often in the form of a copyrighted operations manual that spells out, procedure by procedure, how you are expected to run the business. The manual will include such information as the franchisor's policies and procedures, and cover such details as the hours you must remain open, record-keeping methods and procedures, procedures for hiring and training employees, and, in a restaurant franchise, such matters as recipes, portion sizes, food storage and handling procedures, and menu mix and prices. The franchise agreement may also indicate that operating assistance will be provided in relation to:

1. The selection of inventory for your franchise business
2. Inspections and evaluation of your performance
3. Periodic advice with respect to hiring personnel, implementing advertising and promotional programs, and evaluating improvements in the franchise system
4. Purchasing goods, supplies, and services
5. Bookkeeping and accounting services
6. Hiring and training of employees
7. Formulation and implementation of advertising and promotional programs
8. Financial advice and consultation
9. Such additional assistance as you may require from time to time

CONTRACT DURATION, TERMINATION, AND RENEWAL

The duration of your franchise agreement may be as short as one year or as long as 40 to 50 years. However, the majority of franchise contracts run from 10 to 20 years. Most agreements also contain some provision for renewal of the contract. Be sure you understand these renewal provisions and what the terms, conditions, and costs of renewal will be. Renewal provisions commonly contain requirements for the payment of additional fees and upgrading of the franchise facilities to standards required by the franchisor at that time. The cost of upgrading is usually borne by the franchisee.

You should be aware, however, that not all agreements necessarily contain provisions for their renewal at the expiration of the initial term. Some agreements merely expire at the end of this term, and the rights revert to the franchisor.

The part of the franchise agreement usually considered most offensive by many prospective franchisees are those sections relating to termination of the agreement. Franchisors typically wish to develop a detailed list of conditions in which you might be considered in default of the agreement. *Events of default* typically fall into two categories: (1) critical or material events which would allow for termination of the agreement without notice by the franchisor and (2) events upon which you would first be given written notice with an opportunity to correct the situation.

Most franchise agreements also allow the franchisor the right, upon termination or expiration, to purchase from you all inventory, supplies, equipment, furnishings, leasehold improvements, and fixtures used in connection with the franchise business. The method of calculating the purchase price of such items is entirely negotiable by the parties prior to the execution of the franchise agreement. This has been another area of considerable disagreement between franchisors and franchisees.

When renewing franchise agreements, many franchisors do not require the payment of an additional fee, but they may require franchisees to pay the current, and usually higher, royalty fees and advertising contributions. These increases, of course, reduce your income. In addition, the franchisor may require you to make substantial leasehold improvements, update signage, and make other renovations to your outlet to conform to current franchise system standards. These capital expenditures can be expensive, so it should be clear from the beginning what improvements might be required upon renewal.

SELLING OR TRANSFERRING YOUR FRANCHISE

With respect to the transfer or sale of your franchise, most franchise agreements indicate that you are granted rights under the agreement based on the franchisor's investigation of your qualifications. These rights are typically considered to be personal to you as a franchisee. The contract will usually state that transfers of ownership are prohibited without the approval of the franchisor, but you should attempt to have the franchisor agree that such consent will not be unreasonably withheld.

For self-protection, you should be sure that the agreement contains provisions for the transfer of the franchise to your spouse or an adult child upon your death. Also, it should be possible to transfer the franchise to a corporation that is 100 per cent owned by you and has been set up solely to operate the franchise. These transfers should be possible without the payment of additional fees.

Most franchisors, however, require transfer of your franchise to an external party who meets their normal criteria of technical competence, capital, and character.

Another common provision is for the franchisor to have a *right of first refusal* — the option to purchase your franchise in the event that you receive an offer from an independent third party to acquire your rights. In such a situation you may be required to first offer such rights back to the franchisor under the same terms and conditions offered by the independent third party. If the franchisor declines to acquire your rights within a specified period of time after receipt of your notice of such an offer, you can proceed to complete the sale or transfer to the third-party purchaser.

One problem with this right of first refusal is the response time the franchisor has to exercise this right. In some agreements the allowable period is several months, during which the third-party buyer is left on hold. In your original agreement, you should try to negotiate for a more reasonable period of 15 to 30 days for the exercise of this right of first refusal.

By anticipating these and other problems during the initial negotiations, you may be able to avoid future difficulties and enhance the marketability of your franchise.

SOME EXAMPLES

As mentioned above, the specific terms included in a franchise agreement can vary substantially from situation to situation. For example, under the terms of the Enviro Masters Lawn Care (www.enviromasters.com) franchise agreement for their organic and environmentally considerate lawn care service franchise, franchisees pay $15,000 – $25,000 for an initial franchise fee plus a monthly royalty of 5 per cent of gross sales and 2 per cent of gross sales for the corporate advertising program. The minimum total investment required to get into the business is $25,000 with a total average investment of around $35,000. For this fee the franchisee receives the use of the company's trademark and trade names. The company also provides training, marketing support and field training in turf management and similar areas.

In contrast, franchisees of Quizno's Subs (www.quiznos.com) can expect to make a total investment of around $200,000 to open a typical outlet. This includes their standard franchise fee of $25,000. In addition, they will need further funds for deposits of various types and money for working capital. Royalties amount to 7 per cent of gross sales paid monthly, and the advertising contribution is a further 4 per cent; 1 per cent for national advertising and 3 per cent for expenditures in the local market. Of this amount, franchisees should have at least $60,000 in unencumbered cash. The rest may be financed through one of the national bank's franchise programs with the assistance of the company. Franchisees receive 22 days of intensive initial training, assistance in site selection and lease negotiations, pre-opening and ongoing operational support, and national, local, and grand opening store marketing programs.

The Keg Steakhouse and Bar (www.kegsteakhouse.com) bills itself as Canada's leading steakhouse. A typical new, stand-alone Keg restaurant requires an investment of over $1.4 million to build the facility and cover the necessary start-up costs. This includes the franchise fee of $50,000. Franchisees also pay a royalty of 5% of their gross sales each month and contribute 2.5% to a corporate advertising fund. This enables them to use the "Keg" brand name on their restaurant and the company provides them with training and other support before they open their location, and ongoing support in accounting, marketing, menu development, personnel management, and financial planning.[3]

A sampling of some other popular franchisors indicating their initial franchise or dealership fee, royalty rate, required advertising contribution, and their approximate total average investment to open a typical outlet is shown in Table 5.1.

BUYING A FRANCHISE

FINDING A FRANCHISE BUSINESS

Perhaps the most common source of preliminary information regarding available franchises is newspaper advertisements. Major business newspapers such as the *National Post* and the *Globe and Mail* all have special sections devoted to franchise advertisements. The "Business" or "Business Opportunities" section of the classified advertisements in your local newspaper can also be an important place to look for prospective franchise situations. Business journals and trade magazines may also contain ads for many franchise organizations. Recommendations from friends, trade shows and seminars, and business opportunity shows often held in our larger cities can also be excellent means of contacting franchisors.

Another important source of information is franchise directories, which list franchisors' names and addresses along with information on the type of franchise offered, the costs involved, and other useful information. Some useful directories are the Franchise Annual published by Info Press Inc. (728 Center St., Lewiston, NY 14092 or P.O. Box 670, 9 Duke St., St. Catharines, Ont. L2R 6W8, www.infonews.com) and *The Canadian Franchise & Dealership Guide* (24019 Lasher Lane, Box 97, Baldwin, Ont. L0E 1A0, www.newbusinesscentre.com/cfdg.html).

CHECKING OUT THE FRANCHISE OPPORTUNITY

After sifting through the various choices available, most prospective franchisees narrow their selection down to one or two possibilities. The next step is requesting a promotional kit from each of these franchisors. Normally this kit contains basic information about the company — its philosophy, a brief history, a listing of the number of outlets, where they do business, etc. Most kits also contain an *application form* requesting your name and address, information about your past business experience, the value of your net assets, and other data; for the process to continue with the franchisor, you must complete it in detail. The form may have any one of a number of titles:

- Confidential Information Form
- Personal History
- Confidential Application
- Franchise Application
- Pre-interview Form
- Qualification Report
- Credit Application
- Application for Interview Form
- Request for Interview

3. For further information on these and other franchise opportunities see *The 1999 Franchise Annual*, or *The Canadian Franchise and Dealership Guide*.

TABLE 5.1 A SAMPLING OF CANADIAN FRANCHISORS

Franchisor	Number of Owned Units In Canada	Number of Franchisees /Dealers In Canada	Initial Fee	Royalty	Advertising	Approximate Investment Required	Web Site
Boston Pizza	2	138	$45–60,000	7%	3%	$1–1,200,000	www.bostonpizza.com
Dollar Rent-a-Car	—	24	$15–59,000	7	2	$90–150,000	www.dollar.com
Great Canadian Dollar Store	—	100+	$15,000	4	—	$125,000	www.dollarstores.com
Molly Maid	1	76	$14,000	6	2	$18,000	www.mollymaid.ca
Dairy Queen Canada	—	527	$35,000	4	6	$500—1,200,000	www.dairyqueen.com
We Care Home Health Services	2	52	$40,000	5	2	$150,000	www.wecare.ca
McDonald's Restaurants of Canada	334	771	$45,000	17% including rent, service fees, and advertising	—	$600—800,000	www.mcdonalds.com
Midas Muffler	—	241	$25,000	5	5	$225,000	www.midas.com
Yogen Früz	3	295	$25,000	6	3	$125—150,000	www.coolbrandsinternational.com
Second Cup Coffee Co.	13	226	$20,000	9	2	$250—300,000	www.secondcup.com
Tim Hortons	—	1553	$50,000	3	4	$360—390,000	www.timhortons.com
Kwik Kopy Printing	4	74	$29,500	7	3	$200,000	www.kwikkopy.ca
Shred-It	13	39	$45,000	5	1.5	$300,000	www.shredit.com

Source: Adapted from *The 1999 Franchise Annual*, Info Franchise News Inc., 1999.

OUT OF THE ORDINARY FRANCHISE OPPORTUNITIES

If fast food, oil changes, and lawn care are not your idea of an exciting business, here are some examples of new, imaginative, and extremely unique franchise opportunities that threaten to put an entirely new face on the industry:

- Easyriders – Franchised stores that include retail sales of motorcycles, clothing, and a full range of motorcycle accessories. (www.easyriders.org)
- Everything Garlic – a Vancouver-based franchise concept selling over 800 garlic related products ranging from garlic stuffed olives to garlic shampoo. (www.everythinggarlic.com)
- Interquest – a franchisor of canine training and drug detection services used in high schools, airports, and other public places. (www.interquestk9.com)
- Impressions On Hold International – A franchisor of recording and message services for sale to businesses to increase the productivity of on-hold time for their customers. (www.impressionsonhold.com)
- Moon Land Registry Inc. – A franchised business selling plots of land on the moon, Venus, Mars, or Jupiter's moon, Io, for $15 an acre. (www.moonlandregistry.com)

Source: Lyle Junish, "Out of the Ordinary: Franchise Opportunities that Walk on the Wild Side," Canadian Franchise Business 6, no. 3 (July/August, 2000).

Regardless of which of these titles is used, they are all different ways of describing the same thing and request much the same information. For example, you may be asked for:

1. Personal data such as your name, address, telephone number, age, health and physical impairments, marital status and number of dependents, and the name of any fraternal, business, or civic organizations to which you might belong
2. Business data such as your present business or corporation, your position, the name and address of your employer, how long you have been involved in this business, your present annual salary, and any previous business history you may have
3. References such as your present bank and the name and address of your bank manager, and any other references you may care to provide
4. Financial data such as your average annual income for the past five years, and a total declaration of your current assets and liabilities to establish your net worth
5. Additional data that relate to your particular interest in the franchise

The application form normally requires you to provide a deposit, typically in the range of $2,000 to $5,000. In most cases the form will state that this deposit will be credited toward the initial franchise fee without interest or deduction if the transaction should proceed. However, you should make sure that if you are turned down, all or most of this deposit will be refunded, especially if it is a large amount of money and the franchise is new and unproven.

If your application is approved, the franchisor will interview you to determine your suitability as a franchisee. The focus of this interview will be on assessing your capability according to various objective criteria that have been established by the franchisor. Every franchisor has its own established criteria based on previous experience with various kinds of people. For example, many franchisors will not consider absentee owners and refuse to grant franchises strictly for investment purposes. They feel that the success of their system rests on the motivation created by individually owned and managed outlets.

The personal characteristics desired by the franchisor will vary with the type of business. For example, a different level of education is necessary to operate a management consulting service than is needed to operate a carpet cleaning firm. Research on these selection criteria indicates that many franchisors tend to rank them in the following order:

1. Credit and financial standing
2. Personal ability to manage the operation
3. Previous work experience
4. Personality
5. Health
6. Educational background

While other factors may also be considered by particular franchisors, these criteria tend to dominate the selection process.

This interview is also an opportunity for you to raise questions about the franchisor's financial stability, trademark protection policy, the ongoing services provided to franchisees, information regarding any financial packages that may have been arranged with particular banks, the names and addresses of current franchisees, and any other questions that may occur to you. This is an opportunity for you and the franchisor to assess each other and see if you can work together on a long-term basis.

At this interview, the franchisor will also provide you with a copy of the franchise agreement. At this point, you must evaluate all the available information with the help of your accountant, your bank manager, and your lawyer to ensure that you feel comfortable with the franchisor and that you are happy your investment is secure. If you have any remaining questions or doubts, now is the time to resolve them. Then, if you are still not completely sure in your own mind that you wish to proceed, you should ask for a refund of your deposit.

Well-established and popular franchisors are unlikely to change their arrangements or legal documentation very much in response to a prospective franchisee's requests. They have successful systems in which many would-be franchisees would like to participate. For them, it's a seller's market.

If one of these franchisors accepts you as a franchisee, you may have to make up your mind very quickly. It is important to be decisive. If you are comfortable with the franchisor and the franchise agreement, you should be ready to sign. If not, you should ask for a refund and pursue other opportunities.

Some franchisors will expect you to sign the contract right away. Others wait until they have found a suitable location for your outlet, usually within a predetermined period of time. In some cases, it can take weeks, perhaps even months, for a suitable site to be found or a lease negotiated before you actually sign. It should also be remembered that popular franchisors often have long waiting lists of prospective franchisees, so that one or more years can pass before you will be in business.

FRANCHISE FINANCING

One of the first steps in evaluating any franchise opportunity is to determine the total cost of getting into the business. This could include the initial franchise fee, real estate rental, equipment costs, start-up inventories and expenses, and initial working capital requirements. This total commitment can be substantial. A recent study released by the International Franchise Association in the United States indicated the following average initial investment to start a franchised outlet by industry category. These figures are in U.S. dollars and do not include the cost of real estate.[4]

Baked Goods	$170,000
Business Services	$72,000
Fast Food	$180,000
Lodging	$1,800,000
Printing	$207,000
Restaurant	$559,000
Service Business	$121,000
Sports & Recreation	$471,000
Travel	$73,000

You must also determine how much of this amount must be put up as an initial investment and what kind of terms might be arranged for handling the balance. Most franchisors expect the franchisee to put up 30 to 50 per cent of the total franchise package cost as an initial investment. You must ask yourself whether you have enough unencumbered capital to cover this amount.

Financing of the remainder can sometimes be done through the franchisor, or the franchisor may have previously arranged a standardized financing package for prospective franchisees through one of the major banks or trust companies. Subway, the successful submarine sandwich franchise, offers its new franchisees financing via an in-house equipment leasing program. Compucentre retail stores also has arranged an in-house financing program for franchisees in conjunction with a couple of the major banks. These programs may be somewhat more expensive for the franchisee than arranging an independent bank loan, but they can be more convenient.

The initial investment required for a restaurant franchise can be substantial. A typical fast food take-out restaurant such as Koya Japan has an initial franchise fee of $25,000 and an average total investment of $175,000. The cost of a full service restaurant such as Swiss Chalet Chicken & Ribs includes a franchise fee of $75,000 and a total investment ranging from $1.1 million to $1.4 million. In these cases, equipment and leasehold improvements tend to make up the largest component of the total cost.

In the retail sector, the size of the total investment will vary depending on the nature and location of the outlet. For example, a video store like Jumbo Video will require a franchise fee of $50,000 and a total investment of roughly $400,000, with the franchisee having to provide $150,000 in cash. A computer store like Compucentre has a franchise fee of $25,000 with an average investment of $275,000, while a retail building supply dealership like Windsor Plywood has an initial fee of $35,000 and a total required investment upwards to $1 million. Most of these investments are typically in inventory.

The investment required for a service franchise is usually much lower. Many service franchises can be established for a total investment of less than $50,000. For example, Scharecorp, Canada's largest franchise organization and the operator of Good Turn Systems coin-operated vendors bearing the Muscular Dystrophy Association name and logo, has a franchise fee of $17,500 and a total average investment of $35,000.

4 "The Profile of Franchising: A Statistical Abstract of 1996 UFOC (Uniform Franchise Offering Circulars)", *Info Franchise Newsletter*, International Franchise Association Educational Foundation.

Similarly, Jani-King Canada, the world's largest commercial cleaning franchise, offers its franchises for a fee ranging from $9,900 to $24,900 depending on the territory, with a nominal additional amount of financing for equipment, supplies, and initial working capital. A residential cleaning and maid service franchise like Molly Maid can be established for a franchise fee of $14,000 plus $4-5,000 in working capital. At the other extreme, opening a franchised hotel or motel may involve a total investment of several million dollars, although the initial amount of money required may be much less since the land and buildings for the hotel or motel can often be externally financed.

FUTURE TRENDS IN FRANCHISING

A number of trends have emerged in the past few years and are likely to continue for several years across the United States and Canada. Among the most important of these are:

1. The growth in *conversion franchising*, the conversion of an independent business to a franchise. The idea is not new, and in the past has been used extensively in the franchising of real estate and travel agencies. The movement to conversion franchising is expected to be evident in many other areas, however, especially in construction, home repair and remodelling services, all types of business services, non-food retailing, hotels, and restaurants.

2. Women have become involved in franchising in numbers larger than ever before, both as franchisors and as franchisees. Franchising offers new opportunities for women who are entering the professional and management ranks and want to be part of the business world or to invest in an independent business career. Starting their own businesses through franchising decreases the risk factor for women with little or no previous business experience. Furthermore, women often excel in businesses that cater specifically to the needs or interests of other women.

3. Changing consumer lifestyles and the new status of working women in society have influenced the growth of franchising, particularly in terms of non-food retail stores that provide a variety of services for the home. Accelerated growth is expected in franchise stores providing home furnishings, decorating, picture framing, and other types of accessories for the home. Growth is also expected to take place in all types of general merchandise, video, and electronic stores.

4. Computer technology is having a dramatic impact on the service sector, especially franchising. The computer industry has established new businesses in the form of franchised retail stores and this trend is expected to continue. Although competition will intensify and other distribution channels emerge, franchisors of computer stores will focus on two areas: (1) computer stores specializing in home computers, video games, software, and hardware, and (2) stores providing support services and systems for business.

5. Dental health care and other medical services have become an integral part of franchising as franchised centres have spread to all regions of Canada and the United States. This trend is expected to continue to develop rapidly as medical expenditures rise and the application of modern business methods by franchisors provide increased efficiency, greater service, and lower fees, while meeting the needs of the huge, untapped market.

6. Franchised restaurants of all types are expected to continue to be the most popular sector of franchising. Increased activity is expected in the upscaling of franchised restaurants in terms of exterior and interior decor, service, and quality and variety of food items served. Franchisors of restaurants have been among the fastest-growing, and this trend is expected to continue for the next few years.

7. Franchises that specialize in automotive repairs will continue to grow in many areas of the huge automotive "aftermarket." This trend will continue to expand through the next decade. Traditional sources of automotive repair are disappearing with the continuing decline of new-car dealerships and full-service gasoline service stations. In addition, the automobile population is growing annually in both number and variety and, on average, cars on the road are getting older. Franchise growth will be in specialized automotive centres providing services in tuneup, quick lube, muffler repair and replacement, transmissions, brakes, painting, electrical repairs, and general car care.

8. Other areas of franchising that bear watching over the next few years are automobile leasing, packaging and rapid delivery of parcels, home building, medical centres, temporary health services, and business brokers.
9. Convenience stores, emphasizing speed and service, provide the multiple "fill-in" items that consumers need between their regular trips to the supermarket. To increase their sales volume and compete with fast food restaurants, many convenience stores are offering a wide variety of take-out foods. This segment of the franchise industry is expected to continue to grow dramatically.
10. Businesses engaged in franchising educational services are becoming highly specialized. For example, increased leisure time has created a growing market for dietary, tanning, and exercise training centres that has been successfully exploited by franchise systems. Franchisors have also entered the growing field of early childhood education. Sales of this segment of the franchise industry, too, are expected to continue to increase dramatically.

FYI FOR YOUR INFORMATION

For more information on franchising you might check out the following sources:

1. **CANADIAN FRANCHISE ASSOCIATION**
(www.cfa.ca)
2. **INTERNATIONAL FRANCHISE ASSOCIATION** Check out their "Consumer Guide to Buying a Franchise."
(www.franchise.org/default.asp)
3. **FRANCHISE CONXIONS** A Canadian-based franchise and small-business consulting firm that offers a wide range of services to the Franchise Industry.
(www.franchise-conxions.com)
4. **CHECKLIST FOR FRANCHISEES CANADA BUSINESS SERVICE CENTRES**
(www.cbsc.org/english/search/display.cfm?CODE=4010&Coll=FE_FEDSBIS_E)
5. **FRANNET, THE FRANCHISE CONNECTION** A collection of resource materials and articles that have been featured in various franchise-related magazines and publications.
(www.frannet.com/Research/research.html)
6. **CANADIAN FRANCHISE OPPORTUNITIES** An on-line directory of franchises and franchise business services. (canada.franchiseopportunities.com)
7. **THE FRANCHISE ANNUAL ONLINE** An on-line version of The Franchise Annual with an extensive listing of available franchises.
(www.infonews.com/online.html)
8. **TO FRANCHISE OR NOT TO FRANCHISE** A list of resources to help you make the decision.
(realm.net/hyperlinks/articles/fall00-franresources.cfm)

EVALUATING A FRANCHISE — A CHECKLIST

The checklist shown in Figure 5.1 can serve as an effective tool for you to use in evaluating a franchise opportunity. When reading through the questions, you will notice that some of them require you to do a little homework before you can reasonably respond. For example, you and/or your lawyer will have to review the franchise agreement to assess the acceptability of the various clauses and conditions. You will also have to give some thought to how much capital you have personally and where you might raise additional financing.

Some questions call for further research. Ask the franchisor for the names and addresses of a number of current franchisees. Select a sample of them and contact them to discuss their views of the franchisor and the franchise agreement. Make certain your interview takes place without the franchisor or his representative present. Check the length of time that franchisee has operated in that particular location in comparison to the length of time that franchise has been in existence. If there is a difference try to determine what happened to the earlier franchisee(s). If you have been provided with pro forma financial statements or other information by the franchisor indicating the level of sales and financial performance you might expect, ask these franchisees to confirm that they are reasonably close to reality. In addition, what you may feel you require in terms of training, advertising and promotion support, and ongoing operating assistance may be a function of the type of franchise you are evaluating.

Make a copy of this checklist for each franchise you intend to evaluate. By using a similar outline to assess each opportunity, it will be much easier for you to compare them.

FIGURE 5.1 CHECKLIST FOR EVALUATING A FRANCHISE

THE FRANCHISOR

1. What is the name and address of the franchise company?
Name ______
Address ______
______

2. The franchise company is: Public ______ Private ______

3. What is the name and address of the parent company (if different from that of the franchise company)?
Name ______
Address ______
______

4. The parent company is: Public ______ Private ______

5. On what date was the company founded and when was the first franchise awarded?
Company founded ______ First franchise awarded ______

6. How many outlets does the franchise currently have in operation or under construction?
   a. Of these outlets, how many are franchised and how many are company owned?
      Franchised ______ Company owned ______
   b. How many franchises have failed?
   c. How many of these failures have been within the past two years?
   d. Why did these franchises fail?
      Franchisor's reasons ______
      ______
      ______
      Franchisee's reasons ______
      ______
      ______

7. How many new outlets does the franchisor plan to open within the next 12 months? Where will they open?
How many ______ Where ______
______

8. a. Who are the key principals in the day-to-day operation of the franchisor's business?

Name	**Title**	**Background**
______	______	______
______	______	______
______	______	______
______	______	______

b. Who are the directors of the company, other than those individuals named above?

Name	Title	Background
____________	____________	____________
____________	____________	____________
____________	____________	____________
____________	____________	____________

c. Who are the consultants to the company?

Name	Title	Background
____________	____________	____________
____________	____________	____________
____________	____________	____________
____________	____________	____________

THE FRANCHISE

1. Fill in the following data on each of several present franchisees.

Franchise 1 ____________

Owner ____________

Address ____________

____

Telephone ____________

Date started ____________

Franchise 2

Owner ____________

Address ____________

____

Telephone ____________

Date started ____________

Franchise 3

Owner ____________

Address ____________

____

Telephone ____________

Date started ____________

2. Has a franchise ever been awarded in your area? Yes ________ No ________

a. If Yes, and it is *still in operation,* provide details.

Owner ____________

Address ____________

____

Telephone ____________

Date started ____________

continues

Checklist for Evaluating a Franchise — continued

b. If Yes, and it is *no longer in operation*, provide details.

Person involved ______________________

Address ______________________

Date opened ______________________

Date closed ______________________

Reason for failure ______________________

3. Is the product or service offered by the franchise:

a. Part of a growing market?	Yes ______	No ______
b. Needed in your area?	Yes ______	No ______
c. Of interest to you?	Yes ______	No ______
d. Safe for the consumer?	Yes ______	No ______
e. Protected by a guarantee or warranty?	Yes ______	No ______
f. Associated with a well-known trademark or personality?	Yes ______	No ______
g. Accompanied by a trademark that is adequately protected?	Yes ______	No ______

4. Will you be acquiring:

a. A single-unit franchise? ________

b. An area franchise? ________

c. A master franchise? ________

5. The franchise is: Exclusive ________ Non-exclusive ________

6. What facilities will be required and will you have to own or lease?

a. Business can be operated out of home? Yes ________ No ________

b. Facilities required:	*Yes*	*No*	*Own*	*Lease*
Office	____	____	____	____
Retail outlet	____	____	____	____
Manufacturing facility	____	____	____	____
Warehouse	____	____	____	____
Other (specify)	____	____	____	____

7. Who will be responsible for:	*Franchisor*	*Franchisee*
a. Location feasibility study?	________	________
b. Facility design and layout?	________	________
c. Construction?	________	________
d. Furnishing?	________	________
e. Arranging financing?	________	________

FRANCHISE COSTS

1. Is a forecast of expected income and expenses provided? Yes ________ No ________

a. If Yes, is it:

i. Based on actual franchisee operations? ________

ii. Based on a franchisor-owned outlet? ________

iii. Based strictly on estimated performance? ________

b. If Yes, does the forecast:
   i. Relate directly to your market area? Yes ______ No ______
   ii. Satisfy your personal goals? Yes ______ No ______
   iii. Provide for an acceptable return on investment? Yes ______ No ______
   iv. Provide for an adequate level of promotion and personal expenses? Yes ____ No ____

2. How much money will it require to get started in the business? Itemize.

Item	***Amount***
a. Franchise fee	$ ________
b. Franchisor-provided services	________
c. Supplies and opening inventory	________
d. Real estate	________
e. Machinery and equipment	________
f. Furniture and fixtures	________
g. Opening expenses	________
h. Other	________
Total Initial Investment	**$ ________ (A)**

3. How much other money will be required:

a. To defray operating losses for first few months of operation?	$ ________ **(B)**
b. To cover your personal expenses for the first year of operation?	$ ________ **(C)**

4. Total financial requirements (A + B + C = D) $ ________ **(D)**

5. How much of these total financial requirements do you personally have available? $ ________ **(E)**

6. If the franchisor provides any financial assistance:

a. How much?	$ ________ **(F)**
b. What does this represent as a percentage of your total estimated costs?	________ %
c. What is the interest rate on this financing?	________ %
d. When does the money have to be paid back?	________

7. Where will you be able to obtain the rest of the required funds? Specify sources from the following list:

a. Banks, credit unions, or other financial institutions	$ ________
b. Finance companies	________
c. Friends, relatives, and neighbours	________
d. Other private sources	________
e. Leasing arrangements	________
f. Suppliers' credit	________
g. Government assistance programs	________
h. Other (specify)	$ ________
Total	**$ ________ (G)**

8. Total funds available from all sources (E + F + G = H)

Grand Total **$ ________ (H)**

9. How do the funds available compare with your total estimated requirements? (D – H) $ ________

continues

Checklist for Evaluating a Franchise — continued

THE FRANCHISE AGREEMENT

1. Have you obtained a copy of the franchise agreement? Yes______ No ______

2. Have you given a copy to your lawyer and accountant to review?
Lawyer Yes ______ No ______
Accountant Yes ______ No ______

3. Does the agreement contain clauses that relate to the following areas and activities and are the specified terms and conditions acceptable or unacceptable to you?

	Yes	**No**	***If Yes*** Acceptable	Unacceptable
a. Franchise fee	________	________	________	________
b. Commissions and royalties	________	________	________	________
c. Purchase of products and supplies	________	________	________	________
d. Lease of premises	________	________	________	________
e. Territorial protection	________	________	________	________
f. Training assistance	________	________	________	________
g. Termination	________	________	________	________
h. Renewal	________	________	________	________
i. Selling and transferring	________	________	________	________
j. Advertising and promotion	________	________	________	________
k. Operating assistance	________	________	________	________
l. Trademark protection	________	________	________	________

RUNNING YOUR FRANCHISE OPERATION

1. Does the franchisor provide you with an initial formal training program? Yes ______No______

If Yes: a. How long does it last? ______days

b. Is cost included in the franchise fee? Yes________No ________Partially ______

If No or Partially, specify how much you will have to pay for:

i. Training course $ __________
ii. Training materials __________
iii. Transportation __________
iv. Room and board __________
v. Other __________
Total Costs **$** __________

c. Does the training course cover any of the following subjects?

i. Franchise operations Yes ______ No ______
ii. Sales Yes ______ No ______
iii. Financial management Yes ______ No ______
iv. Advertising and promotion Yes ______ No ______
v. Personnel management Yes ______ No ______
vi. Manufacturing methods Yes ______ No ______
vii. Maintenance Yes ______ No ______

viii. Operations Yes ______ No ______

ix. Employee training Yes ______ No ______

x. Other (specify) ______________________________

______________________________ Yes ______ No ______

2. How do you train your initial staff?

a. Is the training program provided by the franchisor? Yes ______ No ______

b. Does the franchisor make a staff member available from head office to assist you? Yes______ No______

c. What materials are included in the staff training program?

____

____

____

3. Is there any requirement for you to participate in a continuing training program?
Yes ______ No ______
If Yes:

a. Who pays the cost of this program? Franchisee__________ Franchisor __________

b. If you have to pay for this continuing training, how much does it cost? $ __________

4. Is the product or service of the franchise normally sold by any of the following means?

a. In customer's home — by appointment Yes ______ No ______

b. In customer's home — by cold-calling Yes ______ No ______

c. By telephone Yes ______ No ______

d. In a store or other place of business Yes ______ No ______

e. At customer's business — by appointment Yes ______ No ______

f. At customer's business — by cold-calling Yes ______ No ______

g. By direct mail Yes ______ No ______

h. Other (specify) ______________________________ Yes ______ No ______

5. How do you get sales leads and customers?

a. Provided by franchisor Yes ______ No ______

b. Self-generated Yes ______ No ______

c. Through advertising Yes ______ No ______

d. By direct mail Yes ______ No ______

e. By telephone Yes ______ No ______

f. Through trade shows Yes ______ No ______

g. Other ______________________________ Yes ______ No ______

6. Give a brief profile of the types of customers you feel are the best prospects for the products or services offered by the franchise.

____

____

____

continues

Checklist for Evaluating a Franchise — continued

7. a. What is the national advertising budget of the franchisor? $ __________

b. How is this budget distributed among the primary advertising media?

TV	% __________
Radio	__________
Newspaper	__________
Outdoor	__________
Magazines	__________
Direct mail	__________
Other (specify)	__________
Total	**100%**

8. What kind of advertising and promotion support is available from the franchisor for the local franchisee?

	Yes	***No***	***If Yes, Cost***
a. Prepackaged local advertising program	________	________	$ ________
b. Cooperative advertising program	________	________	$ ________
c. Grand-opening package	________	________	$ ________

9. Do you need the services of an advertising agency? Yes ________ No ________

10. a. Who are your principal competitors? Name them in order of importance.

1. ______________________________
2. ______________________________
3. ______________________________

b. Describe what you know about each and how each compares with your franchise.

Competitor 1

Owner______________________________

Address ______________________________

____

Description ______________________________

____

____

Competitor 2

Owner______________________________

Address ______________________________

____

Description ______________________________

____

____

Competitor 3

Owner______________________________

Address ______________________________

____

Description ______________________________

____

____

11. What operating assistance is available from the franchisor if you should need it?

a. Finance and accounting Yes ______ No ______

b. Advertising and promotion Yes ______ No ______

c. Research and development Yes ______ No ______

d. Sales Yes ______ No ______

e. Real estate Yes ______ No ______

f. Construction Yes ______ No ______

g. Personnel and training Yes ______ No ______

h. Manufacturing and operations Yes ______ No ______

i. Purchasing Yes ______ No ______

j. Other (specify) Yes ______ No ______

12. Does the franchisor have a field supervisor assigned to work with a number of franchises?
Yes ______ No ______

If Yes: a. How many franchises is she/he assigned to?

b. Who would be assigned to your franchise?

Name ______________________________

Address ______________________________

____

Telephone ______________________________

Conducting a Feasibility Study

Part 1: Technical and Market Assessment

So far, we have considered and evaluated your new venture primarily from a conceptual point of view. That is, we have concentrated on the following questions:

1. What product/service businesses would you be interested in pursuing?
2. How attractive are these venture ideas?
3. What options should you consider in getting into a business of your own?

Now, in Stage Six, a step-by-step process will be presented to help you transform your *chosen* venture concept from the idea stage to the marketplace. This is accomplished by means of a *feasibility study*.

Before starting a new business you should first conduct a feasibility study to determine whether your idea could turn into a profitable business venture. In many cases, the opposite is true. People get all excited about the prospects of a new business without giving careful consideration to its prospects or thoroughly researching and evaluating its potential. Some time later they may discover that while the idea was good, the market was too small, the profit margins too narrow, the competition too tough, the financing insufficient, or there are other reasons that cause the business to fail. If the individuals involved had thoroughly researched their idea and conducted a feasibility study before starting, many of these failed businesses would never have been started in the first place.

A feasibility study is the first comprehensive plan you need in contemplating any new venture. It proves both to yourself and others that your new venture concept can become a profitable reality. If the feasibility study indicates that the business idea has potential, then you can proceed to write a business plan. A typical feasibility study considers the following areas:

1. The concept for your venture
2. An assessment of your market
3. The technical feasibility of your idea
4. The supply situation
5. Cost-profit analysis
6. Your plans for future action

The first four of these topics will be discussed in this Stage; the last two will be addressed in Stage Seven. Much of the same information can be incorporated into your subsequent business plan (see Stage Eleven) if it appears that your venture warrants commercial development.

The contents of a typical feasibility study are outlined in Figure 6.1. You can use this guide to assist you in evaluating the feasibility of your new venture idea.

YOUR VENTURE CONCEPT

It is critical that you be able to clearly and concisely explain, verbally, the principal concept underlying your venture — what sets it apart from other businesses of similar character. This is what is sometimes called your

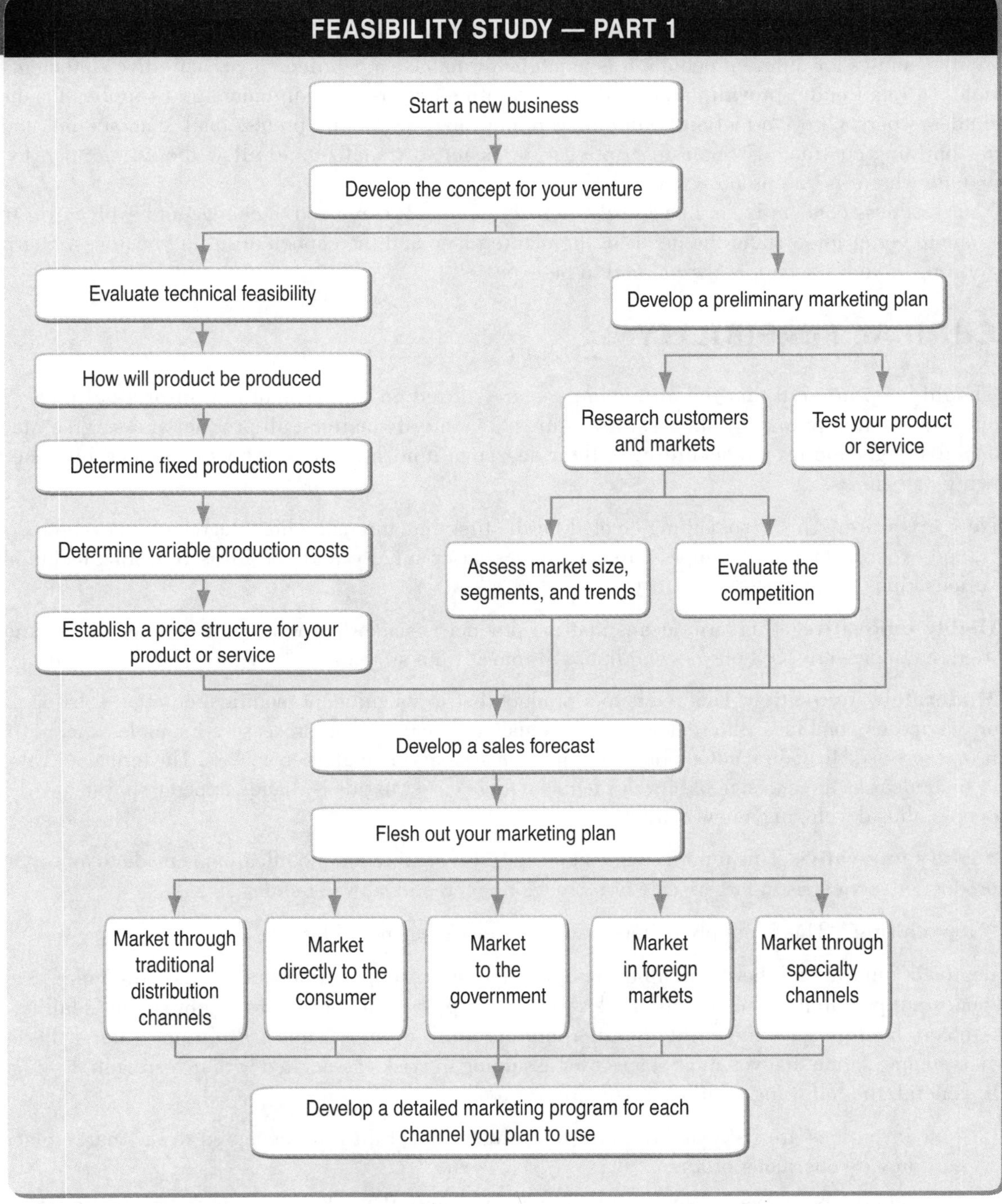

"elevator pitch"—a conversation that begins when the elevator door closes and ends when the door opens at your floor. That means you have only a few seconds to capture your listener's interest, so you had better be able to explain your concept quickly, completely, and confidently. If you have difficulty explaining to other people precisely what it is your business proposes to do, it is a clear sign that your concept still needs development and refinement.

An idea is not yet a concept, only the beginning of one. A fully developed concept includes not only some notion as to the product or service the business plans to provide, but also a description of the proposed pricing strategy, promotional program, and distribution plans. It will also consider such aspects of the business as what is unique or proprietary about your product or service idea, any innovative technology involved in its production or sale, and the principal benefits it is expected to deliver to customers.

Developing a good description of your concept can be difficult. Many concepts are too broad and general, not clearly communicating the really distinctive elements of the venture — for example, "a retail sporting goods outlet" or "a tool and equipment rental store." Other concepts may use words like "better service," "higher quality," "new," "improved," or "precision machined," which are either ambiguous or likely to have different meanings for different people. It is much better to have a detailed, clear, definitive statement — for example, "a retail outlet providing top-of-the-line hunting and fishing equipment and supplies for the serious outdoors person" or "a tool and equipment rental business for the professional, commercial, and residential building contractor." Such descriptions are easier to visualize and allow the uninformed to really understand what it is you propose to do.

Your business concept is not necessarily etched in stone. It may need to change and evolve over time as you come to better understand the needs of the marketplace and the economics of the business. Sharpening and refining of your concept is normal and to be expected.

TECHNICAL FEASIBILITY

You should keep in mind that not all businesses are started on the basis of new or original ideas. Many, in fact, merely attempt to copy successful ventures. To simplify matters, all product and service ideas can be placed along a continuum according to their degree of innovativeness or may be placed into one of the following categories:

1. **New invention** This is something created for the first time through a high degree of innovation, creativity, and experimentation. Examples are fibre optics, laser surgery, and non-invasive testing techniques for various kinds of cancer.
2. **Highly innovative** This term means that the product is somewhat new and as yet not widely known or used. Examples are MP3 players and light rail transit train systems.
3. **Moderately innovative** This refers to a product that is a significant modification of an existing product or service or combines different areas of technology, methods, or processes. Examples include microprocessors used to control automobile fuel injection systems or single-person cars. The term could also refer to such ideas as the redesign of bicycles to make them easier to ride by handicapped or physically disabled people, thus developing a new market.
4. **Slightly innovative** This term means that a small, yet significant, modification is made to an established product or service, as in larger-scale or more exotic recreational water slides.
5. **"Copycatting"** This is simply imitating someone else's business idea.

The degree of innovation inherent in a business idea has strong implications for the risk, difficulty in evaluation, and profit potential of the venture. Risk refers to the probability of the product or service's failing in the marketplace. Evaluation is the ability to determine its worth or significance. Profit potential is the level of return or compensation that you might expect for assuming the risks associated with investing in this business.

In general, the following relationships hold:

1. New inventions are risky and difficult to evaluate, but if they are accepted in the marketplace they can provide enormous profits.
2. For moderately innovative and slightly innovative ideas, the risks are lower and evaluation is less difficult, but profit potential tends to be more limited.
3. In the "copycat" category, risks are often very high and profit potential tends to be quite low. Such businesses usually show no growth, or very slow growth, and there is little opportunity for profit beyond basic wages.

Every new product must also be subject to some form of analysis to ensure that the benefits promised prospective customers will indeed be delivered. In developing a working prototype or an operating model with this in mind, some of the more important technical requirements to consider are:

1. **Keep it as simple as possible** Keep it simple to build, to transport, to maintain, and above all to use.
2. **Make it flexible** There are many examples of products that were unsuccessful in the application for which they were originally developed but were able to be redesigned to satisfy the needs of an entirely different market.
3. **Build a product that will work as intended without failing, or eliminating the need for** regular and constant service, is becoming more important to consumers. They are more inclined than ever before to look for products that are durable, reliable, safe, and easily maintained.

If a product does not meet these technical qualifications it should be reworked until it does.

One key approach for testing a new product is to subject it to the toughest conditions that might be experienced during actual use. In addition to this kind of test there may be standard engineering tests to which the product will have to be subjected to receive Canadian Standards Association (CSA) (www.csa.ca) or Underwriters Laboratory (UL) (www.ul.com) certification. You might also undertake an evaluation of alternative materials from which the product might be made. Further assistance in conducting a technical evaluation may be available from various agencies of your provincial government as well as some colleges and universities, and the Canadian Innovation Centre (www.innovationcentre.ca).

MARKET ASSESSMENT

Assessing the potential market for your concept is a critical part of any feasibility study. At the very least, you need to demonstrate that a market does in fact exist, or there is not much point in developing a full-scale business plan. In some cases the potential market may be large and obvious; in others, considerable research and investigation may be required to demonstrate there is likely to be any significant level of demand. It is essential to determine that there is a sufficiently large market to make the concept financially viable.

WHO IS YOUR CUSTOMER?

To tailor your marketing program to the needs of your market, you must have a very clear idea of who your customers are likely to be. To do this you will need to gather some information in the marketplace. The more information you have about your target market, the better you will be able to develop a successful marketing plan.

TYPES OF MARKETS

The first thing to recognize is that the term "market" does not only refer to a single type of possible customer. A number of different types of markets exist such as:

1. **The consumer market** Individual users of products and services such as you and I.
2. **The institutional market** Organizations such as hospitals, personal care homes, schools, universities, and similar types of institutions.
3. **The industrial market** Other firms and businesses in your community and across the country.
4. **The government market** Various agencies and departments of the municipal, provincial, and federal governments.
5. **The international market** Markets similar to the above examples outside the national boundaries of the country.

WHAT IS *YOUR* MARKET?

Very few businesses initially operate in all of these markets. Most analyze the possibilities available to them in each situation to determine which offers the best potential. This involves asking such broad questions as:

1. How big is the market?
2. Where is it located geographically?
3. How fast is it growing?

FIGURE 6.1 A TYPICAL FEASIBILITY STUDY

Feasibility Study Contents

Feasibility Study Contents	
Concept for your venture	• Explain clearly and concisely the principal concept underlying your venture and what sets it apart from other businesses.
Market assessment	• Describe the profile of your principal target customers. • Indicate current market size, trends, and seasonal patterns. • How do you plan to test your idea? • Describe any market research or customer surveys you plan to conduct. • Assess the nature of your competition. • Estimate your expected sales and market share.
Technical feasibility of your Idea	• Indicate the degree of innovativeness of your venture idea and the risks associated with it. • Does it need to be subjected to some form of technical evaluation or assessment?
Your marketing plan	• Detail the marketing strategy you plan to use. • Describe your marketing plan including your sales strategy, advertising and promotion plans, pricing policy, and channels of distribution.
Managing the supply situation	• How do you plan to assure continuing access to critical supplies of raw materials and component parts at reasonable prices? • Will you produce or subcontract your production?

Conduct cost and profitability assessment	• Determine the funds required to set up your business.
	• Develop short-term financial projections including:
	  • Cash flow forecasts
	  • Pro forma profit and loss statements
	  • Pro forma balance sheet
	  • Break-even analysis

Plan for future action	• What were the strong and weak points of your venture idea? • Did your assessment indicate the business was likely to be profitable? • Is it sufficiently attractive to proceed with the development of a complete business plan?

4. What organizations and/or individuals buy this kind of product or service?
5. Why do they buy it?
6. Where and how do they buy it?
7. How often do they buy it?
8. What are their principal requirements in selecting a product or service of this type?

To determine which of these markets is likely to represent the best opportunity for you, you need to understand just what your product or service has to offer to a group of people or businesses. To do this, you need to understand the primary features of your product or service offering and the benefits it can provide. A feature, for example, is some characteristic of a product or service that is part of its basic make-up, while a benefit is what motivates people to actually buy. If an automobile has air bags or anti-lock brakes, they are features of the car, but the benefit they provide to the consumer is increased safety. By knowing what your product or service has to offer in terms of features and what will make customers buy it, you can begin to determine characteristics that may be common across the members of your potential market. This kind of assessment will serve to identify some broad areas of opportunity for you.

SEGMENT YOUR MARKET

It is natural to want to target as many people and groups as possible with your business offering. However, in most circumstances it is not very practical to do so. For example, you are not likely to have the promotional budget to be able to communicate effectively with many different groups at once. Even if you had a large enough promotional budget, your promotional message would not likely talk directly to any one group, thus having much less impact. So, in addition to doing the broad analysis described above, you also need to question whether within these major market types there are groups of potential customers with different preferences, requirements, purchasing practices, or that are concerned about different benefits. For example, toddlers, teenagers, business people, and older adults all have quite different clothing needs although all are members of the consumer market. Retailers, designers, or manufacturers must take these different needs into account when developing and marketing their product line. Each of these groups should be considered a separate *target market*. This process of breaking large, heterogeneous consumer or industrial markets down into more homogeneous groups is known as market segmentation. Most markets can be segmented on the basis of a number of variables:

1. **Geographic location** such as part of a city or town, county, province, region, or country. If you are selling farm equipment, geographic location is obviously a major factor in segmenting your target markets since you customers will be located in particular rural areas. Or climate is a commonly used geographic segmentation variable that affects industries such as sporting equipment, lawn and garden equipment, snow blowers and snowmobiles, and heating and air conditioning equipment. If this is a factor in your business, you need to identify the geographic area where your market is located and identify the specific boundaries within which you will do business.

2. **Demographic description** such as age, gender, marital status, family size, race, religion, education level, and occupation. Non-consumer markets might be classified on the basis of their total purchases or sales, number of employees, or type of organizational activity. Choose those demographic characteristics of your target market that relate to their interest, need, and ability to purchase your product or service. For example, a market for luxury condominiums would include professional married couples approximately 35–55 years old with incomes of more than $100,000 and either no children or grown children. Similarly, a company like Modrobes might describe its target market as single young men and women between 18 and 25 who are still in school with incomes under $20,000.

3. **Psychographic or sociological factors** such as lifestyle, status, timing and means of purchasing, and reasons for buying products or services similar to yours. The desire for status or enhanced appearance, the pursuit of fun and excitement, or the desire to be socially responsible and environmentally conscious are all examples of these kinds of variables. Many products—like a variety of extreme sports such as skydiving and bungee jumping, organically grown foods, and environmentally friendly insect control methods—would appeal or not appeal to different people largely on the basis of these types of factors.

RESEARCH YOUR MARKET

WHAT IS MARKET RESEARCH?

Market research can be defined as the gathering, processing, reporting, and interpretation of market information. Small businesses typically conduct less market research than larger ones, but it is essential that all businesses engage in this process to some degree to prepare a realistic marketing plan. The market research process involves four basic steps:

- Define the need for information
- Search for secondary data
- Gather primary data
- Interpret the information

We will discuss each of these steps as they relate to obtaining the information you will require to put together your market assessment.

DEFINE THE NEED FOR INFORMATION

Before you take the time to gather any data you need to first decide how you are going to use the information and what you need to demonstrate or show with the information. For example, do you need to:

- Estimate the total expected size of the market for your product or service and the nature and extent of any trends in expected demand?
- Determine the expected level of demand for your product or service?
- Provide a description of whom you feel will be your primary customer?
- Outline how your customers are expected to buy your product or service and with what frequency?
- Understand the nature and extent of the competition you may face in the marketplace?

SEARCH FOR SECONDARY DATA

The easiest place to start to try to answer these questions is by searching through available sources of secondary data. Secondary data is information that others have put together relating to your industry and/or your customers. Secondary data is usually considerably less expensive than gathering new information so you should exhaust all readily available sources of secondary information before moving on to gather new data of your own.

Secondary data can come from a tremendous variety of sources. Often they may not exist in the exact form you require but by combining data from a number of secondary sources you may be able to compile the information you require, and at much lower cost than going out and gathering your own information.

SOURCES OF SECONDARY MARKET INFORMATION

There are a number of sources you might consult to get a handle on the approximate size of the market you are considering entering. Some of these sources are Statistics Canada publications; various industry reports, trade journals, and investment journals; and financial statements of your leading competitors. You must be careful to make some provision for error in your estimate of market size. Most of the information sources you will consult will not be able to provide complete up-to-date figures, and forecasts of future sales are always subject to error. Statistics Canada, for example, breaks the country up into 36 Census Metropolitan Areas (CMAs). (www.statcan.ca/english/census96/list.htm) For each CMA there are a series of referenced maps providing an index for which it is possible to get a tract number for almost any neighbourhood in the country. From this tract number you can get a detailed breakdown of the number of people and their characteristics within a single local neighbourhood or for a combination of tracts comprising a region of a city or for the entire metropolitan area. This data can be a valuable resource providing a wide variety of information on a large number of geographic markets. The major drawback, however, is that it is largely derived from census data and may be a little stale. This should not be surprising, given the constantly changing tastes of consumers and ongoing technological advancement.

Following are listings of some of the more popular sources of market information. Much of this material is available at your local public, college, or university library. In most situations the best place to start is with *the trade publications and trade associations for the industry in which your business will compete.*

TRADE PUBLICATIONS Just to give you an idea of the number and diversity of the trade publications produced in Canada, take a minute to review Table 6.1. It is by no means a listing of all trade-oriented publications, merely a sampling of the range of material available to you. Depending on the nature of your new venture, any one or more of innumerable publications could represent a source of market-related information or a means for you to communicate with potential customers.

GENERAL PUBLICATIONS In addition to trade publications there are numerous general publications that can be extremely useful in compiling relevant market data. Some of the more important of these are listed in Table 6.2 at the back of this Stage. In addition to all these publications, sources that you should look to for information include:

1. Your local chamber of commerce
2. Your city or municipal hall
3. Local or regional development corporations
4. District school board offices
5. Provincial government offices
6. Downtown business associations
7. Shopping centre developers
8. Advertising agencies
9. Newspapers, radio, and television stations
10. Competitors
11. Sales representatives and trade suppliers
12. Similar businesses in another location
13. Other business associates

CANADA BUSINESS SERVICE CENTRES

One prospective source of market information that should not be overlooked is your provincial Canada Business Service Centre (CBSC). The CBSCs are a collaborative effort between federal, provincial, and private sector organizations designed to provide business people with access to a wide range of information on government services, programs, and regulations. Each CBSC offers a broad range of products and services tailored to meet the needs of its particular clients. These include:

- a toll-free telephone information and referral service
- the Business Information System (BIS) database containing information on the services and programs of the participating departments and organizations
- info-FAX service: condensed versions of the BIS products accessed through an automated FaxBack system
- info-Guides: a set of documents that provide brief descriptions of services and programs related to a particular topic (e.g., exporting, tourism)
- a collection of other business services which could include interactive diagnostic software, videos, business directories, how-to manuals, CD-ROM library search capability, and external database access

CBSCs are located in one major urban centre in each province. A complete listing of the location of each Centre and the numbers for telephone referral and FaxBack service at each site can be found in the listing of Useful Contacts at the back of this book (www.cbsc.org).

THE INTERNET

Another place where you may be able to find a good deal of information about any idea you plan to pursue is the Internet. Not everything is available on the Internet yet, but with a little practice even new users can skim the Net's millions of Web pages and thousands of newsgroups for topics of general interest or to help find precise pieces of specific data.

TABLE 6.1 SOME TRADE PUBLICATIONS PRODUCED IN CANADA

Aerospace & Defence Technology
Applied Arts
Architecture Concept
Atlantic Fisherman
Aviation Trade
Bakers Journal
Bath & Kitchen Marketer
Benefits Canada
Boating Business
Bodyshop
Building Renovation
Business to Business Marketing
CAD/CAM & Robotics
Canadian Apparel Manufacturer
Canadian Beverage Review
Canadian Building Owner & Property Manager
Canadian Doctor
Canadian Food & Drug
Canadian Forest Industries
Canadian Funeral News
Canadian Grocer
Canadian Hairdresser
Canadian Heavy Equipment Guide
Canadian Hotel & Restaurant
Canadian Industry Shows & Exhibitions
Canadian Jeweler
Canadian Machinery & Metalworking
Canadian Mining Journal
Canadian Music Trade
Canadian Oil & Gas Handbook
Canadian Pharmaceutical Journal
Canadian Pool & Spa Marketing
Canadian Premiums & Incentives
Canadian Security
Canadian Vending
Computer Dealer News
Construction Canada
Cosmetics
Dental Practice Management
Design Engineering
Eastern Trucker
Electrical Equipment News
Farm Equipment Quarterly
Fleur Design
Floor Covering News
Food in Canada
Food & Drug Packaging News
Footwear Forum
Fur Trade Journal
Gardenland
Gifts and Tablewares
Greenhouse Canada
Group Travel
Hardware Merchandising
Health Care
Industrial Distributor News
Industrial Product Ideas
Jobber News
Lighting Magazine
Luggage, Leathergoods & Accessories
L'Automobile
Machinery & Equipment MRO
Masthead
Medicine North America
Modern Purchasing
Motel/Hotel Lodging
Office Equipment & Methods
Plant Engineering & Maintenance
Plastics Business
Quill and Quire
Sanitation Canada
Service Station & Garage Management
Shopping Centre Canada
Software Report
Sports Business
The Bottom Line
The Business and Professional Woman
The Western Investor
Trade Asia Magazine
Transportation Business
Visual Communications
Water & Pollution Control
Woodworking

What has simplified the job of culling information from the millions of Web pages is the development of a variety of search tools that enable the user to rapidly search through directories or the nooks and crannies of the Web itself to create indexes of information related to a particular topic.

It used to be that search tools could be categorized as either *directories or search engines*. Directories such as Yahoo (www.yahoo.com) enable you to search for Internet sites by category. For example, if you are looking for Web sites on a particular topic such as "home-based business," a particular company or business such as "Spin Master Toys," or if you are looking for a general subject guide to resources available over the Internet, you should probably use a directory. Yahoo! Canada (www.yahoo.ca), for example, contains millions of Web sites organized into a number of categories such as travel, food, and sports, as well as hundreds of subcategories.

Search engines are sites that contain the contents of millions of pages of information from throughout the Web, and are used to find pages containing specific words or phrases. Altavista (www.altavista.com) is one of the most popular. These search engines send out software agents or "spiders" that explore the entire Internet instead of just the Web pages that have been indexed for the directory. The problem with this approach, however, is that search engines are not very discriminating. Sorting through the thousands of matches that may result from any search can be a real chore.

The differences between search engines and directories, however, are becoming very clouded. Each type of search site is taking on more of the characteristics of the other so that directories now include search engines and search engines now include directories. You need to understand the basic characteristics of each type of tool since you will be using both when making any search for information on the Internet, often within the same site.

The major search engines and directories are listed in the FYI box. In addition to these basic tools there are a number of other search tools you should consider as well. These include:

- **All-in-one or "parallel" search engines** such as MetaCrawler (www.metacrawler.com), Dogpile (www.dogpile.com) or Ask Jeeves (www.askjeeves.com). These search engines simultaneously submit your search request to several other search engines and combine the results into one report.
- **Specialized search engines** such as About.com (www.about.com) and Search.com (www.search.com), which will provide you with access to hundreds of other specialized search engines, and Strategis (strategis.gc.ca), the Industry Canada Web site that provides access to almost everything you need to know about starting and running a business in Canada.
- **Search accelerators** such as Copernic 2001 (www.copernic.com), WebFerret (www.ferretsoft.com), and the LexiBot (www.lexibot.com). These programs simultaneously query several search engines for the words or phrases you are searching for and summarize the results in a simple, easy-to-read format. Most of these accelerators are sold as separate programs to be installed on your computer.
- **Subject guides** can be an excellent source of information about a particular topic since someone who has a lot of knowledge about a subject has usually prepared the index. There are literally thousands of subject guides that contain links to a number of other Web sites. Many of them can be found by searching in directories like Yahoo!. Some of the best ones for information relevant to small business include the Web site of the Canadian Youth Business Foundation (CYBF) (www.cybf.ca), the Web site of *PROFIT* magazine (www.profitguide.com), and EntreWorld's Web Site (www.entreworld.com). These guides can be excellent starting points to begin your search for more specific information.
- **Commercial research databases** such as Electric Library Canada (www.elibrary.ca), Encarta Online Library (www.encarta.com), and Northern Light (www.northernlight.com). These databases contain information from newspapers, magazines, journals, and other hard-to-find information sources and make it available for a fee. This can be either a flat fee per month, a per document charge, or a combination of a monthly/annual fee and a per document charge.[1]

Most search engines provide basic instructions as to how to initiate a search as part of their home page. For a beginner, it all starts with you entering a "query." A "query" consists of one or more keywords — a company name, a city or country, or any other topic likely to appear either in the title or the body of a Web page. Most search programs employ Boolean logic, expanding or limiting a search by including "and," "but," and "or" as part of the search process. The more precise your query, the better. For example: if you are interested in a topic like antique automobiles, typing in "antique and automobiles" instead of just "automobiles" will direct you to information regarding older cars, although you may also get sites for antique dealers in general and other related subjects.

With most search engines the process starts with the click of your mouse once you have entered your query. Within seconds, a list of matches is produced, usually in batches of 10, with a brief description and the home page address. A further click on one of the matches gets you to that page or Usenet group.

There are a number of fundamental problems you need to be aware of in gathering research information off the Net. First, the quality of some of the information may be of questionable value or use. There is a lot of useless information on-line since literally anyone can create a Web site. Second, the information you come across may be misleading. Since anyone can set up a Web site and publish information, fraud and misrepresentation have become real problems. Third, the information may be out of date. There is no assurance that information on the Web is the most recent or reflects current research or theory.

To use the Web for research purposes it is essential that you take the time to learn how to do it effectively. Most of us simply do not take the time to learn this skill. We simply connect to the Internet, call up our favourite search engine, plug in a couple of key words, and do a search. Then we begin browsing through the results and start to surf many of the sites that come up. We then give up some time later very frustrated and without having found much relevant information.

Professional researchers, on the other hand, think carefully about the information they are looking for. They plan a specific search strategy and decide which search terms might be the most effective in finding the information they are searching for. It is only then that they log onto the Internet to conduct a preliminary

1. For a more detailed discussion of the use of these search tools see Jim Carroll and Rick Broadhead, *Canadian Internet Directory and Research Guide 2001* (Toronto: Stoddart Publishing Co. Ltd., 2000).

search. Based on what they find they will try some other terms and use other search engines, continually refining their search as they go. Eventually they are likely to find just what they are looking for.

As you can see, the first approach is entirely hit-and-miss while the other involves some careful thought and planning and is likely to be much more effective.

FYI FOR YOUR INFORMATION

Here is a list of the major search engines on the World Wide Web that can be useful for research purposes:

About	www.about.com
AltaVista	www.altavista.com
Excite	www.excite.com
Google	www.google.com
HotBot	www.hotbot.com
Infoseek	www.infoseek.com
Looksmart	www.looksmart.com
Lycos	www.lycos.com
Northern Light	www.northernlight.com
Overture	www.overture.com
WebCrawler	www.webcrawler.com
Yahoo!	www.yahoo.com

GATHERING PRIMARY DATA

Doing your own research—called primary research—may be the best way to get the most current and useful information regarding your potential market. A number of techniques can be used to obtain primary data. These can be classified into two basic research approaches:

OBSERVATIONAL METHODS This is the gathering of primary data by observing people and their actions in particular situations. It may entail such approaches as observing the behaviour of shoppers in a store as they go about purchasing a range of different products, or counting traffic flows through a mall or past a particular location, or observing patterns in traffic flows around a store or other facility.

QUESTIONING METHODS These include both the use of surveys and experimentation that involve contact with respondents. Survey research involves the systematic collection of data from a sample of respondents to better understand or explain some aspect of their behaviour. This data collection can occur by personal contact, through the mail, by telephone, or even over the Internet. In addition, the information may be gathered from people individually as in an individual interview or in a group such as a focus group.

Survey research is the most widely used method of primary data collection. Its principal advantages are its relatively low cost and flexibility. It can be used to obtain many different kinds of information in a wide variety of situations.

However, there are also some problems associated with survey research. Constructing a good survey is not necessarily an easy thing to do. Sometimes people are unable or unwilling to answer survey questions so the response rate is not always as high as you might like to see. In addition there are a number of technical issues relating to survey research such as appropriate sample size, reliability, validity, statistical significance, etc. that need to be considered as well. These issues go beyond the scope of this book but definitely need to be considered when gathering any primary data. However, there are some general guidelines you can follow to help you design effective questionnaires:

- Pre-test the survey on a small group of people to ensure that respondents clearly understand your questions
- Make certain you are actually asking the right questions to get the information you need
- Decide how you intend to use the information you will obtain when designing the questionnaire
- Keep your survey concise and readily understandable

- Ask direct questions that relate specifically to the topic in which you are interested
- If you are providing respondents with a finite range of possible answers (as with a Likert-type scale), try to provide a maximum of five possible responses
- Make sure your questions can be answered easily by your respondents
- Don't offend anyone
- Don't mislead respondents about the purpose of your survey
- Don't answer the questions for them by prompting them for answers
- Give respondents sufficient time to provide an appropriate response
- Don't bias their responses by personally reacting to any answers, either positively or negatively
- Ask all personal information at the end of the survey so the respondent is not discouraged from replying
- Always be courteous; remember they are doing you a favour.

An example of a relatively simple survey developed by a woman who wanted to open a fitness centre and offer one-on-one training is illustrated in the Key Points box.

MARKET-TESTING YOUR IDEA

In addition to obtaining information from prospective customers, there are also a number of primary research methods you can use to gauge likely market reaction to your particular concept or idea. These techniques are more subjective and cannot be analyzed statistically. However, most of them provide instant feedback. Usually one opinion leads to another so that overall you will receive some interesting and useful information. These techniques include prototype development, obtaining opinions form prospective distributors, comparing your idea directly with competitors' offerings, conducting in-store tests, and demonstrating at trade shows.

One or more of these techniques can be employed to assess how the market is likely to react to your concept or idea. The young owners of Spin Master Toys, for example, used a variety of methods to refine and test the idea of the Air Hog, their World War II-era toy jet fighter that flies on compressed air. The English inventors who developed the concept had put together a crude prototype to demonstrate the idea. It was described as "a Canada Dry ginger ale bottle with foam wings" and didn't fly. Subsequent prototypes "flew some of the time — kind of" until after myriad versions, a year and a half, and half a million dollars later they finally had what appeared to be a market-ready product (See Entrepreneurs in Action #21).

At the same time as this product development was taking place, one of the owners took an early prototype of the product to a buyer for Canadian Tire stores. The response was very positive and while the company was not prepared to meet the timeliness for delivery required by the buyer and turned down the sale, the experience did confirm that retailers would be behind their product if they could produce an acceptable, working version.

The company also conducted some focus groups with actual kids to see what they thought of the Air Hog and to assess their ability to use it properly. The initial results were disastrous. The kids couldn't figure out the plane's air-pump system, they turned the propeller the wrong way, and had a variety of other problems. To overcome these difficulties, the company came up with a couple of solutions. One was to set up a 1-800 number to serve as a help line for kids experiencing problems. The other was to include an instructional video with every Air Hog explaining the proper way to use the toy.

All this testing seems to have paid off. The Air Hog was ranked as one of the hottest toys of the 1998 Christmas season by *Time* magazine and touted as one of the year's top achievements in science and technology by *Popular Science*. Three hundred and fifty thousand Air Hogs literally flew off the shelves of major U.S. retailers over that season.[2]

But how do you follow up on the tremendous success Spin Master was able to achieve with the Air Hog? So far their product line has expanded to include the Hydro Vector Rocket, V-Wing Avenger and Renegade planes, Flick Trix replica sports bikes and now the Road Ripper. The Road Ripper is a line of air-pressured cars that race at 200 mph (scale speed). The cars represent the next step in their strategy to create a worldwide brand for air-pressured toys. There idea is to pressurize everything that moves. At the same time the company has continued to rely on the same kind of grass-roots marketing that jump-started the Air Hogs:

2. Shawna Steinberg and Joe Chidley, "Fun for the Money," *Canadian Business* (December 11, 1998): 44–52.

Key points

FITNESS CENTRE QUESTIONNAIRE

1. Do you exercise regularly? YES ___ NO ___
   If NO, please go to Part A.
   If YES, please go to Part B.

PART A. PLEASE CHECK YOUR REASONS FOR NOT EXERCISING:

___ Lack of time ___ Lack of motivation ___ Cost
___ No convenient fitness centres ___ Medical reasons
___ Other. Please specify ________________

PART B. CHECK THE TYPE OF EXERCISE YOU DO:

___ Aerobic ___ Nautilus ___ Free weights
___ Running ___ Swimming
___ Other. Please specify ________________

2. Are you: ___ Male ___ Female
3. What is your age group?
   ___ Under 25 ___ 26–35 ___ 36–50 ___ Over 50
4. Where do you normally exercise?
   ___ At home ___ Fitness centre
   ___ Other. Please specify ________________
5. How far do you live from (town for proposed centre)?
   ___ in town ___ 5–10 kms ___ over 10 kms
6. Do you think your town needs a new fitness centre? YES ___ NO ___
7. Would you be interested in one-on-one training? YES ___ NO ___
8. Do you have any comments or suggestions about the need for a fitness centre in your community?

Source: Adapted from "How to Prepare a Market Analysis," Edward Lowe Foundation, *Entrepreneurial Edge,* http://edge.lowe.org

product demonstrations, unique public relations campaigns, and cultivating relationships with journalists, retailers, and toy-industry insiders.[3]

The company is now looking at the introduction of another radical new innovation with the e-Charger Intruder, the world's first radio-controlled plane with an on-board flight system that lets kids pilot the aircraft with no fear of crashing, priced at less than $100. It is just this type of innovation and effective marketing that makes Spin Master one of Canada's fastest growing companies and enables it to compete with the giants in the toy industry.[4]

DEVELOPING A PROTOTYPE A *prototype* is a "working model" of your product. If you are considering selling a product that, when mass-produced, could cost you $5 per unit to manufacture, prototypes may cost you over $200 each. However, this could be an inexpensive investment, because with just one prototype you can get photographs, make up a brochure or circular, show the idea to prospective buyers, and put out publicity releases. You don't need a thousand or ten thousand units at this stage.

3. Kara Kuryllowicz, "Air Hogs, the Sequel?" *PROFIT: The Magazine for Canadian Entrepreneurs* (September 1999): 10.
4. Kali Pearson, "Why Didn't I Think of That?" *PROFIT: The Magazine for Canadian Entrepreneurs* (May 2001): 28–34.

Even though you are only interested in producing, at most, a few units at this point, it is still important to get manufacturing prices from a number of (around five) different suppliers. You should find out how much it will cost to produce various quantities of the product (1,000 units, 5,000 units, 10,000 units) and what the terms, conditions, and costs of the production process would be. Once you have this information you will be able to approach buyers and intelligently and confidently discuss all aspects of the product.

OBTAINING OPINIONS FROM PROSPECTIVE DISTRIBUTORS A second way to test your product idea is to ask a professional buyer's personal opinion. For example, most major department stores and other retail chains are organized into departments, each department having its own buyer. After arranging to see the buyer representing the product area in which you are interested, arm yourself with the cost information you received from potential suppliers. Remember, a buyer is a very astute person. He or she has seen thousands of items before yours, and in most cases will be able to tell you if products resembling yours have ever been on the market, how well they sold, what their flaws were, etc. You can get a tremendous amount of free information from a buyer, so it is advisable to solicit his or her independent opinion before you become too involved with your product.

COMPARING WITH COMPETITORS' PRODUCTS Most of us have only limited exposure to the vast array of products available in the marketplace and thus could end up spending a lot of money producing a "new" product which is already being marketed by someone else. Test your product idea by comparing it with other products already on the market, before you invest your money.

ONE-STORE TEST Another way to test your product is to run a one-store test. This can be done by arranging with a store owner or manager to put a dozen units of your product on display. The purpose of this test is to learn what the public thinks about your product. You can often get the store owner's cooperation, because the store doesn't have to put any money up front to purchase your product. However, there can be problems associated with such tests. If you are very friendly with the owner, he or she may affect the results of the test in your product's favour by putting it in a preferred location or by personally promoting it to store customers. You should request that your product be treated like any other, because you are looking for unbiased information.

Also, you should keep in mind that one store does not constitute a market; the one store in which you test may not be representative of the marketplace in general. Nevertheless, the one-store test is a good way to gather information on your product.

TRADE SHOWS Another excellent way to test your product idea is at a trade show. It makes no difference what your field is — there is a trade show involving it. At a trade show you will have your product on display and you can get immediate feedback from sophisticated and knowledgeable buyers — people who know what will sell and what will not. There are approximately 15,000 trade shows in Canada and the U.S. every year, covering every imaginable product area. There is bound to be one that could serve as a reasonable test site for you.

CONDUCTING A CUSTOMER SURVEY

A critical factor in successfully launching a new venture is understanding who your customers are and what needs your product or service might satisfy. It is important to consider that not all potential customers are alike or have similar needs for a given product. For example, some people buy a toothpaste primarily to prevent cavities, while others want a toothpaste that promotes whiter teeth, fresher breath, or "sex appeal," or has been designed specifically for smokers or denture wearers. You have to determine which of these segments (i.e., cavity prevention, whiter teeth, etc.) your product or service can best satisfy.

As previously mentioned, most major markets can be broken down into more homogeneous groups or *segments* on the basis of a number of different types of variables. In developing a plan for your proposed business venture you must consider who your potential customers are and how they might be classified, as in the toothpaste example, into somewhat more homogeneous market segments. You should be clear in your own mind just which of these segments your venture is attempting to serve. A product or service that is sharply focused to satisfy the needs and wants of a specifically defined customer group is typically far more successful than one that tries to compromise and cut across the widely divergent requirements of many customer types. Small businesses are often in a position to search for "holes" in the market representing the requirements of particular customer types that larger companies are unwilling or unable to satisfy. Figure 6.2 at the back of this Stage provides a framework you can complete to develop a market profile of your prospective customer.

21 Entrepreneurs in action

Cashing in on Kids

Like a pilot in a death spiral, Ben Varadi was having one of those gut-checking moments. As head of product development for Spin Master Toys, he had flown last January to Scottsdale, Ariz., to film a commercial for a new product that had a lot riding on it. Even though Spin Master had yet to put it in production, the Air Hog promised to be a coup not only for the budding Toronto-based company, but for the industry as a whole: a toy airplane that would run on compressed air rather than gas or rubber bands, and would fly for hundreds of yards rather than piddling out after just a few. In theory, at least, this is what should have happened: the weather should have been cloudless and dry (Varadi chose Arizona as a location because it hardly gets any rain), and the prototype should have flown through the air with the greatest of ease.

So Varadi and the crew are out on a Holiday Inn golf course in Scottsdale — and the sky is cloudy. Too bad, but not awful — who's going to worry about clouds, even a little rain, once this baby is airborne? They get set to fire up the Air Hog, a purple-and-yellow flying machine that otherwise resembles a World War II-era fighter plane. The sophisticated air-compressor engine is primed, the cameras are rolling, the tousle-haired kid hired to star in the ad lets the Air Hog go and — well, a mere four seconds later, the toy's sputtering film début comes to an end on the hard track of the fairway. Crash and burn, baby.

It's a rule in toy advertising that you can't make a product appear to do things in a commercial that it can't do in reality. Trouble was, as with most new toys in the preproduction stage, the Air Hog's abilities were still unknown. Varadi, who's 28, and his Spin Master cohorts, president Anton Rabie and CEO Ronnen Harary, both 27, knew what it was *supposed* to do; they just weren't quite sure that it could actually do it. "Until you're in production, all you've got are theories," Varadi says. "You can spend all this money and at the end of the day, it still doesn't work."

So your company is spending $100,000 filming this commercial — and the Air Hog is performing like a pig. What do you do? You get creative. You shoot the commercial, cutting shots of the plane's brief flights so that it looks like it's flying 100 yards a pop, like it's twisting and turning through the air just the way you want it to. There's nothing dishonest about that — as long as the product, once it's on the market and the object of every 10-year-old boy's desire, lives up to its billing. "So we had a challenge," Varadi says. "We had to make the thing fly like it did in the commercial."

The inverted logic must have worked, because the Air Hog is soaring these days. In an industry dominated by giants such as Hasbro, Mattel and Irwin, five-year-old Spin Master Toys seems to have come up with a bona fide hit. As the Christmas buying season — which accounts for between 60% and 70% of toy sales in North America — gears up, the Air Hog seems poised to be one of the most talked about toys of the year. In October, Time magazine put it next to Tiger Electronics' Furby (an interactive fuzzy doll that is this year's equivalent of Tickle Me Elmo), Hasbro's Tele-tubbies (with a hit kids' show behind them) and Lego's MindStorms (a computerized

THOMAS FRICKE PHOTOGRAPHY

robot kit) as the season's hottest new toys. *Popular Science* magazine stuck the plane on its December "Best of What's New" cover, trumpeting the toy as one of the year's top 100 achievements in science and technology. The Air Hog even made it onto US network television, when the *Today* show featured it in a pre-Christmas "Gadget Guru" segment.

Maybe not surprisingly, the Air Hog has been flying off the shelves of US specialty stores such as FAO Schwarz and Noodle Kidoodle. Since June, Spin Master has sold 350,000 Air Hogs to retailers, who sell it for US$29.99 to US$39.99 ($49.99 in

Canada); by next August, Rabie, Harary and Varadi expect to sell a million more, sending Spin Master's 1998–'99 revenue soaring to $30 million — triple what it was in 1997–'98. Not bad for a product that the major toy companies thought would never fly. And the TV commercial hasn't even aired yet.

They might have been college buddies, but you couldn't ask for three men who seem less like one another to run a company. Varadi, the toy-master, is fittingly a bit of a prankster, his lean face wearing a mischievous perma-grin. Harary? As operations head, he's sort of dour, all business. And Rabie, the ringleader, is the face of Spin Master — all buff and youthful, with a look that could have been ripped from the pages of GQ. Their dynamic is a strangely seamless one —they even finish each other's sentences. But that's not to say they think alike. And as business partners, it's like different pieces of a puzzle coming together to complete the picture.

The history of Spin Master Toys is part Wright brothers, part Roots — a tale of what happens when innovation meets savvy marketing. Childhood pals who met at summer camp a few years after their families moved to Toronto from South Africa, Rabie and Harary both attended the University of Western Ontario in London, where the future company president studied business and Harary took political science. While at school, where they also met biz-student Varadi, the pair established a business under the name Seiger Marketing. Their idea: a campus poster adorned with frosh-week photos and advertising from local businesses. After graduating, Rabie and Harary, then 23, had $10,000 in their pockets from poster sales; all they needed was a product. And when Harary's grandmother brought back a novelty gift from Israel in 1994 — a sawdust-filled stocking with a face that sprouted grass for hair — they knew they had found it. The Earth Buddy was born.

With the Earth Buddy's vaguely environmental cachet, Rabie figured it would be a perfect fit for the urban-adventurer image espoused by Roots Canada Ltd., a company founded by Michael Budman and Don Green (who, coincidentally, also met at summer camp). Budman bit, allowing Rabie and Harary to test-market the nouveaux Chia Pets in Roots stores. The little guys were, in short, a hit. In the US, K-Mart ordered 500,000 Buddies. Operations moved from Harary's kitchen to a factory staffed by 200 employees working around the clock. In six months, the Earth Buddy generated $1.8 million in sales. That's a lot of sawdust and socks.

One hit wonder? No way. In 1994 the company launched a three-rod juggling game called Spin Master Devil Sticks — a higher-tech version of a product Harary sold from the back of his VW Microbus at Grateful Dead concerts when he was 17. In the spring of 1995, the Devil Sticks became the No. 1 non-promoted toy in Canada, selling more than 250,000 units in six months. It broke the company into the US, positioning it for continent-wide distribution, and it gave Rabie and Harary's business a new name — Spin Master — which has proven to be appropriate in more ways than one.

The Air Hog flew onto the scene in February 1996, at the Toy Fair, an annual get-together in New York that attracts hundreds of toymakers, retailers and inventors. There, Varadi was approached by inventors from the English firm Dixon-Manning Ltd., who pitched an idea they had for a plane that ran on air power. Varadi and Harary arranged to meet with Dixon-Manning at 5 p.m. that day to discuss details, but when they arrived, they found the inventors had optioned the concept for 30 days to a major US toy company. "So I made a note to call them in 30 days and see if they passed — and sure enough, they did," recalls Harary. "And when [Dixon-Manning] sent the item to us, I saw why."

Basically, the prototype the inventors sent to Toronto was, Harary says, "a Canada Dry ginger ale bottle with foam wings — it still had the label on it." But the partners at Spin Master saw opportunity. "The one thing that did appeal to me wasn't so much the item itself as the state of the category," Varadi says. Here's the reason: the toy-airplane market didn't have a middle. On the top end were gasoline-powered planes that sold for $80 and up; on the low end were $3 rubber-band-and-balsa-wood "aircraft." Varadi figured that, in that niche market, "there's got to be something in the middle." And the air-pressure technology was something new, holding out the promise of a whole line of toys that ran off its simple-sounding, but hard-to-produce, pneumatic engine. "If we could pull this off, we'd be like pioneers in this category," Varadi says. "We also realized that this would elevate the level of the company in terms of how people saw us."

The trio started talking to buyers within two months of taking on the project in July 1996. Harary took a prototype to a Canadian Tire buyer in October, who said she would place "a big order"— *if* he could ship it for spring. "I had this nagging feeling, what if we make this commitment and can't keep it — will it risk the reputation of the company?" he says. "I looked them in the face and said, 'I don't think we can make it.' No one wants to turn down a challenge, but it was probably one of the best things we've done." Egos still intact, the boys now had confidence that retailers were behind their product. But talking to the buyers led to another revelation: Hasbro, Mattel and, as Varadi says, "everybody and his uncle" had turned down the Air Hog. "You're thinking, if a company like Hasbro turned it down, what were they thinking that we were missing?"

That was gut check No. 1. And for a time, it must have seemed that the no-takers were right. The first prototype Spin Master received from Dixon-Manning didn't fly; the second "flew some of the time — kind of," Harary says.

The three had planned on the development phase taking six months. It ended up taking a year and a half — and costing half a million dollars, money they say came exclusively from company coffers. Rabie remembers getting frantic eureka-style calls from Harary and Varadi, who would be out in a park somewhere testing one of myriad versions of the Air Hog. "There's been another breakthrough!" Varadi would proclaim. Rabie would run out to the park with a camcorder to make a tape to show buyers and — it wouldn't fly, again. "It was Murphy's Law," Rabie says. Meanwhile, focus-group results with actual kids were disastrous: they couldn't figure out the plane's air-pump system, they turned the propeller the wrong way — you name it. Rabie and his team came up with two solutions. One was to set up a 1-800 help line for fledgling pilots; the other was to produce an instructional video (now included with every Air Hog). By showing the video, Varadi says, "we went from a terrible focus group, where one out of five could do it, to a focus group where every kid could do it."

At the end of 1997, Harary was taking his third trip to Asia, learning everything he could about toy manufacturing and negotiating a production deal with a factory in Hong Kong. The next step was to make the moulds for all the parts and set up the machinery to manufacture the planes — a tooling-up that would cost $100,000. Time for another gut check. "It's easy to make one thing work," Harary says, "but to make half a million things work is a totally different ball game." Having already missed one anticipated spring launch, and with another just months away, Rabie, Harary and Varadi decided it was time to fly or get off the plane. But would it work? "When we made the decision to go ahead with it, we didn't know," Rabie says, "We just said, "OK, we're going to tool and debug."

The plan was to launch Air Hogs in May 1998 — since it's an outdoor toy, the Spin Masters figured it would be ideal for a spring début. So they made the ad in Arizona, fixed the design bugs and simultaneously tested two distribution paths in Minneapolis: specialty chains such as Noodle Kidoodle, which concentrate on high-end educational toys, and Target department stores in the area. With air support from the commercial, the plane beat expectations under both retailing models, selling more than 25 units per store per week (eight to 12 units in that price category is considered good). In the end, Spin Master decided to stick with a conservative distribution plan, leaving the Air Hog in specialty stores and as a Sears catalogue item for a year, then releasing it in the mass market with a national ad campaign in the spring of 1999 through major retailers, who usually book their product line a year in advance anyway. "We could go to mass retailers after Minneapolis and say, 'It works!'" Rabie says. "Now we're coming into 1999 with every major retailer's support when we do our TV campaign." (www.spinmaster.com)

Source: Adapted from, Shawna Steinberg and Joe Chidley, "Fun for the Money," *Canadian Business* (December 11, 1998):44-520. Reprinted with permission.

To be successful, you should seek a *competitive advantage* over other firms — look for something especially desirable from the customer's perspective, something that sets you apart and gives you an edge. This may be the quality of your product, the speed of your service, the diversity of your product line, the effectiveness of your promotion, your personality, your location, the distinctiveness of your offering, or perhaps even your price.

To accomplish all this may require some basic market research. This might be thought of as one of the first steps in testing your product or service idea with potential customers.

Since you will want to provide as good a description of your offering as possible (preferably via a prototype), personal, face-to-face interviews are the best method for gathering the information. Figure 6.3 provides an outline for a survey you might conduct. It would be wise to interview at least 30 to 40 potential customers to help ensure that the responses you receive are probably representative of the marketplace in general. This approach can be used effectively for either consumer or industrial products/services.

This customer survey will provide you with important information that will allow you to further develop and fine-tune your marketing strategy. For example, if you discover that the most customers will pay for your product is $10, and you had planned on charging $12, you will have to reconsider your pricing strategy. Similarly, if customers prefer to purchase products like yours by mail, you will have to keep that in mind as you set up a distribution system. The responses to each of the questions posed in the survey should be analyzed and their impact on areas of marketing strategy noted. These will be brought together later in your preliminary marketing plan.

DO-IT-YOURSELF MARKET RESEARCH

Here are some things you should keep in mind when doing your own market research.

1. In conducting a survey, your information will be only as good as your sample. To be useful, your sample group needs to be relevant to and representative of your target population.
2. Design your survey or questionnaire carefully. Make sure it's focused specifically on the information you need to know.
3. Keep your survey or questionnaire as short as possible, preferably a single page.
4. Always provide some opportunity for the respondent to provide detailed answers.
5. Work out how you intend to record the information and analyze the data as you are developing the questionnaire.
6. Before you administer the survey, establish the criteria that you will use to make decisions based on the information obtained from the survey.
7. Remember, market research is needed at all stages of a business's life to keep you in touch with your customers and their needs and desires.

Source: © By J. Susan Ward 2001. (http://sbinfocanada.about.com) licenses to About.com, www.about.com/ All rights reserved.

INTERPRET THE INFORMATION

Once this secondary and primary data has been gathered it must be analyzed and translated into useable information. The research needs to aid you in making management decisions related to such issues as:

Who should be your customer?
What product or service should you be selling?
What is the total size of your potential market and how can it be broken down?
Who are your competitors and what are their strengths and weaknesses?
What is your estimated sales forecast?
Where should you locate your business?
How should you promote, price, and distribute your product?
And so on.

Some conclusions based on the analysis of this data may be obvious. Others may be more difficult to decipher or you may feel the data you need to answer the question are just not available. Nonetheless market research can provide you with some of the information you need to be more proactive and help you decide what you should be doing in the future rather than just relying on what has happened in the past.

ESTIMATING TOTAL MARKET SIZE AND TRENDS

A large part of market assessment is determining the volume of *unit sales* or *dollar revenue* that might flow from a market and what proportion of this you might expect to capture. At first glance "unit sales" seems to mean simply how many potential customers there are in the market for your product/service. However, this would overlook the possibility that some customers may buy more than one unit of the product/service. Estimates of total market size must take these *repeat purchases* into account. Total demand is determined by multiplying the number of customers who will buy by the average number of units each might be expected to purchase. To determine the total market size in dollars, simply multiply this total number of units by the average selling price.

Figure 6.4 at the back of this Stage provides a form you can complete to estimate the approximate total market size (past, present, and future) and the expected trends for your product/service type.

THE NATURE OF YOUR COMPETITION

Unless your product or service is a "new to the world" innovation, which is unlikely, it will have to compete with other products or services that perform a similar function. In the customer survey, your respondents probably identified the names of a number of firms that offer products or services designed to meet the same customer needs as yours. Now you must ask specific and detailed questions concerning your likely competition. The answers will help you get a better understanding of the sales and market share you could achieve, and changes or improvements you should make in your marketing program (pricing, promotion, distribution, etc.).

"Business is lousy. Maybe I should have done more market research first."

You should also be on the lookout for areas where you can gain a sustainable competitive advantage. In other words: Can you provide the best-quality, the lowest-cost, the most innovative, or the better-serviced product?

Figure 6.5 at the back of this Stage provides a form to help you organize your evaluation. Fill out a copy of this form for each major competitor you have identified. Unfortunately, competitors will probably not cooperate in providing you with this information directly. Sources that can be useful in getting the information, however, include published industry reports, trade association reports and publications, corporate annual reports, and your own personal investigation.

DEVELOPING A SALES FORECAST

Sales forecasting is the process of organizing and analyzing all the information you have gathered in a way that makes it possible to estimate what your expected sales are likely to be. Your sales forecast is likely to be one of the most difficult and yet the single most important business prediction you are ever likely to make. If you get it wrong, the error can lead to plenty of unsold inventory and problems generating sufficient cash to keep the business going or to a number of disappointed customers.

But how do you get it right? One way is to consider the following formula:

Sales Forecast = Total Estimated Market Size x Estimated Growth Rate x Market Share Target

ESTIMATING MARKET SIZE

Fairly accurate market data are available from trade associations and other secondary sources for certain industries. However, companies in many other industries have to operate without any concrete information concerning the total size of the market for their products or services. Nonetheless, information on market size is vital to develop a meaningful marketing plan.

It is especially important when introducing new products that you have a good estimate of the size of the total market, but this is exactly the situation for which obtaining an accurate forecast is most difficult. For example, suppose that you were considering setting up a distribution business to sell garbage bags and shopping bags made from recycled plastic (polyethylene) in Halifax. To estimate the total potential market that might be available you would need to know the total demand for such products in the four Atlantic provinces, if that was how you had geographically defined you market. In addition, you would also be interested in determining the size of the various segments of the market. Three obvious segments that should be considered might be: (1) garbage bags for household use sold by retail stores; (2) heavy-duty garbage bags sold in bulk for commercial and industrial use; (3) printed plastic shopping bags for independent retail stores and chains. You may not wish to compete in the entire market but decide to focus on the needs of one particular segment such as printed shopping bags for chain stores.

It is usually much easier to determine market data for established products. Data on total market sales may already exist or they can be developed using either a "*top-down*" or a "*bottom-up*" approach.

TOP-DOWN APPROACH

The "top-down" approach utilizes published data on statistics such as total market size and weights them by an index that may be some factor such as the percentage of the population within your designated geographic area. For example, our distributor of plastic bags needs an estimate of the total size of the potential market for these bags in Atlantic Canada. Since the four Atlantic provinces account for approximately 10 per cent of the total Canadian population, a rough estimate of the size of the plastic bag market in that region would be 10 per cent of the total Canadian market. Data concerning the entire Canadian market may be available from sources such as Statistics Canada, or from trade associations, or other industry sources. One word of caution, however, in using this approach. This estimate of the total market for plastic bags in the Atlantic provinces is only accurate if usage patterns of plastic bags are the same in that region of Canada as they are in the country as a whole.

BOTTOM-UP APPROACH

The "bottom-up" approach involves aggregating information from the customer level to the total market level. Information on past or current purchase or usage of a product or service may be collected from a sample of customers by means of a mail or telephone survey or through personal interviews. For frequently purchased consumer products, like plastic garbage bags, for example, the survey may simply ask how much of the product is used either by individuals or the entire household during an average week or month. These individual or household statistics are then aggregated based upon population or household statistics that are available from Statistics Canada and other sources to develop an estimate of the total size of the potential market. An overview of both these approaches is illustrated in the Key Points box.[5]

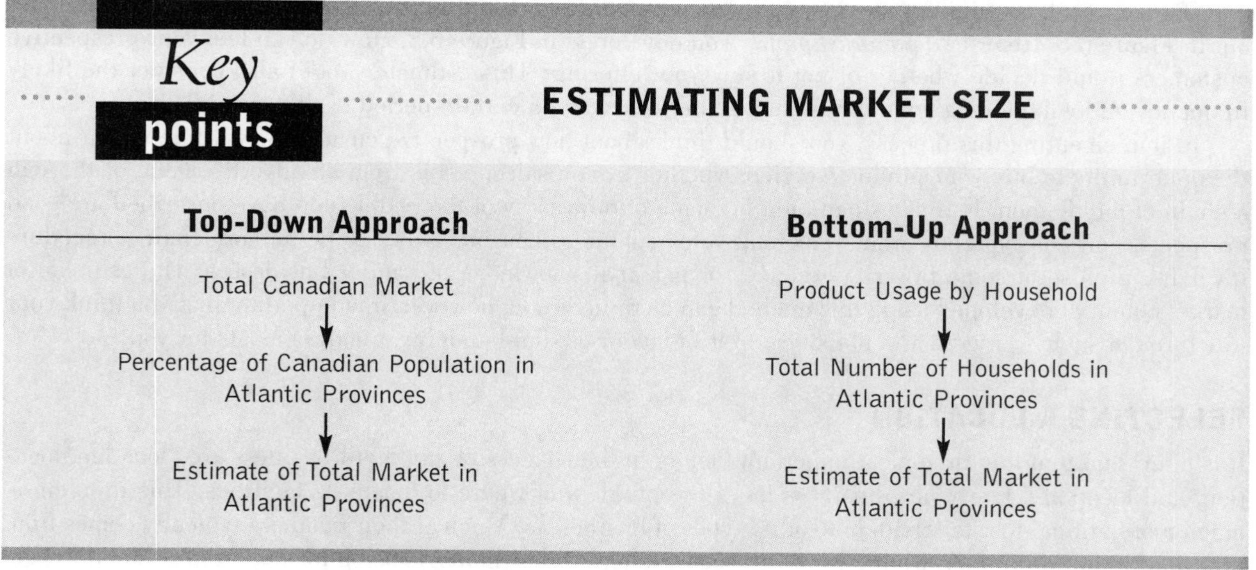

For your business plan, these sales estimates for your first year of operation should be monthly, while the estimates for subsequent years can be quarterly. A serious miscalculation many aspiring entrepreneurs make is to assume that because their new product or service appeals to them, other consumers will buy it as well. It is important to be aware of this tendency. This type of thinking is often reflected in what is known as the "2 per cent" syndrome. This syndrome follows a line of reasoning such as, "The total market for a product is $100 million. If my firm can pick up just 2 per cent of this market, it will have sales of $2 million per year."

There are, however, two things wrong with this line of reasoning. The first is that it may be extremely difficult for you to capture 2 per cent of this market unless your business has a unique competitive advantage. The second is that a 2 per cent market share may still be unprofitable, since competing firms with greater market share may benefit from *economies of scale* — lower unit cost due to mass-production — and other cost advantages unavailable to your firm.

5. Adapted from J.G. Barnes, *Research for Marketing Decision Making* (Toronto: McGraw-Hill Ryerson Ltd., 1991), 84–94.

There are a number of external factors that can affect your sales. These include:

- seasonal changes
- holidays
- special events
- political activities and events
- general economic conditions
- weather
- fashion trends and cycles
- population shifts
- changes in the retail mix.

In addition, there are a number of internal factors that must be considered as well, such as:

- level of your promotional effort
- your ability to manage inventory levels effectively
- the distribution channels you decide to use
- your price level relative to the competition
- any labour and personnel problem you might encounter.

It is impossible to predict all these situations but you should try to take them into account in developing your sales forecast.

One approach to gaining some insight into your business's potential market is to follow the example laid out in Figure 6.6. Refer to the *market profile* you developed in Figure 6.2. How do you feel your prospective customers would decide whether or not to buy your offering? This estimate should also consider the likely frequency and volume of a typical customer's purchases over a certain period of time.

In implementing this process, you should think about how prospective customers will likely hear about the opportunity to buy your product/service, whether from a salesperson, from an advertisement, or through a chain of middlemen. Estimates can then be made of how many of the people you have described are good prospects, and consequently what your total sales volume might be. This can be an "armchair" procedure involving the use of some library references or personal knowledge of similar businesses. The estimate of market potential developed using this method can be quite crude; however, it is important that you think your way through such a process and not sidestep it in favour of simply hoping a market exists for you.

SELECTING A LOCATION

It is often said that the three most important factors in the success of any retail business are "location, location, and location." Every new business faces the problem of where to locate its facilities. This problem is much more critical to retailers than to other types of businesses. Much of their business typically comes from people who are walking or driving by. As a consequence, a customer's decision to shop or not shop at a particular store may depend on such factors as what side of the street you are on, ease of access and egress, availability of parking, or similar concerns. This means that in determining the best location for your business you will have to concern yourself with a variety of issues.

1. **Zoning Regulations** Zoning bylaws govern the kind of activities that can be carried on in any given area. Classifications vary from locality to locality, but many municipalities categorize activities as residential, commercial office, commercial retail, institutional, and industrial. When considering a location, make certain the business activities you plan to pursue are permitted under the zoning restrictions for that area.

2. **Municipal Licences and Taxes** Businesses must typically buy a municipal business licence. In the city of Winnipeg, for example, more than 115 types of businesses require a licence, which costs from $15 to over $2,000. In general, businesses in some amusement fields or that affect public health and safety require a licence.

   Businesses, like homeowners, must usually pay a "business tax" — a tax assessed as a percentage of the rental value of the premises or on the basis of a standard assessment per square foot of space utilized. These requirements vary from municipality to municipality.

3. **Municipal Services** You should make sure that municipal services such as police and fire protection, adequate sewer and water supplies, public transit facilities, and an adequate road network are available to meet your business's requirements.

4. **Other Considerations** Other things to consider are such site-specific issues as:
   - cost
   - the volume and timing of traffic past the location
   - the nature of the location, whether on a downtown street, in a strip mall, or in an enclosed mall
   - the nature of the area surrounding your location and its compatibility with your business
   - the kind and relative location of surrounding businesses
   - the volume of customer traffic generated by these other firms and the proportion that might "spin off" to your store
   - the growth potential of the area or community
   - the number and location of curb cuts and turnoffs

Figure 6.7 at the back of this Stage provides a rating form you can use to help choose the most favourable location for a retail business.

Most of these same location factors also apply to service businesses, although perhaps not to the same degree. If your service business requires you to visit prospective customers at their home or place of business, a central location providing easy access to all parts of your market area may be preferred.

Location has a quite different meaning for manufacturing firms. Manufacturers are principally concerned about locating their plant where their operations will be most efficient. This means considering such issues as the following:

- General proximity to primary market areas
- Access to required raw materials and supplies
- Availability of a suitable labour force
- Accessibility and relative cost of transportation and storage facilities
- Availability and relative cost of power, water, and fuel supplies
- Financial incentives and other inducements available from municipal, provincial, or federal government agencies

The importance of each of these factors in the location decision will depend on the nature of your manufacturing business and your own preferences and requirements.

BUYING OR LEASING FACILITIES

Many new businesses already own or decide to purchase the land and building in which their ventures or the machinery and equipment they will require to operate are located. With today's extremely high costs, however, this may not be a wise decision. The majority of new firms are not principally in the business of speculating in real estate and should not acquire their own property. During their early stages most businesses tend to be short of cash and many have failed because they had their capital tied up in land and buildings when it could have been more effectively used to provide needed working capital for the business itself. In addition, a business that owns its own building may be more difficult to sell at a later date, since a smaller number of potential buyers will have enough capital to buy both the business and the property. While building your own facility enables you to more carefully tailor the property to the specific requirements of your business, it tends to be a much more costly alternative.

If you are planning to rent or lease your facilities it is probably a good idea to have your lawyer review the terms and conditions of the agreement. You will want to ensure satisfactory arrangements in such matters as:

1. **The duration of the agreement** A business lease can last a year, three years, five years, or any other mutually agreed-upon term. A short-term lease may be preferable if your situation is likely to change soon. However, the lease conditions can be a valuable asset of your business, and a short-term lease may reduce the sale value of your business (if you ever sell it) because of loss of the goodwill associated with maintain-

ing your present location. The ideal lease arrangement should enable you to stay in the location for some time, in case your venture is successful, but give you the flexibility to move after a reasonable period of time if it doesn't work out.

You also need to consider the terms and conditions for renewing the lease. Are there provisions for automatic renewal? Is there a maximum to any rent increase applied upon renewal of your lease?

2. **The rent** Rental costs for commercial property are commonly stated in terms of the annual cost per square foot of floor space. For example, a 1,500 square foot location rented for $8 per square foot will cost $12,000 a year, or $1,000 per month. This may be a *net lease*, in which you pay a single monthly fee that is all-inclusive (rent, utilities, maintenance costs, property taxes, etc.), or a "net-net-net" or *triple net lease*, in which you pay a base rent plus a share of all the other expenses incurred by the landlord in operating the building. In the latter situation your operating costs may fluctuate each year because of changing tax, maintenance, insurance, and other costs.

   In retail shopping malls, *participating* (or *percentage*) *leases* are common. Instead of a fixed monthly rent, the landlord receives some percentage of your sales or net profit. There are several types of participating leases. You may pay either a percentage of the total monthly sales of your business, a base rent plus some percentage of your gross sales, or a percentage of your net profit before interest and taxes. Shopping centre leases can be quite complex documents, so be certain to check with your accountant and lawyer before committing yourself.

3. **The ownership of any additions or improvements you might make to the facilities** Under the terms of most leases, all improvements and fixtures that you add to the premises are considered as belonging to the landlord. They immediately become part of the building and cannot be removed without his or her consent. If you need to install expensive fixtures to launch your business, you should try right up front to negotiate permission to remove specific items.

4. **Any restrictions on the use of the property** Most leases specify the kind of business activity you can carry on in the location. Before signing, you should think not only about the activities you now plan to engage in, but also about those you might wish to engage in in the future. Many leases also contain a non-competition clause to protect you from competitive firms' coming into the premises and taking away your business.

5. **Whether you are permitted to sublet some or all of the property to a third party** This is commonly permitted, but only with the prior written consent of the landlord, and it is subject to any use restrictions and non-competition clauses in your agreement.

   A closely related issue is your ability to assign any remaining time left on your lease to another party. If you decide to sell your business, this can be an attractive part of the package. In some cases, assignment of the lease is not permitted; in others, an assignment may be acceptable with the prior written consent of the landlord, which may then not be unreasonably withheld.

6. **The nature of any default and penalty clauses** The lease will spell out the situations which constitute a breach of its conditions and the recourse available to the landlord. Obvious grounds for default include failure on your part to pay the rent, the bankruptcy of your business, violation of the use conditions or non-competition clauses, and so on. Should you default on the lease, the landlord may be able to claim accelerated rent for the time remaining on the lease. For example, if you were to move out two years before your lease expires, the landlord may claim the full two years' rent. In this situation, however, the landlord legally must try to limit his or her damages by renting out your space to another party as soon as possible.

   Your lease may or may not contain a *penalty clause* limiting your exposure should you breach the lease. A penalty of three months' rent is common in many situations, although the landlord will want you or the directors of an incorporated business to sign personal guarantees for the amount of the penalty.

HOME-BASED BUSINESSES

For many kinds of businesses, working out of the home has become a very popular and attractive option. There are a number of advantages to running your business out of your home, the most obvious of which is the cost.

Not only can you save on the rent for your business premises by operating in this manner; the Canada Customs and Revenue Agency will also let you write off part of your home expenses for income tax purposes. Possible write-offs are utility costs, mortgage interest, municipal taxes, and other expenses related to maintaining that part of your premises used for your business. You can also save on the cost and time of travelling to and from work every day, and you have greater flexibility in planning and organizing your work and personal life. In addition, a home-based business may have a number of other benefits such as letting you wear more comfortable clothes and giving you more time to look after and be with your family.

There are, however, a number of disadvantages.

1. It takes a lot of self-discipline to sustain a regular work schedule and resist distractions from family, friends, television, and other sources. You may find that there are too many interruptions to work effectively, that you tend to mix work with family life too much, or become distracted by household chores. Conversely, you may find it very difficult to get away from your work when you would like to, since it is so close at hand, and you may have trouble quitting after a full day.
2. Suppliers and prospective customers may not take you as seriously. You may have to rent a post office box or make other arrangements to give the appearance of operating from a more conventional commercial location.
3. The space available in your home may not be appropriate for your business, and you may not have access to facilities and equipment such as computers and fax machines that you need to conduct your business effectively.
4. If your house is in a typical residential area, operating a business from your home will probably contravene local zoning bylaws.

   It is true that most municipal governments have become reasonably flexible in this regard and do not go looking for violations; they will, however, respond to complaints from immediate neighbours and others in the vicinity. It is probably a good idea to check with these people before starting any kind of visible business activity from your home. Activities that may lead to complaints are posting a large sign on the front lawn, constant noise, a steady stream of customers, suppliers, or others in and out of your home, or the clutter of parked vehicles in your yard or on the street.

In the end, operating a home-based business is really a very personal decision. From a practical perspective, you can probably do what you want, as long as no one complains. However, this mode of operation is not suitable for all types of businesses, and for many people may not be a comfortable decision.

FLESHING OUT YOUR MARKETING PROGRAM

The purpose of this section is to bring together what you have learned about the total market potential for your product or service, customer attitudes toward your particular offering, and the nature of the competitive environment you will be facing. The goal is to put down on paper a preliminary marketing strategy or plan for your new venture concept. This involves making some decisions regarding what you feel is an appropriate *marketing mix* for your business. Put simply, the principal ingredients of your marketing program that must be blended together to form your overall strategy can be grouped under the following headings:

1. Product or service offering
2. Pricing program
3. Promotional plans
4. Method of distribution

PRODUCT OR SERVICE OFFERING

The product area involves the planning and development of the product or service you are planning to offer in the marketplace. This involves defining the breadth and depth of your offering, the length of your line, how it will be packaged and branded, the variety of colours and other product features, and the range of complementary services (delivery, repair, warranties, etc.) that will be made available to the customer.

PRICING PROGRAM

Your pricing strategy involves establishing the right base price for your offering so that it is appealing to customers and profitable to you. This base price may be adjusted to meet the needs of particular situations, such as to encourage early acceptance of your offering during its introductory stages, to meet aggressive or exceptional competition, to provide for trade, functional, seasonal, and other discounts, or to introduce your product/service into new market situations.

There are a number of approaches that can be used to determine a base price for your planned market offering. These include: *cost-based pricing*, *value-based pricing*, and *competition-based pricing*.

COST-BASED PRICING

One of the most commonly used strategies by retailers and small manufacturers is *cost-based pricing or markup pricing*. The cost of your product or service is determined and used as the base, and then a markup is added to determine what your selling price should be. *Markups* are generally expressed as a percentage of the selling price — for example, a product costing $2.50 and selling for $5 has a 50 per cent markup.

To illustrate, let's assume you've come up with a new formula for an automobile engine treatment that will be sold through auto parts jobbers to service stations for use in consumers' cars. Table 6.3 illustrates what the price markup chain for this product might look like.

As you can see, in this illustration a product with a factory cost of $1.50 has a retail selling price of $5 to the final consumer. The markup percentages shown here are merely examples of a typical situation, but in most wholesale and retail businesses standard markups tend to prevail in different industry sectors. Food products and other staple items usually have a low unit cost and high inventory turnover, so the markups tend to be fairly low, 15 to 25 per cent: products such as jewelry and highly advertised specialty products typically have higher markups, perhaps as much as 50 or 60 per cent or even more.

TABLE 6.3 PRICE MARKUP CHAIN

	Per Bottle	Markup
Direct factory costs	$1.00	
Indirect factory costs	0.50	
Total factory cost	$1.50	
Manufacturer's markup	0.50	25%
Manufacturer's selling price	$2.00	
Jobber's markup	0.50	20%
Jobber's selling price	$2.50	
Service station markup	2.50	50%
Service station selling price	$5.00	

This type of markup pricing is simple and easy to apply and can be very successful if all competitors have similar costs of doing business and use similar percentages. On the other hand, this approach does not take into account variations in the demand for the product that may occur with a different final price. For example, how much more or less of the engine treatment would be sold at a price of $4 or $6 rather than the $5 price determined by the standard markup chain?

Most manufacturers do not employ markup pricing in the same way that many wholesalers and retailers do. However, if you plan to manufacture a product that will be sold through wholesalers and various types of retail outlets, it is important for you to know the markups these distributors will likely apply to your product. For instance, in the above example if the manufacturer of the engine treatment thinks $5 is the right retail price, he or she can work backwards and determine that it must be able to sell profitably to the jobbers for $2 to succeed. If that is not possible, perhaps the overall marketing strategy for the product should be reconsidered.

VALUE-BASED PRICING

Instead of using costs, more and more companies are basing their prices on their estimate of the market's perceived value of their market offering. This is particularly true in determining the most appropriate price to charge in a service business. This perceived value is the overall value the customer places on a product or service. The process begins by analyzing customer needs and value perceptions. This may involve much more than just the basic product or service itself and include other features such as availability, image, delivery, after-sales service, warranty considerations, and other issues. With this approach the price is set by determining the price that people are willing to pay while making sure that you can still cover all your costs.

The way businesses are able to price more effectively on "value" is by differentiating themselves in some way from the competition. This differentiation can be based on any number of factors such as promotion and advertising, availability, or the addition of value-added services. People are prepared to pay more for products produced by name designers such as Bill Blass, Calvin Klein, or Tom Hilfiger, for example, than they are for similar items produced by others. Similarly a computer store that provides emergency service to customers on a 24/7 basis might be able to charge more for its computers or extended warranty package than an outlet than is only open from 9:00 a.m. to 6:00 p.m. five days a week.

COMPETITION-BASED PRICING

In some situations consumers base their judgments of a product or service's value on the prices that competitors charge for similar offerings. You might decide to base your price largely on competitor's prices with less attention to your own costs or expected demand. For example, you might decide to charge the same, more or less than your principal competitors. Some of this may depend on the image you are trying to achieve in the market place. If you want to create an image of a bargain or discount operation such as Dollar Store Plus or Ultracuts, for example, then your prices should be consistent with that image. Similarly, if you are trying to establish an image of a luxury type operation such as Holt Renfrew or an exclusive hair salon, people may be prepared to pay more and your prices should be consistent with that position. Your target market might not be attracted to a cheaper product or service.

In addition to establishing a base price for your product or service line, you may permit some customers to pay less than this amount in certain circumstances or provide them with a discount. The principal types of discounts are quantity discounts, cash discounts, and seasonal discounts. *Quantity discounts* are commonly provided to customers who buy more than some minimum quantity or dollar value of products or services from you. This discount may be based either on the quantity or value of each individual order (non-cumulative) or on the total value of their purchases over a certain period of time, such as a month (cumulative).

Cash discounts are based on the typical terms of trade within an industry and permit customers to deduct a certain percentage amount from the net cost of their purchases if payment is made in cash at the time of purchase or full payment is made within a specified number of days. Different types of businesses have their own customary cash discounts. For example, a typical discount is expressed as "2/10 net 30." In this situation, a customer who is invoiced on October 1 for an outstanding bill of $2,000 need only pay $1,960 if payment is made before October 10. This is a 2 per cent cash discount for making payment within the 10 days. Otherwise the full face value of the invoice ($2,000) is due by October 31 or 30 days after the invoice date.

Seasonal discounts of 10 per cent, 15 per cent, 20 per cent, or more on your normal base price may be offered to your customers if their purchases are made during your slow or off-season. This gives you a method of moving inventories that you may otherwise have to carry over to the following year or of providing your dealers, agents, and other distributors with some incentive to stock up on your products well in advance of the prime selling season.

PROMOTIONAL PLANS

The budget that you allocate for the promotion of your new venture must be distributed across the following activities:

1. Advertising
2. Personal selling
3. Sales promotion
4. Public relations

Each of these activities differs along a number of important dimensions such as their cost to reach a member of the target audience and the degree of interaction that can take place with that audience. Table 6.4 summarizes how these activities compare on a number of different criteria.

TABLE 6.4 A COMPARISON OF VARIOUS PROMOTIONAL ACTIVITIES*

	Advertising	Sales Promotion	Public Relations	Personal Selling
Cost per Audience Member	Low	Low	Very Low	Very High
Focus on Target Markets	Poor to Good	Good	Moderate	Very Good
Ability to Deliver a Complicated Message	Poor to Good	Poor	Poor to Good	Very Good
Interchange with Audience	None	None	Low to Moderate	Very Good
Credibility	Low	Low	High	Moderate to High

*Adapted from Gerald E. Hills, "Market Opportunities and Marketing," in William D. Dygrave, *The Portable MBA in Entrepreneurship*, 2nd ed. (John Wiley & Sons, Inc., 1999). This material is used by permission of John Wiley & Sons, Inc.

The distribution of your expenditures should be made to obtain the maximum results for your particular circumstances. It is impossible to generalize about the optimum distribution of your dollars to each of these activities. Different businesses use quite different combinations. Some companies put most of their money into hiring a sales force and their sales promotion program; others put most of their budget into a media advertising campaign. The proper combination for you will depend on a careful study of the relative costs and effectiveness of each of these types of promotion and the unique requirements of your business.

We often think of promotion as being directed strictly toward our final prospective customer, and in fact the largest share of most promotional activity is channelled in that direction. However, promotion can also be used to influence your dealers, your distributors, and other members of your distribution channel. This may persuade them to adopt your offering more rapidly and broaden the breadth of your distribution coverage.

ADVERTISING

Advertising is one of the principal means you have of informing potential customers about the availability and special features of your product or service. Properly conceived messages presented in the appropriate media can greatly stimulate demand for your business and its offerings. A wide range of advertising media are available to carry your messages, of which the most important are those listed in Table 6.5. Which of these media you should choose for your advertising program will depend on the consumers you are trying to reach, the size of the budget you have available, the nature of your product or service, and the particular message you hope to communicate.

ADVERTISING ON THE INTERNET One form of advertising that is rapidly increasing in popularity is the use of the Internet. The World Wide Web is open for business and small firms, particularly retail businesses, are jumping aboard in ever increasing numbers. Before joining this throng, however, you should consider whether a Web presence will really serve your business interests. If so, you need to formulate a clear strategy or plan, rather than just developing another Web page to join the millions that already exist on the Net.

Bud Dickson and Jim Clark (Entrepreneurs in Action #22), for example, have used the Web very successfully over the past few years to expand their canoeing and outfitting business in Ontario's Quetico Provincial Park. Their site receives upwards of 7,500 hits a week and complements the traditional advertising they have always done such as attending sport shows in the United States and placing ads in hunting and fishing magazines and other publications. Their Web site has enabled them to expand their market to eastern Canada and overseas while also providing more information and a higher service level to their clientele.

Should you decide to proceed with implementing a Web site, remember that the Web is not a passive delivery system like most other media but is an active system where the user expects to participate in the experience. Your virtual storefront must be genuinely interesting and the interactivity of the Web should be used to your advantage to attract and hold the ongoing interest of your target consumers.

TABLE 6.5 THE MOST COMMON ADVERTISING MEDIA

1. **MAGAZINES**
   a. Consumer magazines
   b. Trade or business publications
   c. Farm publications
   d. Professional magazines
2. **NEWSPAPERS**
   a. Daily newspapers
   b. Weekly newspapers
   c. Shopping guides
   d. Special-interest newspapers
3. **TELEVISION**
   a. Local TV
   b. Network TV
   c. Special-interest cable TV
4. **RADIO**
   a. Local stations
   b. Network radio
5. **DIRECTORY**
   a. Yellow Pages
   b. Community
   c. Special-interest
6. **DIRECT MAIL ADVERTISING**
   a. Letters
   b. Catalogues
7. **OUTDOOR ADVERTISING**
   a. Billboards
   b. Posters
8. **TRANSPORTATION ADVERTISING**
   a. Interior car cards
   b. Station posters
   c. Exterior cards on vehicles
9. **POINT-OF-PURCHASE DISPLAYS**
10. **ADVERTISING NOVELTIES AND SPECIALTIES**
11. **THE INTERNET**

22 *Entrepreneurs in* action

Canoe Canada Outfitters

BACKGROUND

Ultra light equipment, excellent trail food and the wilderness experience of an outfitter are essential ingredients for a successful wilderness vacation. Canoe Canada is an outfitter for Ontario's Quetico Provincial Park and the White Otter Wilderness Area that attempts to combine these ingredients for its customers. Established in 1974 on a personal service basis so that Bud Dickson and Jim Clark, the company's two founders, could share their knowledge of the Quetico wilderness country with outdoor enthusiasts, Canoe Canada has grown to a staff of eight in the winter and 25 during the summer months.

CONNECTING TO THE INTERNET

A casual conversation with one of their long-time customers, an Internet consultant, convinced both Dickson and Clark to mount a Web site on the Internet. The problem was that, at that time, no Internet access was available in Atikokan. For this reason, and because the consultant had first-hand knowledge of the company, Canoe Canada decided to use the consultant's company in Columbus, Ohio as its Internet service provider (ISP). All e-mail inquiries went to the Internet consultant in Ohio, who would then fax them to Canoe Canada for follow-up. Since 1996, Internet access has been available in Atikokan through Lakehead University which is located 200 km away in Thunder Bay, Ontario — the closest city to Quetico. The company now has the technological infrastructure available to be able to respond directly to the e-mail inquiries.

Despite the exposure Canoe Canada has received by having a Web site — the site currently receives approximately 7,500 hits per week — the company continues to follow up with traditional advertising methods. For example, in addition to attending several sport shows in the United States per year, the company advertises in fishing and hunting magazines, *Canadian Geographic* magazine and *The Financial Post* newspaper. Although the season runs from May to October, reservations are made throughout the year.

In addition to an online trip planning and routing form, an online registration form is available on the site. The former helps give visitors a vision of some of the possibilities a trip to Quetico offers. It also assists Canoe Canada in developing the best route for its customers, although the route remains flexible and can be changed during the trip (i.e., travellers may stay longer in one spot, or extend their planned route). Through the online registration form, customers are able to make payment online with their credit card. However, at this time, it is not a secure line and Canoe Canada has no plans in the near future on making it secure. Finally, the Web site also allows customers to choose their trip menu online so that meals will be packed and ready when they arrive.

While much of the information on the Web site mirrors the information contained in Canoe Canada's print brochures, the Web site does contain additional information and features not found in the brochures. For example, the Web site contains the Online Trip Web page, which is essentially the travelogue of one group's week-long outing. The narrative, accompanied by digital photographs, is presented in a Day 1 ... Day 2 ... format. The Online Trip has been a real attraction to Internet adventure seekers. It is changed annually and is voluntarily written by Canoe Canada customers recounting their experience. The Web site also presents more in-depth information about the area, as well as the equipment and services offered by Canoe Canada, compared to the print brochures.

All in all, Canoe Canada spends about $1,000 a year to maintain and update the Web site. Mr. Clark warns that businesses interested in mounting a Web site should be prepared to update the information regularly, "They can't just establish a home page and leave it. ... If you play this game, don't play it at all unless you play it well." He continues by stating that budgets must be set and time spent in order to keep the content relevant and fresh.

BENEFITS

Canoe Canada's target audience has primarily been American. For example, while the company attends a number of sport shows annually in the United States, it attends none in Canada. When the company was first established, 99% of its clientele was American, with the remaining 1% Canadian. Since the Web site was mounted, its Canadian customers have grown to approximately 5% of the business; Canadians now account for approximately 15% of browsers to the site. Americans account for 84% of browsers to the site, with the remaining 1% made up of visitors from other countries. "The response is actually better than a magazine ad," according to Sandy Dickson. "We reach areas we have not traditionally gotten to before — places like Nova Scotia. The ratio of inquiries to actual booking is about the same as traditional advertising, but it generates enough attention that it is certainly worth it."

The connection to the Internet has allowed customers to ask plenty of questions to the staff about their upcoming wilderness trip. In the past, customers could only contact the company through a long-distance phone call. Regular postal mail and fax were not popular options. Once e-mail became available inquiries have been steadily streaming in. According to Mrs. Dickson who handles the customer inquiries, the advent of e-mail has enabled her to offer a higher level of customer service, although this has made her job more labour-intensive and has increased her workload. She receives an average of 35 e-mail messages daily.

FUTURE PLANS

This upcoming season, the company is expanding its repertoire. It plans to offer kayak trips in the area. While this information will probably not make it to a print brochure for some time, it will most certainly be added to the Web site shortly — at a much lower cost. In addition, information on the fly-in outpost cabins that Canoe Canada owns will be mounted on the site. Mr. Clark feels that the company now has more information on the site than it had in the past. Canoe Canada is no longer as guarded about the "free information" that it offers to its customers and competitors.

Future plans for the Web site may also include pictures from a digital camera mounted on location that would be able to show people the current weather conditions in Atikokan; the company receives many calls each day inquiring about the weather. Mr. Clark is also considering mounting a message board on the site where people could exchange messages and questions about their trips. (www.canoecanada.com)

Source: Adapted from Canoe Canada Outfitters," http//strategis.ic.gc.ca/SSG/ng00057e.html, accessed December 28, 2001.

Opening a successful Web site is not as complicated as it may appear, but it can be expensive to do the job right. You can do it yourself or enlist the expertise of a multimedia production house. Production costs depend entirely upon the size and interactivity of your site, running anywhere from $500 on the cheap to $100,000 for a full-blown corporate site. Maintenance costs are minimal but materials and other aspects of the site's operation should be updated regularly, such as once a month.

Once your page is developed, it is important that you get a domain name and file a registration request. You will also want a reliable Web server to house your site. Try to get as many links leading to your site as possible by listing with directories, hotlinks, and so on where consumers will be able to find you quite easily. You might also give some consideration to joining a Cybermall.

Advertising on the Internet is not for everyone, however. Guitar maker Bob Grierson (Entrepreneurs in Action #23) decided to take his business on-line in 1999 and pulled the plug on his Web site after 18 months. He found that the hands-on individuality of his work didn't translate well into the impersonal e-commerce world. There was lots of activity on his site and it was good for helping people find him, but it didn't translate into a lot of business. In addition, site maintenance was also very time consuming. In addition, he estimates that 95 per cent of those who accessed his site were looking for free information and he didn't want to run a chat line for amateurs. There were some positive benefits to his experience though. He says that it did enable him to find wood and hardware suppliers for his business that he wouldn't have heard about without the Net.

23 Entrepreneurs in action

Net hits the wrong note

Once upon a time, there was a business owner who had a special product.

While there were others in the land who also had special products, he was a smart business owner. He knew that the more people who saw his goods, the more sales he'd make, and the more gold that would flow into his coffers.

So he made himself a Web site to show all that clicked there exactly what they could buy. The clicks came, his coffers grew, and the smart business owner lived happily ever ...

If this fractured fairy tale was really all there was to e-commerce in the 21st century, you'd still be able to access Bob Grierson's Web site.

Grierson, 56, is a Winnipeg-born instrument maker who has repaired, restored and custom-made guitars and other stringed instruments for a living since 1976. He learned his way around tools and fine woodworking from his furniture-making grandfather at a young age. When he discovered popular music as a university student, a lifelong career was born.

"As a left-handed player, I found guitars and instruments were really expensive," says Grierson, who played with local bands such as Black Cat and Bull Rush in the mid-'70s. "Necessity really was the mother of invention here. I just started building them and I've been doing it ever since."

Today, Grierson operates Robert Grierson — Instrument Maker out of his Fort Rouge home. Business is split between repair and custom work for professional musicians (he made the guitar Jim Kale used in the Guess Who's Pan Am Games reunion gig) and restoring stringed instruments for other customers. His is a tactile craft, requiring a well-tuned ear and a sensitive touch.

"It's so very individual. And when you're talking about building an entire instrument, it's even more so," says Grierson. His hourly rate runs from $20 to $60.

"All the materials have to be hand-selected; there's no mass production involved. That's why it can cost from $2,000 to $5,000 to build one guitar. Even guitars mass-produced in Taiwan, Korea and Japan need to be set up correctly for the player. All the fine-tuning work has to be done after the purchase," he says.

Instrument restoration is equally painstaking. Before he can make that old banjo, guitar or fiddle playable, Grierson first determines if the unit is structurally sound.

"Of course, cosmetics are a consideration in restorative work, but most people just want the instrument to work, and work well," he says. "Once I've checked it out structurally and made it playable, then you can decide if you want to spend more money on it."

With a fast-growing reputation as a craftsman with a niche skill, Grierson decided to take his business on-line in 1999 at the urging of a friend who built Web sites.

But he found the hands-on individually of his work didn't translate well into the impersonal e-commerce world. After 18 months, he pulled the plug on his site.

"By virtue of what I do, the Web connection was handy only for posts, really — you know, interested people wanting to reach other people in this business. There was lots of activity on the site and it was good for helping people to find me, but it didn't translate into a lot of business. At least, not like I thought it would," he says, adding that site maintenance also was very time-consuming.

And there was another problem. He estimates that 95 per cent of those who accessed his site were looking for free information.

"Sure, there's a monetary market out there for knowledge, but I didn't want to run a chat line for amateurs. I felt like I was the middle guy between the buyer and seller, or simply a source of information. It wasn't worth maintaining the site when that's all you're getting out of it."

Grierson says he may have deleted his Web site, but there were upsides to his experience.

"I did find wood and hardware suppliers that I wouldn't have heard about as quickly without the Net. That's the shining light of that tool. Yes, it gives a business exposure, but it can also be frustrating, especially for a polarized business like mine.

"If you were able to verify and actually see the damaged instrument, guitar or banjo on-line, that would make a difference.

"The whole idea of e-business is in the infantile stage still," he adds. "I certainly found out what that technology can and can't do. I don't think people have really latched on to the newness of it."

Source: "Net Hits the Wrong Note," Gail Cabana-Coldwell, Monday Business: © Winnipeg Free Press, Mon July 30, 2001. P. B5. Reprinted with permission.

PERSONAL SELLING

Personal selling involves direct, face-to-face contact with your prospective customer. A personal salesperson's primary function is usually more concerned with obtaining orders than informing your customers about the nature of your offering as in the case of advertising. Other types of salespeople are principally involved in providing support to different components of your business or filling routine orders rather than more persuasive kinds of selling. The basic steps involved in the selling process are as follows:

1. **Prospecting and qualifying** Identifying prospective customers
2. **The sales approach** The initial contact with the prospective customer
3. **Presentation** The actual sales message presented to a prospective customer
4. **Demonstration** of the capabilities and features or most important characteristics of the product or service being sold
5. **Handling any objections or concerns** the prospective customer may have regarding your offering
6. **Closing the sale** Asking the prospective customer for the order
7. **Postsales activities** Follow-up to determine if customers are satisfied with their purchase and to pursue any additional possible sales

SALES PROMOTION

Sales promotion includes a broad range of promotional activities other than advertising and personal selling that stimulate consumer or dealer interest in your offering. While advertising and personal selling tend to be ongoing activities, most sales promotion is sporadic or irregular in nature. Sales promotion includes activities related to:

1. Free product samples
2. Discount coupons
3. Contests
4. Special deals and premiums
5. Gifts
6. Special exhibits and displays
7. Participation in trade shows
8. Off-price specials
9. Floats in parades and similar events

As you can see, sales promotion consists of a long list of what are typically non-recurring activities. They are intended to make your advertising and personal selling effort more effective and may be very intimately involved with them. For example, your advertising may be used to promote a consumer contest, or certain special deals and incentives may be offered to your salespeople to encourage them to increase their sales to your dealers or final consumers. These activities can be an effective way for businesses with a small budget and some imagination to reach potential sales prospects and develop a considerable volume of business.

PUBLIC RELATIONS

Public relations relates to your business's general communications and relationships with its various interest groups such as your employees, stockholders, the government, and society at large, as well as your customers. It is concerned primarily with such issues as the image of you and your business within the community rather than trying to sell any particular product or service. Publicity releases, product introduction notices, news items, appearances on radio and television, and similar activities are all part of your public relations program.

METHOD OF DISTRIBUTION

Your channel of distribution is the path your products or service take to market. Physical products typically follow one or more complex paths in getting from the point at which they are produced to the hands of their final consumer. These paths involve the use of several different kinds of wholesalers and retailers who perform a variety of functions that are essential to making this flow of products reasonably efficient. These functions include buying, selling, transporting, storing, financing, risk-taking, and several others.

Distribution channels consist of channel members that are independent firms that facilitate this flow of merchandise. There are many different kinds, and they have quite different names, but the functions they perform may not be that dramatically different. For example, wholesalers are generally classified according to whether they actually take title or ownership of the products they handle (*merchant wholesalers*) or not (*agents*). Merchant wholesalers are further classified as *full-service*, *limited-function*, *drop shippers*, *truck wholesalers*, and *rack jobbers*. Agents are commonly referred to as *brokers*, *manufacturer's agents*, *selling agents*, *food* or *drug brokers*, etc. For small manufacturers, all of these types of wholesalers, alone or in combination, represent possible paths for getting their product to market.

Retailers, too, cover a very broad spectrum, starting with the large department stores that carry a broad product selection and provide an extensive range of customer services, through specialty stores such as electronics, men's clothing, and furniture stores, on down to discount department stores, grocery stores, drug stores, catalogue retailers, and convenience stores. All represent possible members that could be included in your channel of distribution.

In addition to opportunities for marketing your products or services in conjunction with these traditional and conventional distribution channel members, you should not overlook more unconventional possibilities for reaching your potential customers. For example, over the past few years we have seen tremendous growth of various forms of non-store retailing, including:

1. Mail order catalogues
2. Direct response advertising on television, and in newspapers and magazines

3. Direct selling door to door
4. Party plan or home demonstration party selling
5. Direct mail solicitations
6. Vending machines
7. Trade shows
8. Fairs and exhibitions
9. The Internet

Cindy Burton of iWave.com Inc., for example, used to publish an annual directory of prospective donors for non-profit fundraisers that she sold to various clients (Entrepreneurs in Action #24). She now makes that data available to universities, the Red Cross, the United Way and others exclusively over the Net on a subscrip-

24 Entrepreneurs in action

Prospecting for Profits

For Cindy Burton, the Internet was originally a freedom machine: it let her move her book publishing business from busy Vancouver to bucolic Nelson, B.C. But over the past five years, it has driven her company in new directions she never expected.

Burton's Rainforest Publications produced an annual directory of prospective donors for non-profit fundraisers. But when Burton got on the Net in 1995, she realized it offered a huge advantage — continual updates — over print and even the CD-ROM version she'd been planning. The problem: when she asked Canadian clients what kind of modem they had, the usual response was: "A what? How do you spell that?" But some fundraisers were using modems — mainly U.S. universities and large fundraising bodies. Better yet, the U.S. fundraising market is 20 times the size of Canada's.

So Burton started building an online databank for her U.S. clients based on their active participation. What information did they need? How would they want it categorized? "We let the market drive the product, which is what's unique about being online," she says. "It brings the customer directly into your factory." Indeed, clients marvelled at the Net's edge over print: faster, more focussed searches, plus ongoing updates flagged in each search.

As modems proliferated, Burton's new business model proved spot on. Today, her Prospect Research Online service is used by fundraising units at Harvard, most other Ivy League colleges, the Red Cross and the United Way. The price: US$1,500 annually for one user and US$2,500 for workgroups. Canadians get a big break: a flat rate of C$995.

The Net has also driven spinoff ventures for her firm, which relocated to Charlottetown in 1997 and more recently took the name iWave.com after going public. Burton now offers special research on top donors, including such details as education, past contributions and links to charities. At $300 each, Burton hoped some clients might request 10 profiles. Instead, early requests were for 100 and 150 names.

Burton is now leveraging her data into a new field: executive retirement. The executives she profiles for fundraisers are also top prospects for corporate recruiters. After assembling 200,000 profiles, she has unveiled a prospecting service called Executive Alert. "Poaching will become endemic," she says. "And this is the ultimate poaching tool."

Now Burton is determined to extend her fiefdom. Fresh from raising $2.25 million in a private placement in February, her company is bulking up. At the start of the year she had 25 employees, with four devoted to sales. Now the plan is to have a staff of 130, and 45 salespeople. "We can finally go out and sell the product," says Burton. Revenues have been growing quickly — $438,960 for the first three quarters of the current fiscal year, more than double the year-earlier period. But expansion also saw the company lose $1 million in those nine months. By the end of 2000, however, Burton expects her core products to be breaking even.

Burton offers two bits of advice for companies tackling the dot-com world. Involve your customers in developing the product. And don't give in to frills. When her team added fancy graphics to their database, longer download times made users rebel. Let your clients drive your e-business.

Source: "iWave.com Inc.," *PROFIT: The Magazine for Canadian Entrepreneurs* (May 2000): 36–38.

tion basis. This method of distribution enables her clients to make more focused searches as well as giving them more flexibility and ongoing updates. This new system has also opened up a couple of additional ventures for her firm. She can now provide her clients with specialized and more detailed research on top prospective donors for an additional fee and has leveraged her data into a new business in executive recruitment. Her business is now growing rapidly and while still not profitable, she has been able to raise over $2 million in private investment capital.

You should also be aware of market opportunities that may exist for your venture in foreign markets. These may be accessed by direct exporting, using the services of a trading company, licensing or franchising a firm in that market to produce and sell your product or service, setting up a joint venture with a local firm, or some similar strategy.

DEVELOPING A PRELIMINARY MARKETING PLAN

Figure 6.8 presents a framework to help you prepare a preliminary marketing plan for the product or service idea behind your prospective venture. It will guide you through the process and indicate the kind of information you will need to do a thorough job. It will get you thinking about the size and nature of the market opportunity that may exist for your concept or idea. It will also focus your thoughts on the marketing program you will require to take advantage of the opportunity and achieve your personal goals. The marketing plan is a key part of your feasibility study and your subsequent business plan. Much of the work you do here can be incorporated into your business plan.

MANAGING THE SUPPLY SITUATION

A key factor in the success of any new venture is some assurance of continuing access to critical supplies of raw material and component parts at reasonable prices. Many new businesses have floundered due to changing supply situations that impacted their ability to provide products of acceptable quality or that drastically increased their costs of production. These conditions are seldom correctable and tend to be terminal for the smaller firm. It is critical that you investigate the range of possible sources for these key elements well in advance of starting your venture.

Assessing your supply situation requires an understanding of the manufacturing cycle for your product or service and an in-depth appreciation of the market for equipment, materials, and parts. One strategy being followed by more and more smaller firms is to subcontract their production requirements instead of making their own products. This strategy has a number of significant advantages:

- Your business can use the subcontractor's money instead of having to raise the funds to build your own production facilities.
- You can take advantage of the expertise and technical knowledge possessed by the subcontractor without having to develop it yourself.
- Using a subcontractor may enable you to bring your business on stream more rapidly. There is no need to delay while your production facilities are being built and broken in.
- You can concentrate your time on developing a market for your products and running your business rather than on trying to produce a satisfactory product.
- You may be able to benefit from the reputation and credibility of the subcontractor; having your products produced by a firm with an established reputation will rub off on your business.
- A reliable subcontractor can also keep you up to date with technical advances in that field so that your products don't become obsolete.
- Perhaps the most important advantage of using a subcontractor is that it establishes your costs of production in advance, reducing the uncertainty and unpredictability of setting up your own facilities. A firm, fixed-price contract from a reliable subcontractor nails down one of your most important costs of doing business and facilitates your entire planning process.

As you can see, there are a number of strong advantages to subcontracting certain aspects of your operations, but that does not necessarily mean this strategy should be employed in all situations. There are a number of disadvantages that should be considered as well:

- The cost of having a job done by a subcontractor may not be as low as if you did the work yourself. Subcontractors may have antiquated equipment; high cost, unionized labour; or other problems to deal with that make their operations very expensive. Subcontractors also factor in some margin of profit for themselves into a job. The end result may be a total production cost that would make it very difficult for you to successfully compete.
- Your business may be jeopardized if the subcontractor should fail to meet commitments to you or divulge critical trade secrets about your product or process.

In any case, sometimes a suitable subcontractor is just not available. If you want your product produced, you may have no alternative but to do it yourself.

Regardless of the approach you decide to take, to cover your supply situation there are a number of key factors that have to be considered. These include:

- Delivered cost (total cost including transportation, etc.)
- Quality
- Delivery schedules
- Service level

All have to be at an acceptable level for you to have confidence your supply situation is under reasonable control.

FYI FOR YOUR INFORMATION

The following are some helpful Web sites for developing your marketing plan:

FROM IDEA TO MARKET: HOW TO GET YOUR PRODUCT ON THE SHELF THROUGH MARKET RESEARCH
(www.cbsc.org/manitoba/index.cfm?name=idea)

ON-LINE SMALL BUSINESS WORKSHOP
(www.cbsc.org/osbw/workshop.html)

MARKET RESEARCH—WHERE TO FIND THE INFORMATION YOU NEED
(http://www.cbsc.org/alberta/tbl.cfm?fn=market_source)

GUIDES TO CANADIAN INDUSTRY
(strategis.ic.gc.ca/sc_indps/gci/engdoc/homepage.html)

CANADIAN STATISTICS
(www.statcan.ca/english/Pgdb/)

CANADIAN INDUSTRY STATISTICS
(strategis.ic.gc.ca/sc_ecnmy/sio/homepage.html)

CORPORATE INFORMATION CANADA
(www.corporateinformation.com/cacorp.html)

CANADA IN THE TWENTY-FIRST CENTURY
(strategis.ic.gc.ca/sc_ecnmy/mera/engdoc/02e.html)

HOME-BASED BUSINESS
(www.cbsc.org/english/search/display.cfm?CODE=4078&Coll=FE_FEDSBIS_E)

HOME BUSINESS
(www.life.ca/hb/index.html)

EXPORTSOURCE
(exportsource.gc.ca)

TAKE A WORLD VIEW: EXPORT YOUR SERVICES
(strategis.ic.gc.ca/SSG/sc01071e.html)

MARKET RESEARCH REPORTS MRR
(strategis.ic.gc.ca/SSG/bi18355e.html)

TABLE 6.2 OTHER PUBLISHED SOURCES OF MARKET INFORMATION

GENERAL

Gale Directory of Publications and Broadcast Media
Gale Research, Inc.
27500 Drake Road
Farmington Hills, MI, 48331
(www.gale.com)

The Standard Periodical Directory
Oxbridge Communications Inc.
150 Fifth Avenue
New York, NY 10011
(www.mediafinder.com)

Ulrich's Periodicals Directory
R.R. Bowker Company
REWP-North Building
121 Chanion Road
New Providence, NJ, 07974
(www.bowker.com) or
(www.ulrichsweb.com for the online version)

Indexes to books and magazine articles on a wide variety of business, industrial, and economic topics:

Bibliographic Index: A Cumulative Bibliography of Bibliographies
H.W. Wilson Co.
950 University Avenue
New York, NY 10452
(www.hwwilson.com)

Business Periodicals Index
H.W. Wilson Co.
950 University Avenue
New York, NY 10452
(www.hwwilson.com)

Canadian Business and Current Affairs (CBCA)
Micromedia Limited
158 Pearl Street
Toronto, Ontario M5H 1L3
(www.mmltd.com)

A detailed listing of source books, periodicals, directories, handbooks, and other sources of information on a variety of business topics:

Encyclopedia of Business Information Sources
Gale Research Company
27500 Drake Road
Farmington Hills, MI, 48331
(www.gale.com)

A general guide to business publications:

Business Information: How to Find it, How to Use it
Greenwood Publishing Group
BB Post Road W.
Westport CT, 06881
(www.greenwood.com)

Business Information Sources
University of California Press
2120 Berkeley Way
Berkeley, CA 94720
(www.ucpress.edu)

Directories of business-oriented databases:

Gale Directory of Databases
Gale Research Inc.
27500 Drake Road
Farmington Hills, MI, 48331
(www.gale.com)

LEXIS/NEXIS
Reed Elsevier
P.O. Box 933
Dayton, OH 45401
(www.lexis-nexis.com)

INDUSTRY AND MARKET INFORMATION

Data on income, population, expenditures, etc. by major market area:

Survey of Buying Power (annual special issue of Sales and Marketing Management)
Bill Communications, Inc.
770 Broadway
New York, NY 10003
(www.billcom.com)

Information on population size and growth, income, expenditures, prices, and similar data by market area:

FP Markets—Canadian Demographics
Financial Post Data Group
333 King Street East
Toronto, ON M5A 4N2
(www.financialpost.com/product/markets.htm)

Market Research Handbook
Statistics Canada
Ottawa, Ontario K1A 0T6
(www.fedpubs.com/mkthdbk.htm)

COMPANY INFORMATION

Detailed information on most major corporations:

Dun & Bradstreet Million Dollar Directory
Dun & Bradstreet Inc.
The D&B Corporation
One Diamond Hill Road
Murry Hill, NJ, 07974-1218
(www.dnb.com)

Wall Street Research Net
(www.wsrn.com)

Moody's Manuals and Investors Services
99 Church Street
New York, NY 10007
(www.moodys.com)

Listings of Canadian manufacturers by location and product category:

Fraser's Canadian Trade Directory
777 Bay Street
Toronto, Ontario M5W 1A7
(www.frasers.com)

Scott's Directories
Scottsinfo.com
1450 Don Mills Road
Don Mills Ontario M3B 2X7
(www.scottsinfo.com)

Scott's Directories:

- Ontario Manufacturers Directory
- Quebec Manufacturers Directory
- Greater Toronto Business Directory
- Greater Montreal and Laval Business Directory
- Atlantic Industrial Directory
- Western Industrial Directory

MARKETING INFORMATION

Listings of rates and other information on radio, television, consumer magazines, trade magazines, direct mail, and newspapers:

Canadian Advertising Rates & Data
Rogers Media Publishing
777 Bay Street, 5th Floor
Toronto, ON M5W 1A7
(www.cardmedia.com)

SRDS Headquarters
1700 Higgins Road
Des Plaines, IL 60018-5605
(www.srds.com)

SRDS Publications:
- Canadian Rates & Data
- Business Publication Advertising Source
- Consumer Magazine Advertising Source
- Newspaper Advertising Source
- Community Publication Advertising Source
- Out-of-Home Advertising Source
- Direct Marketing List Source
- Technology Media Source
- TV & Cable Source
- Radio Advertising Source
- Interactive Advertising Source
- International Media Guides

A listing of agents and firms representing manufacturers of all types:

Verified Directory of Manufacturer's Representatives
MacRae's Industrial Directories
87 Terminal Drive
Plainview, NY 11803

Manufacturer's Agents National Association Directory of Members
Manufacturer's Agents National Association
20316 Mill Creek Road
P.O. Box 3467
Laguna Hills, CA 92654
manaonline.org

Comprehensive listings of U.S. and Canadian meetings, conventions, trade shows, and expositions:

Conventions & Meetings Canada
777 Bay Street
Toronto, Ontario M5W 1A7
(www.meetingscanada.com)

Trade Shows Worldwide
Gale Research Inc.
27500 Drake Road
Farmington Hills, MI, 48331
(www.gale.com)

A comprehensive listing of mail order firms:

Mail Order Business Directory
B. Klein Publications
P.O. Box 8503
Coral Springs, FL 33065

Directory of Mail Order Catalogs
Grey House Publishing
185 Millerton Road
PO Box 850
Millerton, NY, 12546
(www.greyhouse.com)

Catalogue of Canadian Catalogues
Alpel Publishing
P.O. Box 203
Chambly, QC J3L 4B3

A comprehensive listing of all trade and professional associations in Canada:

Directory of Associations in Canada
Micromedia Ltd.
158 Pearl Street
Toronto, Ontario M5H 1L3
(www.mmltd.com)

FIGURE 6.2 DEVELOPING A MARKET OR CUSTOMER PROFILE

1. Define your target customers in terms of geography, demographic characteristics, or other factors.

2. How many of these target customers are in your trading or relevant market area?

3. What are the principal features and benefits these customers consider in the purchase of a product/service like yours?

4. What psychographic or sociological factors are likely to distinguish your target customers and be important in the purchase of a product/service like yours?

5. Why will they buy your product rather than your competitors'?

FIGURE 6.3 OUTLINE FOR A CUSTOMER SURVEY

Name of Customer ____________________

1. NATURE OF THE CUSTOMER'S BUSINESS OR ROLE

2. CUSTOMERS' REACTION TO YOUR PRODUCT OR SERVICE

a. What advantages/benefits do they see?

b. What disadvantages do they see?

c. What questions do they raise?

3. SPECIFIC NEEDS AND USES

a. What needs and uses do they have for a product/service such as yours?

4. SELLING PRICE, SERVICE, AND SUPPORT

a. What do you believe would be an acceptable selling price?

b. What level of service and support would they expect?

c. What other terms would they expect?

5. CURRENT PURCHASING PRACTICES

a. Where do they currently buy this type of product or service (retailer, wholesaler, direct mail, broker, etc.)?

continues

Outline for a Customer Survey — continued

6. NAME OF COMPETITIVE FIRMS

a. What competing firms' products and services are they currently using?

____

____

____

FIGURE 6.4 FORM FOR ESTIMATING MARKET SIZE

ESTIMATED TOTAL MARKET SIZE

1. DESCRIPTION OF PRINCIPAL MARKET

____

____

	200A	*200B*	*200C*	*200D*	*200E*
Estimated sales in units	______	______	______	______	______
Estimated sales in $000	______	______	______	______	______

2. OVERVIEW OF MAJOR SEGMENTS

a. Description of segment: ______________________________

____

	200A	200B	200C	200D	200E
Estimated sales in units	______	______	______	______	______
Estimated sales in $000	______	______	______	______	______

b. Description of segment: ______________________________

____

	200A	200B	200C	200D	200E
Estimated sales in units	______	______	______	______	______
Estimated sales in $000	______	______	______	______	______

FIGURE 6.5 FORM FOR ANALYZING YOUR COMPETITORS

Name of Competitor ______________________________ **Estimated Market Share** ______%

1. PRODUCT OR SERVICE

a. How does the company's product or service differ from other products and services in the marketplace? ______________________________

____

____

____

b. Do they offer a broad or narrow product line? ______________________________

____

c. Do they emphasize quality? ______________________________

2. PRICE

a. What is their average selling price?

b. What is their profit margin?

c. What type of discounts do they offer?

d. Do they emphasize a low selling price?

3. PROMOTION

a. How much do they spend on advertising and trade promotion?

b. How well known are they (brand recognition)?

c. Through which media do they advertise?

d. What other types of promotion do they use?

e. How many salespeople do they have?

4. DISTRIBUTION/LOCATION

a. What type of distribution intermediaries do they use (brokers, company sales force, direct to wholesaler, etc.)?

b. Where are they located?

c. Is location very important in this industry?

5. MARKETING STRATEGY

a. Does the company cater to any particular segment of the market?

b. Does the company offer some unique product or service that makes it different from other competitors?

c. Do they offer a particularly low price?

d. What is the principal factor that accounts for the success of this firm?

6. MARKET POSITION

a. What is their market share?

b. Have their sales been growing? Stable? Declining?

c. How successful are they?

7. MAJOR STRENGTHS AND WEAKNESSES

a. What are their major strengths?

b. What are their major weaknesses?

FIGURE 6.6 DEVELOPING A SALES FORECAST

1. Provide a summary overview of typical individuals, companies, or organizations that are likely prospects for your product/service offering as described in the market profile you prepared in Figure 6.2. Ask yourself such questions as: How old would these customers be? Where do they live? In what types of activities would they participate? What primary benefits are they looking for in my product or service? Etc.

____

____

____

____

____

2. How many of the people or organizations you have described as good prospects are in your trading area?

____

____

____

3. Describe how you feel these individuals or organizations would go about deciding whether to purchase your product/service rather than a competitor's offering. Would these potential customers be principally concerned with price, convenience, quality, or some other factor?

____

____

____

____

4. How often would prospective buyers purchase your product or service? Daily? Weekly? Monthly? Etc. Where would they look for it or expect to buy it? What kind of seasonal or other patterns are likely to influence sales? How will holidays or other special events affect sales patterns within a month? A year?

____

____

____

____

5. How much (in dollars and/or units) would a typical customer purchase on each buying occasion?

____

____

6. How would your customers likely hear about your product/service offering? Through newspapers? TV or radio advertisements? Word of mouth? Salespeople? Middlemen? Etc.

____

____

____

7. From the above information, estimate your expected annual sales in terms of *dollars* and/or *number of units*:
   By month for the first three years of operation of your business.

	1st Year	2nd Year	3rd Year
January	______	______	______
February	______	______	______
March	______	______	______
April	______	______	______
May	______	______	______
June	______	______	______
July	______	______	______
August	______	______	______
September	______	______	______
October	______	______	______
November	______	______	______
December	______	______	______

FIGURE 6.7 RATING FORM FOR SELECTING A RETAIL LOCATION

FACTOR A: PRIMARY ACCEPTANCE OR REJECTION FACTORS
(RATE YES OR NO)

	Location No. 1	2	3	4
1. Will municipal zoning allow the proposed business?	____	____	____	____
2. Does this site meet the minimum operating needs of the proposed business?	____	____	____	____
3. Do existing buildings meet minimum initial needs?	____	____	____	____
4. Is the rent for this location within your proposed operating budget?	____	____	____	____
5. Is the rent for this location, with or without buildings, reasonable?	____	____	____	____

One "No" answer may be sufficient reason not to proceed with further investigation unless some modification can be achieved.

FACTOR B: SITE EVALUATION
(USE PERCENTAGE SCALE 0 TO 100)

	Location No. 1	2	3	4
6. How does this location compare with the best possible location available?	____	____	____	____
7. What rating would you give the present buildings on the site?	____	____	____	____
8. How would you rate the overall environment of this location with the best environment existing within your trading area?	____	____	____	____
9. How would you rate the availability of parking for automobiles?	____	____	____	____
10. How would you rate the nature and quantity of combined foot and auto traffic passing your location?	____	____	____	____
11. What is the improvement potential of this location?	____	____	____	____
Total	____	____	____	____

continues

Rating Form for Selecting a Retail Location — continued

FACTOR C: TREND ANALYSIS
(COMPARE THE ANSWER FOR EACH LOCATION AND RANK EACH BY NUMBER FROM AMONG THOSE REVIEWED — i.e., 1ST, 2ND, 3RD, OR 4TH)

	Location No. 1	2	3	4
12. Has the location shown improvement through the years?	____	____	____	____
13. Is the owner and/or landlord progressive and cooperative?	____	____	____	____
14. What major patterns of change are affecting this location?	____	____	____	____
a. Streets: speed limits, paving	____	____	____	____
b. Shopping centres	____	____	____	____
c. Zoning	____	____	____	____
d. Financial investment	____	____	____	____
e. Dynamic leadership and action	____	____	____	____
f. Type of shopper or other potential customer	____	____	____	____
15. What businesses have occupied this location over the past 10 years?	____	____	____	____
16. Have the businesses identified in question 15 (above) been successful?	____	____	____	____
17. Why is this location now available?	____	____	____	____
18. Are a number of other suitable locations available?	____	____	____	____

FACTOR D: PRICE-VALUE DETERMINATION

	Location No. 1	2	3	4
19. What is the asking rent for each location?	____	____	____	____
20. What numerical total for each site is developed through questions 6 to 11?	____	____	____	____
21. Is there a "No" answer to any of questions 1 to 5?	____	____	____	____
22. Do the answers to questions 12 to 18 develop a pattern which is:	____	____	____	____
a. Highly favourable?	____	____	____	____
b. Average?	____	____	____	____
c. Fair?	____	____	____	____
d. Questionable?	____	____	____	____
e. Not acceptable?	____	____	____	____
Rank each location according to numerical totals and preferences as to subjective Factors C and D.	____	____	____	____

Adapted from M. Archer and J. White, *Starting and Managing Your Own Small Business* (Toronto: Macmillan Company of Canada, 1978), 38–40. Reproduced by permission.

FIGURE 6.8 **A FRAMEWORK FOR DEVELOPING A PRELIMINARY MARKETING PLAN**

1. DEFINE YOUR GOALS

You need to start this process by defining two sets of goals:

- personal goals, and
- business goals.

a. Your personal goals need to be defined first. You want to be certain that the business you are considering is compatible with the attainment of your personal goals.

Your Personal Goals

How much money do you want, or need, to earn? ______________________________

____

____

What sort of lifestyle is desirable for you and your family? ______________________

____

____

How will your business reflect you and your values? ___________________________

____

____

What are your risk parameters? What is your tolerance for risk?___________________

____

____

What do you want to achieve in five years?____________________________________

____

____

b. Your business goals need to be defined next. These are general statements of business intentions that you are aiming to accomplish, results that your business is committed to achieving over time. You can define your business goals by using such terms as "becoming the leading firm in this industry within this market" or "being the lowest cost or most efficient or most widely recognized business of its type with this area." Goals may also be more modestly defined such as to build "a business large enough to provide an income stream that will enable you to quit your current job."

Your Business Goals

How big do you want your business to be? ___________________________________

____

____

____

What general goals would you like your business to achieve? _____________________

____

____

____

continues

A Framework for Developing a Preliminary Marketing Plan — continued

2. WHAT DO YOU PLAN TO SELL?

You have given some thought to the concept or idea you would like to investigate as a prospective business opportunity. Now you need to translate that notion into a clear definition of your business and a description of the broad range of products and services you plan to offer. If you are able to explain clearly and succinctly what products or services you plan to sell, to whom, and why you think they will buy from you, you are well on the way to developing an effective marketing plan. Generally describe your proposed product/service offerings and whom you see as being your principal target market for each offering or your whole line. If you have many products/services, try to bundle them together into no more than five categories. You can always expand the list later—but for now, keep it simple.

Product/Service Offering

	Product/Service	*Primary Target Markets*
1.	______________	______________
2.	______________	______________
3.	______________	______________
4.	______________	______________
5.	______________	______________

3. ESTABLISH PRELIMINARY SALES ESTIMATES

For each of the products/services in your line, estimate what you feel your sales could be if everything went perfectly after you started up your business. What would your sales be if everything went wrong? What figure in between these two estimates do think represents the most likely case?

Preliminary Sales Estimates

	Sales Goals for Each Product/Service		
	Worst Case	*Most Likely Case*	*Best Case*
1.	$ ______________	$ ______________	$ ______________
2.	$ ______________	$ ______________	$ ______________
3.	$ ______________	$ ______________	$ ______________
4.	$ ______________	$ ______________	$ ______________
5.	$ ______________	$ ______________	$ ______________

Comments:

____

____

____

____

____

4. ESTIMATE TOTAL MARKET SIZE AND TRENDS

A major component of market opportunity analysis and developing a marketing plan is determining the overall volume of unit sales, or dollar revenue, that may flow from a market. When analyzing market potential and size, it is important to refer only to that portion of the market you will be serving. For example, if you are only planning to deal with customers in Edmonton, or part of Edmonton, it does not make sense to include Calgary, Regina, or Toronto in your assessment of market size. On the other hand, if you hope to sell your product regionally or nationally, then those are the relevant market areas to be considered.

In addition to this broad analysis, you might also investigate whether, within this major market area, there are groups of potential buyers with different preferences, requirements, or purchasing practices. This process of breaking large heterogeneous markets down into more homogeneous groups is known as market segmentation. This term should be familiar to you from your reading of Stage 6 in this book.

Most markets can be segmented on the basis of a number of variables:

- geographic location (such as a part of a city or town, county, province, region, or country)
- demographic characteristics (such as age, sex, income, occupation, marital status, race, religion, or education). Institutional, industrial, and government markets can be classified on the basis or their S.I.C. category, their total purchases or sales, number of employees, or the nature of their organizational activity.
- a variety of sociological factors (such as lifestyle, user status, usage rate, timing and means of purchasing, and/or reasons for buying products similar to yours).

You can use the following templates to estimate approximate total market size (past, present, and future) and expected trends in terms of sales for your product or service type. You should do this for both the principal market and the market segments that may pertain to your product/service offering.

To obtain the information needed to complete this worksheet, there are a number of sources you may wish to consult. These have been mentioned earlier in Stage 6, but include:

- trade publications, trade shows, and the trade associations for the industry in which your business will compete
- your local Chamber of Commerce or municipal office
- any local or regional economic development corporations or school board offices
- business resource centres and other agencies of your provincial government
- your Canada Business Services Centre of Industry Canada
- downtown business associations
- advertising agencies, local newspapers, radio and television stations
- your future competitors and prospective customers
- similar businesses in other locations
- prospective suppliers and their sales representatives
- commercial suppliers of industry studies and market research reports
- the Internet

Estimated Market Size—Principal Market

Description of Principal Market

____

____

____

____

____

	Two Years Ago	Last Year	This Year	Next Year	Two Years From Now
Sales in units	______	______	______	______	______
Sales in $000	______	______	______	______	______

continues

A Framework for Developing a Preliminary Marketing Plan — continued

Overview of Market Segments

Describe each major segment and the principal product or service to be offered. Then, complete market size estimates for each segment.

	Description of Segment	*Principal Product/ Service Benefits*
1.	____________	____________
2.	____________	____________
3.	____________	____________
4.	____________	____________
5.	____________	____________

	Two Years Ago	Last Year	This Year	Next Year	Two Years From Now
Sales in units	______	______	______	______	______
Sales in $000	______	______	______	______	______

	Description of Segment	*Principal Product/ Service Benefits*
1.	____________	____________
2.	____________	____________
3.	____________	____________
4.	____________	____________
5.	____________	____________

	Two Years Ago	Last Year	This Year	Next Year	Two Years From Now
Sales in units	______	______	______	______	______
Sales in $000	______	______	______	______	______

	Description of Segment	*Principal Product/ Service Benefits*
1.	____________	____________
2.	____________	____________
3.	____________	____________
4.	____________	____________
5.	____________	____________

	Two Years Ago	Last Year	This Year	Next Year	Two Years From Now
Sales in units	______	______	______	______	______
Sales in $000	______	______	______	______	______

	Description of Segment	*Principal Product/ Service Benefits*
1.	______	______
2.	______	______
3.	______	______
4.	______	______
5.	______	______

	Two Years Ago	Last Year	This Year	Next Year	Two Years From Now
Sales in units	______	______	______	______	______
Sales in $000	______	______	______	______	______

5. ANALYZE YOUR COMPETITION

Unless your product is a "new to the world" innovation, it will have to compete with other products and services that perform a similar function. You have probably identified a number of other firms that offer products and services designed to meet the same customer need as yours. It is important you have a thorough understanding of each of these firms and the way it conducts its business. To obtain this perspective fill in a copy of this worksheet for each major competitor you have identified. This will enable you to get a better understanding of the sales and market share you might achieve, and the nature of the marketing program you could employ, to obtain a comparative advantage.

These competitors will likely not cooperate in providing you with this information directly. You may have to rely on articles in the newspaper and the trade press, corporate annual reports, trade association reports and publications, and your own personal investigation to get all the information you require.

Form for Analyzing Your Competitors

Competitor Name:(Insert name of competitor here) ______

Estimated Market Share (%): ______

1. PRODUCT OR SERVICE

a. How does the company's product or service differ from other products and services in the marketplace? ______
b. Do they offer a broad or narrow product line? ______
c. Do they emphasize quality? ______

2. PRICE

a. What is their average selling price? ______
b. What is their profit margin? ______
c. What type of discounts do they offer? ______
d. Do they emphasize a low selling price? ______

3. PROMOTION

a. How much do they spend on advertising and trade promotion? ______
b. How well known are they (brand recognition)? ______
c. Through which media do they advertise? ______
d. What other types of promotion do they use? ______
e. How many salespeople do they have? ______

continues

A Framework for Developing a Preliminary Marketing Plan — continued

4. DISTRIBUTION LOCATION

a. What type of distribution intermediaries do they use (brokers, company sales force, direct to wholesaler, etc.)? ______
b. Where are they located? ______
c. Is location very important in this industry? ______

5. MARKETING STRATEGY

a. Does the company cater to any particular segment of the market? ______
b. Does the company offer some unique product or service that makes it different from other competitors? ______
c. Do they offer a particularly low price? ______
d. What is the principal factor that accounts for the success of this firm? ______

6. MARKET POSITION

a. What is their market share? ______
b. Have their sales been growing? Stable? Declining? ______
c. How successful are they? ______

7. MAJOR STRENGTHS AND WEAKNESSES

a. What are their major strengths? ______
b. What are their major weaknesses? ______

6. DEFINE A BUDGET

Before spelling out the details of your tentative marketing program, you need to have some idea of the resources needed to implement it. This entails developing some sort of budget indicating what you feel is required to achieve your sales and profit goals, and how these expenditures should be distributed across the range of marketing activities. This worksheet provides a starting point for you to estimate the marketing expenditures you will have to make during your first year to get your business successfully off the ground. This is not an exhaustive list. Use it as a starting point. Your company will use some of these categories plus others peculiar to your marketing needs.

Tentative Marketing Budget

1. Selling (direct costs)
   Sales salaries and commissions: $ ______
   Travel & Entertainment $ ______
2. Selling (indirect costs) Training
   Marketing research $ ______
   Subscriptions and dues $ ______
3. Advertising $ ______
4. Sales promotion other than advertising $ ______
5. Public relations $ ______

6. Marketing administration $ ____________
7. Other items $ ____________

7. FLESH OUT YOUR MARKETING PROGRAM

You are now in a position to bring together everything you have learned about the total market potential for your product or service, customer attitudes toward your offering, and the nature of the competitive environment you will be facing. The goal is to put down on paper a preliminary marketing strategy, or plan, for your new venture concept. This involves making decisions regarding what you feel is an appropriate marketing mix for your business. The principal ingredients that must be blended together to form your overall strategy can be grouped together under the headings of:

- product or service offering
- pricing program
- promotional plans
- distribution strategy

This worksheet provides an outline to help you to lay out your marketing plans and programs.

Outline for a Preliminary Marketing Plan

YOUR CONCEPT

Describe the principal concept underlying your product or service idea.

What is unique or distinctive about your idea? How does it differ from similar concepts already being employed in the marketplace?

Who will be the primary customers for your concept and what are the principal benefits your concept will deliver to them?

How innovative is your concept? How would you categorize it along the continuum from "copycatting" to being an entirely new invention?

continues

A Framework for Developing a Preliminary Marketing Plan — continued

Is your idea technically feasible? Have you built a working model or prototype? Will you have to obtain Canadian Standards Association (CSA) approval or other permissions before the concept can be marketed?

PRODUCTS AND SERVICES

What products or services will you sell? Be specific.

What additional customer services (delivery, repair, warranties, etc.) will you offer?

What is unique about your total product or service offering?

CUSTOMERS

Define your target customers. (Who are they?)

How many target customers are in your trading area?

Why will they buy your product?

COMPETITION

Who are your principal competitors? What is their market position? Have their sales been growing? Stable? Declining?

How does your concept differ from each of these other products or services?

LOCATION

What location have you selected for your business?

Why did you choose that location?

PRICING

Describe your pricing strategy.

continues

A Framework for Developing a Preliminary Marketing Plan — continued

Complete the following table of markups from manufacturer to final customer:

Cost to manufacture	(A)	__________
Manufacturer's markup	(B)	__________
Manufacturer's selling price	(C = A + B)	__________
Agent's commission (if applicable)	(D)	__________
Wholesaler's cost	(E = C + D)	__________
Wholesaler's markup	(F)	__________
Wholesaler's selling price	(G = E + F)	__________
Retailer's markup	(H)	__________
Retailer's selling price	(I = G + H)	__________

How do your planned price levels compare to your competitors?

PROMOTION

What will your primary promotional message to potential customers be?

What will your promotion budget be?

What media will you use for your advertising program?

Will you have a cooperative advertising program? Describe it.

Describe your trade promotion program.

Describe any publicity, public relations, or sales promotion program you will have.

DISTRIBUTION

How do you plan to distribute your product? Direct to the consumer? Through traditional distribution channels? Through specialty channels such as exhibitions, mail order, or trade shows?

Will you employ your own sales force or rely on the services of agents or brokers? How many?

Once you have completed this series of worksheets you will have obtained a better understanding of the likely market opportunity for your concept or idea, and thought through the process of determining how you feel it can be most effectively marketed. This is an essential step in deciding whether the concept really does represent a worthwhile opportunity that ought to be aggressively pursued or should be abandoned. This is also a key part of your business plan. Most of this information represents the foundation upon which the business plan is built and can be directly transferred to that document.

Conducting a Feasibility Study

Part 2: Cost and Profitability Assessment

In addition to determining the size and nature of the market for your new venture idea, it is also important to consider the financial components of your business. The costs associated with operating your business may include labour, materials, rent, machinery, etc. Collecting potential sales and cost information should put you in a better position to make reasonably accurate financial forecasts that can be used not only as a check on the advisability of proceeding with the venture but also for raising capital, if required.

DETERMINE YOUR START-UP FINANCIAL REQUIREMENTS

The process of financial analysis begins with an estimate of the funds required to set up your business. Your start-up financial requirements can be broken down into two components:

1. **One-time expenditures** that must be made before your business can open its doors. These include both *capital expenditures* for the purchase or lease of furniture, fixtures, equipment, or the purchase of your beginning inventory and *soft costs* relating to such items as utility deposits and fees, pre-opening advertising and promotion expenses, and other prepaid expenses. In the case of a retail or manufacturing business, these requirements can be considerable, while a service business may not require a very large initial expenditure to get started. Remember what we are trying to determine here is the amount of *cash* that will be needed to get your business launched. For example, a piece of equipment you require may cost $20,000, but if the seller is prepared to take a deposit of $5,000 and finance the rest or if you will be leasing the equipment for $500/month rather then buying it outright, only your out-of-pocket cash cost needs to be factored in and not the total cost of the item. A typical example showing the estimated one-time financial requirements for the start-up of Tough Guys Sporting Goods is illustrated in Figure 7.1.
2. **Operating expenses** such as payments for your and your employees' wages, rent, operating supplies, telephone and postage, promotion, and other ongoing expenses that must be incurred until the business begins to show a profit. Many new businesses take several months or even years before they operate "in the black." Sufficient funds must be available to cover a minimum of two to three months' operations and provide a cash

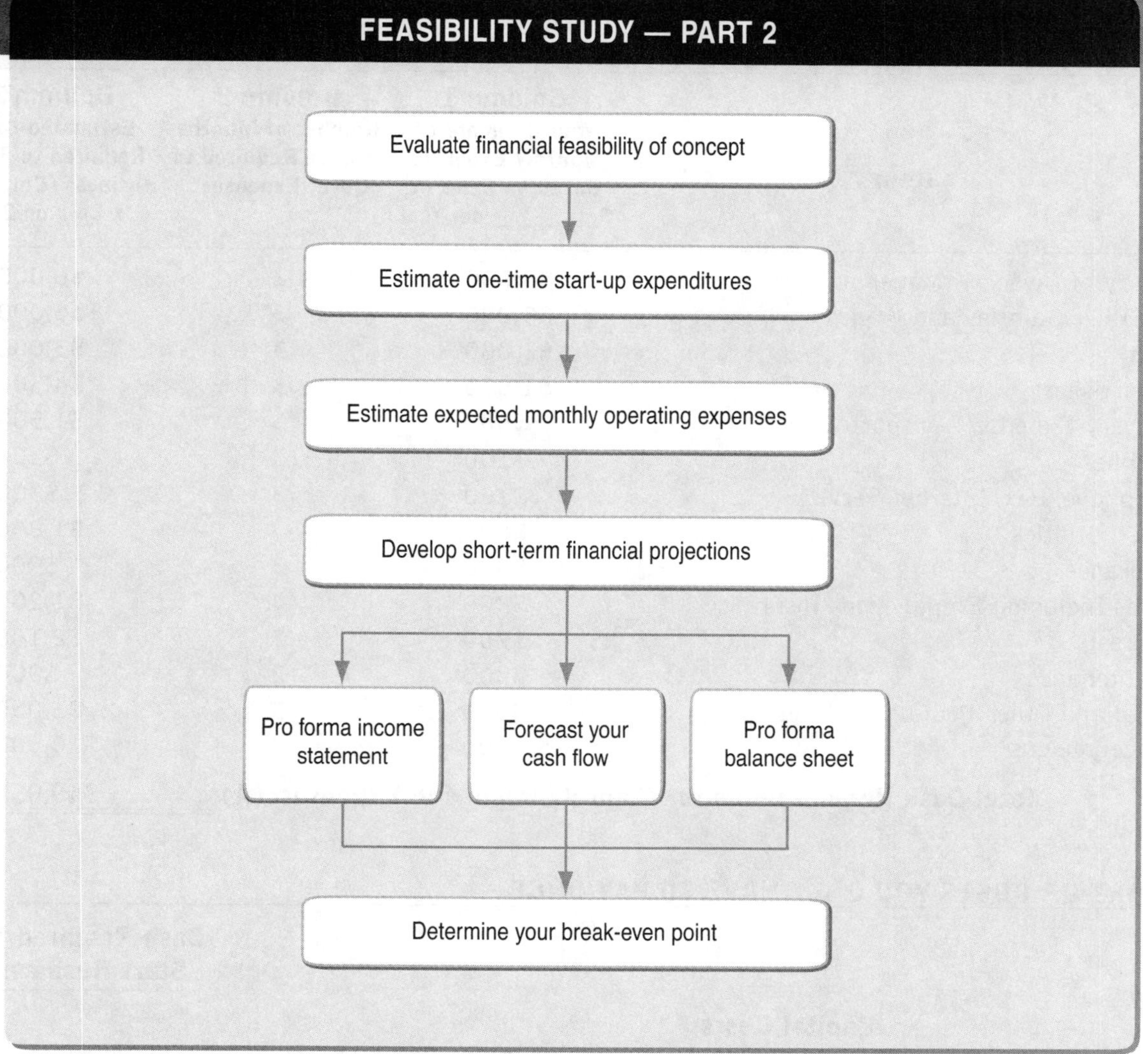

reserve for emergency situations. One way to determine just how much cash you might require is to review your cash flow statement to see how long it takes before your business reaches a positive cash flow situation. If, for example, it is not until the sixth month after you open your doors, you will need enough cash to cover your expected losses up to that time plus some additional cash as a safety factor. An example showing the estimated funds required to cover these initial operating expenses for Tough Guys is also illustrated in Figure 7.1.

Note that a sporting goods store, like many retail businesses, is a relatively capital-intensive business to start. The bulk of the money is required to finance the initial inventory you will need to stock the store, while most of the remaining one-time funds go to decorating and providing the necessary fixtures for the store. In addition, you should have approximately $40,000 available to cover your estimated monthly expenses until the business starts generating a positive cash flow. You do not necessarily have to have the entire cash requirements available strictly from your own resources; $100,000 – $150,000 may be sufficient. Suppliers may be prepared to grant you credit terms so that you do not necessarily have to pay for some of your stock for 30 or 60 days. Or the bank may be prepared to extend a term loan or line of credit to you that you can draw on to meet some of your working capital requirements as they arise.

Insufficient financing is a major cause of new business failure, so you should be certain you have sufficient financing to cover both your estimated one-time and your initial operating expenses.

FIGURE 7.1 ESTIMATED START-UP REQUIREMENTS FOR A SPORTING GOODS STORE

ESTIMATED MONTHLY EXPENSES

Item	Column 1 Your Estimate of Monthly Expenses Based on Sales of $________ per Year	Column 2 Number of Months of Cash Required to Cover Expenses*	Column 3 Estimated Cash Required to Start Business (Column 1 x Column 2)*
Salary of Owner-Manager	$3,000	2	$6,000
All Other Salaries and Wages	$5,000	3	$15,000
Rent	$1,000	3	$3,000
Advertising	$1,500	3	$4,500
Delivery Expense/Transportation	$500	3	$1,500
Supplies	$100	3	$300
Telephone, Fax, Internet Service	$100	3	$300
Other Utilities	$600	3	$1,800
Insurance	$300	3	$900
Taxes Including Employment Insurance	$300	4	$1,200
Interest	$700	3	$2,100
Maintenance	$300	3	$900
Legal and Other Professional Fees	$350	3	$1,050
Miscellaneous	$3,500	3	$10,500
Total Cash Requirements for Monthly Recurring Expenses: (A)			**$49,050**

START-UP COSTS YOU ONLY HAVE TO PAY ONCE

		Cash Required to Start Business
Capital Costs		
	Fixtures and Equipment	$40,000
	Decorating and Remodelling	$10,000
	Installation of Fixtures and Equipment	$5,600
	Starting Inventory	$195,000
Soft Costs		
	Deposits with Utilities	$2,000
	Legal and Other Professional Fees	$1,500
	Licences and Permits	$800
	Advertising and Promotion for Opening	$2,500
	Accounts Receivable	$8,000
	Cash	$5,000
	Other	$5,000
	Total One-Time Cash Requirements: (B)	**$275,400**
	TOTAL ESTIMATED CASH REQUIRED TO START BUSINESS: (A) + (B)	**$324,450**

* These figures may be typical for one kind of business. You will have to decide how many months to allow for your business to offset expected shortages of cash flow.

DEVELOP SHORT-TERM FINANCIAL PROJECTIONS

PRO FORMA INCOME STATEMENT

The next step is to develop your projected operating statement, or *pro forma income statement*. This involves estimating the expected profit or loss by your business. Simply put, the basic formula to calculate profit and loss is:

Revenue – Expenses = Net Profit before Taxes

This means you will have to estimate your total expected revenue and expenses for at least the first year of operation of your business.

An income statement then measures your company's sales and expenses during a specified period of time—usually a month or a year. Its function is to total all sources of revenue for the business and subtract all expenses related to generating that revenue. It shows a company's financial performance over a period of time, and the heading of the income statement should always indicate the time period that is being examined; i.e., for the month ending, for the year ending, etc.

The information you must be able to provide to construct a pro forma income statement includes:

1. Your predicted sales volume for the period for which you are making the forecast or your projected *Net Sales*.
2. How much it is expected to cost to produce or purchase the products you will sell or your projected *Cost of Goods Sold*.
3. Your *Fixed Operating Expenses* such as rent, utilities, insurance premiums, and interest costs.
4. Your controllable or *Variable Operating Expenses* such as advertising and promotion expenses, wages and salaries, and delivery expenses.
5. Your expected *Net Operating Profit or Loss*.

Net Sales is the total sales plus any transportation costs you expect to make during the month or year being examined *minus* any cash discounts, trade discounts, or expected returns.

Cost of Goods Sold is often called Cost of Sales. For retail and wholesale businesses it is the total price paid for the products you expect to sell during the period for which you are developing the forecast. It is just the price of the goods. It does not include selling and other expenses. These are shown elsewhere on the income statement.

For most service and professional businesses, there will be no cost of goods sold. These businesses receive their income from fees, commissions, and royalties so don't typically have inventories of physical products. Their costs to provide these services are included in the fixed and variable operating expense sections of the statement.

Most small retail and wholesale businesses determine their cost of goods sold by:

- determining the value of their inventory at the beginning of the period being projected,
- adding the value of any products purchased during the period, and then
- subtracting the value of any inventory left at the end of the period.

This calculation will provide a value for the amount of inventory actually sold during the period for which you are developing the projection. Net sales minus cost of goods sold yields your expected *Gross Margin* or Gross Profit.

Fixed Expenses are operating expenses or overhead that you must pay regardless of your expected level of sales. These include expenses such as rent, telephone, insurance premiums, business taxes and licences, and interest as well as some provision for depreciation on any capital assets used in the business.

Variable Expenses are those that are expected to rise and fall in proportion to your sales. These include most of your selling expenses such as sales salaries and commissions, travel costs, advertising and promotion, delivery and vehicle expenses, and similar costs.

Net Operating Profit or Loss is the difference between your gross margin and your fixed and variable operating expenses. This is your expected net profit or loss before any consideration of federal or provincial income taxes.

The creation of a pro forma income statement is an important event for a small business. It provides a summary of many of the important activities of the company and provides valuable information to both you as a prospective owner and to others who may be looking to lend money or potentially invest in your business.

One means of developing a pro forma income statement for your business is to follow the Desired Income Approach suggested by Szonyi and Steinhoff.[1] This approach enables you to develop financial projections on the basis of the actual operating performance of firms similar to the business you are contemplating. It also suggests that your business should provide you with not only a return for the time you will spend running the business but also a return on the personal funds you have to invest to launch the business. For example, instead of starting a business, you could keep your present job or obtain another one and earn a salary working for someone else. You could also invest your money in common stocks, bonds, guaranteed income certificates, or other investments, where it would yield some kind of return. Both possibilities should be kept in mind for comparison purposes when determining the expected minimum level of acceptable profit performance of your new venture.

To illustrate this approach, assume you are considering the possibility of opening a retail sporting goods store like the one we discussed before. You have determined that you would like to have a salary of $40,000/year from the business, plus $15,000 as a reasonable return on the investment you will have to make in the business. These represent your desired income and return levels. By referring to Dun & Bradstreet Canada information, Robert Morris and Associates Industry Statement Studies, or the Industry Canada Performance Plus Small Business Profiles you can obtain comprehensive financial data on sporting goods stores as well as dozens of other different lines of business.

Combining the information about your desired income and return goals with some of this published data will enable you to develop a pro forma income statement highlighting the level of operations you will have to reach to achieve your goals. The additional information you require is:

- **The average inventory turnover for this type of business** is the number of times a typical firm's inventory is sold each year. If the business carries an inventory of $25,000 and its overall net revenue is $150,000, inventory turnover is six times per year.
- **The average gross margin** is the difference between the firm's net sales and cost of goods sold, expressed as a percentage. For example, if the business's net sales are $200,000 while cost of goods sold total $140,000, its gross margin is $60,000 or 30 per cent.
- **Net profit** as a percentage of sales is relatively self-explanatory. It can be determined either before or after the application of any federal or provincial taxes. In the case of the Performance Plus Small Business Profiles, it is shown before the application of any taxes.

DEVELOPING THE STATEMENT

With this data and an estimate of your desired salary and return levels, you can construct a pro forma income statement for a sporting goods store. Checking the 1997 Industry Canada Performance Plus Small Business Profiles for SIC code J6541 – Sporting Goods Stores (sme.ic.gc.ca) provides us with the following information:

Inventory turnover	3.4 times per year
Gross margin	34.4% of sales
Net profit as a percentage of sales	2.1%

Figure 7.2 illustrates how this data, along with the information about your desired salary and return, can be used to develop a pro forma income statement. This statement indicates the minimum level of sales your business will have to generate to provide you with your desired salary and level of profitability. Sales above this level will probably provide a higher level of profits, while lower sales will likely mean you will not make as much money as you had hoped. It is assumed in this evaluation that your business will be operated as efficiently, and in a similar manner to, other sporting goods stores across the country.

All the figures in this statement have been computed from our ratio data and our stated desired salary and return on investment. For example:

1. Our $15,000 desired profit is inserted on line (E).
2. Profits for a retail sporting goods store are very slim, at only 2.1% of sales. To determine the sales level required to provide our desired level of profitability, we divide $15,000 by 0.021 to obtain our estimate of the required level of $714,000 for net sales on line (A).

1 A. J. Szonyi and D. Steinhoff, *Small Business Management Fundamentals*, 3rd Canadian ed. (Toronto: McGraw-Hill Ryerson, 1988), pp. 58-65.

3. Our statistics indicate that sporting goods stores typically have an average gross margin of 34.4 per cent of net sales. In our situation this would provide a gross margin estimate of $246,000 on line (C).
4. The difference between our estimated net sales and gross margin has to provide for our cost of goods sold. In this example our cost of goods sold will be $714,000 – $246,000 = $468,000 on line (B).
5. Sporting goods stores have a relatively low level of inventory turnover in comparison with other types of retail business. A typical retail firm will turn over its inventory from six to seven times per year, while our statistics indicate a turnover ratio of only 3.4 times for our sporting goods store. This means we need to have more money tied up in inventory to support our estimated level of net sales than most other retailers. Our projected average inventory level can be determined by dividing our net sales revenue by the inventory turnover rate or $714,000/3.4 = $210,000.
6. The difference between our expected gross margin and the net operating profit (before taxes) necessary to provide our desired income level represents our total operating expenses in line (D). In this case $246,000 – $15,000 = $231,000 should be available to cover such expenses as our salary and that of our employees, rent, insurance, promotion, interest, and similar expenses. Note that our expected salary of $40,000 has to be included in this amount.

FIGURE 7.2 SAMPLE PRO FORMA INCOME STATEMENT

TOUGH GUYS SPORTING GOODS PRO FORMA INCOME STATEMENT
FOR THE YEAR ENDING [DATE]

Net Sales		$714,000 **(A)**
Less: Cost of goods sold		
Beginning Inventory	$195,000	
Plus: Net purchases	483,000	
Goods available for sale	$678,000	
Less: Ending Inventory	210,000	
Cost of goods sold		468,000 **(B)**
Gross margin		$246,000 **(C)**
Operating Expenses		231,000 **(D)**
Net Profit (Loss) before Income Tax		**$15,000 (E)**

This pro forma statement shows you the level of sales, investment in inventory, and similar information you need to know to generate the level of income you feel you need to obtain from the business.

The statement constructed in Figure 7.2 is based upon the distinct financial characteristics of a small, retail sporting goods business and relates only to that situation. A pro forma income statement for a store in another line of business could look very different due to variations in inventory turnover, gross margin percentage, and other factors reflecting the different character of that business.

This is even more true if we are considering the start-up of a service business or a manufacturing company. Service firms, like drycleaners and management consultants, typically do not carry an inventory of goods for resale and so don't have a "cost of goods sold" section on their income statement. Manufacturing companies, on the other hand, may have several types of inventory — raw materials, work in process, and finished goods. Appropriate levels for all three types of inventories should be determined and reflected in the projected income statement. The statement also tries to determine the value of raw materials and components, direct labour, factory overhead, and other inputs required to manufacture a product suitable for sale. This "cost of goods manufactured" replaces the cost of goods sold component on the pro forma statement.

DETERMINING REASONABLE OPERATING EXPENSES

So far, our pro forma income statement has lumped all our business's projected operating expenses together under a single heading. For example, Figure 7.2 shows our overall, estimated operating expenses to be $231,000. This means that all operating expenses must be covered by this amount if we are to achieve our desired level of profitability.

The same statistical sources used to obtain the data for our overall pro forma statement can be used to obtain a breakdown of the typical operating expenses for our type of business. For example, the Performance Plus Small Business Profiles provide data on the operating results of sporting goods stores. It indicates the following breakdown of operating expenses as a percentage of sales for the average firm:

Advertising	2.9%
Delivery expenses	0.8%
Depreciation	1.0%
Wages, salaries, and benefits	15.6%
Insurance	0.5%
Interest and bank charges	1.2%
Professional fees	0.6%
Rent	1.6%
Repairs and maintenance	0.5%
Fuel	0.1%
Utilities	1.0%
Other expenses	6.6%

These expenses total approximately 32.4 per cent of sales. If we translate these percentages to our pro forma income statement, we can obtain an approximation of the detailed breakdown of our operating expenses in dollar terms. Our finalized pro forma income statement would look like Figure 7.3.

This complete pro forma statement can now serve as part of your plan for outlining the requirements of your proposed new business venture or as a guide or schedule to monitor the ongoing performance of your new business during its early stages.

A typical pro forma statement that you can use for projecting the first-year operating performance of your new business is illustrated in the Outline for a Feasibility Study (Figure 7.7) at the back of this Stage.

FORECAST YOUR CASH FLOW

Your next step is to bring the operating profit or loss you have projected closer to reality by developing a cash flow forecast. It traces the expected flow of funds into and out of your business over some period of time. Cash flow is the lifeblood of any business. Therefore, this cash flow analysis is the most important document you will compile in assessing the financial feasibility of your business idea and also enables you to control the financial affairs of your business. It is quite a complex financial statement, so will require you to have some basic understanding of general accounting concepts to prepare it properly. As illustrated in Entrepreneurs in Action #25, failure to plan adequately for their future cash requirements is one of the principal reasons small businesses don't survive. Greg and Kate Williams's failure to estimate accurately the incoming revenue for the one-hour photo shop they purchased caused them not only to lose the business and the money they had invested in it but to have to declare personal bankruptcy as well. An accurate cash flow forecast can be your best means of ensuring continued financial solvency and the survival of your business.

Cash flow statements are similar to but differ from income statements in a number of ways. Cash flow is exactly as the name implies. The statement only measures the flow of cash into and out of the business. Non-cash accounting entries that may show up on an income statement such as depreciation, amortization, and asset transfers are ignored in forecasting the cash flow statement. Similarly, expenses that have been incurred but not yet paid and income that has been earned but not yet received are not included in the cash flow statement either.

The need for a cash flow analysis originates from the reality that in most businesses there is a time discrepancy between when your expenditures are incurred and when the cash is actually realized from the sale of the products or services you provide.

25 Entrepreneurs in action

Over the Edge

Greg and Kate Williams (their names have been changed) were only in their early fifties when Greg took early retirement. Still youthful and vigorous, the Williams had a mortgage to repay, car payments to make and three children in their twenties who still relied on their parents for the occasional handout between jobs. The Williams weren't rich, but they weren't worried either. They'd arrived in Canada from Scotland in 1966 with just $132 between them. Within days of their arrival, they were hard at work. A draughtsman by training, Kate found a job with the provincial government. Greg worked in a beer store, laid floor tile, maintained an apartment building and worked for Sears. Then, in 1969, he joined the city police force. "I was 26 and fit as a fiddle," he recalls.

As the years passed, the Williams saved their money, bought a new house for $19,000, sold it for $30,000 and moved to a larger house farther out of the city. By the late 1970s, their family included two daughters and a son. To earn more money, they opened a video store in the mid-1980s. "It went very well," Kate says, "but with three kids at home, we had to choose finally between running the business and raising our children. The kids were getting neglected."

By then, Greg was within sight of early retirement. He'd served the police force well, as an officer on the beat, a detective and an undercover officer. In 1988, Greg and Kate moved to a resort community about two hours from the city. They paid $119,000 for their one-year-old house, just as real-estate prices in the province began to soar. For the next seven years, until June, 1995, Greg drove back and forth to work.

Before he left the police force "with exemplary service," Greg and Kate found a retail venture that would keep them busy and make some money to augment their savings and pension income. They met the owner of a one-hour photo shop in a nearby town, who wanted to sell out. For $60,000—less than half the price of new equipment alone—the Williams bought the business lock, stock and barrel. The former owner taught them how to operate the developing unit, and the Williams took over in May, 1995. In June, Greg retired. And in November, when the lease expired, the Williams moved the shop from its original location to a newly built shopping mall in their home town.

The move was part of the Williams' plan. Before they invested in the business, they'd learned from their town planners that a photo shop was one of about a dozen businesses the town would need as it expanded over the next few years. Based on the current population of the town — about 11,000 — the Williams calculated the shop could break even if only one in four people in town used their shop to develop photographs, buy film and purchase the occasional picture frame, battery, camera strap or lens. Based on their business plan, the Williams had arranged financing through a local economic-development corporation, which provided a loan of $40,000, and through a local finance company, which provided another $10,000 to cover leasehold improvements. They raised $10,000 privately and scraped together the same amount from their own money. By the time they opened the new store, it had cost the Williams almost $75,000. "The store was beautiful," Kate says. "It was a treat for people to come into."

Unfortunately, not many people came. A couple of local real-estate agents used it to prepare photos and brochures for advertising. But with the resort closed down for the winter, there just weren't enough people walking through the door.

As 1996 began, the Williams realized they were in trouble. Rent alone cost them $1,400 a month. On top of that, they paid taxes and utilities. The Williams also realized they weren't competing on a level field with other one-hour photo services in the area. Department, grocery and drug-store chains have a steady demand for their services; they also pay far less for their equipment and supplies than the Williams since they buy in volume. A roll of developing paper, for example, for which the Williams paid $142 costs the chains about $60. And because of the volume of photographs the big chains develop, they receive the same equipment as the Williams $60,000 unit free of charge. No wonder they could develop a roll of film for $2 to $3 less than the Williams charged.

The fewer people who patronized the shop, the more expensive it became to run the place. The chemicals in the developing unit, which sat unused for days at a time, went bad and had to be replaced almost monthly, at a cost of $600. The rent had to be paid, whether there were customers or not. Greg began siphoning money from a retirement account he'd set up with the contributory surplus from his police pension, then had to find more money to cover the income tax on the withdrawals. By November, 1996, Greg and Kate knew they were in trouble. "Everything that was coming in was going out again," says Greg, "but it still wasn't enough."

A financial consultant suggested they close the store and enjoy their Christmas, but the Williams hung on until February, 1997, when they finally closed the store for good. Even then, they owed only $71,000, excluding their house and equipment. But as Diane Hessel of A. Farber & Partners Inc., observes, "It might as well have been $71 million for the Williams."

Besides, they didn't distinguish between their personal and business debts. No matter how you described it to them, a debt was a debt, and they had a lot of them. In addition to their loan from the local economic-development corporation, they owed another $17,000 to the credit union that had advanced them funds for a previous debt and leasehold improvements, more than $9,500 to their equipment supplier and another $11,000 to Revenue Canada for tax on their previous video business. Along with their own personal debts on their van and house, the Williams owed a total of $229,000; their assets amounted to about $158,000.

On February 27, 1997, the Williams filed for bankruptcy. They expected their bankruptcy to proceed smoothly through the courts, but in October, two of their creditors opposed the Williams' application for discharge—which meant that, unlike the other creditors, they insisted on a court hearing, when they would seek some form of compensation from the estate. Under the stress of their financial predicament and after 25 years of police work, Greg Williams suffered an angina attack. In January, 1998, he underwent triple bypass surgery. The following month, the Williams appeared in bankruptcy court to explain why they could not repay every dollar they owed to their creditors.

After hearing their case, the judge ordered each of the Williams to repay $50 a month for distribution to their unpaid creditors, for a total payment of $2,500, as a condition of the terms for discharge from bankruptcy. They also had to come up with about $4,000 for Revenue Canada, which they arranged to pay off in installments. They can incur further debt, but they have to wait for seven years to have the bankruptcy removed from their credit record. "Pensions are exempt from seizure under the Pension Benefits Act," Hessel points out. "So they're much better off than most bankrupts. And remember, bankruptcy is not a punitive act. It's intended to get people back on their feet."

Slowly but surely, the Williams are doing just that. After closing their shop, Greg found part-time work as a security guard. A couple of months after their appearance in court, he received an invitation to work part-time for the provincial police force. Kate worked long hours in a donut shop for several months until the franchise was sold to a new owner. Now she collects Employment Insurance, which will run out shortly, "the first time in 30 years I've ever claimed it."

"I'm only 56," Greg says optimistically, "but retirement is out the window, at least for another few years. In any case," he adds, "sitting back playing golf and going fishing really wasn't for me."

Source: Bruce McDougall, "Over the Edge," *The Financial Post Magazine* (November, 1998):51–53. Reprinted with permission.

In a typical small business, sales revenue and expenses vary throughout the year. Your cash flow forecast tries to predict all the funds that you will receive and disburse within a certain period of time — e.g., a month, quarter, or year — and the resulting surplus or deficit. It allows you to estimate the total amount of cash you actually expect to receive each period and the actual bills that have to be paid. At times your cash inflows will exceed your outflows; at other times your cash outflows will exceed your inflows. Knowing your expected position and cash balance will enable you to plan your cash requirements and negotiate a line of credit with your bank or arrange other external financing.

Your completed cash flow forecast will clearly show to the bank loans officer what additional working capital, if any, your business may need and demonstrate that there will be sufficient cash on hand to make the interest payments on a line of credit or a term loan for purchasing additional machinery or equipment or expanding the business.

There are three sections to a typical cash flow statement:

- Operating activities
- Investment activities
- Financing activities

These three sections work together to show the expected net change in cash that will occur in the business over a particular period of time. Cash inflows into the business are *added* on the statement while outflows are *subtracted* to determine total net cash flow.

FIGURE 7.3 SAMPLE COMPLETED PRO FORMA INCOME STATEMENT WITH BREAKDOWN OF OPERATING EXPENSES

TOUGH GUYS SPORTING GOODS PRO FORMA INCOME STATEMENT
For the Year (date)

1.	Gross Sales		$714,000
2.	Less: Cash Discounts		0
A.	**NET SALES**		**$714,000**
	Cost of Goods Sold:		
3.	Beginning Inventory	$195,000	
4.	Plus: Net Purchases	483,000	
5.	Total Available for Sale	$678,000	
6.	Less: Ending Inventory	210,000	
B.	**COST OF GOODS SOLD**		**$468,000**
C.	**GROSS MARGIN**		**$246,000**
	Less: Variable Expenses		
7.	Owner's Salary		40,000
8.	Employees' Wages and Salaries		71,384
9.	Supplies and Postage		0
10.	Advertising and Promotion		20,706
11.	Delivery Expense		5,712
12.	Bad Debt Expense		0
13.	Travel		0
14.	Legal and Accounting Fees		4,284
15.	Vehicle Expense		0
16.	Miscellaneous Expenses		46,124
D.	**TOTAL VARIABLE EXPENSES**		**$189,210**
	Less: Fixed Expenses		
17.	Rent		11,424
18.	Repairs and Maintenance		3,570
19.	Utilities (Heat, Light, Power)		7,140
20.	Telephone		1,000
21.	Taxes and Licences		1,000
22.	Depreciation		7,140
23.	Interest		8,568
24.	Insurance		3,570
25.	Other Fixed Expenses		0
E.	**TOTAL FIXED EXPENSES**		**$ 43,412**
F.	**TOTAL OPERATING EXPENSES**		**$231,000***
G.	**NET OPERATING PROFIT (LOSS)**		**$ 15,000**

* Numbers may not match operating expense percentages exactly due to rounding.

CASH FLOW FROM OPERATING ACTIVITIES

Cash flow from operating activities is probably the most complicated section to develop. It is important to distinguish between sales revenue and cash receipts in most businesses. They are typically not the same unless all the business's sales are for cash. Revenues are determined at the time a sale is made. Cash receipts, on the other hand are not recorded until the money actually flows into the business. This may not be for a month or two in the case of sales made on credit, which would be reflected in your *accounts receivable*. Similarly expenses are incurred when materials, labour, and other items are purchased and used, but payments for these items may not be made until sometime later when the cheques are actually issued. These deferred payments would be reflected in your *accounts payable*.

In addition, your net cash flow will typically be different from your net profit. Net cash flow is the difference between your cash inflows and cash outflows. Net profit is the difference between your expected sales revenue and expenses. One reason for this difference is the uneven timing of cash receipts and disbursements mentioned above. Another is that some items on the income statement such as depreciation are non-cash expenses. They represent a change against the business's income for the use of fixed assets owned by the firm but don't involve a direct outlay of cash.

Cash flow from operating activities can be determined from the following formula:

(+) Cash received from customers
(+) Any other operating cash receipts
(=) Total Cash Receipts from Operations (A)
(–) Cash paid to suppliers
(–) Cash paid to employees
(–) Interest paid
(–) Taxes paid
(–) Other cash payments for expenses
(=) Total Cash payments from Operations (B)
Total Net Cash provided by Operations = (A) – (B)

CASH FLOW FROM INVESTMENT ACTIVITIES

Cash flow from investment activities includes changes to your expected cash position owing to the purchase or sale of any assets owned by the business. This might include land and buildings, vehicles, equipment, securities, or anything else the business may have sold or acquired that resulted in the receipt or outlay of cash.

Cash flow from investment activities can be determined from the following formula:

(+) Cash proceeds from the sale of assets
(–) Cash disbursements for the purchase of property or equipment
(=) Total Net Cash provided by Investment

CASH FLOW FROM FINANCING ACTIVITIES

Financing activities on a cash flow statement reflect cash received from borrowing money, issuing stock, or other cash contributions to the business as well as any payments made on loans, dividends paid to shareholders, or other similar payments.

Cash flow from financing activities can be determined from the following formula:

(+) Cash received from bank and other loans
(+) Proceeds from issuing stock
(+) Capital contributions by owners
(=) Total Cash received from Financing (A)
(–) Repayment of principal on loans
(–) Dividends paid to shareholders
(–) Cash withdrawals by owners
(–) Other funds removed from the business
(=) Total Cash payments for Financing (B)
Total Net Cash provided by Financing (A) – (B)

DEVELOPING YOUR CASH FLOW STATEMENT

ESTIMATE YOUR REVENUES

In most small businesses, not all sales are for cash. It is normal practice to take credit cards or to extend terms to many customers. As a result, the revenue from a sale may not be realized until 30 days, 60 days, or even longer after the actual sale is made. In developing your cash flow forecast you must take into account such factors as:

- your ratio of cash to credit card or credit sales
- your normal terms of trade for credit customers
- the paying habits of your customers
- proceeds from the sale of any auxiliary items or other assets of the business

Sales should only be entered on the cash flow forecast when the money has actually been received in payment.

DETERMINE YOUR EXPENDITURES

To estimate your cash outflow you must consider:

- How promptly you will be required to pay for your material and supplies. It is not uncommon that a new business will have to pay for its inventory and supplies up front on a cash on delivery (COD) basis until it establishes a reputation for meeting its financial commitments. Then it may be able to obtain more favourable credit terms from its trade suppliers. These terms of trade should be reflected in the cash flow forecast. For example, if you have to pay your suppliers' invoices right away, the cash payouts would be reflected in the cash flow forecast during the same month in which the purchases were made. However, if you have to pay your suppliers' invoices within 30 days, the cash payouts for July's purchases will not be shown until August. In some cases, even longer-term trade credit can be negotiated, and then cash outlays may not be shown for two or even three months after the purchase has been received and invoiced.

You must also know:

- How you will pay your employees' wages and salaries (weekly, biweekly, or monthly).
- When you must pay your rent, utility bills, and other expenses. For example, your rent, telephone, utilities, and other occupancy costs are normally paid every month. Other expenses like insurance and licence fees may be estimated as monthly expenses but not treated that way for cash flow purposes. Your insurance premium of $1200 annually may have to be paid in three instalments: $400 in April, August, and December. That is how it must be entered on the cash flow worksheet. Your licence fees might be an annual expense incurred in January of each year and would be reflected as part of your estimated disbursements for that month.
- The interest and principal payments that you must make each month on any outstanding loans.
- Your plans for increasing your inventory requirements or acquiring additional assets.

RECONCILING YOUR CASH REVENUES AND CASH EXPENDITURES

To illustrate, let us consider the situation of Tough Guys Sporting Goods, a small retail store, in Figure 7.4. Tough Guys plans to open its doors at the beginning of the new year. Its owner, Bill Buckwold, wants to develop a monthly cash flow forecast for the expected first year of operation of the business and has made the following forecasts:

- Total sales for the year are projected to be $526,000 with a strong seasonal pattern peaking in June and July.
- Of the store's monthly sales, 60 per cent are cash sales and 40 per cent are credit card sales for which the cash is received in the following month.
- Inventory is purchased one month in advance of when it is likely to be sold. It is paid for in the month it is sold. Purchases equal 66 per cent of projected sales for the next month.

FIGURE 7.4 PRO FORMA CASH FLOW FORECAST FOR TOUGH GUYS SPORTING GOODS

12-MONTH CASH FLOW PROJECTIONS

Minimum Cash Balance Required = $5,000

	January	February	March	April	May	June	July	August	September	October	November	December	YEAR 1 TOTAL
Cash Flow from Operations (during month)													
1. Cash Sales	12,000	18,000	22,200	28,000	30,000	36,600	39,000	30,000	24,000	24,000	21,000	30,000	315,600
2. Payments for Credit Sales	0	8,000	12,000	14,800	19,200	20,000	24,400	26,000	20,000	16,000	16,000	14,000	190,400
3. Investment Income	0	0	0	0	0	0	0	0	0	0	0	0	0
4. Other Cash Income	0	0	0	0	0	0	0	0	0	0	0	0	0
A. TOTAL CASH FLOW ON HAND	$12,000	$26,000	$34,200	$43,600	$49,200	$56,600	$63,400	$56,000	$44,000	$40,000	$37,000	$44,000	$506,000
Less Expenses Paid (during month)													
5. Inventory or New Material	−13,200	−19,800	−24,420	−31,680	−33,000	−40,260	−42,900	−33,000	−26,400	−26,400	−23,100	−33,000	−347,160
6. Owner's Salary	−3,000	−3,000	−3,000	−3,000	−3,000	−3,000	−3,000	−3,000	−3,000	−3,000	−3,000	−3,000	−36,000
7. Employees' Wages and Salaries	−2,000	−3,000	−3,000	−3,500	−4,300	−4,300	−4,500	−4,500	−3,000	−2,500	−2,500	−3,900	−41,000
8. Supplies and Postage	0	0	0	0	0	0	0	0	0	0	0	0	0
9. Advertising and Promotion	−2,000	−1,000	−500	−700	−700	−700	−800	−1,000	−500	−800	−800	−1,500	−11,000
10. Delivery Expense	−200	−250	−250	−300	−300	−400	−400	−500	−300	−300	−300	−500	−4,000
11. Travel	0	0	0	0	0	0	0	0	0	0	0	0	0
12. Legal and Accounting Fees	−500	−250	−250	−250	−250	−250	−250	−250	−250	−250	−250	−250	−3,250
13. Vehicle Expense	0	0	0	0	0	0	0	0	0	0	0	0	0
14. Maintenance Expense	−1,000	0	0	−800	0	−1,000	0	−500	−1,000	0	−700	0	−5,000
15. Rent	−1,100	−1,100	−1,100	−1,100	−1,100	−1,100	−1,100	−1,100	−1,100	−1,100	−1,100	−1,100	−13,200
16. Utilities	−450	−450	−450	−450	−450	−450	−450	−450	−450	−450	−450	−450	−5,400
17. Telephone	0	0	0	0	0	0	0	0	0	0	0	0	0
18. Taxes and Licences	−1,000	0	0	0	0	0	0	0	0	0	0	0	−1,000
19. Interest Payments	0	−90	−125	−135	−140	−110	−90	−30	0	0	0	0	−720
20. Insurance	−600	0	0	−600	0	0	−600	0	0	−600	0	0	−2,400
21. Other Cash Expenses	−2,000	−2,000	−2,000	−2,000	−2,000	−2,000	−2,000	−2,000	−2,000	−2,000	−2,000	−2,000	−24,000
B. TOTAL EXPENDITURES	($27,050)	($30,940)	($35,095)	($44,515)	($45,240)	($53,570)	($56,090)	($46,330)	($38,000)	($37,400)	($34,200)	($45,700)	($494,130)
Capital													
Purchase of Fixed Assets	0	0	0	0	0	0	0	0	0	0	0	0	0
Sale of Fixed Assets	0	0	0	0	0	0	0	0	0	0	0	0	0
C. CHANGE IN CASH FROM PURCHASE OR SALE OF ASSETS	$0	$0	$0	$0	$0	$0	$0	$0	$0	$0	$0	$0	$0
Financing													
Payment of Principal of Loan	0	0	0	0	−4,000	−3,000	−7,000	−3,000	0	0	0	0	−17,000
Inflow of Cash from Bank Loan	11,000	4,000	1,000	1,000	0	0	0	0	0	0	0	0	17,000
Issuance of Equity Positions	0	0	0	0	0	0	0	0	0	0	0	0	0
Repurchase of Outstanding Equity	0	0	0	0	0	0	0	0	0	0	0	0	0
D. CHANGE IN CASH FROM FINANCING	$11,000	$4,000	$1,000	$1,000	($4,000)	($3,000)	($7,000)	($3,000)	$0	$0	$0	$0	$0
E. INCREASE (DECREASE) IN CASH	($4,050)	($940)	$105	$85	($40)	$30	$310	$6,670	$6,000	$2,600	$2,800	($1,700)	$11,870
F. CASH AT BEGINNING OF PERIOD	$10,000	$5,950	$5,010	$5,115	$5,200	$5,160	$5,190	$5,500	$12,170	$18,170	$20,770	$23,570	$10,000
G. CASH AT END OF PERIOD	$5,950	$5,010	$5,115	$5,200	$5,160	$5,190	$5,500	$12,170	$18,170	$20,770	$23,570	$21,870	$21,870
MEET MINIMUM CASH BALANCE	ACCEPTABLE	ACCEPTABLE	ACCEPTABLE	ACCEPTABLE	ACCEPTABLE	ACCEPTABLE	ACCEPTABLE	ACCEPTABLE	ACCEPTABLE	ACCEPTABLE	ACCEPTABLE	ACCEPTABLE	ACCEPTABLE

- Cash expenses have been estimated for such items as the owner's salary and employees' wages and salaries, advertising and promotion expenses, delivery expense, rent, utilities, taxes and licences, insurance, and other expenses.
- The store's beginning cash balance is $10,000 and $5,000 is the minimum cash balance that should be available at the beginning of every month.
- The store has negotiated a line of credit with the bank at an interest rate of 10 per cent annually but the interest due has to be paid monthly. This line of credit can be drawn on in order to ensure the business has its $5,000 minimum cash balance available each month up to a limit of $50,000, and will be paid down as surplus cash becomes available.

At the end of each month it shows the cash balance that is available to be carried over to the next month's operations. To this it adds the total of the next month's cash receipts and subtracts the total of the next month's cash expenditures to determine the adjusted balance to be carried forward to the following month. In summary form this relationship can be demonstrated by the following formula:

Forecasted Cash Flow in Month (x) = Cash Balance Carried over from Month (x – 1) + Expected Cash Inflow in Month (x) – Estimated Cash Expenditures in Month (x).

As you can see, cumulative cash surpluses or shortfalls are clearly evident well in advance of their actual occurrence. Knowing this information in advance can assist you in scheduling your initial capital expenditures, monitoring your accounts receivable, avoiding temporary cash shortages, and can enable you to plan your short-term cash requirements well in advance. Tough Guys, for example, does not achieve a positive cash flow until May. The business will be forced to draw on its line of credit in January, February, March, and April to make certain it will have the necessary minimum cash balance available to continue to run the business. Preparing a pro forma cash flow forecast enabled Bill to anticipate these needs and avoid the possibility of any nasty surprises.

A typical cash flow forecast that you can use to project your anticipated cash surplus or shortfall at the end of each month of the first year of operation of your business is illustrated in the Outline for a Feasibility Study (Figure 7.7) at the back of this Stage.

PRO FORMA BALANCE SHEET

One more financial statement should also be developed—*a pro forma balance sheet*. A balance sheet provides a snapshot of your business's health at a point in time. It tells you the value of your business at any point by forecasting what your business will own (*assets*) and what it will owe to other people, companies, and financial institutions (*liabilities*) to determine its *net worth*. The basic formula of the balance sheet is:

Assets = Liabilities + Net Worth

The first section of the balance sheet deals with assets. *Current assets* would include an estimate of your expected average accounts receivable, start-up inventory requirements, available cash, and similar items. *Fixed assets* are typically items like buildings, furniture, fixtures, machinery and equipment, automobiles, and other capital items that you will need to operate your business. Except for land, fixed assets typically get used up over a period of years, and therefore must be gradually *depreciated* in value.

The second part of a balance sheet lists liabilities. *Current liabilities* are debts you expect to incur that will fall due in less than 12 months. These usually include bills from your suppliers for the supplies and raw materials you will need for your initial inventory, short-term loans from banks and other financial institutions, any portion of your long-term debt that must be repaid during your initial year of operation, and so on. *Long-term liabilities* include any outstanding mortgages on land and buildings, notes on machinery and equipment, personal loans that you, your partners, and other stockholders may have made to the business, and any other outstanding loans of a long-term nature.

Net worth represents the value of your investment and equity in the business. Net worth can be comprised of the total capital invested in the business by yourself and any other inside or outside investors plus any profits that have been generated by the business that have been retained within the company rather than being paid out in dividends or other means or minus any losses that may have accumulated in the business.

A typical pro forma balance sheet is illustrated in Figure 7.5.

FIGURE 7.5 SAMPLE PRO FORMA BALANCE SHEET

TOUGH GUYS SPORTING GOODS BALANCE SHEET
End of year 1

ASSETS			
Current Assets:			
1. Cash		10,000	
2. Accounts Receivable		30,000	
3. Inventory		210,000	
4. Other Current Assets		30,000	
A. Total Current Assets			**$280,000**
Fixed Assets:			
5. Land and Buildings	0		
less depreciation	0	0	
6. Furniture and Fixtures	90,000		
less depreciation	5,000	85,000	
7. Equipment	0		
less depreciation		0	
8. Trucks and Automobiles	0		
less depreciation		0	
9. Other Fixed Assets	34,000		
less depreciation	3,000	31,000	
B. Total Fixed Assets			**$116,000**
C. Total Assets (C = A + B)			**$396,000**
LIABILITIES			
Current Liabilities (due within 12 months)			
10. Accounts Payable		123,000	
11. Bank Loans/Other Loans		39,000	
12. Taxes Owed		ø	
D.Total Current Liabilities			**$162,000**
Long-Term Liabilities			
13. Notes Payable (due after one year)		150,000	
14. Other Long-Term Liabilities		68,000	
E. Total Long-Term Liabilities			**$218,000**
F. Total Liabilities (F = D + E)			**$380,000**
NET WORTH (CAPITAL)			
Share Capital			
Common Shares			1,000
Preferred Shares			0
Retained Earnings			15,000
G. Total Net Worth (G = C – F)			**$ 16,000**
H. Total Liabilities and Net Worth (H = F + G)			**$396,000**

HOW TO ANALYZE YOUR PRO FORMA STATEMENTS

Once you have created a pro forma income statement, cash flow statement, and balance sheet for your business there are some easy calculations you can perform that will give you a better understanding of your company. You can calculate a number of *financial ratios* that can help you manage your business and make knowledgeable decisions related to some key questions such as:

- Does the business have the capacity to meet its short-term financial obligations?
- Is the business producing adequate operating profits based on the level of assets it employs?
- Are the owners receiving an acceptable return on their investment?

A ratio shows the relationship between two numbers. It describes the relative size of the two numbers as they relate to one another, and so eliminates the problem of trying to compare things on different scales.

Financial ratios can be used to compare the financial performance of two businesses of different size or to compare the performance of a company with others in the same business or the industry average. This application was previously discussed in Stage 4 relative to analyzing the financial position of a business you might be looking to buy. Financial ratios can also be used to compare your business's performance from one time period to another, and that is the application we will look at here.

Financial ratios can be categorized into three common groups to analyze different aspects of your business:

1. **Liquidity ratios** help you understand your business's ability to meet its short-term obligations and continue to maintain its normal operations. The more liquid assets you have the better, because they can be readily converted into cash.
2. **Profitability ratios** tell you how well you measure up in creating financial value in your business. The money you have invested in the venture could just as easily have been invested in other things such as real estate, bonds, and other securities, so you need to know whether your business can generate the kind of returns that justify the risks involved.
3. **Leverage ratios** measure the level of debt the business has and its ability to pay back this debt over a long period of time.

Examples of some of the more commonly used ratios of each type are illustrated in the Key Points box.

EXAMPLES OF KEY FINANCIAL RATIOS

Liquidity Ratios

1. Current Ratio = Current Assets/Current Liabilities
2. Quick Ratio = (Current Assets – Inventories)/Current Liabilities

Profitability Ratios

1. Gross Margin Ratio = Gross Profit Margin/Net sales
2. Net Profit Ratio = Net Profit before Taxes/Net Sales
3. Return on Assets = Net Profit before Taxes/Total Assets
4. Return on Owner Investment = Net Profit before Taxes/Net Worth

Leverage Ratios

1. Times Interest Earned Ratio = Net Income before Interest and Taxes/Interest Expense
2. Debt-to-Equity Ratio = Long-Term Liabilities/Net Worth

FYI FOR YOUR INFORMATION

For further information on preparing pro forma financial statements to evaluate the financial feasibility of your new venture idea you might check out some of the following Web sites:

1. **CCH BUSINESS OWNER'S TOOLKIT—MANAGING YOUR BUSINESS'S FINANCES** (www.toolkit.cch.com/text/P06_0100.asp)
2. **BUSINESS DEVELOPMENT BANK OF CANADA RATIO CALCULATORS** (www.bdc.ca/scripts/site/function-getchallenge.asp?&chk=1&language=eng&challenge=sec_head_startbiz.gifqk241kq9)
3. **THE ENTREPRENEURIAL EDGE—EDWARD LOWE FOUNDATION—BUSINESS BUILDERS—FINANCIAL STATEMENTS** (edge.lowe.org/fmpro?-db=library.fp5&-format=topics.htm&sortfield=subtopic1&subtopic1=Financial%20Statements&content=Business%20Builder&-find)
4. **PROFITGUIDE, THE BUSINESS RESOURCE FOR CANADIAN ENTREPRENEURS—IT'S ALL IN THE NUMBERS** (www.profitguide.com/inc/print_article.asp?ID=5)

DETERMINE YOUR BREAK-EVEN POINT

As your preliminary financial forecasts begin to clarify the size of the potential opportunity you are investigating, there is one other key question to explore: What sales volume will be required for your business to break even? This *break-even* point indicates the level of operation of the business at which your total costs equal your total revenue. The break-even point is important because it indicates when your business begins to make a profit. If your sales level is less than the break-even point, your business will suffer a loss.

The break-even point is affected by several factors — among them your fixed and variable costs and your selling price. *Fixed costs* are those that remain constant regardless of your level of sales or production. *Variable costs* vary directly with the amount of business you do. For example, your rent is a fixed cost, because it remains the same regardless of your level of sales. Your cost of goods sold, however, is variable, because the amount you spend is directly related to how much you sell. Fixed costs typically include insurance, licences and permits, property taxes, rent, and similar expenses. Variable costs include supplies, salaries and wages, raw material, utilities, and delivery expenses. Variable costs are usually determined on a per-unit or per-dollar of sales basis.

The break-even point can be determined algebraically. The basic formula is:

$$\text{Break-even Point (Units)} = \frac{\text{Total Fixed Costs}}{\text{Contribution Margin per Unit}}$$

where:

Contribution Margin per Unit = Selling Price per Unit – Variable Cost per Unit

and the *contribution margin* ratio can be determined by:

Contribution Margin Ratio = Contribution Margin per Unit Divided by the Selling Price per Unit

Algebraically that relationship can be expressed as:

$$\text{Contribution margin ratio} = \frac{1- \text{Average Variable Cost per unit}}{\text{Selling Price per unit}}$$

Understanding this relationship enables us to also calculate the break-even point in dollars. The basic formula for this determination is:

$$\text{Break-even point (dollars)} = \frac{\text{Total Fixed Costs}}{1 - \dfrac{\text{Average Variable Cost}}{\text{Selling Price per unit}}}$$

$$= \frac{\text{Total Fixed Costs}}{\text{Contribution Margin per Unit}}$$

Or alternatively if we are looking at the global situation for a business:

$$\text{Break-even point (dollars)} = \frac{\text{Total Fixed Costs}}{1 - \dfrac{\text{Total Variable Cost}}{\text{Total Net Sales}}}$$

The following example may help illustrate the break-even concept. Suppose that the financial statements for Gino's Pizzeria, a pizza delivery outlet, indicate that the business's fixed costs every month for rent, utilities, interest expense, insurance, and similar items are roughly \$3,600 per month. In addition, Gino has determined that his variable costs for making a typical large pizza are as follows:

Dough	\$1.40
Tomato sauce	0.35
Cheese	0.75
Toppings	0.75
Delivery box	0.25
Delivery cost	0.50
Total Cost	\$4.00

Rather than take a regular salary, Gino has decided to take any net income the business might generate as his income. In addition, Gino's sells a typical large pizza for \$10.00.

From this information you can see that after the \$4.00 in variable costs have been covered, each pizza sold can contribute \$6.00 towards covering the fixed costs of Gino's business. This is called his *contribution margin.* His contribution margin per unit can then be expressed as follows:

$$\begin{aligned}\text{Contribution Margin per Unit} &= \text{Selling Price} - \text{Total Variable Cost}\\ &= \$10.00 - \$4.00\\ &= \$6.00 \text{ per pizza}\end{aligned}$$

But how many pizzas will Gino have to sell every month in order to break even? This can be determined as follows:

$$\frac{\text{Total Fixed Costs}}{\text{Contribution Margin per Unit}} = \text{Break-even Volume (units)}$$

Or, in this case:

$$\frac{\$3{,}600}{\$6.00} = 600 \text{ pizzas per month}$$

Therefore, Gino must sell a minimum of 600 pizzas every month to cover his fixed costs of doing business. Even at that level of operation, he does not earn any income for himself. It is only after his sales exceed this level that the business starts to generate sufficient revenue to provide him with some compensation for his time and effort and give him a return on the money he has invested in the business. For example, if Gino should sell 800 pizzas one month, that would generate an income of \$1,200 for him as a return on his time and money. On the other hand, if he only sells 500 pizzas his business would incur a loss of \$600.

To determine the volume of sales that Gino will have to achieve each month to reach his break-even point we can use the formula:

$$\frac{\text{Total Fixed Costs}}{\text{Contribution Margin Ratio}} = \text{Break-even Point (dollars)}$$

Or, in this case:

$$\frac{\$3{,}600}{.6} = \$6{,}000 \text{ per month}$$

Therefore, Gino must sell a minimum of 600 pizzas or generate at least $6,000 in sales every month to cover his fixed costs of doing business.

Relating this notion to Tough Guys Sporting Goods store, we can also determine the volume of sales they would require to break even. If we assume all the operating expenses indicated in Figure 7.3 are fixed at least in the short term, including such items as salaries and wages, as well as advertising and promotion expenditures, the financial statement can be summarized as follows:

Projected sales	$714,000
Projected fixed expenses	$231,000
Projected variable expenses (basically our cost of goods sold)	$468,000

$$\text{Total sales needed to break even} = \text{Fixed expenses} \div 1 - \frac{\text{Variable Expenses}}{\text{Sales}}$$

$$= \$231{,}000 \div 1 - \frac{\$468{,}000}{\$714{,}000}$$

$$= \$231{,}000 \div (1 - 0.655)$$

$$= \$231{,}000 \div 0.345$$

$$= \mathbf{\$670{,}000}$$

Therefore the store needs to sell at least $670,000 worth of merchandise its first year to break even based on our estimate of its projected fixed costs and its average gross margin percentage and other variable costs. This concept is illustrated graphically in Figure 7.6 as well.

FIGURE 7.6 GRAPHICAL REPRESENTATION OF THE BREAK-EVEN POINT FOR TOUGH GUYS SPORTING GOODS

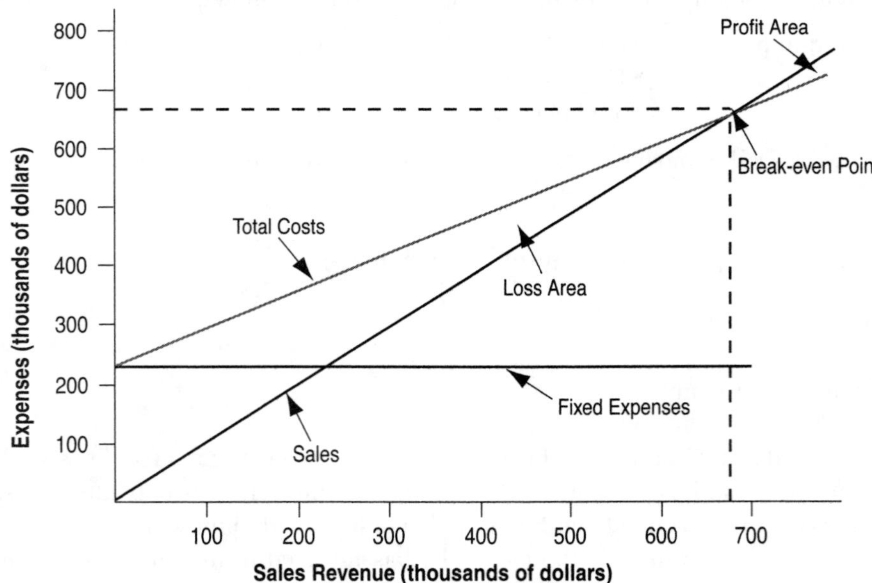

The value of break-even analysis is that it can be used to determine whether some planned course of action — for example, starting a new business, opening a new store, or adding a new item to your product line — has a chance of being profitable. Once you have estimated the break-even point for the action, you are in a better position to assess whether such a sales volume can be achieved and how long it will take to reach it.

It is essential that you determine the break-even level of operation for your business before you proceed very far with its implementation. Bankers and other financial people will expect to see this information as part of the financial documentation for your venture. In addition, if it appears that the break-even volume is not achievable, the business idea is probably destined to fail and should be abandoned before any money is invested.

CONDUCT A COMPREHENSIVE FEASIBILITY STUDY

Figure 7.7 provides a detailed framework that you can use to conduct a comprehensive feasibility assessment of your own new venture idea. Much of the information you have compiled in completing the worksheet in Stage 6 can be incorporated into Figure 7.7 to facilitate your feasibility assessment. When you have completed this evaluation, you need to give some thought to where you go from here. Does the business look sufficiently viable to proceed with the development of a comprehensive business plan? Have you identified all the potential flaws and pitfalls that might negatively impact your business? What role do you expect to play in the growth of the venture? Do you plan to produce and market the concept yourself, or do you hope to sell or license the idea to someone else? How much external money do you need and where do you think you can obtain it? These are the kinds of issues that need to be carefully considered and resolved before you will be in a position to move forward.

In most cases, the next stage is to write a complete *business plan*. This, however, requires a major commitment of time, effort, and money. Make sure your feasibility study indicates that your concept is clearly viable and that a reasonable profit can be expected.

And don't be too disappointed if your feasibility assessment indicates that your concept is not likely to be profitable. Think of all the time and money you have saved by not going forward with the implementation of a business that has a low probability of succeeding. That's why a preliminary assessment is so essential.

FIGURE 7.7 OUTLINE FOR A FEASIBILITY STUDY

YOUR CONCEPT

1. Describe the principal concept underlying your product or service idea.

____

____

____

____

____

2. What is unique or distinctive about your idea? How does it differ from similar concepts already being employed in the marketplace?

____

____

____

____

3. Who will be the primary customers of your concept and what are the principal benefits your concept will deliver to them?

____

____

____

____

4. How innovative is your concept? How would you categorize it along the continuum from "copycatting" to being an entirely new invention?

____

____

____

continued

Outline for Feasibility Study — continued

5. Is your idea technically feasible? Have you built a working model or prototype? Will you have to obtain Canadian Standards Association (CSA) approval or other permissions before the concept can be marketed?

PRELIMINARY MARKETING PLAN

Products and Services

1. What products or services will you sell? (Be specific.)

2. What additional customer services (delivery, repair, warranties, etc.) will you offer?

3. What is unique about your total product or service offering?

Customers

1. Define your target customers. (Who are they?)

2. How many target customers are in your trading area?

3. Why will they buy your product?

Competition

1. Who are your principal competitors? What is their market position? Have their sales been growing? Stable? Declining?

a.

b.

c.

d.

2. How does your concept differ from each of these other products or services?

Location

1. What location have you selected for your business?

2. Why did you choose that location?

Pricing

1. Describe your pricing strategy.

continued

Outline for Feasibility Study — continued

2. Complete the following chain of markups from manufacturer to final customer:

Cost to manufacture	________	(A)
Manufacturer's markup	________	(B)
Manufacturer's selling price (C = A + B)	________	(C)
Agent's commission (if applicable)	________	(D)
Wholesaler's cost (E = C + D)	________	(E)
Wholesaler's markup	________	(F)
Wholesaler's selling price (G = E + F)	________	(G)
Retailer's markup	________	(H)
Retailer's selling price (I = G + H)	________	(I)

3. How do your planned price levels compare to your competitors'?

____

____

____

____

____

Promotion

1. What will your primary promotional message to potential customers be?

____

____

____

____

____

2. What will your promotion budget be?

____

____

____

____

____

3. What media will you use for your advertising program?

____

____

____

____

____

4. Will you have a cooperative advertising program? Describe it.

____

____

____

____

____

5. Describe your trade promotion program.

6. Describe any publicity, public relations, or sales promotion programs you will have.

Distribution

1. How do you plan to distribute your product? Direct to the consumer? Through traditional distribution channels? Through specialty channels such as exhibitions, mail order, or trade shows?

2. Will you employ your own sales force or rely on the services of agents or brokers? How many?

THE SUPPLY SITUATION

1. What raw materials or component parts will you require to produce your product or service? What volume of these materials will you require? Who will be your major source of supply? Do you have alternative supply arrangements or other sources that can meet your requirements?

2. What will be the cost of these materials and components? Are prices guaranteed for any length of time? Are volume or quantity discounts available? What credit terms will your suppliers make available to you?

continued

Outline for Feasibility Study — continued

3. Describe your manufacturing requirements. Will you manufacture the product yourself or use subcontractors? What will it cost to establish your own manufacturing facility?

____

____

____

____

4. If you are planning to use subcontractors, what alternatives are available? What are their capabilities and comparative costs? Will you have to incur any other costs — e.g., for moulds, etc.? Do any of these contractors provide additional services?

____

____

____

____

COST/PROFITABILITY ANALYSIS

1. What do you estimate your costs would be and the funds required to get your business successfully launched?

a. Complete the following chart to determine your one-time financial requirements.

Estimated One-Time Start-up Financial Requirements

Item	*Total Original Cost*	*Estimated Cash Required*
1. Land	$______	$______
2. Building	______	______
3. Improvements:		
I Mechanical	______	______
II Electrical	______	______
III Construction	______	______
4. Machinery and equipment	______	______
5. Installation of equipment	______	______
6. Shop tools and supplies	______	______
7. Office equipment and supplies	______	______
8. Vehicles	______	______
9. Starting inventory	______	______
10. Utility hookup and installation fees	______	______
11. Licences and permits	______	______
12. Pre-opening advertising and promotion	______	______
13. Accounts payable	______	______
14. Cash for unexpected expenses	______	______
15. Other cash requirements	______	______
Total Estimated One-Time Cash Requirements (1+ ... +15)		$______

b. Do you have this much money available or have some ideas as to where you might be able to obtain it?

2. What do you estimate your sales will be, by product or service category, for your first 12 months? What will it cost you to produce those products or provide that service? What do you estimate your gross margin will be for each product or service? How does this compare with the norm for your industry? What operating expenses for such items as rent, travel, advertising, insurance, and utilities do you expect to incur? What profit do you estimate your business will show for its first 12 months?

   Complete the following pro forma income statement for your first year of operation.

3. How are your sales and expenses expected to vary throughout the year? What proportion of your sales will be for cash? On credit? What credit terms, if any, will you provide to your customers? What credit terms do you expect to receive from your suppliers? What other expenses will you have to pay on a regular, ongoing basis?
   a. Complete the following table to estimate your cash flow surplus or deficit for each month of your first year in business.
   b. Can you arrange for more favourable terms from your suppliers, accelerate the collection of your outstanding accounts receivable, negotiate a line of credit with your bank, or take other action to enable your business to continue to operate if cash flow is insufficient?

4. What do you estimate your total fixed costs will be for your first year of operation? What did you estimate your average gross margin to be as a percentage of your total sales in preparing your pro forma income statement in question 2? (This amount is also known as your contribution margin per dollar of sales.)

   Compute your break-even level of sales by means of the following formula:

$$\text{Break-even Point (\$ sales)} = \frac{\text{Total Fixed Costs}}{\text{Contribution Margin per \$ of Sales}}$$

   When do you expect to attain this level of sales? During your first year of business? Your second year? Your third year?

PLANS FOR FUTURE ACTION

1. According to your feasibility study, what were the strong points and weak points of your new venture idea? Can the weak points and potential problems be successfully overcome?

____

____

____

____

2. Does the feasibility assessment indicate that the business is likely to be profitable? Does it look sufficiently attractive that you should write a comprehensive business plan? What other information do you have to obtain, or what additional research do you have to do to develop this plan?

____

____

____

____

3. If you decide not to proceed with the development of a business plan, indicate the reasons why.

____

____

____

____

continued

PRO FORMA INCOME STATEMENT

FOR THE PERIOD ENDING (DATE) ____________

	MONTH												
	1	2	3	4	5	6	7	8	9	10	11	12	TOTAL
1. Gross Sales													
2. Less: Cash Discounts													
A. NET SALES	$	$	$	$	$	$	$	$	$	$	$	$	$
Cost of Goods Sold:													
3. Beginning Inventory													
4. Plus: Net Purchases													
5. Total Available for Sale													
6. Less: Ending Inventory													
B. COST OF GOODS SOLD	$	$	$	$	$	$	$	$	$	$	$	$	$
C. GROSS MARGIN (C=A–B)	$	$	$	$	$	$	$	$	$	$	$	$	$
Less: Variable Expenses													
7. Owner's Salary													
8. Employees' Wages and Salaries													
9. Supplies and Postage													
10. Advertising and Promotion													
11. Delivery Expense													
12. Bad Debt Expense													
13. Travel													
14. Legal and Accounting Fees													
15. Vehicle Expense													
16. Maintenance Expense													
17. Miscellaneous Expenses													
D. TOTAL VARIABLE EXPENSES	$	$	$	$	$	$	$	$	$	$	$	$	$
Less: Fixed Expenses													
18. Rent													
19. Utilities (Heat, Light, Power)													
20. Telephone													
21. Taxes and Licences													
22. Depreciation													
23. Interest													
24. Insurance													
25. Other Fixed Expenses													
E. TOTAL FIXED EXPENSES	$	$	$	$	$	$	$	$	$	$	$	$	$
F. TOTAL OPERATING EXPENSES (F=D+E)	$	$	$	$	$	$	$	$	$	$	$	$	$
G. NET OPERATING PROFIT (LOSS) (G=C–F)	$	$	$	$	$	$	$	$	$	$	$	$	$
H. INCOME TAXES (estimated)													$
I. NET PROFIT (LOSS) AFTER INCOME TAX (I=G–H)													$

1. Expenses and other payments should be entered as negative (–) numbers.
2. This entry should be the same amount as for the beginning of the year. All other rows will be the total for the entire year.

TWELVE-MONTH CASH FLOW PROJECTIONS

	Month 1	Month 2	Month 3	Month 4	Month 5	Month 6	Month 7	Month 8	Month 9	Month 10	Month 11	Month 12	TOTAL
Cash Flow from Operations (during month)													
1. Cash Sales													
2. Payments for Credit Sales													
3. Investment Income													
4. Other Cash Income													
A. TOTAL CASH FLOW ON HAND	$	$	$	$	$	$	$	$	$	$	$	$	$
Less Expenses Paid (during month)[1]													
5. Inventory or New Material													
6. Owners' Salaries													
7. Employees' Wages and Salaries													
8. Supplies and Postage													
9. Advertising and Promotion													
10. Delivery Expense													
11. Travel													
12. Legal and Accounting Fees													
13. Vehicle Expense													
14. Maintenance Expense													
15. Rent													
16. Utilities													
17. Telephone													
18. Taxes and Licences													
19. Interest Payments													
20. Insurance													
21. Other Cash Expenses													
B. TOTAL EXPENDITURES	$	$	$	$	$	$	$	$	$	$	$	$	$
Capital													
Purchase of Fixed Assets													
Sale of Fixed Assets													
C. CHANGE IN CASH FROM PURCHASE OR SALE OF ASSETS	$	$	$	$	$	$	$	$	$	$	$	$	$
Financing													
Payment of Principal of Loan													
Inflow of Cash from Bank Loan													
Issuance of Equity Positions													
Repurchase of Outstanding Equity													
D. CHANGE IN CASH FROM FINANCING	$	$	$	$	$	$	$	$	$	$	$	$	$
E. INCREASE (DECREASE) IN CASH	$	$	$	$	$	$	$	$	$	$	$	$	$
F. CASH AT BEGINNING OF PERIOD	$	$	$	$	$	$	$	$	$	$	$	$	$
G. CASH AT END OF PERIOD	$	$	$	$	$	$	$	$	$	$	$	$	$
MEET MINIMUM CASH BALANCE	ACCEPTABLE	ACCEPTABLE	ACCEPTABLE	ACCEPTABLE	ACCEPTABLE	ACCEPTABLE	ACCEPTABLE	ACCEPTABLE	ACCEPTABLE	ACCEPTABLE	ACCEPTABLE	ACCEPTABLE	ACCEPTABLE

1. Expenses and other payments should be entered as negative (–) numbers.
2. This entry should be the same amount as for the beginning of the year. All other rows will be the total for the entire year.

Organizing Your Business

One of the key issues you must resolve when starting your new venture is the legal form of organization the business should adopt. Making that decision means you should consider such factors as:

1. The complexity and expense associated with organizing and operating your business in one way or another
2. The extent of your personal liability
3. Your need to obtain start-up capital and operating funds from other sources
4. The extent to which you wish ownership, control, and management of your business to be shared with others (if at all)
5. The distribution of your business's profits and losses
6. The extent of government regulation you are willing to accept
7. Tax considerations and implications
8. The need to involve other principals in your venture

The most prevalent forms your business might take are:

- An individual or sole proprietorship
- A partnership (general partnership or limited partnership)
- A corporation

INDIVIDUAL OR SOLE PROPRIETORSHIP

The *individual* or *sole proprietorship* is the oldest and simplest form of business organization. As owner or proprietor you have complete control over the conduct and management of your business. You alone are accountable for all business activities and their consequences. You assume the business's profits and are liable for its debts. You and the business are one and the same. The sole proprietorship is the most common form or organization for small businesses, particularly in the early stages of their development.

ADVANTAGES OF SOLE PROPRIETORSHIP

- **Simple and inexpensive to start** A sole proprietorship is both simple and inexpensive to create and dissolve. It can be brought into existence with a minimum of legal formalities and terminated just as readily. Start-up costs are minimal — usually they are confined to registering your business name with the appropriate authorities and obtaining the necessary licences.
- **Individual control over operations** The operation of the business is coordinated in the mind and actions of a single individual. You are literally your own boss. If the business is not successful you are free to dissolve it. And if the business does well, you can have a strong personal sense of accomplishment.
- **All profits to the owner** If the business does well you will reap the benefits of your efforts; no one will share in the profits of the business. You work for yourself and determine your own destiny. In addition, if your business should incur a loss during its early stages, that loss is deductible from any other income you may have.

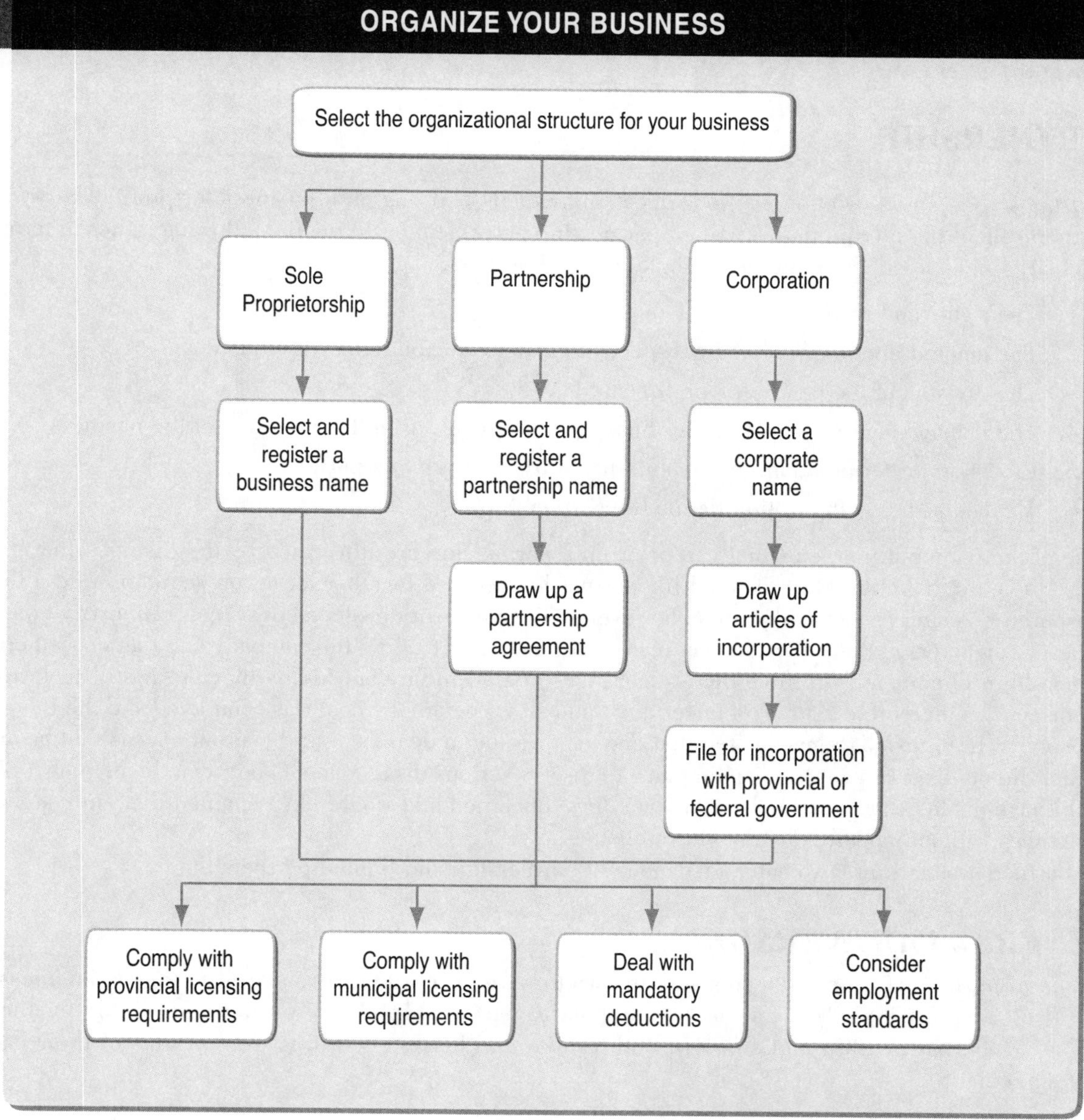

DISADVANTAGES OF SOLE PROPRIETORSHIP

- **Unlimited liability** Since the business and the proprietor are not recognized as being separate by law, you can be held personally liable for all the debts of your business. That means you may have to satisfy business debts with personal assets such as your house and car if the business is unable to meet its obligations. You may be able to protect some personal assets by putting them in your spouse's name before starting your venture but there is no real guarantee against domestic breakdown.
- **More difficult to obtain financing** This obviously limits the capital base of the business unless substantial security is available. It is not uncommon for sole proprietors to obtain the bulk of their initial funding by "maxing out" personal credit cards or by pledging their home, cottage, or other personal assets as collateral for a loan.
- **Limited resources and opportunity** A sole proprietorship usually holds limited opportunity and incentive for employees, as it is not a form of ownership conducive to growth. One person can only do so much and may not have all the skills and knowledge necessary to run all phases of the business.

Employees may have to be hired to perform these tasks. The life of the business in a proprietorship is limited to the life of the proprietor. If you should die, become ill, or encounter serious personal problems, your business is immediately affected, and unless other provisions are made, your business will die with you. This could lead to a forced sale of the business's assets by your beneficiaries, perhaps at a substantial loss.

PARTNERSHIP

A *partnership* is an association of two or more individuals carrying on a business for profit. The *principals* (partners) should jointly prepare a written partnership agreement outlining the following issues in terms that are clearly understood and mutually acceptable to all of them:

1. The rights and responsibilities of each partner
2. The amount and nature of their respective capital contributions to the business
3. The division of the business's profits and losses
4. The management responsibilities of each partner involved in the operation of the business
5. Provision for termination, retirement, disability, or death of a partner
6. Means for dissolving or liquidating the partnership

Some of the potential problems that can occur in a partnership are illustrated by the case of Albert Sanges (Entrepreneurs in Action #26). He and his partner had worked together for seven years to build a thriving transportation company. After that time, however, a disagreement developed over their differing views of one of the key members of their management team that threatened to stifle the company and that caused employee morale to plummet. To resolve the issue Sanges offered to buy out his partner but it still took over six months and an incredible amount of uncertainty and stress before the deal was completed and the issue finally resolved. In hindsight Sanges noted that one major issue in dealing with the situation was that he and his partner did not have any mechanism in place to resolve serious disagreements between them. Such a process would have made things much easier on everyone concerned and would have enabled them to resolve their differences without jeopardizing the entire business.

Partnerships fall into two categories: general partnership and limited partnership.

GENERAL PARTNERSHIP

A *general partnership* is similar to a sole proprietorship except that responsibility for the business rests with two or more people, the partners. In a general partnership all the partners are liable for the obligations of the partnership and share in both profits and losses according to the terms of their partnership agreement.

ADVANTAGES OF A GENERAL PARTNERSHIP

- **Pooling of financial resources and talents** The partnership is useful for bringing together two or more people who can combine their skills, abilities, and resources into an effective group. Management of the business is shared among the principals.
- **Simplicity and ease of organization** A partnership, like a sole proprietorship, is easy and inexpensive to establish and is subject to a minimum amount of regulation.
- **Increased ability to obtain capital** The combined financial resources of all the partners can be used to raise additional capital for the business. Income from the partnership is taxed as part of the personal income of each of the partners.
- **Potential for growth** A partnership has a higher potential for growth than a proprietorship, since a valuable employee may be offered a partnership to dissuade him or her from leaving the firm. Growth, however, is still quite restricted compared to that possible with a limited company.

26 *Entrepreneurs in* action

Division of Labour

For a time, everything seemed to be going smoothly. My business partner and I worked side-by-side each day to develop and grow Link Logistics, the company we so dearly loved. And the company was indeed growing — by over 50 per cent each year. We were making very healthy profits, we were always on the leading edge of technology and we dominated the marketplace for our service. But after seven years of relative harmony, a management disagreement began to sour our relationship. I had a tough decision to make: Should I give in and side with a partner I had worked so well with over the years, or should I do what I felt was best for the company and risk damaging the friendship?

In the beginning, we each had our areas of responsibility, and we established our teams so the company could grow and prosper. My partner was in charge of IT development and the internal system required to run our service. I was responsible for everything else. Together, we made significant advances in all facets of the business, from IT development to sales and marketing. We built a strong company. In fact, after the first two years, our growth began to put us on lists of the fastest growing companies in Canada.

But my partner began to express serious concerns about the way our sales and marketing team was being handled. Clearly, there was a personality clash between him and our VP of sales and marketing. Eventually, my partner decided he could no longer work with this man and insisted on firing him. I, on the other hand, was pleased with the progress being made by our sales and marketing department, and wanted him to stay. With each of us holding equal say in running the business, we were at an impasse. My partner handled the situation by refusing to allow anyone to make normal management decisions without his express agreement. Our business began to suffer and staff morale plummeted.

For six months we struggled as a management team to get things done. I needed to make my choice, and in my heart, I knew that siding with my partner over company interests would affect many more people, including employees, customers and key suppliers, than just the two of us. Link Logistics had become an integral part of the daily trucking industry, and it seemed immoral to just walk away. We had worked way too hard to see the company fail now.

I finally decided to resolve the deadlock by offering to buy my partner's shares. After another six months and an incredibly stressful effort (that remains another story for another time), I completed the buy-out. In the process, we lost 12 employees out of a staff of 25, including our whole development team. Amazingly, we were able to stay focused enough to experience the company's largest growth rate ever — we even set records for the number of customers we signed to our service each month.

Since the buy-out, our new head of IT has put together a fresh, talented team of developers and systems people. The VP involved in the original conflict has formed strategic alliances with several different companies that complement and expand our service offerings. And we continue to expand at a rate that will keep us on the "fastest growth" lists for many years.

In retrospect, I see that my former partner and I did not have in place any mechanism to resolve serious disagreements that might arise between us. As a result, I have restructured the company holdings, and have adjusted the balance of voting rights in our shareholders' agreement to avoid deadlocks that block "business as usual." As unfair as it may seem, I've learned that one partner must have the final say. The deciding vote.

And I've learned the hard way that any partnership agreement should also contain provisions for breaking up the company or shareholders. Under a "shotgun agreement," for example, one shareholder may offer a fair price to buy out another shareholder.

But what do you do if all else fails and a partnership goes sour? If you are determined to keep the business going, as I was, you must stay focused on your objectives. Continue to work within the framework of any agreements that are in place. Do everything in your power to keep your staff loyal and their morale high. And make the success of the company your ultimate priority — even at the expense of a seemingly unshakeable friendship.

Source: Albert Sanges, "Division of Labour." Profit Magazine Online www.profitguide.com/firstperson/F1_sanges.html 12-07-01. Used with permission.

DISADVANTAGES OF A GENERAL PARTNERSHIP

- **Unlimited liability** Partners are personally liable for all the debts and obligations of their business and for any negligence on the part of any of them occurring in the conduct of the business. This is similar to the situation with a sole proprietorship, except that the partners are liable both as a group and individually — i.e., not only for their own actions (severally) but also for the actions of all others in the partnership (jointly).
- **Divided authority** There is less control for an individual entrepreneur in a partnership with divided authority. There may be possible conflicts among partners that can be difficult to resolve and could affect the conduct of the business.

LIMITED PARTNERSHIP

In a *limited partnership*, the partners' share in the liability of the business *is limited to the extent of their contribution to the capital* of the business. In such a partnership, however, there must also be one or more general partners, i.e., partners with *unlimited liability.*

The limited partners may not participate in the day-to-day management of the business of the partnership or they risk losing their limited-liability status. Also, a limited partner is entitled to interest on his or her capital of no more than 5 per cent per year and some agreed-upon share of the profits. Limited partners have one major power — the ability to remove the general partner(s).

ADVANTAGES OF A LIMITED PARTNERSHIP

- **Limited liability** If properly established and registered the liability of the limited partners is restricted to the extent of their investment. Thus, you may find it easier to recruit investors.

DISADVANTAGES OF A LIMITED PARTNERSHIP

- **Centralized management** In a limited partnership only a small subgroup of the owners — the general partners — have decision-making authority and can participate in the management of the business.
- **Difficulty in changing ownership** It is generally difficult to change ownership in a partnership, since the partnership must be dissolved and reconstituted every time a partner dies or wants to retire. So it is important that the procedure for dealing with this issue be laid out in a partnership agreement.

CONTENTS OF A TYPICAL PARTNERSHIP AGREEMENT

1. Names of the partners
2. Name of the business
3. Term of the partnership agreement
4. Extent of each of the partner's interest in the partnership and the capital each has contributed to the partnership
5. The financial records and banking arrangements of the partnership
6. A description of the capital accounts and salary and draw arrangements of each of the partners
7. An outline of each partner's responsibilities for the management of the business and what each can or cannot do without the approval of other partners
8. Partners' responsibilities to work within the business and their ability to assign their interest in the business to others
9. Procedures for the termination or dissolution of the partnership
10. Procedures for the resolution of any disputes among the partners
11. Insurance coverage to be carried by the partnership
12. Any process for amending the agreement

CORPORATION

The *corporation* is the most formal and complex of the various forms of business organization. A firm that is *incorporated* is a separate legal entity from its owners — that is, legally, it is regarded as a "person" with a separate, continuous life. As a legal person, a corporation has rights and duties of its own: it can own property and other assets, it can sue or be sued, and it files its own tax return. Ownership of a corporation is recognized through the purchase of *shares*, or *stock*, which can be held by as few as one or as many as thousands of *shareholders*.

A business need not be large to be incorporated. A sole proprietorship regularly earning in excess of $40,000 to $50,000 of taxable income annually probably should be incorporated.

ADVANTAGES OF A CORPORATION

- **Limited liability** The owner or shareholder of a corporation is liable only for the amount he or she paid or owes for the shares. In case of bankruptcy, creditors are not able to sue shareholders for outstanding debts of the business.
- **Continuity of the business even if the owner dies** Since it is an entity under the law, a corporation is not affected by the death or withdrawal of any shareholder. The shares of its stock can be sold or transferred to other individuals without difficulty. This ease of transfer allows for perpetual succession of the corporation, which is not the case with a sole proprietorship or partnership.
- **Easier to raise capital** Incorporation makes it easier to raise capital, which is done by selling stock. In addition, corporations with some history and a track record can negotiate more effectively with outside sources of financing than either a proprietorship or a partnership.
- **Employee benefits** A corporation has a better opportunity to provide benefits to employees and stockholders in a variety of ways such as salaries, dividends, and profit-sharing plans.
- **Tax advantages** Being an independent entity in the eyes of the law, a corporation receives different tax treatment than either a proprietorship or a partnership, and is taxed separately on its business profits. This may provide you with some opportunity for tax deferral, income-splitting, or the reduction of your actual tax costs through the deductibility of certain personal fringe benefits.

DISADVANTAGES OF A CORPORATION

- **Cost** Corporations are more expensive to start and operate. Initially, incorporation can cost in excess of $1,000 in legal and regulatory fees. In addition, a lawyer may charge upwards of $300 a year to maintain the registered office and keep the corporate *book*, i.e., the record of annual meetings, directors' meetings, etc.
- **Legal formalities** A corporation is subject to more numerous and complicated regulatory requirements than a proprietorship or partnership. Corporations must typically file annual reports, hold annual meetings, and file federal and provincial tax returns. This can be very expensive and time-consuming for a small-business person, and may require the ongoing services of an accountant and a lawyer.
- **Inability to flow losses through** It is not uncommon for a new business to incur substantial start-up costs and operating losses during its first few years. These losses are "locked in" — a corporation must accumulate them for its own use in future years, and cannot use them to offset income a shareholder may have from other sources. If your business should never become very profitable, it is conceivable that its losses could never be used to reduce your tax liability.

  This is in contrast to a proprietorship or partnership, whose early losses would "flow through" to the owners of the business, to be deducted on their personal income tax returns in the year they were incurred. Therefore, it may be more beneficial financially not to incorporate, so you can offset other income for tax purposes. This can improve your overall cash flow when your business is just getting started, and cash flow is most critical. You can always decide to incorporate later without any tax consequences.

- **Guarantee** Lenders often require a personal guarantee. This largely negates the advantage of limited liability.

GETTING INTO BUSINESS

REGISTRATION AND INCORPORATION — MAKING IT LEGAL

For a sole proprietorship, no formal, legal *registration* is required as long as the business is operated under your own name. However, if a specific business name like "Regal Dry Cleaners" or "Excel Construction" is used, or if more than one owner is implied by the use of "and Associates" or "and Sons" in conjunction with your name, your business must be logged with the Registrar of Companies or the Corporations Branch of the province in which the business is located. Registration is a relatively simple and inexpensive process that you can probably take care of yourself. Partnerships must be registered in a similar fashion.

Incorporation is a more complicated and considerably more expensive process that usually requires the services of a lawyer. If your business activities will initially be confined to a single province, you need only incorporate as a provincial company. Should your business plans include expansion to other provinces, however, you will be required to register in each province in which you wish to do business as an extra-provincial company, or register as a federally incorporated company.

Companies can be classified as either private or public. *Public companies* are those like Alcan and Great West Life, which trade their shares on one of the country's public stock exchanges, and with which most of us are familiar. They typically employ professional managers, external directors, and a number of shareholders who are the owners of the business.

Private companies, on the other hand, tend to have only one shareholder, or at most a small number of shareholders. There is some restriction on the transfer of their shares in their *articles of incorporation*, and their shares cannot be offered for sale to the public. A private corporation is sometimes called an *incorporated partnership*, because it usually consists of one, two, or three people who are personal friends, business associates, or family members, each of whom may play two or three roles, serving, for example, as an officer, director, and a shareholder of the company all at the same time.

Calories restaurant, highlighted in Entrepreneurs in Action # 27, is a good example of an incorporated partnership. Janis and Remi Cousyns own 50 per cent of the business and their partner Janet Palmer owns the other 50 per cent. All three work in the business and have quite different responsibilities. Janet is the general manager while Janis serves as the maître d'hotel and Remi the chef de cuisine.

If you choose to incorporate, a private corporation is probably the type you will establish.

CHOOSING A NAME

Like people, all businesses must have a name. The simplest procedure is to name the business after yourself — Harry Brown's Printing, for example. This type of name does not require formal registration for a sole proprietorship, but it does have disadvantages. For example, you might get people phoning you at home at all hours if you and your business's name are the same. In addition, your personal reputation may be tarnished should you experience some financial problems and be forced into receivership or bankruptcy. And if you should ever sell your business, your name would go with it, and the new owner's actions could reflect negatively on your reputation.

For businesses to be registered or incorporated, the most important consideration in selecting a name is that it be acceptable to the Registrar of Companies in your province. All provinces require that a search be conducted of proposed names. Any name that is similar to a name already registered will be rejected to avoid public confusion. It is not uncommon to have to submit several names before one is finally approved. To avoid this problem some individuals use a series of numbers rather than letters for the name of their corporation. On acceptance, the name is typically reserved for your exclusive use for 90 days, so that you can proceed with your registration or the filing of your articles of incorporation.

The best approach is usually to choose a distinctive name for the firm that *accurately describes* the type of business you plan to carry on. That is, a name like "Speedy Courier Service" or "Super-Clean Automobile Washing" is probably much better than one like "Universal Enterprises" or "General Distributing." A good way to check out names is to go through the Yellow Pages or local business directories and get some idea of the range of names currently in use in your business area and perhaps some inspiration for a brilliant new possibility.

27 Entrepreneurs in action

A Recipe for Success

She was a young ballet dancer when he spotted her on the train to Nice 10 years ago. Remi Cousyn, a chef at an exclusive hotel in Switzerland, cast aside his inhibitions and decided to talk to the young, blond Canadian. "I remember thinking I might never get a chance like this again," he recalls. Janis, who had attended the National Ballet School in Toronto and danced with the Royal Winnipeg Ballet, was travelling in Europe. Over the next few years, Remi and Janis spent time together in France, but by 1991, they had moved to Montreal. That same year, they got married in Janis's home town of Saskatoon.

The Cousyns, both 29, spent four years in Montreal, but they eventually returned to Saskatoon, where they now run a restaurant that is not only establishing new culinary standards but turning a profit, too. In fact, their time in Montreal was in many ways a preparation for their current way of life. While Remi worked as a chef, Janis went to university and completed an undergraduate degree in business administration at Concordia. "I knew we would be doing something on our own and I wanted to have a basic knowledge of business," she recalls.

In 1996, during a brief stay in Whistler, B.C., where they worked together in the same restaurant, Janis received the phone call that drew the young couple back to the prairies. In years past, she had waitressed at a café in Saskatoon called Calories. Her former boss, Janet Palmer, who had subsequently become Janis's friend, telephoned to ask her and Remi to come aboard as partners. "Janet said her partner wasn't interested in the business any more and we could slide right in," recalls Janis. "The restaurant wasn't in great shape financially, and I think Janet understood we would be able to provide what was lacking." Janis, who was pregnant at the time with daughter Gabrielle, longed to return home, and Remi, keen to be "master of my own kitchen," also welcomed the move.

Within a year of forming a partnership in 1996, the three had transformed the coffee house into a money-making restaurant. In their first year as partners, Calories went from being in the red to a modest net profit of $9,000; the following year, that figure jumped to $32,000. With a growing clientele and expanded menu, it became clear that more space and a better-equipped kitchen were needed. After preparing a 45-page business plan, the Calories partners applied to a credit union for a loan. To their surprise, they received $175,000 — 90% of the projected renovation costs.

Janis attributes their success to a modest yet sound business plan. "It's pretty well known in the industry that banks aren't interested in financing restaurants. In fact, the credit-union board said they don't lend money to restaurants — ever. But with Calories, the decision to approve the loan was unanimous. We documented how we would cover the costs of paying back the loan in the worst case scenario, and they liked that." Calories is repaying the loan in monthly payments of $3,200 at a fixed rate of 9.8%. On top of the loan, the partners secured another $50,000 for the reno costs through a shareholding plan in which customers bought shares, each valued at $5,000 with a 4% annual yield. The business has no obligation to buy the shares back.

The completed renovations — which include a dining room and new commercial gas stove — made an immediate impact on Calories' bottom line. Not only have the regular theatre and university crowds remained loyal, Remi says they also "see a lot more suits" — a more affluent dinner crowd with money to spend on his international dishes. In March, the first full month after renovating, the business made $75,000, an increase of about 20% over the last full month. Despite being closed for eight weeks for the reno, this year's annual gross for their fiscal year ending in June reached $600,000, compared to $515,000 in 1997. Net profit jumped to $40,000, which is being pumped back into the business "for loans and equipment," reports Remi.

The team uses 30% of the restaurant's gross for food and another 30% goes to paying staff —besides the part-timers, full-time waiters and dishwashers on the payroll, Calories employs a kitchen manager, a bookkeeper, two cooks, a baker and a cleaner. The Cousyns own 50% of the business while Janet Palmer owns the other half. Palmer is general manager, Janis is maître d'hôtel and Remi is chef de cuisine.

The Cousyns are satisfied with the business as it presently exists. "When we first started, sales were about $35,000 a month and we expected $45,000 to be a fairly decent number," says Remi. "Now we've surpassed that—our first month after the renovations we sold $75,000." Janis suggests expanding Calories' small catering line, which now constitutes about 5% of their business, or combining a restaurant with an art gallery, or even franchising, noting that "Calories is a very transportable concept. It appeals to a wide range of people and it has good food." Although they don't own the building Calories occupies, they have made an offer on it, rationalizing that it is smarter to build equity, but they feel that at $300,000, its price is too high.

It's true that running a restaurant comes with long hours and is physically demanding, but both Remi and Janis are happy. It's the independence they find appealing. Remi has always wanted autonomy in the kitchen, and Janis finds the restaurant business gives her a sense of personal control that ballet never did. "In the ballet, if a director doesn't like your style as a dancer, you're finished." In the restaurant business, on the other hand, a strong concept, creative-cooking and a flair for service can make you captain of your own ship. And with the right financial decisions, it can also provide enough money to live a comfortable lifestyle—now and in retirement.

Source: Hugh Lockhart, "Recipe for Success," *The Financial Post Magazine* (September, 1998): 81–84. Reprinted with permission.

Names that are likely to be rejected and which should be avoided are those that:

1. Imply any connection with or approval of the Royal Family, such as names that include the word "Imperial" or "Royal"
2. Imply approval or sponsorship of the business by some unit of government, such as names containing "Parliamentary," "Premier's," or "Legislative"
3. Might be interpreted as obscene or not really descriptive of the nature of the firm's business
4. Are similar to or contractions of the names of companies already in business, even though they may be in a different field, such as "IBM Tailors" or "Chrysler Electronics"

The firm's name can become one of your most valuable assets if your business is successful, as has happened in the case of companies like McDonald's and Holiday Inn. Don't go for the first name that comes to mind. Think it over very carefully.

By permission of Johnny Hart and Creators Syndicate, Inc.

OBTAINING A BUSINESS LICENCE

You may require a municipal as well as a provincial licence to operate your business. Your need for the former depends on the location and nature of your business; requirements for the latter depend solely on the nature of your business.

MUNICIPAL

Not all types of businesses require a municipal licence. Every municipality regulates businesses established within its boundaries and sets its own licensing requirements and fees. In Winnipeg, for example, 114 types of businesses and occupations require a licence. In general, these are amusement operations or ones that may

Key points

SO WHAT'S IN A NAME ANYWAY?

So what's in a name anyway? According to naming experts—everything. Granted, as Shakespeare's Juliet noted, a rose by any other name would smell as sweet...but name it a thugwhistle and see if it sells half as much. There is power in a name. Look at the recall value and daring in a name like Rent-a-Wreck, a Canadian car rental business that's been around for years. Or the name Yahoo! We've all Yahooed even if we didn't know it was a verb. We get it. And we remember.

Some say if you're playing in the big leagues, it's wise to seek a consultant to help come up with a powerful business name. Naseem Javed, a Toronto-based naming consultant and president of ABC Namebank International, emphasizes that "the name of a product, service or company can often make the difference between survival and bankruptcy; between great success and crashing failure."

If there's nothing in the budget for a consultant, check out Industry Canada's Strategis website or books on small business start-up to give you pointers on devising a winner on your own. Many young entrepreneurs across Canada, like Halifax pottery shop owner Laura MacKay, are coming up with their own business names.

To get ideas, MacKay, 24, searched the Internet for names of businesses like hers and hit on a few inventive ones, like You're Fired and Once Upon a Dish. That got her creative juices flowing and she started brainstorming. Since her business invites people to make and paint their own pottery, she wanted to convey something of the process. And then, "It clicked," she says. "Earth, Paint and Fire." The name indicated the elements involved, created vivid images, and had a catchy ring—a play on the name of the '70s band Earth, Wind & Fire. She ran the name by plenty of people "to see if it was cool and if they thought it would stick in their heads," she says. "Everyone was really positive."

Do-it-yourselfers should keep a few points in mind, says naming consultant Henri Charmasson. Through market research, clearly define the message you want to deliver. Then reduce it to a single theme or image and devise a name that conveys that theme. He says distinctiveness is the critical ingredient in a winning name. Distinctiveness will give the name its marketing value, effectiveness and legal power. Take, for example, the name Discount Mufflers. It's not an identifier, he says, but merely a definition. "Since there are hundreds of competitors also selling mufflers at a discount, the phrase is not distinctive. It's neither memorable, nor protectable." But look at the name Midas. It's a distinctive, memorable name, one that can't be copied or easily mimicked by competitors.

The name of a company should also motivate the customer to buy its product or services, and should position these above the competition. Compare the name Cover Girl to Revlon. "Cover Girl," Charmasson notes, "is motivating, conveying what most women want to look like; whereas Revlon is an empty name that requires advertising to communicate what it is."

Arpeggio, for example, targets a different audience than names like Chuck Wagon or Mr. Bubble. As does the name, The Urban Garage. That's the name of a luxury car boutique in West Vancouver that Duncan Pearce, 29, has just opened in what was a garage. The funky name is meant to target high income Baby Boomers, Gen-Xers and car enthusiasts. "I sell performance cars, and I'm targeting enthusiasts who I think will relate to the name," Pearce says. "I was looking for a name that would differentiate my business from the typical car dealership, and one that would lend a feeling that this is a fun, funky place for car enthusiasts."

A memorable name is "catchy, loaded with pleasant evocation, or responsive to some inner desire or need of the customer," Charmasson notes. In Thunder Bay, Ontario, Tanya Wheeler, 34, and Laura McLennan, 27, founders of Blue Loon Adventures, used an evocative symbol in their eco-tour company name, and created a logo to match. "We thought if people couldn't remember the company name, they'd remember the image," says Wheeler. "We wanted a name that was Canadian, as we'd be appealing to international birders and outdoor enthusiasts. The name is memorable because of its association with the song [Blue Moon] and because the loon is identified as a Canadian symbol."

Since many family names are uninspiring and can lead to potential problems if the business is sold, many consultants advise against naming your business after yourself. Also remember, business names that are initials carry no message.

If your business is unincorporated, name registration isn't necessary. However, Vancouver business/intellectual property lawyer and federal trademark agent, Paul Schwartz, advises: "If the new business is to be unincorporated, such as a sole proprietorship or a general partnership, it's still advisable to file the business name with the Registrar of Companies." For businesses to be registered or incorporated, the name must be acceptable to the Registrar of Companies in your province. Getting your corporate name approved at the federal level by the Corporations Directorate offers you added protection of your rights to that name, as this allows your business to operate using its corporate name across Canada. To be approved, the name must be distinctive, must not cause confusion with any existing name or trademark, must include a legal element (usually Ltd., Inc., or Corp.) and must not include unacceptable terms.

For more info, check out Industry Canada's website at [http://www.stragegis.ic.gc.ca].

Source: Excerpted with permission from Realm: Creating Work You Want™ Fall 2000, published by YES Canada–BC. Available online at http://realm.net and in print by calling 1-877-REALM-99. For more information, Phone: (604) 412-4141 Fax: (604) 412-4144. E-mail: info@realm.net.

affect public health and safety. The licensing fees can be as high as several thousand dollars, but in most cases the fees are quite nominal — a few dollars.

In addition, all businesses — whether or not they require a licence — must conform to local zoning regulations and bylaw requirements. In fact, zoning approval is usually a prerequisite to licence approval. Companies operating in their own facilities in most cities must also pay a business tax, assessed as a percentage of the rental value of their business facilities.

PROVINCIAL

Various provincial authorities also require a licence or permit. For example, in Ontario all establishments providing accommodation to the public, such as hotels, motels, lodges, tourist resorts, and campgrounds, must be licensed by the province. Businesses planning to serve liquor, operate long-haul cartage and transport operations, process food products, produce optical lenses, or manufacture upholstered furniture or stuffed toys may also require licensing. You should check with the local authorities to determine the types of licences and permits your business might require.

LAND USE AND ZONING

You should check with the local municipal authorities to ensure that your business conforms to zoning and building regulations.

MANDATORY DEDUCTIONS AND TAXES

If your business has a payroll you will be required to make regular deductions from employees' paycheques for income tax, employment insurance (EI), and the Canada Pension Plan (CPP). These deductions must be remitted to the Canada Customs and Revenue Agency every month.

In addition, you may also be required to pay an assessment to your provincial Workers' Compensation Board. The size of your payment will be based on the nature of your business and its risk classification as well as the estimated size of your annual payroll. These funds are used to meet medical, salary, and the rehabilitation costs of any of your employees who may be injured on the job.

Depending on the size of your venture, you may also be responsible for remitting taxes of various kinds to either the provincial or the federal government. All provinces, except Alberta, apply a retail sales tax to almost all products and services sold to the ultimate consumer. Exceptions in some provinces include food, books, children's clothing, and medicine. The size and the application of these taxes varies from province to province, but if your business sells to final consumers you must obtain a permit and are responsible for collecting this tax and remitting it to the government on a regular basis.

Federal taxes largely fall into the categories of the Goods and Services Tax (GST) and income tax. Several provinces have integrated their provincial sales tax with the federal government's Goods and Services Tax (GST) to create a Harmonized Sales Tax (HST). The GST/HST is levied on virtually all products and services sold in Canada. There are some minor exceptions for certain types of products. If your taxable revenues do not exceed $30,000 you do not have to register for the GST or HST, but you can still choose to register voluntarily even if your revenues are below this level. You should check and see whether these taxes apply in your business. If so, you will be required to obtain a Business Number (BN) and remit any taxes collected on a regular basis.

How income tax is collected depends on the form of organization of your business. Sole proprietorships and partnerships file income tax returns as individuals and the same regulations apply. Federal and provincial taxes are paid together and only one personal income tax form is required annually for both, although payments may have to be remitted quarterly on the basis of your estimated annual earnings.

Corporations are treated as a separate entity for income tax purposes and taxed individually. The rules, tax rates, and regulations that apply to corporations are very complex and quite different from those that apply to individuals. You should obtain professional advice or keep in touch with the local tax authorities to determine your obligations under the Income Tax Act and to keep the amount of tax you have to pay to a minimum.

EMPLOYMENT STANDARDS

All provinces have standards for employment and occupational health and safety that must be adhered to by all businesses within their jurisdiction. These requirements deal with such matters as:

1. Hours of work
2. Minimum wages
3. Statutory holidays
4. Overtime pay
5. Equal pay for equal work
6. Termination of employment
7. Severance pay
8. Working conditions
9. Health and safety concerns

You should contact the office of your provincial Ministry of Labour or its equivalent and request a copy of the Employment Standards Act in effect in your province as well as a copy of the Guide to the Act. This will provide you with specific information on all of these topics, or you can use the services of an accountant or lawyer.

INSURANCE

There are a number of different types of insurance you should consider obtaining for your business and discuss with your insurance agent in arranging an appropriate program:

1. **General liability insurance** covers your liability to customers injured on your premises or off your premises by a product you have sold to them
2. **Business premises insurance** will protect your business premises and equipment from loss due to fire, theft, and other perils
3. **Business use vehicle insurance** must be obtained for cars and other vehicles used in the conduct of your business
4. **Business interruption or loss-of income insurance** will enable you to continue to pay the bills if your business should be closed down by damage due to fire, flood, or other catastrophe
5. **Disability or accident and sickness insurance** can continue to provide you with a source of income if you should become seriously sick or disabled and unable to continue to run your business for a period of time
6. **Key person insurance** can protect your business against the death of its key personnel. It is life insurance purchased by the business with the business being the sole beneficiary
7. **Credit insurance** protects you from extraordinary bad debt losses due to a customer going out of business
8. **Surety and fidelity bonds** protect you from the failure of another firm or individual to fulfill its contractual obligations
9. **Partnership insurance** can protect you against suits arising from actions taken by other partners in your business
10. **Workers' compensation** provides coverage to your employees for compensation they receive due to illness or injuries related to their employment

This kind of program won't protect you from *all* the risks associated with running your business, but it will provide you with some comfort against unpredictable occurrence in several areas that could threaten the survival of your venture.

CONCLUSION

There is no pat answer to the question of the legal form of organization you should adopt. A lot will depend on such issues as the expected size and growth rate of your new venture, your desire to limit your personal liability, whether you plan to start the business on a part-time or a full-time basis, whether you expect to lose or make money from a tax point of view during your first one or two years of operation, your need for other skills or additional capital, and so forth. Take a look at Figure 8.1. It summarizes many of the important differences between the various forms of organization available to you and may help you make your decision.

One word of caution: if you are considering any type of *partnership* arrangement, be extremely careful. In hard reality, partners should fulfill at least one of two major needs for you: they should provide either needed *money* or needed *skills*. If you allow any other factors to overshadow these two essential criteria, you may be taking an unnecessary risk.

One of the primary reasons new venture teams often fail is ill-advised partnerships. Partnerships entered into principally for reasons of friendship, shared ideas, or similar factors can create considerable stress for both the partnership and the individuals involved. It has often been said that a partner should be chosen with as much care as you would choose a spouse. However, in contemporary society, perhaps even greater care should be exercised, since a partnership may be even more difficult to dissolve than a marriage. An unhappy partnership can dissolve your business much faster than you can dissolve the partnership.

FYI FOR YOUR INFORMATION

A GUIDE TO LEGALLY SETTING UP YOUR BUSINESS IN CANADA

Here is a Web site that will help you navigate around some of the government requirements involved is setting up a business in each of the Provinces and Territories of Canada. This is only intended to show you a basic list of some of the most frequent requirements. You should be aware that these requirements will vary from province to province and differ for specific kinds of businesses.
(sade.rcsec.org/scdt/startup/interface2.nsf/engdoc/0.html)

For each province or territory this Web site will provide you with information on the following (and other) topics:

- Canada Business Service Centres
- Getting Started in Small Business
- Market Research
- Business Name, Structure, and Registration
- Business Plan
- Financing
- Taxation
- Hiring Employees or Contractors
- Importing and Exporting

FIGURE 8.1 WHICH FORM OF BUSINESS ORGANIZATION IS BEST FOR YOU?

Figure 8.1 summarizes many of the important differences between the various forms of business available to you. Review each of the alternatives on the dimensions indicated and select which one best fits with your particular circumstances. This may vary from characteristic to characteristic since there are pros and cons of each form. Once you have reviewed all dimensions, you should be able to select the organizational form that appears to be the best overall for your particular situation.

Form of Organization	Initial Requirements and Costs	Liability of Owners	Control	Taxes	Transfer of Ownership	Continuity	Ability to Raise Money
Sole Proprietorship	Minimum requirements. Perhaps only registration of your business name	Unlimited liability	Absolute control over operations	Income from business taxed as personal income	May transfer ownership of assets	Business ceases to exist when owner quits or dies	Limited to what the owner can personally secure
General Partnership	Easy and inexpensive to establish	Each partner is personally liable for all debts of the partnership	Requires majority vote of all general partners	Income from business is taxed as personal income of the partners	Requires agreement of all partners	Dissolved upon withdrawal or death of partner unless specified in partnership agreement	Combined resources of all the partners can be used to raise capital
Limited Partnership	Moderate requirements. Should be registered provincially	Liability limited to the extent of their individual investment	May not participate in the day-to-day management of the business	Same as general partners	May sell interest in the company	Same as general partnership	Limited liability may make it easier to raise capital but can be complicated
Corporation	Most expensive. Usually requires a lawyer to file Articles of Incorporation	Liability limited to investment in company	Control rests with shareholders	Corporation taxed on its income and shareholders taxed on dividends received	Easily transferred by selling shares of stock	Not affected by the death or withdrawal of any shareholder	The most attractive form for raising capital
Which form best meets your needs on each dimension (Select One)	________	________	________	________	________	________	________

Which form of organization do you feel best meets your overall needs? ____________________

Protecting Your Idea

Many entrepreneurs are also inventors. One of the primary problems faced by these inventor/entrepreneurs is how to protect the idea, invention, concept, system, design, name, or symbol that they feel may be the key to their business success. Legislators have long recognized that society should provide some protection for the creators of this "intellectual property." The laws they have developed provide a form of limited monopoly to the creators of intellectual property in return for their disclosure of the details of the property to the public.

Intellectual property is broken down into five components under the law:

1. Patents
2. Trademarks
3. Copyrights
4. Industrial designs
5. Integrated circuit topographies

Protection of your intellectual property can be expensive. While government costs may range from only a small fee for registration of a copyright to several hundred dollars for registration of a patent, many of the procedures can be quite complex and require you to obtain the services of a registered patent agent. This can increase the total cost of obtaining a patent to as much as $10,000, the cost depending on the complexity of the application. Therefore, it is important that you understand the advantages and disadvantages provided by this protection, and its likely impact on the success and financial viability of your business.

APPLYING FOR A PATENT

A *patent* is a government grant that gives you the right to take legal action, if necessary, against other individuals who without your consent make, use, or sell the invention covered by your patent during the time the patent is in force. Patents are granted for 20 years from the date on which the application was first filed and are not renewable. On expiration of its patent, a patented device falls into the *public domain* — i.e., anyone may make, use, or sell the invention.

To be patentable your device must meet three basic criteria:

1. Have "absolute novelty." The invention must be new (first in the world).
2. Be useful. A patent cannot be obtained for something that doesn't work or has no useful function.
3. It must show inventive ingenuity and not be obvious to someone skilled in that area.

A patent may be granted for a product, a chemical composition, an apparatus or machine, or a process. You *cannot* patent a scientific principle, an abstract theorem, an idea, a method of doing business, a computer program, or a medical treatment.

A patent may only be applied for by the legal owner(s) of an invention. You cannot apply for a patent for an invention you may have seen in another country even though that invention may never have been patented, described, or offered for sale in Canada.

Patents are now awarded to the *first inventor to file an application* with the Canadian Patent Office. This means you should file as soon as possible after completing your invention (though not prematurely if certain key elements or features of your idea would be missing from your application). It is also important that you not advertise or display or publish information on your invention too soon, as this may jeopardize your abil-

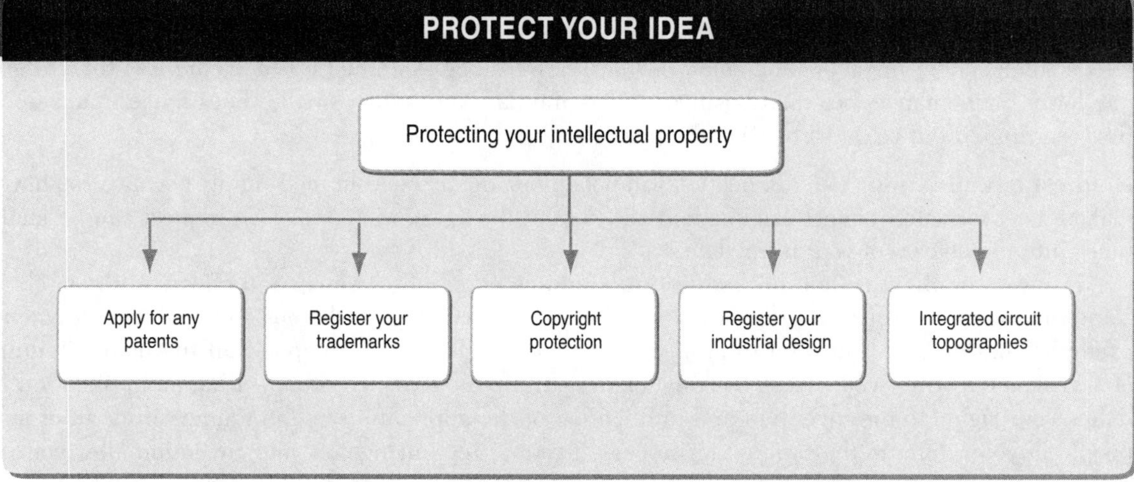

ity to obtain a valid patent later on. There is a one-year grace period for disclosure by an applicant but it is suggested that the following rule of thumb be adopted: *Your application for a patent should be filed before your product is offered for public sale, shown at a trade show, or otherwise made public.*

HOW TO APPLY

If your idea is patentable and you wish to obtain patent protection, you should take the following steps:

1. **Find a patent agent** The preparation and prosecution (assessment) of patent applications is quite complex. You should consult a patent agent trained in this specialized practice and registered to represent inventors before the Patent Office. Though hiring such an agent is not mandatory, it is highly recommended. The Patent Office can provide you with a list of registered agents but will not recommend any particular one to you. Several may also be listed in your local telephone directory, but make certain they are registered with the Patent Office. The address of the office is:
   Patent Office
   Canadian Intellectual Property Office
   Industry Canada
   Place du Portage I
   50 Victoria St.
   Hull, Quebec, K1A 0C9
   (cipo.gc.ca)
   General Inquiries: (819) 997-1936

2. **Conduct a preliminary search** The first step your agent will recommend is a preliminary search of existing patents to see if anything similar to your idea has already been patented, in which case you may conclude the process immediately. This can save you a lot of time and money that might otherwise be spent pursuing a futile application.The search can be conducted in person by visiting the Patent Office in Hull or on the Internet at *cipo.gc.ca* or via the Strategis Web site at *strategis.ic.gc.ca/patents*. The on-line database has descriptions and drawings of patents issued in Canada since 1920.

3. **Prepare a patent application** A patent application consists of an abstract, a specification, and drawings.

   An *abstract* is a brief summary of the material in the specification. The *specification* is a document that contains (1) a complete description of the invention and its purpose and (2) *claims*, which are an explicit statement of what your invention is and the boundaries of the patent protection you are seeking. *Drawings* must be included whenever the invention can be described pictorially. Typically, all inventions except chemical compositions and some processes can be described by means of drawings.

4. **File your application** Filing your application means submitting it along with a petition asking the Commissioner of Patents to grant you a patent. In Canada, filing must be done within one year of any use or public disclosure of the invention.

   If your application is accepted, you will be required to pay an annual maintenance fee to keep it in effect. Independent inventors and small businesses whose gross annual revenues are less than $2 million pay lower maintenance fees than businesses classified as "other than small." Fees range from zero in the first year to $200 in years 15 to 19 of the patent's life.

5. **Request examination** Your application will not automatically be examined simply because you have filed it. You must formally request examination and submit the appropriate fee. This request can be made any time within five years of your filing date.

   Filing an application and not requesting examination can be a cheap and effective way of obtaining some protection for your invention without necessarily incurring all the costs of obtaining a patent. For example, let's assume you want to protect your idea but don't wish to spend all the money required to obtain a patent while you assess the financial feasibility of your invention. Filing an application establishes your rights to the invention and publication of the application by the Patent Office informs other people of your claim to the product or process. Should they infringe on your invention after your application is published, you have five years to decide whether to pursue the grant of a patent and seek retroactive compensation.

   Requesting an examination, however, is no guarantee that a patent will be granted. And if it is not, you will have no grounds to claim damages for infringing on your idea.

   The Canadian Patent Office receives over 35,000 applications a year, mostly from American inventors and companies. As a result, the examination process can be very slow, commonly taking two to three years to complete.

6. **If necessary, file amendment letters** Upon your requesting an examination, the patent examiner will assess your claims and either approve or reject your application. If your application is rejected, you can respond by filing an *amendment letter* with the Commissioner of Patents. The letter will be studied by the examiner. If the patent is not then granted, there may be a request for further amendments. This process will continue until either the patent is granted, your application is withdrawn, or your application is finally rejected.

Key points

BENEFITS OF A PATENT SEARCH

If you are a small business person a patent search can help you:

- identify trends and developments in a particular field of technology
- discover new products that you may be able to license from the patentee or use without needing a licence
- find information that keeps you from duplicating the research
- identify unproductive areas of inquiry by reading about the current state of the art
- keep track of the work of a particular individual or company by seeing what patents they have been granted
- find a solution to a technical problem you may have
- gain new ideas for further research in a particular field

Source: "Summary of benefits of a patent search" — adapted and reproduced as "key Points: Benefits of a Patent Search". Reproduced with the permission of the Minister of Public Worlds and Government Services Canada, 2002.

PROTECTION PROVIDED BY YOUR PATENT

As you can see, the patenting process is complex, costly, and time-consuming. If you have a patent application in process and are concerned that someone else may attempt to patent your invention, you may use the label "Patent Pending" or "Patent Applied For" to inform the public that your application for a patent has been filed. This, however, has no legal significance and does not mean that a patent will necessarily be granted. Of course, it is illegal to use this term if in fact no application is on file.

If your patent application is granted, the onus will be entirely on you to protect your rights under the patent, for the Patent Office has no authority to prosecute for patent infringement. If infringement occurs, you may (1) bring legal action to compel the offender to account for any profits made, (2) seek an injunction to prevent further use of your patent, or (3) obtain a court order for the destruction of any materials produced that infringe on your rights. This, however, can be a very expensive and time-consuming process, which may prohibit a small business from enforcing its rights.

A patent granted in Canada or the United States provides you with no protection outside the country in which it was originally granted. To obtain protection in other countries, you must register your patent in each country within the time limit permitted by law (typically one year from your initial application). You can apply for a foreign patent either from within Canada via the Canadian Patent Office, or directly through the patent office of the country or countries concerned. Under the terms of the Patent Cooperation Treaty, it is possible to file for a patent in as many as 43 countries, including the United States, Japan, and most of Europe, by completing a single, standardized application that can be filed in Canada. Ask your patent agent about these procedures before you decide to file in another country.

You should realize that holding a patent on a worthy idea does not necessarily mean commercial success. Dan Knight and Rick Hilton, whose case is described in Entrepreneurs in Action #28, appear to have an interesting idea with their patented Golf Bag Cooler, but they may never even recover the cost of obtaining their patents.

They are in a similar situation to Mich Delaquis and Fred Coakes and their state-of-the-art, self-draining cookware discussed in Entrepreneurs in Action #29. They have secured patents in the United States and Canada for the locking mechanism on the lid of their pots and invested virtually all of their life's savings and a good portion of their families' and friends' savings. Even though they have managed

28 *Entrepreneurs in* action

A Cool Idea for the Golf Bag

Happiness is pulling a cold beverage out of your golf bag when the clubhouse is four fairways away.

Working up a sweat to get to golf course clubhouses for a cool sip is what prompted Dan Knight and Rick Hilton to invent their Golf Bag Cooler.

It's a skinny tube that fits inside a golf bag and holds six cans. A spring made out of musical instrument wire pushes a fresh can of pop (or beer) to the top of the bag every time one is taken out.

"It was Rick's idea about five years ago. I had an old doodle art tube at home and we tried to come up with a calibrated spring for it," says Knight. "For a while, until we got the right spring, we thought we'd have to put a caution label on the tube in case it shot cans out."

What keeps the cans cold — even in 98 degree Fahrenheit weather — is the air space between two PVC tubes fit one into the other, and small hockey puck-like objects filled with freezable gel which fit in between the cans. "It was the spring and the disks which got us the patent," says Hilton. "There's lots of elongated tube coolers out there, but these two things made ours unique. We got the idea for the disks from a toy hockey puck which we drilled a hole into and filled with gel. We had to use a turkey baster."

They had to turn to engineering companies and a couple of professors at the University of Manitoba to find out what material to build the coolers out of. The parts are manufactured in Boucherville, Quebec and then shipped to Winnipeg.

But as any inventor soon learns, there are three stages to any invention — dreaming it up, getting the patent and then getting it on the market.

Knight and Hilton along with partner Russ Glow have American and Canadian patents on the Golf Bag cooler but they're still trying to find a market with which to share their slice of heaven.

Source: Excerpted from Susie Strachan, "Dreaming of a Cool Million: Inventors Perceive Need, Seek to Cash-in on Fulfilling It," © *Winnipeg Free Press*, 18 February, 1992. Reprinted with permission.

29 Entrepreneurs in action

Feeling the Strain

POT INVENTORS REFUSE TO GIVE UP ON A DREAM

Take two east-end boys who made their living in a city snowmobile plant, lock them in a basement for three years and what do you get?

For Mich Delaquis and Fred Coakes, the answer is a state-of-the-art, self-draining cookware set.

Along the way, the two men exhausted their life savings and a sizable portion of their family's and friends', were knee-deep in flawed designs, fruitlessly wore out welcome mats at city banks, and were turned away by every cookware manufacturer in North America.

But come Feb. 15, the two partners will proudly display their eight-piece EasyStrain Cookware set on The Shopping Channel, every hustling entrepreneur's Valhalla.

"After all we've been through, it feels really good to know we've got a product that's not only good but others see that too," said Delaquis, 30, who has kept his day job as a warranty analyst at Polaris Industries Ltd.

What Delaquis and Coakes have produced is a set of pots and pans that are self-draining and with lids that lock on tight.

The design is simple. When cooking, the straining holes are covered. When it's time to strain, you line up the arrows on the lid with a matching arrow on the handle and turn clockwise; this locks the lid and exposes the holes.

The products are heavy-duty stainless steel with a thick bottom. The larger pots and pans come with an extra handle, making straining easier.

"What struck us was the quality and the unique feature," said Maureen McDermott, merchandise manager at The Shopping Channel. "It's a pretty-looking set. They've used 0.9-millimetre stainless steel. They haven't scrimped on quality.

"It's safe and it's good for either left-handed or right-handed people. I think we'll sell a lot of them."

Delaquis and Coakes are your typical entrepreneurs. Delaquis is the tinkerer; Coakes, the hustler and deal-maker. They saw a need and went about their way to find a product to fill that need.

Delaquis remembers the day three years ago when, still single and living on his own, he scalded his hand while straining a pot of pasta.

"I didn't have a strainer and I had to do it with just lifting the lid a little bit," Delaquis said. "The idea popped into my head that it would be a lot easier to do this if there was a strainer already inside the pot."

It was an idea that wouldn't go away. He went to Coakes, who was then head of the receiving department at Polaris, and told him of his plan.

They went into Coakes' basement and they tinkered. First, using snips and sheet metal, they tried to make their own pots and lids.

Then they concentrated on just designing the lid.

Their first design incorporated a spinning disc and a spring mechanism under the lid.

"The first five manufacturers we showed it to said it couldn't be made," said Coakes, 28. "We had to start all over again."

Along the way, the pair took a 10-week small business course from the Canada Business Service Centre. Then they found a helpful lawyer and an accountant.

Even when they came up with what they believed was a sure thing, they couldn't find anyone in North America to make it.

They secured patents in the United States and Canada for their locking mechanism and got the name trademarked, but 14 manufacturers turned them away.

"They either said it wouldn't work or they were too busy," Coakes said.

Both men credit staff at the Canada Business Service Centre with helping them find contacts in Hong Kong, as well as support here in Winnipeg.

It cost them $30,000 just to get the moulds designed.

"A year ago, I told Mich we've got to start selling some of these and stop writing all these cheques," said Coakes, who now sells Yellow Pages advertising for MTS Advanced.

But don't ask the pair to do a commercial for the Canadian banking industry. They've put $77,000 into the project to date and they need another $100,000 to make the minimum 1,250 sets the Hong Kong manufacturer will produce on a first order. All of that has been money from their own savings and that of family and friends.

"We'd be nowhere if it wasn't for the support and help from our family and friends," Delaquis said.

"One banker had the nerve to tell me that he so admired my tenacity he was certain I'd be a millionaire one day," Coakes said. "I told him I didn't need any lip service. We had two patents, a manufacturer, and now an agreement with The Shopping Channel but not one bank would help us. When we are millionaires, we won't be doing any business with him."

It's not over for Coakes and Delaquis. They're confident they'll find the investors necessary to bring the first 500 sets to The Shopping Channel in February. Once the sales take off, they're planning on larger pots and smaller pans.

After that, they will concentrate on direct marketing, with infomercials in the United States and trade shows. Then they'll go retail.

And Delaquis is not finished.

"I've got an idea or two for some other products." (www.easystrain.com)

Source: Aldo Santin, "Pot Inventors Refuse to Give Up on a Dream," © *Winnipeg Free Press*, 20 November, 1998, B3 – B4. Reprinted with permission.

to interest The Shopping Channel in demonstrating their product, they still need to raise another $100,000 to get the cookware sets produced in Hong Kong, and are still a long way from making a profit on their idea.

An invention succeeds by acceptance in the marketplace. Your patent may be perfectly valid and properly related to your invention but commercially worthless. Thousands of patents are issued each year that fall into this category. A patent does not necessarily contribute to the economic success of an invention. In some high-technology fields, for example, innovations can become obsolete long before your patent is issued, effectively making the patent worthless.

Holding a patent may improve your profitability by keeping similar products off the market, giving you an edge. But there is no guarantee you will be able to prevent all competition. Litigation, if it becomes necessary, can require considerable financial resources, and the outcome is by no means assured. A high percentage of patent infringements challenged in court result in decisions unfavourable to the patent holder.

However, there are many instances where patenting a product concept or idea has led to commercial success. Bill Laidlaw noticed an economic and environmental problem his employer, BC Hydro, was experiencing and invented "Replugs" to solve it (Entrepreneurs in Action #30). Replug sales have gone from $37,000 in 1992 to over $350,000 in 1997 with 75 per cent coming from the United States. Even more impressive has been the market performance of Ron Foxcroft's pea-less whistle, the Fox 40, illustrated in Entrepreneurs in Action #31. Foxcroft developed the whistle after his regular whistle failed to blow while he was refereeing a key basketball game during a pre-Olympic tournament in Brazil. To date they have sold almost 100 million whistles in 126 countries around the world. However, they have also spent $750,000 registering dozens of patents and trademarks in an effort to protect their invention, yet are currently involved in 11 infringement cases against other firms who are either making a cheaper version of the Fox 40, selling an identical product under another name, or are just passing a cheaper imitation off as a genuine Fox 40 whistle.

Bob Dickie of Spark Innovations Inc. has built his whole business around patentable products. He holds 80 patents for his inventions and thinks patent protection is crucial to business success these days. Bob's first product was the FlatPlug, billed as the first innovation in electrical plug design in 75 years. The FlatPlug lies flat against the wall, unlike a conventional electrical plug which sticks out perpendicular to the wall. As a result, it doesn't waste space behind furniture and is more difficult for children to pry out. Bob got the idea when he saw his daughter reach through her crib bars for a conventional plug. FlatPlug is protected by eight U.S. and worldwide patents. Even the package — a cardboard sleeve that keeps the extension cord and the plug in place — is patented.

Bob has a number of strict criteria he feels product ideas have to meet to have commercial potential:

- **It must be ten times better** Rather than evolutionary improvements in product design, he looks for concepts with enough of a "story" to make distribution channels take serious notice.
- **It must be patentable** "If we can't get a patent, the business is absolutely dead," says Dickie.
- **It must be a mass-production item** High-volume products have a higher turnover, reducing much of the risk of holding inventory.

30 Entrepreneurs in action

"Plugging" into the US Market

Bill Laidlaw of Victoria, British Columbia was employed with BC Hydro for 25 years in power line construction and maintenance. He noticed an economical and environmental problem his company was experiencing and invented "Replugs" to solve it. This product has proven its worth to BC Hydro and the novelty of Replugs is spreading to other industries.

The wooden poles used by Hydro companies require maintenance on a regular basis to control rot and insect infestation. Holes are drilled in the poles and preservatives or fumigants are poured into the holes, increasing the life of the pole. The holes then need to be sealed and, traditionally, wooden plugs have been used. Wooden plugs are difficult to pull out and new holes have to be drilled each time maintenance is required. Replugs are removable, reusable plastic plugs and have flexible tapered threads that allow the plug to be pounded into the hole without damaging the hole. The plugs may be removed for maintenance and may be reused.

The result of using Replugs is an increase in the life of the poles—reducing costs. An effective maintenance program combined with the use of Replugs can result in average savings in excess of $5/pole/year for each wood pole subjected to the maintenance program. When the number of poles owned by a utility company is considered, dollar savings enter into the thousands (or even millions for large utilities.) There are an estimated 105 to 110 million wood poles in the United States!

After coming to the Canadian Innovation Centre in March of 1993, Laidlaw had a Critical Factor Assessment done. This assessment told him his product was feasible and recommended that he continue with the commercialization of Replugs.

Laidlaw took early leave from BC Hydro and established W.S. Laidlaw Products to market and manufacture his product. He subcontracted the manufacturing to Scott Plastics in BC and production began in 1990. A Renton, Washington distributor, Materials Procurement sells Replugs to the United States market. He markets them himself in Canada, saying, "it's really just in the starting phases." His market consists mostly of electrical utilities, but that is spreading as he recently filled an order for a jetty maintenance project at the Esquimalt Naval Base. Bill's company has now sold over 4 million Replugs across North America.

Replugs have been tested and approved by BC Hydro. Cost analysis indicates that over the life of a wood pole, removable/reusable Replugs can save about $0.23/installed plug when compared to the wood plug alternative.

Laidlaw has experienced steady growth in sales. In 1992, Replug sales reached $37,000. In 1997, sales were an impressive $350,000. To date, 75% of Laidlaw's sales are in the US, with only 25% in Canada.

Bill Laidlaw has not begun to penetrate middle and eastern Canada, and this is only due to the fact that there has not been a substantial marketing effort yet. As such, the opportunity to expand his market exists.

Laidlaw has the business foresight to see that organizations might not place considerable importance on replacing plugs. As a result, Laidlaw has published a paper which examines the method for evaluating the cost/benefits of wood pole maintenance. This paper serves to highlight the substantial savings a utility can realize.

A simple business idea, simply successful!
(www.replugs.com)

Source: "W.S. Laidlaw Products — A Canadian Business Plugging into the U.S. Market," *Eureka Magazine*, 1998. Reprinted with permission by the Canadian Innovation Centre.

31 Entrepreneurs in action

Defensive Strategy

Summer in Indianapolis can be extremely hot, but it wasn't the temperature that had me on edge as I walked across the floor of the gymnasium to referee a Pan-American basketball game. I was clutching one of the only two operating prototypes of my new Fox 40 pea-less whistle. We had spent three-and-a-half years and $150,000 in production, and the whistle had never been heard by anyone other than our small development group. Would the new whistle work when it counted most?

The idea for a pea-less whistle came to me in 1984 after I needed a police escort out of a gymnasium in Brazil when my regular whistle failed to blow at a crucial point in a pre-Olympic basketball game. Now, as I crossed the floor for the start of the Pan-Am game, I made a mental note of where the exits, security staff and police were located—in case my new invention failed to utter a sound.

The whistle not only worked, it was so loud and clear that it startled everyone in the gym. When the games were over, I came home with orders for 20,000 Fox 40 pea-less whistles, and the funds to put my invention into full production.

Today, we have sold close to 100 million whistles in 126 countries. The Fox 40 whistle is used in almost every professional and amateur league and sports association worldwide, and we have developed variations for dog trainers, hunters, hikers, campers, rescue workers and police departments. We know the whistle works, it's accepted and it sells. Now we're fighting another battle—one that has cost us legal fees in the hundreds of thousands of dollars—with no end in sight. Fox 40, like many companies with useful new products, faces the scourge of imitators supplying cheap rip-offs. But I've learned that with some foresight and planning, any inventor can nip this problem in the bud with proper patent and trademark protection.

When you look for money for a new invention, your bank manager and potential investors always ask those same two questions: 1) Do you have a business plan, and; 2) Do you have a patent? Although you need both to raise money to bring your product to market, most business people never read the full business plan; even fewer understand how patents and trademarks work, or how they protect your product. For the record, patents describe exactly what your products are. Trademarks describe who you are and what your company is all about.

Thousands of patents are filed every year. Few commercial patents ever reach the marketplace and those that do are successful only if the patent is written properly and the product marketed aggressively. Patent searches must be conducted worldwide to protect your invention from infringement by others, and also to protect you from infringing on other patents. The process is incredibly detailed and far too complicated for novices to attempt on their own. Some companies advertise that they can raise money for your invention or help get your invention to market. Get references and check them out thoroughly. Many inventors have learned very expensive lessons trying to get to market using the services of these companies.

I knew we needed help navigating the patent process. The late Chuck Shepherd, from Oakville, Ont., was a guru in the field of developing and patenting new products and ideas. But when I first showed him my concept, he immediately declined to take on the project. He soon changed his mind, not because of the whistle itself, but because he found out I was the guy who owned Fluke Transport Group, the trucking company with the slogan, "If it's on time ... it's a Fluke." He said if I could be successful with that slogan, I could probably sell a pea-less whistle.

We protected our whistle with dozens of patents. Chuck made sure that the technical description of the Fox 40 pea-less whistle was comprehensive and all encompassing. When the whistle design was complete, he took me to meet Stan Rogers of Rogers & Scott, Patent Attorneys, in Oakville. Chris Scott soon joined the team and together we filed world patents for the Fox 40 whistle.

This team prepared me to take my invention to market. They told be that having a patent wouldn't make a product successful. Success would only come from making a better whistle and marketing it more aggressively than the competition. It was simple yet sound advice.

Patents—valuable assets that can be sold or licensed if necessary—are important and are absolutely necessary if you have a product with a world market or a product that can be copied easily. But I soon learned that I also needed trademark protection. Patents have an expiry date and others can patent or introduce similar patents.

Trademarks, however, are yours and provide greater protection against new products. Products are recognized by their name, and as the product becomes more popular so does the value of the trademark. I have never had a customer call me and order two-dozen of a specific patent number. They ask for two-dozen black Fox 40 pea-less whistles. I needed to protect the name.

My team had prepared me for this phase of our development and had filed trademarks in all the markets where we would be doing business. I often say that there is a great deal of Chuck Shepherd in the Fox 40 whistle and there was a great deal of Fox 40 in Chuck Shepherd. I owe a great deal to him and to Stan Rogers and Chris Scott.

We have now spent over $750,000 on patent and trademark registrations to protect our product and our name. We are currently involved with 11 infringement cases against the Fox 40 patents or trademarks. These patent and trademark infringements usually originate from one of three sources:

1. competition who have the capability of making a similar product;
2. companies who see that a large profit can be made by selling a similar product and have the resources to fight us in court, and;
3. companies who get in and out of the market fast, passing their cheap imitation off as our product.

These imitators find it tougher to beat a charge of trademark infringement than one of patent infringement. Companies can argue that their pea-less whistle is different than our pea-less whistle or that their patent does not infringe on ours. But no one can say that they own the Fox 40 pea-less whistle.

Imitation may be the highest form of flattery, but fighting it without the proper protection can also be extremely costly. When all is said and done, our trademarks provide the best long-term protection for our products. My best advice is to patent for design protection and trademark for revenue protection.

(www.fox40whistle.com)

Source: Ron Foxcroft, "Defensive Strategy." Profit Magazine Online, www.profitguide.com/firstperson/F1_foxcroft.html 12-07-01. Reprinted with permission.

- **It should be smaller than a bread box** Small items are easier to make and less costly to design, package, and transport.
- **It must lend itself to distribution through existing channels** Going through established market lines speeds the acceptance of a new product.
- **It should have no government involvement** Spark Innovations stays away from products that are motivated by or are dependent on government support at any level.
- **It must be useful** Dickie only works with products that have long-term, practical usefulness. No novelties, fads, or games.[1]

COMMERCIALIZING YOUR PATENT

Once you have taken steps to protect your idea you will have to give some thought as to the best way to market it and hopefully turn a profit. There are a number of possible options.

- Setting up your own business like the individuals profiled in the Entrepreneurs in Action examples is the option that usually comes to mind. It allows you to retain full control of your idea but also means you assume all the risk.
- Another possibility is to license the invention. With a licence you grant one or more individuals the right to manufacture and sell your innovation in exchange for royalties. The licence can apply generally or only to a specific market or geographic region as long as you have obtained patent protection for that area.
- A third option is to sell your patent. By selling your patent you give up all rights to the idea in return for a lump sum of money. However, then you don't have to worry about whether the product becomes a commercial success.

1. Adapted from Ellen Roseman, "Spark of Genius," The Globe and Mail, 26 September, 1994.

REGISTERING YOUR TRADEMARK

A *trademark* is a word, symbol, picture, design, or combination of these that distinguishes your goods and services from those of others in the marketplace. A trademark might also be thought of as a "brand name" or "identifier" that can be used to distinguish the product of your firm. For example, both the name "McDonald's" and the symbol of the golden arches are (among others) registered trademarks of the McDonald's Corporation.

To *register* a trademark means to file it with a government agency for the purpose of securing the following rights and benefits:

1. Exclusive permission to use the brand name or identifier in Canada
2. The right to sue anyone you suspect of infringing on your trademark to recover lost profits on sales made under your trade name, and for other damages and costs
3. The basis for filing an application in another country should you wish to export your product

To be registerable, a trademark must not be so similar in appearance, sound, or concept to a trademark already registered, or pending registration, as to be confused with it. For example, the following trademarks would not be registerable: "Cleanly Canadian" for a soft drink (too close to Clearly Canadian, a fruit-flavoured mineral water); "Extendo" for a utility knife (too close to Exacto).

The value of a trademark lies in the goodwill the market attaches to it and the fact that consumers will ask for your brand with the expectation of receiving the same quality product or service as previously. Therefore, unlike a patent, a trademark should be registered only if you have some long-term plans for it that will result in an accumulation of goodwill.

It is possible for you to use a trademark without registering it. Registration is not mandatory and unregistered marks have legal status. But registration is advised for most commonly used identifiers, since it does establish immediate, obvious proof of ownership.

Failing to properly register your trademarks can sometimes lead to future problems. Bob Arthurs of the True North Clothing Company in Entrepreneurs in Action #32 learned this lesson the hard way. Despite consulting with a lawyer and a government agency, their failure to do appropriate due diligence and search our previous registrations of the "True North" trade name ended up costing them a lot of money in legal and other fees. In the end they had to buy the rights to use the name from the registered owner despite assurances the term was part of the "public domain" and available for use by anyone.

HOW TO REGISTER YOUR TRADEMARK

In Canada it is possible for you to register your trademark before you actually use it, but the mark will not be validated until it is actually put into service. Registration of a trademark involves the following steps:

1. **A search of previous and pending registrations** As with a patent, a search should be conducted to determine that your trademark does not conflict with others already in use. The search can be conducted at the Trade-marks Office in Hull, Quebec. It maintains a public inventory of all registered trademarks and pending applications. You can also conduct a search electronically at the Canadian Trade-marks Database of the Canadian Intellectual Property Office (http://strategis.ic.gc.ca/cgi-bin/sc_consu/trade-marks/search_e.pl).

2. **An application to register your trademark** This involves filing an application for registration of your trademark.

Once your application is received, it is published in the *Trade-mark Journal* to see if anyone opposes your registration.

Even though registering a trademark is relatively simple compared with applying for a patent, it is recommended that you consult a trademark agent registered to practise before the Canadian Trade-marks Office.

MAINTAINING AND POLICING YOUR TRADEMARK

It normally takes about a year from the date of application for a trademark to be registered. Registration is effective for 15 years, and may be renewed for a series of 15-year terms as long as the mark is still in use.

32 Entrepreneurs in action

The Name Game

We began like so many other young companies, merrily building our company and brand name. Many years and hundreds of thousands of dollars went into laying the groundwork for our name "True North Clothing Company." And like many other young companies, we assumed we were protected against infringing on someone else's trademark. I have since learned that you should never assume.

When we began our company in February 1992, my business partner spoke with a government agency in Hull, Que. regarding the use of trademarks. We were informed that because the phrase "True North" is part of Canada's national anthem, it is public domain and available for anyone's use. Beyond that, without the money for extensive legal advice, we could only briefly consult a lawyer. We were assured that by doing a "poor man's trademark"—sending the designs to ourselves by registered mail and not opening them unless there was a dispute—we were effectively protecting our interest in the name.

In 1996, believing our trademark secure, we started an aggressive advertising campaign in the *Globe & Mail* mail-order section, featuring our new shirt "True North Strong & Free."

After only two days of advertising, we received by registered mail a cease-and-desist letter from lawyers representing a company in Ontario. The company claimed to own the name, and ordered us to stop using their trademark. We spent the next three years involved in faxes, phone calls and face-to-face meetings (with and without lawyers present) in an attempt to come to a peaceful resolution between the Ontario company and ourselves. But it seemed that no matter what solution was proposed, we could not reach an agreement. Our costs were rising. We even made a (five-figure) purchase of a competitor's company and trademark as a safeguard, in case we were forced to stop using "True North" and needed another name. Our legal costs were also into five figures. It reached the point where our lawyer said, "I can't keep taking your money anymore...you guys just can't take these legal bills."

It was clear our competitor had much deeper pockets than we did, and we could no longer afford to fight a strict enforcement of the cease and desist order. We decided to end the dispute by purchasing the trademark from the Ontario company.

So what happened to "public domain"? To this day, nobody has been able to provide us with an answer. Even representatives of the federal government, which is responsible for trademark legislation, have been at a loss for a clear explanation. And over the years, we have received so much mixed and conflicting information from lawyers that we have yet to see one firm support advice another firm has given.

If there is a lesson here, it is that trademark and copyrights should be taken more seriously. We live in an age of corporate branding, and companies have become more vigilant than ever in protecting their trademarks. But more information regarding trademark and copyright laws is available to entrepreneurs today than was available to us, both on the Internet and in libraries across Canada. Many of these resources are absolutely free. My advice to up-and-coming companies is to check out as much material as you can locate. Because even when you think you're right, you can't always win.

(www.truenorthclothing.com)

Source: Robert Arthurs, "The Name Game," Profit magazine Online http://www.profitguide.com/firstperson/F1_arthurs.html, 07-12-01. Reprinted with permission.

As with a patent, it is up to you to police the use of your trademark; the government provides no assistance in the enforcement of your trademark rights. It is your decision whether to take any legal action against an offender.

Registration of a trademark in Canada provides no protection of your trademark in other countries. If you are involved with or contemplating exporting to any other country, you should consider registering your trademark in that country.

MARKING REQUIREMENTS

The Trade-marks Act does not contain any marking requirements. However, trademark owners can indicate their registration through the use of certain symbols, namely ® (registered), ™ (trademark), SM (service mark), MD (marque déposée), or MC (marque de commerce). Although the act does not require the use of these symbols, it is advisable to use them.

OBTAINING COPYRIGHT

A *copyright* gives you the right to preclude others from reproducing or copying your original published work. Materials protected by copyright include books, leaflets, periodicals and contributions to periodicals, lectures, sermons, musical or dramatic compositions, maps, works of art, photographs, drawings of a scientific or technical nature, motion pictures, sound recordings, and computer programs. A copyright exists for the duration of your life plus 50 years following your death.

HOW TO OBTAIN A COPYRIGHT

In Canada, there is no legal requirement that your work be registered in order to obtain copyright; it is automatically acquired upon creation of an original work. Nevertheless, you may wish to apply for voluntary registration. When your work has been registered, a certificate is issued that can, if necessary, be used in court to establish your ownership of the work.

You can register a copyright by completing the required application form and sending it to the Copyright Office along with the appropriate fee. You do not need to send a copy of your work along with the application but you may need to send copies to the National Library of Canada. The registration process typically takes around four weeks but may be longer if amendments are required.

INDICATING COPYRIGHT

There is no requirement to mark your work under the Copyright Act. However, you may choose to mark it with the symbol ©, your name and the year of first publication of the work, for example, © John Doe, 2001. You may use this mark even if you have not formally registered your work with the Copyright Office.

THE PROTECTION PROVIDED BY COPYRIGHT

Your copyright enables you to control the copying and dissemination of your own works. This includes publishing, producing, reproducing, and performing your material. As with patents and trademarks, the responsibility for policing your copyright rests with you.

It is important to understand some of the limitations of copyright protection as well. For example, for purposes of copyright protection, the term "computer program" refers to "a set of instructions or statements, expressed, fixed, embodied or stored in any manner, that is to be used directly or indirectly in a computer in order to bring about a specific result." This means that a specific computer program such as Microsoft Excel can be protected as a literary work but not the idea of spreadsheet programs in general. In addition, any accompanying documentation for a program, such as a user's guide, is considered a separate work and must be registered separately.

Unlike patents and trademarks, a copyright in Canada provides simultaneous protection in most other countries of the world.

REGISTERING YOUR INDUSTRIAL DESIGN

An industrial design is the features of shape, configuration, pattern, or ornament applied to a finished article made by hand, tool, or machine. This may be, for example, the shape of a table or chair, or the shape of the ornamentation of a knife or a spoon. The design must have features that appeal to the eye and be substantially original. Registering your design gives you exclusive rights to the design and enables you to prevent others from making, importing, renting, or selling any article on which the design has been registered and to which the design or a design not substantially different has been applied. Unlike trademark and copyright protection, you can make no legal claim of ownership and have *no legal protection against imitation unless your design has been registered.*

HOW TO REGISTER YOUR INDUSTRIAL DESIGN

You can file your own application for industrial design registration; however, it is generally recommended to hire a patent agent to prepare and follow through on your application. An application for an industrial design must contain:

- a completed application form
- at least one photograph or drawing of the design.

Your application will be examined to ensure that it is original and registerable. It cannot be the same or similar to a design already applied to a similar article of manufacture. Following this assessment the examiner will either approve the application or issue a report indicating what further information or amendments may be required. You have four months to reply to the report. This process can take up to a year, but once registered, designs are valid for 10 years from that date.

MARKING YOUR PRODUCT

You do not have to mark your design to indicate that it has been registered but marking does give you some extra protection. The proper mark is a capital "D" inside a circle along with your name or an abbreviation of it on the article itself, its label, or its packaging. If your product is marked in this way, a court may award a remedy of some kind such as financial compensation if someone is found to be infringing on or violating your design. Otherwise the court can merely issue an injunction to forbid the other party from using your design.

THE PROTECTION PROVIDED BY INDUSTRIAL DESIGN REGISTRATION

As with other forms of intellectual property, you may take legal action against anyone who infringes upon your design in Canada. As the proprietor of the registered design, however, you have exclusive right to use it and may sell all or some of these rights to other people or authorize them to use the design subject to certain conditions. These rights, however, only relate to Canada. To obtain similar rights in other countries you must apply for them in each country separately.

PROTECTING INTEGRATED CIRCUIT TOPOGRAPHIES

The circuits incorporated into an integrated circuit (IC) are embodied in a three-dimensional hill-and-valley configuration called a topography. These designs are protected by the Integrated Circuit Topography Act. IC products, commonly called "microchips" or "semiconductor chips" are incorporated into a variety of consumer and industrial products. The protection associated with the design of a topography is entirely distinct from that of any computer program embodied in the chip. Computer programs are subject to protection under the Copyright Act.

WHAT PROTECTION DOES THE ACT PROVIDE?

The legislation provides exclusive rights in regard to:

- reproduction of a protected topography or any substantial part of it
- manufacturing an IC product incorporating the topography or any substantial part of it
- importation or commercial exploitation of a topography, or of an IC product that embodies a protected topography or any substantial part of it
- importation or commercial exploitation of an industrial article that incorporates an IC product that embodies a protected topography

The Act provides for a full range of civil remedies including injunctions and exemplary damages. Protection for registered integrated circuit topographies is provided for approximately 10 years.

HOW TO PROTECT AN IC TOPOGRAPHY

To protect an IC topography you must apply to the Registrar of Topographies. Applications for "commercially exploited" topographies must be filed within two years of the date of first commercial exploitation anywhere. The application may be rejected if the topography was first exploited outside Canada. Owners must be Canadian or nationals of countries having reciprocal protection agreements with Canada.

FOR MORE INFORMATION ON INTELLECTUAL PROPERTY

Further information on the protection of intellectual property can be obtained from:

Canadian Intellectual Property Office
Industry Canada
50 Victoria St.
Place du Portage, Phase 1
Hull, Quebec
K1A 0C9 Tel: (819) 997-1936 or at (cipo.gc.ca/)

or contact your local Industry Canada, Canada Business Services Centre.

The deadlines for filing, the length of time for which protection is provided, and the current registration fees for several types of intellectual property are summarized in Table 9.1.

TABLE 9.1 INFORMATION ABOUT PROTECTION OF INTELLECTUAL PROPERTY IN CANADA

Type	Application Deadline	Period of Coverage	Government Fees	
Patents	File within 1 year of publication (file before publication for most other countries)	20 years from filing of application	Filing fee	$150
			Examination fee	$200
			Allowance fee (Grant)	$150
			Maintenance fee	
			Year 2, 3 & 4	$ 50
			Year 5 to 9	$ 75
			Year 10 to 14	$100
			Year 15 to 19	$200
Trademarks	(None)	15 years; renewable indefinitely	Filing fee	$150
			Registration fee	$200
Copyright	(None)	50 years plus life of author	Registration fee	$ 65
Industrial Designs	File within 12 months of publication	10 years from date of registration	Examination fee	$160
			Maintenance of registration fee	$215

CONCLUSION

As we have discussed, in addition to various *tangible* assets such as land, buildings, and equipment, your business may also own certain *intangible* assets, such as patents, trademarks, and copyrights. These can be just as important as, or even more important than, your tangible assets. And like tangible assets, with permission of their owner they can be bought, sold, licensed, or used by someone else.

Ideas that are not patentable, and are not otherwise protected, may be protected by contract law either by means of a written *non-disclosure* agreement or by treating them as *trade secrets*. This can be done by taking every precaution to keep valuable knowledge a secret and/or by placing specific provisions in any agreement you may have with your employees that they will neither disclose to anyone else nor use for their own purposes any trade secrets they may acquire while in your employ. The advantages of this type of protection may be even greater than those of patent protection. The success of this approach depends on your ability to control the access of outsiders to the information, as there are no *legal rights* in a trade secret. Typically, once confidential information has been publicly disclosed, it becomes very difficult to enforce any rights to it.

Arranging Financing

Quite a number of sources of financing are available to established businesses. However, there are relatively few sources of *seed capital* for ventures that are just getting off the ground and have no track record. Obtaining such capital can require persistence and determination. Usually you must submit a formal proposal to a prospective source of funding in which you outline your needs, plans for the money, and their expected return and scheduled payment. Many financing proposals have to be revised several times before receiving a positive response. In addition, you may have to be prepared to combine financing from several sources to raise all the funds you require.

Two kinds of funds are potentially available to you: *debt* and *equity*.

DEBT FINANCING

Debt financing is borrowing money that must be repaid in full, usually in periodic payments with interest. Three important parameters associated with debt financing are:

- the amount of principal to be borrowed
- the interest rate on the loan
- the maturity of the loan

Together these three factors determine the extent of your obligation to the creditor. Until the debt has been repaid the provider of the loan has a legal claim against the assets and cash flows of your business. In many case the creditor can demand payment at any time and possibly force your business into bankruptcy because of overdue payments.

The *principal* of the loan is the total amount of money you hope to borrow. This could be the difference between the amount shown on your estimate of your required start-up funding in Figure 7.1 and the sum you are personally able to provide to get your business started.

The *interest rate* is the "price" you will have to pay for the borrowed funds. In most cases it will be tied to the current "prime" rate. This is generally considered to be the rate of interest that banks charge their best customers—those with the lowest risk. For example, a bank might be prepared to offer loans to a small business for prime plus some fixed percentage, perhaps 3 or 4 per cent. The prime rate may fluctuate somewhat due to periodic decisions by the Bank of Canada, so the effective interest rate on your loan may vary somewhat as well.

The *maturity* of the loan refers to the length of time for which you will obtain the use of the funds. This should coincide with your intended use of the money. Short-term needs require short-term financing. For example, you might use a short-term loan to purchase inventory that you intend to sell within a month or two or to finance some outstanding accounts receivables. A short-term loan such as a *line of credit* typically has to be repaid within a year.

Purchasing a building or a major piece of equipment may require a long-term loan or a *term* loan. This is a loan that will be repaid over an extended period of time, typically several years. The purpose of the loan will determine the maturity period.

The primary sources of debt financing are shareholder loans provided by the owners of the business and operating loans and term loans provided by banks and other financial institutions such as trust companies, Alberta Treasury Branches, and credit unions. Providing some funds as a loan rather than as an equity investment can have some advantages for you as the owner of a small business. The interest payments made to you are deductible by the business and it may be easier to withdraw the money if necessary than if it was tied up in equity.

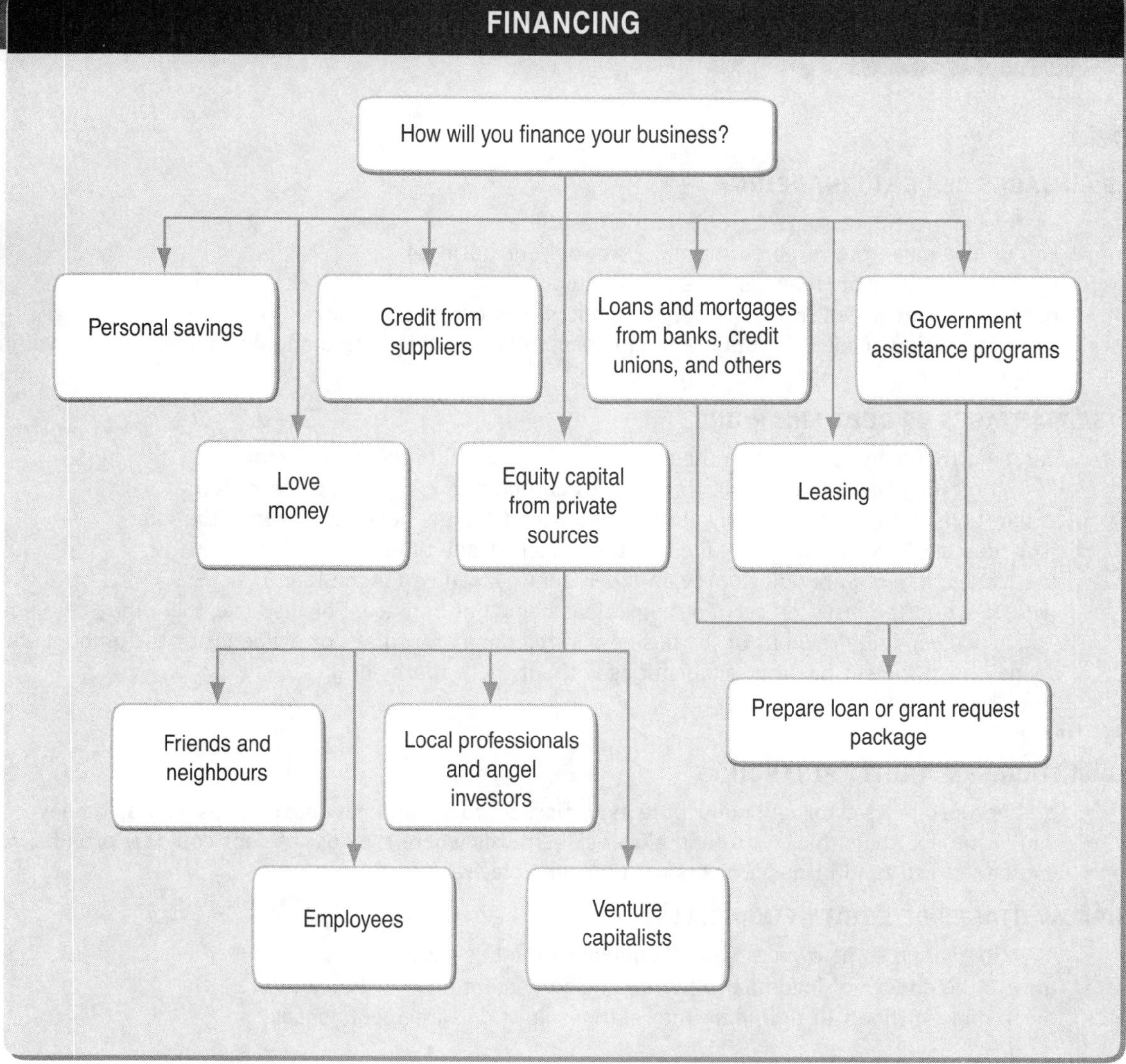

EQUITY FINANCING

Equity funding is money supplied by yourself or investors in exchange for an ownership position in your business. Unlike debt, they don't need to be repaid. Providers of equity capital forego the opportunity to receive interest and periodic repayment of the funds they have extended to your business to share in the profits it is expected to generate. Other than making your own personal investment it is not easy to attract other investors to a new business. No matter how sure you are that your business will be successful, others will not necessarily share your confidence and will need to be persuaded to invest in your idea by your enthusiasm and your business plan.

In addition to providing the funds, equity investors will usually demand a voice in how your business is run. This can substantially reduce your ability to run your business as you would like. They expect to receive their return from any dividends that may be paid out periodically from the net profits of the business or, more significantly, from the increased value of the business as it grows and prospers. They expect to be able to sell all or part of their investment for a considerable profit.

The most common sources of equity financing for start-up businesses are your own personal savings and your family and friends.

The advantages of debt versus equity financing from your perspective as owner of the business are summarized in the Key Points box.

DEBT VS. EQUITY

Debt

ADVANTAGES OF DEBT FINANCING

- useful for meeting a short-term deficit in cash flow
- you do not have to give up or share control of your business
- the term of the debt (loan) is generally limited
- debt may be acquired from a variety of lenders. You can shop around.
- the information needed to obtain a loan is generally straightforward and normally incorporated into a business plan

DISADVANTAGES OF DEBT FINANCING

- can be difficult to obtain when the project is risky and its success uncertain
- taking on more debt than the business needs can be a burden on your cash flows
- if the funds aren't used properly, it may be difficult for the business to repay the loan
- if a "demand" loan, it can be called by the lender at any time
- the lender may require you to provide a personal guarantee for the loan
- lenders will often insist on certain restrictions being put in place. For instance, there may be a limit on how much you can draw out of the business in the form of a salary or dividends or the amount you can spend on equipment or other acquisitions without their approval.

Equity

ADVANTAGES OF EQUITY FINANCING

- an appropriate investor can contribute expertise, contacts, and new business as well as money
- equity may be the only way to fund high-risk ventures where the cost of debt could be prohibitive
- can be used to fund larger projects with longer time frames

DISADVANTAGES OF EQUITY FINANCING

- have to give up some ownership and control of the business
- always the danger of incompatibility and disagreement among the investors
- much more difficult to terminate the relationship if disagreements occur

MAJOR SOURCES OF FUNDS

The major sources of funds for small-business start-ups are personal funds, "love money," banks, government agencies and programs, and venture capital. You may be able to "piece together" the combination of debt and equity funding that you require from a mix of these sources.

PERSONAL FUNDS

The first place to look for money to start your business is your own pocket. This may mean cleaning out your savings account and other investments, selling your second car, postponing your holiday for this year, cashing in your RRSPs, extending your credit cards to the limit, mortgaging the cottage, taking out a second mortgage on the family home, or any other means you may have of raising cash.

"LOVE MONEY"

Once you have scraped together everything you can from your resources and personal savings, the next step is to talk to other people. Additional funds may come from your friends, family, and close personal relations. This is known as "love money."

Recent estimates indicate that, in fact, love money makes up more than 90 per cent of the new business start-up capital in Canada. This personal funding is necessary because banks and other conventional sources usually will not lend money without extensive security. For example, Peter Oliver, whose case is described in Entrepreneurs in Action #33, was able to launch his successful chain of restaurants in Toronto only with the financial support of his wife's parents.

33 Entrepreneurs in action

Love Money — A Helluva Deal for Both Sides

"I've always wanted something I could build into something bigger," says Peter Oliver, explaining why in 1978 he gave up a lucrative career as a real estate agent, and opened Oliver's Old Fashioned Bakery in uptown Toronto. The something bigger is what the 38-year-old has today — four restaurants with anticipated 1987 sales of $12 million and gross profits of 8% to 12%. He also owns two of the four buildings that house his restaurants.

Oliver's success would not have been so swift without the financial support of his wife's parents. They provided the $40,000 down payment on the first building, which was renovated with another $40,000 from Oliver's savings. In exchange for their investment, Oliver guaranteed his in-laws a minimum 12% annual return as well as half ownership in the building. The money has earned them almost 20% every year, and the building has escalated in value from $160,000 to an estimated $1 million. ...

In the beginning he had no formal agreement with his in-laws. But as time went on and they invested more money in his company, proper documents were drawn up, both to arrange bank financing and give everyone concrete evidence of their investment. After nine years, Oliver has built a small empire on a base of love money. And his in-laws have made a superb return on their investments. Oliver sums it up beautifully: "They got a helluva deal," he says, "and I got a helluva deal."

(www.oliverbonacini.com)

Source: Excerpted from Larry Gaudet and Tony Leighton, "Setting Out with Buoyant Backing," *Canadian Business* (October 1987): 76–77. By permission of the authors.

The biggest risk with this source of capital is that if your new business fails and the investors lose money, it can create considerable hard feelings among family and friends. This possibility can be reduced if you lay out all the terms and conditions of the investment in advance, just as you would for any other investors. You should explain the nature of your business, your detailed implementation plans, the risks associated with the venture, and other relevant factors. In fact, it is best if you give both yourself and your investors some measure of comfort by translating your understanding into a formal legal agreement, as Peter Oliver did with his in-laws. If the money is provided to you as a loan, another important reason for putting it into writing is that if, for some reason, you are unable to repay the money and your investor must write it off, the amount of a properly documented loan becomes a capital loss for income tax purposes and can be offset against any capital gains, thereby providing the investor with the potential for some tax relief from the loss.

This most basic kind of financing is often not enough to get the business started, but it is important for external funding sources to see that you and your family are prepared to invest most of your personal resources in the venture. Without a strong indication of this type of individual commitment, it will be extremely difficult to raise any other money. Why should someone not directly involved in the business risk money in your business if you are not prepared to put your own assets on the line?

BANKS, TRUST COMPANIES, CREDIT UNIONS, AND SIMILAR INSTITUTIONS

Banks and similar institutions are the most popular and widely used external source of funds for new businesses. A visit to the local banker becomes almost a mandatory part of any new venture start-up situation. Banks historically have provided debt financing in the form of self-liquidating, short-term loans to cover small businesses' peak working capital requirements, usually in the form of an *operating loan* or *line of credit*.

An operating loan extends credit to you up to a prearranged limit *on an ongoing basis*, to cover your day-to-day expenses such as accounts receivable, payroll, inventory carrying costs, office supplies, and utility bills. If you happen to be in a highly seasonal or cyclical business, for example, such a "line of credit" can be used to purchase additional inventory in anticipation of your peak selling period. An operating loan is intended to *supplement your basic working capital*. An operating loan can also be used to bridge unexpected cash flow interruptions and/or shortfalls. It may also give you the ability to take advantage of supplier discounts for prompt payment.

Operating loans, however, can have some restrictions. For example, your banker may prohibit you from taking retained earnings out of your company during the early stages of your business. In addition, he or she may even veto the purchase of machinery, equipment, and other fixed assets above a certain amount. These operating loans are subject to annual review and renewal by mutual agreement but can often be terminated by the lender at its option unless specific conditions have been incorporated into the loan agreement. Interest on operating loans is usually *tied to the prime rate*. That means it can change either up or down as the prime rate changes. This can be an advantage when interest rates are declining but a major issue if rates are increasing rapidly.

Banks also provide *term loans* to small businesses — loans for the purchase of an existing business or to acquire fixed assets such as machinery, vehicles, and commercial buildings, which typically must be repaid in three to ten years. The "term" is usually linked to the expected lifespan of the asset. Three to four years is common for a truck or computer, while the term of a loan to acquire a building could be considerably longer. Term loans typically have a fixed interest rate for the full term. Therefore your interest cost is predetermined in advance and your budgeting process is simplified. However, the loan amount tends to be limited to a percentage of the value of the asset being financed. In addition, term loans often command a one-time processing fee of 1/2 per cent of the value of the loan.

You should realize that business bank loans, both operating and term loans, are *demand* loans so that regardless of the term, the bank can and will demand they be paid back if it feels the company is getting into trouble. While this usually only occurs when the business has real problems, there is the potential for difficulties; what the banker may perceive as a serious situation may only be perceived as a temporary difficulty by the owner of the business.

Janine DeFreitas and Kevin Fitzgerald, whose situation is described in Entrepreneurs in Action #34 and #35, are typical new business owners. Both were frustrated in their initial efforts to obtain financing from some of the major banks but both recognize they will need bank support to develop and grow their businesses beyond their current stage now that they are more firmly established. Janine, for example, was initially unable to obtain a bank loan despite the fact she had a business plan, love money provided by her father, and a commitment from her principal supplier to provide the necessary inventory for her store. When her request was finally approved on the third try, it was only because it was government guaranteed and co-signed by her father.

Similarly, Fitzgerald's request for start-up funding for his computer resale company was turned down by seven banks and he was forced initially to finance his business by running up charges on his credit card. It wasn't until several years later the company was finally successful in obtaining a line of credit from the Royal Bank. The line of credit has grown significantly over the years, but Fitzgerald and his wife both resent the fact that they must still provide their personal guarantees for the loan despite the fact the business has sales over $5 million.[1]

The bank may ask for your personal guarantee of these loans as well as a pledge of collateral security for the full value of the loan or more. This means that even though your business might be incorporated, your personal liability is not necessarily limited to your investment in the business; you could lose your house, car, cottage, and other personal assets if the business should fail and you are unable to repay your loans to the bank.

To qualify for a loan you must have sufficient equity in your business and a strong personal credit rating. Banks do not take large risks. Their principal considerations in assessing a loan application are the safety of their depositors' money and the return they will earn on the loan. It is critical that you take these factors into account in preparing your loan proposal and try to look at your situation from the banker's point of view.

---

1. "How I raised funds (How savvy entrepreneurs fight for the funding they need)," *PROFIT: The Magazine for Canadian Entrepreneurs* (November, 1998): 35–40.

Key points

ADVICE WORTH BANKING ON

One of the biggest adventures an entrepreneur can undertake is obtaining or renewing business financing—a trail that often determines the survival of many new and small businesses. Unfortunately, the application and approval process for obtaining and renewing commercial credit can be more of a nightmare than an adventure.

In my previous career, I was a branch manager with one of Canada's largest financial institutions. Since I have sat on both sides of the desk, let me share some of my thoughts and advice about seeking bank financing.

As a branch manager supervising the application and investigation process, I believed that assessing the information provided and getting to know my customers were both crucial in making lending decisions. When evaluating potential customers, I made sure not only to review personal credit histories, but I also tried to understand individuals and their personalities. I could usually determine whether I was dealing with a client who would make very effort to repay his or her debt, and I took this factor into account when making the lending decision. Many times applicants did not meet the existing lending criteria or have sufficient collateral for a loan. But if during the interview process they appeared genuine, honest, and hard working, and if they were open about their credit history and how they planned to repay the loan, I would more then likely have approved the loan.

So far, however, as a client applying for commercial credit I have experienced this same flexibility and understanding only twice in seven years. Banks often give the impression that they support and help small business in Canada, but each year our company faces a major challenge to renew credit or obtain new financing. For the approval of commercial loans, it appears that equity, the net worth of borrowers and how much they are risking are more important to banks than the strength of the business plan, the product or the individual.

From my experience as a client, I have learned the importance of being prepared when approaching a bank for commercial financing. Here is my advice:

Provide a solid business plan with financial details of the company and its principals. Include a complete outline of the company's current and projected financial status. But remember, no matter how strong your business plan is or how good your credit history is, if you don't maintain the bulk of the risk, the bank will probably not look at your request seriously. The reality is you must not only sell yourself and your business plan, but you must also be willing to sign everything you own over to the bank.

After jumping through hoops and loops to obtain financing, it is important to establish a good working relationship with your lenders. Provide them with timely and accurate reporting as they request. Share information. And keep the lines of communication open—they need to know you are on top of your operation and that you will present bad news as well as good news to them for discussion. Build the trust factor.

Remember that no matter how strong you feel your relationship with the bank is, there are no guarantees that the staff you deal with now will be involved in future decisions. One year, during our credit renewal process, our file was handed off to a new account manager and branch manager who didn't know anything about our business or the principals. The staff changes resulted in a review of our file, the decision not to deal with our company any more, and a sudden need to seek alternative financing—even after a year of excellent growth and profit.

Prepare for unforeseen financing obstacles by periodically reviewing and updating your business plan, and have strategies ready if you need to seek out new financing. Alternative financing options could include approaching smaller financial institutions such as credit unions or regional banks (which may suit smaller businesses), using the services of companies that trade accounts receivables for cash, or seeking out privately held capital companies. You might also consider finding investment funding, obtained through private placement by selling an equity position in your company, usually to friends, family, or someone willing to take an active role in the business.

Source: Ryan Magnussen, President, WDC Mackenzie Distributors Ltd. Calgary. "Advice Worth Banking On." (www.profitguide.com/firstperson/F1_magnussen.html Used with permission.

34 Entrepreneurs in action

Controlling Interest

JANINE DEFREITAS
The Rubbery Inc., Mississauga, Ont.

Government guarantees, proven products, a 100-page business plan and cold hard cash sounds like a perfect recipe to lure bank financing. Janine DeFreitas knows otherwise.

After the former Rubbermaid Canada sales and merchandising manager watched the company's first full-line retail display sell out in just four weeks, DeFreitas got the urge to open a Rubbermaid-only store. Equipped with her business plan, $50,000 from her father and the promise of product from her supplier, DeFreitas was rebuffed by two banks—and two male loans officers—before a female lender at Toronto-Dominion issued a $110,000 loan. Still, the loan was government-guaranteed and co-signed by DeFreitas' father. "They said I didn't put enough personal equity into it," she says.

The bank should have few worries now: at $3 million a year, sales have doubled projections. DeFreitas is now planning to go national within five years. She's considering franchising to finance out-of-province openings, but is looking at bank debt to fund up to five corporate stores in Ontario. "I wanted to open my own business so I wouldn't have to answer to anybody," DeFreitas explains. "If I go through an investor, I lose a certain amount of control."

(www.therubbery.com)

Source: Excerpted from Charise Clark "How I Raised Funds," *PROFIT* (November, 1998): 35–36. © Charise Clark.

GOVERNMENT

Governments at all levels in Canada have developed a proliferation of financial assistance programs for small business. It is estimated there are more than 600 programs available from both the federal and provincial governments to help people begin a business or assist those that have already started. Many of these programs are aimed at companies in more advanced stages of their development who are looking to grow and expand, but quite a number can be utilized by firms in the start-up stage. Many of these programs offer financial assistance in the form of low-interest loans, loan guarantees, interest-free loans, or even forgivable (non-repayable) loans. Others offer incentives like wage subsidies, whereby the government will pay an employee's wage for a certain period of time. These programs are too numerous to describe in any detail, but let us briefly look at several of the more important ones.

CANADA SMALL BUSINESS FINANCING PROGRAM

New and existing businesses whose gross revenues are less than $5 million may be eligible to obtain term loans from chartered banks, caisses populaires, credit unions, or other lenders and have the loan partially guaranteed by the federal government under the Canada Small Business Financing Act (CSBFA) [(previously known as the Small Business Loans Act (SBLA)]. These loans are provided at a reasonable rate of interest (prime plus no more than 3 per cent for floating rate loans or the lender's residential mortgage rate plus 3 per cent for a fixed-rate loan). In addition, lenders are required to pay a one-time loan registration fee to the government equal to 2 per cent of the amount loaned. This fee is recoverable from the borrower. These loans may be used for any number of purposes, such as the purchase or renovation of machinery and equipment and the purchase and improvement of land and buildings for business purposes. Loan proceeds may be used to finance up to 90 per cent of the cost of the asset, while the maximum value of loans a borrower may have outstanding under the CSBFA cannot exceed $250,000. For more information, contact any private sector lender or:

35 Entrepreneurs in action

Will That Be Cash or Plastic?

KEVIN FITZGERALD, PRESIDENT
Aurora Microsystems Distribution Inc., Sudbury, Ont.

In 1988, physics graduate Kevin Fitzgerald was looking to break into the booming computer resale industry, with a focus on the lucrative corporate, education and government markets. He had just one problem: he had $147 to his name.

Fitzgerald applied to seven banks for startup funds. "In not so many words, they told me I wouldn't succeed," he says. Undaunted, he founded Aurora Microsystems Distribution Inc. with credit cards acquired as a student. In his first year of operations, Fitzgerald ran up $60,000 in charges as he travelled around to drum up clients and bought basic consumables for the office. That figure more than doubled the following year as he put inventory on plastic. Sounds expensive, but by balancing 30-day terms from suppliers and 30 days from credit-card issuers with 60-day payments from customers, Fitzgerald generally paid off his cards promptly while avoiding steep interest charges. All told, Fitzgerald estimates he's charged $1 million in purchases since founding the company — and kept Aurora humming using little capital of his own.

"After years of running on vapor," says Fitzgerald, Aurora won a $50,000 line of credit from the Royal Bank in 1993. The LOC has grown to $500,000 over the years, but both Fitzgerald and his wife — an Aurora employee — guarantee it, despite Aurora's annual revenues of $5 million. That rankles: "If we screw up, the bank has the right to confiscate anything we own," says Fitzgerald. "If she doesn't sign, they pull the line. It's terrible. It's just not right." Fitzgerald was particularly dismayed by one banker with minimal knowledge of the computer business. After explaining that Aurora wanted to emulate Dell Computers, the manager replied, "Who's Dell?" Says Fitzgerald: "If they don't understand the business, how can they possibly understand why you should borrow money from them or how much or what you should do with it?"

As for alternatives, Fitzgerald says building a high-growth business on a shoestring budget leaves little time to scare up funds — a condition he blames for holding Aurora back. But that may soon change as Fitzgerald goes full-throttle to attract outside investors. He's already talked with two venture capitalists, but is willing to consider anyone who "will sit down and work with us," he says. And Fitzgerald figures Aurora would be an attractive investment: "We've never bounced a cheque."

Source: Excerpted from Charise Clark "How I Raised Funds," *PROFIT* (November, 1998): 40.

Small Business Loans Administration
Industry Canada
25 Queen Street
8th Floor, East Tower
Ottawa, Ontario K1A 0H5
Telephone: (613) 954-5540 Fax: (613) 952-0290
(strategis.ic.gc.ca/csbfa)

INDUSTRIAL RESEARCH ASSISTANCE PROGRAM (IRAP)

IRAP provides scientific and technical advice and limited financial assistance for projects designed to enhance a company's technical capability under two program elements:

1. Cost shared small R & D projects provides financial support to cover up to 50 per cent of the costs of subcontractors or consultants to a maximum of $15,000 for small-scale projects of a preliminary nature, for small- and medium-sized companies (up to 500 employees).
2. Cost shared large R & D projects funds 50 per cent of eligible project costs such as staff salaries up to $250,000 for a period of up to 36 months for larger-scale projects and more complex research and development activities.

For more information contact:

Industrial Research Assistance Program
Montreal Road, Building M55
Ottawa, Ontario K1A 0R6
Telephone: (613) 993-5326 or Toll Free: 1-877-994-4727
Fax: (613) 952-1086
(www.nrc.ca/irap)

PROGRAM FOR EXPORT MARKET DEVELOPMENT (PEMD)

PEMD is designed to increase export sales of Canadian goods and services by encouraging Canadian companies to become exporters and helping existing Canadian exporters to develop new markets. PEMD shares the cost of export market development activity these companies would not normally undertake on their own. Market Development Strategies supports a combination of visits, trade fair participation, and market support activities with a repayable contribution ranging from $5,000–$50,000. New exporters may be eligible to receive a maximum of $7,500 for either a market identification visit or for participation in an international trade fair.

For more information contact:

Export Development Division
Department of Foreign Affairs and International Trade
125 Sussex Drive
Ottawa, Ontario K1A 0G2
Telephone: (613) 944-0018
(www.infoexport.gc.ca/pemd/menu-e.asp)

COMMUNITY FUTURES PROGRAM (CFP)

Community Futures is a community economic development program that provides economic planning services to communities as well as business counselling and loans to small business in non-metropolitan communities in Western Canada. Community Futures Development Corporations (CFDC) provide business loans up to $125,000 to assist existing businesses with expansion or to help entrepreneurs create new businesses. CFDCs also deliver two specialized loan programs:

1. The Western Youth Entrepreneurs Program provides repayable loans of up to $25,000 to young entrepreneurs between the ages of 18 and 29, who live in rural areas and have a viable business idea.
2. The Entrepreneurs with Disabilities Program provides repayable loans of up to $125,000 to entrepreneurs with disabilities for a variety of purposes such as:
   - starting or expanding a business
   - applying new technology to their business
   - upgrading their facilities and equipment
   - developing marketing and promotions material
   - establishing working capital for anticipated sales increases

Western Economic Diversification Canada
1500-9700 Jasper Avenue
Edmonton, Alberta T5J 4H7
Telephone: (780) 495-7010
(www.communityfutures.ca)

WOMEN'S ENTERPRISE INITIATIVE LOAN PROGRAM

Western Economic Diversification, through the local Women's Enterprise Initiative in each western province, provides access to a loan fund for women entrepreneurs seeking financing for start-up or expansion of a business. To qualify the business must have a fully completed business plan and be 51 per cent owned or controlled by a woman or women. Loans up to $100,000 are available.

For more information contact the Women's Enterprise Initiative in your province or (www.wd.gc.ca/eng/pos/wei/xindexhtml)

ABORIGINAL BUSINESS CANADA—YOUTH ENTREPRENEURSHIP

Canadian status and non-status Indians, Inuit, and Métis individuals between the ages of 18 and 29 are eligible for support with the preparation of business plans, marketing, and financing the start-up, expansion, modernization, or acquisition of a commercially viable business. The maximum contribution possible is 60 per cent of eligible capital and operating costs to a maximum contribution of $75,000. These contributions are non-repayable.

For more information contact:

Aboriginal Business Canada
235 Queen Street
Ottawa, Ontario K1A 0H5
Telephone: (613) 964-4064 Fax: (613) 957-7010
(www.abc.gc.ca)
or the local provincial office of Industry Canada.

BUSINESS DEVELOPMENT BANK OF CANADA (BDC)

The BDC is a federal Crown corporation that provides a wide range of financial, management counselling, and information services to small business through its broad network of over 80 branches across the country. Its financial services complement those of the private sector by providing funds for business projects that are not available from the commercial banks and other sources on reasonable terms. The BDC will provide term loans for the acquisition of fixed assets, working capital or operating loans, venture loans, and venture capital. Its primary focus is on small- and medium-sized businesses operating in knowledge-based, growth-oriented industries and export markets.

BDC offers an extensive variety of management and financial services including:

1. The Micro Business Program, which combines personalized management support with term financing of up to $50,000 for existing businesses and up to $25,000 for start-ups.
2. The Young Entrepreneur Financing Program will provide term financing of up to $25,000 and 50 hours of business management support to young start-up entrepreneurs between the ages of 18 and 34 to enable them to get their business off the ground.
3. The Student Business Loans Program (SBLP) is offered through Human Resources Development Canada (HRDC) and offers loans up to $3,000 for student entrepreneurs to operate their own businesses during the summer months.

   Michael Vermette (Entrepreneurs in Action #36) was one of the recipients of the SBLP. At the age of 16 he started his own landscaping and lawn care business. Now, five years later, Michael has received a student business loan to get him started each spring and Tri-Star Lawn Care & Landscaping is still growing. The business now has nine employees and has evolved into a year-round enterprise by providing snow-clearing services for local homeowners and businesses while Michael still attends university.
4. The CIBC/BDC Strategic Alliance (Aboriginal Owned Businesses) is one of a number of strategic alliances entered into by the BDC to focus on the special needs of a number of different markets. The CIBC alliance offers improved access to credit and support services for Aboriginal-owned businesses with total combined financing packages of up to $500,000.

   For further information on these and other programs contact:

   Head Office
   Business Development Bank of Canada
   5 Place Ville-Marie
   Suite 400
   Montreal, Quebec H3B 5E7
   Telephone: Toll-free 1-888-463-6232
   (www.bdc.ca)

36 Entrepreneurs in action

Student Biz Blooms with Cash Kick-Start

At the tender age of 15, fast-food restaurant employee Michael Vermette reached one of those life-defining decisions—he resolved that he wasn't going to spend the rest of his life working for someone else.

So the following summer, the then-Winnipeg high school student started up his own lawn-care and landscaping business. Five years later, his Tri-Star Lawn Care & Landscaping is still going strong and the 22-year-old University of Winnipeg administrative studies student and his wife are now considering getting into the property-management business as well.

While that desire to be his own boss has had a lot to do with Vermette's entrepreneurial success thus far, he's quick to also credit much of his success to the federal Student Business Loans Program.

The SBLP has been in operation for more than 15 years and is funded by Human Resources Development Canada and managed by the Business Development Bank of Canada. It offers Canadian high school, college and university students interest-free loans of up to $3,000 to help them start up and operate a summer business. Vermette, who has received a loan from the program in each of the last four years, has applied for a loan again this summer.

During a recent interview, Vermette made no bones about what the student business loans have meant for his fledgling business.

"Without it, most springs I wouldn't have had enough capital saved to afford all the equipment and advertising costs. And I certainly wouldn't have as many customers as I have now."

He noted Tri-Star has grown from a two-person operation with 12 customers that first year to one with between 150 and 160 regular customers and a staff of nine for this summer (including himself and wife Laurie Anne).

In the last few years it's also evolved into a year-round business because in the winter he provides snow-clearing services for local homeowners and businesses.

This year, students have until June 30 to apply for a student business loan.

To be eligible, applicants must be 15 to 30 years of age, be attending a high school, college or university and be prepared to devote an average of 30 to 40 hours per week to their business.

They also cannot have another full-time summer job and their proposed business must provide either a product or a service and be a privately owned business run independently by the students (and partners, if applicable).

© MARC GALLANT/WINNIPEG FREE PRESS. REPRINTED WITH PERMISSION.

Applicants must provide a written business plan detailing their proposed venture, along with a cash-flow forecast. The BDB offers free counselling to help students prepare business plans and to run their companies successfully.

The loans are interest-free until Oct. 1 and students who repay them before Sept. 15 receive a $100 bonus.

Source: Murray McNeill, "Student Biz Blooms with Cash Kick-Start," © *Winnipeg Free Press*, 14 May 2001, B5. Reprinted with permission.

PROVINCIAL FINANCIAL ASSISTANCE PROGRAMS

Most of the provincial governments provide a range of grants, loans, and other forms of assistance to small business. For example, Manitoba offers the Business Start Program that provides a loan guarantee for loans up to $10,000 along with an educational component to assist new entrepreneurs launching their new business. Similarly, Ontario provides the Young Entrepreneurs Program. It is a financing and business training program operated in conjunction with the Royal Bank for youth 18–29 who are not attending school full-time and are interested in starting and operating a business in the province. Upon completion of the Young Entrepreneurs Business Training component, the program will provide them with a loan of up to $7,500 at prime plus 2 per cent.

The number of these programs is much too extensive to discuss here, but you can obtain specific information on the programs offered in your province by contacting the appropriate government department listed among the Some Useful Contacts section.

FYI FOR YOUR INFORMATION

For detailed information on specific federal or provincial programs, you might check the Industry Canada Strategis Web site at (strategis.ic.gc.ca/SSG/so01884e.html), contact your local Canada Business Services Centre, or check out one of the following publications at your local library.

YOUR GUIDE TO GOVERNMENT FINANCIAL ASSISTANCE FOR BUSINESS *IN*: (SEPARATE PUBLICATION AVAILABLE FOR EACH PROVINCE AND TERRITORY)

Productive Publications
P.O. Box 7200, Station A
Toronto, Ontario, M5W 1X8
Telephone: (416) 483-0634

GOVERNMENT ASSISTANCE MANUAL OR CANADIAN SMALL BUSINESS FINANCING AND TAX PLANNING GUIDE

CCH Canadian Ltd.
6 Garamond Court
Don Mills, Ontario, M3C 1Z5
(www.cch.ca)

GOVERNMENT ASSISTANCE PROGRAMS AND SUBSIDIES (GAPS)

Canada Pack
P.O. Box 358
Richmond Hill, Ontario, L4C 4Y6
Telephone: (800) 667-6166

VENTURE CAPITAL

Venture capital involves equity participation in a start-up or growing business situation. Conventional venture capital companies, however, really don't offer much opportunity for firms still in the concept or idea stage. These investors are generally looking for investment situations in proven firms requiring in excess of $1,000,000 and on which they can earn a 40 to 50 per cent annual return. While these companies will often accept high-risk situations, most new venture start-ups don't meet their primary investment criteria.

There are some exceptions to this general rule, however. During the dot-com frenzy of the late 1990s the business press was full of stories of young, Canadian entrepreneurs barely out of school who had received millions of dollars in venture capital financing to launch their latest Internet idea. This situation has cooled considerably over the past year or two. Corporate funds, pension funds, private independent venture funds, and labour-sponsored venture capital funds still have billions of dollars looking for investment opportunities, principally in the high technology sector, but they are being much more careful in determining where it goes.

Christopher Frey, Kisha Ferguson, and Matt Robinson are among the lucky few who have been successful in raising a significant amount of money for a somewhat more traditional business situation. (Entrepreneurs in Action #37) They were looking for a $300,000 equity infusion to help develop their adventure travel magazine, *Outpost*. Sometimes, however, the price can be too high. The initial offer they received to provide the funds demanded a majority stake in the business in return. Though they desperately needed the money to grow their business, they still had sufficient funds to limp along to search out other options so turned the offer down. In the end they connected with a Toronto venture capitalist who provided them with some bridge financing and told them how to beef up their business to make it more attractive to other investors. After 18 months they finally hooked up with another firm in the communications business that provided them with the money they needed to solidify their operations, and they learned a number of valuable lessons along the way.

There are a number of venture capital firms that may be prepared to consider smaller investments. A number of them are listed in the Some Useful Contacts appendix at the back of this book. However, keep in mind that of 100 proposals considered by a typical venture capital firm, only four or five are selected for investment purposes. Therefore, the probability of receiving any financial assistance from this source is very slim. For more information, however, you can contact the:

Canadian Venture Capital Association
234 Eglinton Avenue East
Suite 301
Toronto, Ontario, Canada M4P 1K5
Telephone: (416) 487-0519
(www.cvca.ca)

A new business start-up probably has a better chance of obtaining equity capital from small, private venture capitalists — often called "angels" — or provincially supported venture capital programs. There may be doctors, dentists, lawyers, accountants, and other individuals within your community whom you can approach for investment funds. Many of these people may be looking for situations where they can invest small sums (less than $50,000) with the possibility of earning a larger return than that offered by more-conventional investments, and they are often prepared to invest in start-up situations.

A number of communities and organizations have programs to bring entrepreneurs together with private investors. York University and the MIT Alumni Club of Toronto as well as other organizations sponsor "enterprise forums" in which small companies get an opportunity to tell their story before a group of prospective investors and other experts. The Economic Innovation & Technology Council of the Province of Manitoba periodically sponsors the Invest Manitoba Venture Showcase where local firms who need capital and have a preliminary business plan get the opportunity to make a 10-minute presentation to an audience of prospective investors and others in the community who provide business financing (www.eitc.mb.ca/invest).

37 Entrepreneurs in action

In Search of Adventure Capital

It was the kind of tough call that confronts many entrepreneurs searching for capital. Christopher Frey, Kisha Ferguson and Matt Robinson, partners in adventure travel magazine *Outpost*, badly needed the $300,000 equity infusion being dangled in front of them. The Toronto-based firm was limping along with limited money and had debts to repay. But the investor was demanding a majority stake. Would the trio have to give up control to keep their dream alive?

Frey and Ferguson had launched their quarterly magazine in the spring of 1996 to chronicle Canadians' adventures in exotic locales. But their own 18-month search for capital, as they struggled to secure funding before their cash ran out, was as exciting as any trip from the pages of *Outpost* itself. And, as with any worthwhile quest, what the partners learned along the way—including the power of relationships and the need to think big—was as valuable as the pot of gold that they hoped to discover.

1. YOU NEED A MAP AND A COMPASS

The adventurers started with meagre rations: Frey's experience working on his university newspaper, Ferguson's editorial vision, and $60,000 from savings, family and friends. Frey and Ferguson believed the adventure travel market—growing at an estimated 25% a year—offered a fertile source of readers and advertisers. But that wouldn't be enough. "We knew enough to start, but not enough to have a long-range plan," says Frey. "But we were quick learners, and from the very first day we started, we went about filling in the gaps in our knowledge."

One gap was filled when Matt Robinson joined *Outpost* in June 1997 as a third partner and advertising director. Robinson brought badly-needed marketing savvy from a stint with Toronto publishing giant Maclean Hunter Ltd. Until then, Frey and Ferguson had been traveling without a map. "When I came aboard," recalls Robinson, "Chris was in the process of developing a business plan. It was a living document we developed through the summer and fall." To secure its future, *Outpost* needed ad revenue. To sell ads, it needed to find more readers—an expensive venture. So the trio set out to raise $300,000.

From August until October, the *Outpost* team cold-called more than 200 potential investors culled from a variety of sources, including business and publishing trade magazines. The phone calls yielded a list of some 50 interested people and companies, and the partners mailed promotional packages to them all.

2. BUILD THE VALUE IN YOUR BUSINESS

Meantime, the trio took steps to increase ad revenue, which would make *Outpost* more attractive to investors. "The advertisers are the canaries in our investment world," says Robinson. "Advertisers want value. If they come on board and are singing the praises of the publication, you can translate that to investors as an expression of confidence in the product." The partners relaunched the magazine, doubling the print run to 25,000 copies, adding new editorial sections and more color to the magazine, and producing a media kit to sell

© NADIA MOLINARI

Outpost to advertisers. With finances tight, they funded the improvements in part by an extended overdraft of $12,000—guaranteed against a GIC owned by Frey's parents. The improved magazine debuted in October with $16,000 of advertising—up from $4,000 in the previous issue. Even better, for the first time several brand-name advertisers bought space. "It improved our story [to investors]," says Robinson.

On the financing front, one magazine publisher in Toronto (whom the partners decline to identify) was particularly responsive. The partners met with him six times starting in late summer, 1997. "The first few meetings were a reality check, coming to grips with how difficult the publishing business is," says Frey. The lessons covered both the magazine business and the gruelling requirements of venture capitalists. "It became evident that we had to evaluate every aspect of the company to reach an adequate return to investors," says Robinson. "We learned that the standard return on venture capital is 30% to 40% a year. We did our best to get our projected returns close to that amount."

Outpost was willing to give up a 30% interest for $300,000, but the publisher demanded control. The partners agonized. "We were in an onerous financial situation," says Robinson. "We weren't about to go bankrupt—we could limp along with the three of us putting the magazine out—but the money would have allowed us to repay people who had supported us. And we were sitting on this fabulous market, and we had to get the resources to take advantage of it." But, he says, "We got involved in this project because we wanted to control our destiny. You end up working for someone else and it takes some of that wonderful energy out of your sails." No deal, the trio decided.

Though Frey, Ferguson and Robinson walked away from the money, they had grown as entrepreneurs. "The fact that [the publisher] was willing to talk with us at such length gave us a great deal of confidence in our direction and our ideas," says Robinson. "And he really helped us massage our presentation."

Still, losses for 1997 were $61,000. Robinson gave up his salary for a month and reduced it for the rest of the year. *Outpost* stayed afloat through low overheads, such as renting space for only $450 a month, and by doing what Robinson calls "the 30-60-90 day shuffle," stretching out payments to creditors.

3. LEARN FROM REJECTION

By now the partners had a 25-page business plan which, says Robinson, "was tweaked and morphed many times, not from a lack of focus on our part, but based on an educational process that was going on each time we got feedback from venture capitalists and publishers."

But fishing for investors could be discouraging. "Nothing happens 90% of the time," says Robinson. "You've got to keep your spirits up." Where they couldn't find money, the partners looked for information. "A fair number of people will sit down and listen to you, but often they're doing that just to see what ideas are out there," says Frey. "They may not have any interest at all [in investing]. Then it becomes a smart move to try to turn the meeting to your advantage by getting as much information out of them as possible."

4. ASK FOR MORE THAN YOU NEED

In the spring and summer of 1998, the partners held another important round of meetings, this time with Bob Shoniker, a Toronto venture capitalist. Shoniker asked some tough questions, including, "Do you guys really think $300,000 is enough?" Shoniker noted that it takes as much work to evaluate a $300,000 investment as a $1-million investment. "Up to that point, we had gotten by with the notion of doing as much as possible with as little as possible," says Frey. "But any investor will only invest if they think they're giving you an adequate amount of money." Before their second of three meetings with Shoniker, *Outpost* got the hint and upped the ante—to $1 million.

Shoniker didn't give *Outpost* the $1 million, but he did provide $50,000 in bridge financing. It was a life-saver. "If the bridge capital wasn't there, we would have gone back and negotiated an agreement with the independent publisher and lost control," says Robinson.

Shoniker also challenged *Outpost* to elaborate on its idea for multimedia spin-offs. "The person who just wants to sell a print page of advertising in their publication is going to have a hard time these days," says Robinson. "We really wanted ultimately to develop a brand, with the magazine at the core." *Outpost* had been producing a 10-minute segment for a Toronto community radio station, CJRT, since early 1998. Now, convinced they shouldn't hold off until the magazine was on a sound footing, the partners added plans for a syndicated radio show, website and TV program. *Outpost* was now presented to investors as "an integrated adventure travel communications company that publishes Canada's only adventure travel magazine."

With their new, more aggressive plan and higher revenues—up from $30,000 in 1997 to $150,000 in 1998—the three partners had turned *Outpost* into a promising investment prospect. Still, the company lost $92,500 in 1998, and was rapidly using up its bridge financing. Frey, Ferguson and Robinson slogged on. When the breakthrough finally came at the end of 1998, everything they had learned along the way helped them succeed.

One of the companies they had approached in mid-1997 was BHVR Communications, a Montreal media and entertainment company founded by digital video software entrepreneur Richard Szalwinski. Their approach had gone unanswered. But now Outpost was a substantial property with a vision—and the unreceptive executive who had run BHVR's publishing division was no longer there. Plus, BHVR was looking for new properties after selling its interest in software maker Discreet Logic.

To approach BHVR again, the *Outpost* partners called on their friend Andrew Heintzman, publisher of *Shift* magazine, which had been bought by BHVR in 1996. Heintzman helped arrange a conference call between *Outpost* and BHVR in December 1998. Out of that came a seven-hour meeting in Montreal.

Claude Thibault, vice-president of BHVR subsidiary Normal Net, was impressed. He says BHVR went through "the usual checklist: How much money are they seeking? Where will that take them? Will they need more? What is the valuation? Is it fair? What's their business plan? Does it fit with ours? We were satisfied on all those points rapidly."

Sounds simple, but the partners needed to draw on all they had learned on their journey. They had a sound business plan and were asking for an appropriate investment. They had shown the confidence and the management skills to improve their magazine issue by issue, working on their own. And the multimedia plan urged on them by Shoniker was a perfect fit with BHVR's own vision. BHVR, says Robinson, wanted to leverage content across print and the Net—right up *Outpost*'s alley. *Outpost*'s audience also matched BHVR's target, which Thibault defines as "the edgier half of the 18 to 30 crowd."

There was a discrepancy when it came to valuation. "It's impossible to value a company by any of the standard practices at that stage in its development," says Robinson. He and his two partners valued the company at $1 million; BHVR's number was $700,000. But, with everything else looking positive, BHVR agreed to pay a premium—$1 million for 47% of the company, plus the rights to use *Outpost*'s content on its website.

5. LEVERAGE YOUR RELATIONSHIPS

Robinson believes that Heintzman's recommendation carried weight. "I don't know if we would have had this opportunity if that relationship hadn't been there," he says. He adds this advice: "Adopt an attitude that invites relationships. Don't take any relationships for granted. Any one of them could help."

On December 24, Thibault called to say they had a deal. "We gave a whoop and a holler in the office," says Robinson, "then went home and had a nice Christmas with our families."

The agreement was signed five months later. *Outpost* earmarked the money for investment in circulation, marketing and additional staff. Starting this February, the magazine will come out six times a year. The partners have run a successful direct-mail subscription campaign—with a 3% response rate, according to Robinson—and run a series of TV ads on the Outdoor Network. On the multimedia front, they have obtained an initial commitment from a Canadian broadcaster to partially fund a pilot for a TV series. And they're looking at expanding into Australia, Europe and the United States. *Outpost* has launched a website (www.outpost-magazine.com), and when Normal Net's website launches shortly, *Outpost*'s content will be there too. Robinson forecasts a loss of $130,000 for 2000, but expects to break even for the first time on the November issue. To fund its new initiatives, *Outpost* will need more equity, either from BHVR or outside investors. The quest for financing never ends, but at least Frey, Ferguson and Robinson are now experienced travelers.

(www.outpostmagazine.com)

Source: Sheldon Gordon, "Adventure Capital," *PROFIT: Magazine*, (February-March 2000): 45–48. Used with permission.

Similarly, the federal government started the Canadian Community Investment Plan (CCIP) in 1996 as a means to improve access to risk capital for small- and medium-sized firms in smaller communities located some distance from the country's major financial centres. Each of the 22 demonstration projects across the country, from Pentiction, B.C. to Mount Pearl, Nfld., have developed various innovative strategies aimed at facilitating access to risk capital for their smaller firms. These include arranging investor forums, pre-screening proposals they receive before presenting them to investors, and making their entrepreneurs more investor-ready by offering coaching services and specific seminars (strategis.ic.gc.ca/SSG/cw01000e.html).

Canada's chartered banks are often criticized for not providing this kind of risk capital to small business. Banks, however, are principally low-risk lenders of their depositor's money and traditionally provide debt financing. Venture capitalists and other private investors provide financing in exchange for shares or other interest in the company. Banks have neither the mandate nor the expertise to participate in this specialized market.

Leon Rudanycz, who is profiled in Entrepreneurs in Action #38, is a typical "angel." He had a very successful business of his own, sold it, and used some of the proceeds to invest in other people's ideas. These investments gave him a way to keep involved, to continue to participate in the growth and development of these businesses, to contribute to major company decisions, and an opportunity to make a good financial return on his investments.

Obtaining money from private venture capital sources, however, may pose certain problems for you. You will probably have to give up at least partial ownership and control of your business. In addition, venture capitalists usually have limited resources, so additional funds may not be available if required later. Finally, as amateur investors, these people may not have the patience to wait out the situation if things don't work out as quickly as you originally planned.

ANGEL INVESTORS: THE DEFINITION

Angel investors are individuals who invest in businesses looking for a higher return than they would see from more traditional investments. Many are successful entrepreneurs who want to help other entrepreneurs get their business off the ground. Usually they are the bridge from the self-funded stage of the business to the point that the business needs the level of funding that a venture capitalist would offer. Funding estimates vary, but usually range from $150,000 to $1.5 million.

The term "angel" comes from the practice in the early 1900's of wealthy businessmen investing in Broadway productions. Today "angels" typically offer expertise, experience and contacts in addition to money. Less is known about angel investing than venture capital because of the individuality and privacy of the investments. The Center for Venture Research at the University of New Hampshire which does research on angel investments has developed the following profile of angel investors:

- The "average" private investor is 47 years old with an annual income of $90,000, a net worth of $750,000, is college educated, has been self employed and invests $37,000 per venture.
- Most angels invest close to home and rarely put in more than a few hundred thousand dollars.
- Informal investment appears to be the largest source of external equity capital for small businesses. Nine out of 10 investments are devoted to small, mostly start-up firms with fewer than 20 employees.
- Nine out of 10 investors provide personal loans or loan guarantees to the firms they invest in. On average, this increases the available capital by 57%.
- Informal investors are older, have higher incomes, and are better educated than the average citizen, yet they are not often millionaires. They are a diverse group, displaying a wide range of personal characteristics and investment behavior.
- Seven out of 10 investments are made within 50 miles of the investor's home or office.
- Investors expect an average 26% annual return at the time they invest, and they believe that about one-third of their investments are likely to result in a substantial capital loss.
- Investors accept an average of 3 deals for every 10 considered. The most common reasons given for rejecting a deal are insufficient growth potential, overpriced equity, lack of sufficient talent of the management, or lack of information about the entrepreneur or key personnel.
- There appears to be no shortage of informal capital funds. Investors included in the study would have invested almost 35% more than they did if acceptable opportunities had been available.

For the business seeking funding, the right angel investor can be the perfect first step in formal funding. It usually takes less time to meet with an angel and to receive funds, due diligence is less involved and angels usually expect a lower rate of return than a venture capitalist. The downside is finding the right balance of expert help without the angel totally taking charge of the business. Structuring the relationship carefully is an important step in the process.

What Does an Angel Investor Expect?

There are almost as many answers to what angels expect as there are angels. Each has their own criteria and foibles because they are individuals. Almost all want a board position and possibly a consulting role. All want good communication although for some that means quarterly reports, while for others that means weekly updates. Return objectives range from a projected internal rate of return of 30% over five years to sales projections of $20 million in the first five years to the potential return of five times their investment in the first five years. Most are looking for anything from a five to 25 percent stake in the business. Some want securities—either common stock or preferred stock with certain rights and liquidation preferences over common stock. Some even ask for convertible debt, or redeemable preferred stock, which provides a clearer exit strategy for the investor, but also places the company at the risk of repaying the investment plus interest. Additionally, the repayment may imperil future financing since those sources will not likely want to use their investment to bail out prior investors.

Some angels ask for the right of first refusal to participate in the next round of financing. While this sounds eminently reasonable, some venture capitalists will want their own players only or certain investment minimums so this strategy may limit who future participants might be.

Future representation of the board of directors also needs to be clarified. When a new round of financing occurs, do they lose their board rights? Or should that be based on a percentage ownership—when their ownership level drops below a certain level, they no longer have board representation.

In order to protect their investment, angels often ask the business to agree to not take certain actions without the angel investor's approval. These include selling all or substantially all of the company's assets, issuing additional stock to existing management, selling stock below prices paid by the investors or creating classes of stock with liquidation preferences or other rights senior to the angel's class of security. Angels also ask for price protection, that is anti-dilution provisions that will result in their receiving more stock should the business issue stock at a lower price than that paid by the angels.

To prepare to solicit an angel, several critical factors will aid in making the approach successful. First, assemble an advisory board that includes a securities accountant and an attorney. Two important functions of the board are to recommend angels to contact and to work with the management team to develop a business plan to present to the angel. The business plan itself should define the reason for financing, how the capital will be spent and the timetable for going public or seeking venture capital funding.

Most of all, take your time in forming a relationship with an angel. You are going to be spending a number of years together at a critical time in your business' life. Take the time to assure yourself that this is a person who you are comfortable with through both the ups and downs the future will bring.

ADDITIONAL SOURCES OF FINANCING

PERSONAL CREDIT CARDS

The credit limit extended by financial institutions on personal credit cards can provide you with ready access to a short-term loan, but usually at interest rates that are considerably higher than more conventional financing (upwards of 18–22 per cent). There may be occasions, however, where other sources of working capital are not available and drawing upon the personal line of credit associated with your cards may be the only source of funds available to sustain your business. This can be risky since you are personally liable for the expenditures on the card even though they may have been made for business purposes, but it may be useful if you are expecting a major payment or other injection of cash into the business within a few days.

CANADIAN YOUTH BUSINESS FOUNDATION

The Canadian Youth Business Foundation (CYBF) is a national organization that enables young entrepreneurs (18–29 years old) to pursue their aspirations of building successful businesses by providing them with several forms of business assistance. These include:

- a loan program that will provide up to $15,000 to cover the start-up costs of their business
- mentorship programs like Entre Nous for their loan clients and Odyssey for other young people who do not require a business loan but might like a mentor
- an interactive on-line resource called YouthBusiness.com that provides young entrepreneurs with information, feedback, and other support.

For further information contact their national office at:
Canadian Youth Business Foundation
123 Edward St.
Toronto, ON M5G 1E2
Telephone: (416) 408-2923 Fax: (416) 408-3234
(www.cybf.ca)

38 Entrepreneurs in action

Looks Like an Angel

How do you find an angel? You might hear about him from your lawyer, from an investment company or from somebody at a cocktail party.

"You'd hear that Leon had a business and sold it, and invested in a couple of other ones successfully and has some money to invest," says Leon Rudanycz, a typical contributor to the largely unmeasured pool of informal investment capital that nurtures budding young companies.

Rudanycz, who has degrees in law and engineering, started up a computer distributing company in the mid-'80s. Now called Tech Data Canada Inc., it's one of the country's largest high-tech distributors. Rudanycz sold out, then became an angel by investing some of the proceeds in two other fledgling computer companies.

"Both were started out of people's homes, very lean and mean. I ended up selling my interest in both companies — one within four years, the other three. But they were both profitable from day one."

That's not always the case, and most venture capitalists make their money back when they take the company public, usually seeking an annual return of 30%-40%. In the crapshoot of angel investing, only a few ventures hit the big time, so the winners have to make up spectacularly for the many losers.

"Angel investing, by its nature, is less formal, involves smaller sums of money and usually does not involve a full-time position in the company," says Rudanycz. "It's generally more in the $100,000 range."

Carleton University has carried out the most extensive research into Canada's informal investment market, conducting a survey of 279 angels. "The investors were found to be significantly more wealthy than most Canadians ... and occupy the top one percentile of wealth among Canadian households," says the Carleton report.

In plumbing the angel psychology, the research found that "investors tend to be men with an internal locus of control, very high needs for achievement and dominance."

Almost 90% expected to serve on a board of directors or advisers when investing. A third of them participate directly as an operating principal. And nearly two-thirds also stipulate some sort of operating covenants in the form of periodic reports, authorization of cash disbursements over a certain amount, and control of salaries and dividends.

Rudanycz fits the mould perfectly. "I demand a seat on the board, cheque-signing authority along with the owner, a good handle on the accounting and a hand in major decisions," he says.

His two subsequent high-tech investments were made in the form of a secured loan, and the shares were simply "the kicker, the bonus. I don't always do that, though." For example, Rudanycz says he's considering a straight equity investment in a clothing manufacture and design business. He'd get a piece of the action for a relatively measly $10,000.

"Projected sales in the first year are $100,000 and probably a million in the third, and for them this $10,000 is pivotal," says Rudanycz, describing a deal that's well beneath the threshold of the mainstream venture capital industry.

(www.venturelinkcorp.com)

Excerpted from Gord MacLaughlin, "Divine Intervention," *The Financial Post*, 6 May 1995, p. 7. Reprinted with permission.

SUPPLIERS' INVENTORY BUYING PLANS

In some industries one way of obtaining working capital may be through supplier's financing. Suppliers may be prepared to extend payment terms to 60, 90, or even 120 days for some customers. Other suppliers may offer floor plan financing or factoring options to help their dealers finance inventory purchases, usually in advance of the peak selling season. In addition, many suppliers offer discounts off the face value of their invoice (typically 2 per cent for payment within 10 days) or penalize slow paying customers with interest charges (often 11/2 per cent a month). These programs can impact your financing requirements.

LEASING VS. BUYING

In competitive equipment markets, specialized leasing and finance companies will arrange for the lease of such items as expensive pieces of equipment, vehicles, copiers, and computers. Leasing, often with an option to buy, rather than purchasing can free up your scarce capital for investment in other areas of your business. While the interest rates charged on the lease contract may be somewhat higher than you might pay through the bank, the lease expenses are usually fully deductible from your taxable income. A lease contract will fix your cost of having the equipment for a fixed term and may provide the flexibility to purchase the equipment at a later date at a predetermined price.

LEASEHOLD IMPROVEMENTS

When locating your business in rented premises it is usually necessary to undertake a number of leasehold improvements to make the premises appropriate to your needs. Installing new electrical outlets, adding additional partitions and walls, laying carpet, painting, installing fixtures, and similar modifications can add considerably to the cost of launching your business. Sometimes it may be possible to get the landlord of your location to assist in making these improvements, particularly if there is a lot of other space available to rent. The landlord or property manager may agree to provide a portion (an allowance of a dollar amount per square foot of space) or cover all of your leasehold improvement in return for a longer-term lease (typically three to five years). Reducing your initial expenditures in this way can reduce the start-up cash and equity you require to launch your business, even though you will be paying for these improvements in your monthly rent over the course of the lease.

ADVANCE PAYMENT FROM CUSTOMERS

It may be possible to negotiate a full or partial payment from some customers in advance to help finance the costs of taking on their business. In some industries, construction for example, it is customary to receive a partial payment at certain defined stages during the course of the project rather than waiting until completion. These payments can reduce the cash needs of running your business. Any work that involves special orders or custom designs for products specifically tailored to the requirements of one customer should require a significant deposit or full payment in advance.

With this extensive number of alternatives available to you as potential sources of financing, it may be useful for you to give some thought to the range of possibilities you might tap into in putting together the start-up requirements for your new venture. Figure 10.1 provides a framework for you to identify how much money you think you will need to launch your business and where you think that financing might possibly come from: your personal resources; friends, relations, and other personal contacts; lending agencies; grant programs, and other sources that may be available to you.

EVALUATING YOUR ABILITY TO SECURE FINANCING

Financing is not a business's right. Johanne Dion, the CEO of Trans Hub e Inc. and one of Canada's top women entrepreneurs for 2001 says, "Banks are not there to lend you dollars. They're there to make a profit. If you don't have a good plan, if you don't do your (financial) statements every year, they'll say 'Sorry we need our money.'"[2]

When seeking a loan, it is wise to shop around for the best available terms. This includes comparing obvious features of the loan such as the interest rate but also evaluating:

- size of transaction fees
- prepayment policies
- flexibility of payment terms
- fixed or floating interest rate
- security and personal guarantees required
- quality of overall service provided by the institution
- expected processing time

2. Kara Kuryllowicz, "Learning the Ropes," *PROFIT: The Magazine for Canadian Entrepreneurs* (October 2001): 42.

FIGURE 10.1 WHERE WILL YOU GET THE MONEY?

Starting a business usually requires some money. As we have pointed out in this Stage, there are any number of sources from which this financing can be obtained. You may need to give some thought to approximately how much money you think you will need to launch your business and just where you feel you will be able to obtain it. Completing a form like Figure 10.1 will give you a good estimate of roughly what your start-up financial requirements are likely to be.

How much money do you think you will need to launch your business? **$ ________**
Where can you get the funds?

SOURCE	POSSIBLE AMOUNT	
Personal Sources		
Cash	$ ________	
Stocks/bonds	________	
Mutual Funds	________	
Term Certificates	________	
RRSPs	________	
Cash Value of Life Insurance	________	
Other Investments ________________	________	
Real Estate	________	
Vehicles	________	
Other Assets ________________	________	
Credit Card Limits	________	
Other Personal Sources	________	
Total Available from Personal Sources		$ ________
Personal Contacts		
Family Members	$ ________	
Friends	________	
Colleagues and Acquaintances	________	
Partners	________	
Other Private Investors ________________	________	
Total Available from Personal Contacts		$ ________
Lending Agencies		
Chartered Banks	$ ________	
Business Development Bank	________	
Caisse Populaires and Credit Unions	________	
Finance Companies	________	
Government Agencies	________	
Other Lending Agencies ________________	________	
Total Available from Lending Agencies		$ ________
Grant Programs		
Federal Government Programs	$ ________	
Provincial Government Programs	________	
Municipal Programs	________	
Other ________________		
Total Available from Grants		$ ________
Other Sources		
Suppliers Credit	$ ________	
Customers	________	
Others ________________	________	
Total Available from Other Sources		$ ________
TOTAL AVAILABLE FROM ALL SOURCES		**$ ________**

An important aspect of your financial condition is your ability to obtain financing. In preparing to approach a banker regarding a loan, there are several suggestions you should keep in mind to increase your probability of getting the funds:

- Don't just drop in on your bank manager; make an appointment.
- Start your presentation by briefly describing your business and the exact reason you require a loan.
- Be prepared to answer any questions your banker may have. He or she wants to determine how well you really understand your business. If you can't answer certain questions, explain why and say when you will be able to provide the information.
- Be prepared to discuss collateral and other security you may be required to provide.
- If your business is currently operating, invite the banker to stop by to see it first-hand.
- Ask when you can expect a reply to your request. If there is a delay, inquire whether there is additional information you need to provide.

PROFIT magazine asked entrepreneurs, bankers, and financial consultants their most successful time-tested secrets for getting the best from their banker. Here are their suggestions:

- **Know what your banker is looking for.** Before you set foot inside a bank, you should understand the ground rules of credit. Banks are not in the business of financing risk. Before they sign on the dotted line they need evidence you have a comprehensive plan and the management skills to successfully implement it. Ask yourself the question, "If I were a banker, would I lend money to me?" The bank needs to be reassured that you can repay your loan. The bank will also look for a strong base of equity investment in the company already. Don't expect the bank to invest in something you wouldn't invest in yourself. To reduce its risk the bank will want some form of collateral security. In many cases, the bank will require collateral worth two or three times the amount of the loan.

- **Don't "tell" your banker, "show him."** Don't just tell your banker about the great new product you have devised. Bring it or a prototype of it along to your banker and demonstrate what makes it so great. Bring in a sample of whatever it is you plan to sell and let them see it, taste it, or try it firsthand.

- **Interview your banker.** There are no good banks, only good bankers. Be prepared to shop around. Make certain you are dealing with the right person and the right branch for you. Visit at least three different banks before making a decision. Ask your accountant, lawyer, customers, or suppliers for a referral.

- **Passion makes perfect.** The most persuasive thing an entrepreneur can do when he or she is negotiating a loan is to show how much passion they have for what they are doing. You should try to present the attitude that you are prepared to do everything possible to make the business succeed.

- **Ask for more money than you need.** One of the worst mistakes you can make is to not consider your future requirements when calculating the size of the loan or the line of credit you think you will need. If you have to go back to the bank in five or six months to ask for an increase, the bank is going to be very concerned. It reflects badly on your ability to plan and you are also making extra work for the bank that could be reflected in extra charges for your loan.

- **Get your banker involved in your business.** Invite your banker over, at least every six months, even if it's just for coffee. Make time to get to know your banker. Get them involved and ask them for advice. Take advantage of opportunities to network with bankers and their colleagues. If the bank holds a reception, or open house, make an effort to attend.

- **Increase your credit when you don't need it.** Many entrepreneurs only begin looking for outside financing when their own resources are tapped out. You should start to begin sourcing funds at least 12 months before you need it. Advanced planning will give you time to adequately explore all your options, meet with several banks, and ultimately work out the best deal for your business.

- **Make professional introductions.** Introduce your lawyer and your accountant to your banker. Make sure your accountant gets the bank's proposal outlining the terms and conditions of your loan or line of credit.
- **If all else fails, keep looking.** Finding the money to start or expand a business is hard work. Most entrepreneurs have been turned down many times for financing. The key is continuing to pursue every available means of securing the capital you need.[3]

A financial institution may turn down your loan application for any of a number of reasons, and it is important that you ask what they are. This knowledge may help you in future attempts to secure funding. Some of the most frequent reasons why a loan application can be rejected are as follows:

1. The business idea might be considered ill advised or just too risky.
2. You may not have offered sufficient collateral. Lenders want some assurance that they will be able to recover most or all of their money should you default on the payments.
3. The lender may feel there is insufficient financial commitment on your part.
4. You have not prepared a comprehensive and detailed business plan.
5. Your reason for requesting the loan is unclear or not acceptable to the lender. It is important that you specify the intended application of the requested funds and that this application be outlined in detail. This outline should also show your planned schedule for the repayment of the loan.
6. You do not appear confident, enthusiastic, well-informed, or realistic enough in your objectives. The lender's assessment of your character, personality, and stability are important considerations in their evaluation of your loan application.

The worksheet shown in Figure 10.2 will allow you to assess some of the critical factors that may affect your ability to secure external funding. It will also give you some indication of what aspects of your personal character, development of your business plans, or quality of the basic idea underlying your new venture could be improved. On the worksheet, indicate your assessment of your personal situation on each of the indicated factors as honestly as you can. How do you rate? Could some factors be improved upon? What can you do to strengthen these areas, or how might you overcome these negative factors?

One question you should consider is, "How much can I possibly lose on my venture should it fail?" The losses in some types of businesses can wipe out virtually all of the funds you have invested or personally guaranteed. This tends to be true in situations like a financial planning and counselling business, a travel agency, or a hair salon, in which very little property or equipment is owned by the business. In other situations, such as manufacturing, construction, or real estate, there is usually an opportunity to sell the assets solely or partially owned by the business to recover at least part of your initial investment.

The way to explore this question is to consider alternative scenarios for different ways in which the business might fail and estimate the liquidation value of any residual assets. To the extent that this value falls short of the initial cost of those assets less any outstanding claims, you could lose that amount of money plus the opportunity cost of the time and effort you spent in trying to develop the business.

3. Adapted from David Menzies, "Getting the Best From Your Bank," *PROFIT: The Magazine for Canadian Entrepreneurs* (November, 1998): 26–32. Reprinted with permission.

FYI FOR YOUR INFORMATION

BUSINESS FINANCING

For more information on obtaining financing for your new business you might consult the following Web sites:

SOURCES OF FINANCING—INDUSTRY CANADA

This site contains an extensive directory of Canadian financial providers, a powerful search engine of financial providers, information on different types of financing and financial providers, and tips to help you secure financing.
(strategis.ic.gc.ca/sc_mangb/sources/engdoc/homepage.html)

DOING BUSINESS IN CANADA, CANADIAN BUSINESS GUIDE, MONEY MATTERS

An overview of financial matters as they relate to small business in Canada including financing and insurance.
(www.dbic.com/guide/m5-1.html)

CANADIAN YOUTH BUSINESS FOUNDATION

This organization is a non-profit, private-sector initiative designed to provide mentoring, business support, and loans to young Canadian entrepreneurs who are starting new businesses.
(www.cybf.ca)

CANADIAN BANKERS ASSOCIATION, SMALL BUSINESS FINANCING

This site provides information on sources and types of small business financing.
(www.cba.ca/eng/Tools/Brochures/tools_small_biz_financing.htm)

BUSINESS DEVELOPMENT BANK OF CANADA

This site provides an overview of Business Development Bank financial products aimed at young entrepreneurs, Aboriginal people, and small business in general.
(bdc.ca/bdc/home/Default.asp)

ACOA PROGRAMS

The site provides an overview of a number of programs provided by the Atlantic Canada Opportunities Agency to help local entrepreneurs start new businesses or upgrade existing ones.
(www.acoa.ca/e/financial)

ABOUT CANADA—SMALL BUSINESS, CANADA

Places to find the money and financial information you need to start and grow your Canadian small business, including types of financing, sources of funds, attracting investors, and financial advice from experts.
(sbinfocanada.about.com/cs/financing)

IDEA CAFÉ, IDEA CAFE'S FEAST OF FINANCING: 40+ PAGES OF TIPS AND TOOLS TO HELP YOU GET THE MONEY YOUR BUSINESS NEEDS

This is a U.S. site but with lots of interesting information.
(www.ideacafe.com/getmoney/financing.html)

AMERICA'S BUSINESS FUNDING DIRECTORY

A guide to over 3,600 business loan and venture capital sources of funding (principally in the United States).
(www.businessfinance.com)

BANKS

You might also check the Web site of any of Canada's major chartered banks.

FIGURE 10.2 LOAN APPLICATION ASSESSMENT WORKSHEET

Assessment Factor	Poor 1	2	Good 3	Excellent 4	5
Personal credit rating	____	____	____	____	____
Capacity to pay back loan from personal assets if business fails	____	____	____	____	____
Collateral to pay back loan from personal assets if business fails	____	____	____	____	____
Character (as perceived in the community)	____	____	____	____	____
Commitment (your personal investment of time, energy, and money)	____	____	____	____	____
Clarity and completeness of your business plan	____	____	____	____	____
Viability of business concept (e.g., moderate risk)	____	____	____	____	____
Personal experience in the proposed business	____	____	____	____	____
Successful experience in your own business	____	____	____	____	____
Balanced management team available	____	____	____	____	____
Suitability of your personality to the pressures and responsibilities of the business	____	____	____	____	____

What can you do to improve the weak areas (where you have rated yourself 1 or 2)?

____

____

____

____

Adapted from D. A. Gray, *The Entrepreneur's Complete Self-Assessment Guide* (Vancouver: International Self-Counsel Press Ltd., 1986), p. 123.

Preparing Your Business Plan

The final stage in building a dream for a new venture of your own is developing your business plan. A business plan is a written document that describes all aspects of your business venture — your basic product or service, your prospective customers, the competition, your production and marketing methods, your management team, how the business will be financed, and all the other things necessary to implement your idea. It might be called the "game plan" of your business.

BUSINESS PLANNING — THE "BIG PICTURE"

WHY CONSIDER THE "BIG PICTURE"?

When you start your business you will find that there are many things that happen that you didn't expect, or didn't work out the way you expected. Don't worry. Your experience in this regard won't be unique. This happens to almost everyone. What is important is for you to be prepared for this to happen and ready to make adjustments. In making these changes it is important that you don't lose sight of what it is that you are really trying to do. This means that you need to keep the "Big Picture" in mind. The "Big Picture" is brought together in the business planning process.

THE STEPS IN THE BUSINESS PLANNING PROCESS

The business planning process focuses on the future. It enables you to relate what you wish to achieve to what your business concept or idea can deliver. It entails working your way through each of the following steps in a logical and sequential way:

1. DEVELOP A VISION STATEMENT

A *vision statement* focuses on the "what" of your business. Your *vision statement* should describe your idealized perception of what your business will look like under perfect conditions, if all your goals and objectives have been met. It lays out the "Super Goal" that you would like your business to achieve. The key components of your *vision statement* will be:

- the name of your planned business venture
- the product/service offering you plan to provide
- the target market(s) you intend to serve

Your *vision statement* should be short (a sentence or two). It should also be easy to understand and easy to remember.

For example, a typical *vision statement* for a new sporting goods retailer might be:

The Hockey House plans to provide a wide range of hockey-related products and services to casual skaters, minor hockey players, community clubs and organizations, and competitive hockey teams and players.

2. FORMULATE A MISSION STATEMENT

A *mission statement* focuses on the "how" of your business. It defines the purpose of your venture. It outlines the reason for the existence of your business and provides some understanding of how your business will be operated. It is, in fact, the "Super Strategy" of your business. The key components of your *mission statement* will describe:

BUSINESS PLAN

Prepare your business plan

↓

Develop a vision statement

↓

Formulate your mission statement

↓

Develop clear and specific objectives

↓

Develop a realistic business plan

↓

A typical business plan

- Letter of transmittal
- Title page
- Table of contents
- Executive summary and fact sheet
- Body of the plan
    - Description of the company and the industry
    - Overview of your product/service offering
    - Market analysis
    - Your marketing plan
    - Your development plan
    - Your production/operations plan
    - Your management team
    - Your implementation schedule
    - Your financial plan
- Appendices

- what your business will do
- its market focus, niche, or particular image
- your planned location and the geographic market served
- how you plan to grow the business
- your sustainable uniqueness, or what will distinguish your business from others and will continue to do so on a long-term basis

Your *mission statement* should be a series of short phrases that addresses each of these elements. For example, a *mission statement* for The Hockey House might state:

The Hockey House will provide a broad range of skates, sticks, pads, sweaters, and other related hockey equipment and services intended to meet the requirements of ice and in-line hockey players at all levels of ability; from beginners to semi-professional and professionals. It will also sell related supplies and equipment such as goal nets and timers, with a view to being the one-stop shop for hockey in Manitoba and northwestern Ontario. It will sell to individuals, teams, and community clubs through a retail outlet located adjacent to a major hockey complex in Winnipeg but will also produce a four-colour catalogue and call personally on groups in communities outside the city. Our principal competitive edge will be the breadth of selection we can offer and the quality of service we plan to provide.

3. DEFINE THE FUNDAMENTAL VALUES BY WHICH YOU WILL RUN YOUR BUSINESS

Many arguments, particularly in family businesses or partnerships, occur because the members do not share common values, even when they often assume that they do. For a new business to have a good chance of succeeding all principals should agree on a basic set of values by which they will operate. The process of discussing and trying to achieve agreement on these values is likely to identify points of difference that should be addressed before the business is started. This process can be conducted in two steps. Step 1 requires you and any other principals associated with the business to define their own personal values. Step 2 consolidates the common values by which the business will be operated.

An example of a statement of business values might look like the following:

In conducting our business, we will implement our Vision by conducting our affairs so that our actions provide evidence of the high value we place on:

Integrity *by dealing honestly with our customers, employees, suppliers, and the community*

Responsibility *by taking into account the environment in which we do business, community views, and the common good*

Profitability *by being conscious that an appropriate level of profit is necessary to sustain the business and allow our values to continue to be observed*

Value *by providing quality products that are recognized as delivering value for money*

Employees *by providing quality, equitable opportunities for development in a healthy workplace, with appropriate rewards*

4. SET CLEAR AND SPECIFIC OBJECTIVES

Setting objectives for your business provides you with yardsticks with which to measure your ability to achieve your vision. Objectives define measurable targets whose achievement can also contribute directly to the successful accomplishment of the mission of your business. Unlike "Goals," which provide a broad direction for your business, "Objectives" provide you with the means to measure directly the performance of your business.

Business objectives usually relate to such issues as:

- the return on investment the business should achieve
- a desired level of market position or market share
- projected stages of technological development
- specific levels of financial performance

To be effective an objective should:

- refer to a specific outcome, not an activity
- be measurable
- be realistic and achievable based on the actual capabilities of the business
- contain a specific time deadline

For example, a reasonable set of objectives for The Hockey House might be:

1. *To generate $xxxx in sales by the end of year one*
2. *To achieve $yyy in after-tax profits in year one*
3. *To increase inventory turnover from x times to y times during year one*

Figure 11.1 outlines a framework that will enable you to develop the "Big Picture" for your business.

5. MAKING IT HAPPEN! DEVELOP A REALISTIC BUSINESS PLAN

Your business plan is the most important business document you will ever prepare and it is also probably the most difficult. It takes a lot of time, research, self-discipline, and commitment to complete properly and is not a lot of fun. However, regardless of whether you intend to start a small, part-time business in the basement of your home or launch a sophisticated, high-growth venture, you still need a business plan.

Your business plan is the culmination of all your self-evaluation, ideas, research, analysis, assessment, round-table discussions, bull sessions, schemes, and daydreams. It lays out for everyone to see precisely where you are now, where you are going, and how you plan to get there. It presents everything about you and what you intend to do — your goals and objectives, opportunities and threats facing you, your business strengths and weaknesses, and so on. It is a comprehensive but concise disclosure of all aspects of your business venture.

How you define your business plan, however, affects your approach to writing it. If you view it as a very complex and boring task, your plan will come across that way to any reader. As a result, many business plans are dry, rambling, and highly technical because the entrepreneurs behind them see them largely as some sort of formal academic exercise.

Your business plan should be viewed as a selling document, not unlike a piece of sales literature you would distribute about your company. Except with your business plan, rather than just promoting a particular product or service you are selling the whole company as a package. If you are really excited about your company and the idea upon which it is based, it should come through in your business plan. Your plan should convey to readers the excitement and promise that you feel about your venture.

FIGURE 11.1 DEVELOPING THE "BIG PICTURE"

1. DEVELOP YOUR VISION STATEMENT

a. Write short phrases to describe each of the three elements in your vision statement:
   – the name of your planned venture
   – your product/service offering
   – the target market(s) you plan to serve
b. Combine these phrases into a single sentence

____
____
____
____
____

2. FORMULATE YOUR MISSION STATEMENT

a. Write short phrases to describe each of the following elements of your business:
   – what your business will do
   – its market focus, niche, or particular image
   – its planned location and geographic market served
   – how growth of the business will be achieved
   – your sustainable uniqueness or distinguishing characteristics

continued

Developing the "Big Picture" — continued

b. Combine these phrases into short, linked sentences.

____
____
____
____
____
____

3. DEFINE THE FUNDAMENTAL VALUES BY WHICH YOUR BUSINESS WILL BE RUN

Step 1 Personal Values

Have each principal involved in the business complete the following framework for five values that they hold to be personally important.

a. *Value:* Express as a single word ______________________

What: A brief explanation of what the word means to you.

____
____

Why? Outline why it is important to you that the business operate this way.

____
____

b. *Value:* Express as a single word

What: A brief explanation of what the word means to you.

____
____

Why? Outline why it is important to you that the business operate this way.

____
____

c. *Value:* Express as a single word ______________________

What: A brief explanation of what the word means to you. ______________

____
____

Why? Outline why it is important to you that the business operate this way. ________

____
____

d. *Value:* Express as a single word ______________________

What: A brief explanation of what the word means to you. ______________

____
____

Why? Outline why it is important to you that the business operate this way. ________

____
____

e. *Value:* Express as a single word ______________________

What: A brief explanation of what the word means to you. ______________

____
____

Why? Outline why it is important to you that the business operate this way. ______________

Step 2 Values by Which the Business Will Be Managed

Complete Step 2 from the information provided by each of the principals in Step 1. Include only values that were *common to all principals*. Others should only be included after discussion, negotiation, and consensus among all individuals. Since some values will differ, it is necessary for all parties to agree which will be the common values used to guide the operations of the business. This list should contain five or six values at a maximum and it is important that they be compatible with each other. Each principal will then have to decide whether he/she will be able to work in a business where, perhaps, only some, or none of his/her personal values will be given expression.

a. *Value:* ______________

What: ______________

Why? ______________

b. *Value:* ______________

What: ______________

Why? ______________

c. *Value:* ______________

What: ______________

Why? ______________

continued

Developing the "Big Picture" — continued

d. *Value:* ______________________________

____

What: ______________________________

____

____

____

____

Why? ______________________________

____

____

____

e. *Value:* ______________________________

____

What: ______________________________

____

____

____

____

Why? ______________________________

____

____

____

4. DEFINE YOUR OBJECTIVES

The business's vision will be achieved when the following objectives have been attained:

a. Objective ______________________________
b. Objective ______________________________
c. Objective ______________________________
d. Objective ______________________________
e. Objective ______________________________

Notice in Entrepreneurs in Action #39 the time and effort Kent Groves dedicated to the development of his business plan. He spent over a year researching the mail-order industry, studying the competition, and asking questions of people who were experts in the business. Then, with the assistance of an accountant, he wrote his "road map" to guide him through every aspect of the implementation of his business. With the plan, he was also able to win the confidence of a banker who provided him with the necessary line of credit to carry his seasonal business over its slow periods. His business plan has become a combined operations manual/corporate bible that can be continually referred to so that he knows if, in fact, the business is evolving as he had originally anticipated.

WHY DEVELOP A BUSINESS PLAN?

Your business plan can accomplish many things for you and your proposed venture. These can largely be categorized into two basic areas:

1. **For the internal evaluation of your business**, both as a checklist to see that you have covered all the important bases and as a timetable for accomplishing your stated objectives
2. **For external use** in attracting resources and obtaining support for your venture

From an internal perspective, developing a plan forces you to seriously consider the important elements of your venture and the steps you feel are necessary to get it off the ground. Your plan can be used to inform employees about the goals and direction of your business. It lets everyone know how they fit into the organization and what you expect of them. Your plan can also help you develop as a manager. It requires you to deal with problems relating to competitive conditions, promotional opportunities, and other situations that will confront your business.

39 Entrepreneurs in action

Business Plans: The Lies We Tell Our Bankers?

Some business people call them "the lies we tell our bankers." In this economy, however, a company looking for credit must put a lot more than creative writing in its business plan.

Kent Groves, president of catalogue retailer Maritime Trading Co. of Falmouth, N.S. and a former Nutrilawn International manager who spent a lot of time approving franchises, knows the importance of business plans. "Some of the best plans I saw were put together by people who totally ignored them once the loan was approved. And their franchises were in trouble."

Groves took a year to research the mail-order industry, studying catalogues, trade magazines and reports, and asking questions of industry experts. Then, with an accountant, he spent six weeks writing what he calls a "road map to guide you through every aspect of your operations."

The result: a 68-page plan with 16 appendices. Groves' Rand-McNally approach to mapping business highways offers an executive summary, mission statement ("we are the leader in the direct marketing of the highest quality Maritime products in the world"), profile, industry overview, and bibliography. And he provided details on sales and marketing, operations, and financing. "It helped to have an accountant who would say, 'Those figures don't make sense'," says Groves. "She asked the hard questions."

Most of Groves' efforts were geared to winning a line of credit — essential for a firm that makes all its money at Christmas. But the effort proved frustrating: MTC's application was rejected by Scotiabank, CIBC, and Hongkong Bank. The setback soured Groves: "The banks advertise 'We support small business.' Yeah, until you need money. What a crock!"

After moving to Nova Scotia full-time in June, Groves approached the Royal Bank in Halifax. There he met account manager Earl Covin, who got excited by his plan. "It was a breath of fresh air," says Covin. "I didn't have to do a lot of background work. It had more detail than most bankers ever expect, and it was very realistic." Once past the collateral hurdle — Groves' father helped out — the bank approved a $75,000 credit line in a day.

Beyond winning financial support, MTC's business plan has become a combined operations manual/corporate bible. Says Groves, "We continually check our expenses and they're right on track. We know where we stand." So when he saw catalogue costs coming in 25% below projections, he knew he could boost marketing spending 20%.

More importantly, revenue projections are also on budget. Another catalogue company, using one of the same mailing lists as Groves, received a 1.5% response rate — "dead on" for MTC's projections. MTC forecast an operating deficit of $49,200 at the end of September; the actual amount was $45,000. With his catalogues just hitting the market in October, Groves still expects sales to reach $100,000 by Dec. 31.

Like most road maps, MTC's business plan allows for dirt roads and detours. "When we stray," says Groves, "we know it and at what capacity we're varying. What's important is flexibility that allows you to make changes."

Source: Allan Lynch writes for PROFIT magazine and is author of *Sweat Equity: Atlantic Canada's New Entrepreneurs*.

TIPS FOR DEVELOPING YOUR BUSINESS PLAN

Here are some pointers to consider in developing your business plan:

- **Business planning involves a great deal of work** Be prepared to spend weeks—or months—completing your plan.
- **Work on sections at a time** While this undertaking may appear overwhelming at first, don't get discouraged. Break the project down into manageable chunks and work on each chunk separately.
- **Be brief but complete** Although you may have volumes of important material, aim for a plan that is brief and succinct but includes everything important to the business.
- **Focus on your intended reader** Use your plan to organize your efforts around your objectives to ensure you have all the bases covered.
- **Use layman's terms** Avoid highly technical descriptions of your products, processes, and operations.
- **A business plan is a "living" document** Update it as your knowledge grows and whenever your plans become more concrete.
- **Be realistic** Base your projections on the results gathered from your analysis. Be honest about both positive and negative findings.
- **Discuss your firm's business risks** Your credibility can be seriously undermined if existing risks and problems are discovered by readers on their own.
- **Don't make vague or unsubstantiated statements** Back up your statements with background data and market information.

Adapted from Entrepreneurial Edge, Edward Lowe Foundation, "How to Develop and Use a Business Plan," (edge.lowe.org.)

Externally, your business plan can serve as an effective sales document and is considered by many experts to be the heart of the capital-raising process. Any knowledgeable banker or prospective investor will expect you to be professional in your approach, fully prepared, and armed with a thoroughly researched, well-written business plan when seeking their support. Very little money has been raised for business ideas scribbled on the back of envelopes or on restaurant placemats despite considerable folklore to the contrary.

In the course of attracting external support for your venture a number of people may have occasion to read your plan. These include bankers, suppliers, prospective customers, and potential investors. Each of them will be viewing your business from a slightly different perspective. Bankers, for example, are primarily interested in the business's fixed assets and other available collateral. They want to know if you can pay back their loan at prevailing interest rates. Venture capitalists and other private investors, on the other hand, are more interested in their expected return on investment. They tend to like innovative products and services in growth industries that promise significant returns. These differing viewpoints should be taken into account in developing your plan.

Heidi Lang of the Transatlantic Marketing Group definitely learned the value of having a well-formulated business plan when she went looking for financing to fund the expansion of her business producing and selling photo frames (Entrepreneurs in Action #40). The business was started largely on the basis of what she felt was a market opportunity and her family's economic need at the time. There was no real plan. However, when it came time to look for financing for the business beyond what she could personally provide, Lang discovered that no one would talk to her because she didn't have a clear vision of where she was going with the business and what she planned to do with the money she was seeking. Somewhat frustrated, she got some expert advice and put together a five-year plan. This plan, combined with the strong market performance the company had achieved up to then enabled her to obtain the financing she was looking for. Now business planning has become an integral part of her ongoing activities. It gives her business a clear focus and enables her to look beyond the day-to-day activities and keep on track in relation to the changing environment she sees occurring around the business.

40 Entrepreneurs in action

The Road Ahead

I must make a confession: I did not set out to create a multimillion-dollar business. I mean, like everyone else, I was looking for an opportunity. But I did not have a road map.

And so I find a certain paradox around the subject of planning. I still have grave doubts about the efficacy of making big plans in a world that is shifting gears at G-force speeds. Having said this, I can tell you that the ability at Transatlantic Marketing Group (TMG) to forge cohesive business plans and anticipate shifting market growth has been critical to the success we are currently experiencing.

Our story began in 1993. My husband had just lost his job, and though I was managing a successful independent sales agency, I was certainly not earning enough money to support our household without a second income. We were eating through our savings just to live.

And so necessity became the mother of invention. At work, I had identified a small niche in the marketplace for interesting lines of photo frames, and I decided to try filling it. But after no luck sourcing the product, I thought, "Hey, how tough can this be? I am going to find someone who can make these up for me." So I took the last $10,000 of our savings and waded in. And that's how my company started—there was no grand plan.

Working from home, I found someone who would make up custom frames for me and I began showing them to my retail clients. The product was greeted enthusiastically right from the beginning, particularly in the United States. My background is in sales, and I'm pretty good at it, so I knew how to open the right doors.

I initially capitalized the venture with personal savings and a small grant from the government. The banks were unavailable to us (as they are to many new businesses) so we financed inventory with my Visa card. We also factored our receivables, which was expensive, but it meant we were able to manage our cash flow.

My respect for a well-formulated business plan really grew out of the company's requirements in our second phase of growth. Right from the start, the major retail chains embraced our products. But just over five years into the business, TMG experienced an explosion in sales of over 4,000 per cent. With individual orders in the $50,000 to $80,000 range, it was difficult to find suppliers who would provide TMG with the quality and quantity of materials to meet that kind of demand. Part of the solution lay in finding a reliable source of financing.

My epiphany came when I went out to meet with banks about securing additional financing. No one would talk to me because I didn't have a clearly laid out vision of where I was going and what I wanted to do with the new money I was seeking.

I am nothing if not honest about my own strengths and weaknesses. I have good instincts about the market and I have a ferocious work ethic. But I had no previous experience with systematic marketing analysis. I didn't know anything about long-range business planning and cash flow projections. So I found some expert advice to help put together a five-year projection. We assembled a complete analysis of our competitors to find the windows of opportunity in our category. This plan, combined with our strong track record, helped us win support from a venture capital company that has proven to be a strong financial ally. Even though our business is unusual in their portfolio, our professional approach to management and planning gave them the confidence to go forward with us and our aggressive growth strategy. Our new financing allowed us to move into our own plant and bring production under our direct control.

Of course, all the planning in the world cannot anticipate the unforeseen. There are no rules that lead safely to a predictable outcome. Things change by the day—sales, people and cash flow. But a solid plan can help avoid many of the pitfalls that confront every small business, and can help stabilize problems when they do occur. Exigency plans give us the ability to turn on a dime, quickly and sure-footedly if (and when) our circumstances change. I don't believe in waiting till I have a major problem on my hands; I seek help from experts early. I apply my energies where my skills really count. I stay on the road close to my customers and rely on my advisors to provide professional advice.

Planning is a part of everything I do now. It offers us vision, the ability to clamber over the day-to-day grind and see into the distance for changes and alterations in the terrain ahead. Our map is based on all we know about our existing business and everything we can extrapolate about the future. It reflects the economy and a business environment that is not static but dynamic. You have to be ready to accommodate change and absorb shifts in the marketplace. Planning is the name of the game in a world that is roiling with the forces of economic upheaval. As I see it, there really isn't any other way.

Source: Profit Magazine Online, www.profitguide.com/first-person/FI_lang.html, 12-07-01. Reprinted with permission.

ADVANTAGES OF PREPARING A BUSINESS PLAN

A plan:

- Helps you to face reality and the facts
- Forces you to think ahead and consider the future
- Assists you in summarizing your skills and points out the strengths of others involved in your venture
- Helps you identify and define your product/service, pricing strategy, distribution strategy, and marketing and promotional strategy
- Establishes the amount of financing or outside investment you require
- Outlines the financial future of your business through projected statements such as: cash flow, income and expenses, and balance sheets
- Provides you with an effective sales tool
- Inspires confidence in yourself and projects that confidence to others

Source: Dawn Braddock, "How to Write a Business Plan that Makes Good Business Sense," *Business Sense* (November, 2000): 16–17.

HOW LONG SHOULD YOUR BUSINESS PLAN BE?

Business plans can be broadly categorized into three types: the summary business plan, the full business plan, and the operational business plan.

THE SUMMARY BUSINESS PLAN

Summary business plans commonly run about 10 pages or so; considerably shorter than the 40 or so pages traditional for business plans. Summary business plans have become increasingly popular and accepted for use by early-stage businesses in applying for a bank loan, or they may be all that is required for a small, lifestyle business such as a convenience store, home-based business, graphic design company, or consulting firm. A summary business plan may also be sufficient to whet the appetite of friends, relatives, and other private investors who might subsequently receive a copy of the full plan if sufficiently interested.

THE FULL BUSINESS PLAN

A full business plan similar to the one you would develop by following the samples at the end of this Stage will likely run from 10 to 40 pages. This is the traditional plan. It covers all the key subjects in enough depth to permit a full exploration of the principal issues. The full business plan is most appropriate when you are trying to raise a substantial amount of external financing or if you are looking for a partner or other major private investors.

THE OPERATIONAL BUSINESS PLAN

The operational business plan will usually exceed 40 pages in length but is used only infrequently, such as when a business is planning to grow very rapidly and must try to anticipate a wide variety of issues. Or it might be part of an annual process where it is necessary to get into great detail about distribution, production, advertising, and other areas where it is essential for everyone involved with the organization to understand clearly everything that is going on. Traditional business plans that grow to this length should be avoided as they reflect a lack of discipline and focus.

WHO SHOULD WRITE YOUR BUSINESS PLAN?

You should write your business plan. If someone else develops the business plan for you, it becomes their plan, not yours. If you are part of a management team, each individual should contribute his or her part to the overall project.

Do not under any circumstances hire someone else to write the plan for you. This doesn't mean that you shouldn't get help from others in compiling information, obtaining licences, permits, patents, and other legal considerations, or preparing your pro forma financial statements — only that the final plan should be written by you and your team.

The people who may be assessing your plan want to know that you see the big picture as it relates to your business and understand all the functional requirements of your company, not that you can hire a good consultant. It is very difficult to defend someone else's work. If you put it together yourself, you have a better understanding and feel for the business. Your business plan should be a personal expression written in your own unique style, though of course it should look professional and businesslike.

HOW LONG DOES IT TAKE?

Putting together a business plan does not happen overnight; the process can stretch over several months. Table 11.1 outlines the steps that should be taken to prepare a business plan, and the amount of time it may take to complete each step.

The flowchart in Figure 11.2 indicates how all these steps in developing a business plan interrelate. It shows how certain key steps cannot be undertaken until others have been completed. For example, you cannot effectively research the market (step 4) until you have selected a particular product or service idea (step 3). Similarly, until the market has been researched (step 4), a site chosen (step 6), and a revenue forecast prepared (step 5), you can't develop your detailed marketing plan (step 8).

The 16-week time span shown here is only for illustrative purposes — the actual time required to prepare your business plan will vary with the nature of your venture. A plan for a relatively simple, straightforward business might be completed within a few weeks, while a plan for a complex, high-growth new venture could take many months.

© Jim Toomey, reprinted with special permission of King Features Syndicate.

TABLE 11.1 SUGGESTED STEPS IN DEVELOPING YOUR BUSINESS PLAN

Step	Description	Completion Date
1	Decide to go into business for yourself.	
2	Analyze your strengths and weaknesses, paying special attention to your business experience, business education, and desires.	Third week
3	Choose the product or service that best fits your strengths and desires.	Fourth week
4	Research the market for your product or service.	Seventh week
5	Forecast your share of market if possible.	Eighth week
6	Choose a site for your business.	Eighth week
7	Develop your production plan.	Tenth week
8	Develop your marketing plan.	Tenth week
9	Develop your personnel plan.	Twelfth week
10	Decide whether to form a sole proprietorship, a partnership, or a corporation.	Twelfth week
11	Explain the kinds of records and reports you plan to have.	Twelfth week
12	Develop your insurance plan.	Twelfth week
13	Develop your financial plan.	Fifteenth week
14	Write a summary overview of your business plan, stressing its purpose and promise.	Sixteenth week

FIGURE 11.2 FLOWCHART OF THE STEPS IN DEVELOPING A BUSINESS PLAN

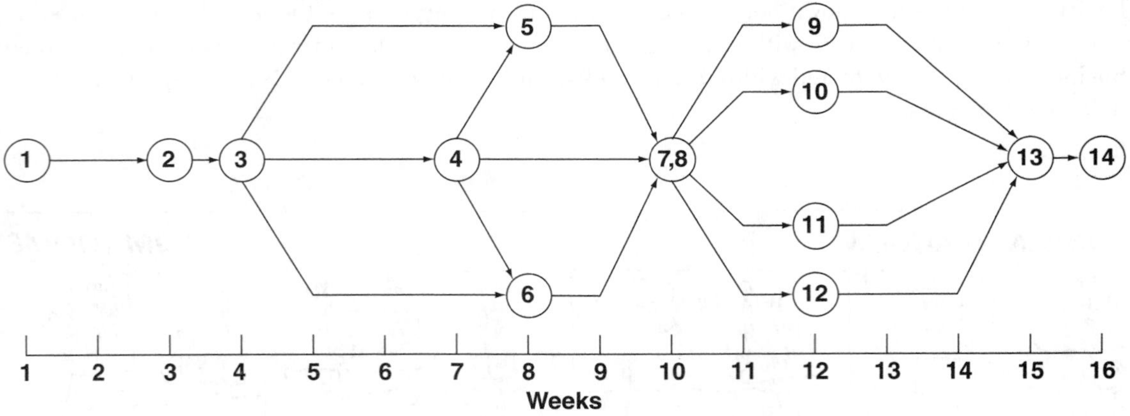

KEY

1. Decide to go into business.
2. Analyze yourself.
3. Pick product or service.
4. Research market.
5. Forecast sales revenues.
6. Pick site.
7. Develop production plan.
8. Develop marketing plan.
9. Develop personnel plan.
10. Decide whether to incorporate.
11. Explain need for records.
12. Develop insurance plan.
13. Develop financial plan.
14. Write summary overview.

Adapted from Nicholas C. Siropolis, *Small Business Management: A Guide to Entrepreneurship*, 2nd ed. (Boston: Houghton Mifflin Co., 1982), 138–141.

WHAT SHOULD YOUR PLAN CONTAIN?

Your business plan is the nuts and bolts of your proposed business venture put down on paper. You will have to decide exactly what information to include, how your plan can be best organized for maximum effectiveness, and what information should be given particular emphasis. All plans, however, require a formal, structured presentation so that they are easy to read and follow and tend to avoid confusion. A number of forms and sample outlines for a business plan are available, but virtually all suggest that business plans contain the following components: (1) letter of transmittal, (2) title page, (3) table of contents, (4) executive summary and fact sheet, (5) body, and (6) appendices. The contents of a typical business plan are outlined in Figure 11.3. You can use this framework as a guideline to assist you in the development of the plan for your business.

FYI FOR YOUR INFORMATION

BUSINESS PLAN OUTLINES AND TEMPLATES

Here are some examples of Web sites that have detailed instructions, outlines, or templates for developing a comprehensive business plan.

Interactive Business Planner

The IBP is a business planning software product designed specifically to operate on the World Wide Web. It uses the capabilities of the Internet to assist entrepreneurs in preparing a three-year business plan for their new or existing business.
(www.cbsc.org/ibp/home_en.cfm)

Ottawa-Carleton Entrepreneurship Centre Business Plan Outline

A brief outline of the requirements of a business plan.
(www.entrepreneurship.com/tools/businessPlanWorkbook.asp)

On-line Small Business Workshop

A well developed business plan outline plus a sample business plan for a fictitious small manufacturing company. Presented by the Canada/British Columbia Business Services Centre.
(www.smallbusinessbc.ca/workshop/workshop.html)

Nova Scotia Business Inc.

An electronic booklet that has been designed to assist and guide you through the steps necessary in preparing your business plan.
(www.novascotiabusiness.com/publications/busplan/index.htm)

Deloitte & Touche, Developing an Effective Business Plan

A guidebook to help you write an effective business plan.
(www.us.deloitte.com/growth/guidebooks/busplan.htm)

BizPlanIt's Virtual Business Plan

This unique and free on-line resource mirrors the major sections of a business plan, and enables you to learn the fundamentals of writing a business plan.
(www.bizplanit.com/vplan.htm)

Money Hunt Business Plan Template

A U.S. site claiming to have the best business plan outline on the Web.
(www.moneyhunter.com)

1. LETTER OF TRANSMITTAL

The letter of transmittal officially introduces your business plan to the reader. It explains your reason for writing the plan, gives the title of the plan or the name of your business, and outlines the major features of your plan that may be of interest.

2. TITLE PAGE

The title page, or "cover page," of your plan provides identifying information about you and your proposed business. It should include the name, address, and telephone number of the business as well as similar information about yourself. The date the plan was finalized or submitted to the recipient should also be included on the title page.

3. TABLE OF CONTENTS

The table of contents is a list of the major headings and subheadings contained in your plan. It provides readers with a quick overview of the contents of your plan and allows them to quickly access the particular sections that may be of primary interest to them.

4. EXECUTIVE SUMMARY AND FACT SHEET

The executive summary may be the most important part of your business plan. It must capture the attention of the reader, stimulate interest, and get the reader to keep on reading the rest of your plan. In two or three pages this summary should concisely explain your business's current status; describe its products or services and their benefits to your customers; provide an overview of your venture's objectives, market prospects, and financial forecasts; and, if you are using the plan to raise external financing, indicate the amount of financing needed, how the money is to be used, and the benefits to the prospective lender or investor.

This summary should give the essence of your plan and highlight its really significant points. In many instances the summary will either sell the reader on continuing to read the rest of the document or convince him/her to forget the whole thing; the game may be won or lost on the basis of the executive summary.

The fact sheet should appear as a separate page at the back of the executive summary. It summarizes the basic information that relates to your venture:

1. Company name
2. Location and telephone
3. Type of business and industry
4. Form of business organization (proprietorship, partnership, or corporation)
5. Principal product or service line
6. Registered patents or trademarks
7. Number and name of founders/partners/shareholders
8. Length of time in business
9. Current and/or projected market share
10. Funds invested in the business to date and their source
11. Additional financing required
12. Proposed terms and payback period
13. Total value or net worth of the business
14. Name of business advisors (legal counsel, accountant, others)

5. BODY OF THE PLAN

The body of your business plan is by far the longest component, because it presents the detailed story of your business proposition. It should be broken down into major divisions using headings, and each major division divided into sections using subheadings. It is probably better to have too many rather than not enough headings and subheadings.

What follows is a typical overview of the kind of material that should be included in the body of your plan.

YOUR COMPANY AND THE INDUSTRY

Describe the start-up and background of your business and provide the reader with some context within which to fit all the information you will be providing later in your plan.

Familiarize the reader with your company; the industry within which you will be competing, your understanding of it, and where it is headed; and what opportunities you see for your business.

YOUR COMPANY

BACKGROUND Give the date your business was started, its present form of organization, its location, and pertinent historical information on the firm. Name the founders and other key people, how your key products or services were chosen and developed, and what success the business has achieved to date.

CURRENT SITUATION Discuss such issues as how you have identified your market opportunity, assessed the competition, and developed some unique factor or distinctive competence that will make your business stand out from the rest.

FUTURE PLANS Discuss your goals and ambitions for the business and your strategy for achieving them.

THE INDUSTRY

PRINCIPAL CHARACTERISTICS Describe the current status and prospects for the industry in which your business will operate. How big is the industry? What are its total sales in dollars? In units? What are typical industry standards, gross margins, seasonal patterns, and similar factors?

MAJOR PARTICIPANTS Identify the major industry participants and describe their role, market share, and other performance measures. What are their principal strengths and weaknesses and how do you feel you will be able to successfully compete in this situation?

INDUSTRY TRENDS Discuss how you feel the industry will evolve in the future. Is it growing or stable? What do you feel industry sales will be five and ten years from now? What general trends are evident and how is the industry likely to be affected by economic, social, technological, environmental, and regulatory trends?

YOUR PRODUCT/SERVICE OFFERING

DESCRIPTION Describe the product or service you plan to sell in detail explaining any unique characteristics or particular advantages. How will features of your product or service give you some advantage over competitors?

Indicate the stage of development your product is at and whether prototypes, working models, or finished production units are available. Include photographs if possible.

PROPRIETARY POSITION Describe any patents or trademarks you may hold or have applied for, or any licensing agreements or other legal contracts that may provide some protection for your product or service. Are there any regulatory or government-approved standards or requirements your product must meet? How and when do you plan to obtain this certification?

POTENTIAL Outline your market opportunity as you see it and explain how you plan to take advantage of it. What are the key success factors in this business and how do you plan to exploit them to your advantage?

MARKET ANALYSIS

This section of your plan should convince the reader that you thoroughly understand the market for your product or service, that you can deal with the competition and achieve sufficient sales to develop a viable and growing business. You should describe the total market and how you feel it can be broken down into segments. You can then indicate the segment or niche you plan to concentrate on and what share of this business you will be able to obtain.

Your analysis of the market may be based on:

1. Market studies available from private research firms and government departments and agencies
2. Statistics Canada or U.S. Bureau of the Census data
3. Information from trade associations and trade publications
4. Surveys or informal discussions with dealers, distributors, sales representatives, customers, or competitors

FIGURE 11.3 A TYPICAL BUSINESS PLAN

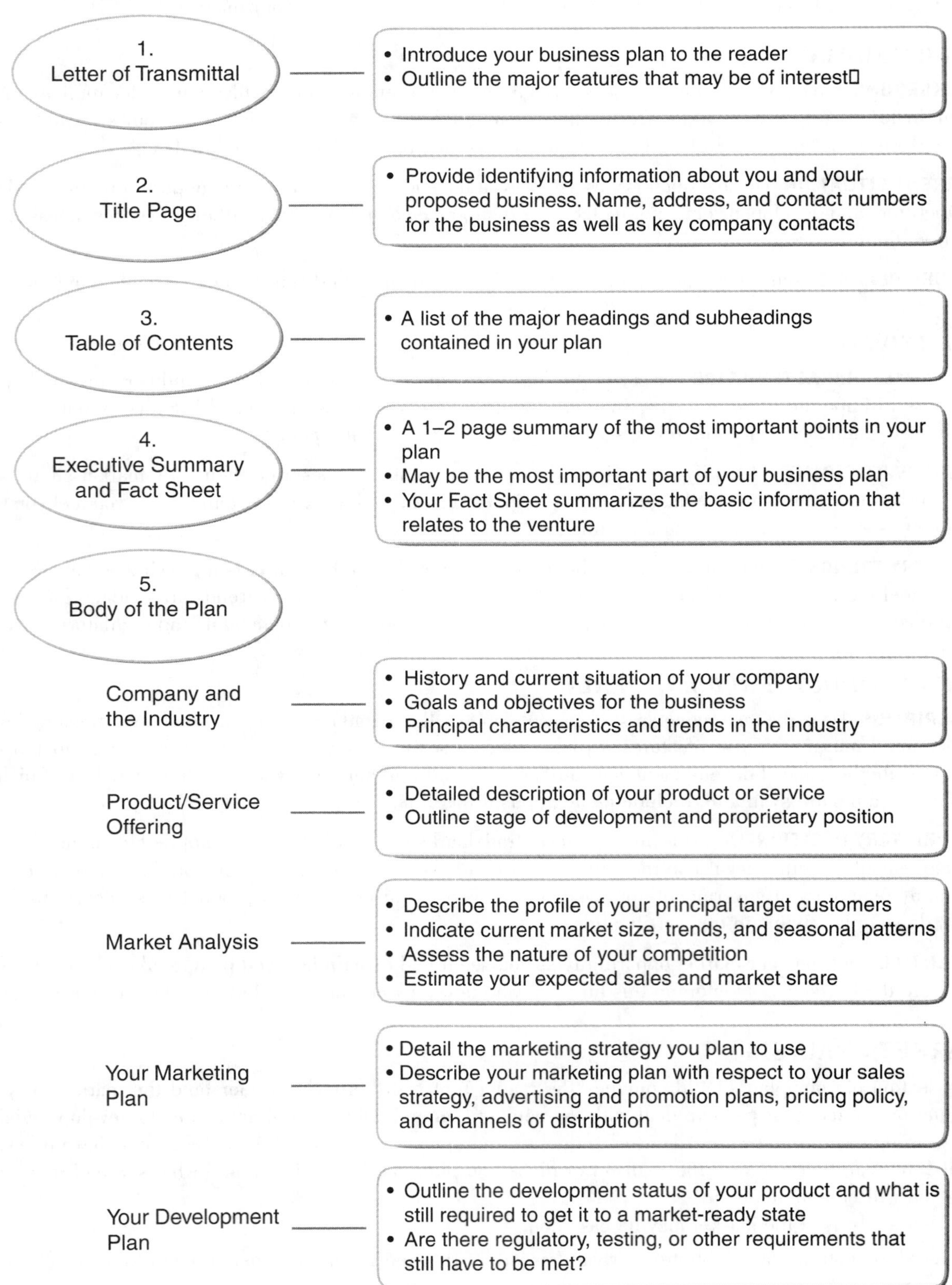

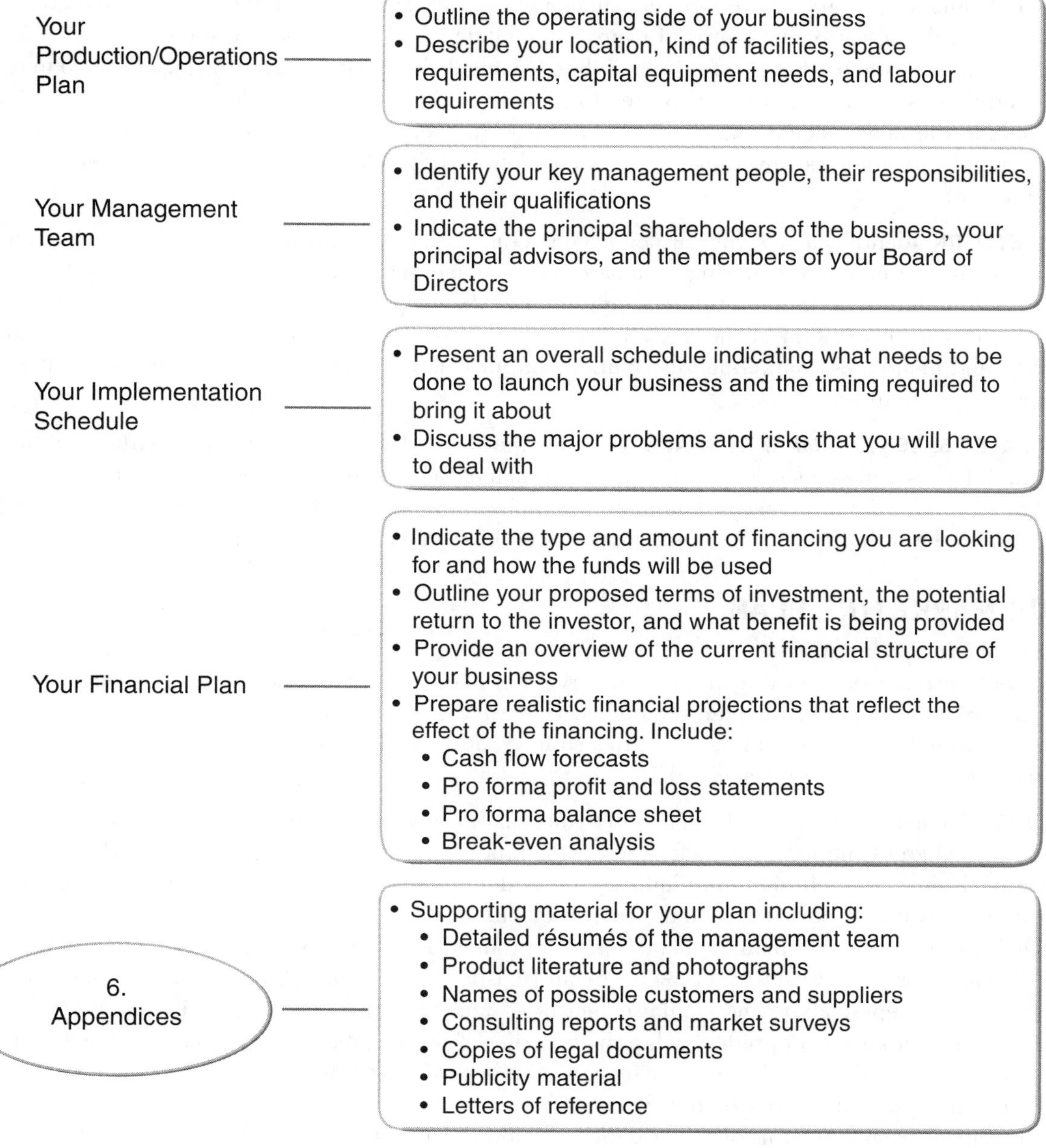

This is often one of the most difficult parts of the business plan to prepare, but it is also one of the most important. Almost all other sections of your business plan depend on the sales estimates developed from your market analysis. The outline described in Stage 6 can help you in this process.

TARGET MARKET AND CUSTOMERS Identify who constitute your primary target markets — individual consumers, companies, health care or educational institutions, government departments, or other groups.

Examine beforehand if these target markets can be segmented or broken down into relatively homogeneous groups having common, identifiable characteristics such as geographic location, age, size, type of industry, or some other factor. Present these facts in the most logical or appropriate format.

Describe the profile of your principal target customers. Who and where are they? What are the principal bases for their purchase decisions? What are their major applications for your product? What principal benefit will they obtain from using your product rather than one of your competitors'?

Identify, if possible, some major buyers who may be prepared to make purchase commitments. If possible, get a purchase order.

MARKET SIZE AND TRENDS Estimate the size of the current total market for your product or service in both units and dollars. How are sales distributed among the various segments you identified? Are there any strong weekly, monthly, or seasonal patterns? Ensure you include answers to these questions.

Describe how the market size for each of these segments has changed over the past three to four years in units and dollars. Outline how it is expected to change over the next three to four years.

Include the major factors that have affected past market growth, i.e., socioeconomic trends, industry trends, regulatory changes, government policy, population shifts, etc. What is likely to happen in these areas in the future?

COMPETITION Identify each of your principal competitors. Make a realistic assessment of each of these firms and their product or service offering. Compare these competing products or services on the basis of price, quality, performance, service support, warranties, and other important features.

Present your evaluation of the market share of each segment by each competitor, their relative profitability, and their sales, marketing, distribution, and production capabilities. How do you see these factors changing in the future?

ESTIMATED SALES AND MARKET SHARE Estimate the share of each segment of the market and the sales in units and dollars that you feel you will acquire for each of the next three to five years. This should be developed by month for the next year and annually for each year thereafter. This information can best be presented in tabular form. Indicate on what assumptions you have based these projections.

YOUR MARKETING PLAN

Your marketing plan outlines how your sales projections will be achieved. It details the marketing strategy you plan to use to establish your product or service in the marketplace and obtain a profitable share of the overall market. Your marketing plan should describe *what* is to be done, *when* it is to be done, *how* it is to be done, and *who* will do it insofar as your sales strategy, advertising and promotion plans, pricing policy, and channels of distribution are concerned.

PRICING Summarize the general financial characteristics of your business and the industry at large. What will be typical gross and net margins for each of the products or services you plan to sell? How do these compare with those of other firms in the industry? Provide a detailed breakdown of your estimated fixed, variable, and semivariable costs for each of your various products or services.

Discuss the prices you plan to charge for your product. How do they compare with your major competitors'? Is your gross margin sufficient to cover your transportation costs, selling costs, advertising and promotion costs, rent, depreciation, and similar expenses — and still provide some margin of profit?

Detail the markups your product will provide to the various members of your channel of distribution. How do these compare with those they receive on comparable products? Does your markup provide them with sufficient incentive to handle your product?

Indicate your normal terms of sale. Do these conform to industry norms? Do you plan to offer cash, quantity, or other discounts?

Indicate how long it will take you to break even, basing your opinion on your anticipated cost structure and planned price.

SALES AND DISTRIBUTION Indicate the methods you will use to sell and distribute your product or service. Do you plan to use your own salaried or commissioned salespeople, rely on manufacturer's agents or other wholesalers and distributors, or utilize a more non-traditional means of distributing your product such as export trading companies, direct mail selling, mail-order houses, party plan selling, or other means of selling directly to the final consumer?

If you plan to use your own sales force, describe how large it will be and how it will be structured. Indicate how salespeople will be distributed, who they will call on, how many calls you estimate it will take to get an order, the size of a typical order, how much you estimate a typical salesperson will sell each year, how he or she will be paid, how much he or she is likely to make in a year, and how this compares with the average for the industry.

If you plan to use distributors or wholesalers, indicate how they have been or will be selected, who they are if possible, what areas or territory they will cover, how they will be compensated, credit and collection policies, and any special policies such as exclusive rights, discounts, and cooperative advertising programs.

Indicate any plans for export sales or international marketing arrangements.

ADVERTISING AND PROMOTION Describe the program you plan to use to make consumers aware of your product or service. What consumers are you trying to reach? Do you plan to use the services of an advertising agency? What media do you plan to use — radio, television, newspapers, magazines, billboards, direct mail, coupons, brochures, trade shows, etc. How much do you plan to spend on each medium? When? Which specific vehicles?

Outline any plans to obtain free publicity for your product or company.

SERVICE AND WARRANTY PROGRAM Indicate your service arrangements, warranty terms, and method of handling service problems. Describe how you will handle customer complaints and other problems. Will service be handled by the company, dealers and distributors, or independent service centres? How do these arrangements compare with those of your competitors?

YOUR DEVELOPMENT PLAN

If your product or service involves some further technical development, the planned extent of this work should be discussed in your business plan. Prospective investors, bankers, and others will want to know the nature and extent of any additional development required, how much it will cost, and how long it will take before your business has a finished, marketable product.

DEVELOPMENT STATUS Describe the current status of your product and outline what still remains to be done to make it marketable. Do you presently have only a concept, detailed drawings, a laboratory prototype, a production prototype, or a finished product? Is further engineering work required? Has the necessary tooling to produce the product been adequately developed? Are the services of an industrial designer or other specialist required to refine the product into marketable form?

COSTS Indicate how much money has been spent on product development to date and where it has been spent. Present a development budget indicating the additional funds required, how they will be spent, and the timing involved in completing the project.

PROPRIETARY ISSUES Indicate any patents or trademarks that you own, have, or for which you plan to apply. Are there any regulatory requirements to produce or market the product? Has the product undergone standardized testing through Underwriter's Laboratory, the Canadian Standards Association (CSA), or some other agency? If not, what are your plans? Have you tested the product at all in the marketplace? What was the result?

YOUR PRODUCTION/OPERATIONS PLAN

Your production/operations plan outlines the operating side of your business. It should describe your plant location, the kind of facilities needed, space requirements, capital equipment needed, and your labour requirements.

If your plan is for a manufacturing business, you should also discuss such areas as your purchasing policy, quality control program, inventory control system, production cost breakdown, and whether you plan to manufacture all subcomponents of the product yourself or have some of them produced for you by someone else.

LOCATION Describe the planned location of your business and discuss any advantages or disadvantages of this location in terms of the cost and availability of labour; proximity to customers; access to transportation, energy supplies, or other natural resources; and zoning and other legal requirements.

Discuss the characteristics of your location in relation to market size, traffic flows, local and regional growth rates, income levels, and similar market-related factors.

FACILITIES AND EQUIPMENT Describe the property and facilities currently used or that will be required to operate your business. This should include factory and office space, selling space, storage space, property size and location, etc. Will these facilities be leased or purchased? What is the cost and timing of their acquisition?

Detail the machinery and equipment that is required for your manufacturing process. Is this highly specialized or general-purpose equipment? Is it leased or purchased? New or used? What is the cost? What will it cost for equipment setup and facility layout? What is its expected life? Will it have any residual or scrap value?

If possible, provide a drawing of the physical layout of the plant and other facilities.

MANUFACTURING PLANS AND COSTS Develop a manufacturing cost outline that shows standard production costs at various levels of operation. Break total costs down into raw material, component parts, labour, and overhead. Indicate your raw material, work-in-process, and finished goods inventory requirements at various sales levels. How will seasonal variations in demand be handled?

Indicate your key suppliers or subcontractors for various raw materials and components. What are the lead times for these materials? Are backup suppliers or other alternatives available?

Outline the quality control procedures you will use to minimize service problems. Do you need any other production control measures?

On the basis of this configuration of facilities and equipment, indicate your production capacity. Where can this be expanded? Do you have any plans to modify existing plant space? What is the timing and cost?

LABOUR Describe the number of employees you have or need and their qualifications. Will they be full-time or part-time? Have you developed a job description for each position? What in-house training will be required? How much will each employee be paid? What kinds of pension plan, health insurance plan, profit-sharing plan, and other fringe benefits will be required? Have you registered with the necessary government departments?

Indicate whether your employees will be union or non-union. If employees will be members of a union, describe the principal terms of their contract and when it expires.

ENVIRONMENTAL AND OTHER ISSUES Indicate any approvals that it may be necessary for you to obtain related to zoning requirements, permits, licences, health and safety requirements, environmental approvals, etc. Are there any laws or regulatory requirements unique to your business? Are there any other legal or contractual matters that should be considered?

YOUR MANAGEMENT TEAM

Your management team and your directors are the key to success. You should identify: who your key people are; their qualifications; what they are being paid; who has overall authority; who is responsible for the various functional areas of the business such as sales, marketing, production, research and development, and financial management; and so forth.

In most small businesses there are no more than two or three really key players — including yourself. Concentrate on these individuals, indicating their education, qualifications, and past business achievements. Indicate how they will contribute to the success of the present venture. Don't hire friends, relatives, or other people for key positions who do not have the proper qualifications.

Many external investors are more concerned about the management of the business than the business itself. They invest in the people rather than the project. They will conduct a thorough and exhaustive investigation of each of your key players to determine whether they are the kind of people in which they wish to invest. This portion of your plan should instill confidence in the management of your business in the mind of the reader.

DESCRIPTION OF MANAGEMENT TEAM Outline the exact duties and responsibilities of each key member of your management team. Prepare a brief résumé of each individual indicating age, marital status, education, professional qualifications, employment experience, and other personal achievements. (You will include a complete, more detailed résumé for each of these individuals in an appendix to your plan.)

DIRECTORS Indicate the size and composition of your board of directors. Identify any individuals you are planning to invite to sit on your board. Include a brief statement on each member's background indicating what he or she will bring to the company.

MANAGEMENT AND DIRECTORS' COMPENSATION List the names of all members of your management team and board of directors and the compensation they will receive in fees or salary. Initially, at least, you and your management team should be prepared to accept modest salaries, perhaps well below what you received in your previous job, if you hope to attract external investors to your business.

SHAREHOLDERS Indicate the name of each of the individual shareholders (or partners) in your business, the number of shares each owns, the percentage of ownership, and the price paid.

Describe any investors in your business other than your management team and members of your board. How many shares do they have? When were they acquired? What price did they pay?

Summarize any incentive stock option or bonus plans that you have in effect or plan to institute. Also indicate any employment contracts or agreements you may have made with members of your management team.

PROFESSIONAL ADVISORS Indicate the name and complete address of each of your professional advisors, for example your lawyer, accountant, banker, insurance broker, and management or technical consultants. Disclose any fees or retainers that may have been paid to any of these people.

IMPLEMENTATION SCHEDULE AND RISKS ASSOCIATED WITH THE VENTURE

It is necessary to present an overall schedule indicating the interrelationship among the various events necessary to launch your business and the timing required to bring it about. This is similar to the type of framework in Figure 11.2. A well-prepared schedule demonstrates to external investors that you have given proper thought to where you are going and have the ability to plan. This schedule can be a very effective sales tool.

Your plan should also discuss the major problems and risks you feel you will have to deal with in developing your business.

MILESTONES Summarize the significant goals that you and your business have already reached and still hope to accomplish in the future. What still needs to be done for the business to succeed? Who is going to do these things? When will they be completed?

SCHEDULE Develop a schedule of significant events and their priority for completion. What kind of strategic planning has been done to see that things occur as necessary? Have you developed a fallback or contingency position in case things don't come off as you have planned?

RISKS AND PROBLEMS You might start by summarizing the major problems you have already had to deal with and how they were resolved. Were any particularly innovative or creative approaches used in addressing these issues?

Identify the risks your business may be faced with in the future. What are you attempting to do to avoid these? How will you deal with them if they arise? How can their impact on your business be minimized?

Summarize the downside risk. What would happen in the "worst case" scenario? What, if anything, could be salvaged from the business for your investors?

YOUR FINANCIAL PLAN

Your financial plan is essential to enable a prospective investor or banker to evaluate the investment opportunity you are presenting. The plan should illustrate the current financial status of your business and represent your best estimate of its future operations. The results presented should be both realistic and attainable.

Your financial plan should also describe the type of financing you are seeking, the amount of money you are looking for, how you plan to use these funds in the business, the terms of repayment and desired interest rate, or the dividends, voting rights, and redemption considerations related to the offering of any common or preferred stock.

FUNDING REQUESTED Indicate the amount and type (debt or equity) of funding you are looking for. For what do you intend to use the money? How will it be applied in your business — to acquire property, fixtures, equipment, or inventory, or to provide working capital?

Give an overview of the current financial structure of your business. Indicate the level of investment already made in the business and where the funds came from. What effect will the additional capital have on your business in terms of ownership structure, future growth, and profitability?

Outline your proposed terms of investment. What is the payback period and potential return on investment for the lender or investor? What collateral, tax benefit, or other security is being offered?

CURRENT FINANCIAL STATEMENTS If your venture is already in operation, you should provide copies of financial statements (profit and loss statement and a balance sheet) for the current year and the previous two years.

FINANCIAL PROJECTIONS In developing your financial plan, a number of basic projections must be prepared. These should be based on realistic expectations and reflect the effect of the proposed financing. The projections should be developed on a monthly basis for the first year of operation and on a quarterly or annual basis for another two to four years. These projections should include the following statements:

1. **Profit and loss forecasts** These pro forma income statements indicate your profit expectations for the next few years of operation of your business. They should be based on realistic estimates of sales and operating costs and represent your best estimate of actual operating results.

2. **Pro forma balance sheets** Your pro forma balance sheet indicates the assets you feel will be required to support your projected level of operations and how you plan to finance these assets.
3. **Projected cash flow statements** Your cash flow forecasts are probably your most important statements, because they indicate the amount and timing of your expected cash inflows and outflows. Typically the operating profits during the start-up of a new venture are not sufficient to finance the business's operating needs. This often means that the inflow of cash will not meet your business's cash requirements, at least on a short-term basis. These conditions must be anticipated so that you can predict cash needs and avoid insolvency.
4. **Break-even analysis** A break-even analysis indicates the level of sales and production you will require to cover all your fixed and variable costs. It is useful for you and prospective lenders and investors to know what your break-even point is and how easy or difficult it will likely be to attain.

   An example of each of these statements and a discussion on how to determine the break-even point for your venture is presented in Stage 7 of this book.

6. APPENDICES

The appendixes are intended to explain, support, and supplement the material in the body of your business plan. In most cases this material is attached to the back of your plan. Examples of the kind of material that might be included in an appendix are:

1. Product specifications and photographs
2. Detailed résumés of the management team
3. Lists of prospective customers
4. Names of possible suppliers
5. Job descriptions for the management team
6. Consulting reports and market surveys
7. Copies of legal documents such as leases, franchise and licensing agreements, contracts, licences, patent or trademark registrations, and articles of incorporation
8. Letters of reference
9. Relevant magazine, trade journal, and newspaper articles

CONCLUSION

It is important that your plan make a good first impression. It should demonstrate that you have done a significant amount of thinking and work on your venture. You should ensure your material is presented to prospective investors, lenders, and others in an attractive, readable, and understandable fashion.

To assist you in completing your business plan, Figure 11.4 provides a business plan outline for a retail or service-type business, while Figure 11.5 provides a similar outline for a manufacturing company. There are some differences in the information that should be incorporated into the plan for each type of business, particularly in describing the distribution strategy for the business and detailing the production/operations plan. These need to be specifically taken into account in preparing your plan. These forms are intended for use as a rough draft only. You can then use them as a basis from which to prepare a formal, professional-looking plan on your typewriter or word processor.

Figure 11.6 provides a checklist that you can use to assess your plan when it is finished for completeness, clarity, and persuasiveness.

The length of your business plan should not exceed 40 double-spaced, typewritten pages, not including appendices. Each section should be broken down into appropriate and clearly identifiable headings and subheadings. Make sure your plan contains no errors in spelling, punctuation, or grammar.

Prepare a number of copies of your plan and number each one individually. Make sure each copy is appropriately bound with a good-quality cover on which the name of your business has been printed or embossed.

FYI FOR YOUR INFORMATION

SAMPLE BUSINESS PLANS

Before starting on your business plan, it may be a good idea to see what a typical plan actually looks like. There are a couple of examples included with this book, but here are some Web sites that have some sample plans as well.

PaloAlto Software

Site contains sample business plans for 60 different businesses including a flower importer, software publisher, tennis pro shop, buffet restaurant, Internet & coffee shop, medical equipment company, and many others. (www.bplans.com)

Moot Corp Competition—The Super Bowl of Business Plan Competitions

A library of different business plans, each of which was a finalist in the Moot Corp competition for MBA students from all over the world.
(www.businessplans.org/mootcorp.html)

SmallBusinessPoint Sample Business Plans

A sample of business plans from existing successful profitable companies and start-ups that are available for sale for a nominal fee.
(www.smallbusinesspoint.com/BusinessPoint/SAMPLEPLANS.htm)

FIGURE 11.4 BUSINESS PLAN OUTLINE FOR A RETAIL OR SERVICE FIRM

1. **LETTER OF TRANSMITTAL**
2. **TITLE PAGE**
3. **TABLE OF CONTENTS**
4. **EXECUTIVE SUMMARY**

Fact Sheet

Company name ____________________

Location and telephone ____________________

____

____

____

Type of business and industry ____________________

____

____

Form of business organization ____________________

____

Principal product or service line ____________________

____

____

continued

Business Plan Outline (Retail or Service) — continued

Registered patents or trademarks (if any) ______

Names of founders/partners/shareholders ______

Length of time in business (if appropriate) ______

Current and/or projected market share ______

Funds invested in the business to date and their source ______

Additional financing required ______

Proposed terms and payback period ______

Total value or net worth of the business ______

NAMES OF BUSINESS ADVISORS

Legal counsel ______

Accountant ______

Banker ______

Other ____

____

5. BODY

A. Your Company and the Industry

THE COMPANY

Date business started ____

Location ____

____

Form of business organization ____

____

Founders and other key individuals ____

____

____

Principal products and services ____

____

____

Success the Business Has Achieved to Date

	Estimated Total Annual Market (year)		*Company Sales (year)*		*Market Share (%)*
Product/Service 1	$__________		$__________		__________
	__________	units	__________	units	__________
Product/Service 2	$__________		$__________		__________
(etc.)	__________	units	__________	units	__________

Future Goals and Plans

____

____

____

____

____

Principal Strategy for Achieving These Goals

____

____

____

____

____

____

continued

Business Plan Outline (Retail or Service) — continued

THE INDUSTRY

Prospects for the Industry

	Total Estimated Industry Sales ($)						
Product/ Service	*Three Years Ago*	*Two Years Ago*	*Last Year*	*This Year*	*Next Year*	*In Two Years*	*In Three Years*
1. ________	$ ______	$ ______	$ ______	$ ______	$ ______	$ ______	$ ______
2. ________	$ ______	$ ______	$ ______	$ ______	$ ______	$ ______	$ ______
3. ________	$ ______	$ ______	$ ______	$ ______	$ ______	$ ______	$ ______
(etc.)							

General industry standards and performance requirements ______________________

____

____

General trends within the industry and factors likely to affect these trends______________

____

____

Major Industry Participants

Name and Location of Competitor	*Estimated Sales*	*Estimated Market Share (%)*	*Principal Strengths and Weaknesses*
____________	$ ____________	____________	____________
____________			____________
____________	$ ____________	____________	____________
____________			____________
____________	$ ____________	____________	____________
____________			____________

B. Product/Service Offering

DESCRIPTION OF PRINCIPAL PRODUCTS/SERVICES

Product/Service	*Description*	*Unique Features*	*Stage of Development*
____________	____________	____________	____________
	____________	____________	____________
____________	____________	____________	____________
	____________	____________	____________
____________	____________	____________	____________
	____________	____________	____________

Patents or trademarks held or applied for ______________________________

____

____

Franchise or licensing agreements and regulatory, certification, or other requirements

Discuss key success factors in your business and how you plan to exploit them

Outline your time frame and schedule for the implementation of your program

C. Market Analysis (repeat for each product/service offered)

TARGET MARKET AND CUSTOMERS

Describe your target market and prospective customers in terms of geography and/or customer type or profile

Describe the principal factors these consumers consider in the purchase of products like yours

Outline the principal benefit they will receive from patronizing your firm rather than one of your competitors

Describe how your target market might be broken down into segments, and outline how these segments have changed over time and how they might be expected to change in the future

Describe any weekly, monthly, seasonal, or other sales patterns

continued

Business Plan Outline (Retail or Service) — continued

COMPARISON WITH COMPETITORS

Factor	Name of Competitor 1. ______	2. ______	3. ______
Price	______	______	______
Convenience of location	______	______	______
Availability of parking	______	______	______
Image	______	______	______
Breadth of product/service line	______	______	______
Depth of product/service line	______	______	______
Credit policy	______	______	______
Display and fixtures	______	______	______
Sales training and effectiveness	______	______	______
Sales support	______	______	______
Availability of delivery	______	______	______
Other:	______	______	______
______	______	______	______
______	______	______	______

Indicate what, if anything, is really unique about your product/service offering or firm situation ______

______

______

______

______

______

______

______

______

SUMMARY OF ESTIMATED SALES BY PRODUCT/SERVICE LINE AND MARKET SEGMENT

Market Segment Description I ______

	Estimated Sales by Month ($ or units)												
Product/Service Line	*1*	*2*	*3*	*4*	*5*	*6*	*7*	*8*	*9*	*10*	*11*	*12*	*Total*
______													
______													
______													
______													______
												Total	______

Market Segment Description II ______________________________

Product/Service Line	Estimated Sales by Month ($ or units) 1	2	3	4	5	6	7	8	9	10	11	12	Total
______________													
______________													
______________													
______________													______
												Total	______

Market Segment Description III ______________________________

Product/Service Line	Estimated Sales by Month ($ or units) 1	2	3	4	5	6	7	8	9	10	11	12	Total
______________													
______________													
______________													
______________													______
												Total	______

(etc.)

D. Marketing Plan

PRICING

Principal Direct-Cost Elements of Your Operation

Material and supplies costs ______________________________

____

Labour costs ______________________________

____

Operating expenses and overhead ______________________________

____

Discuss the prices you plan to charge, and typical gross and net margins for each of your product/service lines and how they compare with those of other firms ______________________________

____

____

Describe your credit arrangements, returns policy, and other terms of sale ______________________________

____

____

____

continued

Business Plan Outline (Retail or Service) — continued

ADVERTISING AND PROMOTION PROGRAMS

Media	Audience Size	Schedule	Frequency of Use x	Cost of a Single Occasion =	Estimated Cost
				$	$
				$	$
				$	$
				$	$
				$	$
				$	$
				Total Estimated Cost	**$**

PUBLIC RELATIONS

Describe any plan to obtain free publicity or other sales promotion activity

Other service and warranty programs you plan to provide and their anticipated costs:

Service	Estimated Cost
	$

E. Operations Plan

Describe your location and its pros and cons:

Location

Advantages

Disadvantages

Traffic flows and patterns

Zoning requirements

Access

Parking ____

____

Visibility ____

____

Cost ____

____

Condition ____

____

Other ____

____

____

____

____

Indicate the major fixtures and equipment you will require:

Type of Fixture or Equipment	*Buy or Lease*	*Number Required*	x	*Unit Cost*	=	*Total Cost*
______	______	______		$ ______		$ ______
______	______	______		______		______
______	______	______		______		______
______	______	______		______		______
______	______	______		______		______
______	______	______		______		______
______	______	______		______		______
				Total Cost		**$** ______

Develop a drawing or floor plan of the physical layout of your store or other facilities.
Where do you plan to buy your floor stock for resale?

Name of Item	*Name of Supplier*	*Price*	*Order Policy*	*Discounts Offered*	*Delivery Time*	*Freight Costs*	*Back-Order Policy*
______	______	$ ______	______	______	______	$ ______	______
______	______	______	______	______	______	______	______
______	______	______	______	______	______	______	______
______	______	______	______	______	______	______	______
______	______	______	______	______	______	______	______
______	______	______	______	______	______	______	______

continued

Business Plan Outline (Retail or Service) — continued

Where do you plan to buy your operating supplies and materials?

Name of Item	Name of Supplier	Price	Order Policy	Discounts Offered	Delivery Time	Freight Costs	Back-Order Policy
		$				$	

Outline your inventory control procedures:

OPENING INVENTORY REQUIREMENTS

Item	Number Required	x	Cost per Unit	=	Total Cost
	$		$		
			Total Initial Inventory	**$**	

OUTLINE OF EMPLOYEE REQUIREMENTS

Job	Qualification Required	Full- or Part-time	Job Description (yes or no)	Compensation	Benefits
				$	

PERMITS OR LICENCES REQUIRED AND NECESSARY INSPECTIONS

Permit, Licences, or Necessary Inspection	Date Received or Completed

F. Management Team

Develop an organization chart indicating who is responsible for each of the major areas of activity in your business; list each function and indicate the name of the individual who will perform that function and to whom he or she will be responsible:

Function	*Performed by:*	*Responsible to:*
Sales		
Marketing		
Operations management		
Bookkeeping and accounting		
Personnel management		

Present a brief résumé of each of these individuals

Outline the size and composition of your board of directors

Present a brief résumé of each individual on your board who is not part of your management team

Indicate the compensation received by each member of your management team and board of directors:

Individual	*Salary*	*Fees or Bonuses*	*Total Compensation*
	$	$	$

Describe the ownership structure of your business:

Individual	*Types of Shares Held*	*Percentage of Total Issued*	*Number of Shares Held* x	*Price Paid per Share* =	*Total*
				$	$

Total Capitalization $

Indicate any options to acquire additional stock that may be held or could be earned by your management team or others

continued

Business Plan Outline (Retail or Service) — continued

Provide complete information regarding your professional advisors:

Advisor	*Name*	*Address*	*Telephone*	*Fees or Retainers Paid*
Lawyer	________	________ ________	________	$ ________
Accountant	________	________ ________	________	________
Banker	________	________ ________	________	$ ________
Other	________	________ ________	________	$ ________

G. Implementation Schedule

Lay out a schedule of milestones or significant events for the implementation of your business and a timetable for completion; indicate who will be responsible for the completion of each task:

Milestone	*Tasks Required to Accomplish*	*Who Is Responsible*	*Scheduled Completion*
________	________	________	________
	________	________	________
	________	________	________
	________	________	________
________	________	________	________
	________	________	________
	________	________	________
	________	________	________
________	________	________	________
	________	________	________
	________	________	________
	________	________	________

Describe the risks your business may be faced with in implementing your plan, and the risk for any prospective investor ____

____

____

____

H. Financial Plan

START-UP COSTS

If yours is a new venture, indicate your estimate of the start-up financial requirements of your business:

ESTIMATED MONTHLY EXPENSES

Item	Column 1 Your Estimate of Monthly Expenses Based on Sales of $_______ Per Year	Column 2 Number of Months of Cash Required to Cover Expenses*	Column 3 Estimated Cash Required to Start Business (Column 1 x 2)*
Salary of Owner-Manager	$0	2	$0
All Other Salaries and Wages	$0	3	$0
Rent	$0	3	$0
Advertising	$0	3	$0
Delivery Expense/Transportation	$0	3	$0
Supplies	$0	3	$0
Telephone, Fax, Internet Service	$0	3	$0
Other Utilities	$0	3	$0
Insurance	$0	3	$0
Taxes Including Employment Insurance	$0	4	$0
Interest	$0	3	$0
Maintenance	$0	3	$0
Legal and Other Professional Fees	$0	3	$0
Miscellaneous	$0	3	$0
Total Cash Requirements for Monthly Recurring Expenses: (A)			**$0**

START-UP COSTS YOU ONLY HAVE TO PAY ONCE

		Cash Required to Start Business
Capital Costs		
	Fixtures and Equipment	$0
	Decorating and Remodelling	$0
	Installation of Fixtures and Equipment	$0
	Starting Inventory	$0
Soft Costs		
	Deposits with Utilities	$0
	Legal and Other Professional Fees	$0
	Licences and Permits	$0
	Advertising and Promotion for Opening	$0
	Accounts Receivable	$0
	Cash	$0
	Miscellaneous	$0
	Total One-Time Cash Requirements: (B)	**$0**
TOTAL ESTIMATED CASH REQUIRED TO START BUSINESS: (A) + (B)		**$0**

* These figures may be typical for one kind of business. You will have to decide how many months to allow for your business to offset expected shortages of cash flow.

continued

Business Plan Outline (Retail or Service) — continued

PRESENT FINANCIAL STRUCTURE

Provide an overview of the current financial structure of your business and the proportion of your total start-up requirements obtained to date:

Source of Funds	*Amount*	*Debt or Equity*	*Repayment Schedule*
Self	$ ________	________	________
Friends, neighbours, relatives	________	________	________
Other private investors	________	________	________
Banks, savings and loans, credit unions, and other financial institutions	________	________	________
Mortgage and insurance companies	________	________	________
Credit from suppliers	________	________	________
Government grants and loans	________	________	________
Other sources:	________	________	________
________	________	________	________
________	________	________	________
________	________	________	________
________	________	________	________
________	________	________	________
________	________	________	________

Additional Funds Required

Indicate the additional funds required and the shares, return on investment, collateral, or other security you are prepared to provide to the prospective lender or investor

____

____

____

____

____

____

____

____

____

Current Financial Statements

If your business is already in operation, provide an income statement and a balance sheet for the current year to date and the previous two years; the following forms will serve as guidelines indicating the basic information to provide for each year:

INCOME STATEMENT FOR
[Name of Company]
for the period ending [date]

Gross sales	$__________		
Less: Cash discounts	__________		
Net Sales		$ __________	(A)
Less: Cost of goods sold:			
Beginning inventory	$__________		
Plus: Net purchases	__________		
Total goods available for sale	__________		
Less: Ending inventory	__________		
Cost of Goods Sold		__________	(B)
Gross Margin (or Profit) (C = A – B)		$ __________	(C)
Less: Operating expenses:			
Owners' salaries	$__________		
Employees' wages and salaries	__________		
Employee benefits	__________		
Rent	__________		
Utilities (heat, light, water, power)	__________		
Telephone	__________		
Supplies and postage	__________		
Repairs and maintenance	__________		
Advertising and promotion	__________		
Vehicle expense	__________		
Delivery expense	__________		
Taxes and licences	__________		
Depreciation or Capital Cost Allowance	__________		
Bad debt allowance	__________		
Interest	__________		
Travel	__________		
Insurance	__________		
Legal and accounting fees	__________		
Other expenses	__________		
Total Operating Expenses		__________	(D)
Net Operating Profit (Loss) (E = C – D)		__________	(E)
Income Tax (estimated)		__________	(F)
Net Profit (Loss) after Income Tax (G = E – F)		__________	(G)

continued

Business Plan Outline (Retail or Service) — continued

BALANCE SHEET FOR
[Name of Company]
as of [date]

ASSETS		
Current Assets		
Cash	$ ______	
Accounts receivable	______	
Inventory	______	
Other current assets	______	
Total current assets		______ **(A)**
Fixed Assets		
Land and buildings	$ ______	
Furniture and fixtures	______	
Equipment	______	
Trucks and automobiles	______	
Other fixed assets	______	
Total fixed assets		______ **(B)**
Total Assets (C = A + B)		**$** ______ **(C)**
LIABILITIES		
Current Liabilities (debt due within 12 months)		
Accounts payable	$ ______	
Bank loans/other loans	______	
Taxes owed	______	
Total current liabilities		______ **(D)**
Long-Term Liabilities		
Notes payable (due after 1 year)	______	
Total long-term liabilities		______ **(E)**
Total Liabilities (F = D + E)		**$** ______ **(F)**
NET WORTH (CAPITAL)		
Total Net Worth (G = C – F)		______ **(G)**
Total Liabilities and Net Worth (H = F + G)		**$** ______ **(H)**

FINANCIAL PROJECTIONS

Develop profit and loss forecasts, projected cash flow statements, and pro forma balance sheets for your business. Each of these statements should be presented for the following time frames:

- **Pro forma profit and loss statements** Monthly for the next year of operation and quarterly or annually for another two to four years
- **Cash flow forecasts** Monthly for the next year of operation and annually for another two years
- **Pro forma balance sheets** Annually for each of the next three to five years

The following forms will serve as guidelines to be followed in developing and presenting this information.

PRO FORMA INCOME STATEMENT

FOR THE PERIOD ENDING (DATE) ____________

	MONTH 1	2	3	4	5	6	7	8	9	10	11	12	TOTAL
1. Gross Sales													
2. Less: Cash Discounts													
A. NET SALES	$	$	$	$	$	$	$	$	$	$	$	$	$
Cost of Goods Sold:													
3. Beginning Inventory													
4. Plus: Net Purchases													
5. Total Available for Sale													
6. Less: Ending Inventory													
B. COST OF GOODS SOLD	$	$	$	$	$	$	$	$	$	$	$	$	$
C. GROSS MARGIN (C=A–B)	$	$	$	$	$	$	$	$	$	$	$	$	$
Less: Variable Expenses													
7. Owner's Salary													
8. Employees' Wages and Salaries													
9. Supplies and Postage													
10. Advertising and Promotion													
11. Delivery Expense													
12. Bad Debt Expense													
13. Travel													
14. Legal and Accounting Fees													
15. Vehicle Expense													
16. Miscellaneous Expenses													
D. TOTAL VARIABLE EXPENSES	$	$	$	$	$	$	$	$	$	$	$	$	$
Less: Fixed Expenses													
17. Rent													
18. Utilities (heat, light, water, power)													
19. Telephone													
20. Taxes and Licences													
21. Depreciation or Capital Cost													
22. Interest													
23. Insurance													
24. Other Fixed Expenses													
E. TOTAL FIXED EXPENSES	$	$	$	$	$	$	$	$	$	$	$	$	$
F. TOTAL OPERATING EXPENSES (F=D+E)	$	$	$	$	$	$	$	$	$	$	$	$	$
G. NET OPERATING PROFIT (LOSS) (G=C–F)	$	$	$	$	$	$	$	$	$	$	$	$	$
H. INCOME TAXES (estimated)													$
I. NET PROFIT (LOSS) AFTER INCOME TAX (I=G–H)													$

continued

ESTIMATED CASH FLOW FORECAST

	Month 1	Month 2	Month 3	Month 4	Month 5	Month 6	Month 7	Month 8	Month 9	Month 10	Month 11	Month 12	Year 1 TOTAL	Year 2 TOTAL	Year 3 TOTAL
Cash Flow from Operations (during month)															
1. Cash Sales															
2. Payments for Credit Sales															
3. Investment Income															
4. Other Cash Income															
A. TOTAL CASH FLOW ON HAND	$	$	$	$	$	$	$	$	$	$	$	$	$	$	$
Less Expenses Paid (during month)[1]															
5. Inventory or New Material															
6. Owners' Salaries															
7. Employees' Wages and Salaries															
8. Supplies and Postage															
9. Advertising and Promotion															
10. Delivery Expense															
11. Travel															
12. Legal and Accounting Fees															
13. Vehicle Expense															
14. Maintenance Expense															
15. Rent															
16. Utilities															
17. Telephone															
18. Taxes and Licences															
19. Interest Payments															
20. Insurance															
21. Other Cash Expenses															
B. TOTAL EXPENDITURES	$	$	$	$	$	$	$	$	$	$	$	$	$	$	$
Capital															
Purchase of Fixed Assets															
Sale of Fixed Assets															
C. CHANGE IN CASH FROM PURCHASE OR SALE OF ASSETS	$	$	$	$	$	$	$	$	$	$	$	$	$	$	$
Financing															
Payment of Principal of Loan															
Inflow of Cash from Bank Loan															
Issuance of Equity Positions															
Repurchase of Outstanding Equity															
D. CHANGE IN CASH FROM FINANCING	$	$	$	$	$	$	$	$	$	$	$	$	$	$	$
E. INCREASE (DECREASE) IN CASH	$	$	$	$	$	$	$	$	$	$	$	$	$	$	$
F. CASH AT BEGINNING OF PERIOD	$	$	$	$	$	$	$	$	$	$	$	$	$	$	$
G. CASH AT END OF PERIOD	$	$	$	$	$	$	$	$	$	$	$	$	$	$	$
MEET MINIMUM CASH BALANCE	ACCEPTABLE	ACCEPTABLE	ACCEPTABLE	ACCEPTABLE	ACCEPTABLE	ACCEPTABLE	ACCEPTABLE	ACCEPTABLE	ACCEPTABLE	ACCEPTABLE	ACCEPTABLE	ACCEPTABLE	ACCEPTABLE	ACCEPTABLE	ACCEPTABLE

1. Expenses and other payments should be entered as negative (–) numbers.
2. This entry should be the same amount as for the beginning of the year. All other rows will be the total for the entire year.
3. These entries should be the same as the ending cash balance from the previous period.

PRO FORMA BALANCE SHEET FOR [COMPANY]

		Opening	End of Year 1	End of Year 2	End of Year3
	ASSETS				
	Current Assets:				
	1.Cash				
	2.Accounts Receivable				
	3.Inventory				
	4.Other Current Assets				
A.	**TOTAL CURRENT ASSETS (A)**	$	$	$	$
	Fixed Assets:				
	5. Land and Buildings				
	less depreciation				
	6. Furniture and Fixtures				
	less depreciation				
	7. Equipment				
	less depreciation				
	8. Trucks and Automobiles				
	less depreciation				
	9. Other Fixed Assets				
	less depreciation				
B.	**TOTAL FIXED ASSETS (B)**	$	$	$	$
C.	**TOTAL ASSETS (C=A+B)**	$	$	$	$
	LIABILITIES				
	Current Liabilities (due within 12 months)				
	10. Accounts Payable				
	11. Bank Loans / Other Loans				
	12. Taxes Owed				
D.	**TOTAL CURRENT LIABILITIES (D)**	$	$	$	$
	Long-term Liabilities				
	13. Notes Payable (due after one year)				
	14. Other Long-term Liabilities				
E.	**TOTAL LONG-TERM LIABILITIES (E)**	$	$	$	$
F.	**TOTAL LIABILITIES (F=D+E)**	$	$	$	$
	NET WORTH (Capital)				
	SHARE CAPITAL				
	Common Shares				
	Preferred Shares				
	RETAINED EARNINGS				
G.	**TOTAL NET WORTH (G=C-F)**	$	$	$	$
H.	**TOTAL LIABILITIES AND NET WORTH (H=F+G)**	$	$	$	$

Indicate the minimum level of sales you will require to cover all your fixed and variable costs and to break even:

$$\text{Break-even Point (in Sales Dollars)} = \frac{\text{Total Estimated Operating Expenses (F in Pro Forma Profit and Loss Statement)}}{1 - \frac{\text{Gross Margin Percentage}}{100}}$$

FIGURE 11.5 BUSINESS PLAN OUTLINE FOR A MANUFACTURING COMPANY

1. **LETTER OF TRANSMITTAL**
2. **TITLE PAGE**
3. **TABLE OF CONTENTS**
4. **EXECUTIVE SUMMARY**

Fact Sheet

Company name ____________________

Location and telephone ____________________

Type of business and industry ____________________

Form of business organization ____________________

Principal product line ____________________

Registered patents or trademarks (if any) ____________________

Names of founders/partners/shareholders ____________________

Length of time in business (if appropriate) ____________________

Current and/or projected market share ____________________

Funds invested in the business to date and their source ____________________

Additional financing required

Proposed terms and payback period

Total value or net worth of the business

NAMES OF BUSINESS ADVISORS

Legal counsel

Accountant

Banker

Other

5. BODY

A. Your Company and the Industry

THE COMPANY

Date business started

Location

Form of business organization

Founders and other key individuals

Principal products and related services

continued

Business Plan Outline (Manufacturing Company) — continued

Success the Business Has Achieved to Date

	Estimated Total Annual Market (year)		Company Sales (year)		Market Share (%)
Product 1	$______		$______		______
	______	units	______	units	______
Product 2	$______		$______		______
	______	units	______	units	______
(etc.)					

Future Goals and Plans

____

____

____

____

____

Principal strategy for achieving these goals ______________________________

____

____

____

____

____

____

THE INDUSTRY

Prospects for the Industry

	Total Estimated Industry Sales ($)						
Product	*Three Years Ago*	*Two Years Ago*	*Last Year*	*This Year*	*Next Year*	*In Two Years*	*In Three Years*
1. ______	$ ______	$ ______	$ ______	$ ______	$ ______	$ ______	$ ______
2. ______	$ ______	$ ______	$ ______	$ ______	$ ______	$ ______	$ ______
3. ______	$ ______	$ ______	$ ______	$ ______	$ ______	$ ______	$ ______
(etc.)							

Describe general trends within the industry and factors likely to affect these trends ______________

____

____

Describe general industry standards and performance requirements ______________

____

____

Major Industry Participants

Name and Location of Competitor	*Estimated Sales*	*Estimated Market Share (%)*	*Principal Strengths and Weaknesses*
________	$ ________	________	________
________	$ ________	________	________
________	$ ________	________	________

B. Product Offering

DESCRIPTION OF PRINCIPAL PRODUCTS

Product	*Description*	*Unique Features*	*Stage of Development*
________	________	________	________
________	________	________	________
________	________	________	________

Describe patents or trademarks held or applied for ________________

Describe franchise or licensing agreements, and regulatory, certification, or other requirements

Discuss key success factors in your business and how you plan to exploit them ________________

continued

Business Plan Outline (Manufacturing Company) — continued

Outline your time frame and schedule for the implementation of your program

C. Market Analysis (repeat for each product or product line offered)

TARGET MARKET AND CUSTOMERS

Describe your target market and prospective customers in terms of geography and/or customer type or profile

Describe the principal factors these consumers consider in the purchase of products like yours

Outline the principal benefit they will receive from patronizing your firm rather than one of your competitors

Describe how your target market might be broken down into segments, and outline how these segments have changed over time and how they might be expected to change in the future

Describe any weekly, monthly, seasonal, or other sales patterns

COMPARISON WITH COMPETITORS

Factor	Name of Competitor 1. ______	2. ______	3. ______
Price	______	______	______
Breadth of product line	______	______	______
Depth of product line	______	______	______
Performance	______	______	______
Speed and accuracy	______	______	______
Durability	______	______	______
Versatility	______	______	______
Ease of operation or use	______	______	______
Ease of maintenance or repair	______	______	______
Ease or cost of installation	______	______	______
Size or weight	______	______	______
Design or appearance	______	______	______
Other characteristics:	______	______	______
______	______	______	______
______	______	______	______

Indicate what, if anything, is really unique about your product offering or firm situation

____

____

____

____

____

____

____

____

____

SUMMARY OF ESTIMATED SALES BY PRODUCT LINE AND MARKET SEGMENT

Market Segment Description I ______________________________

Product Line	Estimated Sales by Month ($ or units) 1	2	3	4	5	6	7	8	9	10	11	12	Total
______													
______													
______													
______													______
												Total	______

continued

Business Plan Outline (Manufacturing Company) — continued

Market Segment Description II ______________________________

Product Line	*1*	*2*	*3*	*4*	*5*	*6*	*7*	*8*	*9*	*10*	*11*	*12*	*Total*
					Estimated Sales by Month ($ or units)								
____________													
____________													
____________													
____________													______
												Total	______

Market Segment Description III ______________________________

Product Line	*1*	*2*	*3*	*4*	*5*	*6*	*7*	*8*	*9*	*10*	*11*	*12*	*Total*
					Estimated Sales by Month ($ or units)								
____________													
____________													
____________													
____________													______
												Total	______

(etc.)

D. Marketing Plan

PRICING

Bill of Material List for Principal Products or Product Lines

Raw Material or Component Part	*Description*	*Supplier*	**Direct Material Costs** *Landed Cost*	x	*No./or Quantity Reqd. per Unit*	=	*Cost per Unit Prod.*
________	________	________	$ ________		________		$ ________
________	________	________	________		________		________
________	________	________	________		________		________
________	________	________	________		________		________
________	________	________	________		________		________

Total Material Costs per Unit $ ________ **(A)**

Assembly or Manufacturing Process	Direct Labour Costs: Estimated Labour Time per Unit	x	Hourly Rate	=	Labour Cost per Unit	
________	________		$ ________		$ ________	
________	________		$ ________		$ ________	
________	________		$ ________		$ ________	
			Total Labour Cost per Unit		**$** ________	**(B)**

Total Direct Manufacturing Cost per Unit (C = A + B) **$** ________ **(C)**

Total Estimated Packaging and Shipping Cost per Unit ________ **(D)**

Total Direct Cost per Unit (E = C + D) **$** ________ **(E)**

Discuss the prices you plan to charge distributors and customers for your product, typical gross and net margins for each of your product lines, and how they compare with those of other firms

____

____

____

Describe your schedule for quantity, cash, functional, and other discounts, credit arrangements, returns policy, and other terms of sale ____

____

____

____

____

____

DISTRIBUTION

Describe the channels of distribution you will use to get your product to the ultimate consumer

____

____

____

____

____

List your principal distributors by name and their expected sales:

Distributor	Address	Territory	Terms of Sale	Exclusive or Non-Exclusive	Total Expected Sales ($ or units)
________	________ ________	________	________	________	________
________	________ ________	________	________	________	________
________	________ ________	________	________	________	________

continued

Business Plan Outline (Manufacturing Company) — continued

List your principal customers by name and the total amount they are expected to buy from you:

Customer		Product	Total Expected Purchases ($ or units)	Share of Your Sales (%)
______	**1.**	______	______	______
	2.	______	______	______
	3.	______	______	______
______	**1.**	______	______	______
	2.	______	______	______
	3.	______	______	______
______	**1.**	______	______	______
	2.	______	______	______
	3.	______	______	______

PERSONAL SELLING PROGRAM

Outline your personal selling requirements — the number and type of people in your sales force and how they will be paid ______

ADVERTISING AND PROMOTION PROGRAM

Describe product packaging requirements and estimated costs for development and use ______

Outline requirements for product brochures and similar descriptive material indicating development costs and expected cost of production ______

Indicate the trade shows you plan to attend to exhibit your product:

Trade Show	Location	Timing	Estimated Cost
______	______	______	$ ______
______	______	______	______
______	______	______	______
		Total Estimated Cost	**$** ______

ADVERTISING PROGRAMS

Media	*Audience Size*	*Schedule*	*Frequency of Use*	x	*Cost of a Single Occasion*	=	*Estimated Cost*
______	______	______	______		$ ______		$ ______
______	______	______	______		$ ______		$ ______
______	______	______	______		$ ______		$ ______
______	______	______	______		$ ______		$ ______
______	______	______	______		$ ______		$ ______
______	______	______	______		$ ______		$ ______
					Total Estimated Cost		**$** ______

PUBLIC RELATIONS

Describe any plan to obtain free publicity or other sales promotion activity ______

______

______

Describe any repair, informational, or other support services you plan to provide and their anticipated costs:

Service	*Estimated Cost*
______	$ ______
______	______
______	______
______	______

E. Production/Operating Plan

Describe your location and its pros and cons:

Location ______

______

Description ______

______

Advantages ______

______

Disadvantages ______

______

Accessibility to suppliers ______

______

Availability of transport services ______

______

Zoning situation ______

______

continued

Business Plan Outline (Manufacturing Company) — continued

Cost ______________________________

____

Condition ______________________________

____

Other factors ______________________________

____

Describe your basic manufacturing processes and list the basic operations your facility will have to perform ______________________________

____

____

____

Indicate the space required or allocated to each of the following activities:

Activity	*Space Required or Allocated (sq. ft.)*
Manufacturing:	
Fabrication	________
Machining	________
Assembly	________
Finishing	________
Inspection	________
Other ________	________
________	________
Storage	________
Shipping	________
Receiving	________
Office area	________
Restrooms and employee facilities	________
Other activities ________	________
________	________
________	________
Total Space Required or Allocated (sq. ft.)	________

Develop a scale drawing or floor plan of the physical layout of your facility.
List the machinery and equipment you will need to perform your manufacturing and other operations:

Type of Machinery or Equipment	*Buy or Lease*	*Number Required*	x	*Unit Cost*	=	*Total Cost*
______	______	______		$ ______		$ ______
______	______	______		______		______
______	______	______		______		______
______	______	______		______		______
______	______	______		______		______
______	______	______		______		______
______	______	______		______		______
				Total Cost		**$** ______

Indicate where you plan to buy your raw materials and component parts:

Raw Material/ Component	*Supplier*	*Price*	*Order Policy*	*Discounts Offered*	*Delivery Time*	*Freight Costs*	*Back-Order Policy*
______	______	$ ______	______	______	______	$ ______	______
______	______	______	______	______	______	______	______
______	______	______	______	______	______	______	______
______	______	______	______	______	______	______	______
______	______	______	______	______	______	______	______
______	______	______	______	______	______	______	______

Indicate where you plan to buy your raw materials and component parts:

Tools or Supplies	*Supplier*	*Price*	*Order Policy*	*Discounts Offered*	*Delivery*	*Freight Costs*	*Back-Order Policy*
______	______	$ ______	______	______	______	$ ______	______
______	______	______	______	______	______	______	______
______	______	______	______	______	______	______	______
______	______	______	______	______	______	______	______
______	______	______	______	______	______	______	______
______	______	______	______	______	______	______	______

Outline your inventory control procedures ______________________________

____

____

____

____

____

____

____

continued

Business Plan Outline (Manufacturing Company) — continued

OPENING INVENTORY REQUIREMENTS

Raw Materials and Component Parts

Item	Quantity Required	x	Cost per Unit	=	Total Cost
			$		$

Total Raw Material Inventory $________(A)

Consumable Tools and Supplies

Item	Quantity Required	x	Cost per Unit	=	Total Cost
			$		$

Total Tools and Supplies $________(B)

Total Opening Inventory Requirements (C = A + B) $________(C)

OUTLINE OF EMPLOYEE REQUIREMENTS

Job	Qualifications Required	Full- or Part-time	Job Description (yes or no)	Compensation	Benefits
				$	

Describe permits or licences required and necessary inspections:

Permit, Licences, or Necessary Inspection	Date Received or Completed

F. Management Team

Develop an organization chart indicating who is responsible for each of the major areas of activity in your business; list each function and indicate the name of the individual who will perform that function and to whom they will be responsible:

Function	*Performed by:*	*Responsible to:*
Sales	______________	______________
Marketing	______________	______________
Operations management	______________	______________
Bookkeeping and accounting	______________	______________
Personnel management	______________	______________
Research and development	______________	______________

Present a brief résumé of each of these individuals.

Outline the size and composition of your board of directors ______________

____

____

____

Present a brief résumé of each individual on your board who is not part of your management team.

Indicate the compensation received by each member of your management team and board of directors:

Individual	*Salary*	*Fees or Bonuses*	*Total Compensation*
______________	$______________	$______________	$______________
______________	______________	______________	______________
______________	______________	______________	______________
______________	______________	______________	______________
______________	______________	______________	______________
______________	______________	______________	______________

Describe the ownership structure of your business:

Individual	*Types of Shares Held*	*Percentage of Total Issued*	*Number of Shares Held*	x	*Price Paid per Share*	=	*Total*
________	________	________	________		$ ________		$ ________
________	________	________	________		________		________
________	________	________	________		________		________
________	________	________	________		________		________
________	________	________	________		________		________
________	________	________	________		________		________

Total Capitalization $________

Indicate any options to acquire additional stock that may be held or could be earned by your management team or others ______________

____

____

continued

Business Plan Outline (Manufacturing Company) — continued

Provide complete information regarding your professional advisors:

Advisor	*Name*	*Address*	*Telephone*	*Fees or Retainers Paid*
Lawyer	____________	____________ ____________	____________	$ ____________
Accountant	____________	____________ ____________	____________	$ ____________
Banker	____________	____________ ____________	____________	$ ____________
Other	____________	____________	____________	$ ____________

G. Implementation Schedule

Lay out a schedule of milestones or significant events for the implementation of your business and a timetable for completion; indicate who will be responsible for the completion of each task:

Milestone	*Tasks Required to Accomplish*	*Who Is Responsible*	*Scheduled Completion*
____________	____________	____________	____________
	____________	____________	____________
	____________	____________	____________
	____________	____________	____________
____________	____________	____________	____________
	____________	____________	____________
	____________	____________	____________
	____________	____________	____________
____________	____________	____________	____________
	____________	____________	____________
	____________	____________	____________
	____________	____________	____________

Describe the risks your business may be faced with in implementing your plan, and the risk for any prospective investor ____

____

____

____

____

____

____

____

____

H. Financial Plan

START-UP COSTS

If yours is a new venture, indicate your estimate of the start-up financial requirements of your business:

ESTIMATED MONTHLY EXPENSES

Item	Column 1 Your Estimate of Monthly Expenses Based on Sales of $______ Per Year	Column 2 Number of Months of Cash Required to Cover Expenses*	Column 3 Estimated Cash Required to Start Business (Column 1 x 2)*
Salary of Owner-Manager	$0	2	$0
All Other Salaries and Wages	$0	3	$0
Rent	$0	3	$0
Advertising	$0	3	$0
Delivery Expense/Transportation	$0	3	$0
Supplies	$0	3	$0
Telephone, Fax, Internet Service	$0	3	$0
Other Utilities	$0	3	$0
Insurance	$0	3	$0
Taxes Including Employment Insurance	$0	4	$0
Interest	$0	3	$0
Maintenance	$0	3	$0
Legal and Other Professional Fees	$0	3	$0
Miscellaneous	$0	3	$0
Total Cash Requirements for Monthly Recurring Expenses: (A)			**$0**

START-UP COSTS YOU ONLY HAVE TO PAY ONCE

	Cash Required to Start Business
Capital Costs	
Fixtures and Equipment	$0
Decorating and Remodelling	$0
Installation of Fixtures and Equipment	$0
Starting Inventory	$0
Soft Costs	
Deposits with Utilities	$0
Legal and Other Professional Fees	$0
Licences and Permits	$0
Advertising and Promotion for Opening	$0
Accounts Receivable	$0
Cash	$0
Miscellaneous	$0
Total One-Time Cash Requirements: (B)	**$0**
TOTAL ESTIMATED CASH REQUIRED TO START BUSINESS: (A) + (B)	**$0**

* These figures may be typical for one kind of business. You will have to decide how many months to allow for your business to offset expected shortages of cash flow.

continued

Business Plan Outline (Manufacturing Company) — continued

PRESENT FINANCIAL STRUCTURE

Provide an overview of the current financial structure of your business and the proportion of your total start-up requirements obtained to date:

Source of Funds	*Amount*	*Debt or Equity*	*Repayment Schedule*
Self	$ ______	______	______
Friends, neighbours, relatives	______	______	______
Other private investors	______	______	______
Banks, savings and loans, credit unions, and other financial institutions	______	______	______
Mortgage and insurance companies	______	______	______
Credit from suppliers	______	______	______
Government grants and loans	______	______	______
Other sources:	______	______	______
______	______	______	______
______	______	______	______
______	______	______	______
______	______	______	______
______	______	______	______
______	______	______	______

Additional Funds Required

Indicate the additional funds required and the shares, return on investment, collateral, or other security you are prepared to provide to the prospective lender or investor

____
____
____
____
____
____
____
____
____
____
____
____
____

Current Financial Statements

If your business is already in operation, provide an income statement and a balance sheet for the current year to date and the previous two years; the following forms will serve as guidelines indicating the basic information to provide for each year:

INCOME STATEMENT FOR
[Name of Company]
for the period ending [date]

Gross sales	$______		
Less: Cash discounts	______		
Net Sales		**$** ______	**(A)**
Less: Cost of goods sold			
Beginning inventory	$______		
Plus: Net purchases	______		
Total goods available for sale	______		
Less: Ending inventory	______		
Cost of Goods Sold		______	**(B)**
Gross Margin (or Profit) (C = A – B)		**$** ______	**(C)**
Less: Operating expenses:			
Owner's salary	$______		
Employees' wages and salaries	______		
Employee benefits	______		
Rent	______		
Utilities (heat, light, water, power)	______		
Telephone	______		
Supplies and postage	______		
Repairs and maintenance	______		
Advertising and promotion	______		
Vehicle expense	______		
Delivery expense	______		
Taxes and licences	______		
Depreciation or Capital Cost Allowance	______		
Bad debt allowance	______		
Interest	______		
Travel	______		
Insurance	______		
Legal and accounting fees	______		
Other expenses	______		
Total Operating Expenses		______	**(D)**
Net Operating Profit (Loss) (E = C – D)		______	**(E)**
Income Tax (estimated)		______	**(F)**
Net Profit (Loss) after Income Tax (G = E – F)		______	**(G)**

continued

Business Plan Outline (Manufacturing Company) — continued

BALANCE SHEET FOR
[Name of Company]
as of [date]

ASSETS		
Current Assets		
Cash	$ ________	
Accounts receivable	________	
Inventory	________	
Other current assets	________	
Total current assets		________ **(A)**
Fixed Assets		
Land and buildings	$ ________	
Furniture and fixtures	________	
Equipment	________	
Trucks and automobiles	________	
Other fixed assets	________	
Total fixed assets		________ **(B)**
Total Assets (C = A + B)		**$** ________ **(C)**
LIABILITIES		
Current Liabilities (debt due within 12 months)		
Accounts payable	$ ________	
Bank loans/other loans	________	
Taxes owed	________	
Total current liabilities		________ **(D)**
Long-Term Liabilities		
Notes payable (due after 1 year)	________	
Total long-term liabilities		________ **(E)**
Total Liabilities (F = D + E)		**$** ________ **(F)**
NET WORTH (CAPITAL)		
Total Net Worth (G = C – F)		________ **(G)**
Total Liabilities and Net Worth (H = F + G)		**$** ________ **(H)**

FINANCIAL PROJECTIONS

Develop profit and loss forecasts, projected cash flow statements, and pro forma balance sheets for your business. Each of these statements should be presented for the following time frames:

- **Pro forma profit and loss statements** Monthly for the next year of operation and quarterly or annually for another two to four years
- **Cash flow forecasts** Monthly for the next year of operation and annually for another two years
- **Pro forma balance sheets** Annually for each of the next three to five years

The following forms will serve as guidelines to be followed in developing and presenting this information.

continued

PRO FORMA INCOME STATEMENT

FOR THE PERIOD ENDING (DATE) ____________

		MONTH												
		1	2	3	4	5	6	7	8	9	10	11	12	TOTAL
	1. Gross Sales													
	2. Less: Cash Discounts													
A.	**NET SALES**	$	$	$	$	$	$	$	$	$	$	$	$	$
	Cost of Goods Sold:													
	3. Beginning Inventory													
	4. Plus: Net Purchases													
	5. Total Available for Sale													
	6. Less: Ending Inventory													
B.	**COST OF GOODS SOLD**	$	$	$	$	$	$	$	$	$	$	$	$	$
C.	**GROSS MARGIN (C=A–B)**	$	$	$	$	$	$	$	$	$	$	$	$	$
	Less: Variable Expenses													
	7. Owner's Salary													
	8. Employees' Wages and Salaries													
	9. Supplies and Postage													
	10. Advertising and Promotion													
	11. Delivery Expense													
	12. Bad Debt Expense													
	13. Travel													
	14. Legal and Accounting Fees													
	15. Vehicle Expense													
	16. Miscellaneous Expenses													
D.	**TOTAL VARIABLE EXPENSES**	$	$	$	$	$	$	$	$	$	$	$	$	$
	Less: Fixed Expenses													
	17. Rent													
	18. Utilities (heat, light, water, power)													
	19. Telephone													
	20. Taxes and Licences													
	21. Depreciation or Capital Cost													
	22. Interest													
	23. Insurance													
	24. Other Fixed Expenses													
E.	**TOTAL FIXED EXPENSES**	$	$	$	$	$	$	$	$	$	$	$	$	$
F.	**TOTAL OPERATING EXPENSES (F=D+E)**	$	$	$	$	$	$	$	$	$	$	$	$	$
G.	**NET OPERATING PROFIT (LOSS) (G=C–F)**	$	$	$	$	$	$	$	$	$	$	$	$	$
H.	**INCOME TAXES (estimated)**													$
I.	**NET PROFIT (LOSS) AFTER INCOME TAX (I=G–H)**													$

continued

ESTIMATED CASH FLOW FORECAST

	Month 1	Month 2	Month 3	Month 4	Month 5	Month 6	Month 7	Month 8	Month 9	Month 10	Month 11	Month 12	Year 1 TOTAL	Year 2 TOTAL	Year 3 TOTAL
Cash Flow from Operations (during month)															
1. Cash Sales															
2. Payments for Credit Sales															
3. Investment Income															
4. Other Cash Income															
A. TOTAL CASH FLOW ON HAND	$	$	$	$	$	$	$	$	$	$	$	$	$	$	$
Less Expenses Paid (during month)[1]															
5. Inventory or New Material															
6. Owners' Salaries															
7. Employees' Wages and Salaries															
8. Supplies and Postage															
9. Advertising and Promotion															
10. Delivery Expense															
11. Travel															
12. Legal and Accounting Fees															
13. Vehicle Expense															
14. Maintenance Expense															
15. Rent															
16. Utilities															
17. Telephone															
18. Taxes and Licences															
19. Interest Payments															
20. Insurance															
21. Other Cash Expenses															
B. TOTAL EXPENDITURES	$	$	$	$	$	$	$	$	$	$	$	$	$	$	$
Capital															
Purchase of Fixed Assets															
Sale of Fixed Assets															
C. CHANGE IN CASH FROM PURCHASE OR SALE OF ASSETS	$	$	$	$	$	$	$	$	$	$	$	$	$	$	$
Financing															
Payment of Principal of Loan															
Inflow of Cash from Bank Loan															
Issuance of Equity Positions															
Repurchase of Outstanding Equity															
D. CHANGE IN CASH FROM FINANCING	$	$	$	$	$	$	$	$	$	$	$	$	$	$	$
E. INCREASE (DECREASE) IN CASH	$	$	$	$	$	$	$	$	$	$	$	$	$	$	$
F. CASH AT BEGINNING OF PERIOD	$	$	$	$	$	$	$	$	$	$	$	$	$	$	$
G. CASH AT END OF PERIOD	$	$	$	$	$	$	$	$	$	$	$	$	$	$	$
MEET MINIMUM CASH BALANCE	ACCEPTABLE	ACCEPTABLE	ACCEPTABLE	ACCEPTABLE	ACCEPTABLE	ACCEPTABLE	ACCEPTABLE	ACCEPTABLE	ACCEPTABLE	ACCEPTABLE	ACCEPTABLE	ACCEPTABLE	ACCEPTABLE	ACCEPTABLE	ACCEPTABLE

1. Expenses and other payments should be entered as negative (–) numbers.
2. This entry should be the same amount as for the beginning of the year. All other rows will be the total for the entire year.
3. These entries should be the same as the ending cash balance from the previous period.

PRO FORMA BALANCE SHEET FOR [COMPANY]

	Opening	End of Year 1	End of Year 2	End of Year3
ASSETS				
Current Assets:				
1.Cash				
2.Accounts Receivable				
3.Inventory				
4.Other Current Assets				
A. TOTAL CURRENT ASSETS (A)	$	$	$	$
Fixed Assets:				
5. Land and Buildings				
less depreciation				
6. Furniture and Fixtures				
less depreciation				
7. Equipment				
less depreciation				
8. Trucks and Automobiles				
less depreciation				
9. Other Fixed Assets				
less depreciation				
B. TOTAL FIXED ASSETS (B)	$	$	$	$
C. TOTAL ASSETS (C=A+B)	$	$	$	$
LIABILITIES				
Current Liabilities (due within 12 months)				
10. Accounts Payable				
11. Bank Loans / Other Loans				
12. Taxes Owed				
D. TOTAL CURRENT LIABILITIES (D)	$	$	$	$
Long-term Liabilities				
13. Notes Payable (due after one year)				
14. Other Long-term Liabilities				
E. TOTAL LONG-TERM LIABILITIES (E)	$	$	$	$
F. TOTAL LIABILITIES (F=D+E)	$	$	$	$
NET WORTH (Capital)				
SHARE CAPITAL				
Common Shares				
Preferred Shares				
RETAINED EARNINGS				
G. TOTAL NET WORTH (G=C-F)	$	$	$	$
H. TOTAL LIABILITIES AND NET WORTH (H=F+G)	$	$	$	$

continued

Business Plan Outline (Manufacturing Company) — continued

Indicate the minimum level of sales you will require to cover all your fixed and variable costs and to break even:

$$\text{Break-even Point (in Units)} = \frac{\text{Total Operating Expenses (F in Pro Forma Profit and Loss Statement)}}{\text{Your Average Selling Price per Unit} - \text{Total Direct Cost per Unit}}$$

$$\text{Break-even Point (in Sales Dollars)} = \frac{\text{Total Operating Expenses (F in Pro Forma Profit and Loss Statement)}}{1 - \frac{(\text{Average Selling Price per Unit} - \text{Total Direct Cost per Unit})}{100}}$$

6. APPENDICES

FIGURE 11.6 CHECKLIST FOR ASSESSING YOUR BUSINESS PLAN

After completing your business plan you should thoroughly review it. This checklist will help you to do so. Decide whether or not you think the answers you have provided are clear and complete. Evaluate the information from the standpoint of a prospective investor or lending agency and ask yourself whether you are satisfied with your responses.

	Answer Is Included (X)	*Answer Is Clear (Yes/No)*	*Answer Is Complete (Yes/No)*
1. YOUR COMPANY AND THE INDUSTRY			
a. Type of business you are planning	______	______	______
b. Products or services you will sell	______	______	______
c. History of the company	______	______	______
d. Why does business promise to be successful?	______	______	______
e. Your future goals and objectives	______	______	______
f. Description of the industry	______	______	______
g. Major participants and significant trends	______	______	______

General Comments

____

____

____

____

____

2. PRODUCT SERVICE OFFERING			
a. Description of your product/service	______	______	______
b. Present stage of development	______	______	______
c. Patent/trademark position	______	______	______

	Answer Is Included (X)	*Answer Is Clear (Yes/No)*	*Answer Is Complete (Yes/No)*
d. Other formal requirements			
e. Growth opportunities and key factors for success			

General Comments

3. MARKETING ANALYSIS AND PLAN

a. Who are your target customers?			
b. What are their characteristics?			
c. How do they buy?			
d. How large is the market and its various segments?			
e. Factors affecting the market			
f. Who are your competitors? How are they doing?			
g. How much of the market will you be able to attract?			
h. What will your principal marketing strategy be?			
i. Have you detailed all aspects of your marketing plan?			
(i) Pricing			
(ii) Sales and distribution			
(iii) Advertising and promotion			

General Comments

4. PRODUCTION/OPERATIONS PLAN

a. Where will your business be located?			
b. What are the characteristics of your location?			
c. Description of machinery and equipment you will require.			
d. What are your costs to produce your product?			
e. What are your inventory requirements?			
f. Who will be your principal suppliers or subcontractors?			
g. Description of your quality control procedures.			

continued

Checklist for Assessing Your Business Plan — continued

	Answer Is Included (X)	Answer Is Clear (Yes/No)	Answer Is Complete (Yes/No)
h. How many employees will you require?	______	______	______
(i) What type?	______	______	______
(ii) How will they be paid?	______	______	______
i. Will you require any licences, permits, or other authorizations?	______	______	______

General Comments

____

____

____

____

____

5. MANAGEMENT TEAM

	Answer Is Included (X)	Answer Is Clear (Yes/No)	Answer Is Complete (Yes/No)
a. Who will manage your business?	______	______	______
b. What are their qualifications?	______	______	______
c. What is the size and composition of your board of directors?	______	______	______
d. What are your managers and directors being paid?	______	______	______
e. What is the ownership structure of the business?	______	______	______
f. Who are your advisors and consultants?	______	______	______

General Comments

____

____

____

____

____

6. FINANCIAL PLAN

	Answer Is Included (X)	Answer Is Clear (Yes/No)	Answer Is Complete (Yes/No)
a. How much money will you need to start the business and sustain it for the first few months?	______	______	______
b. How much money do you have now?	______	______	______
c. How much more do you need?	______	______	______
d. How will this additional money be used?	______	______	______
e. What kind of collateral or security will be provided?	______	______	______
f. How will this money be repaid?	______	______	______
g. Provided financial statements:			
For the current year	______	______	______

	Answer Is Included (X)	Answer Is Clear (Yes/No)	Answer Is Complete (Yes/No)
For the past two years	____	____	____
h. Total estimated net income:			
Monthly for the first year	____	____	____
Quarterly or annually for the next two to four years	____	____	____
i. Estimated cash flow situation:			
Monthly for the first year	____	____	____
Annually for the next two years	____	____	____
j. What is your estimated financial position at the end of each of the next three to five years?	____	____	____
k. What sales volume will you need to break even?	____	____	____

General Comments

____

____

____

____

____

7. APPENDICES

Do you need to include the following appendixes?	*Yes*	*No*
a. Product photographs and specifications	____	____
b. Résumés of your management team	____	____
c. List of prospective customers	____	____
d. List of possible suppliers	____	____
e. Job descriptions for management team	____	____
f. Consulting reports	____	____
g. Market surveys	____	____
h. Legal agreements and contracts	____	____
i. Publicity articles and promotional pieces	____	____
j. Other supporting material	____	____

LifeLink Ventures Inc.

Business Plan

JON MELTZER

JONATHAN DYCK

TYSON CARON

BRAM RAMJIAWAN

TOM HARDER

TABLE OF CONTENTS

EXECUTIVE SUMMARY

Colorectal cancer is the second leading cause of cancer related fatalities in the United States, claiming the lives of 56,000 Americans every year. Currently there is not an accurate, non-invasive, and cost-effective diagnostic test available to the general public. Due to this deficiency, many cases of colorectal cancer remain undetected until they are untreatable forcing approximately 4.2 million patients to undergo unnecessary, invasive and painful procedures, costing the American heath care system $1.68 billion each year. LifeLink Ventures has an exclusive license for AccuScreen™, a non-invasive test that detects colorectal cancer in its earliest stages with an accuracy of 99%. AccuScreen™ was developed by The Institute for Biodiagnostics (IBD), a world leader in non-invasive diagnostic research in collaboration with The University of Texas MD Anderson Cancer Treatment Center.

LifeLink Ventures has signed an agreement to become the commercialization company for many new technologies developed by IBD. LLV is poised to capitalize on this incredible opportunity through its strong management team, stellar advisory board and influential strategic partners. Each member of our team possesses extensive skills and experience related to their respective backgrounds and together will guide LLV to the forefront of the in vitro diagnostic industry.

Investing in LLV at this early stage presents an amazing opportunity as AccuScreen™ has a market potential of $450 million per year in the United States alone and it is just the first test from a very powerful platform technology. An equity investment of $2,000,000 at this early stage will provide investors the opportunity for an ROE of 70% in the fifth year of sales. AccuScreen™ will be distributed across North America in major medical centers and revenue is expected to reach $37,500,000 by year five of sales, with profits of $13,437,333. Starting in the third year of operations it is expected that one new test annually will begin the commercialization process further enhancing the return for our investors.

1. FACT SHEET

Company Name:	LifeLink Ventures Inc.
Contact Information:	435 Ellice Ave. Winnipeg Canada R3B 1Y6 (204) 984-6223 (phone), (204) 983-3154 (fax)
Form of Business:	Corporation
Product Name:	AccuScreen™
Product Description:	Colorectal Cancer screening device designed to analyze stool samples using Magnetic Resonance Spectroscopy (MRS) technology.
Cost to Manufacture:	
• Prototype	$520,000 per device (US)
• Full Scale Production	$328,000 per device (US)
Management Team:	
• President and CEO	Jon Meltzer
• Director of Finance and Operations	Jonathan Dyck
• Director of Marketing and Sales	Tom Harder
• Director of Information Systems	Tyson Caron
• Interim Scientific Director	Tedros Bezabeh
• Director of Clinical Trials and Regulatory affairs	Bram Ramjiawan
• Director of European Operations	Wendy Ero
Total Capital Required:	$2,500,000

2. COMPANY OVERVIEW

2.1 OPPORTUNITY

Colorectal cancer (CRC) is the second leading cause of cancer deaths in the U.S [1]. It is expected that 150,000 Americans will be diagnosed this year with CRC and 56,000 will die due to this disease [2,3]. Even more distressing than the mortality rate is the emotional and physical suffering inflicted by this disease. Although CRC is a devastating disease, it is highly curable if found in the early stages [4]. The U.S. government has also recognized the importance of CRC screening as part of the Balanced Budget Act of 1997, guaranteeing reimbursement for colorectal screening tests. This creates an incredible opportunity for LifeLink Ventures (LLV), due to the fact that there is no screening test for CRC that is accurate, non-invasive and cost effective.

LifeLink Ventures is poised to fill the void in the CRC screening and diagnosis market in North America by developing a test that is accurate, patient friendly and economical. By providing a superior detection method, LLV will reduce mortality rates, and improve the quality of life.

2.2 COMPANY

LifeLink Ventures Inc. is a for profit Canadian company formed with technology licensed from The National Research Council of Canada's Institute for Biodiagnostics **(IBD)**. IBD is a world leader in research and development relating to the non-invasive diagnosis of disease and has an extensive international network of commercial and academic collaborators. IBD has a mandate to conduct research that is of social and economic benefit as well as to foster local technology clusters. Recently, the Director General of IBD, Dr. Ian Smith, has created a prototyping group at IBD to ensure that promising projects have a better chance of commercial success.

The mandate of LifeLink Ventures is to commercially develop IBD platform technologies that have reached the prototype phase. This is an ideal relationship for both entities as IBD can concentrate on world-class research and LifeLink will have access to a continuous pipeline of new products.

The first product, AccuScreen(tm), is a non-invasive method to detect CRC. This platform technology is based on magnetic resonance spectroscopy (MRS) and was co-developed by IBD and The University of Texas M.D. Anderson Cancer Center (Houston, Texas), the top ranked Cancer Treatment Center in the U.S.

2.3 MISSION STATEMENT

LifeLink Ventures Inc. is committed to developing innovative, cost effective medical solutions aimed at improving the quality of life for patients and generating maximum returns to investors.

2.4 STRATEGIC ALLIANCE WITH IBD

The Institute for Biodiagnostics will own 22.5% of LLV through its not for profit holding company, Diaspec Holdings Inc. The IBD's contribution to LLV will include 1200 square feet for four years, development of a prototype, secondment of Dr. Tedros Bezabeh to LifeLink Ventures until the completion of clinical trials, use of IBD's MRS system (equivalent to the LLV prototype) and 100 personnel hours for various tasks on an as needed basis. LifeLink Ventures Inc. will have right of first refusal on an exclusive license for all MRS related technology and an option to negotiate for all other technologies.

LLV will pay all the patenting costs for AccuScreen(tm) and all other commercialized technologies. In addition a 3.5% royalty on gross sales of AccuScreen(tm) will be paid to the IBD and M.D. Anderson. A milestone payment of $20,000 for the timely completion of the prototype device and another $20,000 upon FDA approval will be paid to the IBD.

3. COLORECTAL CANCER

3.1 *THE DISEASE*

Cancer is a disease caused by alterations in a cell's DNA leading to the uncontrolled proliferation of cancerous cells. Currently, cancer is the second leading cause of death in the United States killing over 500,000 people per year. Colorectal Cancer (CRC) is the second leading cause of all cancer deaths accounting for 56,000 fatalities [5]. CRC is curable if found in the early stages thus making early screening imperative. In the early (pre-cursor) stages of CRC small polyps called adenomas are formed inside the colon wall. These adenomas can progress to cancer. This cancer then advances through four distinct stages [6]:

STAGE	CHARACTERISTICS
A	The cancer is only on the inner surface of the colon or rectum.
B	The cancer involves the full thickness of the wall of the colon or rectum.
C	The cancer has spread to lymph nodes.
D	The cancer has spread from the colon or rectum to other places in the body.

If the disease is detected during the first two stages the five-year survival rate is 92%. The survival rate drops to 60% if detection occurs in the third stage, and the chances of survival are only 6% when detection occurs in the fourth stage.

3.2 *DIAGNOSIS AND TREATMENT*

The most common symptoms for Colorectal Cancer are rectal bleeding, blood in the stool, anemia, change in bowel habits and weight loss. If CRC is found in the polyp stage, removal of the polyps during colonoscopy is sufficient, if detected in later stages surgery is the primary treatment.

Studies have shown that 33% of deaths due to CRC are preventable when CRC is detected early. Thus third party insurers like The Health Care Financing Agency (HCFA) and many Heath Maintenance Organizations (HMOs) now cover screening tests for CRC (as mandated by the Balanced Budget Act of 1997). The purpose of mass screening is to select the patient population that requires colonoscopies, which is the gold standard for screening and has therapeutic and diagnostic capabilities. The current screening methods include:

Fecal occult blood test (FOBT) — FOBT is the most commonly used mass screening test for CRC due to its low cost ($3-$25 depending on the estimate) and its low level of invasiveness (a sample of 3 bowel movements in a row spread on a test card that is then analyzed to detect blood in the stool). Physicians recommend that an FOBT test be administered every year; however, there are many problems associated with this test that are well known to the medical community. Many reports demonstrate a low sensitivity for FOBT (as low as 27% [7]) indicating that many cancers go undetected. This is consistent with the inability of the FOBT to detect CRCs that do not bleed. It is common for cancer to remain undetected in the polyp stage, which is the point at which detection is optimal for the patient as the cure rate is high [8-11].

The FOBT also has a low specificity and this results in many people being sent for colonoscopies that don't have CRC (estimates demonstrate a false positive rate as high as 90% [12,13]). This high false positive rate is due to other conditions that can cause blood in the stool and that are much more prevalent than CRC. This exposes the third party-insurers to unnecessary costs.

Flexible sigmoidoscopy — The doctor uses a flexible lighted tube to look at the lining of the rectum and the lower part of the colon. These tests are recommended once every 4-5 years in people over 50 and cost between $150-365 [13]. One major problem with this test is that only the bottom 50-75% of the colon is visualized, excluding the portions of the colon that give rise to at least 40% of CRCs. Another major problem is that flexible sigmoidoscopy is only 75% accurate with polyps under 5mm [13].

Colonoscopy — This test is done under a mild sedative and can visualize the entire colon. During this procedure biopsies can be collected, and the physician can remove polyps. The cost of a colonoscopy can range from $400-$1600 and is used as a screening tool for people at high risk of getting CRC. For people at normal risk and over the age of 50, colonoscopy is recommended every 10 years. Although colonoscopy is the gold standard, it is not perfect. Besides the cost, there is a 10-27% miss rate of adenomas between 5-10mm [14,15] and a complication rate as high as 0.5% [16] (1/500 perforations and 1/5000 deaths[13]). Also, a specialist must perform colonoscopy and it would be impossible for it to become a mass-screening tool as there are currently not enough qualified specialists.

Other tests — Other tests such as MRI, CT, ultrasound, measuring blood levels of carcinoembryonic antigen and barium enema are also used as screening tests for CRC. The problems associated with these tests include one or many of the following: they are not reimbursed for screening purposes, are too expensive, not sensitive enough, and are only effective in certain circumstances.

It is clear that the current screening methods for CRC have many drawbacks and improved methods must be devised in order to better detect CRC and prevent more unnecessary deaths.

4. THE PRODUCT

4.1 OVERVIEW

AccuScreen™ is the most sensitive and cost effective mass-screening tool for colorectal cancer. AccuScreen™ is the pre-eminent screening method due to its ability to:

1) Detect more cancers at early stages when treatment is more effective
2) Significantly reduce the amount of unnecessary colonoscopies
3) Provide the potential to stage the development of CRC thus improving treatment strategies

The major indicators for the efficacy of a diagnostic test are its sensitivity and specificity. A low sensitivity means that many people with CRC are diagnosed as normal and are not treated until later stages, when the disease is less likely to be cured and the cost of treatment is significantly higher. A low specificity means that many healthy people will be classified as diseased, undergoing unnecessary colonoscopies, and will be exposed to unnecessary risk, inconvenience, and costs. Research on 93 patients indicates that AccuScreen™ has a sensitivity of 95% and a specificity of 99-100% (results in preparation for peer reviewed publication). These results exceed all other mass screening tests currently available. We predict that AccuScreen™ will eventually replace FOBT, barium enema and flexible sigmoidoscopy as the method of choice for CRC screening and will reduce the number of colonoscopies for high-risk patients.

4.2 ADVANTAGES

AccuScreen™ has a number of advantages over other screening methods because it is economical, the sample collection is non-invasive, and it has high sensitivity and specificity. AccuScreen™ also has the potential to stage cancers thus giving physicians another tool to help determine the proper course of treatment. LLV has also structured AccuScreen™ in such a way that customers have control over their pricing strategy, thereby enabling them to generate substantial income from the use of AccuScreen™. Another advantage for LLV is that most of the R&D costs for AccuScreen™ will not be absorbed by the customer, as they were part of IBD's research mandate. The most important advantage of AccuScreen™ is the fact that it is platform technology, meaning that future diagnostic tests can be performed from an AccuScreen™ machine for other diseases.

4.3 THEORY

AccuScreen™ uses magnetic resonance spectroscopy (MRS) on liquefied stool samples to differentiate between people with CRC, those with polyps and the normal population. MRS uses a strong magnetic field to characterize the unique profile of a sample (liquid or solid) by determining the physical/chemical properties of the sample's hydrogen atoms. The resulting data is generated as a spectrum and then analyzed by powerful data processing techniques. These techniques/algorithms differentiate between CRC, polyps and the normal population. Despite this complicated technology, AccuScreen™ will be designed with a simple graphical user interface (GUI), an automated sample processing system and a user-friendly read-out so that a person untrained in MRS can easily operate it.

4.4 SAMPLE PROCESSING

Samples will be collected using the LLV stool collection kits and when received by the lab, can be analyzed immediately or stored in a -70°C freezer for up to 6 weeks. Samples will be processed with a special buffer and prior to being analyzed, will be transferred to a disposable micropipette tube. This tube will then be placed into a reusable glass tube specific for MRS. The technician can load up to 24 samples at a time for processing, at which time the automated, bar code driven system will analyze the sample. Results will then be transferred to the patient's chart. The technician will be required only to load the samples, wash and sterilize the MRS tubes and report any problems to LLV. It is predicted that the first version of AccuScreen(tm) will be able to process a sample every 5 minutes.

4.5 COMPONENTS, MANUFACTURING AND MAINTENANCE

As displayed in the picture below, an MRS system contains a super conducting magnet (left), a computer console (right) and a user interface station (middle). AccuScreen(tm) will source these components from Bruker (via Bruker Canada Inc., Milton ON), the leading MRS manufacturer in the world. These components will be integrated with bar code driven, automated sample preparation and sample positioning units. The GUI will be designed for lab technicians not trained in MRS and the classifying software may also have to be refined and adapted accordingly. IBD's prototyping group will complete this step (with help from IBD's informatics department). Manufacturing of the automation units will be sourced to Colorado MED tech Inc. (CMED-Boulder Colorado) which will integrate these items with the MRS system and ship them to the customer.

A service agreement will be built into the lease price/per test price of the machine or calculated separately if the machine is purchased outright. If there is a technical problem with AccuScreen(tm), a representative from CMED, Bruker or IBD will be flown out to service the unit. If portions of the automation system require replacement they will be sent back to CMED for refitting into the next system and a replacement system will be sent to the customer. LLV will keep one system in inventory in case a total replacement is necessary, but this is very rare for a super-conducting magnet. The service agreements will also include quarterly maintenance of the liquid nitrogen and liquid helium levels. LLV will develop online resources for potential and current customers, physicians, technicians and patients and we will be accessible by phone, fax and email. All service work for AccuScreen(tm) service work will be performed at LLV's expense.

4.6 INTELLECTUAL PROPERTY

Applications have been filed to ensure international patent protection and all future patenting costs will be paid for by LLV. Trademarks will be filed by LLV through Dr. Krupnik, who is a member of our advisory board.

4.7 FUTURE DEVELOPMENTS

The proprietary portion of AccuScreen(tm) is the disease classifier developed by IBD. IBD currently has many projects that use MRS to differentiate between various diseases or cancers and the normal population via the analysis of different tissues and fluids. Once the classifiers are developed they can be integrated into the existing hardware and GUI, making AccuScreen(tm) a true platform technology. One other diagnostic test per year is expected to be ready for clinical trials by year 3 of operations and will use the same hardware as AccuScreen™.

5. INDUSTRY ANALYSIS

5.1 INDUSTRY BACKGROUND

AccuScreen™ will compete in the in-vitro diagnostics/medical device industry. This industry is valued at $20 billion and has a 6% growth rate [17]. Recent consolidation has resulted in seven companies (Abbott Labs, Bayer Diagnostics, Becton Dickenson, Dade Behring, Johnson and Johnson, Olympus and Roche Diagnostics) controlling 74% of the market [17]. However, this trend has the potential to reverse in certain segments as new molecular tests may render some of the current tests obsolete [17]. It is also important to note that AccuScreen™ will compete with in-vitro diagnostic tests such as the FOBT, as well as with medical procedures such as flexible sigmoidoscopy and barium enema.

Companies in the U.S. must convince the FDA that their tests are valid and safe in order to gain regulatory approval. Approval is sought once there is sufficient scientific data to demonstrate that the test/device is safe and effective. Without approval medical devices/diagnostics tests cannot be sold in the U.S.

The FDA has three classes for medical devices/tests. Class 1 devices, such as gloves, do not require special regulatory approval, while Class 3 devices (e.g. pacemakers), require very tight scrutiny as they are invasive and present the most potential danger to the patient. Class 2 devices may undergo strict scrutiny depending on whether or not an equivalent device currently exists on the market. If it does then a 510K form is required from the FDA and approval takes an average of 2.4 months from the time of submission [18]. If it is a novel product, then a pre-market approval (PMA) is required. This takes 9 months on average for approval from the time of submission [18]. It is anticipated that AccuScreen(tm) will be classified as a class 2 device.

6. MARKET ANALYSIS

The Balanced Budget Act of 1997 stipulates that every American over the age of 50 can be reimbursed for CRC screening tests. However, only 30-40% of eligible Americans are screened for CRC [19,20]. Some explanations for this low compliance include incomplete knowledge on the part of the patient and the doctor, fear [21], shyness [21] and the high rate of false positives with the FOBT [22]. It is expected that the compliance for screening will increase by 10-20% annually due to cost reimbursements and an aggressive promotion and education about CRC screening by Cancer awareness agencies, HCFA and The Centers for Disease Control and Prevention [13].

6.1 TARGET MARKET

Based on a 40% American compliance rate with FOBT testing, and a population base of 74,375,248 individuals over the age of 50, there is a potential target market of 29,750,099 in the U.S. alone (Exhibit 1). From this data the ten states with the largest population of compliant individuals have been identified. On average each of the ten states has a compliant population of 1,698,555.

In order for an AccuScreen™ unit to be feasible in our market segment, we will initially require a medical facility that has the ability to service a minimum of 45,000 compliant individuals, which represents less than 3% of that specific compliant population (Exhibit 13). As more units are placed, the break-even point decreases dramatically to 20,145 in year 2 and eventually drops to 3,575 in year 5, or 0.21% of the compliant population thus allowing us to target smaller markets.

It is not unreasonable to expect that the initial sales requirement is attainable. M.D. Anderson has outpatient visits in excess of 400,000 each year. In addition, M.D. Anderson has contracts with other area hospitals and labs for performing additional lab work. Therefore M.D. Anderson's outpatient volume will be able to support the required 45,000 tests.

7. MARKETING STRATEGIES

The medical device/in vitro diagnostic sector in the United States is incredibly complex, and consequently forces organizations to target many different groups in order to achieve market acceptance.

AccuScreen™ must be accepted by the most influential hospitals in order to succeed in the U.S. medical market. Initially AccuScreen(tm) will be marketed to the four centers that were used in our clinical trials. These centers are among the highest ranked cancer research facilities in the U.S. according to a report by the U.S. News [23].

LifeLink must convince the gastroenterologists, lab directors and medical specialists that AccuScreen™ is the superior screening method, based on its ability to reduce costs and increase the quality of CRC diagnosis. The recommendations of these specialists will be a determining factor of whether or not AccuScreen™ will be used for mass screening.

In order to reach these individuals LLV will attend numerous conferences relating to CRC, publish the results of studies in peer-reviewed journals, and launch an aggressive mail campaign. The services of Fleishman Hillard International will also be retained to raise awareness of AccuScreen™ in the medical community.

The next critical issue LLV must deal with is obtaining a reimbursement rate from third party insurers such as HCFA and HMOs. The industry standard dictates that the lab should make at least a 30% profit on each test [24]. To determine the reimbursement rate HCFA (which administers Medicare) takes into account safety, efficacy and cost effectiveness [25]. As a result, HCFA has broad discretion in setting reimbursement rates [25]. Since this is perhaps the most critical step in the whole process, LLV will hire a professional consultant to provide guidance.

Another major hurdle LLV will face is determining how to sell the AccuScreen(tm) device to the more than 4,500 hospitals and labs in the United States [18]. Due to considerable consolidation in the industry, most private labs are run by two companies (Laboratory Corporation of America and Quest Diagnostics) while hospital labs (and hospitals in general) belong to or are owned by group purchasing organizations (GPOs). Contracts with GPOs provide a vendor with access to hundreds of labs (some have 900+ members) and the potential for bulk sales. In return, the GPO will get a reduced price for their membership and charge a 1-2% overhead fee on all sales. Obtaining a contract with a GPO will ensure that AccuScreen(tm) will be actively marketed to its members. Consequently, it is of utmost importance to establish strong relationships with these organizations. In order to ensure that this becomes a reality, the services of Corporate Contracts Inc., a company with strong connections to the GPOs, will be retained.

The final influential group is the general public. This group is important because they will be able to create a demand for AccuScreen™. The general public will be reached by launching an awareness campaign that will consist of press releases and a corporate web site. This campaign will be designed under the guidance of Fleishman Hillard.

As the client base for LLV grows, Sales Associates will be hired to maintain superior customer service, as well to develop new relationships with different institutions across North America.

During the development of the North American market, work will also be conducted to begin sales in Europe and Japan. Using Wendy Ero as the LLV representative in Europe will open many doors, and she will be able to initiate dialogue with the appropriate organizations in Europe.

8. PRICING STRATEGY

The evaluation of new screening tests for cancer has traditionally focused almost exclusively on safety and efficacy. However, the emergence of managed care has made costs and cost-effectiveness a legitimate consideration in clinical assessments of new screening techniques.

For these reasons, LifeLink utilized a previously published cost-effectiveness model for colorectal cancer [26] to determine our pricing strategy. The model was used to compare five screening programs: an annual fecal occult blood test (FOBT) alone, a flexible sigmoidoscopy (FS) every five years, FOBT and FS combined, an air-contrast barium enema every five years and the AccuScreen(tm) every two years. The model assumes that all positive test results arising from the above screening methods will be subsequently evaluated with a colonoscopy. The model also assumes that all patients with adenomas will undergo two surveillance exams. Cost-effectiveness was defined as the cost per cancer death prevented [27,28]. LifeLink also considered the total cost of the screening program per patient screened to evaluate its pricing strategy.

Using a 40% compliance level (reflecting current conditions [19, 20]), not only does the AccuScreen™ prevent the highest number of colorectal cancers and deaths, but it also produces the lowest cost per cancer death prevented when the price of the test is less than $200. When the price of the test drops below $50, the AccuScreen™ also yields the lowest cost per patient screened. By examining the costs associated with each screening program, it is revealed that the major cost savings provided by the AccuScreen™ stem from the substantial drop in the cost of cancer care and the significant reduction in unnecessary colonoscopies arising from false-positive results. A summary of the results, a sensitivity analysis for different compliance levels and price per AccuScreen™ test and a breakdown of the total costs for each screening program are displayed in Exhibit 2.

LifeLink will offer the device free of charge and recoup the costs on a per test basis because of the substantial upfront capital outlay required by the AccuScreen™ MRS system. To reduce financial risk, LifeLink will engage in a sale/leaseback agreement with National Medical Leasing, whereby LifeLink will sell to and then lease back the device from the agency. As a result costs will be passed on to individual labs on a per test basis.

To reduce our operating risk, LifeLink will require each lab to guarantee a minimum of 1,000 tests per month before granting a device. Given LifeLink's variable and fixed cost structure, pricing for the AccuScreen™ test will be set at $30 per test and collections will be based on 60 day terms. This pricing strategy is expected to generate exemplary returns for LifeLink, while providing hospital labs with a sufficient margin after reimbursement to cover overhead and a 30% profit.

9. OPERATIONAL TIMELINE

PRIOR TO COMMENCING OPERATIONS

- Source components
- Agree to terms with IBD & Diaspec
- Incorporation of LLV
- Sign agreement with IBD & Diaspec
- Begin dialogue with potential clinical trial sites, suppliers and manufacturers.

JUNE 2001 — BEGIN OPERATIONS — PRE-APPROVAL PHASE

- Solidify relationships with suppliers and manufacturers
- Order MRS system from Bruker for IBD's prototyping group
- Outline clinical trials and regulatory approval stages
  - Design clinical trials with input from clinical trials and reimbursement consultants (*1 month–July 2001*)
  - Begin dialogue with the appropriate regulatory officials (FDA)
  - Sign agreements, finalize the pay structure at clinical trial sites, appoint clinical trial directors
  - Obtain committee approval with respect to clinical trials sites (MD Anderson, Texas; Health Sciences Center, Winnipeg Canada; Memorial Sloan-Kettering Cancer Center, New York and UCLA Medical Center, California – committee approval (*3 months–October 2001*)
- IBD will begin work on the prototype for AccuScreen™'s sample processing units (*1.5 years — complete in January 2003*)
- Begin preliminary work with PR firm
- Formulate reimbursement strategy with consultants

OCTOBER 2001 — COMMENCE CLINICAL TRIALS

- Begin clinical trials (1,500 samples per center) (*6 months–March 2002*)
  - Samples will be obtained from patients that are scheduled to undergo a colonoscopy
  - Test package given to patient by clinical trials coordinator at that site, samples stored at site and shipped to IBD once 50 samples are collected (~once per week)
  - Coded samples received by IBD will be processed by Dr. Bezabeh
- Continue dialogue with regulatory agencies

MARCH 2002 — COMPLETION OF CLINICAL TRIALS AND REGULATORY SUBMISSION

- Tabulate and analyze data (*3 months–May 2002*)
- Prepare final report with regulatory consultant (*1 month–June 2002*)
- FDA submission for regulatory approval (*6 months–December 2002*)
- Implement reimbursement strategy
- Dr. Bezabeh will prepare and submit manuscripts for peer review publication (*5-7 months*)

JANUARY 2003 — COMMENCE SALES TO CLINICAL TRIALS SITES

- Latest expected date for FDA approval
- Automation prototype to CMED for validation and production (*3 months–April 2003*)
- Sale of AccuScreen™ machine to clinical test sites

JUNE 2003 — GROWTH

- Hire Bram Ramjiawan as full-time director of clinical and regulatory affairs
- Expand into smaller U.S. markets and draft a plan for international expansion

JUNE 2004

- Hire Scientific Director
- Start commercialization process with one new product every year

10. COMPETITION

Intense competition exists in most sectors of the health care industry and the in-vitro diagnostic sector is no exception. Currently there are five major companies actively searching for an effective and accurate methods to screen for CRC.

EXACT SCIENCES CORPORATION (NASDAQ:EXAS) www.exactlabs.com: Exact Sciences will attempt to utilize various DNA-based techniques for the detection of CRC and other cancers. Only one of these techniques, the DNA Integrity Assay (DIA), is potentially threatening to AccuScreen™. Exact claims this has the potential to become a platform technology; however, based on the cost of running these tests, the difficulty in automating this technology and the insensitivity of their most recent studies (67-78%), it is unlikely that they pose a major threat to AccuScreen™.

INTERNATIONAL MEDICAL INNOVATIONS (TSE:IMI) www.imin.ca/ IMI has a test (ColorecAlert) for CRC based on detecting markers in rectal mucus. The problem with this test is that it is effective (90% specific) only when combined with another test such as the FOBT test, making the claimed cost benefit unknown at this point. IMI's strengths are that the clinical trials included 670 patients and the technology is conducive to point of care testing (doctor's office) or automation.

PROCYON BIOPHARMA INC. (TSE:PBP) www.procyonbiopharma.com Procyon is also developing a screening test for CRC based on markers present in rectal mucus. The strengths of this test are that it may be conducive for point of care testing or automation and it is sensitive (89%) for detecting polyps, according to their press releases. However, the details of the clinical trials for this product are unknown. Procyon has decided to initially seek approval for and market its product in Canada.

MATRITECH INC. (NASDAQ: NMPS) www.matritech.com/ This company was formed in 1987 and went public in 1992. Its technology is patented and is based on the detection of various types of cancer with antibody-based blood tests. The kit used for the diagnosis of CRC already has FDA approval for bladder cancer screening and is being distributed in Europe and China. Preliminary results on 37 patients show promise, however multi-center clinical trials have not been conducted. It is unknown at this point what the tests cost and if the science is dependable.

LEXON INC. (OTC Bulletin :LXXN) www.lexoninc.com/ Lexon has pending patents on antibody based blood tests for detecting CRC and other types of cancer based on specific proteins present in cancer patients. If successful, this technology poses a threat to AccuScreen™, as there is a higher patient acceptance rate for blood collection as opposed to stool collection. This test may also be conducive to automation, thereby making it quite inexpensive. Lexon has not yet completed clinical trials and it is unknown at this point if this technology is sensitive enough to detect cancer at the polyp stage.

11. MANAGEMENT TEAM

Jon Meltzer, President and CEO: Mr. Meltzer is in his last year as a Ph.D. student in the Faculty of Medicine at The University of Manitoba. He was also founder and CEO of MRR Inc., a University spin-off company that sells reagents for genetic and proteomic research internationally. Mr. Meltzer's combination of science and business experience will guide LLV's present and future objectives and help ensure that LLV meets its target dates.

Jonathan Dyck, Director of Finance and Operations: Mr. Dyck will graduate this year from the I. H. Asper School of Business at the University of Manitoba with a major in Finance. For the past three years, he has sharpened his financial skills in the Treasury and Money Management branch of the City of Winnipeg. Mr. Dyck will be responsible for managing the financial status of LLV, day-to-day operations, communicating with LLV's investors, and ensuring that LLV's pipeline of suppliers and collaborators is on schedule to meet AccuScreen's™ time to market.

Tyson Caron, Director of Information Technology, Faculty of Industrial Engineering: Mr. Caron will graduate this year from the I. H. Asper School of Business with a double major in Management Information Systems and Marketing. He will be responsible for maintaining our website, contact with customers, training AccuScreen's™ users, arranging servicing of AccuScreen™ and helping out with sales, marketing and logistics when necessary.

Tom Harder, Marketing and Sales Director: Mr. Harder will graduate this year from the I. H. Asper School of Business at the University of Manitoba with a double major in Small Business and Marketing. Mr. Harder has worked for The Investment Planning Council of Canada as Director of Marketing and has vast experience as a sales representative. Mr. Harder will be responsible for coordinating the marketing and sales efforts of AccuScreen™ which includes disseminating information on AccuScreen™ (and related research) to physicians, third party insurers (private and government), non-profit agencies, group purchasing organizations (GPOs) and lobby groups.

Tedros Bezabeh, Ph.D, Interim Scientific Director: Dr. Bezabeh is one of the lead researchers that helped developed the AccuScreen™ technology. Dr. Bezabeh will be seconded to LLV until the completion of the clinical trials. Dr. Bezabeh will be responsible for analyzing the samples from our clinical trials, writing up the results for peer-review publication and providing other technical assistance when necessary.

Bram Ramjiawan, Director of Clinical Trails and Regulatory Affairs: Mr. Ramjiawan has much experience with research protocols, clinical trials and regulatory affairs during his training at IBD. He will work part time for LLV until the completion of his degree (Ph.D. student in the Faulty of Medicine at The University of Manitoba), after which he will be hired full time by LLV.

Wendy Ero, Director of European Operations: Ms. Ero will use her specialized training from the Eindhoven University of Technology, faculty of Industrial Engineering and Management Science to assist LLV as it expands into Europe. She will be responsible for making initial contact with European physicians, laboratories, regulatory agencies and potential distributors who are interested in AccuScreen™.

12. BOARD OF ADVISORS

Mr. Don Gales: Mr. Gales is an investment banker with 40 years of experience in business and finance. Mr. Gales has sat on the board of many international companies and is currently on the executive board of Onex Inc., which is a publicly-traded company listed on the Toronto Stock Exchange (TSE). Mr. Gales will bring his many years of financial expertise to LLV and will be instrumental in securing 2nd and 3rd round financing.

Marshall J. Glesby, M.D., Ph.D.: Dr. Glesby is the Medical Director of the Cornell Clinical Trials Unit at Chelsea Center and co-Director of the Cornell Clinical Trials Unit in New York, NY. Dr. Glesby is a well-established clinician-researcher who trained at the most prominent medical schools in North America, has many clinical and academic duties and has reviewed articles for many prominent journals. His knowledge of the clinical trials process, of the U.S. health care system and his contacts with other medical schools will be very beneficial to LLV in the start-up phase.

Eduardo Krupnik, Ph.D., LL.B: Dr. Krupnik has his Ph.D. in the field of colon cancer detection with MRS and is currently practicing intellectual property law at the Canadian firm Borden Ladner Gervais. Dr. Krupnik will advise LLV on various legal issues, including those concerning intellectual property.

Bernard Levin, M.D.: Dr. Levin is the Vice President of Cancer Prevention at The University of Texas M.D. Anderson Cancer Center which was ranked the top cancer care center in the U.S. Dr. Levin is a world renowned gastroenterologist, a co-inventor of LLV's colorectal detection technology, has authored over 200 articles and book chapters on colorectal cancer. As one of the leading authorities in the world on colorectal cancer, Dr. Levin's insight into the disease and its treatment will be invaluable to LLV and he will bring instant credibility to AccuScreen™.

John Saunders, Ph.D.: Dr. Saunders is President and CEO of Innovative Magnetic Resonance Imaging Systems (IMRIS) Inc. Dr Saunders is a physicist with vast experience in magnetic resonance research. He has as over 150 peer reviewed publications and his company has just received approval from the FDA for its movable MRI system. Dr. Saunders will be able to mentor LLV during various points in our development as IMRIS was at a similar stage to LLV five years prior.

Ian Smith, Ph.D.: Dr. Smith is the Director General of the IBD and is a co-inventor of LLV's colorectal detection technology. Dr. Smith has over 100 publications and book chapters and is a leading authority on the use of magnetic resonance in the diagnosis of disease. Dr. Smith also serves on numerous local, national and international committees including the board of a local venture fund, and 4 medical device companies. He has far-reaching, international connections in the industry and will represent IBD's interests on LLV's board. Dr. Smith will be instrumental in all aspects of LLV's development, and in ensuring a consistent product pipeline through world-class research at IBD.

13. CRITICAL RISKS

1. **Technical problems with AccuScreen™:** This is a remote possibility given that AccuScreen™'s software, sample positioning module and sample processing modules will be designed by the experts at IBD and independently validated by CMED prior to launch. MR spectrometers are very reliable devices and they are sourced from the industry leader, Bruker, which has many years in the business. LLV will ensure that CMED, Bruker or IBD will service AccuScreen™ within 48 hours. There will be one AccuScreen™ system at LLV in the unlikely event that there is a system beyond repair.
2. **Difficulties with suppliers and outsourcing partners:** This is a minor risk as our strategic partners are both reliable and reputable. In the event that there are problems, our partners have many reliable competitors. The most critical supplier is Bruker, as there are a limited number of MR Spectrometer manufacturers and the lead time for their product is 5-8 months. However, with consistent sales this is also a minor risk, as the lead-time will be reduced.
3. **Failure of the clinical trials:** This is a minor risk given the strength of our technology and our pre-clinical data. However, if this were to occur it would be a serious setback for LLV and would necessitate a re-evaluation of our strategy (i.e. new trials, development of another product or initiation of our exit strategy).
4. **Failure of regulatory approval:** This is a remote possibility as the FDA has already classified MR spectrometers as class 2 devices. However, constant contact will be maintained with the FDA, HPB of Canada and various consultants at every stage of AccuScreen's™ development to ensure the greatest chance of success. Failure to obtain FDA approval would also necessitate a re-evaluation of our strategy.
5. **Failure to obtain favorable reimbursement:** This is a critical risk that affects all manufacturers of diagnostic tests and can be a devastating setback. It can also occur despite obtaining FDA approval and unlike FDA approval there is no clear process on how to obtain favorable reimbursement from HCFA and other third party insurers like HMOs. We will hire reimbursement consultants (Princeton Reimbursement Group, Minneapolis, Minnesota) prior to the design of clinical trials and throughout the regulatory and reimbursement process in order to minimize this risk. If an unfavorable reimbursement rate is received, LLV may have to consider dissolution.

6. **If AccuScreen™'s patents are rejected:** The patents for AccuScreen™ are currently in the PCT application process, which may take many years (4-7) to complete. Based on the preliminary assessments it is likely that they will issue; however, even if they do not issue, AccuScreen™ will have first mover status for a product that has a high entry barrier. Also, the critical part of our technology is the classification software that will be protected by copyright and trade secret.

7. **Low market acceptance for AccuScreen™:** Failure to gain market acceptance could occur for various reasons, and would be very damaging to LLV, as all resources would have been placed into the commercialization of AccuScreen™. We will minimize this risk as much as possible by an early, aggressive marketing campaign that will include extensive help from external consultants and a PR firm (Fleishman Hilllard International Communications). These efforts will focus on promoting the benefits of AccuScreen™ to physicians, third-party insurers, lobby groups, purchasing officials, and the general public.

8. **The emergence of new technologies:** This is always a concern in highly competitive, technologically-based industries. However, any new technology would have to make it past the proof of concept stage to significantly match AccuScreen™ on its medical and economic benefits for CRC screening and its potential as a platform technology. LLV must be efficient in its commercialization efforts, as some competitors are at a similar stage of development and they have secured sufficient financing for their objectives.

9. **Lawsuits from patients:** This is a reality in all areas of the health care industry. However, since AccuScreen™ will primarily be used as a screening tool for more invasive procedures such as colonoscopies, lawsuits are a remote possibility. However, $10,000,000 of liability insurance will be purchased.

10. **Disputes over patents and copyrights:** This is also a common occurrence in the health care industry and can lead to bankruptcy irrespective of whether a company has launched the suit or is the defendant. Thus we have diligently investigated these issues and found no apparent conflicts. Any potential situation will be analyzed and decisions will be made on a case-by-case basis as to whether to litigate or settle out of court. IBD has some obligations to assist in the prosecution of parties infringing on their patents.

11. **Inexperienced management team:** This is not a major concern as LifeLink has an experienced board, experienced consultants, reliable suppliers and outsourcing partners at every stage of commercialization. Should the board determine that there is a problem with LLV's management, its members will not hesitate to bring in senior help to remedy the situation. Due to the high potential value of AccuScreen™ technology, LLV will be able to be sold at a substantial profit should the management team prove to be ineffective.

14. FINANCIAL SUMMARY

In the first two years of operations, LifeLink Ventures (LLV) expects to incur $1,526,687 in losses as the Company guides the AccuScreen™ device through development, clinical trials and regulatory approval. Upon approval, LLV reasonably expects to place two AccuScreen™ devices in its third and fourth year of operations, which will generate sales of AccuScreen™ tests of $2,073,600 and $5,184,000 respectively. Profit margins in year 3 and year 4 are 2.67% and 33.58%, translating into a return on equity of 20.14% and 160.92% respectively.

Sales of AccuScreen™ devices and subsequent tests are expected to expand significantly after year 4, as the Company benefits from improved awareness, experience in operations and established connections within the medical community. LifeLink expects to sell an additional six devices in year 5, which will lead to a 120% year-over-year increase in AccuScreen™ test sales. Overall, LifeLink expects to place 27 AccuScreen™ devices over five years, and realize a profit of $13,357,432 in year 7 on total sales of $37,562,400 for a return on equity of 70%.

15. COMPANY OFFERING

LifeLink will require $2,469,794 to finance operations during its two-year startup phase. Funding will be provided as follows:

- The National Research Council's Industrial Research Assistance Program (IRAP) will contribute $214,345 in forgivable loans

- The Canadian Federal and Manitoba Provincial Governments will reimburse $155,449 in the form of research tax credits
- Each member of LifeLink's management team will contribute $20,000 of personal funds for a total of $100,000. In return, each member will receive 180,000 common shares of LifeLink, which represents a combined 75% of the Company. Each member of LLV's board of advisors will be offered 5,000 common shares for a combined 2.5% of the company. The remaining 22.5% of the Company or 270,000 common shares will be held by Diaspec Holdings.
- LifeLink will raise the remaining $2,000,000 by issuing 800,000 preferred shares at $2.50 per share. The holder of each preferred share is entitled to receive an 8% cumulative dividend. Each preferred share is convertible into one common share at the option of the holder or upon the closing of an underwritten public offering.

16. HARVEST STRATEGY

LifeLink recognizes the uncertainty of our proposed strategy and has considered possible exit strategies that will lead to the dissolution of the company.

- Unfavorable clinical trial results — If the outcome of the clinical trials is unfavorable, the Company will pursue dissolution pending a review.
- Inability to obtain FDA approval or favorable reimbursement rates — If the company is unable to gain FDA approval or favorable reimbursement rates for AccuScreen™, the Company will pursue dissolution pending a review.

LifeLink also recognizes the incredible potential of this device and has considered possible harvest strategies in the interest of maximizing shareholder wealth.

- Selling the Company — If the outcome of the clinical trials is favorable, management strongly believes that LifeLink could be sold at a substantial premium to competitors such as SmithKline Beecham, Helena Laboratories or Bayer who may want to enhance or defend their positions in the colorectal cancer screening market.
- Initial Public Offering — If the Company is successful at commercializing the AccuScreen™ test in North America, management believes that the incredible potential of the test could warrant a public offering on a biotechnology-orientated exchange such as the NASDAQ or the CDNX, with the proceeds being used to finance international expansion and additional development projects.

17. ASSUMPTIONS

1. LLV will receive $30 for each test performed
    - Payment will be received 60 days after the test has been performed
2. Investment income is calculated by multiplying the beginning monthly cash balance by a monthly investment rate of 0.5%.
3. Advertising and Promotion is based on the cost of a public relations firm, three medical conferences per year, promotional material, marketing video, market research and other related expenses.
4. AccuScreen™ device sales incorporates the cost of a Bruker MRS ($230,000), Colorado MEDtech manufacturing costs for the automated sample preparation ($60,000) and sample positioner ($20,000), supply of 500 MRS tubes ($5,000), Reimer Trucking shipping costs ($5,000), installation ($4,300) and training ($4,500). Both Bruker and Colorado MEDtech have expressed a willingness to provide favorable payment terms dependent on the eventual sale to National Medical Leasing. Reimer Trucking requires payment before shipment is received.
5. To combat lengthy lead times from Bruker (5 months), LLV will also lease an additional device for inventory purposes, commencing February 2003. This enables LLV to ship, install, and train lab staff within one month of a sale.

6. AccuScreen™ Test Kits include the variable costs of a capillary test tube ($0.01), labels ($0.0176), patient test tube ($0.343), ice pack ($0.95), packaging box ($2.31) and saline reagent ($1.00). It is assumed that suppliers will provide 30-day payment terms.

7. Shipping costs for AccuScreen™ tests during clinical trials are based on Fedex quotes for shipping a 20lb box ($130) and a 50lb box ($250) and local courier rates per test ($5). It is assumed that Fedex will provide 30-day payment terms. Shipping costs for AccuScreen™ equipment are estimated to be $5,000 per sale.

8. Service & Maintenance assumes four service calls per year ($2,800/call) and four nitrogen and helium refills per year ($300/refill), performed through a local contractor.

9. Licensing Fees required by the IBD and M.D. Anderson include 3.5% of gross sales, and milestone payments to the IBD of $20,000 upon completion of a working prototype and $20,000 upon FDA approval (January 2003). Payment terms will reflect receivables.

10. Sales Commissions amounting to 2.0% of sales are required by Group Purchasing Organizations. Payment terms will reflect receivables.

11. Insurance policies will be provided by Hallmark Insurance Brokers and cover clinical trials ($5,000) and a $10 million liability insurance policy ($5,500).

12. Patent costs reflect international filing, maintenance, prosecution and exam fees for the United States, Canada, the European Union, Japan and Great Britain.

13. Clinical Trials involve committee approval ($24,000), clinical trial coordinators ($180,000) and hospital overhead ($51,000).

14. Consulting services are required for Food and Drug Administration, Health Care Financing Administration and Group Purchasing Organizations.

15. Interest Payments are calculated by multiplying the beginning monthly cash balance by a monthly borrowing rate of 0.75%.

16. Income Taxes are based on an effective tax rate of 45%. Note that losses in previous years can be carried forward to offset current profits.

17. The AccuScreen™ device has the capacity to analyze 8,640 samples per month. It is assumed that baseline utilization will be 50% of capacity.

18. LLV will incur costs for commercializing new products (R&D) starting in year three of operations.

18. REFERENCE LIST

1. Markowitz AJ, Winawer SJ: Screening and surveillance for colorectal cancer. Semin.Oncol. 1999; 26: 485–498.

2. Baquet CR: Colorectal cancer epidemiology in minorities: a review. J Assoc.Acad.Minor.Phys. 1999; 51–58.

3. Conley BA, Kaplan RS, Arbuck SG: National Cancer Institute Clinical Trials Program in Colorectal Cancer. Cancer Chemother.Pharmacol 1998; 42 Suppl: S75–S79

4. Dashwood RH: Early detection and prevention of colorectal cancer (review). Oncol.Rep. 1999; 6: 277–281.

5. U.S.Department of Health and Human Services Centers for Disease Control and Prevention. Chronic Diseases and Their Risk Factors: The Nation's Leading Causes of Death, 1999. 2001.

6. Kumar V, Cotran RS, Robbins SL: The GI Tract. In: Basic Pathology. 1992; 473–522.

7. Brevinge H, Lindholm E, Buntzen S, Kewenter J: Screening for colorectal neoplasia with faecal occult blood testing compared with flexible sigmoidoscopy directly in a 55–56 years' old population. Int J Colorectal.Dis 1997; 12: 291–295.

8. Fattah AS, Nakama H, Kamijo N, Fujimori K, Zhang B: Colorectal adenomatous polyps detected by immunochemical occult blood screening. Hepatogastroenterology. 1998; 45: 712–716.

9. Sieg A, Scheida M, John MR, et al: Validity of new immunological human fecal hemoglobin and albumin tests in detecting colorectal neoplasms — an endoscopy-controlled study. Z.Gastroenterol. 1998; 36: 485–490.

10. Nakama H, Abdul FA, Zhang B, Kamijo N, Fujimori K, Miyata K: Detection rate of immunochemical fecal occult blood test for colorectal adenomatous polyps with severe dysplasia. J Gastroenterol. 1997; 32: 492–495.

11. Nakama H, Fattah A, Zhang B, Uehara Y, Wang C: A comparative study of immunochemical fecal tests for detection of colorectal adenomatous polyps. Hepatogastroenterology. 2000; 47: 386–389.

12. Simon JB: Fecal occult blood testing: clinical value and limitations. Gastroenterologist. 1998; 6: 66–78.

13. Kearney, B. Colorectal Cancer Diagnostics: Current Status and Emerging Approaches. 3–1–3–17. 2001. Decision Resources Inc.

14. Rex DK, Cutler CS, Lemmel GT, et al: Colonoscopic miss rates of adenomas determined by back-to-back colonoscopies [see comments]. Gastroenterology 1997; 112: 24–28.

15. Hixson LJ, Fennerty MB, Sampliner RE, McGee D, Garewal H: Prospective study of the frequency and size distribution of polyps missed by colonoscopy. J Natl.Cancer Inst. 1990; 82: 1769–1772.

16. Markman M: Intraperitoneal chemotherapy in the management of colon cancer. Semin.Oncol. 1999; 26: 536–539.

17. Kadens, D. Sales of In Vitro Diagnostic Products to 2004. 8–1–8–11. 2001. Decision Resources Inc.

18. Standard and Poor's Industry Surveys. Medical Devices. 1–28. 1999. McGraw Hill.

19. Vernon SW: Participation in colorectal cancer screening: a review. Journal of The National Cancer Institute 1997; 89: 1406–1422.

20. Winawer SJ, Zauber AG: Colorectal Cancer Screening: Now is the time. Canadian Medical Association Journal 2000; 163: 543–544.

21. Li T, Nakama H, Wei N: Reasons for non-compliance in colorectal cancer screening with fecal occult blood test. Eur J Med Res 1998; 3: 397–400.

22. Delco F, Sonnenberg A: Limitations of the faecal occult blood test in screening for colorectal cancer [see comments]. Ital.J Gastroenterol.Hepatol. 1999; 31: 119–126.

23. Cancer center rankings. U.S.News . 2001. http://www.usnews.com/usnews/nycu/health/hosptl/speccanc.htm

24. Clinical Chemistry Instrumentation. 1998. Theta Reports.

25. Bagley, G. P. A Primer of the Medicare Program: Coverage and Payment for Laboratory Tests. 7–1–7–12. 2001. Decision Resources Inc.

26. Lieberman DA: Cost-effectiveness Model for Colon Cancer Screening. Gastroenterology 1995; 109: 1781–1790.

27. Schrag D, Weeks J: Costs and cost-effectiveness of colorectal cancer prevention and therapy. Semin.Oncol. 1999; 26: 561–568.

28. Wagner JL: Cost-effectiveness of screening for common cancers. Cancer Metastasis Rev 1997; 16: 281–294.

LIFELINK VENTURES — EXHIBIT 1

CENSUS DATA AND ESTIMATED COMPLIANCE RATES FOR TOP TEN STATES (2000)

	Total Population	Total Population over 50	FOBT Compliance Rate (%)	Total FOBT Compliance
California	33,145,121	7,940,431	33.5%	2,657,016
New York	18,196,601	5,196,962	50.6%	2,629,708
Florida	15,111,244	5,057,065	49.0%	2,476,373
Texas	20,044,141	4,798,635	40.0%	1,919,023
Pennsylvania	11,994,016	3,727,561	44.9%	1,673,223
Michigan	9,863,775	2,664,036	45.7%	1,217,571
Ohio	11,256,654	3,179,636	37.5%	1,193,717
North Carolina	7,650,789	2,111,627	55.5%	1,171,905
New Jersey	8,143,412	2,349,583	44.3%	1,040,296
Massachusetts	6,175,169	1,755,890	57.3%	1,006,723
United States	**272,690,813**	**74,375,248**	**40.0%**	**29,750,099**
			Total Compliance of Top Ten States:	**16,985,555**
			Average Compliance of Top Ten States:	**1,698,555**

LIFELINK VENTURES — EXHIBIT 2

COST-EFFECTIVENESS SUMMARY AND SENSITIVITY ANALYSIS

COST-EFFECTIVENESS SUMMARY (AT 40% COMPLIANCE AND $30 PER ACCUSCREEN™ TEST)

	Cancers Prevented	Deaths Prevented	Unnecessary Colonoscopies	Cost per Death Prevented	Cost per Screenee
FOBT	15.0%	23.0%	8.0%	$343,530	$ 790
FS	15.0%	21.0%	0.0%	449,048	943
FS/FOBT	20.1%	26.5%	6.0%	374,830	992
Barium Enema	15.0%	23.0%	4.0%	442,765	1,018
AccuScreen	**27.0%**	**31.9%**	**0.0%**	**235,795**	**753**

EFFICACY OF SCREENING PROGRAMS

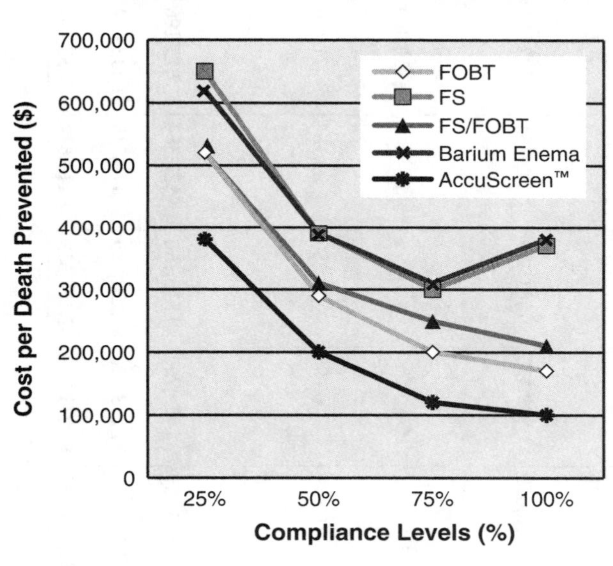

COST EFFECTIVENESS OF ACCUSCREEN™

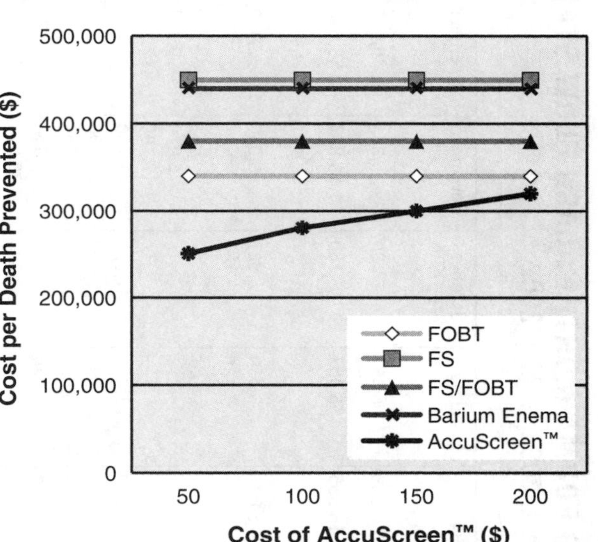

TOTAL COST BREAKDOWN OF EACH SCREENING PROGRAM

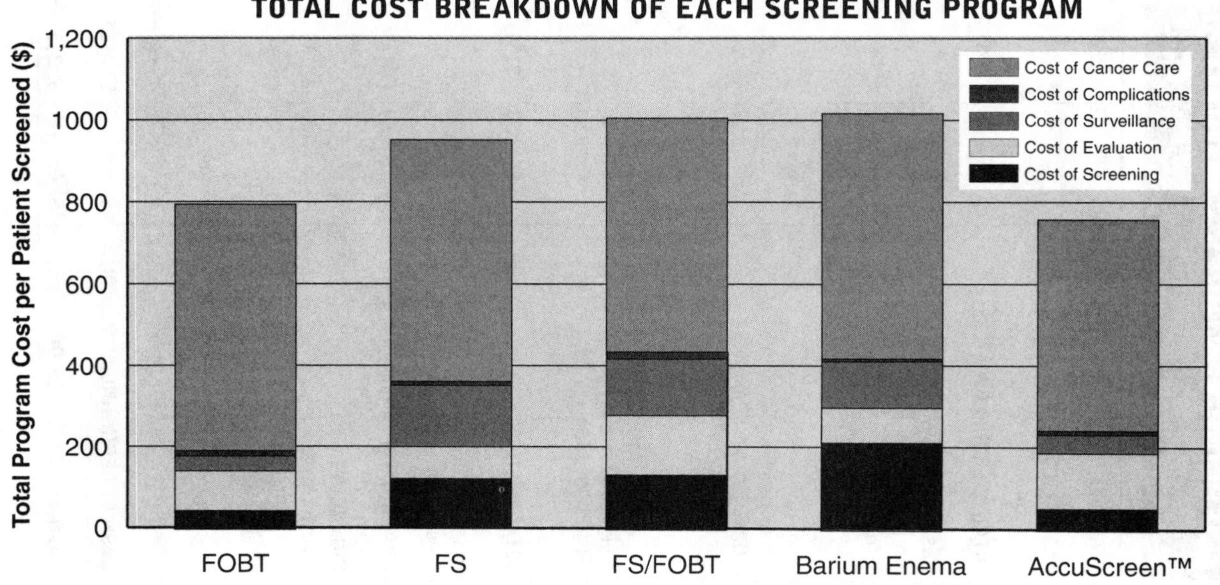

LIFELINK VENTURES — EXHIBIT 3 PRO FORMA MONTHLY CASH FLOW STATEMENTS FOR START UP PHASE
June 1, 2001 to May 2002

	June	July	August	September	October	November	December	January	February	March	April	May
CASH INFLOWS												
Investment Income	-	7,250	6,565	6,357	6,180	5,883	5,558	3,677	3,307	2,922	2,321	2,074
TOTAL CASH INFLOWS	**$ -**	**$7,250**	**$6,565**	**$6,357**	**$6,180**	**$5,883**	**$5,558**	**$3,677**	**$3,307**	**$2,922**	**$2,321**	**$2,074**
CASH OUTFLOWS												
Advertising and Promotion	15,300	100,300	6,823	6,050	6,823	6,050	7,330	6,300	5,300	5,300	5,300	5,300
Travel -	4,800	2,400	-	7,200	-	-	7,200	7,600	14,800	-	7,600	
Lease Payments	-	-	-	-	-	-	-	-	-	-	-	-
AccuScreen Test Kit Purchases	-	-	-	-	-	6,014	5,454	5,454	5,454	5,454	5,454	-
Shipping	-	-	-	-	-	12,700	12,700	12,700	12,700	12,700	12,700	-
Wages and Benefits	21,250	21,250	21,250	21,250	21,250	21,250	21,250	21,250	21,250	21,250	21,250	21,250
Office Supplies & Equipment	700	700	700	700	700	700	700	700	700	700	700	700
Insurance	-	-	-	5,000	-	-	-	-	-	-	-	-
Communications	438	438	438	438	438	438	438	438	438	438	438	438
Clinical Trials	-	12,000	12,000	-	30,000	30,000	30,000	30,000	30,000	81,000	-	-
Consulting Costs	12,500	12,500	12,500	12,500	12,500	12,500	12,500	12,500	12,500	12,500	12,500	12,500
Licensing Fees	-	-	-	-	-	-	-	-	-	-	-	-
Legal & Accounting Fees	4,650	2,500	2,500	2,500	2,500	2,500	2,500	2,500	2,500	2,500	2,500	2,500
Interest Payments	-	-	-	-	-	-	-	-	-	-	-	-
TOTAL CASH OUTFLOWS	**$54,838**	**$154,488**	**$58,610**	**$48,438**	**$81,410**	**$92,151**	**$92,871**	**$99,041**	**$98,441**	**$156,641**	**$60,841**	**$50,288**
CAPITAL												
Purchase of Fixed Assets	-	-	-	-	-	-	310,000	-	-	-	-	-
CHANGE FROM CAPITAL	**$ -**	**$ -**	**$ -**	**$ -**	**$ -**	**$ -**	**$310,000**	**$ -**	**$ -**	**$ -**	**$ -**	**$ -**
FINANCING												
Contributions from IRAP	6,750	10,350	10,350	6,750	15,750	21,364	21,196	21,196	18,196	33,496	9,196	3,750
Research Tax Credits	-	-	-	-	-	-	-	-	-	-	-	126,048
Bank Line of Credit	-	-	-	-	-	-	-	-	-	-	-	-
Issuance of Common Shares	100,000	-	-	-	-	-	-	-	-	-	-	-
Issuance of Preferred Shares	1,400,000	-	-	-	-	-	-	-	-	-	-	-
CHANGE FROM FINANCING	**$1,506,750**	**$10,350**	**$10,350**	**$6,750**	**$15,750**	**$21,364**	**$21,196**	**$21,196**	**$18,196**	**$33,496**	**$9,196**	**$129,798**
CASH AT BEGINNING OF PERIOD	**$ -**	**$1,451,913**	**$1,315,025**	**$1,273,330**	**$1,237,999**	**$1,178,519**	**$1,113,614**	**$737,497**	**$663,329**	**$586,391**	**$466,167**	**$416,843**
CASH AT END OF PERIOD	**$1,451,913**	**$1,315,025**	**$1,273,330**	**$1,237,999**	**$1,178,519**	**$1,113,614**	**$737,497**	**$663,329**	**$586,391**	**$466,167**	**$416,843**	**$498,428**

LIFELINK VENTURES — EXHIBIT 4 PRO FORMA MONTHLY CASH FLOW STATEMENTS FOR START UP PHASE
June 1, 2002 to May 2003

	June	July	August	September	October	November	December	January	February	March	April	May
CASH INFLOW												
Investment Income	2,482	2,119	1,891	1,607	1,346	1,079	814	542	3,074	2,760	2,425	2,126
TOTAL CASH INFLOW	**$2,482**	**$2,119**	**$1,891**	**$1,607**	**$1,346**	**$1,079**	**$814**	**$542**	**$3,074**	**$2,760**	**$2,425**	**$2,126**
CASH OUTFLOWS												
Advertising and Promotion	5,300	5,300	6,823	6,050	6,823	6,050	7,330	6,300	5,300	5,300	5,300	5,300
Travel -	2,400	12,000	-	-	-	-	-	7,600	7,600	-	7,600	
Lease Payments	-	-	-	-	-	-	-	-	6,849	6,849	6,849	6,849
AccuScreen Test Kit Purchases	-	-	-	-	-	-	-	-	-	1,736	1,736	1,736
Shipping	-	-	-	-	-	-	-	-	-	5,700	5,700	5,700
Wages and Benefits	57,500	27,500	27,500	27,500	27,500	27,500	27,500	27,500	27,500	27,500	27,500	27,500
Office Supplies & Equipment	700	700	700	700	700	700	700	700	700	700	700	700
Insurance	-	-	-	-	-	-	-	-	-	-	-	-
Communications	438	438	438	438	438	438	438	438	438	438	438	438
Clinical Trials	-	-	-	-	-	-	-	-	-	-	-	-
Consulting Costs	12,500	12,500	12,500	20,500	20,500	20,500	20,500	20,500	13,000	13,000	13,000	13,000
Licensing Fees	-	-	-	-	-	-	-	40,000	-	-	-	-
Legal & Accounting Fees	2,500	2,500	2,500	2,500	2,500	2,500	2,500	2,500	6,000	2,500	2,500	2,500
Interest Payments	-	-	-	-	-	-	-	-	-	-	-	-
TOTAL CASH OUTFLOWS	**$78,938**	**$51,338**	**$62,460**	**$57,688**	**$58,460**	**$57,688**	**$58,968**	**$97,938**	**$67,386**	**$71,323**	**$63,723**	**$71,323**
CAPITAL												
Purchase of Fixed Assets	-	-	-	-	-	-	-	-	-	-	-	-
CHANGE FROM CAPITAL	**$ -**	**$ -**	**$ -**	**$ -**	**$ -**	**$ -**	**$ -**	**$ -**	**$ -**	**$ -**	**$ -**	**$ -**
FINANCING												
Contributions from IRAP	3,750	3,750	3,750	3,750	3,750	3,750	3,750	3,750	1,500	1,500	1,500	1,500
Research Tax Credits	-	-	-	-	-	-	-	-	-	-	-	29,400
Bank Line of Credit	-	-	-	-	-	-	-	-	-	-	-	-
Issuance of Common Shares	-	-	-	-	-	-	-	-	-	-	-	-
Issuance of Preferred Shares	-	-	-	-	-	-	-	600,000	-	-	-	-
CHANGE FROM FINANCING	**$3,750**	**$3,750**	**$3,750**	**$3,750**	**$3,750**	**$3,750**	**$3,750**	**$603,750**	**$1,500**	**$1,500**	**$1,500**	**$30,900**
CASH AT BEGINNING OF PERIOD	**$498,428**	**$425,723**	**$380,254**	**$323,435**	**$271,105**	**$217,740**	**$164,882**	**$110,478**	**$616,833**	**$554,021**	**$486,958**	**$427,160**
CASH AT END OF PERIOD	**$425,723**	**$380,254**	**$323,435**	**$271,105**	**$217,740**	**$164,882**	**$110,478**	**$616,833**	**$554,021**	**$486,958**	**$427,160**	**$388,863**

LIFELINK VENTURES — EXHIBIT 5

PRO FORMA ANNUAL CASH FLOW STATEMENT FOR START UP PHASE
June 1, 2001 to May 31, 2003

	Year 1	Year 2
CASH INFLOW		
Investment Income	52,093	22,265
TOTAL CASH INFLOW	**$52,093**	**$22,265**
EXPENSES		
Advertising and Promotion	176,175	71,175
Travel	51,600	37,200
Lease Payments	-	27,396
AccuScreen Test Kit Purchases	33,284	5,209
Shipping	76,200	17,100
Wages and Benefits	255,000	360,000
Office Supplies & Equipment	8,400	8,400
Insurance	5,000	-
Communications	5,250	5,250
Clinical Trials	255,000	-
Consulting Costs	150,000	192,000
Licensing Fees	-	40,000
Legal & Accounting Fees	32,150	33,500
Interest Payments	-	-
TOTAL EXPENDITURES	**$1,048,059**	**$797,230**
CAPITAL		
Purchase of Fixed Assets	310,000	-
CHANGE FROM CAPITAL	**$310,000**	**$ -**
FINANCING		
Contributions from IRAP	178,345	36,000
Research Tax Credits	126,048	29,400
Inflow of Cash From Bank Loan	-	-
Issuance of Common Shares	100,000	-
Issuance of Preferred Shares	1,400,000	600,000
CHANGE FROM FINANCING	**$1,804,394**	**$665,400**
CASH AT BEGINNING OF PERIOD	**$ -**	**$498,428**
CASH AT END OF PERIOD	**$498,428**	**$388,863**

LIFELINK VENTURES — EXHIBIT 6 ACCUSCREEN SALES PROJECTIONS

June 1, 2003 to May 31, 2008

MACHINE CAPACITY	
Minutes per Sample	5
Samples per Hour	12
Samples per Day	288
Samples per Month	8,640
Samples per Year	103,680

Baseline Utilization Rate	50%

2003 – 2004	June	July	August	September	October	November	December	January	February	March	April	May
Machines	1	-	-	-	-	-	1	-	-	-	-	-
Tests	-	4,320	4,320	4,320	4,320	4,320	4,320	8,640	8,640	8,640	8,640	8,640

2004 – 2005	June	July	August	September	October	November	December	January	February	March	April	May
Machines	1	-	-	-	-	-	1	-	-	-	-	-
Tests	8,640	12,960	12,960	12,960	12,960	12,960	12,960	17,280	17,280	17,280	17,280	17,280

2005 – 2006	June	July	August	September	October	November	December	January	February	March	April	May
Machines	1	-	1	-	1	-	1	-	1	-	1	-
Tests	17,280	21,600	21,600	25,920	25,920	30,240	30,240	34,560	34,560	38,880	38,880	43,200

2006 – 2007	June	July	August	September	October	November	December	January	February	March	April	May
Machines	1	-	1	1	-	1	1	-	1	1	-	1
Tests	43,200	47,520	47,520	51,840	56,160	56,160	60,480	64,800	64,800	69,120	73,440	73,440

2007 – 2008	June	July	August	September	October	November	December	January	February	March	April	May
Machines	1	1	-	1	1	1	-	1	1	1	-	1
Tests	77,760	82,080	86,400	86,400	90,720	95,040	99,360	99,360	103,680	108,000	112,320	112,320

Total	Year 3	Year 4	Year 5	Year 6	Year 7	Total
Machines	2	2	6	8	9	**27**
Tests	69,120	172,800	362,880	708,480	1,153,440	**2,466,720**

LIFELINK VENTURES — EXHIBIT 7 PRO FORMA MONTHLY CASH FLOW STATEMENTS
June 1, 2003 to May 2004

	June	July	August	September	October	November	December	January	February	March	April	May
CASH INFLOW												
Payments for AccuScreen Equipment Sales	328,800	-	-	-	-	-	328,800	-	-	-	-	-
Payments for AccuScreen Tests Conducted	-	-	-	129,600	129,600	129,600	129,600	129,600	129,600	259,200	259,200	259,200
Investment Income	1,934	1,172	654	16	-	0	0	-	-	-	-	-
TOTAL CASH INFLOW	**$330,734**	**$1,172**	**$654**	**$129,616**	**$129,600**	**$129,600**	**$458,400**	**$129,600**	**$129,600**	**$259,200**	**$259,200**	**$259,200**
CASH OUTFLOWS												
Advertising and Promotion	5,300	5,300	6,823	94,650	6,823	6,050	7,330	6,300	5,300	5,300	5,300	5,300
Travel	2,400	-	-	-	-	-	2,400	-	7,600	7,600	-	7,600
AccuScreen Test Kit Purchases	-	-	20,004	20,004	20,004	20,004	20,004	20,004	40,008	40,008	40,008	40,008
AccuScreen Equipment Costs	310,000	-	-	-	-	-	310,000	-	-	-	-	-
MRS Tubes	5,000	-	-	-	-	-	5,000	-	-	-	-	-
Shipping	5,000	-	-	-	-	-	5,000	-	-	-	-	-
Installation & Training	8,800	-	-	-	-	-	8,800	-	-	-	-	-
Service & Maintenance Expense	-	-	-	3,500	-	-	3,500	-	-	7,000	-	-
Licensing Fees	-	-	-	4,536	4,536	4,536	4,536	4,536	4,536	9,072	9,072	9,072
Sales Commisions	-	-	-	2,592	2,592	2,592	2,592	2,592	2,592	5,184	5,184	5,184
Lease Payments	13,698	13,698	13,698	13,698	13,698	13,698	20,547	20,547	20,547	20,547	20,547	20,547
Wages and Benefits	104,167	74,167	74,167	74,167	74,167	74,167	74,167	74,167	74,167	74,167	74,167	74,167
Office Supplies & Equipment	700	700	700	700	700	700	700	700	700	700	700	700
Rent	-	-	-	-	-	-	-	-	-	-	-	-
Communications	438	438	438	438	438	438	438	438	438	438	438	438
Insurance	5,500	-	-	-	-	-	5,000	-	-	-	-	-
Patent	10,000	-	2,000	-	900	-	9,000	-	1,700	-	2,000	-
Consulting Costs	8,000	8,000	8,000	8,000	8,000	8,000	8,000	8,000	8,000	8,000	8,000	8,000
Legal & Accounting Fees	4,100	2,500	2,500	2,500	2,500	2,500	4,100	2,500	2,500	2,500	2,500	2,500
Research & Development	-	-	-	-	-	-	-	12,000	12,000	-	30,000	30,000
Interest Payments	-	-	-	-	690	731	759	1,010	1,157	1,518	939	419
Income Taxes	-	-	-	-	-	-	-	-	-	-	-	-
TOTAL CASH OUTFLOWS	**$483,102**	**$104,802**	**$128,329**	**$224,784**	**$135,046**	**$133,415**	**$491,872**	**$152,793**	**$181,245**	**$182,033**	**$198,854**	**$203,934**
FINANCING												
Contributions from IRAP	-	-	-	-	-	-	-	3,600	3,600	-	9,000	9,000
Research Tax Credits	-	-	-	-	-	-	-	-	-	-	-	20,580
Bank Line of Credit	-	-	-	91,977	5,446	3,815	33,472	19,593	48,045	(77,167)	(69,346)	(55,835)
Issuance of Common Shares	-	-	-	-	-	-	-	-	-	-	-	-
Issuance of Preferred Shares	-	-	-	-	-	-	-	-	-	-	-	-
Preferred Dividends	-	-	-	-	-	-	-	-	-	-	-	-
CHANGE FROM FINANCING	**$ -**	**$ -**	**$ -**	**$91,977**	**$5,446**	**$3,815**	**$33,472**	**$23,193**	**$51,645**	**$(77,167)**	**$(60,346)**	**$(26,255)**
CASH AT BEGINNING OF PERIOD	**$388,863**	**$236,495**	**$132,866**	**$5,192**	**$2,000**	**$2,000**	**$2,000**	**$2,000**	**$2,000**	**$2,000**	**$2,000**	**$2,000**
CASH AT END OF PERIOD	**$236,495**	**$132,866**	**$5,192**	**$2,000**	**$2,000**	**$2,000**	**$2,000**	**$2,000**	**$2,000**	**$2,000**	**$2,000**	**$31,011**

LIFELINK VENTURES — EXHIBIT 8 PRO FORMA MONTHLY CASH FLOW STATEMENTS
June 1, 2004 to May 2005

	June	July	August	September	October	November	December	January	February	March	April	May
CASH INFLOW												
Payments for AccuScreen Equipment Sales	328,800	-	-	-	-	-	328,800	-	-	-	-	-
Payments for AccuScreen Tests Conducted	259,200	259,200	259,200	388,800	388,800	388,800	388,800	388,800	388,800	518,400	518,400	518,400
Investment Income	145	215	544	761	1,370	2,313	3,266	3,997	4,818	5,480	6,759	8,013
TOTAL CASH INFLOW	**$588,145**	**$259,415**	**$259,744**	**$389,561**	**$390,170**	**$391,113**	**$720,866**	**$392,797**	**$393,618**	**$523,880**	**$525,159**	**$526,413**
CASH OUTFLOWS												
Advertising and Promotion	5,300	5,300	6,823	6,050	6,823	6,050	7,330	6,300	5,300	5,300	5,300	5,300
Travel	2,400	-	-	-	-	-	2,400	-	10,000	7,600	2,400	7,600
AccuScreen Test Kit Purchases	40,008	40,008	60,013	60,013	60,013	60,013	60,013	60,013	80,017	80,017	80,017	80,017
AccuScreen Equipment Costs	310,000	-	-	-	-	-	310,000	-	-	-	-	-
MRS Tubes	10,000	-	-	-	-	-	10,000	-	-	-	-	-
Shipping	5,000	-	-	-	-	-	5,000	-	-	-	-	-
Installation & Training	8,800	-	-	-	-	-	8,800	-	-	-	-	-
Service & Maintenance Expense	7,000	-	-	10,500	-	-	10,500	-	-	14,000	-	-
Licensing Fees	9,072	9,072	9,072	13,608	13,608	13,608	13,608	13,608	13,608	18,144	18,144	18,144
Sales Commisions	5,184	5,184	5,184	7,776	7,776	7,776	7,776	7,776	7,776	10,368	10,368	10,368
Lease Payments	27,396	27,396	27,396	27,396	27,396	27,396	34,245	34,245	34,245	34,245	34,245	34,245
Wages and Benefits	104,167	74,167	74,167	74,167	74,167	74,167	74,167	74,167	74,167	74,167	74,167	74,167
Office Supplies & Equipment	700	700	700	700	700	700	700	700	700	700	700	700
Rent	-	-	-	-	-	-	-	-	-	-	-	-
Communications	438	438	438	438	438	438	438	438	438	438	438	438
Insurance	5,500	-	-	-	-	-	5,000	-	-	-	-	-
Patent	-	-	1,000	-	-	-	-	-	2,000	-	3,000	-
Consulting Costs	8,000	8,000	8,000	8,000	8,000	8,000	20,500	20,500	20,500	20,500	20,500	20,500
Legal & Accounting Fees	4,100	2,500	2,500	2,500	2,500	2,500	4,100	2,500	4,100	2,500	4,100	2,500
Research & Development	30,000	30,000	30,000	81,000	-	-	-	12,000	12,000	-	30,000	30,000
Interest Payments	-	-	-	-	-	-	-	-	-	-	-	-
Income Taxes	-	-	-	-	-	-	-	-	-	-	-	350,009
TOTAL CASH OUTFLOWS	**$583,064**	**$202,764**	**$225,291**	**$292,146**	**$201,419**	**$200,646**	**$574,575**	**$232,245**	**$264,849**	**$267,977**	**$283,377**	**$633,987**
FINANCING												
Contributions from IRAP	9,000	9,000	9,000	24,300	-	-	-	3,600	3,600	-	9,000	9,000
Research Tax Credits	-	-	-	-	-	-	-	-	-	-	-	62,475
Bank Line of Credit	-	-	-	-	-	-	-	-	-	-	-	-
Issuance of Common Shares	-	-	-	-	-	-	-	-	-	-	-	-
Issuance of Preferred Shares	-	-	-	-	-	-	-	-	-	-	-	-
Preferred Dividends	-	-	-	-	-	-	-	-	-	-	-	-
CHANGE FROM FINANCING	**$9,000**	**$9,000**	**$9,000**	**$24,300**	**$ -**	**$ -**	**$ -**	**$3,600**	**$3,600**	**$ -**	**$9,000**	**$71,475**
CASH AT BEGINNING OF PERIOD	**$31,011**	**$45,092**	**$110,743**	**$154,196**	**$275,910**	**$464,661**	**$655,128**	**$801,418**	**$965,570**	**$1,097,939**	**$1,353,841**	**$1,604,623**
CASH AT END OF PERIOD	**$45,092**	**$110,743**	**$154,196**	**$275,910**	**$464,661**	**$655,128**	**$801,418**	**$965,570**	**$1,097,939**	**$1,353,841**	**$1,604,623**	**$1,568,524**

LIFELINK VENTURES — EXHIBIT 9

PRO FORMA ANNUAL CASH FLOW STATEMENTS
June 1, 2003 to May 31, 2008

	Year 3	Year 4	Year 5	Year 6	Year 7
CASH INFLOW					
Payments for AccuScreen Equipment Sales	657,600	657,600	1,972,800	2,630,400	2,959,200
Payments for AccuScreen Tests Conducted	1,555,200	4,665,600	9,460,800	19,310,400	32,270,400
Investment Income	3,777	37,681	162,003	465,830	1,079,140
TOTAL CASH INFLOW	**$2,216,577**	**$5,360,881**	**$11,595,603**	**$22,406,630**	**$36,308,740**
CASH OUTFLOWS					
Advertising and Promotion	159,775	71,175	71,175	71,175	71,175
Travel	27,600	32,400	39,600	44,400	44,400
AccuScreen Test Kit Purchases	280,059	760,159	1,560,327	3,140,658	5,161,082
AccuScreen Equipment Costs	620,000	620,000	1,860,000	2,480,000	2,790,000
MRS Tubes	10,000	20,000	50,000	90,000	135,000
Shipping	10,000	10,000	30,000	40,000	45,000
Installation & Training	17,600	17,600	52,800	70,400	79,200
Service & Maintenance	14,000	42,000	91,000	182,000	301,000
Licensing Fees	54,432	163,296	331,128	675,864	1,129,464
Sales Commisions	31,104	93,312	189,216	386,208	645,408
Lease Payments	205,467	369,841	698,588	1,260,198	1,972,484
Wages and Benefits	920,000	920,000	1,390,000	1,390,000	1,390,000
Office Supplies & Equipment	8,400	8,400	8,400	8,400	8,400
Rent	-	-	24,000	24,000	24,000
Communications	5,250	5,250	5,250	5,250	5,250
Insurance	10,500	10,500	10,500	10,500	10,500
Patent	25,600	6,000	5,500	9,600	35,700
Consulting Costs	96,000	171,000	120,000	120,000	120,000
Legal & Accounting Fees	33,200	36,400	41,200	44,400	36,400
Research & Development	84,000	255,000	255,000	255,000	255,000
Interest Payments	7,223	-	-	-	-
Income Taxes	-	350,009	2,719,787	6,238,236	10,877,692
TOTAL CASH OUTFLOWS	**$2,620,209**	**$3,962,342**	**$9,553,471**	**$16,546,290**	**$25,137,155**
FINANCING					
Contributions from IRAP	25,200	76,500	76,500	76,500	76,500
Research Tax Credits	20,580	62,475	62,475	62,475	62,475
Bank Line of Credit	-	-	-	-	-
Issuance of Common Shares	-	-	-	-	-
Issuance of Preferred Shares	-	-	-	-	-
Preferred Dividends	-	-	(648,000)	(160,000)	(160,000)
CHANGE FROM FINANCING	**$45,780**	**$138,975**	**$(509,025)**	**$(21,025)**	**$(21,025)**
CASH AT BEGINNING OF PERIOD	**$388,863**	**$31,011**	**$1,568,524**	**$3,101,631**	**$8,940,946**
CASH AT END OF PERIOD	**$31,011**	**$1,568,524**	**$3,101,631**	**$8,940,946**	**$20,091,506**

LIFELINK VENTURES — EXHIBIT 10

PRO FORMA ANNUAL INCOME STATEMENTS
June 1, 2001 to May 31, 2008

	Year 1	Year 2	Year 3	Year 4	Year 5	Year 6	Year 7
SALES							
AccuScreen Test Sales ($)	-	-	2,073,600	5,184,000	10,886,400	21,254,400	34,603,200
AccuScreen Equipment Sales ($)	-	-	657,600	657,600	1,972,800	2,630,400	2,959,200
TOTAL SALES	**-**	**-**	**2,731,200**	**5,841,600**	**12,859,200**	**23,884,800**	**37,562,400**
COST OF GOODS SOLD							
Cost of AccuScreen Tests Sold:	-	-	320,067	800,168	1,680,352	3,280,687	5,341,119
Cost of AccuScreen Equipment Sold:	-	-	620,000	620,000	1,860,000	2,480,000	2,790,000
TOTAL COST OF GOODS SOLD	**-**	**-**	**940,067**	**1,420,168**	**3,540,352**	**5,760,687**	**8,131,119**
GROSS MARGIN	**$ -**	**$ -**	**$1,791,133**	**$4,421,432**	**$9,318,848**	**$18,124,113**	**$29,431,281**
VARIABLE EXPENSES							
Travel	51,600	37,200	27,600	32,400	39,600	44,400	44,400
MRS Tubes	-	-	10,000	20,000	50,000	90,000	135,000
Shipping	76,200	17,100	10,000	10,000	30,000	40,000	45,000
Installation & Training Expense	-	-	17,600	17,600	52,800	70,400	79,200
Service and Maintenance Expense	-	-	14,000	42,000	91,000	182,000	301,000
Licensing Fees	-	40,000	72,576	181,440	381,024	743,904	1,211,112
Sales Commissions	-	-	41,472	103,680	217,728	425,088	692,064
Lease Payments	-	27,396	205,467	369,841	698,588	1,260,198	1,972,484
TOTAL VARIABLE EXPENSES	**127,800**	**121,696**	**398,715**	**776,961**	**1,560,740**	**2,855,990**	**4,480,260**
FIXED EXPENSES							
Advertising and Promotion	176,175	76,384	159,775	71,175	71,175	71,175	71,175
Wages and Benefits	288,284	360,000	920,000	920,000	1,390,000	1,390,000	1,390,000
Office Supplies and Equipment	8,400	8,400	8,400	8,400	8,400	8,400	8,400
Rent	-	-	-	-	24,000	24,000	24,000
Communications	5,250	5,250	5,250	5,250	5,250	5,250	5,250
Insurance	5,000	-	10,500	10,500	10,500	10,500	10,500
Consulting Costs	150,000	192,000	96,000	171,000	120,000	120,000	120,000
Legal and Accounting Fees	32,150	33,500	33,200	36,400	41,200	44,400	36,400
Research and Development	255,000	-	84,000	255,000	255,000	255,000	255,000
Interest Expense	-	-	7,223	-	-	-	-
Depreciation	46,500	79,050	55,335	38,735	27,114	18,980	13,286
TOTAL FIXED EXPENSES	**966,759**	**754,584**	**1,379,683**	**1,516,460**	**1,952,639**	**1,947,705**	**1,934,011**
NET OPERATING PROFIT (LOSS)	**$(1,094,559)**	**$(876,280)**	**$12,735**	**$2,128,012**	**$5,805,469**	**$13,320,417**	**$23,017,009**
OTHER INCOME							
Contributions from IRAP	178,345	36,000	25,200	76,500	76,500	76,500	76,500
Investment Income	52,093	22,265	3,777	37,681	162,003	465,830	1,079,140
TOTAL OTHER INCOME	**230,438**	**58,265**	**28,977**	**114,181**	**238,503**	**542,330**	**1,155,640**
TOTAL TAXABLE INCOME	**$(864,120)**	**$(818,015)**	**$41,712**	**$2,242,193**	**$6,043,971**	**$13,862,747**	**$24,172,650**
Income Tax	-	-	-	350,009	2,719,787	6,238,236	10,877,692
Research Tax Credit	126,048	29,400	20,580	62,475	62,475	62,475	62,475
NET INCOME	**$(738,072)**	**$(788,615)**	**$62,292**	**$1,954,659**	**$3,386,659**	**$7,686,986**	**$13,357,432**
Preferred Dividends	-	-	-	-	648,000	160,000	160,000
TO RETAINED EARNINGS	**(738,072)**	**(788,615)**	**62,292**	**1,954,659**	**2,738,659**	**7,526,986**	**13,197,432**

LIFELINK VENTURES — EXHIBIT 11

PRO FORMA ANNUAL BALANCE SHEET
June 1, 2001 to May 31, 2008

	Year 1	Year 2	Year 3	Year 4	Year 5	Year 6	Year 7
CURRENT ASSETS							
Cash	498,428	388,863	31,011	1,568,524	3,101,631	8,940,946	20,091,506
Accounts Receivable	-	-	518,400	1,036,800	2,462,400	4,406,400	6,739,200
TOTAL CURRENT ASSETS	**498,428**	**388,863**	**549,411**	**2,605,324**	**5,564,031**	**13,347,346**	**26,830,706**
FIXED ASSETS							
Patents	-	-	25,600	31,600	37,100	46,700	82,400
Equipment	310,000	310,000	310,000	310,000	310,000	310,000	310,000
less depreciation	46,500	125,550	180,885	219,620	246,734	265,714	278,999
TOTAL FIXED ASSETS	**263,500**	**184,450**	**154,715**	**121,981**	**100,366**	**90,986**	**113,401**
TOTAL ASSETS	**$761,928**	**$573,313**	**$704,126**	**$2,727,305**	**$5,664,397**	**$13,438,332**	**$26,944,107**
CURRENT LIABILITIES							
Accounts Payable	-	-	68,520	137,041	335,474	582,423	890,765
Bank Loans	-	-	-	-	-	-	-
TOTAL CURRENT LIABILITIES	**-**	**-**	**68,520**	**137,041**	**335,474**	**582,423**	**890,765**
LONG TERM DEBT							
Long Term Debt							
TOTAL LONG TERM DEBT	**-**	**-**	**-**	**-**	**-**	**-**	**-**
TOTAL LIABILITIES	**-**	**-**	**68,520**	**137,041**	**335,474**	**582,423**	**890,765**
SHAREHOLDERS' EQUITY							
Common Shares	100,000	100,000	100,000	100,000	100,000	100,000	100,000
Preferred Shares	1,400,000	2,000,000	2,000,000	2,000,000	2,000,000	2,000,000	2,000,000
Retained Earnings	(738,072)	(1,526,687)	(1,464,395)	490,264	3,228,923	10,755,909	23,953,342
TOTAL SHAREHOLDERS' EQUITY	**761,928**	**573,313**	**635,605**	**2,590,264**	**5,328,923**	**12,855,909**	**26,053,342**
TOTAL LIABILITIES AND SHAREHOLDERS' EQUITY	**$761,928**	**$573,313**	**$704,126**	**$2,727,305**	**$5,664,397**	**$13,438,332**	**$26,944,107**

LIFELINK VENTURES — EXHIBIT 12

SELECTED FINANCIAL RATIOS
June 1, 2003 to May 31, 2008

	Year 3	Year 4	Year 5	Year 6	Year 7
Annual Sales Growth	N/A	113.88%	120.13%	85.74%	57.26%
Gross Margin	65.58%	75.69%	72.47%	75.88%	78.35%
Operating Margin	0.47%	36.43%	45.15%	55.77%	61.28%
Profit Margin	2.28%	33.46%	26.34%	32.18%	35.56%
Current Ratio	1.39	4.17	16.59	22.92	30.12
Return on Assets	9.75%	113.93%	80.71%	80.48%	66.15%
Return on Equity	17.48%	162.22%	91.15%	84.54%	68.66%

LIFELINK VENTURES — EXHIBIT 13

BREAKEVEN ANALYSIS
June 1, 2003 to May 31, 2008

	2003	2004	2005	2006	2007
Fixed Costs ($)	$1,379,683	$1,516,460	$1,952,639	$1,947,705	$1,934,011
Contribution Margin Ratio	50.98%	62.39%	60.33%	63.92%	66.43%
Level of Sales Required to Breakeven (Annually)	$2,706,220	$2,430,682	$3,236,534	$3,046,907	$2,911,548
Number of Tests Required to Breakeven (Annually)	90,207	81,023	107,884	101,564	97,052
Number of Machines Sold	2	4	10	18	27
Number of Tests Required per Machine to Breakeven (Monthly)	3,759	1,688	899	470	300
Number of Tests Required per Machine to Breakeven (Annually)	45,104	20,256	10,788	5,642	3,595

LIFELINK VENTURES — EXHIBIT 14

SENSITIVITY ANALYSIS FOR SELECTED VARIABLES ON ANNUAL NET INCOME
June 1, 2003 to May 31, 2008

MACHINE UTILIZATION	NET INCOME				
	Year 3	Year 4	Year 5	Year 6	Year 7
80%	$1,059,687	$2,912,041	$6,331,561	$13,479,466	$22,886,224
70%	727,902	2,592,631	5,349,941	11,548,653	19,709,974
60%	395,480	2,273,485	4,368,308	9,617,828	16,533,711
50%	62,292	1,954,659	3,386,659	7,686,986	13,357,432
40%	(271,340)	1,449,503	2,555,511	5,754,914	10,179,881
30%	(604,972)	585,643	2,089,663	3,823,065	7,002,561
20%	(938,604)	(283,485)	617,094	2,800,316	3,821,751
10%	(1,272,236)	(1,152,613)	(1,252,065)	(425,185)	789,697

PRICE PER TEST	NET INCOME				
	Year 3	Year 4	Year 5	Year 6	Year 7
$50.00	$1,387,178	$3,227,571	$7,300,903	$15,386,424	$26,023,526
$40.00	725,801	2,590,672	5,343,802	11,536,727	19,690,502
$30.00	62,292	1,954,659	3,386,659	7,686,986	13,357,432
$20.00	(603,030)	590,263	2,092,482	3,834,965	7,022,005
$10.00	(1,268,353)	(1,143,372)	(1,231,907)	(385,868)	854,690

Alfa-B Pollination Services, Inc.

A Business Plan by:

Joel Lemoine
Lindsay Robison
Brandi Smith

TABLE OF CONTENTS

ALFA-B POLLINATION SERVICES INC.

Ste-Agathe, Manitoba
PO Box 233
R0G 1Y0

Ph: 204-555-2600
Fax: 204-555-2827
http://www.alfa-b-pollination.ca.com

MISSION STATEMENT

"To help farmers increase the quality and yield of alfalfa crops by providing custom pollination services using leafcutter bees. Alfa-B Pollination Services will maintain the highest standard of quality and customer service, while improving agricultural production in an environmentally friendly manner."

COMPANY MANAGEMENT

Name	Position	Experience	Share
Joel Lemoine	General Manager	International Business Marketing Farming Operations	22%
Lindsay Robinson	Director of Marketing	Marketing Human Resource Management	22%
Brandi Smith	Director of Finance	Finance/Marketing Leafcutter bee operation	22%

BOARD OF ADVISORS

Name	Position	Experience
David Booth	Beekeeper/Farmer	Booth Farms
Art Chaput	Accountant	Chartered Accountant
Ron Collins	Banker	Commercial Banker
Dave Smith	Beekeeper/Farmer	Booth Farms
Kirk Windsor	Lawyer	Commercial Law

EXECUTIVE SUMMARY

Alfa-B Pollination Services has identified an excellent business opportunity to service Manitoba's agricultural sector by providing custom pollination services to help increase crop yields for alfalfa seed producers. Through the process of using leafcutter bees to pollinate alfalfa seed crops, Alfa-B's services are able to improve the quality of seed and increase alfalfa producers, yields by over twenty times.

Alfa-B is an incorporated business committed to providing high quality custom pollination to Manitoba alfalfa growers. Alfa-B will work side by side with alfalfa producers by acting primarily as beekeepers, placing leafcutter bees on crops in the early summer, managing the bees during the pollination season, as well as caring for and storing the bee larvae during the winter months. This business plan outlines the management team, as well as their objectives and strategies for running a highly successful business. Alfa-B Pollination Services will combine the skills, experience and agricultural backgrounds of three partners to supply producers with the first commercialized custom leafcutter bee pollination service in Manitoba.

Several agricultural organizations have begun to encourage farmers to diversify their operations away from common crops such as wheat, oats and barley. With the price of alfalfa at a high stable level, and the increasing global use of alfalfa seed in herbal remedies and for medicinal purposes, the demand for alfalfa seed has begun to increase. These trends in the agriculture sector have provided Alfa-B Pollination Services with an excellent opportunity to enter the industry to help serve alfalfa producers. Alfa-B is confident in its ability to serve growers by using the highest standards of quality and service.

The three members of the Alfa-B management team have committed $105,000 to the start-up of this new venture. The Bank of Montreal has endorsed the plan by committing $250,000 of debt financing through a Farm Improvement Loan. Alfa-B also provides an excellent opportunity for outside investors as the company will issue an additional $55,000 of preferred shares to complete the financial requirements. Ten percent of net income will be paid out as preferred dividends to outside investors at the end of the third year of operation. By the sixth year, Alfa-B will purchase the shares at an anticipated return on investment of over 35%.

From the beginning of operations, Alfa-B has strong income levels. With forecasted year one pollination contracts for 1200 acres, the company has retained earnings of over $28,000. In year two, with an increase of a conservative 300 acres of alfalfa, Alfa-B's net income increases by 40% to over $41,000. In year three, net income again doubles providing the company with a strong financial position to begin paying shareholders dividends. By the end of year five, gross profit will have a five year growth rate of over 400% to reach $155,500.

Alfa-B's management team consists of three partners whose rural backgrounds have led them to an interest in and understanding of the agricultural industry. Joel Lemoine, General Manager, brings his knowledge of farming along with his educational and practical experience in administration. Lindsay Robinson, Director of Marketing, brings her skills in public relations and marketing, as well as her knowledge of human resource management to the team. Brandi Smith, Director of Finance, brings to Alfa-B her experience working with leafcutter bees and knowledge of financial issues in the agricultural sector. The management team has also recruited a strong Board of Advisors who all bring extensive knowledge in their area of expertise.

ALFA-B POLLINATION SERVICES

Alfa-B Pollination Services is an incorporated business specializing in providing custom pollination services to Manitoba farmers through the use of alfalfa leafcutter bees. Alfalfa seed producers rely heavily on the use of leafcutter bees for pollinating the alfalfa flowers and increasing crop yield. Without a pollination mechanism, there are no economical benefits for farmers to harvest alfalfa seed. The alfalfa leafcutter bee is the only bee that can be relied upon to efficiently and effectively pollinate alfalfa and increase yields. Their natural instincts make them an ideal insect to efficiently pollinate large areas.

Alfa-B is proposing a service that aims to enhance the yield of crops, while offering a streamlined service. Alfa-B's quality service stems from the ability to rent the finest bees and our initiative to work side by side with the farmer on a weekly basis throughout the pollination season to ensure optimal pollination, thus resulting in high crop yields. The absence of commercial leafcutter bee services in Manitoba will give the business the opportunity to develop and expand among sparse competition. Alfa-B will work to promote and expand the alfalfa seed market within Manitoba by educating producers on the advantages of crop diversification, and the benefits of pollination with leafcutter bees. Custom pollination provides an opportunity for non-alfalfa farmers to diversify into alfalfa seed on a crop rotational basis, without committing large amounts of capital to leafcutter bee operations. The lack of direct competition within Manitoba also gives Alfa-B the benefit of setting the standard for reliable, quality service for other companies entering the market.

For the farmer, the availability of Alfa-B's service offers the ability to more than double crop yield without the extra work and expense of taking care of their own leafcutter bee operation. With leafcutter bees, yields can average from 200 to more than 500 pounds of seed per acre, with high yields producing up to 800 pounds per acre. Data from Agriculture Canada indicate that without the presence of leafcutter bees in alfalfa fields, a seed farmer would experience an 85 percent loss of yield, meaning only 30 to 80 pounds per acre would be produced. In addition to placing the bee larvae in the field during spring and removing them before harvest, Alfa-B will take part in continuous checking of bee houses, caring of bees and interacting with the farmer to ensure proper care is taken during spraying and other crop applications. The expertise Alfa-B has with regard to leafcutter bees and pollination will be an asset in offering the best care to our bees, and ensuring a healthy inventory of bees for the following year.

THE AGRICULTURAL INDUSTRY

Agriculture is the largest industry sector in the Manitoba economy. Over 19.1 million acres of land are dedicated to crop products. In 1998, sales in Manitoba relating to crop production were $2.76 billion, which accounted for 4% of the province's GDP.

Among the crops grown in Manitoba is alfalfa. In Canada, alfalfa is primarily cultivated either for forage (feed for livestock) or for seed. Approximately 1.2 million acres of Manitoba farmland is planted for alfalfa forage each year, while 36,000 acres are planted for its seed (21). Over $8.3 million of production was attributed to alfalfa seed sales in 1998, with $4.3 million of this being exported out of Manitoba to the United States.

The annual yields and quality of alfalfa can fluctuate tremendously from year to year because of variations in weather, pest populations and the presence or absence of natural pollinators. These fluctuations can cause growers to alter their use of alfalfa from year to year between forage and seed. In a good season, when conditions are optimal and prices of the alfalfa seed have risen due to the demand, farmers may opt to sell their seed to the market to achieve higher gains.

Regardless of whether the grower provides quality crop management and the best genetic stock, a bountiful harvest cannot be achieved without adequate pollination. Therefore, the availability of quality forms of pollination is a major concern for farmers, as it determines the quality and yield of a crop, and thus the profit the grower receives. Wind is the primary source of pollination for plants, with water, mammals, birds, insects and artificial agents also acting as pollinating mechanisms. Bees have made their name in the agricultural industry as a provider of quality pollination at a reasonable price to farmers. Particularly, leafcutter bees have become synonymous with the pollination of alfalfa on the Canadian Prairies (14).

IMPORTANCE OF LEAFCUTTER BEES IN THE AGRICULTURAL INDUSTRY

With good management, leafcutter bees are credited with increasing alfalfa seed yield by as much as twenty times, yielding up to 800 pounds of seed per acre (2). These remarkable results are a result of the bees' ability to work in hotter weather and cover an area of land more thoroughly than other pollinating insects, such as honeybees. Leafcutter bees are the most important alfalfa pollinators in Canada, with their presence increasing in importance throughout the rest of the world as well (14).

THE NEED SATISFIED BY ALFA-B POLLINATION SERVICES

Custom pollination through the use of leafcutter bees is widely known among farmers. Although some producers house their own bees, custom pollination is preferred by many farmers because the beekeeper provides total bee management and care, leaving more time for the farmer to concentrate on crop management and farm operations. Quality care and management of bees by experienced beekeepers enables more effective bee pollination and makes custom pollination a desirable service for growers. This system allows for the bee larvae to hatch under controlled conditions with the supervision of experienced beekeepers, easy removal of the bee cells from nesting material and the control of parasites and predators.

CURRENT TRENDS IN THE AGRICULTURAL INDUSTRY

The Manitoba Department of Agriculture, as well as farm organizations such as KAP (Keystone Agricultural Producers) have begun to recognize the importance of crop diversification and in turn have begun to encourage farmers to diversify their crop production. Agricultural associations are encouraging a movement away from standard crops such as wheat, oats and barley because these prices have dropped to levels that have not been seen since the 1930s (21). Also, transportation prices have risen drastically, causing growers to absorb higher costs when transporting their seed. Exhibit 3 illustrates the forecasted year 2000 prices for common seeds such as flax at $0.69 per pound compared to alfalfa seed's expected average price of $1.12 per pound. Alfalfa's comparably high price will make it the seed of choice for many farmers in the years to come.

MARKET PROFILE

Alfalfa seed is grown in two varieties. Many farmers grow the common alfalfa seed, which is a lower quality seed selling for approximately $.80 to $1.01 a pound depending on supply and demand. The second type of seed grown consists of pedigree or commercial alfalfa seed. This seed is of premium quality and has sold on average over the past five years for $1.00 to $1.28 a pound (24). In 1999, Manitoba Crop Insurance indicated that 12,200 acres of common alfalfa seed was grown and insured and an additional 2,440 acres was also seeded but not insured. Seventeen thousand two hundred acres of pedigree or commercial alfalfa seed were grown and insured, plus 3,440 acres of uninsured alfalfa. In conclusion, the current market for common alfalfa seed is 14,640 acres and 20,640 acres of pedigree or commercial alfalfa seed, for a total of 35,280 acres.

As mentioned earlier, prices for alfalfa seed play an important role when analyzing the potential market. In 1998, studies from Manitoba Crop Insurance showed 200,000 acres of alfalfa used for forage had been insured and grown, while an additional 800,000 acres of uninsured forage was seeded. Of these 1,000,000 acres of alfalfa forage, some was grown because prices didn't seem inviting to grow common or pedigree seeds. Many farmers grow alfalfa for forage primarily to use as nutritious feed for livestock. If seed prices seem attractive and higher yields are expected, farmers will be convinced to allocate greater acreage to seed production. The market is likely to guarantee 30,000 acres of alfalfa seed growth but it also enables Alfa-B to set its sights on some of the 1,000,000 acres of farmland driven by fluctuating market prices for alfalfa seed of both common and pedigree or commercial seeds.

Studies from Manitoba Agriculture and information from seed companies, such as Brett Young Seeds, confirm there is an increasing demand for leafcutter pollination services. Seed companies do not have the time to set up pollination services but are more than willing to hire outside sources because for them, more pollination services equal more yields and more seed to sell. Alfalfa seed growers must put leafcutter bees in their fields to maximize results. Growers will be inclined to pay a pollination company in order to increase their yields from 30 pounds per acre to over 300 pounds per acre.

INDUSTRIAL USES OF ALFALFA

Aside from alfalfa being used as a forage crop for use as livestock feed, alfalfa seed has many industrial uses, particularly in the health industry. As Canada and the rest of the world begin to move into holistic medicines and alternative methods of healing, the ingredients used will be highly sought after for this purpose. Alfalfa seed acts as an important ingredient in many alternative remedies for a variety of illnesses (4). This crop, which is used to produce such products as alfalfa tablets, helps ease swelling associated with arthritis, aids in detoxifying the liver, is valuable to the heart and helps with muscle cramps.

Also, alfalfa is known to help such problems as bad breath, acne, allergies, peptic ulcers, bladder infections and tooth decay. The plant acts as an excellent source of nutrients, especially vitamin A, C, thiamine and niacin. The value associated with the alfalfa seed, along with the current trend toward holistic healing, will cause continuous growth in the production of alfalfa seed in order to supply the wealth of demand that exists in the medical industry (1).

THE MANAGEMENT TEAM

Joel Lemoine is the General Manager of Alfa-B Pollination and will be in charge of the daily operations of the business. Joel is completing his Bachelor of Commerce degree at the University of Manitoba, focusing on Marketing and International Business. He has previously obtained a Business Administration diploma from College de St. Boniface. Having been raised on a farm, Joel has an extensive background in agriculture and farming operations. He has been employed in the agribusiness sector with organizations such as the Canadian Grain Commission and Manitoba Pool Elevators (Agricore). Joel has experience working in the agricultural finance sector through employment with Caisse Populaire Provencher. At this position, Joel assisted in the administration and financing of farming accounts.

Lindsay Robinson graduated in December 1999 from the Bachelor of Commerce (Honours) program at the University of Manitoba, with a focus on Human Resource Management and Marketing. Lindsay grew up in a farming community in southwestern Manitoba, and is familiar with the Manitoba agricultural industry. She was previously employed with the Public Affairs department at the University of Manitoba where she has gained experience in both marketing and human resource activities. Currently Lindsay is working for Westman Human Resources. Lindsay will hold the position of Director of Marketing, as well as oversee all aspects of human resource management. She will handle the promotion at all agricultural fairs and will head the personal selling to farmers program.

Brandi Smith graduated from the University of Manitoba's Bachelor of Commerce (Honours) program with a double major in Finance and Marketing. Brandi is currently employed with National Leasing Group Inc., as Finance Analyst. She also has experience working in the agricultural industry through employment in the finance department of the Canadian Wheat Board. She will take on the position of Director of Finance for Alfa-B, responsible for all aspects of finance including managing debt and equity financing, and projecting future cash flows. Through family involvement in beekeeping, Brandi has a knowledgeable background in the use and care of alfalfa leafcutter bees for crop pollination.

BOARD OF ADVISORS

To run a successful service business in the agricultural sector, Alfa-B requires the assistance and direction of a Board of Advisors. The Board has been selected based on their extensive knowledge in their respective industry, and their ability to guide the management team in areas with which they are not familiar.

David Booth and Dave Smith bring to Alfa-B extensive knowledge and practical experience in leafcutter bee operations. They are the co-owners of Booth Farms in Lac du Bonnet, Manitoba, and have been raising bees and pollinating alfalfa for over 15 years. Mr. Booth and Mr. Smith will work closely with Alfa-B's management team to help establish strong contacts in the Manitoba agricultural sector, as well as provide overall direction and guidance in beekeeping operations.

Kirk Windsor practises commercial law as a partner of the Winnipeg firm Swystun Kararsevich Windsor. He has been retained by Alfa-B to provide all legal advice and draw up legally binding contracts between Alfa-B and it customers. An example of a short form legal contract Alfa-B will use is found in Exhibit 1.

Alfa-B Pollination Services has consulted Ron Collins, Commercial Banker from the Bank of Montreal in securing funds to begin operations, as he has helped Alfa-B's management determine the appropriate financing for the business. Mr. Collins is familiar with financing agricultural related businesses, as over 50% of his customers are involved in agriculture.

Art Chaput is the final member of Alfa-B's Board of Advisors. He is a partner and tax specialist in the Winnipeg office of BDO Dunwoody LLP Charter Accountants and Consultants. Mr. Chaput provides advisory services, both accounting and tax, to numerous agriculturally based businesses.

OPERATING STRATEGY

HEADQUARTERS AND FACILITIES

Alfa-B plans to purchase a 32 x 41 x 16-foot Westeel building for $20,000 in Ste-Agathe, Manitoba. Ste-Agathe is on the southern tip of Manitoba's alfalfa producing region and provides Alfa-B with a cost-efficient business facility.

The building will provide ample room for winter storage of shelters and nests. The machine shed is currently equipped with one office, which will be used as the primary location from which the business operates. Alfa-B will set up necessary business equipment, such as computers and phones to facilitate daily business operations. A temperature-controlled 10 x 14-foot insulated room will be built to house bee cocoons (larvae) in the wintertime. The room will contain various monitoring and stabilizing equipment to ensure the most beneficial storage conditions for the bee larvae. Estimates have been acquired from an electrician and carpenter for the required renovation to the storage facility. Costs of approximately $37,000 have been budgeted to complete all renovations, which include the installation of a temperature monitoring system, heat exchanger, cooling unit, and back-up generator.

CAPITAL ASSETS

Alfa-B will purchase a 16-foot trailer from Rainbow Trailer Sales in Cartwright, Manitoba for $3,400. This trailer will be used for the transportation of bees, nests and shelters to customer fields. After reviewing costs in used truck magazines and contacting various dealerships, Alfa-B has budgeted $18,000 to purchase a ¾ ton, late 90s model pick-up truck. The truck will be depreciated over ten years and the trailer over twenty years, at a straight-line rate. A second truck and trailer are scheduled to be purchased in year 4, or at the time Alfa-B has been contracted to pollinate at least 2,100 acres, to accommodate the projected increase in demand and subsequent travel.

Approximately twenty-four million bees will be purchased from International Pollination Systems in Fisher Branch, Manitoba during Alfa-B's first year. Information gathered from a variety of published materials recommends between 10,000 and 15,000 bees be placed per acre for efficient alfalfa pollination (2). Discussions between Alfa-B's board of advisors and management have decided to use 20,000 bees per acre in order to obtain the highest potential pollination results. The costs associated with this initial bee purchase are estimated at $0.006 per bee, for a total of $144,000.

Wood shelters, 6x4x4 feet are used to house the leafcutter bees once they are placed in a field. Nests, containing styrofoam grooves, house the bees and provide a beneficial environment for the leafcutter bee to lay larvae during the pollination season. One shelter will be placed every three acres, requiring Alfa-B to purchase 600 shelters in year one. The shelters have an initial cost of $160 per house, and the nests are $20 each. Approximately eleven nests are required for one bee shelter, bringing the total cost per shelter area to $380. These assets will be amortized over a 12-year period, at a yearly rate of $13.33 for shelters and $1.67 for nests. Exhibit 6 provides a detailed summary of Alfa-B's start-up capital costs.

MARKETING PLAN

CUSTOMER ANALYSIS

Farmers represent a unique segment in Canada and Manitoba, and their needs must be completely understood to build a successful marketing plan and achieve our anticipated reach and frequency in the market. Many farmers are very interested in agricultural development, but are often hesitant to try new techniques due to capital commitments and fluctuating costs. However, reference groups are able to influence the views and beliefs that farmers hold. These reference groups include fellow farmers, Manitoba Agriculture, Agriculture Canada and other related agriculture organizations (21). Alfa-B's marketing plan includes interacting with all the above-mentioned agriculture groups, and utilizing their networks and resources to reach our target market.

Alfa-B has conducted marketing research to answer these questions by contacting ten farming operations from a variety of regions in Manitoba concerning their needs and views on the use of leafcutter bees for pollination. Results were interpreted to indicate alfalfa seed growers are aware of the practice of pollination with leafcutter bees, and many of its benefits. Conversely, all alfalfa forage growers are aware of pollination with bees, but some are skeptical about switching crops from the purpose of forage to seed, as this market is volatile and very dependent on demand and commodity pricing. The majority of alfalfa growers can be found in the areas surrounding Winnipeg where deep, well-drained soil is found.

MARKETING STRATEGY

From the information obtained, Alfa-B has developed a marketing strategy that is based not only on building company awareness among growers, but on informing alfalfa forage growers about the numerous benefits of the practice. Advertising to forage growers will play a strong role in the advertising plan due to the potential for such growers switching crops from forage to seed. In recent years, alfalfa seed prices have risen, contributing to the degree to which some growers shift from producing alfalfa for forage to growing it for the purpose of selling the seed.

The company will strive to create a perceived difference in the minds of consumers between the high quality of service and results obtained with Alfa-B and that obtained by farmers who own their own bees. Alfa-B will position itself as a company that offers superior service while obtaining top-quality results. The marketing strategy will emphasize bee management and strong relations with alfalfa farmers.

In the initial two years of Alfa-B, marketing will be a vital aspect of the entire company strategy. It is crucial that potential customers become aware of the company, and educated about the benefits of custom pollination. Alfa-B Pollination will promote the further education of farmers about the advantages of custom pollination through advertisements in a variety of agricultural journals, forage seed grower newsletters and exhibits at various trade shows throughout the Prairie Provinces. This strategy will be focused primarily in Manitoba, since there are no other corporations that currently specialize in custom pollination services here. In the peak business months of May, June, August and September, it estimated Alfa-B will be travelling 2,500 km per month and require accommodations for five nights per month at an average rate of $50 per night, at an approximate cost of $1,000 during these months.

PERSONAL SELLING

Marketing will be focused through the use of personal selling to farmers through trade fairs, direct mailings and rural agriculture representatives. A booth will be set up at the Brandon Ag Days held in January and at the Manitoba Alfalfa and Forage Seed Growers Association's annual convention. Also, a booth will be arranged at the "Canadian Association of Agri-Retailers Convention and Trade Show" at the Winnipeg Convention Centre in February. These events showcase many different services in the agriculture industry, and each is attended by over 30,000 farmers from Manitoba. Prices to set up a booth at these trade shows range from $452 at the Brandon Winter Fair to $656 at the Canadian Agri-Retailers Convention in Winnipeg.

Having direct contact with consumers will enable Alfa-B to address specific concerns and questions growers have about their pollination strategy and the business itself. To address the issue of clutter at the fair, Alfa-B will bring in sample shelters, larvae and nests to attract attention to their booth. As well, short videos, stressing the related benefits of leafcutter bee pollination, which Alfa-B will produce through a contract with a Web page designer, will be shown on television sets to answer any general inquiries the public may have.

Alfa-B's Director of Marketing will develop contacts and work closely with agriculture representatives from specific regions of the province. The reps will have contact with farmers and be able to inform them of the services Alfa-B can provide.

Pamphlets and posters will be developed for distribution to agricultural representatives and growers. The pamphlets will contain information on the practice of pollination using leafcutter bees (including its benefits for the grower), a description of Alfa-B and its specific services and contact information for customers. The pamphlets will stress the advantages of leafcutter bees and describe the focus of Alfa-B's business. The costs of designing and printing pamphlets and posters are included as 10% of advertising costs. Advertising costs for Alfa-B's first year of operations are approximately $9,500. By year two this will increase to a projected $14,000.

ADVERTISEMENTS

Alfa-B will purchase print advertisements in agricultural journals, magazines and newspapers that circulate in Manitoba such as *Grainews*, *The Cooperator*, *Western Producer*, and rural newspapers such as *The Beausejour Clipper*, *Lac du Bonnet Leader* and *The Sentinel Courier*. Advertising will be aggressive in the late winter and early spring when farmers are looking for seed and planning their crop management for the year, and non-existent during the summer, when contracts have already been arranged. Advertising costs for the first year will be approximately $7000, and will be maintained at that level in subsequent years. Advertisements will gain consumer awareness, introduce the concept of custom pollination, and explain how farmers receive the benefits of leafcutter bees pollinating their alfalfa without having to deal with the hassle and issues related to beekeeping.

WEB SITE

Consumers in general are becoming more computer savvy and are using the Internet more frequently in order to search for information from the comfort of their home. As a result, establishing company web sites is becoming an increasingly efficient medium by which to advertise and inform consumers. Farmers, as business operators, are using computers as a communication media (e-mail), an information source (the Internet), to manage all their financial information, and to track inventory. Sameer Hasan, who has experience in the development and management of Web sites, will do the initial Web site design and subsequent updates. Sameer has quoted Alfa-B an initial cost of $1000 to design a quality site, with monthly payments of $50 for continuous updating. Server fees of $70 per month will also be a part of the costs necessary to support a web site for Alfa-B. This Web site will be used to supply general information about Alfa-B's services, as well as serve as a medium through which customers can contact the company.

PRICING STRATEGY

Alfa-B will adopt a two-tiered pricing strategy reflecting the risks involved with agriculture-related businesses. The average price charged to farmers for a type of pollination service similar to Alfa-B is about 33% of yield at season's end. Alfa-B Pollination feels they will be able to charge an alfalfa grower more than the average 33% of yield because of the superior service it will offer such as accurate and timely set-up of leafcutter bees and shelters, and follow-up measures to improve operations from year to year. By charging a rate of 35%, Alfa-B can sell the idea of the worry-free service the company offers, in addition to the no-risk clause for the farmer. On an average field of 300 acres of alfalfa, the use of leafcutter bees will help increase yields to 350 pounds of seed per acre. With seed costs estimated at $1.00 per pound total sales of seed would be approximately $105,000. At a rate of 35%, Alfa-B's income for an average field will equal $36,750.

Contracts will clearly explain and stipulate the payment conditions of Alfa-B's service. Before Alfa-B places shelters and bee larvae in fields, a down payment of $52 an acre is required. The remainder of the payment will not be determined until harvest is complete and the total yield of the crop has been calculated. At this time, the remaining 35% of the yield (less the down payment) will be due to Alfa-B to be paid no later than the end of November of the current harvest year.

Alfa-B will also generate income from the sale of bee larvae at the end of the pollination season. Through the course of the summer, leafcutter bees lay larvae in the styrofoam nests, which result in an end-of-year bee population of over one and a half times the beginning bee population. The excess larvae not needed for the following year's pollination will be sold to Canadian bee brokers at an average price of $0.005 per bee. In Alfa-B's first year of operations, the beginning of season bee population of 24 million will increase to approximately 38.4 million bees. At the end of year one, we will have an excess of 8.4 million bees to sell at forecasted revenue of $42,000.

HUMAN RESOURCE PLAN

Due to the physical demands of the agricultural industry, all members of the management team will be involved in handling custom pollination operations. In the spring, all partners will work together in preparing the shelters and nests to be placed in the fields. From June through September, all partners will be working in the fields, setting up shelters, monitoring bees to produce optimal pollination, and collecting larvae in the fall. All partners will receive an initial annual salary of $25,000, or $1,042 bimonthly before taxes, and will share equally in the profits or losses of Alfa-B. In each subsequent year of operations, the management team will receive an annual salary increase of $1,000. In the fifth year of business, the salary will top out at $29,000. At this level, the personal income tax rate will be the lowest for members of the management team. Additional income will be dependent on the success and profitability of Alfa-B, as it is paid out in the form of dividends to common shareholders based on a percentage of net income.

STAFF

In view of the seasonal nature of the pollination business, one term employee will be hired for six months (May to October) during the first year of Alfa-B's operations. The one full-time employee, Darrell Fast, who Alfa-B plans to hire, has previous experience working with leafcutter bees outside of Lac du Bonnet, Manitoba. Mr. Fast's knowledge of the pollination process and leafcutter bee management will be a great asset to Alfa-B's staff, as he will act as a mentor for the part-time workers in future years. It is imperative all other full-time employees hired in the future have experience with bee pollination and the agricultural industry as well. As demand increases, more full-time seasonal employees will be hired to join the "pollination team."

Mr. Fast will be responsible for preparing the bees and nests to be placed in the fields in May and June. During the summer pollination months, he will continually travel throughout Manitoba to visit the contracted farmers in order to inspect nests and bees. Because of his previous work with leafcutters, he will be in charge of stripping the larvae from the nests in September along with decontamination and cocoon testing.

Alfa-B Pollination plans to undertake its summer recruitment efforts at the University of Manitoba to hire Agriculture students who are pursuing a major in entomology or have prior experience working with bees. Two students will be hired during the second summer as "pollination assistants." This number is projected to double (four employees) in subsequent years as a result of increased demand. Training of new employees will be conducted on the job by the management team and the full-time employees. The bulk of Alfa-B's work will be done in teams; therefore timely and pertinent feedback can be given to employees throughout the course of their employment to improve their skills and task behaviour.

Each student will take part in such tasks as placement of houses in fields during spring, removal in the fall, general maintenance and care of bees and shelters during the season. It is also critical employees maintain constant communication with the growers to ensure proper spraying techniques are undertaken. As each student's experience with the leafcutting operation grows, he or she may also be responsible for aiding with some marketing aspects of the business. Employees will attend information sessions in rural communities with one of the business owners to inform farmers of the practice of leafcutter bee pollination.

EMPLOYEE COMPENSATION

Each summer student position will be placed at a wage of $9 per hour, which is the standard wage paid by leafcutting operations in other provinces. These positions will last from the beginning of May to the beginning of September. Hours of work will be 7:30 am to 4:00 p.m., Monday to Friday, for a total of 35 hours per week. Occasionally, farmers will require service during the weekend. In these circumstances the management team of Brandi, Lindsay and Joel will take on the job. If additional assistance is needed under these conditions, the students will be called upon to assist the management team. If term employees exceed 40 working hours in one week, overtime will be paid out at a rate of time and one-half, or $13.50 per hour.

Alfa-B Pollination Services is conducting research into provincial government assistance for paying summer students. Career Start is a program run by the provincial government that offers some monetary assistance (approximately 33% of minimum wage) to businesses that hire summer student employees. This aid from the government will allow Alfa-B to offer wages that are competitive with the industry standard, while maintaining lower annual labour costs. The company's current financial plan does not include this type of government assistance in the budgeted labour costs, but will be updated in the future if Alfa-B qualifies for the program next year when summer students are hired.

Mr. Fast will be paid $2,000 per month, or $12,000 for the first year six-month term position. Each additional year Mr. Fast returns to a term position with Alfa-B, he will qualify for a 6% wage increase. Additional full-time term employees will be paid a starting salary of $12,000 for six months of service with Alfa-B Pollination. Term employees will work 40 hours per week, and be compensated at time and a half for any reported overtime.

Turnover is expected to be low for Alfa-B's full-time term employees due to the limited number of jobs available for pollination specialists. The management team will fill out employee evaluations at the end of each summer in order to record the skills and behaviours of all employees. These evaluations will be used as a means of awarding bonuses or raises to well-deserving employees. As well, the evaluations will aid in deciding which term employees to ask back for the following summer. It is beneficial for Alfa-B to hire the same summer students year after year if possible. This would allow the business to avoid training costs that would be incurred if new employees were hired every year. Also, previous employees will be familiar with Alfa-B's operations and will be in tune with the company's goals.

BENEFITS

Full-time employees will be offered non-monetary benefits above their salary, making the positions more competitive with other job opportunities. The benefits package supplied by Alfa-B will include 4% paid holidays during the six-month term position, as well as various certificates for dinners and entertainment used to reward good performance. Treating employees as valuable resources will maintain employee performance and morale.

FINANCING

Alfa-B Pollination will be financed through a combination of debt and equity. The management team will contribute a total of $105,000 from personal funds and each will receive 33.3% of the common shares position in the corporation. Additional equity of $55,000 will be raised through issuing shares to outside sources. The outside investors of Alfa-B will receive preferred, non-voting shares in the company.

Alfa-B forecasts paying dividends to preferred shareholders and common shareholders at the end of the third year of operations. Preferred dividends will be paid out at a rate of 10% of the end-of-year net income. End of year three has preferred dividends of $8,000. At a constant rate of 10% of net income, preferred dividends have a three-year growth rate of 94% to over $15,500 at the end of year five. It is forecasted the preferred shares will be purchased back by Alfa-B and retired at the end of the sixth year of operations with a return on investment of over 35%.

An initial bank loan of $250,000 is required to start Alfa-B Pollination. A Farm Improvement Loan (FIL) has been approved from the Bank of Montreal and will carry an interest rate of prime plus 1%. Under a Farm Improvement Loan, the Bank has limited its risk, as the federal government provides a guarantee on 85% of the outstanding loan balance over the life of the loan up to $250,000. The loan will be repaid over ten years through a monthly principal payment of $2,083 plus interest. Currently the Canadian prime rate is 7.0%, thus the interest rate on the FIL would be 8.0%. The debt interest rate is floating and will be recalculated each time the bank prime rate fluctuates. Exhibit 5 is a copy of the term sheet between the Bank of Montreal and Alfa-B Pollination Services. The agreement provides a detailed description of the agreement of the loan.

Due to the seasonal cash inflows of the corporation, a revolving line of credit will be established with the Bank of Montreal to help cover daily expenses and cash shortfalls. The line of credit will be priced at 1% over prime, with a maximum outstanding balance of $25,000. The line of credit will only be required to help Alfa-B during the first three years of operations. Exhibit 4 details the financial structure of Alfa-B Pollination Service, including the lenders, rates and collateral required.

REVENUE

The initial funds raised will allow Alfa-B to purchase the fixed assets required to begin business for the 2001 crop year. Shelter, nests and bee stock will be purchased in the spring, while other funds will be set aside for renovating the machine shed as a winterized storage facility later in the year.

The initial financing requirements are dedicated to providing adequate funds for Alfa-B to custom pollinate 1,200 acres of alfalfa. This is an estimated 3% of the 1999 production of alfalfa seed crops. Over the course of the first five years, Alfa-B has projected an increase in demand by a conservative 300 acres per year (approximately one new customer per year). Through this level of service, Alfa-B has no difficulty making repayments on their Farm Improvement Loan, and is building strong retained earnings to finance future operations of the company.

Forecasted statements, shown in Exhibits 7 to 14, provide a detailed financial summary of Alfa-B's first five years of operation. The Bank of Montreal Farm Improvement Loan and shareholder investment are sufficient to fund the first year of operations, with the line of credit required only in year two and three to help cover the seasonal nature of Alfa-B cash flows.

End of first year financial statements show before-tax net income of slightly under $37,000, and net income of $29,000. Alfa-B qualifies for the small business corporate tax rate of 22%. This rate will not change until the company's before-tax net income increases to over $200,000.

With an increase in pollination volume of 300 acres in year two, end-ofyear net income increases by over 40% to $41,000. This trend continues over the next three years, with net income reaching $156,000 and retained earnings of $270,000 in the fifth year of business. Alfa-B has a net operating profit margin of 39% by the fifth year of operations.

Alfa-B Pollination Services is in a strong financial position by the end of the third year of business. At this time, the company will begin paying dividends to both its preferred and common shareholders. As stated previously, preferred shareholders will receive 10% of the end-of-year net income. Common dividends are forecasted to start at 25% of net income in year three. These dividends will be paid to the three members of Alfa-B's management, and will act as additional personal income from the company. The common dividends are anticipated to increase by 5% each subsequent year of operation, until Alfa-B can no longer maintain a current ratio of 2:1. These dividends may fluctuate from year to year depending on commodity prices of alfalfa, and Alfa-B's expansion opportunities.

RISK FACTORS

In undertaking any new business venture, there are external risks that must be identified and contended with. Alfa-B Pollination Services has identified the key risks present in the agriculture sector, as well as risks associated with a company of this nature.

COMMODITY PRICES

Alfa-B's yearly profit potential is based on promoting effective pollination from the use of leafcutter bees, as well as the commodity price of alfalfa. By charging a maximum price of 35% of the producers crop yield, Alfa-B is sharing the risks associated with uncertain commodity prices. When the seed is in demand and alfalfa prices are high, the alfalfa producer, as well as Alfa-B will benefit. Alfa-B is somewhat protected by charging customers an upfront service fee of $52 per custom pollinated acre. In the event alfalfa prices fall to an unfavourable level, the company will still be able to cover its expenses.

THREATS INVOLVED WITH LEAFCUTTER BEES

The greatest current concern to leafcutter beekeepers is the present of chalkbrood disease, which infects the larva stage of development and causes the bee to die before reaching maturity. The cocoons become hardened, and appear chalky, cream coloured, grey or black. Studies in the United States have shown if chalkbrood disease is present, beekeepers can lose 50% or more of their bee stock (9). By conducting proper decontamination of equipment in the fall, Alfa-B Pollination will prevent diseases and parasites from affecting their bees. All nests and trays will be decontaminated in the spring to prevent parasites from entering. Also, bees will be purchased from a trusted source in Manitoba, where populations are carefully monitored to ensure disease-free bees.

The second most important problem facing leafcutter bee management is loss of bees from parasites. At least eight parasitic species are known to infest leafcutter bees or their nest materials. Through conducting cocoon testing in the fall, Alfa-B will be capable of detecting parasites in their early stage of development, which will enable them to deal with the problem before it gets out of hand (26). As well, the bee stock will hatch in a controlled environment, which will be protected from parasites.

ENVIRONMENTAL RISKS

Alfa-B will limit its liability by purchasing maximum insurance policies to protect the bee stock from such things as windstorms, hail, frost, fire, theft and vandalism. This will greatly reduce the risk to Alfa-B if something unforeseen was to damage the bee stock. As well, insurance will be purchased on all the other assets belonging to the company, including bee shelters, nests and the winterized complex. The insurance policy for the first year of operation will cost slightly over $2,000. Exhibit 2 provides a more detailed summary of the policy and identifies all threats Alfa-B Pollination is protected against.

COMPETITION

There are no commercial businesses within Manitoba offering leafcutter bee pollination services, which is a large advantage for Alfa-B. Although Alfa-B Pollination will have no direct competition within Manitoba, its indirect competition may force the business to overcome some obstacles in gaining market share.

DIRECT COMPETITOR ANALYSIS

The major source of direct competition within Manitoba will be independent farmers who own their own leafcutter bees. Many of these farmers will offer neighbours the use of their bees for pollination purposes. A key obstacle will be convincing farmers of the advantages of using Alfa-B's services over managing their own bees. These advantages will be highlighted prominently in the company's marketing strategy. Alfa-B will focus on the high quality of its service and focus predominantly on bees.

Independent farmers may find they save money by managing their own bees, but the process is very time consuming and as a result, bees are often neglected or do not reach their full pollination potential. By focusing solely on bee management and care, Alfa-B can provide a more concentrated effort to supply top quality and healthy bees. Alfa-B will work in conjunction with farmers to coordinate the most effective pollination schedule.

INDIRECT COMPETITION

Alfa-B has identified honeybee pollination operations as a source of indirect competition. There are approximately 100 commercial honey beekeepers in Manitoba. Although these businesses will not act as direct competition for Alfa-B, they could still hold some of the potential market share. Growers may see honey bees as an advantage over leafcutter bees due to their ability to produce honey as a by-product, which can be sold commercially. This may pose as a threat to Alfa-B Pollination. It will be one of Alfa-B's objectives to inform farmers about the capabilities of leafcutter bees in comparison to honeybees. Leafcutter bees are able to pollinate an area 15 times more efficiently than honey bees and work better under hotter working conditions (2).

Saskatchewan produces over 50% of the Canadian acreage for alfalfa; therefore, leafcutter bee operations are predominant in this area. Saskatchewan leafcutter operations act as a source of indirect competition for Alfa-B due to their size and ability to service some of the Manitoba market for the pollination of alfalfa. Northern Saskatchewan is a rich area for the use of leafcutter bees. As a result, many operations have been established to serve this market. These businesses have the advantage of years of experience in the agricultural industry and the ability to move into available markets with ease. For this reason, Alfa-B must be aware that some of its northern market could be swept away by Saskatchewan pollination businesses. To directly combat this issue, advertising campaigns for the southern part of Manitoba will focus on Manitoba pride, as well as gaining awareness of Alfa-B Pollination and its benefits.

HARVEST/DIVESTITURE STRATEGY

In the event that Alfa-B management desires to exit the business, the company will sell all its bee stock to bee brokers and sell the equipment to local farmers involved with leafcutter bee pollination. There are also areas to list leafcutter bee equipment on the Internet, which may be used if a sale cannot be made locally. All liquidated assets and available cash will be divided equally among the three members of Alfa-B Pollination. This stipulation will be outlined as part of the incorporation agreement made among the parties.

If market growth becomes stagnant for reasons beyond the control of management (e.g. alfalfa prices fall, a recession occurs), Alfa-B will attempt to engage in other pollination-related business. Services could expand to include fruit crops in British Columbia or Nova Scotia, as well as other forage crops, as described in the following section.

THE FUTURE

There are several options for future expansion available for Alfa-B Pollination:

BEE SALES TO CANADIAN BEE BROKERS

Alfa-B Pollination plans to start selling excess bee populations to Canadian bee brokers in its second year of business. If high chalkbrood levels, high labour costs and high equipment costs associated with hygienic management of leafcutter bees continue in the United States, U.S. farmers will continue buying from Canadian sources. Also, with a ban in place on importing bees from American pollinators, and the majority of American farmers purchasing bee stock from Canada, leafcutter bees will continue to be in high demand in Canada. The infected bee populations in the United States make Canada an important supplier of bees, and thus bee brokers will be in a continuous need of leafcutter bees. Alfa-B will sell excess bee stock to Canadian brokers at the going market rate. Currently, prices are holding steady at $0.005 per bee.

The use of an effective, short residual, pre-bloom insecticide only when pests are a problem will keep bee-poisoning cases to a minimum. The development of new, more specific insecticides that are safe for bees will also reduce the bee losses. With increased emphasis on sustainable agriculture and integrated pest management, bee poisoning by insecticides should become less frequent. Alfa-B will be able to benefit from new and improved leafcutter bee management practices that control the insect enemies of alfalfa leafcutter bees.

EXPANSION INTO DIVERSE CROPS

The leafcutter bee is also used to pollinate forage legume species such as clover, and has recently been used to successfully pollinate blueberries, strawberries, Saskatoon berries and a new hybrid canola variety on a large enough scale to show promising results (3, 22). This may enable Alfa-B to diversify its pollination expertise to other crops and geographic areas. Within four years, Alfa-B will market themselves in regions of Canada that produce fruit, nut crops and vegetable crops. Alfa-B can continue to benefit from forage crops, and also introduce its service to oilseed crops and even many garden flowers, which will represent a large expansion of their target market.

MOVEMENT TO OTHER PROVINCES

As mentioned above, there are a number of possibilities to expand Alfa-B Pollination Services into fruit crops. These types of crops are predominately grown in British Columbia, as well as Nova Scotia. Alfa-B Pollination hopes to begin work with fruit crops in British Columbia within seven years.

Saskatchewan is a province with a large market for pollination by leafcutter bees. After Alfa-B Pollination becomes well established (within 5 years of its operation), it will consider entering the Saskatchewan market. This move must be done after the business has become well developed and recognized among growers in the Prairie Provinces, or survival in the competitive Saskatchewan market will be difficult.

A full-scale marketing plan will be the primary objective in Alfa-B's first years in order to gain the market awareness needed to survive in the future. Expansion is only possible if sales are sustainable and there is demand by consumers. Opportunities will always be available as long as Alfa-B attracts farmers who are interested in the potential of increasing their crop yields.

PURSUE ACCELERATED GROWTH STRATEGY

Alfa-B has the ability to pursue an accelerated growth strategy. Instead of selling excess bees to bee brokers, Alfa-B will retain a large stock of bees to provide us the opportunity to custom pollinate an additional 500 acres of alfalfa in the second year of business. If the demand is substantial for Alfa-B's services, this strategy will be pursued. Under this type of scenario, further capital financing is required to help purchase the extra shelters and nests required to meet the increased demand.

ALFA-B — EXHIBIT 1

RENTAL AGREEMENT
ALFA-B POLLINATION SERVICES INC.

Ste-Agathe, Manitoba
P.O. Box 233
R0G 1Y0
(204) 882-BEES
www.alfa-b pollination service.ca.com

Rental No.
Customer No.
Commencement Date:

NOTICE: THIS IS A NON-CANCELABLE BINDING CONTRACT. THIS CONTRACT WAS WRITTEN IN PLAIN LANGUAGE FOR YOUR BENEFIT. IT CONTAINS IMPORTANT TERMS AND CONDITIONS AND HAS LEGAL AND FINANCIAL CONSEQUENCES TO YOU. PLEASE READ IT CAREFULLY. FEEL FREE TO ASK QUESTIONS BEFORE SIGNING

(Lessor)

CUSTOMER			Telephone No.
	Marketing Contact:	Billing Contact:	Facsimile No.
ADDRESS			
CITY & PROVINCE	POSTAL CODE	COUNTRY:	
LOCATION OF CROP (if different than above)			
CUSTOMER OWNS PREMISES ☐	NAME AND ADDRESS OF LANDLORD IF EQUIPMENT IS TO BE PLACED IN RENTED PREMISES.		
# of ACRES	CROP DESCRIPTION (Include Hybrid, Quantity and Expected Yield)		

TERM (NO. OF COMPLETE MONTHS)	DOWN PAYMENT WILL BE MADE IN ADVANCE	☐ MONTHLY ☐ QUARTERLY ☐ OTHER	NO. OF PERIODIC RENT PMTS. DURING TERM	PERIODIC RENT AMOUNT	P.S.T	G.S.T./H.S.T	TOTAL RENT PAYMENT

TERMS AND CONDITIONS

1. RENTAL CHARGES You (the customer or lessee) agree to lease from us (Alfa-B Pollination Services Inc.) the equipment and leaf cutter bees for the terms stated above. You will pay partial payment at the time of delivery, with further payment due at the above specified date and interval. If any payment is late, we will charge a late fee of $10.00 or for each month or partial month during which the payment is unpaid plus interest at the rate of 24% per annum, calculated monthly. You agree the shelters, nests, and larva will be removed from the field after the pollination period is completed at our convenience. If the equipment and larva can not be retrieved, you will be charged that market value of all assets unattainable.

2. OTHER IMPORTANT TERMS: THIS LEASE CANNOT BE CANCELED BY YOU FOR ANY REASON, INCLUDING WEATHER, LOSS OR DAMAGE OF BEES, FAILURE OF BEES TO POLLINATE CROP. YOU MAY NOT REVOKE ACCEPTANCE OF THE EQUIPMENT. WE ARE NOT RESPONSIBLE FOR EQUIPMENT DAMAGE. YOU ARE LEASING THE EQUIPMENT "AS IS", AND WE DISCLAIM ALL WARRANTIES, EXPRESS OR IMPLIED. WE WILL BE RESPONSIBLE FOR SERVICE REPAIRS, AND MAINTAINING THE EQUIPMENT IN THE SAME STATE AS DELIVERED. You certify to us that the equipment and bees will be used by you solely for business purposes of pollination and improving crop yields.

3. TITLE. We will have title to the equipment, bees, and larva during this lease. We will file a financing statement or similar registration evidencing this lease under the applicable personal property legislation. The time for attachment of the security interest granted by this agreement has not been postponed.

4. PAYMENT PLAN. A downpayment of $52 an acre is to be paid at the beginning of the term of the rental agreement. The remainder of the payment is due no later than November, 30 of the same harvest year.

5. LOSS, DAMAGE, INSURANCE. You are responsible for and accept the risk of loss or damage to the equipment, bees and larva. You agree to keep the equipment insured against all risks of loss in an amount at least equal to the replacement cost, and you will list us as loss payee and give us written proof of this insurance. IF YOU DO NOT GIVE US SUCH PROOF, WE MAY (BUT WILL NOT BE OBLIGATED TO) OBTAIN OTHER INSURANCE AND CHARGE YOU A FEE FOR IT.

6. DEFAULT. If you fail to pay us as agreed, we will have the right to (i) sue you for all past due payments and all payments to become due in the future for the unexpired term, plus the residual value we have placed on the equipment and other charges you owe us, and (ii) repossess the equipment. You will also pay for our reasonable collection and legal costs. This lease is governed by the laws of the Province where the equipment is located and any disputes will be referred to the courts of that Province. To the extent permitted by law, you waive the benefit and protection of any legislation that restricts or limits our rights under this lease, including the provisions of The Limitation of Civil Rights Act of Saskatchewan, if applicable.

7. ASSIGNMENT. YOU AGREE THAT YOU MAY NOT ASSIGN (TRANSFER) THIS LEASE OR SUBLEASE THE EQUIPMENT TO ANYONE ELSE. YOU AGREE THAT WE MAY SELL OR ASSIGN ANY OF OUR INTERESTS TO A NEW OWNER OR A SECURED PARTY ("THIRD PERSON") WITHOUT NOTICE TO YOU. In that event, the Third Person will have such rights as we assign to them but none of our obligations (we will keep those obligations), and the rights of the Third Person will not be subject to any claims, defenses or set-offs that you may have against us or another person.

8. TAXES AND OTHER FEES, INDEMNIFICATION. You agree to reimburse us for all taxes, charges and administration costs of $100.00 in connection with the ownership and use of the equipment. UNLESS WE HAVE GIVEN YOU A WRITTEN OPTION TO PURCHASE THE EQUIPMENT FOR 10% OF ORIGINAL EQUIPMENT COST OR LESS AT THE END OF THE LEASE, YOU AGREE THAT WE ARE ENTITLED TO ANY AND ALL TAX BENEFITS (SUCH AS DEPRECIATION AND TAX CREDITS), AND YOU WILL NOT DO ANYTHING INCONSISTENT WITH THIS UNDERSTANDING. IF YOU DO, YOU WILL INDEMNIFY (REIMBURSE) US FOR OUR RESULTING LOSSES. YOU ALSO AGREE TO INDEMNIFY US FOR ALL LOSSES AND LIABILITIES ARISING OUT OF THE OWNERSHIP OR YOUR USE OF THE EQUIPMENT. THESE PROMISES WILL CONTINUE AFTER THIS LEASE ENDS.

9. MISCELLANEOUS. You authorize us to share credit and other information about you and your company with our affiliates. For your convenience, we may accept a facsimile copy of this lease with facsimile signatures. You agree a facsimile copy will be treated as an original and will be admissible as evidence of this lease. The parties agree that this document will be written in the English language. Les parties aux presentes conviennent a ce document soit redige en anglais.

x ______________________________
AUTHORIZED SIGNATURE TITLE

____
FULL LEGAL NAME OF LESSEE

X ______________________________
AUTHORIZED SIGNATURE TITLE

PRE-AUTHORIZED PAYMENT PLAN

DELIVERY AND ACCEPTANCE CERTIFICATION

The lessee hereby certifies that all equipment refferred to above has been delivered, is fully installed and it is in good operating order. Lessee unconditionally accepts the equipment and requests that leasing company sign this lease and pay the equipment vendor.

X ______________________________
AUTHORIZED SIGNATURE

ACCEPTED BY CUSTOMER FOR OFFICE USE ONLY

______________________________ By ______________________________ Date

/Short form Rental Contract **Rev. 06/99**

ALFA-B — EXHIBIT 2

INSURANCE POLICY

LEAFCUTTER BEEKEEPERS FORM COVERAGE—RIDER FP12
FARM INSURANCE POLICY

If the Coverage Summary Page indicates that Rider FP-12 applies, Barnabe/Saurette Insurance (B/S) provides the insurance described below in return for payment of the premium.

A. Property insured and amounts of insurance. B/S insure:

1. $XXXXX on nesting boards or shelters.
2. $XXXXX on bees or cocoons in all stages of development.
3. $XXXXX on beekeeping equipment and supplies used in connection with beekeeping operations, excluding farm equipment and machinery.

B. Insured perils.

Cover Code A: If this Rider specifies Cover Code A, you are insured against direct loss or damage caused by Fire, Lightning or Explosion of natural, coal or manufactured gas.

Cover Code K: If this Rider specifies Cover Code K, you are insured against direct loss or damage caused by the perils insured by Cover Code A, plus the following named perils:

1. **Smoke.** This peril means smoke due to a sudden, unusual and faulty operation of any heating apparatus flued to a chimney.
2. **Riot, Vandalism or Malicious Acts.** This peril does not include loss or damage caused by:
   (i) any tenant, tenants' guests tenants' employees or members of their households;
   (ii) you or any person employed by you;
   (iii) or resulting from theft or attempted theft.
3. **Theft or attempted theft.** This peril does not include:
   (i) theft or attempted theft by any person employed by you or a member of his or her household;
   (ii) theft or attempted theft by any tenant, tenants' guest, tenants' employees or members of their household;
   (iii) any mysterious disappearance or unexplained loss.
4. **Windstorm or Hail. This peril does not include:**
   (i) loss or damage to property in a building, unless damage is concurrent with and result from an aperture caused by windstorm or hail;
   (ii) loss or damage by windstorm to an outside shelter or property within an outside shelter, unless the shelter was properly anchored;
   (iii) loss or damage to property in an outside shelter, unless the shelter sustained damage by the windstorm or hail;
   (iv) caused by water, waterborne objects, ice, waves whether or not driven by wind;
   (v) loss or damage to adults bees in the open field, including while in hive or shelters.
5. **Ravaging by bears.** B/S will only pay in excess of any amount payable under any government assistance program.

C. Loss of damage not insured-applicable to Cover Codes A and K.
B/S do not insure loss or damage:

1. caused by electrical currents other than lightning, but if there is resulting fire or explosion, we will pay only for the resulting damage to the insured property caused by the fire or explosion;
2. caused by dishonesty of an employee or any other person to whom the property is entrusted;
3. caused by death resulting from or contributed to by disease, illness, parasites, predators or poisoning whether consequent upon an insured peril or not.

D. Co-insurance clause.
B/S will not pay for a greater portion of any loss than the applicable amount of insurance bears to 80% of the Actual Cash Value of the insured property at the time of the loss. If this Rider specifically insures two or more items, this condition will apply separately to each item.

E. Deductible.
In case of damage to insured property while located in the open field caused by any of the following perils:

(a) windstorm or hail;

(b) riot, vandalism or malicious acts;

(c) theft, or attempted thefts; or

(d) ravaging by bears;

B/S is responsible only for the amount by which the loss or damage exceeds $1,000 or the "Deductible Amount" of this Rider, whichever is the greater. Otherwise, the "Deductible Amount" of this Rider will apply.

F. Conditions.
This Rider is subject to all the terms and conditions of the policy to which it is attached.

ALFA-B — EXHIBIT 3

SEED NAME	1999 PROJECTED PRICE PER POUND
Alfalfa	$1.00 – $1.25 *
Wheat	$0.39
Barley	$0.23
Canola	$0.78
Flax	$0.69
Oats	$0.29

*$1.25 is the price for high quality pedigree alfalfa seed

ALFA-B — EXHIBIT 4

FINANCING STRUCTURE

LENDER	AMOUNT	USE	RATE	COLLATERAL
(FIL) Farm Improvement Loan Bank of Montreal	$250,000	Direct loan on capital assets	Prime + 1%	Fixed Assets, personal guarantees, accounts receivable
Bank of Montreal	up to $25,000	Revolving line of credit	Prime + 1%	All inventory and personal guarantees
Equity Investment	$160,000	Funding start-up costs	Payback outside investors within 8 years	Unsecured

ALFA-B — EXHIBIT 5

TERM SHEET

BORROWER:	**ALFA-B POLLINATION SERVICES INC.**
FACILITY #1:	**FirstBank Operating Account (FBOA).**
Amount:	$25,000
Purpose:	For operating purposes.
Availability:	By way of overdraft.
Margin Requirement:	None.
Repayment:	On demand. From operating cash flow.
Pricing:	Bank of Montreal Prime Rate plus 1%, floating, payable monthly in arrears. Note: Prime Rate is the floating annual rate of interest established from time to time by the Bank of Montreal as the base rate it will use to determine rates of interest on Canadian Dollar loans to customers in Canada. Currently the Prime Rate is 6.50%.
Facility Fee:	$50 per month. Facility fee to include all monitoring fees, cheques, deposits and statements. Facility fee to be subject to review and adjustment annually.
FACILITY #2	**Farm Improvement Loan (FIL)**
Amount:	$250,000
Purpose:	To assist with purchase of leafcutter bees, machinery and equipment in the amount of $378,000. Detailed list attached.
Availability:	By way of promissory note. Financing limited to 80% of eligible costs. Copies of invoices/cancelled cheques to be provided for each draw request.
Term:	Maximum 10 years.
Repayment:	From cash flow at approximately $2,083.33 per month plus interest amortized over 10 years. Payments to commence 30 days from drawdown. Blended option available. Payments to be adjusted annually to reflect interest rate changes to respect original term.
Pricing:	Bank of Montreal Prime Rate plus 1%, floating, payable monthly in arrears.

Reporting Requirements: The Borrower will deliver to the Bank:

1. Externally prepared financial statements annually, within 120 days of each fiscal year end. (Minimum Review Engagement)
2. Internally prepared monthly financial statements within 25 days of each month end.
3. Other information as the Bank may reasonably require, from time to time.

General Terms and Conditions:

1. All legal costs and related expenses incurred by the Bank will be for the account of the Borrower.
2. Facilities will be subject to the Bank's right of periodic and at least annual review.
3. Adequate insurance will be kept in force.

Conditions Precedent:

1. All security to be in place to the satisfaction of the Bank and its solicitors as appropriate.

Security and Documentation to Be Provided:

1. Proper current account and borrowing authorities.
2. FBOA overdraft borrowing agreement.
3. General Assignment of Book Debts registered as required.
4. General Security Agreement providing for a first fixed charge over fixed assets being financed. Detailed list of fixed assets to be provided.
5. Full covering guarantees from each of the shareholders. Updated personal financial statements to be provided annually.
6. Farm Improvement application/documentation as required under program.
7. Assignment of full covering insurance over equipment.

Acknowedged and accepted this _____ day of December, 1999.

Alfa-B Pollination Services Inc.

Per: ______________________________

Per: ______________________________

ALFA-B — EXHIBIT 6

ALFA-B POLLINATION SERVICES
Capital costs*

	Cost
Leafcutter Bees [1]:	**$144,000**
Building:	
Wintering Complex	**20,000**
Machinery and Equipment:	
Flatdeck Trailer	4,500
3/4 ton truck	18,000
Bee Stripper	3,000
Total:	**$25,500**
Shelters and Nests:	
Shelters [1]	64,000
Nests [1]	88,000
Total:	**$152,000**
Incubation & Fumigation:	
Fumigation Chamber	4,000
Trays	21,600
Humidifier	200
Racks	500
Monitoring System	500
Heat Exchanger	1,100
Wiring and Thermostat	250
Black Lights	150
Cooling unit	3,000
Dehumidifier	1,000
Back-Up Generator	2,000
Banding Machine	2,200
Total:	**$36,500**
Total Capital Costs:	**$378,000**

(1) Gives Alfa-B Pollination the ability to custom pollinate 1,200 acres of alfalfa in first year of operations.

* Guidelines for Establishing Pollination Costs

ALFA-B — EXHIBIT 7

CASH FLOW STATEMENT—ALFA-B POLLINATION SERVICES
For the Year Ending 2001

	Jan	Feb	Mar	Apr	May	Jun	Jul	Aug	Sep	Oct	Nov	Dec	TOTAL
CASH INFLOW													
Shareholders investment	-	-	160,000	-	-	-	-	-	--	-	-	-	$160,000
Bank of Montreal Loan	-	-	-	250,000	-	-	-	-	-	-	-	-	$250,000
Bank of Montreal Line of Credit	-	-	-	-	-	-	-	-	-	-	-	-	$ -
Revenue from pollination service	-	-	-	-	31,200	31,200	-	-	-	42,300	42,300	-	$147,000
Sale of bees	-	-	-	-	-	-	-	-	-	-	-	21,000	$21,000
TOTAL CASH INFLOW	**$ -**	**$ -**	**$160,000**	**$250,000**	**$31,200**	**$31,200**	**$ -**	**$ -**	**$ -**	**$42,300**	**$42,300**	**$21,000**	**$578,000**
CASH OUTFLOWS													
Bees	-	-	-	144,000	-	-	-	-	-	-	-	-	$144,000
Building	-	-	-	-	-	20,000	-	-	-	-	-	-	$20,000
Shelters	-	-	-	-	64,000	-	-	-	-	-	-	-	$64,000
Nests	-	-	-	-	88,000	-	-	-	-	-	-	-	$88,000
Trucks	-	-	-	-	18,000	-	-	-	-	-	-	-	$18,000
Flatdeck trailer	-	-	-	-	3,400	-	-	-	-	-	-	-	$3,400
Bee Stripper	-	-	-	-	-	-	-	3,000	-	-	-	-	$3,000
Winterizing complex	-	-	-	-	-	-	3,250	33,400	-	-	-	-	$36,650
Incorporation	-	-	330	-	-	-	-	-	-	-	-	-	$330
Legal & Accounting	-	-	-	1,785	500	500	500	500	1,000	1,000	1,000	500	$7,285
Insurance & Licencing	-	-	-	-	696	-	-	696	-	-	696	-	$2,087
Salaries[1]	-	-	-	6,250	8,250	8,250	8,250	8,250	8,250	8,730	6,250	6,250	$68,730
Advertising	-	-	2,790	1,503	600	600	-	-	-	-	600	600	$6,694
Web Page	-	-	-	1,000	100	100	100	100	100	100	100	100	$1,800
Trade Show	-	-	-	-	-	-	-	-	-	-	-	-	$ -
Utilities	-	-	-	100	100	100	100	100	400	400	400	400	$2,100
Telephone	-	-	-	500	350	350	350	350	350	150	150	150	$2,700
Fuel[2]	-	-	-	200	700	700	700	700	700	700	200	200	$4,800
Travel[3] -	-	-	-	-	-	500	500	500	500	-	-	-	$2,000
Administration and Banking Fees	-	-	-	100	100	100	100	100	100	100	100	100	$900
Miscellaneous	-	-	500	500	500	500	500	500	500	500	500	500	$5,000
Interest on long-term debt	-	-	-	1,563	1,563	1,563	1,549	1,536	1,523	1,510	1,497	1,484	$13,791
Principle on long-term debt	-	-	-	-	-	-	2,083	2,083	2,083	2,083	2,083	2,083	$12,498
Income Tax	-	-	-	-	-	-	-	-	-	-	-	8,094	$8,094
Payroll tax	-	-	-	-	-	-	-	-	-	-	-	-	-
TOTAL CASH OUTFLOWS	**$ -**	**$ -**	**$3,620**	**$157,501**	**$186,859**	**$33,263**	**$17,982**	**$51,815**	**$15,506**	**$15,273**	**$13,576**	**$20,462**	**$515,858**
TOTAL MONTHLY CASHFLOW	**$ -**	**$ -**	**$156,380**	**$92,499**	**($155,659)**	**($2,063)**	**($17,982)**	**($51,815)**	**($15,506)**	**$27,027**	**$28,725**	**$539**	**$62,142**
TOTAL CASH AVAILABLE	**$ -**	**$ -**	**$156,380**	**$248,879**	**$93,220**	**$91,157**	**$73,174**	**$21,359**	**$5,853**	**$32,880**	**$61,604**	**$62,142**	**$62,142**

(1) Salary expense includes salary of $25,000 per owner, and wages of all other full-time and part-time employees of Alfa-B Pollination Services Inc.
(2) Fuel expense is for an estimated 2500 km in peak months.
(3) Travel expense is for an estimated 5 nights per month in hotels and trip expenses.

ALFA-B — EXHIBIT 8

ALFA-B POLLINATION SERVICES—INCOME STATEMENT
For the Year Ending 2001

	Q1	Q2	Q3	Q4	TOTAL
REVENUE					
Pollination Contracts	-	62,400	-	84,600	147,000
Sale of bees	-	-	-	21,000	21,000
TOTAL REVENUE	**$ -**	**$62,400**	**$ -**	**$105,600**	**$168,000**
EXPENSES					
Incorporation	300	-	-	-`	300
Legal/Accounting	-	2,785	2,000	2,500	7,285
Insurance	-	696	696	696	2,087
Salaries	-	22,750	24,750	21,230	68,730
Advertising	2,790	2,704	-	1,200	6,694
Web Page	-	696	300	300	1,296
Trade Show	-	-	-	-	-
Utilities	-	300	600	1,200	2,100
Telephone	-	1,200	1,050	450	2,700
Fuel	-	1,600	2,100	1,100	4,800
Administration and Banking Fees	-	300	300	300	900
Travel	-	500	1,500	-	2,000
Depreciation	-	3,923	4,534	4,534	12,992
Miscellaneous	500	1,500	1,500	1,500	5,000
Debt Servicing	-	4,689	4,609	4,492	13,791
Payroll tax	-	-	-	-	-
TOTAL EXPENSES	**$3,620**	**$44,147**	**$43,939**	**$39,502**	**$131,207**
Net Income Before Taxes	(3,620)	18,253	(43,938)	66,099	36,793
Income Tax					8,094
NET INCOME	**($3,620)**	**$18,253**	**($43,939)**	**$66,098**	**$28,698**
Retained Earnings	(3,620)	14,634	(29,305)	28,698	

ALFA-B — EXHIBIT 9

CASH FLOW STATEMENT—ALFA-B POLLINATION SERVICES
For the Year Ending 2002

	Jan	Feb	Mar	Apr	May	Jun	Jul	Aug	Sep	Oct	Nov	Dec	TOTAL
CASH INFLOW													
Bank of Montreal Line of Credit	-	-	-	-	-	-	-	9,000	14,650	-	-	-	$ -
Revenue from pollination service	-	-	-	-	39,000	39,000	-	-	-	52,875	52,875	-	$183,750
Sale of bees	21,000	-	-	-	-	-	-	-	-	-	-	30,000	$51,000
TOTAL CASH INFLOW	**$21,000**	**$ -**	**$ -**	**$ -**	**$39,000**	**$39,000**	**$ -**	**$9,000**	**$14,650**	**$52,875**	**$52,875**	**$30,000**	**$258,400**
CASH OUTFLOWS													
Shelters	-	-	-	-	16,000	-	-	-	-	-	-	-	$16,000
Nests	-	-	-	-	22,000	-	-	-	-	-	-	-	$22,000
Incorporation	30	-			-	-	-	-	-	-	-	-	$30
Legal & Accounting	500	500	500	500	500	500	500	500	500	500	500	500	$6,000
Insurance & Licencing	1,074	-	-	1,074	-	-	1,074	-	-	1,074	-	-	$4,296
Salaries	6,250	6,250	6,250	6,250	8,370	8,370	8,370	8,370	8,370	8,879	6,500	6,500	$88,729
Labour	-	-	-	-	2,520	2,520	2,520	2,923	-	-	-	-	$10,483
Advertising	2,790	2,483	2,790	1,503	600	600	-	-	-	-	-	-	$10,767
Web Page	100	100	100	100	100	100	100	100	100	100	100	100	$1,200
Trade Show	502	1,158	-	-	-	-	-	-	-	-	-	-	$1,660
Utilities	400	400	400	400	400	100	100	100	400	400	400	400	$3,900
Telephone	150	150	350	350	350	350	350	350	350	150	150	150	$3,200
Fuel	100	100	100	100	300	700	700	700	700	300	100	100	$4,000
Travel	300	200	50	50	50	500	500	500	250	100	100	-	$2,600
Administration and Banking Fees	100	100	100	100	100	100	100	100	100	100	100	100	$1,200
Miscellaneous	500	500	500	500	500	500	500	500	500	500	500	500	$6,000
Interest on long-term debt	1,471	1,458	1,445	1,432	1,419	1,406	1,393	1,380	1,367	1,354	1,341	1,328	$16,797
Principal on long-term debt	2,083	2,083	2,083	2,083	2,083	2,083	2,083	2,083	2,083	2,083	2,083	2,083	$24,996
Interest on line of credit	-	-	-	-		-	-	-	56	148	-	-	$204
Principal on line of credit	-	-	-	-	-		-	-	-	23,650		-	$23,650
Income Tax	-	-	-	-	-	-	-	-	-	-	-	11,654	$11,654
Dividends	-	-	-	-	-	-	-	-	-	-	-	0	$ -
TOTAL CASH OUTFLOWS	**$16,350**	**$15,483**	**$14,668**	**$14,443**	**$55,292**	**$17,829**	**$18,290**	**$17,606**	**$14,776**	**$39,338**	**$11,874**	**$23,415**	**$259,366**
TOTAL MONTHLY CASHFLOW	**$4,650**	**($15,483)**	**($14,668)**	**($14,443)**	**($16,292)**	**$21,171**	**($18,290)**	**($8,606)**	**($126)**	**$13,537**	**$41,001**	**$6,585**	**$966**
Carried over cash $62,142													
TOTAL CASH AVAILABLE	**$66,792**	**$51,309**	**$36,641**	**$22,198**	**$5,906**	**$27,076**	**$8,786**	**$179**	**$53**	**$13,590**	**$54,591**	**$61,176**	**$61,176**

ALFA-B — EXHIBIT 10

ALFA-B POLLINATION SERVICES—INCOME STATEMENT
For the Year Ending 2002

	Q1	Q2	Q3	Q4	TOTAL
REVENUE					
Pollination Contracts	-	78,000	-	105,750	183,750
Sale of bees	21,000	-	-	30,000	51,000
TOTAL REVENUE	**$21,000**	**$78,000**	**$ -**	**$135,750**	**$234,750**
EXPENSES					
Incorporation	30	-	-	-	30
Legal/Accounting	1,500	1,500	1,500	1,500	6,000
Insurance	1,074	1,074	1,074	1,074	4,296
Salaries	18,750	22,990	25,110	21,879	88,729
Labour	-	5,040	5,443	-	10,483
Advertising	8,063	2,704	-	-	10,767
Web Page	300	300	300	300	1,200
Trade Show	1,660	-	-	-	1,660
Utilities	1,200	900	600	1,200	3,900
Telephone	650	1,050	1,050	450	3,200
Fuel	300	1,100	2,100	500	4,000
Administration and Banking Fees	300	300	300	300	1,200
Travel	550	600	1,250	200	2,600
Miscellaneous	1,500	1,500	1,500	1,500	6,000
Debt Servicing	4,375	4,258	4,197	4,172	17,001
Depreciation	4,584	5,376	5,376	5,376	20,712
TOTAL EXPENSES	**$44,836**	**$48,692**	**$49,800**	**$38,450**	**$181,778**
Net Income Before Taxes	(23,836)	29,308	(49,800)	97,300	52,972
Income Tax					11,654
NET INCOME	**($23,836)**	**$29,308**	**($49,800)**	**$97,300**	**$41,318**
Retained Earnings	4,862	34,171	(15,629)	70,017	70,017

ALFA-B — EXHIBIT 11

ALFA-B POLLINATION SERVICES—CASH FLOW STATEMENT
For the Years Ending 2003-2005

	2003	2004	2005
CASH INFLOW			
Bank of Montreal Line of Credit	-	-	-
Revenue from pollination service	220,500	257,250	294,000
Sale of bees	69,000	87,000	105,000
TOTAL CASH INFLOW	**$291,950**	**$344,250**	**$399,000**
CASH OUTFLOWS			
Truck	-	18,000	-
Trailer	-	3,400	-
Shelters	16,000	16,000	16,000
Nests	22,000	22,000	22,000
Incorporation	30	30	30
Legal & Accounting	6,000	6,000	6,000
Insurance & Licencing	5,612	4,500	4,500
Salaries	92,521	96,614	100,506
Labour	10,483	10,886	10,886
Advertising	9,567	9,567	9,567
Web Page	1,200	1,200	1,200
Trade Show	1,660	1,660	1,660
Utilities	3,900	3,900	3,900
Telephone	3,520	3,696	3,882
Fuel	4,900	5,145	5,515
Travel	2,780	2,780	2,780
Administration and Banking Fees	1,200	1,200	1,200
Miscellaneous	6,000	6,000	6,000
Interest	14,922	13,087	11,329
Principal on long-term loan	24,996	24,996	24,996
Interest on Line of Credit	15	-	-
Principal on Line of Credit	2,450	-	-
Income Tax	22,652	33,124	43,881
Dividends	28,109	46,976	77,789
TOTAL CASH OUTFLOWS	**$280,517**	**$330,761**	**$353,620**
TOTAL ANNUAL CASH FLOW	**$11,433**	**$13,489**	**$45,380**
TOTAL CASH AVAILABLE	**$72,609**	**$86,098**	**$131,477**

ALFA-B — EXHIBIT 12

ALFA-B POLLINATION SERVICES—INCOME STATEMENT
For the Years Ending 2003-2005

	2003	2004	2005
REVENUE			
Pollination Contracts	220,500	257,250	294,000
Sale of bees	69,000	87,000	105,000
TOTAL REVENUE	**$289,500**	**$344,250**	**$399,000**
EXPENSES			
Incorporation	30	30	30
Legal/Accounting	6,000	6,000	6,000
Insurance	5,612	4,500	4,500
Salaries	92,521	96,614	100,506
Labour	10,483	10,886	10,886
Advertising	9,567	9,567	9,567
Web Page	1,200	1,200	1,200
Trade Show	1,660	1,660	1,660
Utilities	3,900	3,900	3,900
Telephone	3,520	3,696	3,882
Fuel	4,900	5,145	5,515
Administration and Banking Fees	1,200	1,200	1,200
Travel	2,780	2,780	2,780
Miscellaneous	6,000	6,000	6,000
Debt Servicing	14,937	13,087	11,329
Depreciation	22,227	27,420	30,587
TOTAL EXPENSES	**$186,537**	**$193,685**	**$199,542**
Net Income Before Taxes	**$102,963**	**$150,565**	**$199,458**
Income Tax	22,652	33,124	43,881
NET INCOME	**$80,311**	**$117,441**	**$155,577**
Preferred Share Dividends	8,031	11,744	15,558
Common Share Dividends	20,078	35,232	62,231
Retained Earnings	$122,220	$192,684	$270,473

ALFA-B — EXHIBIT 13

ALFA-B POLLINATION SERVICES—BALANCE SHEET
Forecasted for 2000

	Q1	Q2	Q3	Q4
Assets				
Cash	156,380	91,157	5,854	62,145
Accounts Receivable	-	-	-	-
Bee Stock	-	144,000	144,000	144,000
Total Current Assets	**$156,380**	**$235,157**	**$149,854**	**$206,145**
Building	-	20,000	20,000	20,000
Trucks	-	18,000	18,000	18,000
Trailer	-	3,400	3,400	3,400
Shelters	-	64,000	64,000	64,000
Nests	-	88,000	88,000	88,000
Bee Stripper	-	-	3,000	3,000
Winterizing Complex	-	-	36,650	36,650
Accum. Depreciation	-	(3,923)	(8,457.50)	(12,992)
Net Depreciable Assets	-	189,477	224,593	220,058
Total Long-Term Assets	**-**	**189,477**	**224,593**	**220,058**
TOTAL ASSETS	**$156,380**	**$424,634**	**$374,447**	**$426,203**
Liabilities				
Current Portion of Long-term debt	-	12,498	6,249	24,996
Line of Credit	-	-	-	-
Total Current Liabilities	**$ -**	**$12,498**	**$6,249**	**$24,996**
Bank of Montreal loan	-	237,502	237,502	212,506
Total Long-Term Liabilites	**$ -**	**$237,502**	**$237,502**	**$212,506**
Equity				
Preferred Stock	55,000	55,000	55,000	55,000
Common Stock	105,000	105,000	105,000	105,000
Retained Earnings	(3,620)	14,634	(29,304)	28,700
Total Shareholders Equity	**$156,380**	**$174,634**	**$130,696**	**$188,700**
TOTAL LIABILTIES AND EQUITY	**$156,380**	**$424,634**	**$374,447**	**$426,203**

ALFA-B — EXHIBIT 14

ALFA-B POLLINATION SERVICES—BALANCE SHEET
For the Years Ending 2001-2005

	31-Dec-01	31-Dec-02	31-Dec-03	31-Dec-04	3-Dec-05
Assets					
Cash	62,145	61,176	72,609	86,098	131,477
Accounts Receivable	-	-	-	-	-
Bee Stock	144,000	144,000	144,000	144,000	144,000
Total Current Assets	**$206,145**	**$205,176**	**$216,609**	**$230,098**	**$275,477**
Building	20,000	20,000	20,000	20,000	20,000
Trucks	18,000	18,000	18,000	36,000	36,000
Trailor	3,400	3,400	3,400	6,800	6,800
Shelters	64,000	80,000	96,000	112,000	128,000
Nests	88,000	110,000	132,000	154,000	176,000
Bee Stripper	3,000	3,000	3,000	3,000	3,000
Winterizing Complex	36,650	36,650	36,650	36,650	36,650
Accum. Depreciation	(12,992)	(33,703)	(55,930)	(83,350)	(113,937)
Net Depreciable Assets	220,058	237,347	253,120	285,100	292,513
Total Long-Term Assets	**220,058**	**$237,347**	**$253,120**	**$285,100**	**$292,513**
TOTAL ASSETS	**$426,203**	**$442,523**	**$469,729**	**$515,198**	**$567,990**
Liabilities					
Current Portion of Long-term debt	24,996	24,996	24,996	24,996	24,996
Line of Credit	-	-	-	-	-
Total Current Liabilities	**$24,996**	**$24,996**	**$24,996**	**$24,996**	**$24,996**
Bank of Montreal loan	212,506	187,510	162,514	137,518	112,522
Total Long-Term Liabilites	**$212,506**	**$187,510**	**$162,514**	**$137,518**	**$112,522**
Equity					
Preferred Stock	55,000	55,000	55,000	55,000	55,000
Common Stock	105,000	105,000	105,000	105,000	105,000
Retained Earnings	28,700	70,017	122,219	192,684	270,472
Total Shareholders Equity	**$188,700**	**$230,017**	**$282,219**	**$352,684**	**$430,472**
TOTAL LIABILTIES AND EQUITY	**$426,203**	**$442,523**	**$469,729**	**$515,198**	**$567,990**

REFERENCES

Norman Barnabe	Barnabe-Saurette Insurance, Ste-Agathe, Manitoba
David Booth	Booth Farms, Lac du Bonnet, Manitoba
Art Chaput	Chartered Accountant, BDO Dunwoody
Ron Collins	Commercial Banker, Bank of Montreal
Brian Dorge	Agricore, Ste-Agathe, Manitoba
Kerry Dusik	Brett Young Seeds, Oakbluff, Manitoba
Darrell Fast	Winnipeg, Manitoba
Dave Green	Dave's Pollination, Hemingway, South Carolina
Lee Gregory	International Pollination System & Gregory Farms, Interlake, Manitoba
Ron Haccke	Fine Art Student, University of Manitoba
Sameer Hasan	Management Information Systems Student, University of Manitoba
Candyce Henschell	Swystun, Karasevich, Windsor, Winnipeg, Manitoba
Janet Honey	Manitoba Department of Agriculture
Rheal Lafreniere	Entomology, Manitoba Department of Agriculture
Pierre Lanoie	Dairy Farmer, La Salle, Manitoba
Ernie Lemoine	Alfalfa Farmer, Ste-Agathe, Manitoba
Roger Penner	Rainbow Trailer Sales, Cartwright, Manitoba
Jeff Robinson	Graphic Designer, Winnipeg, Manitoba
Dave Smith	Booth Farms, Lac du Bonnet, Manitoba
Robert Warren	Director, Asper Centre for Entrepreneurship, University of Manitoba
Bob Wilson	Northstar Seed, Neepawa, Manitoba
Kirk Windsor	Swystun, Karasevich, Windsor, Winnipeg, Manitoba
Geoff Young	Manitoba Department of Agriculture

BIBLIOGRAPHY

1. **Alfalfa: Historical Uses and Notes**, http://www.gulfstream-group.com/abdominalcramps/alfalfa.htm
2. **Alfalfa Leafcutting Bee**, http://www/pollination.com/IPSalfbee.html
3. **Alfalfa leafcutter bee management in Western Canada**, Agriculture Canada
4. **Alfalfa Leafcutter Bees for Blueberry Pollination**, http://data.ctn.nrc.ca/marit/content/type/org336/div1212/listings/r1956.htm
5. **Alfalfa: System: General Nutrition**, http://www.dmi.net/basics/pi-alfalfa.htm
6. **Allstar Seed Processing Operation**, http://www.abatti.com/allstar/cutter.htm
7. **Canadian Associations**, http://www.seedquest.com/countries/america/canada/associat.htm
8. **Canadian Foot Inspection Agency**, http://www.strategis.ic.gc
9. **Controlling Chalkbrood Disease in Alfalfa Leafcutter Bees**, Manitoba Alfalfa Seed Producers' Association
10. **Cyndi's List**, http://city.net/img/tra/mag/map/manito.gif
11. **Darting Lamp Company**, Business Plan
12. **Economics and Agronomics of New Crops — Alfalfa Seed**, http://eru.usask.ca/agec/Alfalfa/intro.htm
13. **Entomology Leaflet: Dewey M. Caron**, http://www.cybertours.com/midnitebee/html/pollination_html
14. **Farm Business — Grainews**, http://www.agcanada.com/gn/gnfarmbiz.htm
15. **Gryba's Pollination Service**, http://www.zipzone.com
16. **Guide to Managing Bees for Crop Pollination**, Canadian Association of Professional Apiculturists
17. **Guidelines for Establishing Pollination Costs**, http://gov.mb.ca/cgi-bin/print_hit_bold.pl/agriculture/business/cac13s01.html?alfalfa#first_hit
18. **Hyper Penguin**, Business Plan
19. **Importance Alfalfa**, http://genes.alfalfa.ksu.edu/alfalfa/importance/html
20. **Lenny's Back Yard**, Business Plan
21. **Manitoba Ag Days**, http://www.agdays.com
22. **Manitoba Agriculture**; various pamphlets and information
23. **Manitoba Agriculture — Beekeeping**, http://www.gov.mb.ca/agriculture/honey/index.html
24. **Manitoba Agriculture — Fruit Crops**, http://www.gov.mb.ca/agriculture/fruit/bld01s00.html
25. **Manitoba Department of Agriculture**, http://www.gov.mb.ca/agriculture
26. **Manitoba Forage and Grass Seed Production Guide 1999**, http://www.gc.mb.ca/cgi-bin/print_hit_bold.pl/agriculture/forages/bjb00s24html?alfalfa+seed#first_hit
27. **Ostriches On Line**, http://ostrichesonline.com/search.html
28. **The Pollination Home Page**, http://pollinator.com
29. **Pollination Contracts**, ftp://members.aol.com/pollinators/polentrs/txt

Further Information

FURTHER READING

BANKS

ROYAL BANK OF CANADA
(www.royalbank.com)

PUBLICATIONS

- Definitive Guides to…
  - Small Business Financing in Canada
  - Exporting for Small Business in Canada
  - Personal Financial Management
  - Managing Human Resources
  - Understanding Business Cycles for Growing Companies
- The 10 Minute Guides to…
  - Managing Foreign Exchange Risk
  - Internet and Electronic Commerce
  - Market Trends
  - Agricultural Business Reviews
  - Today's Entrepreneur
  - Trade Views

ON-LINE (www.royalbank.com/sme/index.html)

- Small Business & Entrepreneurs
  - Products & Services
  - Managing Your Business
  - Women Entrepreneurs
  - Your Internet Strategy (www.royalbank.com/sme/articles/index.html)
  - Understanding eCommerce (www.royalbank.com/sme/articles/index.html)

BANK OF MONTREAL
(www.bankofmontreal.com) *OR* (www.bmo.com)

PUBLICATIONS

- Small Business Problem Solver Series
  - The Cycles of Your Business
  - Using Other People's Help
  - Sources of Capital
  - Developing Your Business Plan
  - Making Sense of Terms and Jargon
  - Cash Flow Planning
  - Measuring Performance
  - Managing Your Cash Flow
  - The Financial Proposal
  - Dealing with Your Banker
  - Are You an Entrepreneur
  - Marketing Your Business
  - Becoming a People Manager
  - Computers for Your Business
  - Doing Business Internationally

ON-LINE (www.bmo.com/business/business.html)

- The Life of Your Business
  - I Have an Idea
  - I'm Starting a Business
  - My Business Is Growing
  - My Business Is Well Established
  - I'm Expanding into New Markets
  - My Business Could Use Some Help
- Business Plan Essentials
- Personal Strengths and Weaknesses
- Setting up a Business Account
- Sources of Capital
- Long Term Goals

TORONTO DOMINION BANK
(www.tdbank.ca or www.td.com)

- Publications
  - Canada Small Business Financing Loans
  - Small Business Accounts
  - Protect Your Business
  - Payment Power for Merchants
  - Agriculture Credit Products
  - Payroll Services for Your Small Business

ON-LINE

- TD Marketsite (www.tdmarketsite.com/main/main.html)
  - Bricks to Clicks
  - Electronic Commerce
  - Canadian Business News
  - Economic Indicators
  - BuySite
  - SupplySite
  - Auction Services

***SCOTIABANK* (www.scotiabank.ca)**

ON-LINE (www.scotiabank.com/)

- Small Business & Professionals
  - Planning and Starting Your Business
  - Building and Growing Your Professional Career
  - Expanding Your Business
  - Managing Business Challenges
  - Your Business & Personal Rewards
  - Scotia*business* Plan Writer

BUSINESS DEVELOPMENT BANK OF CANADA (www.bdc.ca)

PUBLICATIONS

- Growth Potential Assessment
- Arranging Financing
- Credit and Collection Tips
- Evaluating the Purchase of a Small Business
- Forecasting and Cash Flow Budgeting

ON-LINE (www.bdc.ca/bdc/home/Default.asp)

- Growth
- Quality
- Export
- eBusiness

ACCOUNTING FIRMS

ERNST & YOUNG (www.ey.com)

PUBLICATIONS

- Guide to Taking Your Company Public
- The Next Level: Essential Strategies for Achieving Breakthrough Growth
- What's Luck Got to Do with It? Twelve Entrepreneurs Reveal the Secrets Behind Their Success
- Women Entrepreneurs Only: 12 Women Entrepreneurs Tell the Stories of Their Success
- Making Sure Internal Controls Work
- Web Certificates and Privacy
- Stay Focused Without Developing Tunnel Vision
- The New Basel Accord: Sizing Up Risk
- Building the Future: The "Talent Triangle" for Start-up Success

ON-LINE (www.ey.com/global/gcr.nsf/Canada/Serv_ES_Welcome)

- Managing Personal Finance and Wealth Building
- Going Public – IPO Journey
- Financing and Raising Capital
- Buying, Selling, and Strategic Partnering
- International Expansion
- Minimizing Tax Liability
- Managing Employee Services, Recruiting, and Retention
- Operating as an eBusiness

KPMG (www.kpmg.com)

VARIOUS PUBLICATIONS AND ON-LINE ARTICLES ON:

- Enterprise risk management
- eCommerce and cyber crime in Canada
- Developing winning strategy

ANDERSEN CONSULTING (www.andersen.com)

- Formerly Arthur Andersen
- Case studies

VARIOUS PUBLICATIONS AND ON-LINE ARTICLES ON:

- Transforming business
- eBusiness
- Customers & Channels
- Digital Markets & Supply Chain
- Enterprise Technology
- Strategy & Value

DELOITTE, TOUCHE, TOHMATSU (www.deloitte.com)

VARIOUS PUBLICATIONS AND ON-LINE ARTICLES ON:

- Consulting
- Human Capital
- Research
- Industry Analysis
- eViews

FEDERAL GOVERNMENT

INDUSTRY CANADA (www.ic.gc.ca)

PUBLICATIONS

- Access to Financing for Small Business Series
    - Assessing the Changing Needs
    - Meeting the Changing Needs
- Roadmap to Exporting – Second Edition
- Loans for Small Business Enterprises
- Aboriginal Entrepreneurs in Canada: Progress and Prospects
- Dealing with Debt: A Consumer's Guide
- Choosing a Name… for your Federally Incorporated Company
- Quality Assurance in Services: An ISO 9000 Workbook for Small Professional Service Firms
- Sector Competitiveness Frameworks
    - Management Consulting
- Connectedness in Manufacturing
- A Guide to Integrated Circuit Topographies
- A Guide to Patents
- A Guide to Trade-marks
- A Guide to Copyright
- A Guide to Industrial Designs
- What's in a Name? Using Trade-marks as a Business Tool
- Interactive Business Planner
- Become Investor Ready – Build Investor Relationships: Steps to Growth Capital (Book)
- Electronic Commerce (Newsletter)
- Small Business Quarterly (Newsletter)

- The Canadian Entrepreneur's Guide to Securing Risk Capital – Steps to Growth Capital (Pamphlet)
- The Winning Formula at Work: Investment Facilitation Techniques – Developed by the 22 Pilot Projects Under the Canada Community Investment Plan (Book)
- The Winning Formula: Facilitating Investment in Small Business Growth – Lessons from 22 Pilot Projects Under the Canada Community Investment Plan (Booklet)
- Your Guide to Government of Canada Services and Support for Small Business, 2000 (Booklet)
- Your Internet Business – Earning Consumer Trust (Booklet)
- Small Business Guide to Federal Incorporation
- Bankruptcy
- Consumer Protection

ON-LINE

(www.ic.gc.ca/cmb/welcomeic.nsf/icPages/IndustryCanada OnLine#online14)

- Business Diagnostic and Benchmarking Tools
- Coffee Break Listserv
- Interactive Business Planner
- Lease or Buy Calculator
- Performance Plus
- SME Financial Service Charges Calculator
- Sources of Financing
- Strategis Registration

FOREIGN AFFAIRS AND INTERNATIONAL TRADE CANADA (www.infoexport.gc.ca)

PUBLICATIONS

- Market Reports
  - Aboriginal Products, Services and Technologies
  - Advanced Manufacturing Technologies
  - Aerospace and Defense
  - Agricultural Technology and Equipment
  - Agriculture, Food and Beverages
  - Arts and Cultural Industries
  - Automotive
  - Bio-Industries
  - Building Products
  - Chemicals
  - Consumer Products
  - Electric Power Equipment and Services
  - Environmental Industries
  - Fish and Seafood Products
  - Forest Industries
  - Health Industries
  - Information and Communication Technologies
  - Metals, Minerals and Related Equipment, Services and Technologies
  - Oil and Gas Equipment and Services
  - Plastics
  - Rail and Urban Transit
  - Service Industries and Capital Projects
  - Space
  - Tourism

ON-LINE

- CanadExport Trade Newsletter (www.dfait-maeci.gc.ca/english/news/newsletr/canex/menu.htm)
- ExportSource (www.exportsource.gc.ca/dindex2_e.html)
  - Preparing to Export
  - Researching Countries and Sectors
  - Marketing Your Exports
  - Entering the Market
  - Financing Exports
  - Getting the Product or Service to Market
  - Preventing and Resolving Problems
  - Understanding the Global Marketplace

CANADA CUSTOMS AND REVENUE AGENCY – CUSTOMS AND EXCISE (www.ccra-adrc.gc.ca/)

PUBLICATIONS

- Welcome to Canada – Your Guide to Bringing a Convention, Meeting, Trade Show, or Exhibition Across the Canadian Border
- Guide to Importing Commercial Goods
- Exporting Goods from Canada
- SERVE - Industrial Awareness Program
- Doing Business in Canada – GST/HST for Non-Residents
- Employee or Self-employed?

ON-LINE (www.ccra-adrc.gc.ca/customs/business/menu-e.html)

- Guide for Canadian Small Business
- Small Business Information Seminar
- Business Gateway (www.businessgateway.ca/)
  - Business Start-Up
  - Tax
  - Regulations
  - Business Statistics and Analysis
  - Mergers / Acquisitions / Bankruptcy
  - Financing
  - Human Resources Management
  - Exporting / Importing
  - Innovation / R&D / Technology
  - Selling to Government / Tenders

PUBLIC WORKS AND GOVERNMENT SERVICES CANADA **(www.pwgsc.gc.ca)**

PUBLICATIONS

- Doing Business with Public Works and Operations Canada (Newsletter)

ON-LINE

- Serving Business (www.pwgsc.gc.ca/text/business/index-e.html)
  - Opportunities
  - Doing Business
  - Publications

ON-LINE INFORMATION

PROVINCIAL GOVERNMENTS

PRINCE EDWARD ISLAND ECONOMIC DEVELOPMENT AND TOURISM
(www.peibusinessdevelopment.com)

- Invest in PEI
- Sectors of Excellence
- Starting or Expanding Your Business
- Trade & Export Development
- Media Centre
- Business Parks

NEW BRUNSWICK BUSINESS
(www.gov.nb.ca)

- Marketing a Small Business
- Key Steps to Business Improvement
- Corporate Directories
- Going Public
- Invest New Brunswick (www.gnb.ca/nbfirst/e/)
  - Workforce
  - Business Costs
  - Infrastructure
  - Sectors
  - Business Climate
  - Community Profiles

GOVERNMENT OF QUEBEC
(www.gouv.qc.ca/Index_en.html)

- Starting a Business
- Foreign Investors
- Immigrant Investors
- Direct Assistance Abroad
- Quebecers Wishing to Start a Business
- Portrait of Quebec

ONTARIO MINISTRY OF ECONOMIC DEVELOPMENT AND TRADE
(www.gov.on.ca)

- Starting Your Business
  - Starting a Small Business in Ontario
  - Business Start-Up
- Relocating Your Business to Ontario
  - Ontario Investment Service
  - Investments in Ontario
- Doing Business
  - Doing Business in Ontario
  - Ontario Salutes Small Business
  - Ontario Business Connects
  - Agricultural Business Development
- Licensing and Registration
  - Business Information
- Laws and Taxes
  - Corporations Tax
  - Retail Sales Tax
  - E-Laws
- Trade
  - Ontario Exports

MANITOBA DEPARTMENT OF INDUSTRY, TRADE, AND MINES
(www.gov.mb.ca/itt/index.html)

INFORMATION PAMPHLETS

- Starting a Small Business in Manitoba
- Monter une petite enterprise au Manitoba

SMALL BUSINESS MANAGEMENT SYSTEMS

- Retail Business Plan
- Service Business Plan
- Construction Business Plan
- Manufacturing Business Plan
- Small Business Finance Plan
- Marketing
- Bookkeeping

MANITOBA BUSINESS
(www.gov.mb.ca/business.html)

- AgriBusiness Development
- Business Events Calendar
- Business Resources
- Export Services
- Manitoba Markets
- Small Business Information

SASKATCHEWAN DEPARTMENT OF BUSINESS AND ECONOMIC DEVELOPMENT
(www.gov.sk.ca/topic-picklists/?13)

- Agribusiness
- Business Development
- Business Resource Centre
- Canada/Saskatchewan Business Service Centre
- Small Business

ALBERTA CANADA
(www.alberta-canada.com/index.html)

- Investing in Alberta
- Locating Your Business in Alberta
- Exporting Your Products
- Alberta Products and Services
- Starting Your Business

BRITISH COLUMBIA MINISTRY OF SMALL BUSINESS, TOURISM, AND CULTURE
(www.gov.bc.ca)

- Home-Based Business
- Small Business Resources
- Small Business Training
- Small Business Programs and Initiatives

ASSOCIATIONS AND OTHER ORGANIZATIONS

CANADIAN FRANCHISE ASSOCIATION
(www.cfa.ca)

The following can be ordered from www.cfa.ca/bookstore.html

- CFA Franchise Canada (Magazine)
- CFA Franchise Canada – The Official CFA Directory
- CFA "Investigate Before Investing" Information Kit
- Franchise Annual
- Franchising for Dummies
- Franchise Law that Matters
- Franchising Your Business
- Franchising: So You Want to Be on the Leading Edge
- Growth Hormones for the Franchise Sector
- How to Make Your Numbers Talk
- Make Sure It's Deductible
- Negotiate Your Commercial Lease
- Networking Is More than Doing Lunch
- Protecting Trade Secrets
- Selected Articles and Papers on Franchising
- So You Think You Need a Lawyer
- So You Want to Buy a Franchise
- Start and Run a Profitable Home-Based Business
- Start and Run a Profitable Coffee Bar
- What to Say When Your Customers Won't Pay
- Where to Go When the Bank Says No

DUN AND BRADSTREET
(www.dnb.ca/resources/index.html)

- Credit
    - Establish Credit Terms
    - Monitor Accounts
    - Assess Collections
- Marketing
    - Locate Markets
    - Target Prospects
    - Expand Customer Base
- Purchasing
    - Identify Suppliers
    - Evaluate Risk
    - Maintain Supplier Relationships
- Receivables
    - Collect and Manage Receivables

SOME USEFUL CONTACTS

FEDERAL GOVERNMENT

INDUSTRY CANADA (www.ic.gc.ca)
Chief Information Office
235 Queen St.
Ottawa, ON K1A 0H5
(1 800) 328-6189
Phone: (613) 954-5031
Fax: (613) 954-1894
E-mail: strategis@ic.gc.ca

FOREIGN AFFAIRS AND INTERNATIONAL TRADE CANADA (www.dfait-maeci.gc.ca)
125 Sussex Drive
Ottawa, ON K1A 0G2
(1 800) 267-8376
Phone: (613) 944-4000
Fax: (613) 996-9709
E-mail: enqserv@dfait-maeci.gc.ca

STATISTICS CANADA (www.statcan.ca)
Statistical Reference Centre
R.H. Coats Building, Lobby
Holland Ave.
Ottawa, ON K1A 0T6
(1-800) 263-1136
Phone: (613) 951-8116
E-mail: infostats@statcan.ca

CANADIAN INTELLECTUAL PROPERTY OFFICE (www.cipo.gc.ca)
Industry Canada
Place du Portage, Phase 1
50 Vicoria St., 2nd Floor
Hull, QC K1A 0C9
Phone: (819) 997-1936
Fax: (819) 953-7620
E-mail: cipo.contact@ic.gc.ca

CANADA BUSINESS SERVICE CENTRES (www.cbsc.org/main.html)

CANADA/BRITISH COLUMBIA BUSINESS SERVICE CENTRE
(www.sb.gov.bc.ca/smallbus/sbhome.html)
601 West Cordova St.
Vancouver, BC V6B 1G1
Phone: (604) 775-5525 or (1-800) 667-2272 (within BC)
Fax: (604) 775-5520
InfoFax: (604) 775-5515 or (1-800) 667-2272
E-mail: askus@cbsc.ic.gc.ca

- Interactive Business Planner
- Interactive Export Planner
- Online Workshop
- Links

THE VIRTUAL BUSINESS LINK
(www.cbsc.org/alberta/index.html)
Business Service Centre
100 – 10237 104th St. NW
Edmonton, AB T5J 1B1
Phone: (780) 422-7722 or (1-800) 272-9675
Fax: (80) 422-0055
E-mail: buslink@cbsc.ic.gc.ca

CANADA/SASKATCHEWAN BUSINESS SERVICE CENTRE (www.cbsc.org/sask/index.cfm)
122 3rd Ave. N.
Saskatoon, SK S7K 2H6
Phone: (306) 956-2323 or (1-800) 667-4374
Fax: (306) 956-2328
InfoFax: (306) 956-2310 or (1-800) 667-9433
E-mail: saskatooncsbsc@cbsc.ic.gc.ca

Other regional addresses accessible at
www.cbsc.org/sask/regional_partners.cfm

CANADA/MANITOBA BUSINESS SERVICE CENTRE
(www.cbsc.org/manitoba/index.html)
PO Box 2609
250 – 240 Graham Ave.
Winnipeg, MB R3C 4B3
Phone: (204) 984-2272 or (1-800) 665-2019
Fax: (204) 983-3852
InfoFax: (204) 984-5527 or (1-800) 665-9386
E-mail: manitoba@cbsc.ic.gc.ca

Other regional addresses accessible at
www.cbsc.org/manitoba/index.cfm?name=satellit#top

CANADA/NOVA SCOTIA BUSINESS SERVICE CENTRE
(www.cbsc.org/ns/index.html)
1575 Brunswick St.
Halifax, NS B3J 2G1
Phone: (902) 426-8604 or (1-800) 668-1010
Fax: (902) 426-6530
TTY: (902) 426-4188 or (1-800) 797-4188
InfoFax: (902) 426-3201 or (1-800) 401-3201
E-mail: halifax@cbsc.ic.gc.ca

Other regional addresses accessible at
www.cbsc.org/ns/english/local.cfm

CANADA/NEWFOUNDLAND & LABRADOR BUSINESS SERVICE CENTRE (www.cbsc.org/nf/index.html)
PO Box 8687, Station A
90 O'Leary Ave.
St. John's, NF A1B 3T1
Phone: (709) 772-6022 or (1-800) 668-1010
Fax: (709) 772-6090
InfoFax: (709) 772-6030
E-mail: info@cbsc.ic.gc.ca

Other regional addresses accessible at
www.cbsc.org/nf/people/commun.html

CANADA/ONTARIO BUSINESS SERVICE CENTRE
(www.cbsc.org/ontario)
City Hall, Main Floor
100 Queen St. W.
Toronto, ON M5H 2N2
Phone: (416) 392-6646 or (1-800) 567-2345
Fax: (416) 392-1794
E-mail: info@cobsc.org

Aboriginal Business Service Network
Phone: (877) 699-5559
Fax: (416) 973-2272
Team Canada Trade Enquiries
Phone: (888) 811-1119

Regional site addresses can be accessed at
www.cbsc.org/ontario/regions.cfm

INFO ENTREPRENEURS
(www.infoentrepreneurs.org/eng/index.html)
5 Place Ville Marie
Plaza Level, Suite 12500
Montreal, QC H3B 4Y2
Phone: (514) 496-4636 or (1-800) 322-4636
Fax: (514) 496-5934
InfoFax: (514) 496-4010 or (1-800) 322-4010
E-mail: infoentrepreneurs@cbsc.ic.gc.ca

CANADA/NEW BRUNSWICK BUSINESS SERVICE CENTRE (www.cbsc.org/nb/index.htm)
570 Queen St.
Fredericton, NB E3B 6Z6
Phone: (506) 444-6140 or (1-800) 668-1010
TTY: (506) 444-6166 or (1-800) 887-6550
Fax: (506) 444-6172
E-mail: cbscnb@cbsc.ic.gc.ca

CANADA/PRINCE EDWARD ISLAND BUSINESS SERVICE CENTRE (www.cbsc.org/pe/index.html)
PO Box 40
75 Fitzroy St.
Charlottetown, PE C1A 7K2
Phone: (902) 368-0771 or (1-800) 668-1010
Fax: (902) 566-7377
TTY: (902) 368-0724
E-mail: pei@cbsc.ic.gc.ca

CANADA/YUKON BUSINESS SERVICE CENTRE (www.cbsc.org/yukon/index.html)
PO Box 1006
Dawson City, YT Y0B 1G0
Phone: (867) 993-5274
Fax: (867) 993-6817
E-mail: yukon@cbsc.ic.gc.ca

CANADA/NWT BUSINESS SERVICE CENTRE (www.cbsc.org/nwt/index.html)
PO Box 1320
8th Floor Scotia Centre
Yellowknife, NT X1A 2L9
Phone: (867) 873-7958 or (1-800) 661-0599
Fax: (867) 873-0101
InfoFax: (867) 873-0575 or (1-800) 661-0825
E-mail: yel@cbsc.ic.gc.ca

CANADA/NUNAVUT BUSINESS SERVICE CENTRE (www.cbsc.org/nunavut/index.html)
PO Box 1000, Station 1198
Parnaivik Building
Iqaluit, NU X0A 0H0
Phone: 877.499.5199 or 867.979.6813
Fax: 877.499.5299 or 867.979.6823
E-mail: cnbsc@gov.nu.ca

PROVINCIAL GOVERNMENTS

BRITISH COLUMBIA
Ministry of Competition, Science and Enterprise
PO Box 9046
Victoria, BC V8W 9E2
Phone: (250) 356-7411
Fax: (250) 356-6376
E-mail: cse.minister@gems7.gov.bc.ca
Web: www.gov.bc.ca/cse/Default.htm

ALBERTA
Alberta Economic Development
Economic Development Authority
6th Floor, Commerce Place
10155 102nd St.
Edmonton, AB T5J 4L6
Phone: (780) 415-1319
Web: www2.gov.ab.ca/home/business_and_economy/

SASKATCHEWAN
Department of Economic Development
Head Office
1919 Saskatchewan Dr.
Regina, SK S4P 3V7
Phone: (306) 787-2232
Fax: (306) 787-3872
E-mail: bburnett@ecd.gov.sk.ca
Web: www.gov.sk.ca/topic-picklists/?13

MANITOBA
Department of Industry, Trade and Mines
Small Business & Co-operative Development Branch
PO Box 2609
250 – 240 Graham Ave.
Winnipeg, MB R3C 4B3
Phone: (204) 984-2272 or (1-800) 665-2019
E-mail: manitoba@cbsc.ic.gc.ca
Web: www.gov.mb.ca/itt/trade/index.html

ONTARIO
Economic Development and Trade
900 Bay St.
Hearst Block
Toronto, ON M7A 2E1
Phone: (416) 325-6666
Fax: (416) 325-6688
E-mail: medtt@edt.gov.on.ca
Web: www.ontario-canada.com

QUEBEC
Ministere de l'Industrie et du Commerce
710, Place d'Youville
Québec, QC G1R 4Y4
téléphone: (418) 691-5650
télécopieur: (418) 643-8853
E-mail: info@mic.gouv.qc.ca
Web: www.mic.gouv.qc.ca/index.html

Or

380 West, Saint-Antoine St.
5th Floor NE
Montréal, QC H2Y 3X7
téléphone: (514) 499-2552
télécopieur: (514) 873-1788

NEW BRUNSWICK
Business New Brunswick
PO Box 6000
5th Floor, Centennial Building
Fredericton, NB E3B 5H1
Phone: (506) 453-3984
Fax: (506) 444-4586
E-mail: wwwedt@gov.nb.ca
Web: www.gnb.ca/BNB-ENB/Index.htm

NOVA SCOTIA
Nova Scotia Business
520 - 1800 Argyle St.
Halifax, NS B3J 2R7
Phone: (1-800) 260-6682 or (877) 297-2124 (within Nova Scotia)
E-mail: nsbi@gov.ns.ca
Web: www.novascotiabusiness.com

PRINCE EDWARD ISLAND
Development and Technology
First and Second Floors
94 Easton St.
PO Box 910
Charlottetown, PE C1A 7L9
Telephone: (902) 368-6300
Facsimile: (902) 368-6301
E-mail: rkscales@gov.pe.ca
Web: www.peibusinessdevelopment.com

NEWFOUNDLAND
Department of Industry, Trade, and Rural Development
PO Box 8700
Confederation Annex
4th Floor
St. John's, NF A1B 4J6
Phone: (709) 729-5600 or (1-800) 563-2299
Fax: (709) 729-5936
E-mail: ittinfo@mail.gov.nf.ca
Web: www.success.nfld.net

NORTHWEST TERRITORIES
Community Economic Development Services
Department of Resources, Wildlife, and Economic Development
PO Box 1320
Yellowknife, NT X1A 2L9
Phone: (867) 873-7272
Fax: (867) 873-0434
E-mail: michele_irving@gov.nt.ca
Web: www.gov.nt.ca/RWED/subject_bus.htm

YUKON TERRITORY
Yukon Economic Development
PO Box 2703
Whitehorse, YT Y1A 2C6
Phone: (867) 667-8422
Fax: (867) 667-8409
E-mail : scott.kent@gov.yk.ca
Web: www.economicdevelopment.yk.ca/

NUNAVUT
Communications
PO Box 1000, Station 204
Iqaluit, NU X0A 0H0
Phone: (867) 975-6000
Fax: (867) 975-6099
E-mail: icon@nunanet.com
Web: www.gov.nu.ca

OTHERS

CANADIAN FRANCHISE ASSOCIATION
300 – 2585 Skymark Ave.
Mississauga, ON L4W 44L5
Phone: (905) 625-2896 or (1-800) 665-4232
Fax: (905) 625-9076
E-mail: info@cfa.ca
Web: www.cfa.ca

INTERNATIONAL FRANCHISE ASSOCIATION
900 - 1350 New York Ave. NW
Washington, DC 20005-4709
United States of America
Phone: (202) 628-8000
Fax: (202) 628-0812
E-mail: ifa@franchise.org
Web: www.franchise.org

CANADIAN VENTURE CAPITAL ASSOCIATION
301 - 234 Eglinton Avenue East
Toronto, ON M4P 1K5
Phone: (416) 487-0519
Fax: (416) 487-5899
E-mail: cvca@cvca.ca
Web: www.cvca.ca

HELPFUL WEB SITES

GENERAL INFORMATION

ABOUT THE HUMAN INTERNET (www.about.com)

- Choose the small business link from the list of links
- Everything from marketing and management to small business in the UK

***CANADA/BRITISH COLUMBIA SMALL BUSINESS WORKSHOP* (www.sb.gov.bc.ca/smallbus/workshop/workshop.html)**

- Everything from starting, planning, and financing through marketing and regulations for the small business
- A must-see for anybody looking into business

***SMALL- AND HOME-BASED BUSINESS LINKS* (www.bizoffice.com/index.html)**

- American site
- Covers the areas of news, franchising, marketing, opportunities, and financing
- Links to different sites
- TalkBoard: Small- and Home-Based Business Forum
- Bookstore, Library
- Tips on how to grow your business

***YOUR OFFICE MAGAZINE* (www.youroffice.ca)**

- A magazine for small business
- Articles and features to help business people
- Interesting, insightful

***BANK OF MONTREAL'S BUSINESS SITE* (www.bmo.com/business/business.html)**

- A good site to browse and pick up tidbits of information
- Tips and hints on what to do and what to watch out for
- To help you during the conception phase, look at the "I have an Idea" page
- If you are in start-up mode, take a look at "I'm Starting a Business"

***ROYAL BANK'S SMALL BUSINESS AND ENTREPRENEUR SITE* (www.royalbank.com/sme/index.html)**

- Links to other sites
- Feature articles on topics such as e-commerce and creativity

***ROYAL BANK'S 'TODAY'S ENTREPRENEUR' WEBSITE* (www.royalbank.com/sme/te/index.html)**

- Covers everything modern entrepreneurs might be wondering about
- Informative radio spots
- Archived transcripts
- Covers customer service, competition, networking, finance, operations, marketing, and start-up

***THE CANADIAN TECHNOLOGY NETWORK* (www.nrc.ca/ctn/questionnaire/ctn_orig.html)**

- This site tells you how you can join, network, and benefit from the experience of others in the CTN
- If you are looking at starting a technology-related business (not just computers) this is a site for you to look into

***ENTREPRENDRE* (www.entreprendre.ca/)**

- A French site with research information, archives, and other up-to-date information that may be of interest to browsers wanting to get a feel for the culture and business
- No English option

***BUSINESSTOWN.COM* (www.businesstown.com/)**

- Daily business ideas, bookstore, small business forum, franchising, SOHO, continuously changing topics on all aspects of your business

***THE GLOBE AND MAIL'S REPORT ON BUSINESS MAGAZINE* (www.robmagazine.com)**

- Updated monthly
- Good general information for people trying to keep track of the Canadian economy and news as well as get some insight into different sectors

***PROFIT GUIDE* (www.profitguide.com)**

- Rated links to sites that help you determine the best way to start your own business

***ON-LINE COMMUNITY CENTRE FOR CANADIAN BUSINESS STUDENTS* (www.businesssense.com)**

- Magazine
- Contests and Scholarships
- Campus Reps
- Events

***WESTERN ECONOMIC DIVERSIFICATION CANADA* (www.wd.gc.ca)**

- Information on starting and planning a business
- General information of use to any small business owner

***HUMAN RESOURCES DEVELOPMENT CANADA – SMALL BUSINESS SITE* (www.hrdc-drhc.gc.ca/common/employr.shtml#market)**

- On-line Business Week Magazine
- Market and industry information
- Human resources planning
- Additional business links

***CANADIAN ASSOCIATION OF FAMILY ENTERPRISE* (www.cafeuc.org)**

- Find the chapter nearest you at www.cafeuc.org/about/chapters.html
- Personal advisory groups, mentoring, family councils – CAFE tries to look out for the *family* in family business
- Associate members welcome (those who would be of service to members)

***CANADAONE* (www.canadaone.com)**

- On-line magazine, business and resource directory, links to other great sites

***WALL STREET JOURNAL ONLINE* (www.wsj.com)**

- Mainly American information, but a comprehensive site, easy to navigate

***CNN SMALL BUSINESS WEBSITE* (www.cnnfn.com/smbusiness/)**

- American site
- General background information on business news
- Links to the CNN main site to see the headlines of the day

***FORTUNE MAGAZINE* (www.fortune.com/)**

- American site
- Excellent for background business information and to get ideas
- Try the small business site at netbusiness.netscape.com/

***THE SMALL BUSINESS JOURNAL* (www.tsbj.com/)**

- American site
- Covers areas of interest to all small business owners
- Updated consistently

***MOREBUSINESS.COM BY ENTREPRENEURS FOR ENTREPRENEURS* (www.morebusiness.com/)**

- An American site with good updated links and daily news about building a business, starting a business, getting more profit from your business, and business planning

***GLOBENET: THE GLOBE & MAIL HOMEPAGE* (www.globeandmail.ca)**

- Report on Business
  - All kinds of general information on business and industry in Canada
  - Updated continuously

***STRATEGIS* (strategis.ic.gc.ca)**

- Huge site contains information on everything you would ever want to know about business and markets. A must-see, but don't get lost in the site
- Main areas of interest are:
  - Company Directories
  - Trade and Investment
  - Business Information by Sector
  - Economic Analysis and Statistics
  - Research Technology and Innovation
  - Business Support and Financing
  - Licences, Legislation, and Regulation
  - Employment and Learning Resources
  - Consumer Information

***CIBC SMALL BUSINESS INFORMATION EXCHANGE* (www2.cibc.com/english/business_services/small_business/index.html)**

  - Links to other sites based on industry and geographic location

***ERNST & YOUNG ENTREPRENEURIAL BUSINESS SITE* (www.ey.com/global/gcr.nsf/Canada/Serv_ES_EBC_Welcome)**

- Must view. Excellent site for everything from industry to specific interests
- Always changing

***QUICKEN SMALL BUSINESS CENTRE* (www.quicken.ca)**

- Free software, marketing hints, tips on developing a home office, on-line advice about small business and taxing
- Small Business Café
- The Quicken.ca Consultant
- Links to financing
- Easy to read and browse – appealing

ASSESSING YOUR PERSONAL POTENTIAL

THE BUSINESS GUIDE: STARTING A SMALL BUSINESS
(www.businessguide.net/starting.htm)

- Covers all areas involved in start-up – from assessment of ability to insuring your business

WESTERN ECONOMIC DIVERSIFICATION CANADA
(www.wd.gc.ca/eng/tools/default.htm)

- "Am I an entrepreneur?": Self-assessment quiz
- Links to the Canada/British Columbia Business Service Centre On-Line Small Business Workshop

CANADA BUSINESS SERVICE CENTRES
(www.cbsc.org/main.html)

  - Links to all the CBSCs, covering all areas of business
  - Interactive Business Planners
  - On-line small business workshop
  - Electronic commerce info-guide
  - Local information
- Canada/British Columbia Service Centre
- The Business Link
- Canada/Saskatchewan Business Service Centre
- Canada/Manitoba Business Service Centre
- Canada/Nova Scotia Business Service Centre
- Canada Business Service Centre – Newfoundland
- Canada/Ontario Business Service Centre
- Info entrepreneurs (Quebec)
- Canada/New Brunswick Business Service Centre
- Canada/Prince Edward Island Business Service Centre
- Canada/Yukon Business Service Centre
- Canada NWT Business Service Centre
- Canada/Nunavut Business Service Centre

NEW BUSINESS OPPORTUNITIES

THE BUSINESS GUIDE: STARTING A SMALL BUSINESS
(www.businessguide.net/starting.htm)

- Covers all areas involved in start-up—from assessment of ability to insuring your business

BUSINESSTOWN.COM
(www.businesstown.com/businessopps/newbiz.asp)

- Daily business ideas (www.businesstown.com/)
- A list of businesses you can start with differing amounts of start-up capital

WESTERN ECONOMIC DIVERSIFICATION CANADA – SELLING TO GOVERNMENT
(www.wd.gc.ca)

- From the home page choose the Business Tools and Guides link and then choose the Guide to Selling to Government
- Becoming a supplier
- Should you be selling to government? What does it take to win a government contract?

CANADIAN COMPANY CAPABILITIES
(strategis.ic.gc.ca)

- Connecting buyers and sellers
- Links to other on-line directories
- Search for companies
- Register your company
- Update your company information

BUSINESS OPPORTUNITIES HANDBOOK
(www.busop1.com)

- Links, opportunities, listings, articles, shows
- Excellent links, although most are in the United States

FRANCHISING

SCOTIABANK'S GUIDE TO PURCHASING A FRANCHISE **(www.scotiabank.ca)**

- From the home page choose the Small Business and Professionals link and then choose the Franchising link from the drop down menu under Small Business
- Order the guide from here

BUSINESSTOWN.COM
(www.businesstown.com/businessopps/franchises.asp)

- Are you considering a franchise? This site goes through some pros and cons of franchising and allows you to communicate with 'Bob' to get answers to your questions that weren't handled in the articles supplied

CANADIAN FRANCHISE ASSOCIATION
(www.cfa.ca)

- Excellent list of publications, access to associates, member lists

INTERNATIONAL FRANCHISE ASSOCIATION **(www.franchise.org)**

- Check out their "Consumer Guide to Buying a Franchise"

FRANNET, THE FRANCHISE CONNECTION
(www.frannet.com)

- A collection of resource materials and articles that have been featured in various franchise-related magazines and publications

THE FRANCHISE HANDBOOK ON-LINE
(www.franchisehandbook.com)

- Franchise information
- Directory of franchise opportunities
- News from the franchise industry
- Expert advice
- Business opportunities

STARTUP JOURNAL
(www.startupjournal.com/franchising/)

- Links to other companies providing franchising opportunities – a good all-around site

PROTECTION OF INTELLECTUAL PROPERTY

***CANADIAN INTELLECTUAL PROPERTY OFFICE* (www.cipo.ic.gc.ca/)**

- Search patents on-line
- Trademarks
- Copyrights
- Industrial designs
- News
- Canadian and international links
- Events
- Frequently asked questions, background on intellectual property
- An excellent site for anyone considering the possibility of protecting intellectual property

THE BUSINESS GUIDE: STARTING A SMALL BUSINESS
(www.businessguide.net/starting.htm)

- Covers all areas involved in start-up – from assessment of ability to insuring your business

FINANCING

FIRST NATION'S BANK OF CANADA
(www.firstnationsbank.com/)

- Deposits, investments, credit, loans, and cash management

ROYAL BANK SMALL BUSINESS AND ENTREPRENEUR FINANCING
(www.royalbank.com/sme/financing.html)

- Shows types of financing available for small business and entrepreneurs
- Brief descriptions of what each type of loan is normally used for
- Links to other funding and venture capital sites

ROYAL BANK FINANCING: LEASING
(www.royalbank.com/business/services/leasing.html)

- Various types of business leases for the entrepreneur or small business owner
- Description of what leasing is, how it can help your business, and what you need to complete a lease

ROYAL BANK: FINANCING FOR KNOWLEDGE BASED INDUSTRIES
(www.royalbank.com/kbi/index.html)

- Royal Bank defines Knowledge Based Industries (KBIs) as being in the science and technology sector
- Worth looking into

ENTERWEB FINANCE AND BANKING SITE
(www.enterweb.org/finance.htm)

- Links to all kinds of finance and banking sites, all rated from fair to outstanding. A place to look when you understand your financing needs and want to look for companies that might meet those needs

THE BUSINESS GUIDE: ACCESSING GOVERNMENT FUNDING
(www.businessguide.net/articles.htm)

- This site covers information that you would require when looking for government funding. The site tells you what the government criteria are when looking at projects they will fund

BUSINESSTOWN.COM
(www.businesstown.com/finance/money.asp)

- This site goes through the pros and cons of all the financing alternatives
- Are you already in business but experiencing some of those small business money crunches? Look for some ideas at www.businesstown.com/finance/problem.asp

***PROFIT GUIDE* (www.profitguide.com/profitcentres/)**

- Rated links to small business banking and finance sites

***WESTERN ECONOMIC DIVERSIFICATION CANADA – ACCESSING CAPITAL* (www.wd.gc.ca)**

- Links to different lenders and the Canada Small Business Loans Act
- Especially noteworthy is the Steps to Capital Growth link under the Tools & Guides link

***BUSINESS DEVELOPMENT BANK OF CANADA* (www.bdc.ca)**

- Links to the location nearest you, entrepreneur awards, student business loans, Profit$ e-zine
- Descriptions and links to Young Entrepreneur financing and Youth Business programs (www.bdc.ca/scripts/site/function-get-challenge.asp?&chk=1&language=eng&challenge=sec_head_youthbiz.gifqk248kq16)

***ABORIGINAL BUSINESS CANADA* (http://abc.gc.ca)**

- A list of Aboriginal Capital Corporations by region
- Entrepreneurship development, financial and business development, strategic business development

***ATLANTIC CANADA OPPORTUNITIES AGENCY – VENTURE CAPITAL* (www.acoa.ca)**

- Choose the Sources of Financing link to open a page full of financing alternatives

***CANADIAN VENTURE CAPITAL ASSOCIATION* (www.cvca.ca)**

- Address and contact information is on the site

***CIBC'S SMALL BUSINESS SITE* (www.cibc.com/solution/hom.jsp)**

- Choose Business Services then navigate to your site of interest
- Covers the areas of PC Banking, E-commerce, Internet Banking, Small Business Services, and Information Exchange

***QUICKEN SMALL BUSINESS CENTRE* (www.quicken.ca)**

- Free software, marketing hints, tips on developing a home office, on-line advice about small business and taxation
- Small Business Café
- The Quicken.ca Consultant
- Links to financing
- Easy to read and browse – appealing

***STRATEGIS* (www.strategis.ic.gc.ca)**

- Choose the "Business Support, Financing" link to open the portal to an extensive database of links to financial providers for small- and medium-sized business

***MONEYHUNT* (www.moneyhunter.com)**

- Site for a popular American TV show that helps businesses find capital

DEVELOPING A BUSINESS PLAN

***PALOALTO SOFTWARE* (http://pasware.com/)**

- Software for business plans, marketing plans, toolkits, as well as an opportunity to ask the software designers pertinent questions
- The different sections tell you about the product and what you can expect
- Sample plans and demo software available

***SCOTIABANK SCOTIABUSINESS PLAN WRITER* (www.scotiabank.ca)**

- Download or order the diskette
- Brief answers as to what a business plan is and why you need one

***BANK OF MONTREAL'S BUSINESS PLAN ESSENTIALS* (www.bmo.com/business/business.html)**

- Walks you through not only what should be in your business plan, but also why you need one – likely the most important question you should be asking yourself

***ROYAL BANK'S THE BIG IDEA – A GUIDE TO WRITING A BUSINESS PLAN* (www.royalbank.com/business/bigidea/)**

- Good to ensure the information requested on the disk is in your plan if you are going to be approaching the Royal Bank

***THE BUSINESS GUIDE: STARTING A SMALL BUSINESS* (www.businessguide.net/starting.htm)**

- Covers all areas involved in start-up – from assessment of ability to insuring your business
- Preparing a Business Plan
- Download a Word '97 Business Plan Template from www.businessguide.net/

***BUSINESSTOWN.COM* (www.businesstown.com/planning/creating.asp)**

- Lists of topics to cover in a business plan, on-line consulting (Ask Bob), links to other sites, and describes why a business plan is very important

***EPEI START UP CHECKLIST AND SMALL BUSINESS GUIDE* (www.peibusinessdevelopment.com/starting/index.php3)**

- Everything from how to start a business, to where to gather reference material, to how to run your business

***PROFIT GUIDE* (www.profitguide.com)**

- Choose the ProfitCentre link from the home page
- Links to business plan generators. All rated.

***BUSINESS DEVELOPMENT BANK OF CANADA BUSINESS PLAN* (www.bdc.ca)**

- What is a business plan?
- Why do you need a business plan?
- Template
- Good especially if you are approaching BDC — they will want a well-thought-out business plan. You can structure a business plan in literally thousands of different ways, so giving a plan to them in a format that they suggest is half the battle

***ENTREPRENEURSHIP INSTITUTE OF CANADA - BUSINESS START-UP GUIDES AND RESOURCE BOOKS* (www.entinst.ca)**

- A list of guides and paperback books covering everything from starting and financing your business to business plans for particular industries
- Books must be purchased

***DELOITTE AND TOUCHE LLP: DEVELOPING AN EFFECTIVE BUSINESS PLAN* (www.us.deloitte.com/growth/guidebooks/default.htm)**

***CANADA BUSINESS SERVICE CENTRES* (www.cbsc.org)**

  - Links to all the CBSCs, covering all areas of business
  - Interactive business planner
  - On-line small business workshop
  - Electronic commerce info-guide
  - Local information
- Canada/British Columbia Business Service Centre
- The Business Link
- Canada/Saskatchewan Business Service Centre
- Canada/Manitoba Business Service Centre
- Canada/Nova Scotia Business Service Centre
- Canada Business Service Centre – Newfoundland
- Canada/Ontario Business Service Centre
- Info entrepreneurs (Quebec)
- Canada/New Brunswick Business Service Centre
- Canada/Prince Edward Island Business Service Centre
- Canada/Yukon Business Service Centre
- Canada NWT Business Service Centre
- Canada/Nunavut Business Service Centre

***MOREBUSINESS.COM* (www.morebusiness.com/templates_worksheets/bplans/)**

- An American site with good updated links and daily news about building a business, starting a business, getting more profit from your business, and business planning

***BIZPLANIT* (www.bizplanit.com)**

- Provides a complete guide to creating a business plan

***ERNST & YOUNG* (www.ey.com)**

- From the home page choose Canada, then choose Services and finally take the link to Entrepreneurial Services

YOUTH ENTREPRENEURS

L'ASSOCIATION DES SERVICES D'AIDE AUX JEUNES ENTREPRENEURS DU QUEBEC (SAJE) **(www.quebecaffaires.com/saje/)**

- The site describes the association and what they do. If you are a resident of QC, between the ages of 18 and 35, and an entrepreneur or small business owner, you might want to contact them and see how they can help you with your business
- Site is in English and French

CANADIAN FEDERATION OF INDEPENDENT BUSINESS – LINKS **(www.cfib.ca/youth/links/Default_e.asp)**

- Links to such sites as the Marketing Resource Centre, Entrepreneurship Centre

ASSOCIATION OF COLLEGIATE ENTREPRENEURS **(www.acecanada.ca)**

- Site is dedicated to providing students with skills, resources, and contacts to make sure their ventures are successful
- Links to other excellent sites for business start-ups and small business owners

CANADIAN YOUTH BUSINESS FOUNDATION **(www.cybf.ca)**

- Nicely laid out site dedicated to those considering starting a new business or young entrepreneurs with questions about improving their current business

REALM **(www.realm.net)**

- On-line or paper business magazine for the young entrepreneur
- Mentorship, classifieds, etc.

BUSINESS DEVELOPMENT BANK OF CANADA YOUTH BUSINESS SITE **(www.bdc.ca)**

- Click on the Youth Business link

ABORIGINAL YOUTH BUSINESS COUNCIL **(www.aybc.org)**

- Business profiles
- Directories
- Networking eMail directory

WOMEN ENTREPRENEURS

CANADIAN WOMEN'S BUSINESS NETWORK **(www.cdnbizwomen.com/)**

- Links, news, networking, and resources

THE CHANGING FACE OF BUSINESS **(www.youroffice.ca/mag9902/9902women.html)**

- From the Your Office.ca site, an article about women business owners

ENTERWEB ENTERPRISE DEVELOPMENT WEB SITE: WOMEN AND ENTERPRISE DEVELOPMENT **(www.enterweb.org/women.htm)**

- Rated sites for Women business owners. Ranges from general topics about women in business to sites about women in business in Southeast Asia

BEYOND BORDERS: CANADIAN BUSINESSWOMEN IN INTERNATIONAL TRADE **(www.infoexport.gc.ca/businesswomen/specialinfo-e.asp)**

- 7.6MB downloadable document in PDF format. Looks at the unique challenges faced by women involved in international trade
- Advice from successful women exporters
- Summary of findings

CENTRE FOR WOMEN'S BUSINESS RESEARCH **(www.nfwbo.org)**

- Characteristics of women business owners
- Financing and business issues
- Home-based, women-owned businesses

ABORIGINAL ENTREPRENEURS

SCOTIABANK ABORIGINAL BANKING **(www.scotiabank.ca)**

- Choose Aboriginal Peoples from the Small Business Professionals drop down menu
- Managing investments, financing your business, business planning software

FIRST NATION'S BANK OF CANADA **(www.firstnationsbank.com/)**

- Deposits, investments, credit, loans, and cash management

ABORIGINAL BUSINESS CANADA **(http://abc.gc.ca)**

- Entrepreneurship development, financial and business development, strategic business development

CIBC'S ABORIGINAL BANKING SITE **(www.cibc.com/aboriginal/home.html)**

- CIBC's holistic approach to banking with the aboriginal peoples of Canada

BUSINESS DEVELOPMENT BANK OF CANADA **(www.bdc.ca)**

- Choose the "Aboriginal business" link from the home page
- Aboriginal finance programs
- Links to other financial institution's Aboriginal finance programs

E-COMMERCE

STRATEGIS **(www.e-com.ic.gc.ca/eteam/)**

- Electronic commerce in Canada
- Using electronic commerce
- What is it?

STARTUP JOURNAL **(www.startupjournal.com)**

- Choose the technology link to find articles and other links about use of technology in your business

WEBCOM **(www.webcom.com/)**

- E-commerce, web hosting, how to make money with WebCom

PROFIT GUIDE **(www.profitguide.com)**

- Choose the ProfitCentres link and then choose the Buying and Selling Online link
- Rated links to helpful export sites

BUSINESSTOWN.COM **(www.businesstown.com/internet/index.asp)**

- Information about getting on-line incrementally, building traffic
- The site doesn't cover true e-commerce, but it gets you started

ERNST & YOUNG ECOMMERCE **(www.ey.com)**

- From the home page choose Canada, then choose Services and finally take the link to Entrepreneurial Services
- Case studies, alliances, solutions and descriptions of e-commerce

ATLANTIC CANADA OPPORTUNITIES **(www.acoa.ca)**

- From the home page search for "Electronic Commerce"
- Growing Business Through eCommerce
- Innovation Through eCommerce

MARKET INFORMATION

KPMG MARKET FOCUS **(www.kpmg.ca)**

- Snippets of market information in the areas of biotechnology, health care and life sciences, high technology, hospitality and tourism, information, communications, entertainment, and insurance

GD SOURCING **(www.gdsourcing.com/)**

- The GD stands for Government Data
- Web site provides links to many other sites where you can gather statistical information. There are both fee-based and free services for specific requests

STRATEGIS BUSINESS INFORMATION BY SECTOR **(strategis.ic.gc.ca)**

- From the home page choose "Business Information by Sector"
- Contains information on business sectors, strategic information guides, guides to Canadian industries, and changing articles

HUMAN RESOURCES DEVELOPMENT CANADA – MARKET AND INDUSTRY INFORMATION **(www.hrdc-drhc.gc.ca)**

- From the home page choose "Employers & Entrepreneurs" then choose "Market & Industry Information"
- Links to other sites where you can gather information

***EXPORT DEVELOPMENT CORPORATION* (www.edc-see.ca/index_e.asp)**

- Economic research and foreign market information
- "Are You Export Able?" assessment questionnaire
- Links to related web sites

***ATLANTIC CANADA OPPORTUNITIES AGENCY* (www.acoa.ca)**

- Market trends and opportunities in Atlantic Canada
- Financial Help

***CANADIAN FEDERATION OF INDEPENDENT BUSINESS RESEARCH* (www.cfib.ca)**

- From the home page click "Research & Publications"
- Provides provincial outlooks, publications, research reports

***PR NEWSWIRE* (www.prnewswire.com)**

- From the home page choose "Industry Focus"
- Excellent site to gather up-to-the-minute news when doing market or industry research
- Canadian news can be found at www.newswire.ca

***CIBC ECONOMICS ONLINE* (www.cibc.com)**

- From the home page click on "Business Services" then choose "Economics Online"
- A look at economic indicators in the provinces
- Provincial forecasts
- Industry reviews

***EXPORT SOURCE FOREIGN MARKET RESEARCH* (http://exportsource.gc.ca/)**

- Provides information from government and other sources
- Country information
- Trade statistics and leads
- List of potential exporting partners

Glossary of Financial Terms

Accounts payable Money owed by a firm to its suppliers for goods and services purchased for the operation of the business. A current liability.

Accounts receivable Money owed to a firm by its customers for goods or services they have purchased from it. A current asset.

Amortization To pay off a debt over a stated time, setting aside fixed sums for interest and principal at regular intervals, like a mortgage.

Angels Private individuals with capital to invest in business ventures.

Assets The resources or property rights owned by an individual or business enterprise. Tangible assets include cash, inventory, land and buildings, and intangible assets including patents and goodwill.

Bad debts Money owed to you that you no longer expect to collect.

Balance sheet An itemized statement that lists the total assets and total liabilities of a given business, to portray its net worth at a given moment in time.

Bankruptcy The financial and legal position of a person or corporation unable to pay its debts.

Break-even point The level of sales in either units or dollars at which sales revenue and costs are equal so that a business is neither making nor losing money.

Capital asset A possession, such as a machine, that can be used to make money and has a reasonably long life, usually more than a year.

Capital costs The cost involved in the acquisition of capital assets. They are "capitalized," showing up on the balance sheet and depreciated (expensed) over their useful life.

Capital requirement The amount of money needed to establish a business.

Capital stock The money invested in a business through founders' equity and shares bought by stockholders.

Cash discount An incentive provided by vendors of merchandise and services to speed up the collection of accounts receivable.

Cash flow The movement of cash in and out of a company. Its timing is usually projected month by month to show the net cash requirement during each period.

Cash flow forecast A schedule of expected cash receipts and disbursements (payments) highlighting expected shortages and surpluses.

Collateral Assets placed by a borrower as security on a loan.

Cost of goods sold The direct costs of acquiring and/or producing an item for sale. Usually excludes any overhead or other indirect expenses.

Current assets Cash or other items that will normally be turned into cash within one year (accounts receivable, inventory, and short-term notes), and assets that will be used up in the operation of a firm within one year.

Current liabilities Amounts owed that will ordinarily be paid by a firm within one year. Such items include accounts payable, wages payable, taxes payable, the current portion of a long-term debt and interest, and dividends payable.

Current ratio Current assets divided by current liabilities. Used as an indication of liquidity to show how easily a business can meet its current debts.

Debt Money that must be paid back to someone else, usually with interest.

Debt capital Capital invested in a company that does not belong to the company's owners. Usually consists of long-term loans and preferred shares.

Debt-to-equity ratio The ratio of long-term debt to owner's equity. Measures overall profitability.

Demand loan A loan that must be repaid in full, on demand.

Depreciation A method of writing off the costs to a firm of using a fixed asset, such as machinery, buildings, trucks, and equipment, over time.

Equity The difference between the assets and liabilities of a company, often referred to as net worth.

Equity capital The capital invested in a firm by its owners. The owners of the equity capital in the firm are entitled to all the assets and income of the firm after all the claims of creditors have been paid.

Financial statements Documents that show your financial situation.

Fiscal year An accounting cycle of 12 months that could start at any point during a calendar year.

Fixed assets Those things that a firm owns and uses in its business and that it keeps for more than one year (including machinery, land, buildings, vehicles, etc.).

Fixed costs or expenses Those costs that don't vary from one period to the next and usually are not affected by the volume of business (e.g., rent, salaries, telephone, etc.).

Franchise The right to sell products or services under a corporate name or trade mark, usually purchased for a fee plus a royalty on sales.

Goodwill The value of customer lists, trade reputation, etc., which is assumed to go with a company and its name, particularly when trying to arrive at the sale price for the company. In accounting terms it is the amount a purchaser pays over the book value.

Gross margin or gross profit margin The difference between the volume of sales your business generates and the costs you pay out for the goods that are sold.

Income statement The financial statement that looks at a business's revenue, less expenses, to determine net income for a certain period of time. Also called profit-and-loss statement.

Industry ratios Financial ratios established by many companies in an industry, in an attempt to establish a norm against which to measure and compare the effectiveness of a company's management.

Intangible asset Assets such as trade names or patent rights that are not physical objects or sums of money.

Interest A charge for the use of money supplied by a lender.

Inventory The supply of goods, whether raw materials, parts, or finished products, owned by a firm at any one time, and its total value.

Inventory turnover The number of times the value of inventory at cost divides into the cost of goods sold in a year.

Investment capital The money set aside for starting a business. Usually this would cover such costs as inventory, equipment, pre-opening expenses, and leasehold improvements.

Lease An agreement to rent for a period of time at an agreed price.

Liabilities All the debts of a business. Liabilities include short-term or current liabilities such as accounts payable, income taxes due, and the amount of long-term debt that must be paid within 12 months; long-term liabilities include long-term debts and deferred income taxes. On a balance sheet, liabilities are subtracted from assets; what remains is the shareholders' equity.

Line of credit An agreement negotiated between a borrower and a lender establishing the maximum amount of money against which the borrower may draw.

Liquid assets Cash on hand and anything that can easily and quickly be turned into cash.

Liquidation value The estimated value of a business after its operations are stopped and the assets sold and the liabilities paid off.

Liquidity A term that describes how readily a firm's assets can be converted into cash.

Long-term liabilities Debts that will not be paid off within one year.

Markup The amount vendors add to the purchase price of a product to take into account their expenses plus profit.

Net worth The value of a business represented by the excess of the total assets over the total amounts owing to outside creditors (total liabilities) at a given moment in time. Also referred to as book value.

Operating costs Expenditures arising out of current business activities. What it costs to do business — the salaries, electricity, rental, deliveries, etc., that are involved in performing the operations of a business.

Operating loan A loan intended for short-term financing, supplying cash flow support, or to cover day-to-day operating expenses.

Overhead Expenses such as rent, heat, property tax, etc. incurred to keep a business open.

Pro forma A projection or estimate. A pro forma financial statement is one that shows how the actual operations of the business will turn out if certain assumptions are realized.

Profit The excess of the selling price over all costs and expenses incurred in making the sale. Gross profit is the profit before corporate income taxes. Net profit is the final profit of the firm after all deductions have been made.

Profit-and-loss statement A financial statement listing revenue and expenses and showing the profit (or loss) for a certain period of time. Also called an income statement.

Profit margin The ratio of profits (generally pre-tax) to sales.

Quick ratio Current cash and "near" cash assets (e.g., government bonds, current receivables, but excluding inventory) compared to current liabilities (bank loans, accounts payable). The quick ratio shows how much and how quickly cash can be found if a company gets into trouble. Sometimes called the acid test ratio.

Retained earnings The profits that are not spent or divided among the owners but kept in the business.

Return on investment (ROI) The determination of the profit to be accrued from a capital investment.

Term loan A loan intended for medium-term or long-term financing to supply cash to purchase fixed assets such as land or buildings, machinery and equipment, or to renovate business premises.

Terms of sale The conditions concerning payment for a purchase.

Trade credit The credit terms offered by a manufacturer or supplier to other businesses.

Turnover The number of times a year that a product is sold and reordered.

Variable expenses Costs of doing business that vary with the volume of business such as manufacturing cost and delivery expenses.

Venture capital Funds that are invested in a business by a third party either as equity or some form of subordinated debt.

Working capital The funds available for carrying on the day-to-day operation of a business. Working capital is the excess after deduction of the current liabilities from the current assets of a firm, and indicates a company's ability to pay its short-term debts.

Index